D0992056

The Urge to Mobilize

GEORGE YANEY

The Urge to Mobilize

AGRARIAN REFORM IN RUSSIA, 1861-1930

University of Illinois Press

URBANA   CHICAGO   LONDON

Harriet Irving Library

\UG 23 1983

University of New Brunswick

Publication of this work was supported in part by grants from the National Endowment for the Humanities and the University of Maryland

©1982 by the Board of Trustees of the University of Illinois
Manufactured in the United States of America

Library of Congress Cataloging in Publication Data

Yaney, George L.
  The urge to mobilize.

  Bibliography: p.
  Includes index.
  1. Land reform—Soviet Union—History.
2. Stolypin, Petr Arkad'evich, 1862-1911.
I. Title.
HD1333.S65Y36   333.3'1'47   81-11527
ISBN 0-252-00910-X   AACR2

To the Memory of

WALTER RATHENAU,

Tragic Prophet

Figure 1. The Gubernias of European Russia.

Preface

This is a large book and, I am told, a complex one, so a few preliminary remarks about its organization are in order. First, there is a glossary at the end. Most of the terms in it are familiar to specialists in Russian history, but since the book might conceivably be of interest to people outside the field, I have provided explanations of important terms and abbreviations.

Then there is the matter of source citation. It may dismay historians to find that most references to sources are incorporated parenthetically in the body of the text instead of being placed in footnotes. This arrangement has its disadvantages, but it saves space. Moreover, it serves in most cases to tell a reader something about the nature of each source without forcing him to shift his glance to bottoms of pages or ends of chapters. A student who does not care much about sources will grow accustomed to skipping over parentheses without undue fatigue. The young in heart will rejoice to discover that all Latin abbreviations have been dispensed with. Where I use the same source in several places consecutively, I do not repeat the author's name (or short title). Likewise, consecutive references to archival materials from the same *delo* (volume or box), *opis* (catalog), or *fond* (collection) omit the identifying numbers after the first citation except in cases where it seems clearer to repeat them.

A few remarks on mechanics. I have followed the Library of Congress's system of transliteration from Russian but without diacritical marks. Familiar terms—e.g., gubernia and kolkhoz—I use as if they were English to avoid excessive italicizing. Dates prior to 14 February 1918 are Julian; from then on they are Gregorian. I have tried to render quotations from administrative documents in simple English, though the originals are often in very turgid Russian.

A preface is as good a place as any to express gratitude to those who have helped put the book together. It has been a process of 20 years, and I am indebted to many people, but I can list only a few here. Lev Magerovsky of the Russian (now Bakhmetev) Archive at Columbia University provided me with very useful sources. Serafima Grigorevna Sakharova of the Central State Historical Archive in Leningrad was enormously helpful in finding materials, and I am obliged to IREX and the U.S. Office of International Education for making it possible for me to work in Leningrad in 1977, especially for keeping up their support in the face of an initial Soviet rejection. Once I got to Leningrad, the Academy of Sciences—especially Andrei N. Nadirov—was the kindest of hosts. A number of Soviet scholars have given me valuable help, especially Vera Romanovna Leikina-Svirskaia, who generously and patiently shared her ideas and her masterful knowledge of bibliography with me. A number of students at the University of Maryland have rendered indispensable aid with their relentless criticisms: Bruce Adams, Joseph Clarke, Karen Leibert, and Lillian Liu. I am also very much indebted to Steven Grant, Roderick McGrew, Walter Pintner, and S. Frederick Starr for reading the book in manuscript and commenting extensively on it. Bonnie Depp of the University of Illinois Press has vastly improved the text with her thoroughgoing editorial work, and Richard Wentworth, director of the Press, should receive some sort of medal for keeping the faith. I am grateful to the General Research Board of the University of Maryland and to the National Endowment for the Humanities for contributing substantially to defray the costs of publication. Finally I want to thank my wife Ann for helping so much to sustain an effort that has brought her so little benefit.

Contents

Illustrations

Every minute, every second, we
feel on ourselves the terrible pressure of the masses.... This
pressure completely paralyzes the
intelligentsia.... They say that the
people are not an active element,
but a blind, passive force. Be this
as it may, the fact is plain: it is not
we, the intelligentsia, who act on
the peasant, but he on us.

A. Efimenko (1884: vii)

CHAPTER 1

Introduction

> But what Russian doesn't like fast driving?... How can he not like
> fast driving when there's something so exalted and wonderful
> about it, when it makes you feel as though some unseen force has
> swept you up and is carrying you off and you find yourself flying,
> everything is flying: the milestones, the merchants' carts coming
> toward you; and the forest on either side is flying too,... the
> whole road is flying, God knows where, into the hazy distance,
> and there's something sinister about flashing past objects that
> disappear even before they've come into focus.
>
> Nikolai Gogol (1961: 277)

A. THE PURPOSE OF THIS BOOK

This book attempts to describe the implementation of the so-called
Stolypin Land Reform, named after Petr Stolypin, prime minister of
Imperial Russia from 1906 until his assassination in 1911. It was an
agrarian reform, involving an elaborate attempt by the government to
foster social change among the 70-80% of its subjects who lived in peasant villages and made their livings chiefly by farming. The general
purposes were to: (1) convert subsistence agriculture into commercial
farming, (2) replace patriarchal social structures with communities of free
citizens, and (3) redivide the peasants' land so that each household would
possess a single, integral plot.

The Stolypin Reform presents an unusually well-documented example of a government attempting to impose social change on a people
through administrative means. A study of its implementation, therefore,
permits a close look at the impact of administrative process on the
decisions it is intended to carry out. Theoretically, the enactors and
directors of a reform establish ends, whereas the administrative "machinery" provides the means to achieve these ends. It is my central purpose to
question this assumption. The following chapters investigate the actual
relation between the intentions of the reform's enactors and directors on
the one hand and the practices of local agents on the other. By focusing
attention on the locales, I suggest that the reform was not, in essence, an

intellectual exercise conducted in the capital cities by self-styled political "leaders" and administrative "heads." It emerged, rather, from interaction between officials and peasants in the countryside.

Historians habitually assume that the essence of a government-imposed reform is to be found in statutes and official commands emanating from legislatures and central offices. According to unshakeable scholarly convention, these ordinances proceed from the intentions of the men who write them, and therefore the history of a reform must show what these men wanted to accomplish and make some evaluation of their success or failure. Seen in this light, the Stolypin Reform was, principally, a few statutes enacted in late 1906. If these statutes achieved the purposes of their enactors, the reform succeeded; if not, the reform failed. End of history. According to this neat formulation administrative organization played no active role. We need not inquire what its officials did; we have only to ask whether or not the intentions expressed in the statutes were carried out. I have something to say about scholars who write history within this conventional framework, and it may clarify things if I say it here at the outset. They do not know what they are talking about.

As will be seen in the following chapters, the enactors of the Stolypin Reform had no coherent idea of what they wanted officials in the countryside to do, and therefore the statutes they wrote did not contain enforceable commands. Capital-city intentions—including administrative programs, ideological proclamations, political platforms, and class interests—took form during the course of elaborate rhetorical exercises, in which various groups and individuals strove to formulate philosophically attractive statements without regard for actual conditions in rural Russia. These conditions had been much studied by 1906, but since the results did not lend themselves to glib statement, they were generally ignored by would-be authors of reform programs. So it does not matter very much what the statutes said, or what their authors said they intended to accomplish or what we might conceive their material interests to have been. The Stolypin Reform proceeded not from capital-city schemes but from the process of implementation, which created and achieved purposes of its own.

Conceiving of the Stolypin Reform as an interaction between government and peasantry does not make its study easier. We must confront a number of questions. First: what did the reform actually do? If officials and peasants in the provinces did not carry out the central government's programs, what changes, if any, did they effect in rural Russia? In order to deal with this question properly, the book extends beyond the time of the reform. It describes the Russian government's experiments with agrarian reform during the period 1861-1930, from serf liberation up to

Stalin's forced collectivization. The first part, the years from 1861 to 1906, brings in the whole process by which the government came to conceive of its "duty" to change peasant society. The years after 1914 continue the story of interaction between peasantry and reform organization to its end. This expanded time frame serves primarily to show the significance of the changes that took place—or were taking place— during the Stolypin Reform proper. We are able to see somewhat more clearly the actual conditions that were to be changed and also the direction agrarian reform ultimately took.

The second question has to do with the motivation and direction behind the reform. If statutes, ideologies, and the power of government did not inspire and guide the participants, what did? If the government administration was not simply a machine to be turned on and off by "authority," what actually provoked it into action? I have suggested that interaction between officials and peasants guided the Stolypin Reform, but this does not tell us what moved officials to engage in this interaction to begin with.

To answer this question, the book elaborates the concept introduced by its title, "urge to mobilize." As will be suggested numerous times in the pages to come, actual officials in the countryside did not ordinarily interact with peasants out of careerist self-interest, respect for higher authority, zeal for legality and regulation, or some inspiring vision of a future utopia. When such motives operated under the circumstances prevailing in rural Russia, they discouraged interaction more often than encouraging it. Thus, if we are to ask what made administrators work, we cannot find our answer in the forms of administration, or the correctness of some philosophy, or even in the practicality of some program. We must seek out the reformers' motivation in the attitudes of the reformers themselves, and it is in these attitudes that we discover an impulse driving them into sustained interaction with the peasantry, come what may. As the book attempts to show, capital-city visions and schemes fell apart in the villages, yet the reformers' impulse survived and actually grew stronger throughout the period under consideration. To me, this suggests that administrators and technicians in the countryside were seeking primarily not to bring benefits to peasants but to satisfy their own inner need to force the rural population into conformity with "modern" assumptions regarding human nature.

Let me emphasize that I introduce the idea of an urge to mobilize for the purpose of answering a question, and the question has arisen because I am rejecting conventional assumptions about the workings of government-imposed agrarian reform. I am sure the reader will find the urge an awkward concept, and so it is. On the other hand, he will agree that it fills a need, if only he grant that the quesiton of motivation and direction behind agrarian reform is indeed an important one and that it cannot be answered satisfactorily by a conventional discussion of capital-city schemes.

To sum up this brief explanation of how a book about the Stolypin Reform came to extend over a period of 70 years and bear a title like "urge to mobilize," it all comes from studying local officials and gradually becoming dissatisfied with the assumption that they did their work because something called an "organization" compelled them to do it. It is not hard to see that the government plunged into interaction with the peasants after 1906, but if we wish to follow the course of this interaction and understand it, we must say something about earlier developments in rural Russia and we must ask why officials actually desired to mobilize peasants.

It may be useful if I present a brief outline of the book's contents. Chapter 2 deals with official attempts to gather information about peasant society in the early 1870s. Chapter 3 takes up the 1880s, when the government first undertook to establish agencies of agrarian reform in the countryside. The general idea at that time was to set up officials who could operate in the virtual absence of information or guiding policy. Chapter 4 describes the implementation of this reform during the 1890s and 1900s, and Chapter 5 presents a survey of peasant agriculture as the government saw it in about 1900. Chapter 6 describes the enactment of the Stolypin Reform itself during the period 1902-6, and the following three chapters discuss the reform's implementation up to 1914. They show how the officials sent out at the end of the 1880s were displaced after 1906 by surveyors, agronomists, and other forms of agricultural specialist. Chapter 10 shows how the new organization of specialists fared during World War I, when it gave up reform and took on the task of supplying grain to the army and towns. This fateful step all but destroyed the reform organization in 1917. Chapter 11 describes the conditions under which it survived through the civil war, and, finally, Chapter 12 traces the brief reawakening of agrarian reform during the 1920s until its final destruction, along with that of peasant society, in 1930.

B. A BRIEF EXPLANATION OF THE TITLE

As said before, the term "urge to mobilize" refers to a characteristic feature of modern minds, i.e., minds formed within or heavily influenced by modern European culture. It manifests itself in association with a belief in a systematic universe, which in Russia began to take hold in the capital cities in the late seventeenth century. As I suggested in an earlier work, Russia's ruling elite consciously strove to organize their government systematically from about 1700 on. Inspired (obsessed) by European writings, they set out to base Russian law on constitutional principles, organize Russian administration around a precise division of functions, and subject the use of Russian resources to the discipline of double-entry bookkeeping. For a generation or two they kept up their quest out of a belief in its necessity, but from the 1760s on, they generally spoke as if the rule of system embodied virtue as well as practical expediency. In Catherine's reign and thereafter, the "best" minds in the country operated on the assumption that human nature fitted into a universal system and should therefore be systematic. They themselves aspired to behave systematically, and they were in the habit of condemning any behavior they regarded as unsystematic—e.g., using bribes, hiring relatives, owning serfs—as evil. Thus Russians began their systematization by shouldering an unpleasant burden but soon learned to turn their burden into a crusade. By 1800 the idea of carrying the crusade for system to all the Russian people had come into circulation. By 1860 all right-thinking Russians accepted this idea as holy truth, and it had become impossible to disagree with it openly in polite society (Yaney, 1973: 32-36).

On the basis of these considerations, I suggested in my first book that the systematization of Russian government was not so much a process of imposing the forms of system as the spread of a belief that both individual and society should be systematic. This faith did not require its disciples actually to behave systematically, only to struggle against the profoundly unsystematic methods of governing and doing business that prevailed everywhere in Russia except in the imaginations of the "enlightened." Systematization, then, did not necessarily lead to the gradual establishment of system but only ensured that believers in system would continue to struggle against the custom of doing business through personal relationships. Actually, the nature of this struggle militated *against* the establishment of systematic organization. Those who struggled to impose system habitually employed unsystematic means; those who found themselves struggling against the constraints of system were not averse to employing system and shouting its slogans. Moreover, since everyone had to manage his affairs in the traditional fashion, no matter how fanatically devoted to system he might be, systematization could not help but create inner tensions in capital-city Russians. They could easily learn to loathe both themselves and their country. More important for our purposes, they could easily learn to hide the unsystematic elements in their behavior under a facade of rational method; that is, they could *repress* their inclinations to be unsystematic. Historically, then, the systematization of Russian government was the spread of a collective neurosis.

I said in my earlier book that when this neurosis reached a certain intensity, it drove capital-city Russians into the countryside to reform peasant society. I had not yet thought up the term "urge to mobilize," but this was what I was talking about when I said that the systematization of Russian government drove its officials into "a massive effort to impose social change on the peasantry" (p. 36).

The above discussion rests on the assumption that faith in the power and truth of system precedes and causes the urge to mobilize. This assumption is not necessarily true, but it does simplify things. It liberates us from the necessity of pondering the pre-cartesian world. Simplicity is certainly desirable, and so I stick by my definition throughout the following pages. I wish to point out, however, that one could conceive of the urge to mobilize more broadly. One could argue in a Weberian spirit that an urge to mobilize was operating in such phenomena as the early Christian campaign to convert Europe, the Crusades of the 1100s, and the rise of the mendicant orders in the 1200s. It might be possible to proceed from such considerations to an analysis that showed faith in system evolving out of an originally Hellenic-Hebraic urge to mobilize. Fortunately, we need not perform any such exercise here, but it is important to recognize the possibility of performing it, because this will help us to keep in mind the real complexity of the relationship between system and mobilization.

I should not like the reader to think of this book as a condemnation of modernity and its fantasies. The last thing I want is to give comfort to the yokel-worshipping nincompoopery associated with Lev Tolstoi in his declining years. To be sure, the word "mobilize" has a negative ring. It conjures up visions of soldiers marching away from weeping wives and mothers, government agents seizing buildings, sergeants pushing civilians out of trains, miserable evacuees standing in line with tin plates in their hands. "Mobilize" promises no rewards; it only demands obedience and sacrifice. It is, in short, a relatively honest word. One rarely sees it in advertisements or hears it in political speeches. This is why I use it. I do not wish to glorify the phenomena we customarily describe as reform, enlightenment, economic development, or progress. "Systematization," I might add, has the same advantage. It has the same dull, harsh sound, promising little good and perhaps even boding ill. Admittedly "sytstematize" and "mobilize" come often from the mouths of officious persons, the sort who delight in reminding everyone that "there's a war on." But nothing is perfect. On balance, I trust such words. It sometimes seems to me that if I could persuade everyone to say "systematize" each time he wanted to say "liberate," and to say "mobilization" every time he wanted to say "reform" or "progress," I would not have to write long books about government-peasant interaction in Russia.

But I am *not* implying that modernization is a regrettable, catastrophic phenomenon. I do not sympathize with the tiresome romantics who have so long flooded the world with shoddy illusions of lost Edens destroyed by industry, bureaucracy, money, public schools, totalitarian dictators, and the like. I do not join hands with the crowd of fatuous pseudo-academics who concoct twaddle about "natural" ids, "innocent" children, and "noble" savages. I have no use for the horde of essentially suicidal ideologues who have successfully persuaded civilization not merely to stop imposing itself on barbarians but to go the whole way and to restore itself to barbarism: to shed its neuroses, as the jargon has it. I hasten to assure the reader that I am wholly on the side of progress. I acknowledge my dependence on window screens and air conditioners. I am in favor of adulthood and civilization. I like sophisticated and courteous people even if they are hypocritical. I generally support administrators who are doing their jobs, even when I think them pompous and humorless. On the other hand, I detest bigoted peasants, scrofulous barbarians, and ill-mannered children, and I have no objection to mobilizing them. On the contrary, I enthusiastically recommend their mobilization. As I go on to describe the "progress" of the Russian peasant, however, I do wish to remind myself and others that in spite of all advantages this progress has a distinctly sinister aspect. One of the biggest conceptual obstacles hindering our understanding of Russia is our extreme proneness, almost our compulsion, to ignore this.

CHAPTER 2

The Information Problem

And already there's nothing to see but dust rising in the distance.

Nikolai Gogol (1961: p. 278)

A. INTRODUCTION

During the 1860s and '70s many government servitors and other varieties of capital-city Russian convinced themselves that something was wrong with the newly liberated peasantry, and as a result they felt a great thirst for information about life in the villages. The government was now pretending to be a bureaucracy, after all, and properly bureaucratic reforms had to be based on solid data. Unfortunately, as this chapter will attempt to show, the tsarist government's local agencies were incapable of furnishing useful data regarding rural society as a whole. The gubernias and uezds had no apparatus to do the necessary counting, and local administrators had long been accustomed to composing their reports on the basis—at best—of remarks solicited in the most casual manner from peasant elders. In about 1870, therefore, would-be bureaucrat-reformers began casting about for new ways to gather information.

But the information problem was much more serious than a mere lack of data. In all countries at all times, the acquiring of useful information may produce more than one impact on would-be reformers. On the one hand, an investigation of peasant households in a certain area may reveal concrete problems: a lack of firewood, appallingly low wages for farm hands resulting from a heavy influx of migratory workers from neighboring territories, insufficient protection against fire hazards in village dwelling areas. Such discoveries provide a basis for drafting useful, purposeful programs. They point the way to action and allow costs to be calculated. On the other hand, growing familiarity with peasant life may reveal serious obstacles to reforms conceived in the capital cities: government efforts to supply firewood to peasants who need it may encourage speculation in the lumber market and cause prices to rise rather than fall; new laws to restrict the movement of migratory labor may impede promising progress in agriculture and cottage industries in some areas; the sale of fire insurance may lead to an orgy of arson, as policy-holding peasants take to burning their huts in order to convert them to ready cash. In short, valid information may serve to block reforms as well as direct them. This chapter will suggest that in post-Liberation Russia the gathering of information revealed obstacles much more abundantly than workable programs. The tsarist government's would-be reformers invariably decided that peasant reform was necessary *before* they possessed information, and therefore the fundamental assumptions underlying their investigations and programs always lacked empirical bases. The main source whence they derived their proposals was almost never an expression of demand coming from the peasants. Usually their thinking began with scenarios for progress borrowed from the works of European intellectuals. When these ethereal proposals came up against more or less solid information, they manifested a distressing tendency to collapse. Worse, each collapse of this sort threatened to carry away the scenarios themselves and with them the capital city's sense of purpose. The basic problem of information, then, was that data could corrode the impulse to reform.

This disconcerting state of affairs was reflected in the efforts of several "commissions" that Tsar Alexander II set up in the early 1870s to investigate rural Russia and come up with ideas for what the government might do about its difficulties. Commissions of high-level bureaucrats had existed before. In the late 1850s and early '60s some of them had succeeded in producing some important legislation: chiefly the Liberation Statutes, the law on zemstvo institutions, and the judicial reform. These earlier bodies, however, had not compiled data systematically. A typical one usually began its work by drafting a proposed law and then, almost as an afterthought, inviting local authorities to send in comments on the draft. Thus "information" in the early 1860s had consisted largely of essays composed in the governors' offices, setting forth ad hoc opinions already current in the gubernia capitals and adding on whatever data happened to be at hand. By contrast, the commissions of the early 1870s possessed relatively broad powers to prescribe the methods by which gubernia officials were to gather evidence. In two cases, as we shall see, commission members actually went out to rural areas to get information for themselves.

The commissions failed to produce significant legislation, and so they have not received nearly so much scholarly attention as their predecessors of the Liberation years. Nevertheless, our account of agrarian reform begins with these "failures." They represent the Russian government's first more or less systematic attempts to gather information about the countryside. They also mark the beginning of bureaucracy's direct involvement in rural society and its first serious encounter with the information problem.

B. THE COMMISSION ON GUBERNIA AND
UEZD INSTITUTIONS

History

The *komissiia o gubernskikh i uezdnykh uchrezhdeniiakh* began its work in 1859 as part of the government's effort to do something about serfdom. For about three years it performed heroic legislative labors, among them enactment of the zemstvo statute of 1 January 1864. Then it virtually ceased to meet (Garmiza, 1957: 132-36, 154-55; Starr, 1972: 322-24). In April 1870 Alexander ordered his minister of internal affairs (MVD), A. E. Timashev, to set the *komissiia* to work again, this time to reform police organization in the gubernias and uezds. On 24 May Timashev issued an instruction to comply with the tsar's command, and on this basis our *komissiia* returned to action.[1]

The *komissiia*'s new quest for information began inauspiciously. Timashev, it seems, was not really concerned to inform himself. What he wanted, for the most part, was to impose changes in local administration that he had already decided were needed. This, at least, is the most obvious inference to be drawn from the sequence of events that preceded the instruction of 24 May.

The story begins in December 1869, when Timashev made a report to the tsar calling for a renewed effort to reform police organization in the gubernias and uezds (TsGIAL, f. 1316, op. 1, d. 4, ll. 2-4). Since 1859, said the report, new law courts and zemstvoes had been introduced with their own independent spheres of action under new sets of rules. The police, on the other hand, were still floundering along under a mishmash of outdated statutes and ad hoc temporary rules dating from Nicholas I's reign. This, said the report, was no small matter: the police were still the bulwark of government administration in the countryside. If they ceased to function, the entire apparatus of government would be helpless. Timashev urged that the MVD-police organization be reconstituted so that it might perform its proper functions under the new circumstances created by the Liberation. But the MVD was not calling for a mere reorganization *within* the police. Timashev's idea of police

[1]The instruction of 24 May 1870 is in TsGIAL (Tsentralny Gosudarstvennyi Istoricheskii Arkhiv Leningrada), f. 1316, op. 1, d. 4, ll. 354-55. The tsar's order of 16 Apr. is referred to in Timashev's instruction to the gubernias of 15 June (d. 12, l. 3).

reform was to put *all* government agencies and local institutions in each gubernia under the control and direction of the governor, which is to say that he wanted the head of the police (and the MVD's own agent) in each gubernia to become a kind of territorial commander-in-chief. Zemstvoes, law courts, and a variety of agencies from other ministries had broken free from the governor's domination; the MVD wanted them back. So said Timashev in December 1869. Five months before the tsar ordered him to summon the *komissiia*, Timashev already knew what he wanted the *komissiia* to decide (ll. 5-46, 181-96).

The minister worked rapidly. His report to the tsar was dated 26 December 1869, and on 10 January 1870 he laid a list of 32 propositions before the Committee of Ministers, setting forth the views expressed in his report. Unfortunately, none of the ministers approved his ideas. On 27 January they decided to write up their respective objections in detail, and it was only on 16 April that they met once again to consider Timashev's propositions. Since most of the ministers had opposed them from the beginning, the result was foreordained. The committee decided to leave local administration to its chaos until further study had been made (ll. 197-294, 359-75).

So much for the preliminary steps. Until 16 April, the day the Committee of Ministers rejected Timashev's propositions, the government's information gathering, such as it was, had followed the old pattern of the 1850s and early '60s; that is, the central offices had drawn up statements on the basis of information already at hand. Now, however, the government began to take a new tack. Alexander II signed the committee's verdict on the same day it was rendered and appended a command to Timashev to set the old *komissiia* in motion. About a month later, as we have seen (n. 1), Timashev compiled, and it was at this time that the *komissiia* began to gather information.

Methods

On the whole, the *komissiia*'s methods were less than impressive. At no time in its lifespan did any member actually go outside the capital city to obtain information for himself. In effect, Timashev merely told the governors to write down what they thought about gubernia administration and submit their essays to the *komissiia*. Presumably the members could consider these recommendations from the field as they drafted their reform proposals. Despite its modest dimensions, however, the idea of seeking information in advance represented an important innovation. In form, at least, the *komissiia* of 1870 resembled an authentic fact-finding body. Moreover, its members were drawn from all ministries involved in domestic adminstration, not only the MVD. They were not subordinate to Timashev. Each of them could draw on the materials coming in from the gubernias to support the views of his own organization.

Gubernia "investigations" began in June. Timashev had his department send out circulars on the 15th and 26th, ordering his governors to report on the "inadequacies of the existing order" and to suggest "appropriate measures to establish gubernia administration on a workable basis." Responses were due by 15 August (TsGIAL, f. 1316, op. 1, d. 12, ll. 3, 15). This left very little time for fact finding. On the other hand, the unprecedented scope of the assignment did allow an enormous degree of freedom to the governors to select their topics of discussion. All aspects of domestic administration stood defenseless before their pens. But the governors showed very little inclination to be free. After all, they were Timashev's subordinates (Yaney, 1973: 330-37); thus it should not surprise us to learn that the vast majority followed Timashev's line with little variation. The main "inadequacy" in gubernia administration, they said, consisted of the governor's inability to cope with the new institutions and agencies. Gubernia administration was in chaos, and therefore the governors' powers as territorial overlords should be restored to them. The newly freed serfs should be subordinated more directly to the police, the governors should have broad powers of supervision over the zemstvoes, and the jurisdiction of the law courts should be restricted so as to get them out of the MVD's way (TsGIAL, f. 1316, op. 1, dd. 13-14).

The *komissiia* found these replies unsatisfactory. According to a statement drafted in early October, the governors' reports had provided "only general considerations regarding the bases on which it would be useful to develop gubernia administration, without giving any indication of the circumstances that made change necessary" (d. 12, l. 71). What the *komissiia* wanted was "facts that would provide convincing evidence of the harm resulting from the local organs' lack of freedom of action" (l. 72). The governors were not to suggest that the reforms of the 1860s be abandoned. Restoring the governors' absolute power would be more likely to undermine the new institutions than to bring the police in line with them. The *komissiia* desired "to perfect the existing legislation on administration in order to fit it into the reforms, not in any way to diminish the significance of the reforms" (l. 72). In effect, our commission was directing the governors *not* to agree with Timashev. The members, coming from all the ministries involved in domestic administration, must have had orders from their respective chiefs to oppose him. Apparently they were successful. Reports continued to dribble in from the governors after October 1870, but no one in St. Petersburg seems to have pursued the matter further.

Even if we leave aside the vagaries of St. Petersburg politics, it must be admitted that the *komissiia*'s methods of inquiry in 1870-71 left much to be desired. For one thing, no one told the governors *how* to collect information. Circulars requesting reports did not stipulate what data were to be collected or by whom. For another, the governors were not allowed enough time to prepare their reports. As noted above, they had only two months to conduct investigations, and this did not allow them to do anything but consult their own archives. Obviously the *komissiia* did not worry much more than Timashev had about the merit of the governor's proposals or the validity of the information they submitted.

As we shall see in the following pages, the governors' reports to the *komissiia* were not altogether useless. A few governors seem to have made an effort to conduct serious investigations, and some even offered valuable insights. But how was a minister to distinguish honest reports from fabrications designed to please a superior? Even if he could make such a distinction, how could he persuade his fellow ministers to accept his judgment? In short, what good were the governors' reports of 1870-71 to would-be reformers?

Significance

Perhaps the best answer may be found in the reports themselves. For one thing, they were by no means uniform. Despite the fact that a majority of the governors hastened to agree with their superior, their reports, taken individually, expressed a wide variety of views. Among other things the *komissiia* received: an opinion from Riazan to the effect that gubernia administration was just fine as it was and needed no basic changes (TsGIAL, f. 1316, op. 1, d. 13, l. 412), a suggestion from Samara that the new zemstvoes and peasant institutions had actually strengthened gubernia administration (ll. 418-31), a series of recommendations from Saratov saying nothing at all about zemstvoes or peasant institutions (ll. 439-43), and a more or less typical statement from Simbirsk to the effect that governors should be given control over all local institutions and ministerial agenices (d. 14, ll. 83-93).

The diversity in the governors' reports must have been a little bewildering to the central offices, but it permitted some instructive comparisons. Take, for example, the reports from Archangel and Astrakhan gubernias. The governor of Archangel took sides with Timashev. Gubernia administration, he said, was in chaos. Ministerial agencies and the new local institutions were operating in virtual isolation from each other. A governor could not impose either policies or commands on ministerial agents except by appealing to their respective superiors in St. Petersburg, and such appeals were usually futile. Likewise, he could not influence the zemstvoes' activities without appealing to the Senate. As for the local judges, appointed for life in accordance with the judicial reform of 1864, he could not influence them at all. Thus, when he received complaints against administrative arbitrariness, or the slowness of law courts, or the zemstvoes' misuse of their funds, he was generally unable to respond effectively. Not surprisingly, people were losing confidence in the governors, which meant that they were losing confidence in government per se. The solution to the problem, said Archangel, was to give the governors supervisory power *(nadzor)* over all institutions and agencies in their gubernias. (d. 13, ll. 2-8).

The governor of Astrakhan saw things differently. He, too, felt that the presence of independent ministerial agencies rendered governors unable to administer their territories properly, but he disagreed with his colleague in Archangel regarding local institutions. In Astrakhan's opinion, zemstvoes and city dumas with legally defined prerogatives could actually help the governor to unify his administration. Only define the powers and responsibilities of all institutions and agencies with precision in a new, all-inclusive statute, and government would become orderly in the provinces. There would be no need for all-powerful governors (d. 12, ll. 17-33; d. 13, ll. 12-14).

A comparison of these two reports suggests, among other things, that the governor of Archangel did not give much consideration to the practical problems of administration. When he recommended that the governor be granted new powers, he never raised the question of how these powers were to be implemented. He was content to advance the suggestion that gubernia ministerial agencies should become, in effect, the governor's own little council of ministers (d. 13, ll. 8-10). Astrakhan, on the other hand, described the practical limitations of gubernatorial authority in some detail. He admitted openly, as few governors did, that he himself was not doing his job satisfactorily, mainly because he had too many responsibilities. If he were given yet more power, he said, his work would become even less effective.

An honest report like Astrakhan's was surely useful to the central government, but its value and significance might not have been clear without some context in which to judge it. This was what reports like the one from Archangel provided. The Astrakhan report exposed the superficiality of the Archangel report, but it was Archangel's report that provided the basis for recognizing Astrakhan's value.

It must be admitted that both reports reflected a lack of critical standards and an inclination to indulge in hollow expertise. Both Archangel and Astrakhan spoke of zemstvo institutions, yet neither gubernia had them. Similarly, the governors of Vilna and Kurliand did not hesitate to praise the new law courts and zemstvoes, though neither existed as yet in their gubernias.[2] The governor of Olonets had had direct experience with the new courts, but his reasoning about them was

2D. 13, ll. 37-38; d. 12, ll. 45-46.

shoddy. He recommended in all seriousness that if judicial institutions had their own separate sphere of activity, the governors ought to have theirs. In other words, law was all right so long as it did not interfere with administration. On this ludicrous basis he was able to pose as a supporter of the new courts and still agree with Timashev that the governor's personal power should be set above the law.[3]

In a word, the reports received by the *komissiia* were sloppy. We should not assume, however, that sloppiness was altogether a bad thing. Had the reports been prepared efficiently and systematically, they would only have parroted Timashev with more perfect harmony. As it was, their variety provided a basis of sorts for distinguishing relatively intelligent and meaningful analyses from the products of shiftless and/or subservient governors. Interministerial squabbling and weak communications with the countryside allowed room in the gubernias not only for incompetence but also for independence of judgment. In the central offices it produced not only confused and random information but also a basis for assessing the value of information.

Admittedly there was no clear standard or precise measure by which the reliability of this or that report could be measured. An official in the central offices simply had to get the feel of them, as a wine taster does with his wine, before he could estimate their quality. He could not assume, for example, that all governors who followed the MVD's line were unintelligent, spineless, or reactionary. Nor were those who opposed their superior necessarily perceptive, courageous, and liberal. There was, after all, an argument for the governor's authority.

Consider the report submitted by the governor of Orel (TsGIAL, f. 1316, op. 1, d. 13, ll. 287-322). It started off with the standard Timashev line that the governor had been rendered helpless by the proliferation of institutions and ministerial agencies not subject to his authority. In the past only gentry marshals, bishops, and generals had been independent; now there were peaceful arbitrators, zemstvoes, law courts, city dumas, and an ever-growing number of bureaucrats from St. Petersburg. Like Timashev, the governor of Orel thought all these new entities should be under the governor's control. But Orel went further and dealt with the more basic question of the nature of law in Russia. Most reports, both for and against Timashev, had little to say about the question of law. They merely repeated the tired old hope that if only laws could be written to prescribe everyone's rights and duties with precision, all would be well with the government. The governor of Orel dismissed this old saw as empty verbiage. He said that the statutes of the 1860s had come primarily from theory—necessarily so, otherwise they would not have

---

[3]D. 13, ll. 257-64. Olonets complained huffily that the law did not empower him to tell judges how to dress when they appeared before him (l. 258).

brought any serious changes. These revolutionary statutes had carried Russia forward "gigantic steps," and this was good, but now it was time to consolidate. The laws would have to be changed to conform to practice. Each statute, he said, came "...from its own theoretical basis, and this rendered them mutually inconsistent....Now the time has come to apply these laws: to render them consistent with one another, eliminate unnecessary rules and add necessary ones that are now lacking" (l. 322).

The very need for change in the law demanded that there be an authority with the power to make changes. In a time of rapid social development detailed and exact statutes were out of place, as was the whole idea that each governmental function could be precisely identified in advance. Laws, said Orel, should be broad in scope and vague in wording, not detailed and specific. Theories and legal enactments were alike only guesses about the future, and it would not do to force field administrators to operate strictly in accordance with guesses, however educated. If statutes had to develop in accordance with practical requirements, agents would have to recognize and respond to these requirements—thus the need for powerful governors.

Of course the Orel report was far from a perfect solution to the problems of government-peasant interaction. It did constitute, however, an unusually honest and intelligent recognition of them. Unlike most of the governors' reports, Orel's was not merely an expression of opinion but also an attempt to point out implications and practical consequences. It certainly reflected a keener understanding of Russian realities than Timashev's own writings. To my knowledge, Timashev never stated openly that his idea of governor power meant setting the police above the law. The governor of Orel, on the other hand, explicitly recognized the weakness of law in the gubernias and acknowledged that governors with arbitrary power would be outside the law.

The most sophisticated of the governors' reports of 1870 came from Pskov (ll. 392-411). It is of special interest not only because of its intrinsic merit but also because the governor of Pskov was none other than Mikhail Kakhanov. Eleven years later, in 1882, Alexander III would appoint Kakhanov a deputy MVD and entrust him with the drafting of a thoroughgoing reform of governing institutions in rural Russia.

Kakhanov's opinion was directly opposite to that of Orel's governor. Far from supporting Timashev's proposal to concentrate authority in the hands of the governors, the governor of Pskov wished to take yet more of it away from them. He began his report by pointing out the weaknesses of a system of government that depended on the governor's arbitrary power. In the pre-Liberation era, he said, the law had held the governor responsible for just about everything that occurred in his gubernia. As a result he had been physically unable to meet his responsibilities. "Even under the most advantageous circumstances," said Kakhanov, the sheer weight of official duties, the general lack of resources, the low moral level of the servitors, and the absence of public opinion had compelled the governor "to neglect his duties, to allow officials to exceed their authority, and to look tolerantly on blatant evils." There had been effective and enlightened governors before the Liberation, but they had had to find their strength in their own personalities and in their personal connections in the capital cities, not in the law. Despite these weaknesses, Kakhanov opined, the governor's power had been necesssary before the 1860s. "The whole pattern of life" had called forth the need for arbitrary personal authority. "Circumstances had created not only the possibility of arbitrariness but the necessity for it" (ll. 393-95):

> A governor who was accessible received all kinds of requests and demands: complaints against...neighbors, lords, officials, and law courts. But this did not reflect the people's confidence in him; only the widespread conviction that everything depended on the whims of persons in authority. This conviction was so firm that whenever a new governor was appointed, old cases, already decided, were once again resubmitted....Along with the conviction that the governor could do anything, there grew up in the people an inclination to put their hopes in his power and at the same time an actual lack of confidence in him. (Ll. 395-96)

In short, the people had come to believe that the governor could do anything, and therefore his failures to solve the problems of society could only be explained by ascribing evil intentions to him. The inescapable need for the governor's power had trapped tsarist administration in a vicious circle.[4]

The reforms of the 1860s provided a way out of the dilemma, Kakhanov continued, but they also gave rise to new problems:

> Since the reforms, zemstvoes and judicial institutions have freed the administration to a considerable extent from its responsibilities for matters not properly the concern of executive officials, such as the local economy and the judicial system. These reforms have altered the significance of gubernia administration but not its nature....Its powers are no longer indefinite but are precisely delimited by the strict rules governing the new institutions. The administration is not accustomed to limits, and in recent times, with the new institutions not yet fully established, it has kept within them only with difficulty. On the other hand, the populace distrusts the government's desire to keep itself within legal limits....(Ll. 396-97)

---

[4]Field (1976: 1-26, 208-14) has suggested that the peasantry were caught in the same circle by their faith in arbitrary power.

Worse, the administration itself was beginning to lose its cohesion: "Purely administrative offices are going their own ways, and the governor's supervisory powers are no longer sufficient to discharge his responsibilities.... This administrative disunity is the source of the government's massive correspondence...and the extreme slowness of its operation" (l. 398).

Such was Kakhanov's analysis of the situation in 1870. Admittedly none of his concepts was original in itself, but his statement of them was exceptionally clear and realistic. So far as I know, it is the most succinct exposition of the problems of rural administration that we have from Alexander II's reign. The recommendations Kakhanov made on the basis of his analysis, however, are less impressive. In essence they were the same as the ones he would advance as deputy MVD in the early 1880s. The governor's powers and duties should be precisely defined in law, "down to the minutest relationships and activities"; the zemstvoes should retain their independence; and ministerial agencies should be subordinated to gubernia administration rather than to their superiors in St. Petersburg.[5] These assertions begged more questions than they answered. If official powers and functions could have been separated merely by writing a proper document, Peter I would have done so at the beginning. As it was, Russia in Kakhanov's day had already been governed for over 150 years by officials clamoring for precise regulations that would tell everyone what to do. Whatever the weaknesses in Kakhanov's ideas of reform, however, his report did have great value as information. Moreover, its value was perceptible to any official in the central offices who had read the other governors' reports, which is probably why Kakhanov was brought to St. Petersburg in 1872 and ultimately appointed deputy MVD.

To sum up, the *komissiia*'s investigation of 1870 was the first of its kind, the first, that is, to ask for general views and specific reform proposals from gubernia agencies rather than comments on existing projects. Its method were primitive but not entirely unproductive. If information from the gubernias produced no conclusive recommendations, at least it afforded some basis for making the *komissiia*'s deliberations realistic. On the other hand, the inexactness and diversity of the information allowed each minister to choose only the items that suited his own interests and to use these items to formulate his arguments. Since the ministries were at least as concerned to undermine each other as they were to inform themselves, merely suggestive insights, however profound, were not much help in producing interministerial decisions. Scattered statements of opinion supplied ammunition for conflicts rather

[5]TsGIAL, f. 1316, op. 1, d. 13, ll. 401-8. The quotation is on l. 401.

than resolving them. This is one reason why the *komissiia*'s work produced no concrete reforms.

It will not do, however, to account for the *komissiia*'s "failure" merely by referring to disunity in the ministries. Such an explanation would imply that Alexander II had only to hire like-minded ministers, and his government could instantly have enacted reforms. But Kakhanov's perceptive report—among other documents of the time—suggests that the basic problem was not in St. Petersburg but in the uezds. If the governor of Pskov was correct, even a unified bureaucracy could not have imposed reform on rural Russia. Leave it to the zemstvoes, Kakhanov said. Rely on them to direct government operations in the uezds, because the government had no viable administrative means to unify its own agencies. What is this if not a declaration that the government could not impose reform on rural society? Here, then, is one case where information from the countryside told the central offices more about obstacles to its programs than means for carrying them out.

C. THE COMMISSION FOR REFORMING THE VOLOST COURTS

The *kommisiia po preobrazovanniiu volostnykh sudov* offers a much clearer illustration of the negative impact of information on reform aspirations. Its methods, though by no means flawless, were far closer to satisfactory than Timashev's, and its information came from far deeper levels of rural society than governors' reports could reach, especially governors' reports compiled within a 60-day period. As a result, this commission could do much more damage to St. Petersburg's visions of reform than the MVD's *komissiia* had.[6]

History

Volosts were set up by the Liberation statute as institutions of peasant government. They had existed before in one form or another as far back as Paul's reign (1796-1801), but it was only in the 1860s that they were extended to all peasant villages. Each one comprised several villages and was staffed entirely by peasants elected from among these villages. The volost court formed a part of volost government. In the early 1870s, it was made up of four members elected for one-year terms. Its function was to judge petty crimes and civil disputes and, when appropriate, to impose sentences on offenders.[7]

[6]The Russian word for "commission" was spelled variously in the 1870s.
[7]The Liberation statute required volost court members to serve one year. They were to receive no pay except what their electors saw fit to provide (*VPSZ,*

In 1867, only a very short time after the courts came into being, the minister of justice announced to Tsar Alexander II that he was dissatisfied with them. Alexander responded by appointing a commission to look over his minister's statement, and in due course this commission submitted an opinion. The tsar read the opinion and on 16 December 1871 ordered the minister of justice to set up another commission to study the volost courts. The members, said the tsar's order, were to be officials from the central offices of justice and the MVD, and they themselves were to visit volosts in a few selected areas in European Russia in order to investigate the courts directly. The tsar wanted them to observe courts in operation, inspect their records, solicit opinions about their work from the peasants, and take statements from local officials who had had experience with peasant justice (*Trudy*, 1873-74: I, i). The official purpose of the investigation was to determine whether or not the volost courts were so "completely superfluous" that their functions could be turned over to the justices of the peace.[8] Soon after the tsar's order came out, seven men were appointed to this commission: five from justice, one from the MVD, and one from the Senate. The senator, M. N. Liuboshchinskii, was to be chairman.

Methods

The new commission lost no time getting to work. In the early months of 1872 it compiled a list of 28 questions as a basis for peasant interviews and selected the areas its members would visit. The questions were devised partly to elicit local opinion and partly to compile statistical information: e.g., the number of cases tried per year by each volost court, the number of judges on each court, the percentage who were literate, how many cases each court handled and which kinds, the percentage of cases that were appealed to higher courts (*Trudy*, 1873-74: I, ii-viii).

Originally the commission intended to visit a selection of volosts scattered over 17 gubernias. The idea was to get a cross-section of geographical conditions, nationalities, village sizes, categories of pre-Liberation legal status, and degrees of involvement in commerce and

---

36657, arts. 93-110). In 1887 the term was lengthened to three years (Yaney, 1973: 360-61). As of 1872, most of the volosts the commission visited did not pay their peasant judges, though in many places judges were freed from other obligations *(natural'nye povinnosti)* during their terms of office. In the central "industrial" gubernias many volosts paid each judge a small amount, usually around 20-30 rubles per year. The highest salary the commission found was 75 rubles per judge per year (in two volosts: one in Moscow gubernia and one in Iaroslavl. See *Trudy*, 1873-74: II, 122-23; III, 73.

[8]The justices of the peace *(mirovye sudi)* were local judges appointed by the uezd zemstvo assemblies (Yaney, 1973: 232, 236).

industry. As it turned out, the members managed to talk with local officials in 17 gubernias but visited volosts in only 13 (pp. viii-xi).

The members of the commission left St. Petersburg on 20 June 1872. They traveled together from gubernia to gubernia and split up in each one to cover their own separate volosts. The extent and nature of their work varied from one gubernia to another. They visited 82 courts in Tambov and 53 in Kiev, but in the other gubernias they averaged only 20 to 30. In some volosts they were accompanied by one or more local dignitaries—usually an arbitrator, sometimes a gentry marshal or police commandant—but they often conducted interviews on their own. In almost all cases their interviews were conducted in the presence of volost elders and clerks. Their standard procedure was to call their interviewees into the volost offices and talk to them there. They never visited the outlying villages, and apparently they witnessed very few courts in actual operation. Their reports include only a very few descriptions of court sessions (pp. viii-xiii). The commissioners returned to St. Petersburg in September, and in the following year the government published their findings in seven massive volumes. This done, the commission passed into administrative oblivion.

The published works of the commission fell far short of the original plan. In essence they were no more than a haphazard accumulation of official reports and records of interviews. They contained no statistics of the sort that could be usefully compiled into a single table. A careful reader could, of course, have compiled his own figures, but information was not sufficiently standardized to provide a basis for quantitative comparison or generalization regarding all volost courts. Even such a simple quantity as the volost elder's salary did not lend itself to statistical summarization. Not all interview reports included it, and even if they had, a compilation would have been of doubtful value. The significance of each salary depended on a number of factors—volost population and area, standard of living, number and salary of volost clerks, amount of administrative expense the elder was expected to bear, the functions he performed—that are not recorded consistently in the commission's materials. Not only was it impossible to compile meaningful statistics; it was extremely difficult even to arrive at broad generalizations about the provisions of peasant law. As will be seen, the investigators found that such concepts as "school," "election," "priest," "house," "field," "law," and even "family" had no commonly accepted meanings in peasant society.

This is not to say that the commission's methods were ineffective. However crude they were by modern standards, they produced the best collection of information on peasant society that St. Petersburg had ever had up to that time. One must keep in mind that the members had no

way to prepare themselves for the exigencies of village interviewing.
Judging from a bibliography of works on the "peasant question" published in 1865 (Mezhov), scholarly study of the Russian peasantry had
begun only in 1858. By 1870 the available materials were already
voluminous, but as yet they covered only formal law and agriculture.
They offered little or no insight that would allow investigators to foresee
the difficulties they would encounter. It is not so surprising, then, that
the commission was unprepared to cope with the virtual absence of
consistent concepts in village social structure, and that as a result it could
draw no conclusions and make no recommendations. One of the members, M. I. Zarudnyi, wrote a monograph on the investigation, in which
he consciously avoided any attempt to summarize the commission's findings in statistical form. The *Trudy* represent an honest and objective
study, he said, but their contents are obscure and difficult to analyze
(Zarudnyi, 1874: 10). But if the members had no basis for planning an
orderly study ahead of time, we may say that when they finished their
work, such a basis did at last exist. A growing scholarly debate on the
nature of peasant law drew heavily on the commission's materials during
the 1870s and '80s, and in the 1880s the Kakhanov commission would
find them very valuable (TsGIAL, f. 1317, op. 1, d. 71, l. 63). Peasant
society was still a mystery after 1872, but the problems involved in studying it were now much better understood, and investigators could at least
take them into account.

Findings

Officially the justice commission set out to answer such questions as:
should volost court members serve longer terms and receive a salary? Did
the peasants want the courts preserved or abolished? How competent
were the court members? How subject were they to outside influence?
Should litigants be allowed to appeal court decisions? To whom? On
what basis? These questions were indeed asked and answered in the
interviews, but the answers were less than satisfying to would-be reformers of peasant law. They suggested overwhelmingly that the peasant
legal order did not lend itself to specific changes in rules. Legal rules
could not be changed because they did not exist to begin with. As
virtually all students of peasant law would agree in subsequent decades,
the only way to "improve" peasant law was to introduce general reforms
into peasant society as a whole (e.g., Efimenko, 1884: 136; Brzheskii,
1902: 4). By and large, then, peasant answers to the commission's
questions were valuable not in themselves but as indications that the
questions were irrelevant.

The commission's unprecedented attempt to storm the peasant
volosts raised many questions apart from the ones the members asked

the peasants. Perhaps most important were the questions the commission's materials begged: those regarding method. A clerk in St. Petersburg, reading through the interviews, could not get very far without asking himself how reliably they reflected the peasants' actual views. How useful, for example, was the commission's standard procedure of interviewing peasants in groups in the presence of the volost elders? Were these hand-picked interviewees trying to convey information or merely to satisfy what the elder took to be the expectations of his distinguished visitors? Did statements by elected peasant officials reflect the views of their constituents? Unfortunately, the commission's volumes did not discuss its interviewing procedures. Thus it was difficult for a reader to decide what the information in them meant.

The materials also contained statements from a variety of local officials. Most governors put in brief comments, and each one of these was accompanied by remarks from a smattering of gentry marshals, *prokurory,*[9] justices of the peace, chairmen of zemstvo directorates, police commandants, arbitrators, etc. On the whole the arbitrators' statements were the most useful of these (concerning the arbitrators, see ch. 3, sec. C).

Statements from officials did not come from the "horse's mouth," so to speak. They were, at best, pale reflections of peasant law, not descriptions. Still, we might at least expect them to reflect some common point of view. However ignorant the contributors may have been of peasant conditions, they worked for the same government. In fact, however, the most striking feature of these official comments is the utter lack of agreement among them. In only one gubernia out of 17 did every statement reflect the same point of view.[10] In all the rest officials described conditions in radically different ways. The governors, it seems, made no effort to impose a single official doctrine on their subordinates. In Kiev and Novgorod some effort was made at the gubernia level to read the statements and consolidate them into a single report. In Kiev the governor-general did it (*Trudy,* 1873-74: VII, 403-8); in Novgorod it was the gubernia board for peasant affairs (pp. 449-52). These efforts, however, did not involve any correction or amendment of the statements themselves. In other gubernias, it seems, the governors did not even read what their subordinates had to say. Contrary to received opinion in St. Petersburg regarding slavelike subservience among low-level administrators, the main difficulty facing any would-be compiler of information was not official conformity to established views but the absence of any

[9]In the late nineteenth century the gubernia *prokuror* was essentially a district attorney (Morgan, 1962: 17-21).

[10]All officials in Vologda gubernia disapproved of the volost courts and recommended their abolition (*Trudy,* 1873-74: VII, 505-25).

common view at all. This generalization applies not only to the officials'
beliefs about policy but even to their concepts of what was going on in
the areas where they worked. One surmises that the information coming
from officials was by and large authentic, but it was incoherent.[11]

Consider some typical statements from administrators. An arbitrator
in Tambov gubernia asserted unequivocally that volost courts worked
well in all respects. They served the interests of both peasants and
government, and peasants never complained against them (*Trudy,* 1873-
74: VII, 16-17). In the same uezd, however, a chairman of the uezd
congress of justices maintained that peasants never used their volost
courts and had no inclination to use them. Court members, said the
chairman, neither knew nor abided by local custom, mainly because
there was no such thing as a uniform customary law extending over an
entire volost. In the absence of either state law or custom, they had no
basis for deciding cases except their whims. Consequently, he opined, it
would be best for all concerned to abolish the volost courts (p. 25). The
same divergence of opinion can be observed elsewhere. In one uezd in
Moscow gubernia two arbitrators reported that the courts were working
well, while the police commandant thought they were in desperate need
of reform (pp. 128-30). In another Moscow uezd an arbitrator said that
the members of volost courts worked well but were hampered by the
interference of volost clerks, who generally drifted from job to job and
took little interest in their responsibilities. In the same uezd the police
commandant reported that the courts were staffed by short-term ignoramuses, whereas the clerks, many of whom remained at their jobs for long
periods of time, generally performed their duties honorably and competently (pp. 133-35).

Despite sharp disparities among the local officials' descriptions, their
statements reflect general agreement on a few matters. No one denied
that most of the judges were illiterate. One chairman of an uezd congress
of arbitrators compiled figures on the subject. Of 138 volost judges in the
uezd, he said, only 46 were literate; of the 46, more than half could do no
more than sign their names (p. 69). A few observers were not troubled by
the judges' illiteracy (see, e.g., pp. 229-30). Most comments, however,
declared illiteracy to be an unqualified evil. Judges who could not read
had to rely on other persons to explain the law to them and were
therefore susceptible to outside influence. Most often it was the volost
elders and clerks who exercised this influence, but it could also be a rich
peasant, or government official, or anyone at all with vodka to dispense
(e.g., pp. 2-3, 8).

[11]See especially the statements from Samara and Smolensk gubernias (pp.
537-69, 613-40).

Most statements stressed the pre-eminent significance of personality in the working of the courts. Procedures for hearing witnesses varied with each witness, and the gravity of a sentence depended on who was being punished. Some administrators considered the predominance of personal influence to be malign (pp. 4-5); others suggested that the courts were at their best when capable and honest persons influenced them unofficially (p. 10). Most statements indicated that the peasants wanted some powerful individual to dominate the courts and, if necessary, force the judges to do the right thing (e.g., pp. 403-4, 424-25).

Almost all the official statements noted or implied—some approvingly, some disapprovingly—that volost judges strove primarily not to enforce rules of law but instead to persuade disputing parties to resolve their disagreements. An anti-court *prokuror* in Vologda gubernia indicated that many hearings on theft (with breaking and entering) involved nothing more than the court and the interested parties getting drunk at the expense of the accused and resolving the matter by persuading the injured party to forgive and forget (p. 511). Even so, punishments were meted out now and then, the most common one being the birch. One arbitrator in Kiev gubernia provided figures: whipping was used in 968 out of 1,090 cases in which punishment was inflicted (p. 415).[12] But if the volost courts handed down sentences, does this not suggest some awareness on their part of laws violated? What was being punished if not the breaking of rules? Unfortunately, the statements of local officials do not delve into this question. They simply allow us to observe that although volost courts did impose punishments, they consistently sought to decide each case as if it were a dispute between individuals.[13]

So much for the statements of officals. I hope the preceding paragraphs convey an impression of their value as information and also their limitations. We should note that in spite of their overall ambiguity, some of them were suggestive and insightful. An astute official in the central government who read through the *Trudy* could discriminate between more or less valid assertions. He could recognize, for example, the stupidity of an arbitrator in Samara gubernia who claimed piously that volost elders and clerks *never* influenced the courts (*Trudy,* 1873-74: VII, 537). Likewise, our official could detect the inanity of an arbitrator in Tambov who deplored the general illiteracy and ignorance of peasant judges but then recommended that they be ordered to judge cases

[12]Alas, this exceptionally diligent gatherer of quantities neglected to say what area or period of time he was describing.

[13]Strictly speaking, this was contrary to law. The Liberation Statute (*VPSZ,* 36657, art. 107) provided that the court should strive to make peace between contending parties in civil suits but not in criminal cases.

regarding property and inheritance in accordance with the government's enormously complex statutes (pp. 2-3).[14]

Statements from nonpeasants were only a by-product of the commission's investigations. Less than one-fifth of the *Trudy* is devoted to them. The remainder consists of materials gathered in the volosts themselves: volost court records, interviews with peasants, and a few descriptions of actual court sessions. These materials represent the truly unique part of the commission's information gathering. It is appropriate, therefore, to give particular attention to them and to the value of the information they contain.

At first glance they indicate that peasant custom varied considerably from volost to volost. Some courts said they only rarely sentenced anyone to be beaten (I, 3, 12, 15, 124, 499; III, 243; IV, 13, 243; V, 47, 415), but the majority thought beating was the most suitable and frequent punishment (I, 293, 313; II, 32, 228; III, 160, 178, 309; V, 228; VI, 18, 30). With regard to inheritance, the interviews reveal an astonishing variety of practices, indicating seemingly fundamental differences from place to place in the nature of the family itself. There were some volosts where an adopted son *(priemysh)* received no share in the family inheritance (I, 205, 259-62; III, 145; V, 52, 73), others where he was treated the same as sons by blood (I, 391, 541; II, 219; III, 2, 233-234, 323; IV, 119; V, 177; VI, 3, 29), others where he was treated like a son by blood only after living and working with the family (I, 3, 12; II, 29, 430; III, 75, 189; VI, 44), and yet others where his "rights" depended entirely on the "situation" (I, 339, 505; III, 161; V, 332; IV, 46). In one volost the peasants said that an adopted son might or might not share in the inheritance, but a bastard invariably did (I, 505). Many volosts reported that bastard sons had the same rights as their legitimate brothers (II, 363, 603; III, 2, 79, 381; IV, 29; V, 177; VI, 29, 44), but in many others bastards were explicitly denied a share in the inheritance (II, 324; III, 244; V, 52, 87; VI, 19, 41).

These descriptions probably suggest more variation among volosts than actually existed. In one volost in Ekaterinoslav gubernia the peasants simply denied knowledge of any customs regarding inheritance (V, 390). Similarly, the peasants in a Tambov volost testified that a widow might or might not get a share of her husband's property, "depending on what kind of person she is" (I, 77). These were not typical responses, but I have the impression that they reflected peasant thinking far more accurately than the more definite answers I have listed above. Peasants who

---

[14] A more consistent report from an arbitrator in Kostroma noted that laws imposed on illiterate judges would simply render them all the more dependent on outside help (*Trudy*, 1873-74: VII, 229-30).

ostensibly recognize the "right" of a bastard or adopted son to "inherit" were simply acknowledging that they had no precise basis for defining membership in a household. If most interviewees tried to describe inheritance customs in the form of rigid rules, this was probably because the interviewers from the capital city urged them to do so.[15]

These remarks concerning the commission's information on inheritance may be applied equally well to all subjects touched on in the interviews with peasants. The practice of conducting group interviews imposed an artificial uniformity on what the peasants said in each one, and this false uniformity *within* each volost exaggerated the apparent variation *among* them. Peasant custom was too amorphous to be clearly identified anywhere (Zarudnyi, 1874: 92-94; Leontev, 1894: 29-31, 41-47).

Perhaps the clearest evidence for this characteristic amorphousness lies in the "procedures" by which the peasants decided their legal cases. There was no single formula. The peasants could and did take their disputes and accusations to any official or esteemed neighbor who seemed able to negotiate an acceptable agreement, regardless of his formal role in government. Usually, however, the cases came first to the village authorities, either the elder or the assembly (*Trudy,* 1873-74: I, 57, 389; II, 283, 329-30; III, 74; IV, 264; V, 1, 66, 498; VI, 52, 121, 461). Every effort was made to decide the matter in the village, though the Liberation statutes did not authorize village institutions to render judicial decisions except in civil disputes (*VPSZ,* 36657, arts. 51, 99). But the statutes assumed that village authorities would distinguish between criminal acts and civil damages, and this was not the case. It was often hard to tell when judicial decisions made in the villages were legitimate or not. Only a very few interviewees flatly denied that village elders and assemblies acted in a judicial capacity (*Trudy,* 1873-74: I, 1; III, 115). Virtually all interviewees acknowledged that the elders and/or assemblies tried to handle *all* cases before taking them to the volost, regardless of their character.

Cases the village could not resolve went to some higher official, most often the volost elder, who had no formal authority to decide cases but who often did so in practice (I, 76-77; II, 91, 428; III, 30, 50, 199; V, 318; VI, 30, 300, 461, 627). When it was not the elder, it was often some official from outside peasant society (e.g., II, 388; III, 187; IV, 236; V, 333; VI, 28; VII, 585-86). Only after these erstwhile executive authorities failed or refused to decide a matter to the satisfaction of both parties did it come before the volost court. When it did, the court usually sought the advice of the volost elder or clerk in arriving at its decision (II, 59, 123,

[15]Useful studies in depth of peasant attitude toward inheritance are Dovnar-Zapolskii (1897: XXXII, 82-142; XXXIII, 1-16) and Semenova (1914: 21-57). See also below, ch. 5, sec. B.

256; IV, 105, 118; V, 340; VI, 40-41, 50). The clerk explains the law, said one peasant judge, "and then we know how to decide" (I, 47). The Liberation statutes (*VPSZ*, 36657, art. 104) made it strictly illegal for the elder or clerk to influence the court's decisions in any way, but circumstances conspired to render this formal provision inoperable.

In any case, it was an exceptional clerk who knew the statutes, and he was a rarity indeed if he could actually impose his knowledge on court procedure with any consistency. How could peasant judges have comprehended modern notions of evidence and rules of debate? They may have deferred to the clerk, as so many of them claimed, but one doubts they were deferring to his knowledge of law. What the interviews revealed was a general inclination to resort to traditional methods of deciding cases that bore no relation to any rules of law, either statutory or customary. These methods included casting lots,[16] compromise by awarding the injured party only half his claim,[17] and requiring one of the parties to swear by God that he was telling the truth.[18] In some cases there probably was a real difference between courts which claimed to rely on the clerks' relatively formal notions of law and courts in which custom prevailed. More often than not, however, the apparent difference between clerk-dominated courts and those utilizing lots and oaths was merely an expression of two facets of peasant legal procedure coexisting in all volosts.

In one revealing interview (*Trudy,* 1873-74: I, 273-75) some volost judges in Tambov gubernia claimed that the clerk really did the deciding in their cases, since he knew the law and they did not. This made it sound as if law prevailed in the court (though obviously it did not prevail in the court's relations with the clerk). The judges said, however, that they made most of their decisions by persuading the disputants to agree.

[16]In general, lots *(zhrebii)* were cast to decide a case only if both parties agreed. Lots seem to have been used frequently in Tambov gubernia (see, e.g., *Trudy,* 1873-74: I, 234, 424, 441) but only rarely in the other gubernias surveyed by the commission.

[17]E.g., I, 340-41; II, 46, 228; III, 31, 287, 329; IV, 20; V, 3, 161; VI, 29, 95-96, 274. This method *(grekh po polam)* was reported frequently in all gubernias except Iaroslavl, Kharkov, and Poltava. In Iaroslavl it was reported relatively rarely; in Kharkov and Poltava its use was explicitly denied.

[18]This was not merely a way of formalizing testimony but an actual method for arriving at a decision. Usage seems to have varied, but swearing by oath generally decided a matter when (and only when) one side challenged the other to swear his story was true and the other side accepted the challenge. Once an oath was taken under these circumstances, the court assumed that the oathtaker's account was true (e.g., I, 298; II, 60, 255; III, 267, 309, 329; V, 6, 100, 293; VI, 29, 74, 274). The volosts of Kharkov and Poltava generally denied using this method. So did a few volosts in other gubernias (e.g., III, 144, 188; V, 37, 161; VI, 43, 595).

This contradicted any implication there may have been in their first statement that law prevailed. To make matters worse, the clerk broke in abruptly to assert that all decisions were made in accordance with the Liberation statutes. His interruption brought an end to the discussion. The clerk's statement was absurd, since the statutes prescribed that the volost court's *decisions* should be governed by custom (*VPSZ*, 36657, arts. 103, 107). Only procedure was to follow legal rules. Apparently, then, the clerk was as anxious as the judges to make all volost operations appear legal; equally apparently, none of them understood the government's law. The testimony also suggests that neither custom nor clerk consistently dominated the process of making judicial decisions.[19]

The main factor determining whether custom-legality or clerk-legality would prevail in a given volost at a given time was personality, usually the elder's or the clerk's. Peasant interviews, like the statements of local officials, give the impression that personality was the primary element in all phases of the judicial process. I have already referred to the practices in some volosts of deciding questions of inheritance according to the "kinds of persons" involved or the "situation." Similarly, many peasant judges said that they never punished anyone for falling behind in his taxes unless he lived a "dissolute life" (*Trudy*, 1873-74: I, 3; II, 440; III, 129, 153; V, 67; VI, 74), and some asserted openly that they made it a rule to sentence men of bad reputation to be beaten regardless of their offense (I, 234; III, 13, 84, 178, 200). In many interviews the peasants testified explicitly that all sentences were imposed "according to the man being punished" (I, 313, 339; II, 28, 33, 143; III, 219, 287; IV, 25, 243; V, 308; VI, 19, 395).

It should also be pointed out that personal influence—chiefly that of the volost elder—could play a major role in determining whether or not litigants and witnesses would be forced to attend court and whether or not sentences, once imposed, would ever be carried out. The latter issue did not come up in many interviews, but it seems that most elders did not keep records of punishments, and they frequently neglected to impose them (I, 275, 390-91; II, 323, 330, 352, 439; V, 48, 289; VI, 293).

In sum, peasant interviews portrayed the following elements in peasant "law": (1) any person of influence could judge a legal case; (2) instead of judging in accordance with norms, he normally aimed to secure agreement between disputants on any acceptable basis; (3) when he did judge, he judged the personality of the accused rather than his

---

[19] A fair number of judge-interviewees vigorously denied being influenced by outside persons (e.g., *Trudy*, 1873-74: III, 152, 266; V, 100, 175, 256-57). In all likelihood, this signified a collective desire to appear proper before visiting bureaucrats. In one Iaroslavl volost the elder broke up some playacting of this sort by contradicting the judges' glib denial to their faces (III, 187, 190).

deed; and (4) when a court imposed a sentence, its implementation depended largely on the whim of the volost elder. Peasant law, then, was not rigid, nor was it sanctified by long-established traditions carefully handed down from generation to generation. Perhaps most important, it contained no rules whose legitimacy and force derived from abstract principles. This was the essential message the *Trudy* conveyed to the government.

Significance

Supposing the *Trudy*'s message was valid, what government measures were now to be adopted? Did the message actually tell the government what to do with the volost courts?

For those high government officials who wished to dispense with the courts, as the minister of justice apparently did, the message was clear: write a new statute abolishing them, and order peasants to bring all legal actions before the government's courts. Those who shared this conviction emphasized the courts' disorderliness, pointing with particular relish to scenes such as the following, which took place in August 1872 in a volost court in Riazan gubernia (I, 814-18). A member of the commission was present, along with an arbitrator and two justices of the peace.

The judges and the volost elder were all drunk. The first case involved a 75-year-old widow who wanted her son-in-law to return a cow to her. She presented her argument regarding the cow. The volost elder then interrupted to inform the court of some circumstances she had neglected to mention. The central question, he said, was not the cow but some oats and rye in the son-in-law's possession. When the elder finished, the son-in-law spoke up, denying that he owed the widow anything and claiming that she had slaughtered the cow in question. Having heard all this, the judges ordered the son-in-law to return the oats and rye to the widow. He refused. This seems to have confused the judges. They asked the elder what to do. At first the elder replied that it was not his business to judge, but after some further interchange between the judges and the son-in-law, he asserted that statutory law *(zakon)* required the son-in-law to return the oats and rye.

At this point a man came forward and abruptly introduced an entirely different case. Apparently he had been sentenced to a beating by the court at an earlier session and had run away to avoid it. After some incoherent wrangling the elder, ignoring all that had been said, announced that the arbitrator wanted this man beaten for taking oats. The judges decided to have the man beaten, whereupon his mother stood up to protest, asking to be beaten in his place. Suddenly the son-in-law from the first case broke in to repeat his refusal to give his mother-in-law oats and rye. The elder replied that the son-in-law had to give her the oats and rye, though now this old legal expert abandoned his stand on *zakon* and asserted simply that the court had already decided the matter (in fact the record did not show any decision). The son-in-law began shouting. The elder ordered him to leave the court. The son-in-law responded by calling the judges fools. One judge ordered that he be held under arrest for two days, whereupon the son-in-law was removed. The court then returned to the case of the man who had run away to avoid being beaten. The arbitrator intervened (illegally) to remind the elder to record the sentence before administering the beating. There was some argument among the judges about the number of strokes. Apparently the elder had originally suggested 20 (the legal maximum). Some judges thought this would be too many. The elder said it was up to them, but then he proceeded to order 20. Thus ended the court's deliberations on the two cases.

Not all descriptions of peasant trials in the commission's materials indicated disorder of this magnitude. A very few courts appear to have been well regulated and quite capable of doing orderly work (e.g., VI, 647-48). Clearly, however, a vast majority of the courts suffered from procedural incoherence (e.g., II, 145-46; III, 104-6; VI, 273, 299, 677-78). A capital-city clerk might well have concluded from reading the materials that the minister of justice's desire to get rid of peasant judges was well conceived.

But there was another side to the question. The virtual absence of systematic procedure did not preclude the possibility of the courts' being useful. A substantial number of statements from both volosts and local officials favored their continuation even while recognizing their procedural irregularities. There were some categories of disputes and offenses, chiefly those involving landholding, that could not conceivably have been resolved by any legal order except the peasants' own.

Consider a case mentioned in an arbitrator's report from Vitebsk gubernia (VII, 585-86). A former serfowner held one of the strips in a village field. Instead of farming it himself, he rented it out to one of the villagers. His tenant chose to plant rye in the strip in a year when the other stripholders—his fellow villagers—left their land fallow. This created grave difficulties for the villagers. It was customary to let the village's farm animals graze on fallow fields, and this would be impossible in a field with a strip of grain extending across it. Sooner or later the animals would get into the rye, and the villagers would be liable for damage.

If this had been a simple question of village land, the matter could have been settled by the peasants themselves, but since the strip in question was not peasant land, it was not formally subject to volost authority. Peasant stripholders had no legal way to compel the landowner's tenant to follow customary procedures. The villagers complained to the arbitrator. The arbitrator resolved the problem by simply ignoring the statutes and referring the complaint to the volost court on his own authority. There was no other apparent way to settle the matter satisfactorily. Government law did not provide for the intricacies of open-field farming. In this case, then, the volost court filled a real need. Had it not existed, the agricultural scheme of an entire village could have been disrupted by a single man. True, there was a reverse side of the coin. So long as a village could impose traditional landholding practices on its members, sound agricultural methods were not likely to develop. Even so, peasant custom did perform socially useful functions within the context of peasant life, and in 1872 it seemed to many that appropriate institutions, such as the volost courts, were needed to uphold it. Eliminating such institutions would not necessarily ease the transition to a modern legal order, as many bureaucrat-reformers assumed. Without the volost courts peasant life might have become much *less* orderly than it was.

What, then, could the commission recommend regarding the volost courts? Should the peasants be taught to understand modern law, or be freed from its burdens? Should the volost courts be compelled to operate more systematically, or allowed more leeway to adapt themselves to the peasants' way of life? Would the guarantee of legal rights by modern courts make it easier for a few money lenders, tavern keepers, and millers to exploit the peasant masses, or would it "free" these masses from oppressive backwardness? The *Trudy* offered no convincing answers. Even if the commission's methods had been scientifically sound, its information would have suggested no clear direction for government action.

It is of more than passing interest that the tsarist government never conducted this sort of investigation again. Bureaucrats from the central government did not reappear in peasant villages in their official capacities until the 1900s, and then their purpose was not to investigate peasants but to inspect their own subordinates (see ch. 4, sec. B). There may be any number of explanations for this, but one of the most important ones is the paradoxical relationship between information and reform.

Nowhere is this paradox so apparent as in the work of the ministry of justice's commission. Despite all the defects and inadequacies in the commission's work, its interviews with peasants probed more deeply into peasant society and shed more light on the peasant way of life than any previous study. One would think the ministries would have intensified their efforts to investigate peasant society directly and perhaps given correspondingly less attention to reports from local officials and gentry. In fact, the ministries did just the reverse. In ensuing decades they itensified their efforts to accumulate statements of opinion from rural administrators and left the business of making empirical village studies to scholars and radicals. The central government did not actively prevent the further investigation of peasant villages. The ministers were by no means afraid to have scholars study the peasant way of life directly and publish reports on their work. There are grounds, however, for suggesting that the government's would-be agrarian reformers simply did not see much value in gathering information directly from peasants. The most interesting feature about the information provided by the commission on volost courts is not its defects but the fact that even if it had had no defects at all, it would still have been of very little value to administrators who were engaged in imposing reform of rural society. The paradoxical relationship between information and reform may be stated as follows: a would-be reformer must seek information but he does not really want to find it. What he wants, rather, are clear answers to specific questions, answers that can be used to uphold specific policies and plans.

Statements from local administrators did provide relatively clear answers to the questions the government asked. Were the questions irrelevant and the official answers usually superficial? This was not of primary importance to the central offices. The government was not a scholarly institute seeking truth but a state organization committed to act in the name of general welfare—to act, that is, whenever it decided that general welfare was in jeopardy *whether it knew what it was doing or not.* No one would have disagreed that informed action was preferable to blind groping, but these were not the alternatives actually confronting the government in rural areas. The choice lay between blind groping and no action at all. In this situation a collection of statements from local officials had the distinct advantage of telling a minister what his agents wanted him to hear. Moreover, the local agents' statements committed them to a program and, in a sense, made them responsible for it. Most important, the statements allowed the central offices to present a facade of orderly, scientific decision making. Peasant interviews, on the other hand, contained only raw information not readily assimilable into a coherent program of action. Indeed, direct knowledge of peasant society actually disorganized the government. It created an impression of impenetrable disorder not only in the volosts but also in the government's own thinking, thereby casting doubt on all administrative efforts to cope with peasant problems. No matter what program might be proposed, its opponents could find in peasant interviews abundant evidence to demonstrate its futility and dangerous consequences. In short, the post-Liberation government did not need information so much as a unifying ideology. This is probably the main reason it did not again resort to peasant interviews (see Elenev, 1870: 20-26).

D. THE VALUEV COMMISSION

History

When Petr Valuev became minister of state domains in early 1872, he was accepting what amounted to a demotion. From 1861 until 1868 he had been MVD, a much more important post. Now, in 1872, his return to state domains (he had served there in a subordinate post during 1857-61) branded him as a man clearly past the peak of his career. State domains had never been as big or important as the MVD, and in the years after 1866, when the state peasants were "liberated" from its supervision, it fell to a nadir of insignificance. Its budget for 1867 was 44.7 million rubles; in 1868 this figure decreased abruptly to 11.8, representing a level of operation from which it would not rise until 1874, when Valuev managed to expand his ministry by bringing in two additional departments, mining and horse breeding (*Istoricheskoe,* 1888: I, pt. 1, 98-99).

Valuev was undaunted by the relatively low status of his ministry, for he knew that the tsar had big plans for him. The new minister was to use his position to open a campaign for the improvement of Russian agriculture. If Valuev could formulate such a campaign and get it in motion, he would enjoy the full support of the imperial will. Given such lofty backing, Valuev's hitherto miniscule ministry could hope to assume a leading role in domestic administration, and the minister himself would acquire leverage to uphold and further the agrarian policies he had developed as MVD, especially his beliefs concerning the peasantry.

A recent study reveals yet deeper motives. According to a Soviet scholar, V. G. Chernukha, Valuev's fundamental aim was not to improve agriculture but to induce the tsar to set up a moderately constitutional regime, embodying an elected parliament with consultative powers. As Chernukha points out, Valuev was closely associated with Petr A. Shuvalov, head of the Third Section of His Majesty's Own Imperial Chancellery and, in 1872, Alexander's right-hand man. Shuvalov's plan was to use Valuev's investigation to show that agriculture was in a bad way. He hoped the tsar would be persuaded that serious measures for agricultural advance were necessary and that their formulation would require the calling of delegates from the gentry-dominated zemstvoes to form a Russia-wide assembly. In due course the assembly would develop an agrarian reform program, the tsar would approve it, and a general atmosphere of good feeling would prevail. Under these circumstances the assembly would not be likely to disband. Properly manipulated, it would create enough momentum to transform itself into a constituent assembly, capable of drafting a constitutional reform. The tsar, full of confidence in his gentry, would accept it. As Chernukha describes Valuev's commission, then, it was primarily intended not to *bring about* agrarian reform but rather to *use* agrarian reform to enmesh the tsar in a public discussion of constitutional reform (Chernukha, 1972: 142-55; 1978: 79-92).

Chernukha's analysis is convincing up to a point. It is true that Shuvalov was striving to reorganize the gentry in order to keep them in control of things, and he believed that the best way to accomplish this was to form a parliamentary government based on a gentry-zemstvo constituency. This was also one of the ideas rattling around in Valuev's head during the 1860s and '70s. But Chernukha goes on to relate the whole story of Valuev's commission as if constitutional government were the only motive behind it (1972: 148-58), and here she is wrong. Valuev was much more a bureaucrat than a political leader. At no time in his career did he ever achieve that condition of simple-minded semiconsciousness which would allow him to follow a single purpose to the end without regard for the exigencies of administration. He never lost sight of the contradictions and complications in the government's operation and in his own thinking. In particular, he did not risk his ministry or endanger the cause of agrarian reform in 1872-73 in an attempt to hoodwink the tsar. His report did not, as Chernukha claims (1972: 158), call for massive government action to achieve peasant reform. As we shall see, it only expressed a pious hope that everyone might cooperate and somehow make reform take place over a long period of time. Shuvalov's schemes notwithstanding, Valuev's final report on his investigation warned against any drastic moves to change peasant society.[20]

Whatever his motives, Valuev did become minister of state domains in early 1872, and he received an official assignment to study the condition of Russian agriculture. Not surprisingly, he asked the tsar to set up a study commission, and on 26 May 1872 Alexander granted his minister's request (*Ocherk*, 1887: 122-23). The official name of Valuev's group was the tsar's commission for the investigation of the present state of agriculture and rural productivity in Russia *(vysochaishe utverzhdennaia komissiia dlia issledovaniia nyneshnego polozheniia selskogo khoziaistva i selskoi proizvoditelnosti v Rossii)*. There were ten members in addition to Valuev himself: five of his own subordinates from state domains, two each from the MVD and MF (ministry of finance), and one from the ministry of crown lands.[21]

[20]Chernukha (1972: 158) refers to p. 42 in the conclusions to the Valuev commission's report when she interprets its essential meaning. She should also have considered p. 40, which depicts agrarian reform as a gradual unfolding that would only take place as part of broad social progress. These conclusions appear in a separate 52-page section of the report. Hereinafter I shall cite them as *Doklad* proper, to distinguish them from the rest of the commission's materials. Concerning citations of the report *(Doklad)* as a whole, see the Glossary.

[21]The commission's full report *(Doklad)* takes up seven volumes, some of

The commission did its fieldwork during the summer of 1872. Its materials, assembled in a series of appendices to its report, included: (1) statements by rural officials and people who lived in the countryside in answer to a standard questionnaire; (2) "expert" testimony before the commission during its meetings in St. Petersburg; (3) a collection of budgets for landed estates, showing their annual income and expenses; and (4) statistical tables concerning Russian agricultural production. Nine hundred fifty-eight men were interviewed in the countryside. Among them were 45 governors, 37 gentry marshals, 283 estate owners, 51 estate stewards, 25 estate tenants,[22] 21 priests, 94 elected volost officials, 17 peasant heads of household, 8 grain merchants, and 254 "miscellaneous" interviewees (*Doklad* proper, 1873: 1-2). In addition, 181 "experts" testified before the commission in St. Petersburg at a series of about 50 meetings that began in November 1872 and ran until March 1873. These experts included professors, agronomists, grain merchants, and estate owners (pp. 2-3).

Two impressions emerge from a reading of the Valuev commission's materials: the investigators took far more interest in large estates than in villages, and they were far more interested in hearing from officials and estate holders than from peasants. Even in the questions specifically regarding peasant agriculture, only 80 out of 330 responses came from peasants (*Doklad,* 1873: I, pt. 1, 161-200). Nevertheless, the commission's final report had quite a bit to say about peasant society and administration. Despite the commission's official assignment to study agriculture, despite the investigators' failure to give more than cursory attention to the peasantry, the final report expressed unequivocal disapproval of two major aspects of peasant society that had no direct relation to agriculture. One was periodic land repartition in communal villages; the other was the tendency for large peasant families to break up into nuclear units. Moreover, the report strongly implied that the village and volost institutions established in 1861 were hopelessly inadequate (*Doklad* proper, 1873: 36-40, 49-51).

Curious, after all the academic fanfare accompanying Valuev's investigation, that the members of his commission should have agreed to slip these irrelevant, off-the-cuff remarks into their final report. One supposes that the explanation is to be found in the close resemblance between these utterances and Valuev's own notions about peasant soci-

---

which are divided into several separately paged sections. Almost all these volumes consist of appendices containing materials gathered by the commission. The members are listed on p. 1 of the *Doklad* proper.

[22] In this connection the term "tenant" refers to an investor who rented large areas and then subleased them to peasants in small lots.

ety.[23] Evidently the chairman was able to impose these notions on his commission, or perhaps he selected agreeable members to begin with. In either case Valuev was able to conduct the meetings in a high-handed manner. We have the "Journals" *(Zhurnaly)* of the last meetings, during March and April 1873, when the final report was being drawn up. Judging from their contents, Valuev was the only one present who enjoyed the privilege of digressing from the subject of agriculture. On one particularly glaring occasion a member other than Valuev tried to depart from the agenda. He ventured to suggest that peasants paid more than their share of zemstvo taxes,, i.e., the taxes collected by zemstvoes to support their own operations. As we have seen, Valuev was a supporter of the zemstvoes. He shut off the member's remarks concerning their flaws. Peasant taxation, said the minister, was of no concern to the commission (*Doklad,* 1873: *Zhurnaly,* 36). But somehow the size of peasant families was of vital concern to an investigation of agriculture. So Valuev believed, and therefore the commission reported on the subject.[24] It is not surprising, then, that the materials collected by the commission did not support the conclusions that appear in the report. Insofar as the Valuev commission produced definite conclusions regarding peasant reform, they were bogus. This is not to say they were necessarily unwise or invalid, but they did not originate in the information the commission gathered.

In the end, the commission's recommendations about peasants were very modest. As said before, Valuev believed that agricultural development could only come slowly. The government could do little more for the time being than to adopt piecemeal measures (see n. 23). Peasant custom could not be swept away overnight. Better to bring the backward masses under the influence of their relatively progressive gentry neighbors and let them become modern at their own pace (*Doklad,* 1873: *Zhurnaly,* 34-35; *Doklad* proper, 36-40, 49-51). Above all, maintain private property rights. Even the need to protect the forest cover and prevent soil deterioration was not sufficient to justify any infringement of them (*Zhurnaly,* 27). Nothing suggests radical reform here. Indeed, Valuev's conclusions precluded any general reform program. His commission produced only a very few proposals for legislation, and these were uniformly petty (*Ocherk,* 1887: 126-27).

Valuev's practical intent, it seems, was to separate agricultural reform from broader areas of social change, thereby making agricultural

[23]Valuev's own views are recorded in *Doklad* (1873: V). Notes in this volume are paged separately. Valuev's is the first.

[24]The *Zhurnaly* are not included in any of the seven volumes. They are only summaries, not verbatim records, and they cover only the meetings of the commission proper. The meetings with experts are reported in vol. VI.

improvement amenable to management by a single government agency and avoiding all the fuss involved in any administrative reorganization. To be sure, he took pains to express disapproval of communal land repartition and the breakup of peasant families, but this does not mean that he wanted to enact government programs to cope with these evils. He was outlining the direction in which he believed society should move, not undertaking to move it. Throughout his career in government Valuev believed more or less consistently that the key to peasant uplift was not some government-sponsored reform but gentry leadership. He did not mean the sort of leadership exercised by a serfowner or police captain. What he had in mind was the setting of good examples. Given proper encouragement by an enlightened ministry of state domains, Valuev hoped that gentry landowners would improve their agricultural practice and make their estates profitable. Then, with edifying models of productive citizenship before their eyes, the peasants would strive to join in the general advance. So Valuev envisioned it (Czap, 1967: 394-402). It may be said, then, that Valuev wanted not merely to separate agricultural improvement from social reform but to keep the government out of social reform entirely. Social development, he thought, would only go forward as a natural result of increased agricultural productivity. It would be disastrous to try to bring it about in any other way.

Methods

But if Valuev achieved very little in the way of reform, his commission's methods are not without interest. Like the commission on volost courts, Valuev's group went out to the countryside themselves and conducted their own interviews on the basis of a standard questionnaire. Unlike the commission on volost courts, they got virtually all their information, including their materials relating to peasant society, from nonpeasants. In St. Petersburg the commission met as a body to hear testimony from "experts," something the justice commission could not have done even had its members wanted to. In 1872 there were no experts on peasant law. The Valuev commission's manner of presenting information was also unique. Answers to the questionnaire were not simply compiled word for word in each locale, as in the justice commission's volumes. Instead, responses to each question from all gubernias were reported together in the form of topical, more or less coherent summaries, drawn up in St. Petersurg. Only the hearings with "experts" were presented verbatim.

The variety of subjects covered by the Valuev commission's materials was enormous. The members did not probe as deeply into rural society as the justice commission had, but the answers they got ranged beyond their questions and offered information that ventured outside the framework of conventional capital-city images. From a statistician's point of view, this probably did more harm than good, for breadth has a way of disturbing quantitative measure. Still, a careful reader of the Valuev materials was likely to learn a great deal about the countryside that he didn't know before. Take, for example, the reports about horse thieves. Theories about rural development and ethnographic studies of folkways never reflected much interest in the matter, but Valuev's materials show horse stealing to have been a major fact of life in rural Russia. In many gubernias the countryside concealed massive gangs capable of terrorizing all who tried to oppose them. Some were so well organized as to resemble governments in miniature. They had market outlets of their own where a peasant could go to buy back his stolen horse. Far from avoiding such groups, many villages and estate managers cooperated with them and sought their protection. It was expedient in many areas to have at least one gang member in residence in one's village or on one's estate.[25]

Another topic that interested the commission was the migrant laborer. According to a fair number of interviewees, a peasant who left his village to do agricultural labor in other areas had no reliable way to find out in advance where work was available. Many migrants traveled long distances without ever getting work. An area would have a good harvest one year and wages would be high. Report of this would spread, and the next year laborers would pour in from the most remote places, only to find that the harvest was bad and no jobs were available. According to one report, unscrupulous landholders were not above planting fake rumors of high wages on their estates in the inns along the roads, thereby attracting unwitting migrants in large enough numbers to keep wages low (*Doklad,* 1873: I, pt. 1, *dopolnenie,* 6).

Then there was the problem of holidays. Since the Liberation many villages had declared new holidays on various pretexts, usually religious. According to a statement from Smolensk gubernia, there were 77 legitimate holidays in the Russian calendar, including the 52 Sundays. The actual number celebrated by Smolensk peasants, however, was 131, many of them during the summer when field work reached its greatest intensity (pp. 24-25). Reports for other areas ranged from 85 in Novgorod up to 148 in Nizhnii Novgorod (*Doklad,* 1873: I, pt. 1, 201-4).

[25]Statements about horse thievery are scattered throughout vols. I and VI of the *Doklad;* see, e.g., VI, pt. 1, 12, 18-19, 26, 35, 42, 198. They came from such diverse areas as Simbirsk (where the Tatars were supposedly to blame), Minsk, Moscow, St. Petersburg, Vilna, Voronezh, and Samara. All but one interviewee who referred to the problem thought it was serious and getting worse. The one was A. A. Polovtsov (p. 161), who would later become head of the Imperial Chancellery. He said there was no problem with horse thieves in the vicinity of his estates in St. Petersburg gubernia, nor had there ever been.

Some villages added yet more to the usual number for their territory by participating in the celebrations of neighboring communities, and it happened with depressing frequency that a single holiday was extended into a spree lasting several days. Taking all these possibilities into account, the number of working days per year often went as low as 200. Most reports suggested that this state of affairs had come about since the end of serfdom and was getting worse. Typically, Ekaterinoslav reported an increase from 85 holidays in 1862 to 117 a decade later (pp. 213-14). A few reports, however, presented quite different views. According to interviewees in Tavrid and Chernigov gubernias, holidays had not increased in number since the Liberation (pp. 213-14).

The actual effect of holidays varied. In most places the peasants absolutely refused to work, e.g., Kaluga gubernia, where the villages punished any members who worked (p. 204). In a few gubernias peasants worked on holidays only when it seemed "necessary," e.g., Tula (p. 211). In either case local landowners suffered, for most of them depended on labor from surrounding villages. As the estate owners saw it, declaring a holiday was equivalent to welching on a contract, especially when the peasants had been paid a lump sum for a season's labor. Such collective refusal to work, with the blessing of holy custom, caused many landholders to take a jaundiced view of peasant "tradition" and even the Orthodox church itself. Certainly the abundance of holidays was one factor behind the widespread conviction among landholders and administrators that custom was nothing more than a cover for laziness, barbarism, and above all drunkenness. Interviewee-landowners frequently remarked that drunkenness had been spreading since the Liberation, mostly on holidays.[26]

Some topics were brought up and discussed in the interviews quite spontaneously, without having been suggested by the prepared questions. The malign influence of Jews, for example, was an almost universal theme in the reports from the western gubernias. It seems that the Jews ran many of the landed estates, either as stewards or as tenants. Moreover, they operated most of the taverns and monopolized the buying and selling of grain. According to all reports that mentioned Jews, they did only harm. They reaped their profits heedless of consequences, while gentry, peasantry, and soil all went to ruin (pp. 31-33, 70-72, 81-83). As substantive information such reports were of doubtful validity, to say the least, but they were informative. Apart from their value as a reflection of anti-Semitic sentiment, they indicated clearly the ineptitude and irresponsibility of the Polish gentry in the western gubernias. The

---

[26]For remarks disapproving of priestly influence, see *Doklad* (1873: I, pt. 1, 217, and *dopolnenie,* 28). On increasing drunkenness, see especially I, pt. 1, 201-24.

gentry's own references to their helplessness before Jewish "chicanery" constitute an unconscious but unequivocal admission of their inability to function in a modern economy.[27]

Speaking generally, it is not hard to detect the ex-serfowners' point of view in these reports, and it is true that Valuev himself saw the problems of Russian agriculture through gentry eyes. The commission's materials convey the impression that its members concurred with their chairman in his belief that large private holdings would be the focal point of agricultural progress in Russia. A large section (vol. VII) is devoted to operating budgets of landed estates, and the reports of interviews are filled with references to peasant failings. Taken together, they convey the impression that landed estates would indeed function well if only peasants could be made to work, preferably for low wages.[28]

Significance

The Valuev commission's materials do not support any single point of view consistently. As with the other commissions, the very disorderliness of the investigators' work provided a check of sorts on preconceptions, their own and those of their interviewees. As said above, unsolicited remarks about the baneful influence of Jews offered a revealing glimpse into the farmers' own weaknesses. To mention another example, the information in the commission's report failed to support the widespread belief that agriculture had been going downhill since the Liberation. To be sure, statements from interviewees in the countryside were full of laments about the disastrous decline in crop production since 1861. All over Russia, so most statements described it, fields were being left unplowed or, at best, farmed in careless, unproductive fashion. The most common explanation was that the peasants had been deprived of much needed guidance from the gentry. The commission tacitly accepted this view in its report to the tsar, wherein it "concluded" that agriculture had suffered profound "dislocations" in the early 1860s (*Doklad* proper, 1873: 4). But the commission's statistical tables cast serious doubt on these "firsthand" accounts. They show agricultural production and numbers of farm animals rising from 1861 on (vol. IV, tables 1 and 2). Thus, although the eclectic nature of the commission's information rendered all conclusions ambiguous, the product was nonetheless more valid and use-

[27]See especially the "expert" statement of one A. M. Bazhanov from Grodno gubernia (*Doklad,* 1873: VI, pt. 1, 220-21).

[28]In a more self-critical vein, a number of reports and experts considered landlord absenteeism to be the major obstacle to agricultural development. This, however, was only the other side of the same coin. If the landlords' vices were responsible for peasant backwardness, it still followed that gentry estates were the hope of Russian agriculture.

ful than an orderly parroting of Valuev's views would have been. In general, Valuev's group produced the same result as the justice commission: a pile of rich and suggestive materials, useful to scholars but not very helpful to administrators trying to devise programs.[29]

E. ELIMINATING THE SOUL TAX

Taken together, the above descriptions of government investigations suggest that reliable information about rural problems in Russia did not furnish a basis for remedial action but only made clear the administration's inability to impose any solution to them. This generalization is borne out by the experience of yet another investigation of the early 1870s, this one conducted jointly by the MF and MVD. The purpose was to find out what local administrators and zemstvoes thought of an MF project to eliminate the soul tax and replace it with a tax on dwellings and landed property. Actually, the ministries were conducting an inquiry rather than an investigation. The central offices had already decided what to do, and they were asking for opinion rather than seeking information. Nevertheless, the study of the soul tax commission is of interest to us because local institutions had to answer relatively specific questions relating to a single issue.[30]

The project was drafted in an atmosphere of apparent interministerial harmony and then sent out to the governors in the summer of 1871, together with a list of questions about it. The governors were ordered to present project and questions to the gubernia zemstvo assemblies for their consideration. The assemblies were to write down their considerations and send them to the gubernia "boards for peasant affairs" (see Glossary) for study and comment.

During the following months zemstvoes and boards duly produced their considerations and comments, and the governors compiled them and sent them off to St. Petersburg along with their own conclusions. Surely this was as orderly a process of policy formulation as any admin-

---

[29]It is of interest that Iu. E. Ianson got much of the data for his pioneering statistical study of peasant society from the Valuev commission's materials (1881: xiv). Ianson was Russia's first serious student of agricultural statistics. His book, first published in 1877, relied heavily on figures compiled by zemstvoes, and he complained of the general inadequacy of the central government's figures. His favorable remarks about the Valuev commission's materials may be interpreted to mean that they were, after all, the best information the government had in the 1870s.

[30]The soul tax was a direct tax, levied (in theory) on each village in proportion to the number of male inhabitants. It increased sharply in amount during the 1860-70s before it was finally abolished in the 1880s. (Gindin, 1960: 33-35).

istrator could wish. Reports from several sources in each gubernia would serve as a check on each one, thereby forcing the governors to do more than repeat what their superiors wanted. At the same time the specific nature of the subject matter would assure that the assembled answers and proposals would not be too diverse to be usable. Best of all, the central offices, having already agreed unanimously to the project, would be unlikely to use the inquiry's results as a basis for mutual squabbles.

But even this very orderly process failed to produce any reform. Here again the government received useful information. Materials from the gubernias contained descriptions of the peasant economy and the impact of taxation on it. The relatively clear message the reports conveyed, however, was that the government could not improve its tax system without introducing fundamental changes in rural administration and society.

To be sure, there was no lack of proposals scattered through the various reports, but they were all general. None of them offered any practical suggestions as to how this or that type of tax might actually be collected. Take, for example, the idea of an income tax. Many zemstvoes and local officials favored the introduction of a tax levied on all inhabitants in proportion to their income without regard for social status (*Svod,* 1873-74: I, 13-14, 86, 278-88, 324-25). However, only two gubernia reports so much as mentioned problems of implementation. One of them, from St. Petersburg gubernia, referred cursorily to the possibility that people might conceal their incomes (pp. 324-25). The other, from Nizhnii Novgorod, was unique in that it not only expressed a desire for an income tax but also discussed the difficulties involved in its collection. The gubernia board for peasant affairs attempted to draw up practical measures, but in the end the members concluded reluctantly that they could not discover any (pp. 13-14). After studying the board's deliberations, the governor opined that in the absence of reliable records of income in the villages, an income tax would only bring "constant interference, futile investigations, great inequities, and perhaps abuses" (p. 14). This was *all* the reports had to say about the implementation of an income tax. None of the other proposals said anything whatever, only that they liked the idea of an income tax. A careful reader must have found such statements meaningless. So it was with all the positive proposals from the gubernias, which must have been all the more discouraging, since they were accompanied by convincing descriptions of the weaknesses in the government's project for a tax on dwellings and land.[31]

---

[31] B. Veselovskii's explanation of zemstvo enthusiasm for the income tax in the 1870s is of interest (1909-11: I, 154-55). He says it represented above all a desire on the part rural gentry to shift the tax burden from farmers to urban businessmen.

The zemstvo assemblies were generally agreed that the peasants' tax burden was far too heavy. They also agreed that the essence of the problem lay not in the total amount of the tax paid by the peasantry but in the way the burden was apportioned among individual families. Somehow the government was going to have to change the basis on which each village taxed its members. But, said most zemstvoes, the government never had regulated the apportionment of its direct taxes on the villages. It had ordered the soul tax to be paid according to the number of males, but this prescription had never had much bearing on actual collections. Each village and volost apportioned its collective tax burden according to its own peculiar procedures. A formal change in the government's tax base, therefore, would not be likely to produce any real effect. Actual redistribution of the tax burden required that the government intervene in peasant society itself, limiting or destroying the power of the village administrations and replacing them with either government officials or all-class local institutions. This, said most zemstvoes, was why the MF's project would not have any practical effect by itself. If the government wanted to improve its revenue system, it would have to embark on a broad program of social and administrative reform (*Svod,* 1873-74: I, 3-14). In particular, the government would have to relieve the villages of collective responsibility for the personal taxes and private obligations of their members. So long as the villages had to make good their members' financial obligations, the processes of taxation would have to be left entirely in the villagers' hands; not only the processes of taxation but all aspects of political and economic life would escape government control (pp. 13, 209-11).[32]

Many reports merely recommended the elimination of collective responsibility and left it at that. The Moscow assembly, for example, submitted a resounding denunciation but did not take up the subject of implementation at all, which led the governor to remark that their proposal had no practical value. Until the government had some alternative basis for assessing and collecting taxes and debts, collective responsibility could not be dispensed with (*Svod,* 1873-74: I, 100-115). This was the consideration that led the Voronezh board for peasant affairs to assert that eliminating collective responsibility would demand a yet deeper reform: the abolition of common land ownership in the village (p. 21). But even this was not enough. Most reports said that any peasant tax reform would do more harm than good, because a reform affecting only peasants would perpetuate their isolation from the rest of society. What was needed was a general tax reform that would subject all classes to the same revenue system (pp. 88-89, 94-95), and according to many reports

---

[32]Concerning the effects of collective responsibility on peasant society, see Yaney (1973: 137-43, 233-34) and Aleksandrov (1976: 142-88, 298-316).

any general reform of this sort would demand all-class governing institutions. The peasant volost would have to give way to a territorial institution involving all inhabitants whether they belonged to villages or not (pp. 38, 76). It seems, then, that in order to abolish the soul tax in 1872, it would have been necessary to destroy the peasant village as an institution and, in effect, subordinate the peasants to gentry-dominated zemstvoes. Indeed, many reports recommended that uezd zemstvo assemblies assume direct responsibility for apportioning taxes in the villages (e.g., p. 38).

The government could not accept these counterproposals. It could not very well re-establish the power of ex-serfowners over peasant villages with the Liberation not yet completed, especially in view of the hostility between peasants and gentry that resounded through the materials the Valuev commission collected. It appeared that the government would have to carry out its own reform. How? The reports on soul tax reform—and many responses to the other investigations of the early 1870s—suggested that it was no use trying to change one segment of peasant life at a time. The only remaining possibility, then, was for the government's own organization to carry out sweeping changes in peasant institutions, setting aside in one grand act the peasants' law, their agricultural practices, their economic arrangements, and their political system. Who did the government have available to carry out all these measures? In 1872 it had only the arbitrators, and most reports agreed they were useless (pp. 177, 182-83). The government had recently rejected an MVD proposal to extend the arbitrators' responsibilities, and in 1872 it was on the verge of deciding to abolish them entirely (see ch. 3, sec. C).

It is not surprising that a few reports from the gubernias reluctantly acknowledged the necessity for collective responsibility (e.g., pp. 205-6). The central government agreed, and it had also to agree that it could not tell villages how to apportion taxes. In the case of tax reform, as with all other proposed reforms in the early 1870s, the government had to do either everything or nothing. It felt compelled, therefore, to do nothing.

F. CONCLUSIONS

Alexander II's investigations of rural Russia in the early 1870s suggest a number of conclusions. The *komissiia* on uezd and gubernia institutions found that official reports from gubernia-level administrators often (but not always) reflected the sentiments of ministerial superiors rather than observations of reality. The justice commission on volost courts and the Valuev commission on agriculture amassed useful information, but this produced only the discouraging realization that the government was unable either to formulate or to direct reforms in rural

Russia. Any student of Russian history knows that there was an ample supply of ideas for agrarian reform kicking around St. Petersburg in the 1870s and thereafter. Russia did not lack would-be leaders, within the administration and outside of it, who were sure they had solutions to all rural difficulties. As far as I know, however, no one in that day could conceive of a reform program on the basis of systematic observation. No such reform could be formulated because observation only suggested the impossibility of reform. By 1874 the government had learned that it was unable to act in rural Russia, and this was the key reason for eliminating the arbitrators in that year. Instead of acting upon rural society, the government withdrew from it.

It would be possible to go on from here to show how information from the countryside increased in quantity and improved in quality after the 1870s. This, however, would be beside the point. The basic problem of communication between government and peasantry was not a lack of information but the fact that capital-city society was undertaking to destroy peasant society without acknowledging that destruction was its aim. The basic purpose of communication with the peasants was never to inform them or find out about them but somehow to keep in touch with them while pulling them out of their mysterious village worlds and rendering them intelligible to "modern" men. The government began to work more actively along this line after about 1880, and it is the resultant interaction, not merely the flow of information, that will be the focus of our attention in succeeding chapters. As we shall see, it was more or less in the nature of things that when and if the government did act, it would have to initiate its action on the basis of fantasy, which is why the ministries would need unity of belief among their servitors more than valid information.

CHAPTER 3

The Beginnings of Action, Part One: Enactment of the Statute on Land Captains

> The only excuse I can offer, if accused of dull and unattractive characters, is that it's never possible to see a thing in its entirety at the start.
>
> Nikolai Gogol (1961:271)

A. INTRODUCTION

The government's first post-Liberation effort at active agrarian reform came in the 1880s, with the statute on land captains, which was enacted in 1889. The statute set up a new rural official, the land captain (*zemskii nachalnik*), and it gave him two outstanding features: he was to govern his territory in explicitly formal independence from all other government agents except the governors; and he was expressly endowed with broad executive, judicial, and even legislative powers over the peasants and craftsmen who resided in or were legally attached to the volosts under his jurisdiction. He was, in brief, a tsar in miniature.[1]

[1]The "statute" on land captains actually comprised several documents, only one of which is formally entitled the *Polozhenie* [statute] *o zemskikh uchastkovykh nachalnikakh*. This *Polozhenie* was enacted on 12 July 1889 along with the following: (1) an introductory decree, (2) a set of rules on the structure of the judiciary in areas where the land captains would be operating, (3) another set of rules regarding the volost courts in these areas, and (4) yet another set of rules governing the introduction of the *Polozhenie*. The introductory decree is in *TPSZ*, 6195; the rest of the above, including the *Polozhenie*, are all together in *TPSZ*, 6196, though the clauses in each one are numbered separately. These enactments of 12 July are only about half the legislation customarily referred to as the statute on land captains. On 29 Dec. 1889 another decree (*TPSZ*, 6482) came out, followed by a voluminous set of rules (*TPSZ*, 6483) regulating the conduct of judicial affairs under land captains and urban courts respectively. As used here, the term "statute on land captains" includes all the above legislation taken together.

The statute called forth a large-scale enterprise. During the six years following its enactment about 2,000 of the new officials began operating in 36 gubernias of European Russia and in a few uezds of a 37th. The first ones took up their posts on 1 February 1890 in six gubernias, all in central Russia: Vladimir, Kaluga, Kostroma, Moscow, Riazan, and Chernigov. The next lot began operating on 1 September 1890 in ten gubernias, more widely dispersed than the first six: Ekaterinoslav, Kursk, Nizhnii Novgorod, Poltava, Pskov, Novgorod, Simbirsk, Smolensk, Tula, and Kharkov. It bears mentioning that these 16 gubernias were the only ones to get their captains prior to the onset of the great famine of 1891. The next lot of 12 gubernias—Vologda (five uezds), Voronezh, Viatka, Kazan, Orel, Penza, Samara, Saratov, St. Petersburg, Tambov, Tver, Iaroslavl—got their captains on 1 July 1891, too late for the new officials to warn the government but in time to help with relief measures. Bessarabia, Tavrid, and Kherson got theirs much later, on 1 September 1892; Perm received hers on 1 September 1893; and on 1 October 1894 land captains took up their duties in Astrakhan, Olonets, Orenburg, Ufa, and Stavropol (*Sbornik,* 1901: I, 399-400). Stavropol was not on the original list; it was added by the law of 6 June 1894 (I, 3, 400).

In the following decade the number of captains and the territory they covered continued to expand, though somewhat more gradually. In 1899 they were set up in five additional uezds of Vologda gubernia (p. 3); in 1901 they entered the Belorussian gubernias (Vitebsk, Mogilev, and Minsk), and in 1903 they were extended to Vilna, Grodno, and Kovno (*TPSZ,* 18854, 19530, 23106). In 1904, 95 new *uchastki*—subdivisions of the uezd over which the land captains ruled—were established in the gubernias where the statute was already in force (*IZO,* 1904: 6-7). By 1908, then, about 2,500 land captains covered 42 gubernias and most of a 43d (*Kratkii,* 1908: 22). Each one received an annual salary of 1,000 rubles and an additional allowance of 1,200 to cover living and office expenses (*TPSZ,* 6196, *Prilozheniia,* 249).

Besides the captains themselves, a number of land captain-like officials came into being in the late nineteenth century. In 1898 "peasant captains" (*krestianskie nachalniki*) were established in several Siberian gubernias on much the same basis as the land captains (*TPSZ,* 15503; Volkov, 1910: 1211-42). In 1901-2 they were extended to almost all of western and central Siberia, so that in 1908, 89 of them were spread out over eight provinces (*TPSZ,* 19990, 21505, 21640; *Kratkii,* 1908: 22). In addition to the land captains and peasant captains, 14 peasant commissioners (*osobye chinovniki po krestianskim delam*) were working in Archangel gubernia in 1908 (Volkov, 1910: 1209-10). Kiev, Volyniia, and Podoliia gubernias still had the "peaceful arbitrators" that had been established in 1861 (see below, sec. C). Transcaucasia had acquired arbitrators of the same sort with a few local modifications. Some *stanovye pristavy* (see below, sec. C) in northeastern Siberia were charged with most of the tasks and responsibilities of land captains; 80 peasant supervisors (*komissary po krestianskim delam*) were working in Congress Poland, and 35 in the Baltic gubernias (*TPSZ*, 6188). Some of these latter officials predated the land captains, and in any case the resemblance between them and the captains was remote. There was, however, a family relationship among all the above-named officials. They were all agents of the MVD, and the MVD held them responsible for the proper operation of peasant institutions in their territories (*Kratkii*, 1908: 22; "Krestianskoe pravo," 328-29). These rural guardians represented the MVD's belief that the central government had somehow to protect peasant institutions from the rest of society and to guide them through the travails and pitfalls of modernization.

The purpose of this chapter is to discuss the process by which the ministry decided to use agencies of this sort to bring agrarian reform to Russia. Two questions are at issue: what did the MVD seek to accomplish, and why did it decide to use this method to accomplish it?

B. THE NATURE OF GOVERNMENT ACTION

Alexander III's Approach to Agrarian Reform

The tsarist government's information gathering during the 1870s had resembled in some respects the struggles of a motorist who finds that water will not run his car and then undertakes to correct this deficiency by purifying the water. Information was the water, and the ministries, like the motorist, clung to the belief that it would turn into fuel for the engines of reform if only it could be blended properly. Had the government held rigidly to this belief, it might never have moved at all, but in fact it did move. In the 1880s it began to carry out some of the peasant reforms it had discussed in the 1870s. Peasants who had not yet taken possession of their allotment land under the terms of the Liberation were permitted (or compelled) to do so, and a bank was established to lend money to peasants who wished to buy additional land. The salt and soul taxes were abolished, and the government issued a few statutes designed to discourage peasant families from dividing into small units and to prevent farm laborers from welching on their work assignments.

Admittedly, these modest measures were less than breathtaking, but they betokened a growing determination in the capital cities to move into the countryside come what may. After 1880 or so the ministers no longer asked whether the peasants should be subjected to reform, only how the job should be done.

It took almost all of the 1880s for the government to decide on an approach to agrarian reform, and in the end the central offices were unable to make the decision. They proposed a number of projects, but, as in the previous decade, their best efforts were devoted to blocking each other rather than gathering support for positive action. At last, Alexander III had to intervene personally to make his government move, though he did not know any better than his officials where he was heading. The project he adopted, the statute on land captains, was based largely on fantasy.

Alexander III's fantasy of rural reform differed significantly from that which had motivated his father in the 1850s. The tsar-liberator had dreamed primarily of paper. Loyal citizens and conscientious administrators would join together to write out a perfect reform program, one based on the best available data and comprehending all projects in one unified system. Once this system was properly drawn up and printed on paper, it would allow rural society to throw off the bonds of tradition and move forward into prosperous modernity. A single golden document would give just recognition to all legitimate points of view, make clear each citizen's rights and duties, and tell each government official exactly what he should and should not do. Properly instructed about this prodigy of print, a grateful people would accept its authority with joyous confidence. All Russia would toil together in budgeted harmony toward prosperity and national power.

Alexander III rejected this image. Instead of a paper structure uniting central offices with local institutions, he envisioned virtuous knight-servitors, each of whom would ride out alone to rule over the peasants in his district as a patriarchal chieftain. Most of these chieftains would be of the gentry class, but they would stand high above gentry interests. They would serve the government, but they would not be subject to commands from bureaucratic offices and courts. Each of them would govern as he himself thought best, and the captains in each gubernia would be personally responsible to the governor alone for the effectiveness of their work. Personal links between superiors and subordinates would tie government and peasantry together much more effectively than paper. Such was Alexander III's basic idea of agrarian reform.

The key authors of the statute on land captains were Dmitrii A. Tolstoi and A. D. Pazukhin. The former was MVD from 1882 until his death in April 1889; the latter was head of the MVD chancellery from 1885 until 1891, when he too died in office. For both men it was an article of faith that the government had failed to cope with peasant society since the Liberation. The reason: bureaucracy was rendering the government unable to influence the villages. Institutions and agencies of government "worked on the basis of statutory law," said a note of February 1887, signed by Tolstoi but probably authored by Pazukhin; *therefore,* these institutions and agencies "could not directly influence peasant affairs." How did statutory law prevent the government from interacting with peasants?

> The attitudes of the majority of local institutions and officials toward their duties are extremely formalistic. They fear more than anything else that they will transgress the limits of their official functions. They almost always prefer to avoid taking part in any matter that could possibly be construed to fall within the province of another agency and in the execution of which they might be subject to accusations, however preposterous, of exceeding their authority. Under the circumstances it often happens that a peasant or even a landowner...is shuttled from one official to another and receives no satisfaction. (TsGIAL, f. 1149, 1889g., op. vol. XI, d. 44, ll. 10-11)

The reader will observe that the Tolstoi-Pazukhin note did not complain of inadequacies in the statutes or corruption and ineptness among the government's servitors. It did not recommend measures to repair laws or discipline officials. It was the very nature of bureaucracy and statutory law they were after. Bureaucratic organization created obstacles to proper government in rural Russia by working well, not by failing to work, and therefore the problem was not to correct it but to free the government's agents from its baneful influence.

It will not do to conclude that Tolstoi's note expressed an atavistic romanticism of the sort often attributed to his contemporary, Dostoievskii. Tolstoi and Pazukhin were speaking not about the philosophy of law in general but about the situation in the Russian countryside in particular. The authors of the statute on land captains had no fundamental, ideological objection to modern administration. The only point they were trying to make in their note of February 1887 was that modern administrative methods were not appropriate at that time for governing peasant villages in Russia.

Pazukhin had expounded this view at some length in the fall of 1886, during the meetings of an MVD committee set up to study an early draft of the statute on land captains. He had persuaded most of the committee that administrators and judges in rural Russia did not maintain their formalistic indifference to the peasantry merely out of laziness. They could not take an active interest in the peasants even if they wished, he said, because there were no commonly accepted laws governing peasant society. During the previous 25 years Senate decisions on appeals from peasant courts had been inconsistent because they had been based on what the Senate took to be custom in the particular village where the case originated. Each decision was designed to fit its own case; consequently the accumulating decisions were not giving rise to consistent rules of law that might guide administrators and protect peasant rights. Legal system was not evolving in rural Russia, nor was it likely to evolve if the government continued simply to stand by and wait for peasants and law courts to produce it by themselves. A new kind of official would be needed in the countryside, one who would be able to govern effectively in the absence of law, whose responsibility to both peasants and tsar would not be limited by either bureaucratic regulations or peasant customs. According to the MVD committee, the new official would need not only executive and judicial powers but legislative as well. Such a man, Pazukhin hoped, would neither stifle the villages with official rigamarole nor allow the persistently nonsystematic villages to disrupt the government's organization (TsGIAL, f. 1282, op. 2, d. 1838, ll. 414-16, 429-31, 456-58).

To put the case another way—as one of the first land captains did— rural administrators who insisted on working within a systematic framework threatened to undermine the peasants' faith in law. Most peasants were not familiar with the government's statutes (*zakony*), but, left to themselves, they cherished the belief that these statutes were "just"; which is to say, they corresponded exactly to peasant ideas of justice (*pravo*). So strong was this conviction, said our captain, that when a government official decided a case in a way contrary to what local peasants considered just, the peasants were likely to come away with the impression that the official had violated the government's statutes. As a result, peasants often opposed a formally legal action in the name of their convictions regarding legality. They denounced *zakon* in the name of *zakon*. Given this puzzling state of affairs, a serious effort on the government's part to impose *zakon* on villges systematically would compel the villagers to recognize that formal *zakon* and their own *pravo* were at odds. The result would be not the victory of one over the other but the simultaneous destruction of both (Beer, 1894-95: II, x). Was it not, therefore, a wise idea to begin the campaign for legal system in the villages by establishing an official empowered to set the government's *zakon* aside now and then, whenever he sensed that it was threatening to undermine the peasants' belief that *zakon* was indeed right? Pazukhin and Tolstoi thought so, and Tsar Alexander III agreed with them.[2]

Line-over-Staff Organization

To comprehend Alexander III's approach to rural administration in somewhat more familiar terms, it will be useful to resort to a model. I call it line-over-staff organization. A model, of course, does not describe any actual administration. Like Max Weber's "ideal" bureaucracy, the

---

[2]The above considerations about peasant attitudes toward law and administration are analogous to Daniel Field's analysis of peasant attitudes toward the tsar (1976: especially 208-14).

concept of line-over-staff organization is only an abstraction, one aspect of reality extrapolated from others in order to give an added dimension to description.

Perhaps the best way to visualize line-over-staff organization is to contrast it with Weber's ideal. Weber's bureaucracy is an organization in which regulations and schedules confine all officials to their own proper functions. A line officer—i.e., an official who directs actual operations— is obliged to follow these regulations and schedules, and therefore the scope of his "power" is very narrow. The members of his own staff take most of their orders from staff officers on higher echelons, and these orders are binding on all line officers regardless of echelon. In effect, line officers do their work under overall staff direction. Indeed, insofar as they compel each other to stick to their own respective functions, they themselves perform essentially staff functions. A minister of rail transport, for example, is a line officer within his own organization because he directs the operations of railroads. In the eyes of the other ministers, however, he is a member of the staff, because he imposes his regulations upon them whenever they need his equipment. In my terms, then, Weber's ideal bureaucracy is a staff-over-line organization.

The contrast between Weber's model and a line-over-staff organization is nowhere more sharply drawn than in military organization. Ordinarily, when it is not engaged in combat, a modern army strives to organize itself according to Weber's model. Its regulations bristle with provisions for the sanctity of line-officer authority, but since the days of Louis XIV, staffs have had things pretty much their own way. Line officers spend virtually all their time implementing directives that originate with staffs.

Once in a while, however, an army must fight, and when it does, the staff-over-line quality tends to disappear. Army units in the midst of battle confront a situation wherein the necessity for immediate action predominates over all other considerations. Reliable information is often unavailable; commands from one's superior may be impossible to carry out or entirely lacking. On all echelons, men become conscious that they must do something, but they do not know what to do. At such times line officers are likely to seize the initiative and to begin directing staffs solely on the basis of immediate, ad hoc considerations. One unit may seize supplies that have been set aside for another; a lower-echelon commander may disregard his superior's operational plans and develop his own tactics as he goes along; superior officers may subject their subordinates to punishments that are entirely illegal. It can happen that a small unit commander—or even a private soldier who momentarily seizes command—may find himself in a position to direct the staff machinery of an entire army (see Marshall, 1947: 48-49, 61-63, 68-70, 88-99, 116-17, 131-32).

No modern military organization makes explicit provision for line-over-staff operation. Theoretically, the "chain of command" continues to operate throughout the hottest battle. In practice, however, line officers in combat are generally held responsible for winning or losing, and nothing else matters. If their gambits work, anything they have done, however illegal or contrary to orders, is likely to be considered acceptable and even praiseworthy. But they may suffer defeat, in which case anything they have done—however legal, proper, or well intended—may be criticized or denounced. The fact is that no staff, however elaborate, can direct combat. At best, it can only make preparations that it hopes will prove to be adequate when combat begins. A modern army in the midst of battle may come very close to being a line-over-staff organization.[3]

Ideal bureaucracy and line-over-staff organization do not negate each other except as theoretical formulations. In practice, they are complementary, for line-over-staff organization is unthinkable apart from an extant administration that affects to be staff-over-line. Staff and line oppose each other primarily in order to identify their respective roles, not because they serve contrary purposes.

Generally speaking, the disadvantages of line-over-staff organization are more formidable than the advantages. If it allows a unit commander to respond rapidly to a changing and unpredictable situation, it also deprives commanders on higher echelons of systematic control over their subordinates' activities. Lacking effective coordination from the center, unit commanders will sooner or later run into one another and quickly become entangled in meaningless, destructive disputes. This is bad enough in a simple, nonspecialized organization where all units are doing the same thing. In a modern army, where artillery, transport, infantry, communications, and engineering units must coordinate precisely and continuously in order not to destroy each other, line-over-staff organization in pure form is virtually an impossibility. Obviously it is not an arrangement to which a modern military commander resorts out of conscious preference. A competent officer is driven to it only when he himself does not know what is happening or what to do, when he is compelled, that is, to allow his subordinates' judgment to govern his own.

[3]Professional studies of military organization cannot acknowledge this fact of life except as an evil to be opposed or a flaw to be corrected. Hence they tell us little about the workings of line-over-staff organization. Even so, one may find an occasional insight in their pages. Alvin Brown, for example, has stumbled upon the principle that staff should never be involved in implementing the plans it makes (1953: 119-27, 173-74). Brown would not admit under torture that he is recognizing the need for line-over-staff organization, but his principle brings him closer than most of his kind.

Military combat is not by any means the only area wherein line-over-staff operation comes into play. Any organization, military or civil, may arrive at a point where staff becomes incapable of formulating and issuing commands or line officers feel compelled by their circumstances to ignore staff commands. In a word, any organization may experience uncertainty. When this happens, line-over-staff operation may become appropriate and even necessary. In his work on German economic administration during World War II, A. S. Milward suggests that a heavily line-over-staff approach to management—which he calls the "blitzkrieg strategy"—was employed with some success in the mobilization of Germany's economy up until 1941. Admittedly, says Milward, the blitzkrieg strategy was not effective for long-run development, but Germany's experience showed that it can have significant advantages over long-range planning under certain circumstances (1965: 7-14). In a similar vein, a recent study of Germany's war organization during World War I shows how the breakdown of Walter Rathenau's planned economy in 1916 led German military and industrial leaders to adopt General Ludendorff's essentially blitzkrieg methods (Feldman, 1966: 149-65). Ludendorff's approach proved to have serious drawbacks (pp. 253-66), but its employment resolved some serious problems and may well have been the best path the government could have taken. Rathenau himself approved of the change, though he was basically a believer in planned (staff-over-line) organization (pp. 164-65, 266; also Rathenau, 1967: 210-12). Perhaps it is not so unusual, then, that many would-be agrarian reformers in Russia have considered line-over-staff organization appropriate.

C. THE LESSONS OF EXPERIENCE: PEASANT
ADMINISTRATORS PRIOR TO 1880

Alexander III's fantastic notion of a countryside governed by solitary patriarchs was already assuming embryonic form in the offices of the MVD before he came to the throne. Long before the Liberation it was becoming apparent that the introduction of a modern legal system in the villages would require more than the simple printing of statutes. In 1859 a member of the *komissiia* on uezd and gubernia institutions made the following observations:

> Virtually the only means for publishing laws and administrative directives to the people...is the reading of manifestoes and decrees in churches and public squares.... But public reading not only fails to accomplish its purpose...it is positively harmful. Manifestoes and decrees are read unintelligibly by deacons or police officials; most of the people cannot hear; barely five percent are present; and,

finally, even the most attentive and informed listeners are seldom
able to get a true understanding of the substance of a decree or
manifesto from a single reading....Priests and police officials not
only do not care about the correct meaning of the law but,
unfortunately, are sometimes prepared to confuse the people intentionally in hopes of serving their own interest. (*Raboty,* 1859: I,
73-75)

The author of the above lines did not go so far as to recommend line-
over-staff organization in the countryside, but his description conveys the
clear implication that rural administrators would have to grapple with a
profound, perennial uncertainty. By 1880 administrators in the MVD's
central offices had advanced somewhat further. "During the last twenty-
five years," said an official history of the ministry published in that year,
"the ministry of internal affairs has been under constant strain" (*Kratkii,*
1880: 1). The new social-legal order established by Alexander II's legislation had heightened tensions within society and given rise to antigovernment sentiment. Disputes were increasing in frequency and intensity (pp.
2-3), and the press's new habit of publicizing famines was causing people
to lose confidence in the government (pp. 3-4). During the past few years
the government had been attempting to cope with these new, disturbing
problems, and, as a result, the MVD "has been transformed little by little
from a general caretaker of society into an active leader." The ministry
stood ready to play its new role. It had amassed "exact information" and
this gave it "firm ground for leadership" (p. 8). Judging from its own
account, then, the MVD had not yet decided in 1880 what it was to do,
but it certainly felt called upon to do something about the mess in rural
Russia. We might inquire into the antecedents of this compulsion. Why
did the MVD feel in 1880 that there was a mess, and why did it feel
obliged to cope with it?[4]

The *Stanovoi Pristav* (Police Captain)

The *stanovye* were the MVD's first salaried officials in rural Russia.
Nicholas I set them up in 1837, and in the 50-odd years from their
establishment until the coming of the land captains, they were virtually
the only ranking agents the central government had below the uezd level.
Originally the *stanovoi* had been conceived in terms that conveyed a
vaguely line-over-staff sense. He had been, said the MVD's self-history of
1880, "an investigator, judge, and protector of local interests all at
once" (*Kratkii,* 1880: 73). During the 1860s, however, his powers suffered

---

[4]Apparently the MVD was not as ready to act as its history claimed. Two
decades later the ministry would explicitly acknowledge that its organization had
not been at all prepared to govern peasants in 1880 (*Trudy,* 1903-4: I, 4-6).

severe curtailment, and by 1880 he had become something of a disappointment to the central offices. Whatever the MVD decided to accomplish in the countryside, mere *stanovye* could not do the job.

The police captain's inadequacies notwithstanding, he was a part of that foundation in practical experience on which Tolstoi and Pazukhin erected their concept of the land captains. The *stanovye* had failed to handle the peasants, but in the 1880s their experience suggested, if nothing else, a fairly clear idea of what the land captain should *not* be. Thus, if we are to understand why the government introduced the land captains and continued to uphold them, we should begin with its first would-be peasant protectors. If Alexander III's fantasies about rural reform had any connection with the MVD's experience, the history of the land captains began with the *stanovye*.

In the year 1837 the government had not yet made up its mind whether serf estates were obstacles to peasant reform or agencies of it. For those who viewed them as obstacles, the *stanovoi* represented an extension of central government power into a backward countryside: the first substantial check on the political power of privileged serfowners. In short, he was potentially an agency of reform. Admittedly, the letter of the law described him as essentially a conservative institution, designed to regulate an existing order rather than to change it. The law of 3 June 1837 (*VPSZ,* 10305) expressed the hope that property-holding gentry would serve as *stanovye* in the vicinity of their own estates, and this, presumably, would assure the local populace, especially the estate holders, of an officialdom devoted to their welfare. The local gentry assemblies were even allowed to nominate candidates. Even so, the very presence of the *stanovoi* in the hinterland outside the uezd centers, whither no sort of bureaucrat had ever ventured, constituted a serious threat to the autonomy of serf estates. The new policeman operated in the *stan,* a territorial subdivision that extended, in 1860, over roughly a third of an uezd (*Trudy,* 1860: bk. 2, 54): still rather far from intimate contact with peasants but much closer to them than any government agent had ever been before on a regular basis. On balance, the *stanovoi* boded no good for serfowners.

No statutory provision explicitly granted absolute authority to the *stanovoi*. His power, such as it was, rested on his duty to enforce a mass of regulations that the peasants neither knew nor obeyed. Since Catherine II's reign the government had been interjecting legal rules into the countryside at will, and although these rules were almost never published in the villages, let alone enforced, their existence made all the peasants outlaws. Any administrator had abundant pretexts for arresting and penalizing anyone he wished, and thus the very presence of a *stanovoi,* however idle and ineffectual he might be, tremendously expanded opportunities for arbitrary action. This is not to say that the new policeman's authority was absolute. No single official could hold absolute authority in the Russian countryside, because there were always others who were just as capable of throwing dead-letter regulations around. But the *stanovoi* had a distinct advantage over other officials in that he was physically much closer to the peasants than they were. With the coming of the *stanovoi,* serfowners and their stewards had for the first time to cope with an emanation from the central government somewhat more substantial than paper commands. They had to rub elbows with an actual power locus. This, at least, was what the legislation of June 1837 implied.[5]

In the end, the police captain did not prove to be a benevolent protector. To the extent that he involved himself in peasant life, he had to resolve whatever disputes the peasants brought before him, and the very best he could do in the absence of consistent legal rules was to extend the government's "benevolence" to some peasants—that is, decide in their favor—while "oppressing" others. Ordinarily the recipients of benevolence thought themselves deserving and therefore were not grateful to the *stanovoi,* whereas the oppressed—those who lost their cases— usually resented his "arbitrary interference." Not surprisingly, real-life police captains generally showed little inclination to involve themselves in peasant life.

The MVD was disappointed. In the late 1850s the ministry's central offices investigated the *stanovye.* Their report, which came out in 1860, pronounced the authority of the *stanovoi* "a source of abuses and disorders." Even if a particular *stanovoi* were virtuous, said the report, he had "neither the time nor the inclination" to look after the local population. At best, he sought only "to satisfy the demands of higher authority or the formal requirements of the law." As for *stanovye* who were not so virtuous, the absence of effective regulations "opened a wide area for them to satisfy their personal desires" (*Trudy,* 1860: bk. 2, 47-54). According to the MVD, then, the *stanovye* brought very little benefit to the peasants. Worse, they were not much good to the ministry's central offices. Apparently they could not even perform the routine functions of rural administration. "As a result of his extremely broad and indefinite responsibilities," said the report of 1860, the *stanovoi* "has

---

[5]Engelgardt gives an excellent description of the state of affairs created in the villages by dead-letter laws (1937: 315-43). Writing in the late 1870s, he cited many archaic regulations, such as those requiring peasants to change their shirts twice a week and plant birch trees in the village streets. He noted with dismay that although recent laws on health and sanitation were more intelligently conceived, they had the same effect in actuality as the old paternalistic laws. Thus he actually dreaded the time when the government would begin issuing laws regarding proper agricultural practice, although he himself devoted his life to improving peasant agriculture.

operated too arbitrarily, and at the same time he has been unable to perform his proper duties" (pp. 50-51).[6]

But perhaps the MVD's investigators were too harsh. By their standards, an effective *stanovoi* would have had to be a superman. Once he set up housekeeping in his *stan*, he had not only regulations to enforce but also orders to carry out. His office was the only government agency out there, so all commands for rural Russia went out to him, and all reports back to the capital city had to come from him. Every program, every policy, every capital-city fantasy about rural reform ended up (or threatened to end up) in what passed for his office. Very quickly, therefore, the *stanovoi* was loaded down with duties, which meant in practice that he had to do an inordinate amount of paperwork in order to give the impression that he was performing these duties. He had no time to formulate a coherent structure for rural administration or exert a wholesome influence on rural society, even if he had been so disposed.

By 1860 the *stanovoi* had gone through a cycle of sorts. He had started off as an honorable aristocrat on a general mission to the peasantry, but he had turned out to be a clerk. The government began by ostensibly relying on his virtue but ended by demanding his obedience. Having observed this sorry state of affairs in 1860, did the MVD get rid of the *stanovye*? Nothing of the sort. The *komissiia* discovered that virtually all governors wanted to retain their agents in the *stany*, with the proviso, however, that their activities be regulated and their spheres of responsibility clearly delimited (pp. 97-98). Here is the *komissiia*'s view: "The commission suggests that the authority and responsibility of the police be delimited as clearly as possible....The more precisely their activities are defined the stronger will be their legal authority and the less likely will they be to act arbitrarily" (p. 114). This marked the end of the cycle. Twenty-odd years of virtuous service had failed to establish the authority of government in rural Russia. Now the *komissiia* proposed another myth, that of paper power. Where personal virtue had failed, consistent regulations would succeed. To express this cycle in my terms, bureaucracy began in 1837 to insert itself into the countryside by resorting to line-over-staff methods and then strove to reduce the incoherence made visible by these methods (pp. 96-110).[7]

But the cycle ended only to begin again. At the same time the *komissiia* on uezd and gubernia institutions was reducing the *stanovye* to

---

[6]On the defects in rural police organization in the 1840s and '50s, see Abbott (1971: 19-40). Nicholas seems to have had little faith in the *stanovye* in his latter years. In 1848 he told an audience of serfowners: "I have no police.... You are my police and each of you is a manager of my affairs" (quoted in Chernyshev, 1918: 2).

[7]See Abbott (1971: 54-60) on the capital cities' general dissatisfaction with rural police during Alexander II's early years.

mere policemen, it was drafting the statute establishing "peaceful arbitrators" (*mirovye posredniki*) (*VPSZ*, 36660, arts. 2-96). These new knight-servitors would possess virtually absolute authority over villages undergoing "liberation" from serfdom. Indeed, the *komissiia* made the arbitrator's freedom from formal regulation explicit. Peasant affairs were so diverse, said the *komissiia*, that the arbitrator had to have as much freedom as possible to act decisively according to the requirements of each situation. If he was to command the peasants' confidence, he would have to make quick, meaningful judgments. Only under "real necessity," therefore, was he to work with written reports and correspondence (*VPSZ*, 36660, arts. 37, 56, 64).[8] These considerations came from the same legislators who were deploring the arbitrariness and helplessness of the *stanovye* and demanding that paper replace virtue as the basis for rural government. The *stanovye*, it seems, had become a part of the tangle the government wanted to reform; now it would be up to a new set of line-over-staff agents to do the reforming.

It should be pointed out that the cycle from arbitrary agent to clerk and back to arbitrary agent took place not in the actuality of the *stany* but in the central offices: in capital-city imaginations, where such fantasies as "virtuous heroes of service" and "exact codes of law" had meaning. Real-life *stanovye* did not cease to be despotic in the 1860s. They went on as before, disregarding paper reforms, proclaiming law and ignoring it as they saw fit, obstructing as well as serving the government's purposes in haphazard fashion. In the post-Liberation countryside authority continued to emanate from persons and to be limited by other persons.

The Arbitrator

In some ways the arbitrator was different from the *stanovoi*. Although he was appointed to his post by the MVD, he did his work largely on his own, unsupervised by any ministry. Only the Senate could remove him from his post, and then only if a court convicted him of violating the law. Moreover, he was initially closer than the *stanovoi* to the peasants with whom he worked. Approximately 1,700 arbitrators took up their positions in early 1861 (Chernukha, 1972: 32), whereas in 1859 there were only 1,227 *stanovye* on duty (*Trudy*, 1860: bk. 2, 54). The arbitrator's territorial unit, the *uchastok*, was somewhat smaller than a *stan*, and until 1863 he had charge only of ex-serfs, i.e., less than half the peasant population (Chernukha, 1967: 205). Then, too, the arbitrator had more "honor" than the *stanovoi*. The Liberation statute required him to have a certain minimum amount of property and/or education—

---

[8] *Trudy* (1860: bk. 2, 1st *prilozhenie*, 16; 2d *prilozhenie*, 40).

1,350 acres, or 405 acres plus sufficient education to qualify for the twelfth *chin* (rank) in government service—and he served without pay (*VPSZ*, 36660, arts. 6-11). The *stanovoi*, by contrast, was not formally required to achieve any specified level of schooling or possess any amount of property, and he received a salary.[9] Another difference was that the arbitrator did not do the same sort of work as the *stanovoi*, at least not in theory. He was not a governor in miniature, responsible for supervising all aspects of peasant life. To be sure, he possessed broad powers, but as the authors of the Liberation statute saw it, he had only to accomplish two tasks: to preside over the breakup of serf estates, and help ex-serfs establish their new volost and village administrations. These jobs finished, he was supposed to disappear (*Trudy*, 1860: bk. 2, 1st *prilozhenie*, 6-7). Finally, it may be said that the general purpose of the arbitrator was different from that of the *stanovoi*. The arbitrator was explicitly ordered to preside over a change in rural society, whereas the *stanovoi*'s official mission was to preserve the "law" as it was.

These differences proved to be minimal. The MVD could not discharge arbitrators who displeased him, but he could and did eliminate *uchastki* in which undesirable arbitrators happened to be working. By November 1871 the MVD's activities along this line had reduced their number from the original 1,700 to 864, while at the same time the arbitrators' jurisdiction within their ever-growing *uchastki* expanded to include all the peasants, not merely ex-serfs (Chernukha, 1972: 32, 45, 64). In practice, then, the MVD's administrators could impose their will on arbitrators about as easily as on the *stanovye*, and the arbitrators found themselves saddled with even more peasant villages—on the average—than their police counterparts. As to the arbitrator's honor, it rested on very weak grounds. The law allowed him no salary, but it did order the local zemstvo to provide him with 1,500 rubles each year to cover expenses. As to the high standards of landholding and education, they applied only so long as candidates came forth who met them. If such candidates were not available, men with much lower qualifications could be appointed. In gubernias lacking resident Great Russian gentry, the MVD employed military officers and civil officials to fill arbitrator positions whether they were gentry or not (*VPSZ*, 36660, arts. 6-11; Chernukha: 1967, 225-27; 1972: 56-57; Kataev, 1911: II, 69-71, 79-81). Moreover, the arbitrator did not turn out to be nearly as temporary as had been intended, and as "honorable" men lost interest in the job (Chernukha, 1972: 43-44), the duties attached to it expanded rapidly to encompass all manner of clerk-work. The central offices, always glad to

[9]Before 1859 he received 224 rubles/year plus 198 for expenses. In 1859 his salary went up to 600 rubles plus 300 for expenses (*Trudy*, 1860: bk. 2, 53-54; 2d *prilozhenie*, 1).

find agents with wide-ranging authority to accomplish the capital cities' purposes, showered the arbitrators with new responsibilities and functions, and the erstwhile knight-servitors quickly came to resemble the *stanovye*. After 1863, when the initial agreements *(ustavnye gramoty)* between serfs and serfowners were largely completed, the unfortunate heroes of virtue turned into general managers of peasant affairs (Chernukha, 1967: 221-24; 1972: 25-69; Kataev, 1911: II, 32-44). Indeed, one member of the editing commissions, K. I. Gechevich, pointed out even before 1861 that the Liberation statutes gave the arbitrator more duties than he could possibly handle, thus burying him from the outset in trivial routines (Kataev, 1911: I, 93-94).

As for the theoretical difference between presiding over change and preserving the existing order, it had little practical significance. True, the *stanovye* had not been established explicitly to reform serfdom, but Nicholas I had had such a reform clearly in mind when he set them up. Nor, on their side, were the arbitrators wholeheartedly on the side of reform. They were not set up to alter peasant society by their own action, only to keep it in order while the serfowners were being extracted from it. The letter of the law allowed the arbitrator to act only on the basis of appeals from individual peasants, not according to any plan or inclination of his own. The law offered no formal pretext for the arbitrator to intervene consistently in peasant institutions or even to manipulate them. The most he could do was to preside over them (*VPSZ,* 36660, art. 40; Kataev, 1911: II, 50-56). It may be said, then, that the arbitrators resembled the *stanovye* in their relations with peasant society. Both began their careers with the same promise: that they would bring the tsar's protection directly to the lowliest inhabitants of the land. Both evolved through much the same cycle: from tsar's personal henchman to tool of the government organization.

Not surprisingly, the MVD grew increasingly dissatisfied with the arbitrators. From about 1863 on the ministry strove continually in two directions at once: to subordinate the arbitrator to its formal authority and, failing this, to eliminate him. On the one hand, the MVD set forth a string of proposals to put arbitrators under the direct authority of the governors and establish clear limits to their authority. On the other hand, and at the same time, the ministry kept complaining that arbitrators interfered with the regular police and that therefore they should be done away with. MVD Timashev said in 1873 that the police could get along better without arbitrators in the way. In most cases, he complained, the would-be knights "not only fail to discharge their duties but often make it difficult by their wrangling for the police to perform theirs" (*Zapiska,* 1873: 26). As it happened, the MVD failed to get control over the arbitrators, and in the early 1870s it settled for eliminating them. Obviously, then, the arbitrators' development differed from that of the *stanovye* only because the MVD was unable to make it the same. The MVD tried to reduce the arbitrators to the status of *stanovye;* having failed, it eliminated them.[10]

The early 1870s saw the government at the end of its second cycle. The third did not begin immediately, mainly because this was a time when interest in experiments with rural administration reached a very low ebb. The law of 27 June 1874 (*VPSZ,* 53678), which eliminated the arbitrators, was intended to preserve and even enhance the independence of peasant institutions from government supervision (Kataev, 1911: II, 86-88).[11] The failings of the *stanovye* and arbitrators, the findings of the investigations of 1870-73, the ghosts of Arakcheev and Kiselev: all suggested that any attempts by the government to direct peasant society by administrative means were doomed to failure.[12] In 1870 Dmitrii Tolstoi himself declared his opposition to any reform that would central-ize control of gubernia administration in the hands of the governors or extend the police further into peasant society. He was minister of education then, and, like all his colleagues in the Committee of Ministers, he thought the MVD was already too powerful (TsGIAL, f. 1316, op. 1, d. 4, ll. 226-27, 360). Thus the end of the arbitrators' cycle did not immediately call forth another specimen of virtuous, line-over-staff re-former. Instead, it reflected the government's passivity in rural affairs.

We might sum up the lessons of the MVD's experience with quasi-line-over-staff reform during the 1860-70s with the observation that heroic individuals did seem to be the only device available to the central ministries for intervening in the countryside, yet heroes tended in practice to become overburdened clerks. In future, the government would either have to give up trying to impose reform through its own organization or else develop some arrangement that would sever line more fully from staff.

[10]Timashev's note suggests that the MVD had pursued only one goal with regard to the arbitrators since May 1863: to abolish them and thereby begin to bring the peasantry into the same legal order with everyone else (*Zapiska,* 1873: 1-3). In fact, the ministry continually strove to acquire the arbitrators at the same time it was moving to abolish them (Chernukha, 1967: 211, 224-37; 1972: 57-63; Kataev, 1911: II, 56-58; Strakhovskii, 1905: 389-404.

[11]The 1874 law did not eliminate the arbitrators in Perm, Bessarabia, and the gubernias of western Russia. In these areas they had been MVD agents from the beginning, i.e., clerk-despots imposed from the outside on the areas and societies in which they served (Kataev, 1911: II, 59-82, 101-3).

[12]On Arakcheev's and Kiselev's attempts at peasant reform, see Yaney (1973: 164-68). The committee for the management of rural society referred disapprov-ingly to Kiselev's interference in peasant society (Kataev, 1911: II, 96).

It must be added that the arbitrators left behind them not only lessons but a legacy. According to M. M. Kataev, the MVD's own historian, this legacy took form in the following manner.

In 1860 the *komissiia* on gubernia and uezd institutions completed its first draft of the law establishing the arbitrators. According to this document, the arbitrators were to be elected by the gentry and peasants of their respective locales, and they would function for only a short time (*Trudy*, 1860: bk. 2, 1st *prilozhenie*, 6-7). Most members of the *komissiia* really did not wish to set up institutions of peasant government separate from the rest of the population, and they especially disapproved of officials with power to act arbitrarily. The idea of liberation included— indeed, demanded—legal equality for all citizens, ex-serfs and ex- serfowners alike, and if the former were thrust into separate institutions, progress toward equality would be endangered if not blocked entirely. The members of the *komissiia* were keenly aware of this issue, and although they felt compelled to respect existing peasant modes of gov- ernment, they took pains to make the way easy for evolution toward full legal-administrative system. They only consented to empower the arbi- trator "to act as an executive agency without the constraints of formal law" because they were assured that he would be a representative institu- tion and would not be around very long (Kataev, 1911: I, 15). In short, the *komissiia* found itself compelled to use an administrative device that contradicted its own concept of peasant government, and it resolved the contradiction by separating this device from the central administration (II, 48-50).

We should note that the *komissiia*'s express recognition of the contradiction in its proposed measures was quite unprecedented. The mixing of would-be legal system and agents with arbitrary power had been a regular practice in Russia since Peter I's time, and various statesmen had noticed it throughout the eighteenth and early nineteenth centuries. To my knowledge, however, no statute had ever provided for self-contradiction in so many words.

The *komissiia*'s punctiliousness indicated that something new was happening in 1860. A serious commitment to bureaucratic organization was emerging among government servitors. Precisely because the *komis- siia* felt compelled to establish a legal-administrative system, with central administration and local institutions all connected by a single code of laws, it had to separate the arbitrators from this system *explicitly*. Unlike the *stanovye*, the arbitrators would not operate arbitrarily simply by virtue of their de facto situation in their locales. Their separateness had to be stated and justified officially (I, 12-16, 47-62). This was the source from which the "mess" of 1880 arose.

Despite the abiding faith of most *komissiia* members in the saving virtue of democratic elections, they decided to have the governors appoint the first arbitrators for three-year terms. This, said the *komissiia,* was necessary because elections would take too long (I, 22, 37-40). When the *komissiia*'s project came before the editing commissions for approval, however, idealism triumphed. The commissions voted eighteen to three to elect the first arbitrators from among both peasants and serfowners. But idealism did not flourish for long. The project went from the editing commissions to the chief committee on peasant affairs, and there the idea of elected arbitrators disappeared as abruptly as it had appeared. Herein, Kataev tells us, we may behold the work of Nikolai Miliutin, chairman of the *komissiia* and one of the minority of three in the editing commissions who had voted against instant democracy. Miliutin strongly believed that elections would create disorder among the peasants and discredit the whole idea of participatory government. He also wanted to be sure the first arbitrators would be men who favored the Liberation (Chernukha, 1972: 28-32; Rose, 1976: 94-96), and he did not trust local constituencies to select such men with the unerring accuracy he desired. Such was Miliutin's influence that he was able to persuade the chief committee to strike out *all* provisions regarding the election of arbitrators. In its final form the Liberation statute called for the MVD and its governors to appoint the arbitrators, and the question of how they were to be reselected was left to the future. In this seemingly inadvertent way, the concept of a temporary expedient for peasant government quietly faded out of the Liberation Statute. The way was open for the arbitrator to become an institution (Kataev, 1911: I, 99-109). New selection procedures were never adopted. When many arbitrators quit their jobs after two years and returned to their former occupations (*Kratkii,* 1880: 28), the governors simply replaced them by fiat.

Institutionalization of the arbitrators sharpened the separation between peasant government and the nonpeasant population. Instead of preventing the entrenchment of a peasant administration outside the government's law, as most authors of the legislation of 1861 had wished, the Liberation inadvertently helped to seal the peasants off from modern law. This, says Kataev, marked the origin of the MVD's notion that peasants *required* a separate administration. As the new villages and volosts evolved, their separation became more pronounced, until at last separateness became an important element in the peasant way of life. Peasants became more dependent than ever on institutions that did not fit the government's law, and for this reason there gradually evolved in the MVD "a firm policy not to introduce peasant administration into the general system of all-class government" (I, 40).

The MVD's futile attempts to subordinate the arbitrators to its police hierarchy kept the problem of separate peasant administration in the open but did not resolve it. During the 1860s and early '70s the government neither accepted the MVD's proposals to strengthen the separation nor formulated an alternative arrangement. Instead, it side-stepped the issue. It replaced the arbitrators with an uezd-level college for managing peasant affairs. The new college included the gentry marshal (as chairman), the uezd police commandant, and a permanent member. The permanent member was selected by the governor, with MVD approval, from among candidates nominated by the local zemstvo (*VPSZ*, 53678; Yaney, 1973: 368-69). The main effect of this arrangement was to reduce drastically the number of officials involved in managing peasant institutions. About 400 permanent members of uezd colleges replaced about 800 arbitrators. The MVD probably had closer control over the new officials than it had exercised over the arbitrators, but its ability to work directly with peasant society certainly did not increase (Kataev, 1911: II, 105-9). As for the peasants' separateness, it persisted. The 1874 law did not eliminate special organs of peasant management but only rendered them ineffectual. The new colleges, working away on their reports in the uezd capitals, relatively far from the villages, would be unable to carry out any reform, but they would still allow peasant institutions to float along under their own separate regime.

To sum up Kataev's account of the "mess" the MVD faced in 1880, he indicates that after 1861 the development of relationships between government and peasant went entirely contrary to the intentions behind the Liberation. In order to preserve the autonomy of peasant institutions, the government took measures that not only failed to bring the peasants into the imperial legal-administrative system but actually widened the gap between modern and peasant legal orders. By 1880 the arbitrators had either disappeared or followed the *stanovye* into clerkdom, and peasants were still notably disinclined to participate in the government's legal-administrative system on their own initiative.

D. THE DEBATE ON PEASANT ADMINISTRATION, 1880-89

The Kakhanov Commission

In 1880, when the government began again to speak seriously of rural reform, a strong sentiment manifested itself among some high-level officials—so Kataev says—in favor of reinstating the arbitrators (1911: II, 113-14). But it was not a good year for proposals that dealt only with peasant administration. A more general debate was underway among the tsar's statesmen, ranging over all facets of government and political order, and many of the most influential participants insisted on reforming Russia's constitutional order before adopting specific reforms in peasant administration. For several years the government would consider the possibility of turning rural Russia over to the zemstvoes, and until this possibility of constitutional reform had been either accepted or rejected, the question of *how* to manage peasants had to be set aside.

Two ministers of internal affairs were involved in the debate on general governmental reform: Mikhail Loris-Melikov (April 1880–April 1881) and Nikolai Ignatev (May 1881–May 1882). During his year of office Loris-Melikov ordered senatorial inspections of zemstvo institutions in eight gubernias, and he called upon zemstvoes and gubernia boards for peasant affairs in all 34 zemstvo gubernias to submit reform proposals (TsGIAL, f. 1317, op. 1, d. 102, ll. 2-4). When Ignatev took over, the resultant reports and proposals were pouring in. He formed a commission under Mikhail Kakhanov to consider them and draft suitable legislation. Ignatev's concepts of government were not profound. In a characteristically fantastic statement he indicated that he wanted Kakhanov's project to "unify the activities of all gubernia institutions and agencies, cut down on burdensome formalities, and strengthen all authorities in the locales that preserve order and protect both public and private interests" (ll. 2-3). In other words, Ignatev wanted a piece of paper that would eliminate all the bad features of bureaucracy and preserve all the good ones. He also mentioned the peasants: "Peasant institutions are only a part of gubernia administration, and the particular question of their structure can only be dealt with satisfactorily in connection with the main problem of reforming the whole of gubernia organization" (l. 4).

A subcommittee of Kakhanov's commission drafted a project reform in 1882-83. In general, it reflected the views Kakhanov had already expressed ten years before, when he had been governor of Pskov (see ch. 2, sec. B). The project did not call for administrative programs managed by bureaucrats but instead proposed new constitutional arrangements that would bring peasants and nonpeasants together in local autonomous institutions, identified and protected by a single legal system. Villages, volosts, and zemstvoes were to be organized under a common set of principles; traditional status distinctions were to be minimized and ultimately done away with.[13]

I have argued elsewhere that Kakhanov's project would have produced the practical effect of solidifying gentry predominance in the countryside. The sleepy uezds, still dominated to a considerable extent by networks of local families, might well have ossified yet more than they already had. More likely, the disparate elements in a crumbling traditional order would have broken out into violent conflict much sooner than they did, and the government would ultimately have been compelled

[13]The subcommittee's project is in TsGIAL, f. 1317, d. 71. Detailed studies of the Kakhanov commission's work are in Gessen (1904: 172-207), Zaionchkovskii (1970: 217-33), and Strakhovskii (1903: 94-110).

(or invited) to resort to administrative intervention long before it actually was, in spite of its palpable inability to make such intervention effective (Yaney, 1973: 346-51).[14]

But history will never know the outcome of Kakhanov's proposals. Dmitrii Tolstoi, who succeeded Ignatev as MVD in 1882, did not believe in zemstvo autonomy. He packed Kakhanov's commission with new members unsympathetic to the subcommittee's project, and they managed, in November 1884, to block it. In April 1885 Tolstoi dismissed the commission outright. Its materials and projects were filed away in the MVD archives for the benefit of future scholars (Kataev, 1911: II, 116; Gessen, 1904: 179-99).

Tolstoi's Vision

As MVD, Tolstoi no longer saw rural administration in the same light as he had in the early 1870s, when he had opposed Timashev's attempt to expand the ministry's powers in the countryside. Now, in the mid-1880s, he was quite prepared to set up agencies to conduct rural reform. Toward Kakhanov's general concept of rural reform, Tolstoi remained consistently negative throughout his ministerial career. He wanted no part of any effort to enact one single reform that would bring all society under a common set of institutions. Neither society nor government was ready to work within a single scheme. The government should cope with necessities, not theories, said Tolstoi in November 1887. If there was to be a workable legal system, it could not be drafted in advance but would have to arise in the course of ad hoc interaction between populace and government (TsGIAL, f. 1149, 1889g., op. vol. XI, d. 44, l. 472). Tolstoi and Kakhanov did agree on one point: the government's domestic administration was not governing the peasants properly. Therefore, said Kakhanov, get it out of the way and allow local institutions to do the job. Therefore, said Tolstoi, abandon the futile effort to formulate grand schemes, subordinate zemstvo and urban institutions more firmly to the central administration, and then clear the whole lot out of peasant society so that MVD agents can act freely on the basis of practical experience to confront actual problems as they arise (Kataev, 1911: II, 115-20).

Tolstoi was fond of renouncing theory and exalting "experience." Indeed, his rhapsodies on the theme of spontaneous practicality sometimes brought him to the very edge of existentialism. "General plans...

[14]A number of recent Soviet works have commented on the disadvantages of government institutions dominated by landholders; see, e.g., Anfimov (1969: 84-89, 108-9, 294-98). A Western view that reaches much the same conclusion by a different route is Nötzold (1966: 48, 59-97).

cannot be based on actual needs," he once said, "and it is extremely difficult to avoid basing them on considerations of a more or less theoretical character." Schemes and systems drafted in St. Petersburg had to be based on theory; ergo, they could not furnish a viable basis for government in rural Russia (TsGIAL, f. 1149, 1889g., op. vol. XI, d. 44, ll. 467-68). One could hardly ask for a more explicit profession of faith in line-over-staff administration.

Tolstoi's vision proceeded in large part from his contact with A. D. Pazukhin, who first came to St. Petersburg in 1884 as one of the men Tolstoi used to pack Kakhanov's commission. By origin an uezd gentry marshal from Simbirsk gubernia, Pazukhin had already expressed some ideas on "spontaneous" agrarian reform in 1880-81, during the zemstvo debates being conducted at that time in response to Loris-Melikov's proposals (Gessen, 1904: 195-98). By 1884, therefore, he was prepared to play a leading role in blocking Kakhanov's proposals (Zaionchkovskii, 1970: 219; Gessen, 1904: 174-88). While he was at it, he published a short monograph on rural administration wherein he set forth most of the concepts that would be embodied in the statute on land captains. Tolstoi was so happy about Pazukhin's achievements that he made the erstwhile country crusader head of the MVD chancellery and ordered him to draft a project for the reform of peasant society and rural administration. Thus began the process of articulating "Tolstoi's" vision.[15]

What exactly did the "vision" involve? I have already suggested a general answer in terms of a model: the land captain was intended to be a line-over-staff official. It is time, however, to set aside abstract considerations and to investigate the terms and concepts that informed the imaginations of the founding fathers themselves. We must consider the concrete evidence in order to see what indication it may offer that Pazukhin and Tolstoi had line-over-staff officials in mind during their time of close cooperation.[16]

One element in the vision is reasonably clear: the labels used to express it. It pleased Tolstoi and Pazukhin to portray themselves as conservatives. They often spoke of the land captains as maintainers and restorers of order in the countryside. The peasants needed pacifying, guidance, and protection—"guardianship" was the word used in the decree announcing the statute of 1889 (*TPSZ*, 6195). The land captains would guard and guide, and the peasants would prosper in peace.

[15]Pazukhin's monograph first appeared in serial form in the pages of *Russkii Vestnik,* a journal published by the "reactionary" Mikhail Katkov.

[16]I have discussed Pazukhin's and Tolstoi's concept of the gentry elsewhere (1973: 369-76). The account that follows is to some extent repetitive, in that it comes to much the same conclusion. The approach here, however, is somewhat different. I am attempting to show how the concept of the land captain *developed* during the process of enacting the statute of 1889.

Sometimes Pazukhin even sounded reactionary. On at least one occasion, in September 1886, he and some of his supporters said explicitly that what they wanted in essence was "a return to the old order as it had been prior to the Liberation" (TsGIAL, f. 1282, op. 2, d. 1838, l. 415).

But labels were the least significant element in the vision. It is very doubtful that Pazukhin's fond references to "restoration" are reliable indicators of his beliefs. More characteristic of his real attitude were the frequent comparisons he made between his proposed land captains and the arbitrators. As Pazukhin saw it, those good old knights of virtue had given peasant society better protection and guidance during their golden years right after 1861 than it had ever had before or since (f. 1149, 1889g., op. vol. XI, d. 44, l. 8). As Pazukhin said in his (and Tolstoi's) note of February 1887, the original arbitrators, "residing in their *uchastki*, heard appeals verbally...and either told petitioners what office could handle their problems, or, in cases that came under their jurisdiction, decided disputes then and there in the presence of both sides" (l. 10). Now, however, in the 1880s, the arbitrators were no more. The peasants were drifting helplessly, victimized by *kulaki, advokaty,* and other sharp operators (l. 12). The land captain would put a stop to this. He would work on a personal and informal basis with the peasants, and this would enable him to pit the full power of the state against would-be exploiters (l. 15). Pazukhin never ceased to believe that he was creating land captains in the arbitrators' image, and the statute of 1889 did in fact borrow heavily from the legislation on the arbitrators (*TPSZ*, 6196, *Polozhenie,* art. 22). This tells us what Pazukhin meant by "guardianship." Far from being a preserver of old verities, real or imagined, Pazukhin's land captain was basically a crusader for progress. Pazukhin used his labels a little carelessly, but he was looking forward, not back.

Pazukhin's memory of the arbitrators was not altogether accurate. Their success, such as it was, had come only while they were carrying out a specific mission. As institutions of government, they had not been any more effective than the *stanovye.* Instead of bringing the government's system to the countryside, they had become part of the society the government had to cope with. Even so, Pazukhin did not give up the idea of using officials with arbitrary authority to govern peasant society *and* to change it. This is the point. It does not matter whether Pazukhin's memory served him well or not; what does matter is that his vision of the land captains was firmly associated with the model of a rural chief who used his authority to inflict change on peasant society while guarding the peasants from the worst consequences of the change he was inflicting. He recognized the inadequacies of the *stanovye* and arbitrators, but he remained convinced that arbitrary authority was a necessary element in rural administration if rural society was to develop. The failure of the land captain's predecessors had stemmed not from arbitrariness but from the government's failure to maintain their arbitrariness. Pazukhin and Tolstoi feared that the land captain, like his predecessors, might be compelled to fritter away his powers performing petty functions and struggling against other officials. Thus their primary concern was to ensure that their statute would guarantee the new captain's freedom of action. Whether or not this was a viable purpose, it was certainly not a reactionary or conservative one. Insofar as the land captain would differ from the arbitrator, the purpose of making him different—i.e., more arbitrary—was to make him a more effective agent of social change. For the enactors of the statute on land captains, the chief lesson of the MVD's experience since 1837 was that any new patriarchal guardian would have to be *explicitly* independent from peasant custom and *explicitly* invulnerable to interference by bureaucracy. Pazukhin's and Tolstoi's idea was to use legal-administrative system to guarantee their captains' independence from legal-administrative system for the purpose of introducing legal-administrative system to the peasantry.

It is important in this connection to stress that Pazukhin was very little concerned about reserving the position of land captain for the landed gentry. In 1880-81, when he was still out in Simbirsk, he conceived of his captain as an elected official, and he still cherished this concept in 1884, after he had come to St. Petersburg to help lay Kakhanov's project to rest (Gessen, 1904: 195-98). In practice, the landholding gentry would dominate any elections held in rural areas, and therefore elected land captains would very likely be drawn from their ranks, but Pazukhin only accepted this as a fact. He did not make it a cause for which he urged his followers to struggle. He believed in the gentry's predominant role because they were political leaders, not the reverse. So far as I have seen, he had no desire to guarantee the gentry political leadership in order to perpetuate their privileges or preserve their wealth. On the contrary, in 1884 Pazukhin did *not* agree with those who wished to restrict political leadership to landholding gentry, and he *did* vote to make education as important a qualification for a land captain as landholding (pp. 175, 179). As for his original project—the one he wrote for Tolstoi in 1886—it did not call for gentry at all but only stressed the need to select the "best man" in each locale as land captain (TsGIAL, f. 1282, op. 2, d. 1838, l. 407). Of course, the "best men" were assumed to be gentry, but if an occasional nongentry landholder or educated bureaucrat turned up, Pazukhin was perfectly willing to let him be a captain, provided only that he possessed the heroic qualities captains were supposed to possess. The MVD committee that revised Pazukhin's project in late 1886, just before Tolstoi brought it to the tsar, took a similar view. The members specified the land captain's qualifications in terms of experience in government service, not birth (ll. 407-9). It was only in 1887-88 that the term "local gentry" replaced the concept of experienced servitor, and in January 1889 the statute still read "local gentry." Not until the last debates in the State Council did Tolstoi's *opponents* manage to change the statute to read "local hereditary gentry" (f. 1149, 1889g., op. vol. XI, d. 44, ll. 1066-67).[17]

Consider also Pazukhin's project for zemstvo reform. Admittedly, one of the enactors' aims was to expand gentry influence in the zemstvoes. Pazukhin often spoke of "allowing gentry estate owners to play "a greater role in local affairs" (Zaionchkovskii, 1970: 370), and he dressed up his project with some statements about granting them "rights." But how did Tolstoi and Pazukhin visualize this "greater role"? The clearest answer to this most significant of questions may be found in their initial project for the statute on zemstvoes. It provided, among other things, that members of uezd zemstvo assemblies were to be subject to punishment if they refused to accept their membership or failed to attend meetings (TsGIAL, f. 1282, op. 2, d. 1837, ll. 2, 45-47). This provision never became law, but it does tell us something about Pazukhin's thinking: namely, that he did not intend the granting of "rights" to be any great favor. The zemstvo assembly, as Pazukhin saw it, was more like a company of militia than an autonomous institution, and membership in it was a duty, not a distinction. Existing zemstvo and town institutions, said Pazukhin, were based on an erroneous concept: that of self-government *("obshchestvennoe samoupravlenie")*. This notion was bad for Russia. It should be replaced by another: "state administration by means of and with the cooperation of representatives of the local population" (quoted in Zaionchkovskii, 1970: 370). When Pazukhin spoke of increasing gentry influence in the zemstvoes, he meant that the gentry should be encouraged and compelled to serve the government as agents of bureaucracy.

We may say, then, that when Pazukhin referred wistfully to the qualities of the gentry and the glories of pre-Liberation days, he was not thinking of the privileges the gentry serfowners had enjoyed. On the contrary, he was reviving a pre-Liberation fantasy in which serfowners played the role of government agents. "The Russian gentry," he (and Tolstoi) said in 1887, "have always been, and still are, more an organ of government *(gosudarstvennoe ustanovlenie)* than a social group" (TsGIAL, f. 1149, 1889g., op. vol. XI, d. 44, l. 17). In his book of 1886 he set forth the opinion that the Liberation Statute had been a good thing on the whole because many serfowners had forgotten their true calling, which was to serve the state (Pazukhin, 1886: 8-9). The Liberation

---

[17]"Local hereditary gentry" was the term finally adopted in the statute (*TPSZ*, 6196, *Polozhenie*, arts. 6-7). The original term, "local gentry," had opened the way for merely "personal" gentry to compete on an equal basis for the new jobs. See the Glossary concerning the meanings of these terms.

had not solved this problem. The gentry were still not doing their job. Russia, he said, would not be "normal" until the gentry "again became servitors as well as landholders" (p. 60). He composed a short history of the Russian gentry, showing that throughout Russia's development she had been primarily a "military camp," concerned primarily with staving off external enemies. So she still was, and the gentry existed solely to man the defenses (pp. 44-57).[18]

We shall see in Chapter 4 that the hopes of the land captains' creators proved to be illusory. For all practical purposes, the captains soon lost their freedom of action and followed essentially the same path to clerkdom as the *stanovye* and arbitrators had. Thus the significance of the land captains lies not in their success but, rather, in the basic vision they embodied. Their purpose from the beginning was bureaucratic, statist, and progressive, not reactionary, aristocratic, or exploitative. Pazukhin and Tolstoi were not counter-reformists, as virtually all historians insist; for better or worse, they were the initiators of agrarian reform in Russia.

The Russian Gentry's Role in Government

I cannot simply assert that agrarian reform began in the MVD in the 1880s and leave it at that. The weight of scholarship, carried along by the cliché "era of reaction," is so overwhelming, inside and outside of Russia, before and after the Revolution, that no one can simply wave a little evidence at it and hope it will tiptoe away. We must dwell a little longer on the gentry before continuing with the adventures of Tolstoi and Pazukhin.

Petr A. Zaionchkovskii, the Soviet Union's leading student of nineteenth-century Russian government, sees in the statute on land captains a "vision" very different from the one I have described. He suggests that it sprang from the brains of sinister, reactionary journalists, chiefly V. P. Meshcherskii and Mikhail Katkov, who were able to manipulate the presumably stupid Alexander III and thereby impose their shoddy ideas on a helpless bureaucracy (Zaionchkovskii, 1970: 388-401). In particular, Zaionchkovskii maintains that Katkov brought about Pazukhin's rise to high position and was able to influence him while he was drafting his statutes (pp. 71-72).

To be sure, Katkov showed favor to Pazukhin by publishing his monograph (n. 15), and the two men did correspond until Katkov's death in 1887. This, however, is hardly sufficient evidence to demonstrate Katkov's role in enacting the statute on land captains. In addition to this

---

[18]Pazukhin's view of the gentry is by no means without historical basis; see S. B. Veselovskii (1969: 465-70, 474-76).

circumstantial evidence, Zaionchkovskii has little to offer except the gossip of bureaucrats. This is understandable; what other kind of evidence would there be regarding behind-the-scenes influence on the tsar and his favorites? But even the most intelligent gossip is highly tenuous, especially when it comes to the private remarks of Alexander III's administrators regarding the evil Katkov and the sinister Meshcherskii.

Zaionchkovskii relies particularly heavily on the diary of A. A. Polovtsov, Alexander III's imperial secretary until 1892. To some extent his reliance is justified, for Polovtsov was an unusually careful writer. Yet when it came to Katkov and Meshcherskii, Polovtsov invariably abandoned his critical faculties. On one occasion E. M. Feoktistov, director of the chief administration for press affairs, told Polovtsov that Meshcherskii had persuaded Alexander III to make I. A. Vyshnegradskii the new minister of finance (Polovtsov, 1966: II, 40). As Polovtsov tells it, Feoktistov's story depended entirely on the word of Meshcherskii himself and on that of K. P. Pobedonostsev, procurator of the Holy Synod. Polovtsov was suspicious of Pobedonostsev and frequently referred to his shiftiness and confused thinking. As for Feoktistov and Meshcherskii, Polovtsov not only distrusted but scorned them (p. 41). In this case, however, when a story about Meshcherskii's "power" was concerned, he believed what Feoktistov, Meshcherskii, and Pobedonostsev said without the slightest reservation. This is an expression of Polovtsov's paranoia, not evidence of Meshcherskii's influence. Polovtsov and his fellow bureaucrats lived in a world where the tsar's favor meant power to decide and command. One thing none of them ever showed any sign of grasping (except, perhaps, Tolstoi—see Feoktistov, 1975: 214, 240-41) was that the tsar's favor could also be a device to shield the press from bureaucratic interference. For all his much advertised stupidity, Alexander III seems to have understood the value of an autonomous press much better than any of his servitors. Like Bismarck, he supported certain journalists not because he agreed with them and intended to follow their guidance but because he found this an excellent way to keep his administrators on their toes. Administrators like Polovtsov assumed that the tsar was dominated by the journalists he protected; likewise the journalists believed him to be dominated by bureaucrats. But surely the historian should not take this unvarying chorus of outrage for facts. Katkov and Meshcherskii favored the statute on land captains and supported Pazukhin, but I have seen no convincing evidence to show that they fed Tolstoi and Pazukhin their ideas or, in general, that journalists of any kind influenced Tsar Alexander III. The only basis Zaionchkovskii has for making much of Katkov's and Meshcherskii's malevolent influence is his unquestioning, a priori acceptance of the metaphor "era of reaction." Zaionchkovskii's eagerness to associate himself with this metaphor in no way distinguishes him from other historians. His distinction is that he is the best qualified of the lot to get free of old dogmas. Unfortunately, he has shown no desire to do so.

For those who agree that Katkov and Meshcherskii dominated Alexander III, the next building block in the conventional metaphor is the virtually a priori postulate to the effect that these "reptiles" favored the restoration of gentry privilege and generally functioned as oracles for gentry "interests." And from this pseudo-foundation we may proceed easily to the conclusion that the land captains were part of a scheme to solidify the rule of an archaic, exploitative, parasitic, greedy gentry class over an oppressed, poverty-stricken peasantry.

Admittedly Katkov and Meshcherskii set forth a variety of views on the nature of the Russian gentry. Sometimes they sounded as if they were protectors of gentry economic interests. In 1896, for example, the evil Meshcherskii applauded a conference of gubernia gentry marshals that had voted to award gentry status to anyone who acquired a certain amount of land. This same conference also approved a proposal to make it more difficult to attain gentry status through government service (Solovev, 1967: 255-58). Considered in isolation, Meshcherskii's response to the marshals' votes—like many other "reptile" writings—can be interpreted as an expression of concern for maintaining the narrow interests of landholders against the state's needs and the people's welfare. On balance, however, Meshcherskii's occasional support for landholders' privileges seems to have come from his concern to unify the Russian gentry, not to please them. His writings, taken together, reflect an abiding conviction that the gentry were essentially instruments of the state. For Meshcherskii, a good government was one in which a strong tsar compelled the gentry to serve and awarded privileges only to those who served well. His real convictions are accurately reflected in his lifelong admiration for two heroes of autocratic service: P. A. Kleinmikhel, protégé of Arakcheev and fully his equal in tyrannical determination to do the tsar's will at any cost; and D. G. Bibikov, whose unrelenting pressure on the serfowners of the southwest made him a symbol of Nicholas I's despotism in the eyes of liberal and conservative gentry alike during the mid-nineteenth-century reform era (Meshcherskii, 1897-1912: I, 38-41). Meshcherskii's heroes were destroyers of gentry privilege and symbols of gentry duty, and his own view, if he could be said to have held one consistently, was that of a prophet to Russian bureaucrats, not a defender of landholders' interests.[19]

Whatever the reader may wish to conclude about Katkov's and Meshcherskii's views, we may be certain that Pazukhin's notions about the role of the Russian gentry in the state were widely held among the

---

[19]Concerning the tyrannical, anti-gentry ways of Kleinmikhel, see the second volume of Delvig (1912-13). On Bibikov, see Yaney (1973: 169-75).

government's leading administrators. With the possible exception of Kakhanov and a few of his erstwhile supporters, notably Polovtsov, no one in the higher levels of government was especially concerned with maintaining the position or the privileges of the gentry per se. Tolstoi's opponents agreed with him that the central government's business was to employ the gentry to mobilize the peasantry. Their differences with him arose solely over the question of *how* to employ the gentry.

Take, for example, A. P. Nikolai, chairman of the State Council's department of laws, and B. P. Mansurov, member of the department of laws and one of the council's most active debaters. Both these men consistently distrusted landholders and disapproved of local autonomy. They both opposed the rule that land captains should be local gentry. Nikolai wanted the position left open to anyone the MVD chose to appoint, regardless of status (Zaionchkovskii, 1970: 387). Mansurov actually wished to rule out the use of resident gentry estate holders on the grounds that they were inherently corrupt when they governed their own locales (TsGIAL, f. 1149, 1889g., op. vol. XI, d. 44, ll. 765-68). Nikolai and Mansurov opposed Tolstoi's statute as long as they could, but their main reason was that he insisted on separating his captains from the rest of the bureaucracy, thereby (they believed) weakening the bureaucracy as a whole. In other words, these two "conservatives" wanted to strengthen and extend bureaucracy at least as badly as Tolstoi did.

Much the same may be said of I. I. Vorontsov-Dashkov, minister of the imperial court and Tolstoi's leading opponent in the State Council. One of those rare men, a politically conscious Russian capable of consistent thought, Vorontsov led the opposition to Tolstoi's statute on land captains and then enthusiastically supported Tolstoi's zemstvo statute of 1890. He took both of these seemingly contradictory positions for the same reason. He believed in a unified, centralized bureaucracy that would operate by its own rules and compel Russian society to accept its authority. Thus he opposed the creation of agencies empowered to operate outside the law, and he favored the subordination of the zemstvoes to the central administration (Mamulova, 1960: 76, 79; Chernyshev, 1918: 232-37). At least two of Tolstoi's ostensible supporters, Pobedonostev and M. N. Ostrovskii (minister of state domains), took essentially the same view of rural administration as Vorontsov, though they voted with Tolstoi out of loyalty to the tsar. These two notorious "reactionaries" did not stand consistently on either side of the debate between Tolstoi and his opponents, but they certainly agreed with both sides that gentry and local institutions should serve the central government (TsGIAL, f. 1282, op. 2, d. 1836, ll. 91-99, 102-13).[20]

[20] At least two of Tolstoi's opponents in the State Council, A. A. Polovtsov

To be sure, the imperial government did regard the gentry with favor in the 1880s and thereafter. Members of the gentry were generally given preference over nongentry in school admissions and selections for government posts. Alexander III and Nicholas II both sincerely wished for the gentry to hold land and to prosper. In 1896 Nicholas officially agreed with the governor of Vologda that the government should maintain gentry estates where they were and help extend them to areas where they did not exist (*Svod vysochaishikh,* 1895: 27-28). In the same year he endorsed the governor of Tomsk's hope that gentry estates might soon be extended into Siberia (p. 170).

The government's favor, however, proceeded from the belief that gentry worked more reliably and effectively than nongentry. Well or ill conceived, gentry privilege was a technique for utilizing manpower, not a concession to anyone's economic interests. The establishment of the land captains represented a setback to gentry status in the countryside, for it set a (theoretically) very powerful government agent in charge of the laborers and tenants who farmed gentry land. One could argue, of course, that gentry *attitudes* dominated the government and also produced the statute on land captains, but the views underlying Tolstoi's vision dominated just about all segments of the Russian political spectrum. Nikolai Chernyshevskii, a son of a priest who grew up to be a radical journalist, wrote a novel, *What Is to Be Done,* in which the main character perfectly typified Pazukhin's ideal gentry-servitor, though the author's intent was to inspire revolutionaries. Vladimir Lenin, one of the many who found Chernyshevskii's novel inspiring, was himself as typical a *dvorianin* in his attitude toward state service as the best of land captains. Thus it means very little to say that the gentry ideology of state service dominated the tsarist government and then infer gentry *class* domination. In general, the government's favor toward the gentry did not give rise to its actions and policies; on the contrary, actions and policies gave rise to a demand for manpower that the gentry seemed best able to satisfy. Alexander III "favored" his gentry in approximately the same way Lenin and Stalin would "favor" their workers.

The Evolution of Tolstoi's Vision

Tolstoi and Pazukhin did not insist on combining executive and judicial authority in the land captain's hands merely because he had virtue. The main reason, as noted earlier, was that their vision of the

and Kakhanov, strove to block the statute on land captains because they thought it furthered the purposes of bureaucracy at the expense of gentry landholders. Both of these men scorned gentry who attained their status through government service, and they believed in the virtues of hereditary estate owners (Polovtsov, 1966: I, 314-15, 447; II, 106, 431-32). See also Yaney (1973:369-76).

captain called upon him to *mobilize* peasants and revolutionize their society. As we shall see, this key element in the vision of the enactors grew steadily more apparent as the process of enactment unfolded.

It seems to me that the evolution of Tolstoi's vision of line-over-staff administration may be observed in two places: inside the MVD and in the State Council. Inside the ministry it underwent discussion among a group of servitors—the Gagarin committee—who shared the vision. Their contribution was to compel Pazukhin to elaborate upon his ideas by identifying some of the problems his land captains would face. In the interministerial discussions that arose when the statute came before the State Council, on the other hand, Tolstoi and Pazukhin had to contend with men who did *not* share their vision. Instead of compelling Tolstoi to describe the captains in greater detail, his opponents stressed theoretical problems, thereby leading him into an attempt to articulate theoretical premises for the land captains. In both places we shall be able to see somewhat more clearly what the authors of the statute wanted and what they were willing to sacrifice to get it.

The Gagarin Committee, 1886

The statute on land captains first achieved written form in the spring of 1886, when Pazukhin, acting on Tolstoi's orders, drafted a project for the reform of peasant society and rural government. Its central ideas were the land captain and a reorganization of the zemstvoes designed to subordinate the gubernia and uezd directorates—i.e., the zemstvoes' executive agencies—to the central government administration.[21] Tolstoi rushed to show Pazukhin's draft to a few of his fellow ministers: Pobedonostsev, Ostrovskii, and N. A. Manasein (minister of justice). They raised some objections. Pazukhin reworked his project, presumably to win their support, and in the fall an MVD committee met to consider the result.

There were ten members, including the chairman, Konstantin D. Gagarin. Nine of them—all but Gagarin—could claim to be in close touch with the problems of local government. They included four governors, one ex-governor, three gubernia marshals, and Pazukhin himself, an ex-uezd gentry marshal (TsGIAL, f. 1282, op. 2, d. 1838, l. 403). They were handpicked, it seems, to make sure they were in fundamental sympathy with Pazukhin's ideas. Nine approved the basic idea of giving the land captain both judicial and executive powers (Zaionchkovskii, 1970: 369), and at least five (besides Pazukhin) sup-

---

[21] Unfortunately the original draft of Pazukhin's project has not come down to us, but there is a description of it in Pobedonostsev's note to the tsar, dated 18 Apr. 1886 (Zaionchkovskii, 1970: 366). Mamulova (1960: 65-66) lists other epistolary and memoir sources that discuss Pazukhin's first draft.

ported the Pazukhin-Tolstoi line throughout. P. A. Krivskii had already spoken in favor of establishing *"uchastkovye nachalniki"* with combined executive and judicial powers (p. 196), and he, like Pazukhin, believed his *nachalnik* could be any qualified person, regardless of social status (Polovtsov, 1966: 130). G. V. Kondoidi and A. E. Zarin had been appointed to Kakhanov's commission in 1884-85 along with Pazukhin as part of Tolstoi's effort to block the subcommittee's project of zemstvo reform (Zaionchkovskii, 1970: 219). They had been uezd marshals then but had since risen in rank, doubtless as a result of their performance for Tolstoi in the commission. Kondoidi was now a gubernia marshal and would shortly be elevated to a post in the MVD's central offices. Zarin had become a governor (TsGIAL, f. 1282, op. 2, d. 1838, l. 403). N. P. Dolgovo-Saburov, formerly a governor, had just been appointed head of the land section in the MVD. Finally there was Gagarin, Tolstoi's immediate subordinate in the MVD. These five, six if we add Pazukhin, were Tolstoi's boys, so to speak, virtually sure supporters of the Tolstoi-Pazukhin version of reform.

The committee members were practical men; at least this was their pose: Rasputins of sorts, bearing with them the aura of honest reality from the provinces, unsullied by capital-city rot. They all seem to have had great respect for immediate problems and a concomitant scorn for broad theories. To some extent, then, we may assume that they really did have similar attitudes toward agrarian management. Doubtless there was some competition among them to see who could be Tolstoi's best boy, but on the whole their personal aims coincided with the common purpose of their meetings: to render Pazukhin's draft into a workable project.

We need not follow the committee's discussions clause by clause through Pazukhin's entire project. My purpose is much less ambitious. I only want to consider the concrete rules the members proposed in order to ensure that the land captain would be above the toils of peasant custom and also free from bureaucratic interference. As we shall see, the business of formulating these rules represented the first important step in the evolution of Tolstoi's vision.

The whole committee believed that the captain had to maintain a position outside peasant custom. "Peasant institutions," they said, "cannot operate without active and authoritative leadership by government servitors, close to the peasants but standing outside peasant society, knowing all the intricacies and conditions of village life but not constrained by complex formalities" (l. 430).

Nine members took this to mean that the land captains, unlike the *stanovye* and the arbitrators, had to have both judicial and executive authority (Zaionchkovskii, 1970: 369). But the committee went further than this. In matters regarding land use, the captains were even to have legislative powers. The peasants had shown themselves unable to devise consistent regulations of their own to govern landholding. They were redistributing their land more often than ever—so thought the committee— and redistribution was an inherently disorderly and primitive practice. Thus far the government had been unable to improve the situation. The Senate had not produced any perceptible principles to guide land use in the village (TsGIAL, f. 1282, op. 2, d. 1838, ll. 414-16, 456-68). It would be up to the land captains, therefore, to compel their villages to draw up regulations for themselves. Then the captains would have something to enforce, and the peasants would learn to rely on legal system—rather than the vagaries of their personal relationships—as the basis for their land rights (ll. 414-15). None of these notions about the land captain's power to enact rules of land usage got into the 1889 statute. The committee approved them, however, and its approval is significant as an authentic expression of what the authors of the statute envisioned when they spoke of "protection" and "preservation."

The land captain's intended relationship with the peasant legal order came up in another context. Pazukhin's original project allowed a captain to alter the substance of any volost court decision at any time, even if it was not appealed by any of the parties involved. Five members objected to this extreme abandonment of limits to the captains' power because, they said, it would render the courts' decisions eternally contingent. Old disputes could be reopened whenever the local captain was replaced or persuaded to change his mind. Under such conditions property ownership would become meaningless. Once an item of property became the subject of a formal dispute, title would always be contingent on a land captain's change of heart, no matter how many times the matter had been settled. Unlimited power to alter judicial decisions would make the very existence of legal rules impossible, and therefore Pazukhin's provisions on the volost courts would hinder the emergence of consistent principles of law in the volosts. So said the five opposing members (ll. 432-34).

These five members, only one of whom (Zarin) was a "sure supporter," were taking a stand on much the same grounds as the whole committee had when it had agreed on the need to establish firm regulations for land use. Consistency, however, had no virtue for Pazukhin when it conflicted with experience. He, together with Krivskii, Kondoidi, Dolgovo-Saburov, and Gagarin, snapped back with the old Tolstoi line: "What you say is all very well in theory but experience shows, etc., etc." In this case, said the supporters of Tolstoi's vision, experience showed that the volost court was in hopeless chaos and could not be allowed any prerogatives whatever in practice. A peasant, especially a poor one, could easily be intimidated by his fellow villagers and prevented from appealing against an unjust decision. If the volost court were allowed to decide on its own, it would possess de facto arbitrary power. It could be used by powerful individuals—kulaks et al.—as a tool to dominate the villages and frustrate the good intentions of the land captains. Such in fact was the situation in 1886, said Pazukhin and the loyal four (ll. 434-37). The land captains would need full powers over the volost courts in order to cope with them.

Here again is an illustration of what the enactors meant by "protecting" law in the villages. They wanted the land captains to have enough power to obliterate peasant institutions if need be in order to make the peasants "normal" (modern) and bring them "justice."[22]

So much for the land captains' separation from peasant custom. We have now to consider the Gagarin committee's treatment of their freedom from bureaucratic (staff) interference. This subject came up in a discussion of the captain's authority to approve elections of volost elders. As one would expect, Pazukhin's project required the captain to confirm all elections of volost elders in his *uchastok*. No elder could take his post without the land captain's approval, and once this approval was forthcoming, no one below the gubernia level could remove the new official. One member of the committee wanted to amend this provision so that the uezd police commandant would also have to approve elections of volost elders. In other words, the captain was not to be allowed to act entirely on his own responsibility. Elders-elect could not take office until both captain and commandant had been consulted. This idea the committee voted down. The majority believed that the land captain's responsibility for volost administration should be "undivided" (ll. 411-12). If *any* government official below the gubernia level had the power to block *any* of the captain's actions or hear *any* complaints against them, this would open the door to all the evils of uezd politics and render the captain's position untenable. By blocking the election of a volost elder, a police commandant, like a modern-day hijacker, could compel a captain to negotiate on any matter, whether it had to do with the elder in question or not.

This view of uezd politics also found expression in Pazukhin's provision requiring *all* appeals against the land captain to go to the gubernia board (see Glossary). Ideally the captain was to have no superior but the board, and he could take no action that would not be subject to review by the board (ll. 452-55). One member of the committee opposed this idea in part. He suggested that the captain's executive decisions be appealed to the uezd congress instead of the gubernia

---

[22]Tolstoi reaffirmed his belief in the land captain's right to interfere in volost courts even when no one appealed to him as late as Feb. 1887 (TsGIAL, f. 1149, 1889g., op. vol. XI, d. 44, ll. 94-98), but this extreme notion was never enacted into law.

board.[23] The committee voted him down on the grounds that if a body of uezd administrators heard appeals against individual land captains, its unity would be broken by "intrigues" and "conflicts" among the members, and the captains would be trapped in politics. To keep the captain clear of the tangles of uezd administration, the committee prescribed a unique arrangement in which certain types of decisions were to be made by individual land captains, while other types would go directly to the uezd congresses for decision, and these two areas of command would be separate (ll. 413-15). Pazukhin's project had been more extreme than this, having assigned virtually all matters to the individual captains rather than the uezd congress. This was one instance when the committee ventured to moderate Pazukhin's revolutionary fervor. A majority voted to transfer a few categories of decisions to the congress. In general, however, the committee agreed wholeheartedly with Pazukhin that there should be no interference with the MVD "line" by any official or institution below the gubernia level. The authority of the capital-city "staff" was to stop abruptly in the governors' offices (ll. 439-40).[24]

To some extent, the gubernia board weakened the governor's personal "line" authority over the land captains. The officials on it were indeed "staff," and when they heard appeals against the land captains' decisions, they were, seemingly, interfering with the "line." The board's influence, however, was severely limited by provisions that allowed the governor to appeal its decisions to his superior, the MVD. According to Pazukhin's project, a governor's appeals against his board were to be heard either in the MVD itself or in the Senate. The ministry would pass on the expediency of the board's decisions, and the Senate would pass on their legality (ll. 456-58). What this meant, however, was that the ministry would act as a final court of appeal, for the project granted it the prerogative of deciding which matters involved legality and which involved expediency. The Senate was only to get cases when and if the MVD chose to pass them on. According to the committee's project, then,

---

[23] According to the statute on land captains, the uezd congress *(sezd)* consisted of two different boards *(prisutstviia):* one to handle administrative affairs, the other for judicial cases. The board for administrative affairs included the gentry marshal (as chairman), all land captains of the uezd, police commandant, treasurer, and chairman of the zemstvo board. In cases involving taxes and land repartitions, the uezd tax inspector *(podatnoi inspektor)* also attended as a voting member. The board for judicial cases also included the marshal and captains, but the other members were different. They were: the uezd member of the *okrug* court, the "honorary" *(pochetnye)* justices of the peace, and the town judges *(gorodskie sudi).* The deputy *prokuror* of the *okrug* court could participate in cases that involved the procuracy. (*TPSZ*, 6196, *Polozhenie*, arts. 69-76).

[24] It was indeed true in practice that no single authority could separate himself from the amorphous clutter of local politicians and government agents that prevailed in uezd administration (Yaney, 1973: 338-45).

the gubernia board's power to interfere in the MVD's "line" was to be minimal. Governors and land captains were not only to be free to do their work without outside supervision; they could also decide for themselves what their work consisted of. No law, or plan, or policy was to hover above the MVD's agents to guide them or provide an abstract basis for criticizing them. The "staff" would have no function but to serve the line when and if the line demanded its services. This was the general principle of organization underlying the vision of the MVD committee of 1886.[25]

The Rise and Fall of the Opposition, 1887-89

Here, in brief, is a narrative of the statute's progress from the time it left the MVD committee until its enactment into law. In November 1886, when the committee completed its deliberations, Tolstoi promptly submitted the result to the tsar. Alexander welcomed it with enthusiasm and just as promptly ordered the State Council to consider it. That is, he ordered the council to consider the part dealing with the land captains. By this time Pazukhin's original two-fold proposal had been divided into two separate parts, only one of which went to the council. The second, concerning zemstvo reorganization, was held back to await passage of the first. It would come before the council only in March 1890, almost a year after Tolstoi's death (Mamulova, 1960: 68, 72-73, 79-80).

The council's deliberations on the captains took much longer than the impatient tsar anticipated. On 24 February 1887 the members decided that Tolstoi's project required further study, and in the ensuing months the ministers and several other members wrote up their opinions at length. To these Pazukhin-Tolstoi wrote lengthy replies, and this flurry of paper lasted until December 1888, when at last the combined departments of law, economy, and religious and civil affairs received the project once again.

By this time the bureaucracy had organized itself to oppose Pazukhin's land captains under the leadership of Vorontsov-Dashkov. In September 1888 the minister of the imperial court wrote to Tolstoi that while he approved the idea of powerful officials ruling over uezds with subordinate captains in the *uchastki,* he firmly believed that these territorial chieftains should not be separate from uezd administration. Following an

[25]In the end, the statute did not fully realize Pazukhin's hope to free the land captains from uezd-level supervision. The additional law of 29 Dec. 1889 provided that the uezd congress would hear "protests" against some types of his judicial decisions (*TPSZ,* 6483, *Pravila o proizvodstve sudebnykh del, podvedomstvennykh zemskim nachalnikam i gorodskim sudiam,* art. 240). The July statute had provided that most of the captain's acts could be appealed only to the gubernia level, but in the ensuing months Pazukhin seems to have lost his fight to free his knights entirely from uezd influence.

idea originally set forth in the summer of 1887 by E. P. Staritskii, a member of the council, Vorontsov proposed to set up a chief administrator *(uezdnyi nachalnik)* with governor-like authority over all offices and institutions in his uezd, including zemstvoes and peasant volosts. Working directly under his supervision would be a network of district captains *(uchastkovye nachalniki),* each of whom would be responsible for governing his respective area as an agency of uezd administration. Vorontsov's captains differed from the Pazukhin-Tolstoi variety in two ways: they did not possess judicial power, and their executive responsibilities extended over the entire population in their *uchastki.* This arrangement, said Vorontsov, would extend the central administration's influence into rural Russia without setting the peasants apart from the rest of society or breaking up the government's organization into separate, uncoordinated components. By contrast, Pazukhin's project would fragment local administration more than it already was. It would reform only one area of administration and leave the rest untouched, thus perpetuating the unsatisfactory practice of introducing reforms by patchwork. In Vorontsov's view, Pazukhin was proposing to free the peasants from disorderly administration by separating them from all administration. Vorontsov preferred to unify uezd administration and render it orderly (TsGIAL, f. 1149, 1889g., op. vol. XI, d. 44, ll. 579-623, 840-42).

The combined departments endorsed Vorontsov's general idea at their December meeting by a vote of 18 to 7, and on 16 January 1889 the State Council as a whole followed suit by a vote of 39 to 13. This meant, in effect, that the tsar's ministers, his chief advisors, and some members of his family were tactfully, but firmly and publicly, suggesting that he drop the land captains. Alexander emphatically rejected this suggestion. He backed the minority, and this ended all open resistance. During the first half of 1889 there were sporadic attempts to delay Tolstoi's project, but at last, in July 1889, it came once again before the council, wherein it passed without further ado. Thus ends the narrative.

The State Council's opposition in January 1889 deserves further consideration here, if for no other reason than its remarkable strength. The 39 who were pushed aside when Alexander supported the minority included some of the best-informed and most influential men in the capital cities: Valuev, former MVD and erstwhile chairman of the commission on peasant agriculture; Liuboshchinskii, former chairman of the commission on volost courts; Reitern, Abaza, and Bunge, Russia's ministers of finance during the preceding three decades; Timashev, former MVD and a long-standing believer in the use of special MVD agents to rule the peasants; Ignatev, MVD in the first year of Alexander III's reign; Grand Duke Mikhail Nikolaevich, president of the State Council and uncle of the tsar, usually subservient and even obsequious before his strong-willed nephew but now untypically rebellious; and the Grand Dukes Vladimir and Aleksei Aleksandrovich, the tsar's own brothers. The opposition also included six incumbent ministers: Vannovskii of war, Chikhachev of the navy, Girs of foreign affairs, Solskii of state control, Pauker of communications, and Vorontsov of the imperial court (TsGIAL, f. 1149, 1889g., op. vol. XI, d. 44, 1. 840). Surely this was no crowd of raving liberals, willing to let the state collapse for the sake of their doctrines. All were faithful upholders of autocracy, and several of them stood high in Alexander III's favor. It would be no exaggeration to call them pillars of the government organization.

Even the statute's 13 supporters in the State Council gave Tolstoi and the tsar only the smallest comfort. The three most important ones— Pobedonostsev, Ostrovskii, and Manasein—had consistently opposed the statute before it reached the final stages of the legislative process, and they only voted for it in the council out of personal loyalty to the tsar (Polovtsov, 1966: II, 95, 102, 103, 117, 129-30, 136). Manasein expressed his discontent officially (albeit vaguely) as late as March 1887 (TsGIAL, f. 1149, 1889g., op. vol. XI, d. 44, ll. 139-63), and in 1888 he and Pobedonostsev only affected to back Tolstoi while delaying his project as long as possible in hopes that he would die soon and with him his statute (Polovtsov, 1966: II, 92-93, 136). Pobedonostsev went further. He wrote at least two personal letters to Alexander expressly disapproving of the statute, the last one on the very day (29 December 1888) that he was voting *for* it in the combined departments of the State Council (Pobedonostsev, 1926: II, 104-6, 204-8).[26]

This left only three ministers who supported the statute throughout the enactment process: Tolstoi himself; Vyshnegradskii, the incumbent MF; and Delianov, the minister of education. Practically speaking, however, these were not three independent statesmen but only one, Tolstoi, and two of his henchmen (Johnson, 1971: 26-27, 34-35, 275-76; Polovtsov, 1966: I, 540-41).

In the final analysis, then, Tolstoi and Alexander got the statute on land captains enacted virtually by themselves. Indeed, since Tolstoi was a dying man during the time the statute was being debated, Alexander had to do the job pretty much on his own. Certainly he finished it on his own. I. N. Durnovo, Tolstoi's successor as MVD, told Polovtsov on 30 April 1889 that when Alexander appointed him, the impatient tsar insisted on pushing the statute on land captains through the State Council before the summer. Durnovo protested his ignorance of the matter and his inability to defend Tolstoi's work, but the tsar brushed aside all objections (Polovtsov, 1966: II, 193). In the spring and summer

---

[26]On Ostrovskii's attitude, see Mamulova (1960: 75).

of 1889 Alexander III stood virtually alone against the united opposition of his highest servitors.

Given the very real force behind the opposition to Tolstoi, it is not surprising that it had some impact on Tolstoi's vision. Despite their failure to block the statute on land captains, its opponents did succeed in compelling the authors to express their beliefs more fully and to confront the contradictions in their thinking more directly. Pazukhin's initial project of early 1886 had not provided explicitly for a line-over-staff organization. Only in the course of his struggle with the opposition did the old man from the uezd find himself compelled to articulate in detail the vision that his more complaisant committee of 1886 had had only to imply.

The main issue in January 1889 was peasant separateness, the legacy of serfdom, preserved in rural administration by the arbitrator and by the habits of 30 years. Pazukhin and Tolstoi found themselves upholding it; the opposition protested that it should come to an end. But Pazukhin had not always been a believer in peasant separateness. Quite to the contrary: in the early 1880s he had dreamed of a land captain who would govern not only the peasantry but the entire rural population. In many respects this older idea resembled the captain of 1889. He was to have both judicial and executive powers. He would be explicitly set apart from courts of law and would not be hampered by other administrators. Local, sub-uezd courts—the justices of the peace—were to be eliminated, thus emptying the countryside of all other sub-uezd officials except the MVD's police. But in 1880-81 Pazukhin visualized a staff of sorts. Uezd administration was to be united with the zemstvoes into one organization, and the land captains were to be subordinated to it (Gessen, 1904: 194-98). In early 1886, when Pazukhin wrote up the first draft of his statute, he still visualized the uezd in much the same terms (Zaionchkovskii, 1970: 367). This concept, uniting all uezd institutions and including the whole population in something like a regiment of militia, resembled the proposal Vorontsov advanced in 1888 to *oppose* the Pazukhin-Tolstoi project! At first Pazukhin had wanted not to perpetuate the separate status of the peasant but only to mobilize the countryside, thereby uniting it. The only important difference between his early vision and Vorontsov's idea of late 1888 was that the latter did not give his captains both judicial and executive powers.

We already know that in fall, 1886, Pazukhin and his supporters in the Gagarin committee strenuously resisted all measures that might have allowed uezd administration to intervene in the land captains' affairs. By this time, then, Pazukhin's vision had undergone a change. Uezd administration was to retain the conventional separation between judicial and executive powers, the local justices of the peace were to be left in peace, and the land captains were to be set apart from this old bureaucratic, staff-over-line arrangement to work on their own with the peasants.

How did this change occur? The evidence does not admit of any definitive answer, but the best guess is that Pazukhin and Tolstoi amended their project during the summer of 1886 in response to opposition from Manasein, the minister of justice. Manasein wished above all to maintain the legal system established in 1864, including the justices of the peace. He protested the idea of combining executive and judicial powers in any one official and he objected strenuously to the elimination of his local judges (Zaionchkovskii, 1970: 367-68). Tolstoi and Manasein arrived at a compromise. The MVD got his line-over-staff agents; Manasein retained his justices. In order to keep them from running into one another, the captains would be expressly confined to peasant affairs, while the justices would be expressly excluded from them. This arrangement brought Manasein, Pobedonostsev, and Ostrovskii together with Tolstoi in an uneasy agreement, which was incorporated into the project the Gagarin committee considered in the fall of 1886. Manasein continued to voice his opposition to Tolstoi's project as late as March 1887, but he refrained from attacking its provisions. His note of that month confined itself to vague generalities and asked for delay (TsGIAL, f. 1149, 1889g., op. vol. XI, d. 44, ll. 139-63). He voted on Tolstoi's side in the State Council.

Obviously Manasein's opposition had an important impact on Pazukhin's vision. Instead of working as a line-over-staff agent under a powerful uezd commander, the captain would work directly under the governor. Instead of governing everyone, the new knight of rural management would oversee only the peasants. Confronted with a choice between the omnipotence of their captains and the unity of uezd administration, Pazukhin and Tolstoi agreed to sacrifice the latter in order to keep the former. Above all, they wanted line-over-staff administration in the countryside.

The reasoning underlying the Tolstoi-Manasein compromise remains mysterious. Polovtsov's diary offers a bizarre explanation, based on a conversation Polovtsov allegedly had with Manasein on 19 December 1888. On the day before, Manasein had cast his vote with Tolstoi in the meeting of the combined departments of the State Council, and Polovtsov asked him why he had done this despite Manasein's long-standing opposition to the land captains. The minister of justice replied that he expected the tsar to back Tolstoi's project no matter what it contained; thus there was no point in trying to stop it head on. Instead, Manasein said, he had tricked Tolstoi into the compromise described above, hoping that the combined rule of land captain and justice of the peace was so patently unworkable that it could not possibly be put into effect.

Alexander would sign the statute, but it would remain only a piece of paper. In short, Manasein set out to stop Tolstoi by rendering his project absurd. So said Polovtsov (1966: II, 131).

But the question of *how* Manasein and Tolstoi made their compromise is not of primary importance here. The significant thing is that it was Manasein who forced Pazukhin to accept a separate peasant administration. Peasant separation was not one of the cornerstones of Pazukhin's thinking. He had often spoken of the peasants' need for special attention (Pazukhin, 1886: 37; Weissman, 1976: 10), but he had not meant to split the government itself into parts. The separate village, like the land captain of pure gentry stock was not a dogma to which Pazukhin clung but simply a fact of life he accepted and with which he intended his new line-over-staff agents to deal. He only agreed to gentry preference and peasant separation because he feared that his basic idea, line-over-staff administration, would not be accepted on any other terms.

Whether he intended it or not, Manasein certainly did set Pazukhin up for the State Council's opposition. In mid-1887, when the council's initial response to the proposed statute began to take form, one of the members, E. P. Staritskii, openly accused Tolstoi of undermining the government's unity (TsGIAL, f. 1149, 1889g., op. vol. XI, d. 44, ll. 278-89). This was a formidable challenge indeed. So long as the MVD had had only believers in local autonomy, representative institutions, and constitutions to deal with, it could brush them off as parasitic landholders, doctrinaire liberals, and subverters of Russian unity. Now, however, Tolstoi found himself cast as a revolutionary, and he was compelled to make the radical essence of his vision clear—especially the embarrassing fact that his and Pazukhin's line-over-staff arrangement could only extend bureaucracy by undermining it. In November 1887 Tolstoi's reply to Staritskii appeared (ll. 459-68). It was at this point that he began to utter his existentialist remarks about the impossibility of governing by law or acting by plan. He could get away with these remarks because he had the tsar's unwavering support. On the other hand, he had to make them, because even the tsar's support did not free him from the necessity of conferring with his fellow statesmen and responding to their accusations regarding the revolutionary implications of his vision. We may say, then, that the debate over Vorontsov's proposal brought into the open the absurdity of Pazukhin's compromise with Manasein. It would indeed be awkward to have a land captain and a justice of the peace in each *uchastok:* a despot for the peasantry and a court of law for everyone else. Not only would it widen the gap between peasants and citizens, it would split the government bureaucracy into two sections that would be wholly separate and yet would have to operate in unison. A number of council members, notably Timashev and Solskii, would have supported Pazukhin's original idea of a single chain of command incorporated into the government organization as a whole, but they voted with Vorontsov because they could not accept either of the extremes the statute on land captains embodied: peasant separateness and virtually absolute line-over-staff authority.[27]

Why, we might ask, did Pazukhin and Tolstoi insist on peasant separateness in the face of all the opposition it created? Pazukhin had not wanted it to begin with. It had only entered into his project as part of an attempt to gain Manasein's allegiance, and since Tolstoi enjoyed the unwavering support of the tsar, one would think he could have scuttled the minister of justice easily enough. Why, instead, did he and Pazukhin now begin to attack the concept of unified uezd administration as such and to uphold peasant separation as a positive good?

Insofar as the answer to this question lies in substantive issues, it is that Tolstoi and Pazukhin had learned something new in the course of their debates. When Pazukhin composed his first draft, he did not see very clearly what line-over-staff organization would entail in practice. He and Tolstoi seem to have imagined that all Russians would join hands to follow their local captains into reform. The spirit of common striving would overcome all obstacles and smooth over all conflicts. As they worked their project through the MVD committee and the long inter-ministerial debates, however, the authors perceived that line-over-staff agents would be incapable of governing citizens. Indeed, they could not *govern* anyone. The land captains, like the arbitrators, would be useful only for the purpose of *imposing* reform, which meant that their line-over-staff operation would only be suitable, if at all, in the volosts. If line-over-staff organization was actually to be put into practice, it would demand peasant separation. Carried to an extreme, line-over-staff organization implied nothing less than the destruction of the government at the hands of its own agents; therefore the existing bureaucratic-systematic institutions had to be roped off, so to speak, from the supposedly all-powerful captains. The *idea* of a bureaucratic agent independent from bureaucratic control is logically absurd, and a bureaucracy cannot consciously and formally base itself on absurdity any more easily than a bishop can pray to Satan at high mass. Yet this was what Tolstoi was trying to do in 1886-89. When he became aware of this, he recognized that peasant separation was indeed a precondition for line-over-staff operation, and so he and Pazukhin became advocates of it.

The significance of this development in Tolstoi-Pazukhin's thinking is that it reveals yet more clearly the revolutionary essence of their vision.

[27]One may infer Timashev's and Solskii's views from Polovtsov's report of their statements in the council debates (1966: II, 119-20, 130, 146). On Timashev's earlier views regarding government organization, see *Zapiska* (1873) and also Abbott (1971: 182, 185-86, 204-5).

They frequently tried to mask this essence even from themselves, but, when pushed to the wall, they had at last to assert in so many words that their primary purpose was to *move* peasant society. They had to specify the price they were willing to pay in order to bring effective leadership to rural Russia. Far from being a conservative trying to preserve gentry privilege or traditional peasant communities, Pazukhin was setting out to drive the gentry into the unpleasant task of ripping peasant society apart.

One can find grounds for doubting Pazukhin's radicalism before 1886, but this was only because no one had yet forced him to express it clearly. In the beginning the enactors had not pretended to think logically. They had had no intention of erecting their dream into a system of government. What they had wanted, in essence, was to set their captains in motion and then ride with the result. Manasein spoiled this plan by treating the statute as a system of government and then pointing out its logical conclusion, thereby forcing Pazukhin and Tolstoi, who despised theoretical standpoints, to try to talk like theoreticians. In order to prevent a tangle between bureaucratic order and their independent "line," they accepted peasant separateness. They took a theoretical position, and Vorontsov had only to point to the contradiction in the position. With the peasantry explicitly set apart in order to preserve the land captain's independence, the disadvantages of this independence stood out in sharp outline. "Tolstoi," the opposition asked, "do you want independent line agents in the *uchastki* so badly that you are willing to split up the population into two separate societies to get them?" And Tolstoi had to answer. He had to articulate matters he would rather have left unarticulated. Legality, social stability, and bureaucratic propriety were only peripheral matters, he found himself replying. The main purpose, Russia's most desperate need, was to *move* (Polovtsov, 1966: II, 104, 151-52).[28]

Alexander III agreed. Delay disturbed him far more than contradictions. In early 1889 the emperor of Russia was in a mood for visions, not analyses, and he tended to regard the statesmen who pointed out Tolstoi's inconsistencies as contemptible clerks. Lacking the courage to fight the tsar in the open, they were seeking to entangle him and his henchmen in pointless quibbles. Two years before, in early 1887, Tolstoi had reported to the council that Alexander wanted the project finished before the summer holidays (TsGIAL, f. 1149, 1889g., op. vol. XI, d. 44,

---

[28]Pobedonostsev may have grasped the situation more clearly than anyone else at the time. He never ceased to think Tolstoi's project was a poorly constructed affair (1926: II, 204-8). On the other hand, as he said more than once to Polovtsov, Tolstoi was the closest thing to a strong leader the government had (Polovtsov, 1966: II, 97). This, it seems, was Pobedonostsev's—and the tsar's—principal reason for supporting Tolstoi no matter how inconsistent his arguments were.

1. 1). By early 1888 the tsar was already impatient. Polovtsov was so afraid of the royal anger that he resorted to elaborate maneuvers, involving almost all the ministers and council members, before he ventured to put off the council's consideration yet another year (Polovtsov, 1966: II, 92-97). Not surprisingly, Alexander's impatience was all the greater in 1889, as he said on several occasions (pp. 161, 180, 192). Two years had already passed; now a third was about to follow; and still the State Council debated. This deliberate obfuscation was intolerable.

In late January 1889, shortly after the 39-13 vote in favor of Vorontsov's counterproposal, Alexander sent a note to his long-suffering uncle, the Grand Duke Mikhail Nikolaevich, president of the State Council, saying that the royal will agreed with Tolstoi and his 12 supporters. This was not unusual in itself. The tsar could support a minority in his council if he chose, and all the post-Liberation tsars did it on occasion. In this case, however, the royal will went further and added a new proviso, one that had not yet appeared in any proposal before the council. *This* was unusual (Yaney, 1973: 265-74).

Alexander's note read as follows:

> Being in agreement with the opinion of the thirteen members, I desire that the justices of the peace in the uezds be eliminated in order to make available a sufficient number of reliable land captains and to lighten the uezds' financial burden. Part of the justices' cases can be handed over to the land captains and the volost courts, and a lesser part—the more serious cases—can be transferred to the *okrug* courts. In any case I insist that these changes not interfere with the final consideration of the project before the summer holidays. (Quoted in Polovtsov, 1966 : II, 485)

The Grand Duke Mikhail was thrown into confusion. What did his nephew have in mind? To eliminate the justices of the peace was virtually to destroy the government's judicial system outside the cities. The rural population would no longer have courts of law in the *uchastok* or even in the uezd. The nearest judge would be in the capital city of the *okrug* (region), an administrative unit about the size of a gubernia. Who would take over the justices' functions? The *okrug* court would take on some, but obviously it could not do the work of the more than 50 justices in each *okrug* (on the average). Alexander's note did not spell it out, but the implication was clear. Most of the justices' work would be taken over by land captains and volost courts. Not only the peasants but the entire rural population would come under the captains, just as Pazukhin's original project had suggested. Thus perished Manasein's compromise. Administration was to be unified after all. Moreover, the job was to be done quickly. Nothing was to impede the completion of the State Council's deliberations before it adjourned for the summer.

If the tsar's note bewildered his uncle, it infuriated Polovtsov. As imperial secretary and general manager of the State Council, he took this blatant disregard for the council's prerogatives as a personal attack on himself. He reacted with an unusual action of his own: he went directly to Alexander and protested. We have Polovtsov's own account of this meeting as he wrote it down in his diary (pp. 154-58). Alexander received him and Tolstoi, and the three of them wrangled through the better part of a Saturday afternoon. Polovtsov was at a disadvantage. He could not challenge the tsar's power to write notes as he pleased, nor could a mere imperial secretary venture to disagree with what the tsar chose to write. Polovtsov had to confine himself to claiming that the tsar's command was unenforceable.

He argued as follows. The imperial note was self-contradictory. On the one hand, it decided an argument about whether the land captains were to be exclusively rulers over peasants or parts of uezd administration. By agreeing with the "thirteen," it accepted the former position unequivocally. On the other hand, it made the land captain a judge in certain types of civil and criminal cases over the entire population of his *uchastok*. These two facts did not go together. The tsar's decision for the minority and his proposed amendment could not be incorporated into a single body of legislation. Worse, Tolstoi's project did not make the land captain a court per se but only gave him power to manipulate the volost courts. By implication, therefore, anyone desiring justice from the land captain—according to a strict interpretation of the tsar's note—would first have to present himself to the volost court and be judged. In short, Alexander III was ordering that the entire rural population be subjected to exclusively peasant courts. The tsar was inadvertently going a long way toward meeting the objections to peasant separation, though in a way no one had foreseen or desired. As Polovtsov saw it, Alexander was making it impossible for the council to legislate. The whole purpose of bringing the division over Vorontsov's proposal before the tsar was to get a clear decision. The imperial note had not only failed to provide one but it had thrown the whole foundation for the debate into disarray. Polovtsov argued in vain. The tsar's note to the State Council was left unchanged. Clearly Alexander was not going to tolerate any further opposition, no matter how good its logic might be. The tsar, it seems, was at least as passionate a revolutionary as his henchmen.

It took time and cut into the summer holidays, but at last the council produced Alexander's statute. The most appalling discrepancies introduced by the imperial note were compromised away. Each uezd got its own judge—officially styled the uezd member of the *okrug* court— which would provide the nonpeasant population outside the cities with courts of law. The rural gentry would not have to bow to the volost courts after all. On the negative side, however, legal separation between peasant and nonpeasant was fortified all the more.[29]

In the end the land captain did not get his independence. Pazukhin's and Tolstoi's vision did not in fact come to dominate government organization on any level. But, then, their vision is significant to the history of agrarian reform not because of its immediate effects but because it shows us the purpose underlying the statute on land captains. The enactors did not consciously see themselves mobilizing peasants, nor, in the event, did the land captains actually prove capable of mobilizing anyone. For all their failings, however, the land captains did reflect a far more insistent urge to mobilize than any administrative reform since the time of the Emperor Paul. Unlike the arbitrators, they were explicitly authorized to intervene in the villages and volosts *on their own initiative,* not merely when individual peasants requested it. Moreover, they were coming to the villages as agents of bureaucracy, not merely as benign preservers of old ways. In theory, they were intended to protect the villages from bureaucracy; in practice, however, they had much more to do in their *uchastki* than to keep bureaucrats out. To justify his existence to the capital cities, each captain would have to perform all the functions bureaucracy aspired and/or pretended to perform. After all, he was not out in the villages because bureaucracy was bad per se, but only because bureaucrats had not been able to function effectively there on their own terms. In brief, the land captain had to serve bureaucracy's purposes. He was not an antidote for bureaucracy—as his creators had occasionally claimed—but a missionary from it, a symbol of it, and a surrogate for it.

Saddled with all these roles and expectations, the captains never had a chance to become an institution of government. After 1889 bureaucracy hastened to press its demands upon them, and they fell rapidly into the same sterile clerkdom as had their predecessors. It might not be true, however, that the captains failed to achieve their purpose. If we accept the proposition that the main aim of the captain's creators was to augment and extend the power of government, then he may have done his work well, for it was the nature of his position that he should strive to eliminate himself. Tolstoi and Pazukhin intended him to prepare the way for joining the peasantry together with the other inhabitants of Russia in a common citizenship, and his success at bringing this to pass had,

---

[29]Since the *okrug* was approximately as large as a gubernia, the establishment of an uezd "member" did extend the central government's judicial system much further into the countryside, though not far enough, of course, to replace the justices of the peace that Alexander was eliminating.

perforce, to reduce him to the position of an ordinary bureaucrat. The captains were the vanguard of the capital-city movement to invade and destroy peasant society, and in this sense they made a contribution. They began the advance, and this is what a vanguard is supposed to do.

CHAPTER 4

The Beginnings of Action, Part Two: The Land Captains at Work

...the poor virtuous man must be given a well-earned rest, because the very phrase *virtuous man* is beginning to sound shallow on people's lips, because the virtuous man has been turned into a sort of horse and there's no author who hasn't ridden him, urging him on with his whip or whatever comes to hand. And so, they've exhausted the virtuous man; there's not even a trace of virtue left in him.

Nikolai Gogol (1961: 251)

We have seen that the government's earliest efforts at agrarian reform repeatedly called forth the idea of an all-powerful agent, possessing virtue, whose general purpose was to establish legal system in the villages. The presumption was that legal system would allow and encourage the peasants to modernize their agriculture and become useful, prosperous citizens. With the land captains this idea reached—or almost reached—its quintessential form: line-over-staff organization. The captains, unlike any of their predecessors, operated in the presence of a legal system and depended upon it to guarantee their power to disregard it. Given this paradoxical arrangement, the captains had either to take over and eliminate the system on which they depended or else suffer the elimination of their own nonlegal powers. This chapter will show that the second course was the one followed—as it must always be if an organization is to go on existing.

A. THE DISAPPEARANCE OF THE GENTRY

Before describing the dissolution of the captains' line-over-staff position, we must add yet one more brief chapter to our discussion of gentry privilege. Gentry participation in land captainry underwent important changes during the decades following 1889, and a brief description of these changes will conclude our demonstration of the MVD's utter indifference to the matter of gentry status.

The statute on land captains established two sets of minimal requirements for aspiring land captains. One was in articles 6 and 7 of the *Polozhenie* (*TPSZ,* 6196), which provided that the captains had to be local hereditary gentry with certain minimal amounts of landed property, education, and service experience. This set of requirements was imposed in 31 of the original 37 gubernias where captains were established—all, that is, except Astrakhan, Viatka, Perm, Olonets, Stavropol, and Vologda, where very few gentry estates existed. In these 31 gubernias land captains in each uezd were nominated by the uezd gentry marshal with the approval of the uezd gentry assembly. The gubernia marshal compiled nominations from the uezds into a gubernia list and submitted it to the governor. All candidates had to meet the standards set forth in articles 6 and 7 unless the marshal and governor could not find enough qualified candidates, in which case candidates who met only the second set of requirements could be appointed.

These much lower standards were set forth in articles 15 and 16, which allowed candidates to be appointed without either gentry status or landed property. All an article-15 captain had to have was a high school education or a certain number of years in government service. The decree of 29 December 1889 added a special provision "temporarily" allowing the MVD to appoint anyone it thought suitable under article 15, even candidates who did not meet any formal education or service requirements whatsoever (*TPSZ,* 6482, pt. III).

As it happened, the majority of initial appointments in the 31 gubernias met the requirements set forth in articles 6 and 7. Exact figures regarding initial appointments are not available for all gubernias, but in six whose records happen to provide reliable totals, 249 land captains—87% of the total number in these gubernias—met the standards, while 36, or 13%, had to be appointed under article 15.[1]

Figures for other gubernias do not lend themselves to exact compilation, but in the 31 where candidates were supposed to meet the standards of articles 6 and 7, it is safe to say that at least 75% were local herditary noblemen. A fair number of captains appointed in the other six gubernias were also hereditary gentry, and some of them had considerable experience as servitors in the locales where they were appointed. In

---

[1]The six gubernias were Moscow (TsGIAL, f. 1291, op. 30, 1889g., d. 37, pt. 1, ll. 42-48), Kaluga (d. 39, ll. 55-61), Tula (1890g., d. 22, pt. 1, ll. 87-91, 105), Vladimir (d. 26, ll. 45-47), Pskov (d. 53, pt. 1, ll. 67-68), and Riazan (1889g., d. 38, pt. 1, ll. 72-79).

a sense, therefore, they could be conceived of as local hereditary gentry, though they held no land in their uezds. But even if we were to assume that *no* appointees in these six gubernias were either gentry or local, the overall proportion of local hereditary gentry among the initial contingent of captains would still be at least two-thirds. We may say, then, that the captains of the early 1890s generally bore out the hope that rural "virtue"—i.e., willingness to serve the government—resided in the gentry.[2]

In ensuing years, especially after 1905, land captains who qualified under articles 6 and 7 became steadily scarcer. All laws extending the captains to new areas required candidates to satisfy only article 15 (*Sbornik,* 1901: II, 1, 5). Likewise, the peasant captains of Siberia had to qualify only under article 15. They too needed to have a high school education or three years' experience in rural administration, nothing more (Volkov, 1910: 1212). By 1905 only 31 of 51 gubernias with land captains were attempting, with diminishing success, to hire local gentry landholders. Twenty were not even trying. It is safe to assume that the number of these would-be patriarchs who were still *local* hereditary gentry was well under half the total. In 1902 the MVD reported to the State Council that only 20% of the captains in service met the standards of articles 6 and 7 (Weissman, 1976: 34).

But it is difficult to express gentry disappearance in figures. Not all captains appointed under article 15 were necessarily of low social status. Some, at least, were university educated, and some were landholding hereditary gentry serving in a gubernia other than the one in which their estates were located. Even if we did know the qualifications of every captain accurately, the land section's records still do not tell us reliably how many positions were vacant at any one time. Thus even the total number of land captains in service is not knowable with precision, let alone the percentage of them who fell into any particular category.[3]

It is obvious, however, that the percentage of captains who met the standards of articles 6 and 7 declined with time. The records are full of complaints from governors to the MVD regarding the difficulty of find-

---

[2]Moreover, the gentry played a key role in selecting most captains, though a governor could reject their nominees. If the MVD's central offices backed the governor, the rejection stood (*Svod,* 1903: 19-20).

[3]The land section *(zemskii otdel)* was the department of the MVD that exercised direct supervision over the land captains and all the other types of peasant managers who worked for the MVD (as described in ch. 3, sec. A). This is not to say that the land section was the sole directorate of peasant affairs; in fact, there were a great many departments and sections in the various ministries that participated in peasant "direction." We may say, however, that the land section was the only government department to be concerned solely with the management of the peasantry. From the time of its establishment in the late 1850s, its officials drew up much of the legislation having to do with peasant administration and/or reform.

ing suitable candidates. Most appointments made in Moscow gubernia during the 1890s met only the requirements of article 15, and a substantial number of captains in Kharkov came in on this basis during the same period (TsGIAL, f. 1291, op. 30, 1889g., dd. 36-37). The governor of Smolensk reported a shortage of captains qualified under articles 6 and 7 as early as September 1894, although, he said, there had been no lack of them in the beginning (op. 39, 1894g., d. 5, l. 5). An MVD circular of 18 December 1898 complained that many positions throughout European Russia were remaining vacant for long periods of time for lack of replacements (*Sbornik,* 1901: I, 14-15), which indicates that the difficulty of finding suitable candidates had become general by then. An official MVD paper of 1903 stated explicitly that the "downfall" of the landholding gentry had given rise to a serious shortage of qualified land captains (*Trudy,* 1903-4: I, 66).

The downfall speeded up in 1906. The decree of 5 October ordered, among other things, that all positions in the government be opened to all classes on an equal basis (*TPSZ,* 28392). No exception was made for land captains—the decree did not mention them—and the implication was clear that rural knights could now be drawn from any class. Governors were now free to nominate candidates who were not of the gentry class even where gentry were available, and they did this frequently. They even put up an occasional peasant for the job (TsGIAL, f. 1291, op. 32, dd. 21, 23). Nevertheless, articles 6 and 7 of the 1889 statute were never formally revised to conform to the 1906 decree, and although the number of landholding gentry who served in their own locales continued to shrink, gentry appointments to land captainry continued until 1917 to exceed those from other classes (dd. 21, 23, 29).[4]

Certainly the MVD did not push very hard to democratize its rural agents after 1906. So far as I know, the land section's earliest reference to the impact of the 5 October decree on land captains came in May 1913, six and a half years after the decree was published. Readers of the section's journal for that month confronted the "news" that, as a result of the 1906 decree, gentry no longer enjoyed preference over nongentry in the selection process (*IZO,* 1913: 232). It seems, then, that although the "civil rights" legislation of 1906 foreshadowed the end of gentry land captainry, it had little immediate impact.

What did change dramatically in 1905-7 was the appointment process. Local landholders with the qualifications set forth in articles 6 and 7 ceased almost entirely to present themselves as candidates, and as a result

[4]With regard to the above citations, the items in *delo* 21, covering 1912, are not paged. The reference to *delo* 23, which covers 1913, is in *spisok* 34. *Delo* 29 covers appointments in 1916, and its contents show a clear majority of hereditary gentry, almost none of whom resided in the areas where they served.

the MVD began to take over the job of finding, training, and appointing its captains on its own. Before 1906, says an official historian of the MVD, the governors seldom asked the ministry to send men to fill vacancies. Thereafter, this became common practice (Boianus, 1911: 15). The records I have seen tend to confirm this generalization. The governor of Nizhnii Novgorod, for example, reported an especially acute shortage of captains in September 1905, and from then on he kept up a stream of requests for replacements (TsGIAL, f. 1291, op. 30, 1890g., d. 57, pt. 3, e.g., ll. 37, 42-43). In August 1906 the governor of Chernigov asked the MVD to supply candidates, and he continued this practice in ensuing years (1889g., d. 41, pt. 2, l. 85). World War I brought on an extreme shortage of captains by any standard. The governor of Tula reported in April 1915 that 20 of his 57 captains had gone into the army and would have to be replaced from outside the gubernia (1890g., d. 22, pt. 2, l. 188). By 1917 land captains no longer had any direct association with gentry institutions.[5]

No one in the MVD made any serious effort to hinder the gentry's disappearance. I. N. Durnovo, who was minister from 1889 to 1895, was anxious for his captains to have good relations with local gentry institutions. When he confronted disagreements between uezd gentry marshals and governors regarding appointments to captaincies, he usually resolved them by allowing the governors to shift the candidates they favored to other uezds, where, presumably, they would not tangle with the marshals (see, e.g., pt. 1, ll. 82-83). It cannot be said, however, that either Durnovo or any of his successors adhered consistently to this principle. The central offices did not hesitate to cross with the local gentry in cases involving land captains.

Consider the case of A. A. Silin, a captain of Kharkov gubernia. In 1900 the governor liked him well enough to recommend him for a promotion in rank. In 1908, however, the head of the land section, Ia. Ia. Litvinov, denounced Silin for laziness and ordered the governor to "request" his "voluntary" retirement. The gubernia board rejected Litvinov's demand, saying that Silin had worked diligently for 18 years. In particular the board referred to a report from the uezd gentry marshal, commending Silin for his steadfastness in the face of great difficulties during the critical years of 1905-6. But the MVD swept all this aside. In May 1909 Silin resigned because of "illness" (d. 66, ll. 8-26).

Not that Silin's case was typical. After reading through a fair number of MVD decisions regarding complaints against land captains, I confess that I would not recognize a typical case if I saw one. Nor have I

[5]Dubrovskii (1963: 164-67) conveys the impression that most land captains were still local gentry after 1905 and that the MVD had no trouble finding men to fill the positions. He is quite wrong on both counts.

been able to identify a typical MVD attitude. Many servitors believed that local hereditary gentry made better land captains. Litvinov, who was so hard on poor Silin, often made passing reference to the solid qualities of experienced captains—or officials of any kind—who were local gentry. Litvinov did not favor hereditary gentry per se (see below, sec. B), but when he found a competent captain who was of this class, he felt that the world was as it should be.[6] By contrast, Litvinov's long-time co-worker in the land section, D. I. Pestrzhetskii, apparently disapproved of men with lineages, especially those who served as captains in the vicinity of their own estates. Pestrzhetskii stated his feeling quite plainly when he reported on his inspection of peasant administration in Novgorod gubernia in 1910. Surprisingly, his unusually blunt remarks were published in the land section's journal in 1911. Ever since 1889, he opined, the worst feature of the land-captain organization had been the involvement in it of uezd gentry marshals. They had always been unreliable. Now, in 1910, in Novgorod gubernia, only two of them were still performing their administrative functions, and a fair number did not even reside in the gubernia, let alone in their uezds. As for the Novgorod captains, most of them were local hereditary gentry, he said; *"nevertheless"* they were doing good work (*IZO,* 1911: 412-13). Litvinov would have said "therefore." The point, however, is that no land-section bureaucrat really cared what social status the captain possessed, regardless of attitudes. The MVD was no upholder of the gentry, only a utilizer.

B. THE DWINDLING OF LINE-OVER-STAFF ADMINISTRATION

The point to be made in the following pages is that the land section's line-over-staff organization eroded away primarily because of its inherently self-destructive nature. Before describing this erosion, however, I must acknowledge that opposition to the captains continued to be strong in the capital cities throughout the tsarist government's last years, so strong that one is tempted now and then to erect it into an explanation for the demise of the captains' line-over-staff authority.

Let us consider this opposition for a moment. It is common knowledge among historians of modern Russia that the captains were among the favorite targets of all opponents of the government, left-wing, liberal, and right-wing alike. Less well known but perhaps more significant was the continuing opposition within the tsarist bureaucracy. Alexander and his loyal successor, Nicholas II, stifled all overt opposition, but neither of these champions could eliminate or even weaken the prevailing sentiment

[6]For typical Litvinov remarks, see, e.g., *IZO* (1910: 128-30, 176).

of hostility toward the captains throughout virtually all government offices in St. Petersburg. As Alexander stood against his officials in 1887-89 to enact his statute, so also did Nicholas have to stand against them to keep the captains in being.

Nicholas was ready to fight for his captains at the drop of a hat. Whenever the subject came up, he began snarling, as if fearful that the slightest sign of weakness on his part would release a wave of attacks. Typical of his conduct was his reaction to some remarks by the governor of Mogilev in his annual report for 1895. The bureaucracy was preparing to introduce the captains into his gubernia, and he was foolhardy enough to express doubt concerning the wisdom of combining judicial and executive prerogatives in one official. When this heresy came under Nicholas's scrutiny, he wrote in the margin, "I do not permit such doubts" (*Svod vysochaishikh,* 1897: 90-91). More to Nicholas's liking was the annual report from the governor of Bessarabia for the same year, proclaiming unrestrained enthusiasm for the land captain's powers. If the captain were deprived of his judicial power, warned Bessarabia, he would be reduced to the level of a mere *stanovoi.* "Businesslike report," Nicholas scribbled approvingly, and he underlined some of Bessarabia's remarks about the awful consequences that would ensue if the captains lost their judicial power. "About this," said the imperial scrawl, "there can be no discussion" (pp. 12-13). Nicholas II left many such comments on the land captains. Doubtless his continuing defensiveness reflected his awareness of continuing opposition to them among his high-level officials. In 1898 he was so afraid of this opposition that he published the statute establishing peasant captains in Siberia without allowing the State Council to discuss it.

Despite the strength of the opposition during the decades after 1889, I do not believe it was the main force reducing the captains to clerkdom. As I shall suggest here, the dwindling of line-over staff administration had no direct connection with the opposition. It was the MVD itself that strove to throttle its own agents and bring them under control.

The Land Captains' Decline to Clerkdom after 1905

In 1906 the government decided with unusual abruptness to do away with peasant separation. Its most direct attack came with the decree of 5 October, a bold pronouncement enacted on the basis of article 87 (see Glossary) of the new fundamental laws, allowing individual peasants to do a number of things without having to get permission from their households, villages, or volosts. An adult peasant no longer needed anyone's permission to attend school or take up a variety of occupations. Moreover, he could do these things and still remain a member of his original village. He could even acquire land in other villages and be a member in all of them. He could break with his family on the same basis as nonpeasants could, he was no longer required by law to obey direct orders from land captains, and he was no longer subject to any punishments except those imposed on other classes of the population (*TPSZ,* 28392). Now the land section was able to say officially that the government had adopted a new aim in rural Russia: "to establish a common system of rights and administration that would unite villages with the other citizens of the Empire" (*Kratkii,* 1908: 28). The direct effect of the October decree was to loosen the formal authority of traditional peasant institutions over their members, and since the land captain's power was exercised in large part through these institutions, it too suffered limitation. In 1912 the captains lost all their exceptional power, at least on paper. The law of 15 June re-established *uchastok* justices of the peace and set them over the volost courts, thus stripping the captains of their judicial functions and leaving them only such executive functions as the law assigned them. The road to clerkdom had reached its end.[7]

Legislation was by no means the only weapon bureaucracy used to bring the land captains under staff control. The MVD's land section exerted itself strenuously after 1905 to put the erstwhile knights in their proper, bureaucratic place. The section's official history, written in 1908, notes sadly that the decree of 5 October aroused opposition among the

[7]The 15 June law is in *TPSZ,* 37328. The law itself, setting up the justices, is in XXXII, sec. 1, 622-705. The new rules on the volost court are in *prilozhenie* 1 to the law, printed in XXXII, sec. 2, 212-18. Post-1912 justices, unlike the pre-1889 ones, had full jurisdiction over peasants and nonpeasants alike. There were special rules for the peasants, but they applied only when and if all the disputants in a particular case desired to be governed by them (pp. 683-84).

It would be more precise to say that the end of the road to clerkdom was in sight. The new judicial institutions did not spring up immediately. Implementation of the 15 June law went slowly before the outbreak of World War I and slower yet during the war years. By 1917 the new institutions covered at most only 20 gubernias. They were first established in June 1913 in ten gubernias: Chernigov, Ekaterinoslav, Kharkov, Kherson, Kiev, Kursk, Podoliia, Poltava, Tavrid, and Volyniia (*IZO,* 1913: 313-25). This establishment, however, was only on paper. The new justices did not begin operating until 1914 (p. 528). Another ten gubernias—Bessarabia, Grodno, Kovno, Minsk, Mogilev, Orel, Tambov, Vilna, Vitebsk, and Voronezh—were scheduled in 1913 to have the new institutions by 1915 (p. 295). On 16 Sept. 1914, however, the government ordered a delay of one year (1914: 392). Meanwhile, an MVD circular of 14 May 1914 had announced plans to extend the new institutions to 15 more gubernias, including, at last, Moscow and St. Petersburg (pp. 237-38). But these plans, it seems, were never carried out.

Moreover, it must be kept in mind that the 5 Oct. decree was also slow to take effect in the countryside. A note of 8 Aug. 1917 from the MF to the land section refers to a case in which government officials had successfully upheld a village in its efforts to prevent two men from becoming members in it (TsGIAL, f. 1291, op. 51, 1917g., d. 81, ll. 137-40).

captains. Some recalcitrant knights did not comprehend the new limitations on their authority (p. 19). In order to deal with this surly and undesirable conservatism, the MVD held a congress of selected permanent members of gubernia boards in the fall of 1907. Not surprisingly, the selected permanent members joined section officials in showering the captains with abuse. *Most* captains are lazy, declared the chairman of the congress. With few exceptions, they do not try to acquaint themselves with the peasants in their *uchastki*. Their sloth and passive formalism have created a gap between government and peasants, one result of which was the rural violence of 1905-6. Obviously, said the chairman, the captains require supervision, and the section is going to see to it that they get it (*Trudy*, 1908: 89-91).[8]

It is certainly true that the land section took a keen interest in its captains after 1906. It stepped up its inspections of them drastically. In 1906 section officials devoted 150 man-days to inspecting gubernia boards, uezd congresses, and land captains; in 1908 and thereafter the annual rate rose to well over 1,000 (Boianus, 1911: 10). Many reports of these inspections were published in the section's journal *(IZO)*. Individual captains and board members who were found wanting were identified and their misdeeds graphically described. In a more constructive vein the section began to play a greater role in selecting new captains, and it introduced training programs for candidates. By 1909 all newly appointed land captains were receiving some kind of training (*Kratkii*, 1908: 20-21; Boianus, 1911: 15-18; *Programma*, 1914). There can be no doubt that after 1905 the MVD itself wanted its captains to be clerks.[9]

[8]Concerning the office of permanent member *(nepremennyi chlen)* of the gubernia board, see Yaney (1973: 325-26, 369, 377-79) and the Glossary.

In one respect, at least, the congress's criticisms were unfair. From the very beginning the expectation that a captain could acquaint himself thoroughly with the peasants in his *uchastok* was preposterous. The grotesque fantasy of a land captain "close" to the peasants had been a basic element in Pazukhin's thinking ever since 1880, and it had been one of the chief justifications for line-over-staff authority. But actual captains were never close to actual peasants, not even in theory. The Gagarin committee had called for *uchastki* with a *minimum* population of 10,000 males (TsGIAL, f. 1282, op. 2, d. 1838, l. 407), and actual *uchastki* were not far from this ideal. They varied in population from about 20,000 to 40,000 men and women. As B. P. Mansurov indicated back in 1888, no captain could possible get "close" to 40,000 people (f. 1149, 1889g., op. vol. XI, d. 44, ll. 765-68).

[9]For examples of the land section's public attacks on its captains, see almost any issue of the *IZO* up to Mar. 1912 (e.g., 1910: 125-30). Then the *IZO* ceased publishing harsh personal attacks against deficient captains. Inspections continued, but published reports confined themselves to general statements— doubtless as a result of Stolypin's death in Sept. 1911 and his replacement as MVD by less energetic supporters of bureaucratic order and expansion.

Rejection of Line-over-Staff Administration in the Central Offices,
1896-1906

Many historians have assumed that the government's attack of 1906
on the traditional villages and volosts marked an abrupt end to the land
captains' arbitrary authority. This assumption has very little foundation
in fact. If the personal views of the directors of the land section are any
indication of the MVD's policies, it may be said that the dwindling of
line-over-staff administration was well underway by the late 1890s. The
first two men who managed the land section after 1889 actually believed
the land captains should be autonomous chiefs over a separate peasant
society. These were Dolgovo-Saburov, who ran the section from 1886 to
1893, and A. S. Stishinskii, who ran it from 1893 to 1896. As we have
seen, Dolgovo-Saburov was an early supporter of Pazukhin and a fellow
nobleman from Simbirsk (ch. 3, sec. D). He took over the section immediately after his helpful participation in that tidy little MVD committee
of 1886, wherein Pazukhin's dreams achieved their purest expression.
Stishinskii had also been associated with the Gagarin committee, not as a
voting member but as its recording secretary. In 1890-93 he assisted
Dolgovo-Saburov, and apparently he worked very closely with his chief.
His signature appeared very often on the section's orders relating to captains. Stishinskii's loyalty to the old Pazukhin vision during his tenure of
office cannot be doubted. Much later, in the early 1900s, he still cherished the belief that peasants needed the patriarchal guardianship of all-
powerful knights (Gurko, 1939: 146-47). In 1905-6 the exigencies of
intragovernment politics forced him into some unlikely alliances, and he
supported a bewildering variety of proposals, but his voice could still be
heard opposing any assault on peasant "custom" as late as 1909. This
seems to have been his authentic viewpoint.[10]
    In 1909 Stishinskii had few allies, but during his tenure as head of
the land section his way of thinking enjoyed fairly solid support in the
MVD organization. In late 1894, when the MVD asked the governors
how they felt about the land captains' combined judicial and executive
powers, the response was overwhelmingly favorable.[11] In 1894-95 the
MVD published a two-volume work by one V. A. Beer, a land captain of
Orel gubernia, which was designed to serve as a manual for land captains. In addition to a mass of laws and official instructions, Beer offered

[10]On Stishinskii's opposition to Stolypin and his reforms, see Gurko (1939:
486-87) and Chernyshev (1918: 352-60). On his compromises in 1905-6, see ch. 6,
sec. D.
    [11]See, e.g., letters from Smolensk (TsGIAL, f. 1291, op. 39, 1894g., d. 5, ll.
1-5), Pskov (d. 7, ll. 1-4), Kazan (d. 3, l. 2), Kaluga (d. 8, ll. 1-3), and
Ekaterinoslav (d. 9, ll. 1-3).

some general comments on the nature of the captain's work. He said, among other things, that the job of overseeing volost courts put the captain in a position that could not be defined by any consistent law or policy. He had to choose each day between the equally harmful alternatives of allowing a court to disgrace itself by operating on its own, or destroying the court's prestige and authority among the peasants by interfering in its operation. A conscientious captain had to make judgments in one direction or the other from day to day, and he had no basis for these judgments except in his own personal integrity and in his direct relationships with the peasants involved (Beer, 1894-95: II, x). In Beer's mind, then, the captain had to be a line-over-staff administrator, else he could not guide peasant society, and in the mid-1890s this view still had the land section's blessing.

It is difficult to assess the views of Stishinskii's successor, Georgii G. Savich, who headed the land section from 1896 to 1902. There is one item of evidence, however, that gives us some idea of how he envisioned peasant society. This is a study he made of a peasant village in Nizhnii Novgorod gubernia, published in 1906. Judging from his description of Pavlovo village, Savich thought more like a zemstvo statistician than an official of the MVD. He depicted the zemstvo as a vital source of help and encouragement to the villagers (1906: 31-32, 38-43), whereas the land captain and governor often appeared in his book to be annoyances (e.g., pp. 73-79). Yet the period Savich was discussing included the very years when he himself headed the land section. Savich, it seems, did not trust his captains. During his term of office the land section began to renounce Stishinskii's faith in arbitrary patriarchs. According to the land section's official history, Savich was the first director to inspect captains in the field (*Kratkii,* 1908: 21), and under his directorship the section prepared its 1899 draft of the 1905 *nakaz* (instruction) to the captains, which, as we shall see, reflected a very strong inclination to impose regulations upon them.

There can be no question aout the views of Savich's successor, V. I. Gurko, who directed the section from 1902 through 1906. Gurko was an outspoken bureaucratizer of the Vorontsov school from the begining. He believed that the chief defect in the land captains was their possession of judicial authority, and his abiding purpose as director, say his memoirs, was to make the work of the captains "strictly legal." In 1904 he introduced the practice of publishing negative inspection reports about delinquent captains in the land section's journal (Gurko, 1939: 144-46). Gurko's regime encompassed the enactment of the Stolypin Land Reform and will be discussed at some length in Chapter 6. Suffice it to say here that when he left office in late 1906, the captains were undergoing a decisive transfiguration. Later, under Stolypin, the MVD would squeeze its agents even more tightly to compel them to carry out the new reforms. By 1906, however, the ground had already been well prepared. Pazukhin's co-believers had lost control of the land section a full decade before.[12]

Early Efforts to Bureaucratize the Land Captains, 1896-1905

During the 1890s the MVD initiated two major campaigns to subordinate the captains to systematic regulation. The first was a massive investigation of peasant society as a whole, reminiscent of the efforts to gather information in the early 1870s though much more elaborate than those relatively primitive exercises. The second was a more modest enterprise: the compilation of an instruction to the captains designed to introduce a measure of uniformity and regularity into their operations. The following two sections present a few glimpses of these efforts, reflecting the change in the MVD's attitude toward bureaucratic administration prior to 1905.

The MVD Strives to Overhaul Peasant Society, 1894-1905

In 1894 the MVD sent out to the gubernias a list of 66 questions about the nature of peasant society. Predictably, the governors convened meetings of local officials to discuss these questions, and in due course reports were submitted to the central government. They were published in 1897 in three volumes plus one supplementary volume (*Svod*, 1897; *Dopolnitelnyi*, 1897). A few years later, in 1901, Tsar Nicholas asked his MVD, D. S. Sipiagin, to submit his "considerations" on what should be done with all the material left over from this investigation. Sipiagin's response must have been optimistic, because on 14 January 1902 the tsar ordered him to prepare a draft reform of the legal-administrative order through which the government administered peasant villages. In April Sipiagin was assassinated, and this delayed the execution of the tsar's order, but in June the new MVD, V. K. Pleve, reconvened the editing commission that had originally launched the investigation of 1894-97. Stishinskii, now a deputy MVD, was put at its head and ordered to produce new statutes designed to rearrange peasant society (*Trudy*, 1903-4: I, 8-9). This task the commission accomplished by October 1903, whereupon the MVD printed its projected laws and the land section began preparations to obtain comments on them from the gubernias. The MVD decree of 8 January 1904 ordered the governors to form

---

[12]See Gurko (1939: 146-47). Gurko tells us that when he took over the land section he was able to rely on the men Savich had appointed and, indeed, Savich himself, who continued to serve in the MVD (pp. 144, 153).

conferences to discuss the project and told them approximately how to do it (*Svod...o nadelnykh zemliakh,* 1906: vii-viii).[13]

According to the MVD's official statement, the last move the editing commission made before the outbreak of the Russo-Japanese War was to assemble the governors in St. Petersburg on 25 January 1904 to receive instructions from Stishinskii in person. At that time, says the official statement, Stishinskii told them to form subcommittees within each gubernia conference to deal with particular questions and sections of the project, and he specified how the work was to be divided between these subcommittees and their parent conferences (pp. viii-x). Gurko's memoirs present the matter somewhat differently. He says the governors were invited to St. Petersburg in groups of 15, and the meeting of 25 January involved only the first 15 (1939: 168-69). Unfortunately for bureaucratic regularity, the exigencies of war mobilization prevented any more governors from coming to St. Petersburg and also delayed the formation of gubernia conferences and subcommittees. In short, the investigation began badly.

Things got worse as it went along. When the land section gathered its materials together in 1905, many reports were missing, and those which did come in were confused and inconsistent. In part, this was because of war and growing turbulence in the countryside, but the primary reason for the confusion seems to have been the rapid flow of constitutional legislation, beginning with the manifesto of 12 December 1904. New laws, enacted more or less arbitrarily and haphazardly, continually changed the basis on which the conferences were working (Yaney, 1973: 272-73). Some conferences met before the flow began and submitted reports on the basis of the old legal order, though they knew it was about to disappear. Others tried to change their reports to take the new legislation into account, although in the absence of clear instructions they wrangled much and accomplished little. Some others simply did not submit reports. In the end, only 31 out of 46 gubernia conferences were heard from. Twelve of the 31 submitted incomplete reports; that is, the conferences answered only a few of the questions and sent in subcommittee reports to cover the rest. Two of the 31, Grodno and Chernigov, sent in relatively complete reports, but they were accompanied by remarks to the effect that the conferences no longer endorsed them. When in the fall

[13] According to Gurko, the editing commission was "fictitious" and Stishinskii played only an ornamental role in the formulation of the project. Gurko claims that he and his land section were the real authors (1939: 153-56, 163; Simonova, 1965: 216-17). In any case the projects attributed to the commission were printed in *Trudy* (1903-4: I, 109-443). Richly annotated versions, full of relevant information, were published in *Trudy* (1903-4: II-VI).

of 1905 the land section began to compile these bewildering materials, the October Manifesto confused the matter even further. In the end, the land section was only able to publish two volumes of the reports, those dealing with sections five and six of the MVD's project.[14]

Despite this distinctly whimpering end to the MVD's pre-1905 efforts at peasant reform, there was some significance to them. If nothing else, the draft project of 1902-3 tells us with unusual clarity where the MVD stood at that time. It stood, said the editing commission's introductory essay, for the basic principle of keeping the peasantry and their separate legal order under a special administration but also for allowing individual peasants to take themselves and their lands out of this separate order to join the modern world of private property (*Trudy*, 1903-4: I, 11-18). Moreover, the peasants' separate legal-administrative order was to be altered and limits imposed on the land captains' authority. New, much more detailed rules regarding volost court procedure were to be enacted (p. 73). Peasant-elected boards were to be set up (with the captains as chairmen) to hear appeals against the volost courts. Elected peasant representatives were to have voting membership in uezd congresses (pp. 73-83). By 1903, then, the MVD intended to subordinate its line-over-staff "guardians" to laws and institutions.

The Land Section Undertakes to Instruct the Captains, 1898-1905

The second of the MVD's early efforts to regulate the land captains was no more successful than the first. It began in 1898, when the land section drafted a *nakaz* (instruction) spelling out the captains' duties in some detail. As usual, the section sent its draft out to the governors so they could convene conferences to discuss it article by article. The conferences did indeed conduct their discussions, and the gubernia boards then submitted reports to the land section, which printed two volumes of selected extracts from them in 1899 (*Sbornik*, 1899). For some reason the instruction was very long in appearing. It came out at last in August 1905, just in time to be rendered at least partly obsolete by the October Manifesto and the reform legislation of the following year.[15]

Like the frustrated peasant reforms of 1894-1905, the land section's project *nakaz* tells us something about the MVD organization's image of the land captains. Take, for example, article 2 of the project, which dealt

[14]The reports on section five were in *Svod...o nadelnykh zemliakh* (1906). Those on section six were published separately in *Svod...po proektu pravil* (1906). The difficulties of the gubernia conferences are described in the latter volume on pp. i-vii, and in the former on pp. x-xv.

[15]Curiously, the land section continued to take this document seriously even after the legislation of 1905-6. The section's history, published in 1908, said that the *nakaz* was a "reference book for each land captain, prescribing the formal procedures to be followed in all his activities" (*Kratkii*, 1908: 20).

with the captains' role in volost and village assemblies. It suggested that the captain had to be present only at a few volost assembly meetings, those at which certain important matters were to be discussed. Otherwise he should attend volost (and village) meetings only when he considered it necessary. When he did attend a meeting, he should only appear at the beginning and then leave immediately after the peasants began their deliberations (*Sbornik*, 1899: I, 13). The idea was that the peasants would then be able to conduct their discussions without any outside constraint. For believers in patrimonial guardianship this was heresy. What were the captains good for if not to keep order in the peasants' meetings—to prevent drunkenness and protect the weak members of the village from the strong? Of course an individual patriarch might decide on his own to let a particular village conduct one or more assemblies without him, but no administrative fiat should prescribe his behavior in such matters, not if he was an authentic guardian. Predictably, the gubernias' reaction to article 2 was negative (I, 13-79).[16]

In a similar vein, the gubernia conferences overwhelmingly rejected article 18 of the land section's draft because it suggested that the captains' discretionary powers should be limited by law. Tambov's response summed up the feeling of most local administrators. The conference stated that the original statute gave the captain the right to change any sentence by a volost court "according to his inner conviction, unaccountable to anyone," and therefore the proposed *nakaz* contradicted the law (I, 237). Such a response was quite in keeping with the old Pazukhin spirit. A considerable number of gubernia boards expressed similar sentiments. By 1899, then, the land section was somewhat at variance with the MVD's local agencies. It wanted to limit the captains' authority over the peasants, whereas the local agencies wanted the captains to keep their power to push peasants around.

On the other hand, the gubernia conferences had little to say against the multiplying of bureaucratic directives to the captains. Articles 36 through 45 of the project required the weary knights to perform an incredible variety of functions. They had to gather statistics in the villages, handle all cases in which peasants and/or villages fell into arrears, assume responsibility for all income and expenditures of village and volost administrations, and also take charge of such matters as fire protection, orphans, schools, churches, and zemstvo expenditures in the volosts. In other words, they were to oversee and in some cases to manage virtually all village activities.[17]

[16]According to A. S. Ermolov's study of the famine of 1891-92, one of the land captain's most important contributions had been to keep order at peasant assemblies (1892: 251).

[17]The draft *nakaz* missed a few functions that had already been assigned to the captain. For example, the law already required him to oversee the selling of

To these provisions the gubernias made very little objection. Only a few conferences even alluded to the futility of St. Petersburg's demands. Olonets slyly pointed out that since no one could possibly perform all these duties, they should not be understood literally as concrete instructions but only as general indicators of the close contact the captains were expected to maintain with their people (II, 68-70). The Kherson conference stated its protest more flatly. The captains were already overburdened with work, it said, and therefore the proposed *nakaz* would simply not be enforced (p. 390). In Nizhnii Novgorod an uezd gentry marshal put it more tactfully. He suggested that the *uchastki* be reduced in size, thereby reducing each land captain's work load (pp. 356-57). The Samara gubernia board noted that peasant society had grown much more complex since the Liberation, making it impossible for the captains to impose such detailed procedures on village and volost institutions (pp. 8-9). Finally, Poltava argued that if the captains had to do all these things, they would no longer be captains (pp. 70-72). This was all. Of about 40 conferences, only 5 commented on the captains' burdens.

Of course, one could argue that these vast responsibilities actually augmented the captain's authority. Taken by itself, the *nakaz* sometimes made the captain sound like a fatherly chieftain looking after all the needs of his flock. In fact, however, the *nakaz* was referring to reports the land captain *had* to make, records he *had* to keep and/or check, and petitions of various sorts he *had* to process, regardless of his own estimate of the need for all this or his own preference as to what else might be more important for him to do. The instruction was not a description of the things a good land captain might find himself doing. It was, rather, a formidable list of formal requirements imposed upon him.

One wonders why officialdom in the gubernias made no fuss about the burdens being imposed on the erstwhile knights. Two explanations suggest themselves. First and most obvious, they had as much reason as the central ministries to prefer a vulnerable clerk, however ineffectual, to a freewheeling savior, especially a clerk who could be held responsible for all the ills of rural life. Less apparent, but just as important, a land captain saddled with ostensibly vast responsibilities was preferable to the host of new bureaucrats who might well be sent out to take his place if it were admitted that he could not do all his jobs by himself. So long as the captains could go on absorbing the continuing stream of commands from St. Petersburg, the uezds would at least be left more or less as they

---

stamps and the collecting of taxes on official documents (*Sbornik*, 1901: II, 195-315). He also sat on examining committees for the local schools (Maiborodov, folder 2, 39), recorded all criminal convictions in volost courts and reported them with commentaries to the minister of justice (*Sbornik*, 1901: II, 455-58), and supervised all redistributions, sales, and rentals of village lands.

were. So long as the captains did not make trouble for local administration, local administration would not make trouble for them, and so long as this happy balance was left unshaken, vast responsibilities could accumulate on paper without seriously upsetting anyone in the countryside. Any office wishing to give the impression of being involved in rural administration had only to send out orders to the land captains. These orders, neatly compiled in chronological sequence, accompanied (ideally) by reports indicating that the countryside had heard and was obeying, were the visible sign of the office's activity. Should someone discover this fraud and denounce one or more uezd offices for hiding their witless passivity behind a screen of formal documents, the respective managers had nothing to fear, because they could justify themselves simply by pointing to the failure of the captains to carry out their legally assigned tasks. Here was the essence of the gubernias' faith in the captains' "power." Very few local administrators actually wanted independent knights of virtue out in the *uchastki,* but the captain's power made him a convincing scapegoat, so they affected to believe in it.

The *nakaz* of August 1905 did not turn out to be as demanding as the land section's project of 1899. Even so, it seems to have been ignored in practice (Maiborodov, folder 2, 94). It had to be ignored, because the land captains already had duties that were quite beyond their capacity to perform. Another piece of paper adding a dozen tasks not to be performed to a hundred that were already not being performed could not have had much impact in the *uchastki.*

But I am not concerned at this point with the central government's impact on its local agencies. My purpose here is only to indicate that the captains' line-over-staff authority did not last very long, despite the intentions of Pazukhin and Tolstoi. The authors of the statute of 1889 failed to make the legal-administrative system guarantee the captains' independence. The discussions that produced the *nakaz* in 1898-99 show that virtually all the captains' superiors were distinctly hostile toward any sign of independent operation. There was as yet no adequate staff to manage the line in the uezds, so we should not say that Weber's bureaucracy prevailed. But if the MVD's quasi-bureaucracy was not yet managing its minions in the countryside in 1905, neither was it supporting any knightly aspirations they may have cherished. A captain who ventured to play the hero was likely to end as the land section's fall guy, and so it behooved him to play the clerk. This was the way the section wanted it.

The Land Captains' Attempts to Cope with Peasant Poverty

We can observe the captain's subjection to quasi-staff more directly by focusing on one area of his operation: the development of government policies regarding peasant poverty.

In their first years of service the captains received some applause for their knightly qualities. To take one example, A. S. Ermolov's description of the famine of 1891-92 suggests that the captains had some success in compelling villages to distribute relief supplies only to those villagers who really needed it. In so doing, says Ermolov, the newly appointed knights were challenging the "kulaks" and making it possible for the first time for the government to deal directly with individual peasants on its own terms. He makes the point that the government could not have made this successful invasion of village society under a regime of formal law. A modern legal system, with independent judges, could not have compelled the villages to use their famine relief funds "properly" (Ermolov, 1892: 180-81).[18]

But the government did not rely for long on independent line agents to take care of peasant poverty on their own. The first law telling local officials how to cope with peasant tax arrears came out on 7 February 1894. It allowed needy peasants to put off paying arrears in their redemption debts (see Glossary) and land taxes (*Sbornik,* 1901: II, 45-61). Subsequent laws—those of 13 May 1896 and 31 May and 23 June 1899—provided for yet more radical relief measures (pp. 62-89). They allowed captains to recommend the lowering of payments and even cancel arrears entirely in hardship cases. These unquestionably benign acts did not merely tell the captain to grant relief to any deserving peasants he happened to find. He was not to sit in his office waiting for this or that household or village to come in with a petition. He had, rather, to go out and visit all households and villages with arrears greater than a given maximum amount, and to obtain information about them. He had to determine the area and fertility of their land and to estimate the value of their buildings and movable property. In addition, he had to calculate their annual income and expense. He did not do this just once. He had to keep it up year after year, as long as the families and households remained in arrears, and he had to make regular reports, in which he either recommended some measure of relief or explained why he was withholding relief.

The new laws not only buried the captain under a mountain of paperwork; they also subordinated him to a new set of superiors. Now he would have to coordinate with local agencies of the MF—chiefly the fiscal chamber (see Glossary)—and his massive reports would have to gain their approval. Worse, the MF's own agents, the tax inspectors, were to take a far more active part in peasant government. The MF's

[18]It should be mentioned that Ermolov was no wholehearted supporter of the land captains. He favored the introduction of all-class local institutions à la Kakhanov as the ultimate solution to the problems of peasant management (1892: 251-53).

instruktsiia of 4 December 1899 assigned them a clearly dominant role in the business of collecting taxes from villages (pp. 128-68). This did not free the captain from any responsibilities; it simply forced him to discharge them under the distinctly unknightly eye of the MF's local agent.[19]

Another area of the captain's welfare operations had to do with famine relief. During the 1890s the government dramatically expanded its programs for making loans to peasants in areas struck by famine, and with the increased numbers of borrowers came a more than corresponding increase in those who fell into arrears on their payments. Some famine debts were simply canceled en masse in general clemency decrees, such as the manifesto of 14 November 1894 celebrating Nicholas II's marriage (*TPSZ*, 11035), but the loans still outstanding had to be dealt with. Article 5 of the above manifesto authorized the MF and MVD to reduce payments on outstanding famine debts in specific cases, provided they acted in agreement, and the law of 12 June 1900 erected this authorization into the same sort of general welfare program as obtained for peasants who failed to pay their taxes. According to the 1900 law, volost administrations were to bear the brunt of the clerical and investigative labor, but of course this meant that the captains had to oversee it. Formal responsibility rested with the uezd congress, and the congress simply passed the burden along to its individual captain-members.

Famine relief gave the captains yet another set of superiors. The 1900 law made all officials in the zemstvo directorate voting members of the uezd congress whenever it considered matters relating to grain reserves and famine relief (*Sbornik*, 1901: I, 105). Now the captains would have to negotiate with uezd zemstvo administrators in order to get their reports approved and their tasks accomplished. Strangely, the law of June 1900 is commonly believed to have transferred responsibility for famine prevention and relief from the zemstvoes to the land captains. Actually, the captains had always been responsible for the distribution and collection of relief loans. Zemstvo assemblies had made policy, but zemstvo servitors had had to work through the captains or else accept their supervision. After 1900 the zemstvoes lost their policy-making role to the MVD, but their administrators began to exercise supervision over the captains' day-by-day work.[20]

---

[19] To be precise, the law held the gubernia boards responsible for performing these functions, and they could use any official to do the work. In practice, however, the captains would have to do the job. They would be responsible whenever it was not done properly.

[20] For a detailed discussion of the law of 12 June, see Robbins (1976: 25-37), who accepts the view that the 12 June law took the zemstvoes out of famine relief. It seems to me, however, that he neglects the enhanced powers the law granted to zemstvo *administrators*.

In sum, by 1900—long before the "revolutionary" changes of 1906—
the land captain had lost his independence from the "staff." He was a
clerk, and the offices under which he worked—of which there were now
quite a few—consciously aspired to multiply his tasks while limiting his
power to act on his own initiative. The MVD's editing commission noted
in 1903 that village and volost institutions had become fully subordinate
to uezd-level government agencies (*Trudy,* 1903-4: I, 44). In effect, the
captain had lost his original *raison d'etre.* He had become merely an
all-purpose servant for any government administrator who had anything
to do with rural Russia.

A Captain's View

Another way of looking at the land captains' loss of independence is
to consider their own statements. We have the memoirs of a man who
held the job during the Stolypin era, and his experience, while not typical, is at least suggestive. This was Vladimir Maiborodov, nobleman of
Chernigov gubernia and alumnus of St. Petersburg University. He served
as captain from 1904 until the Revolution, first in Bessarabia gubernia
and then in Kherson.

As his years of service went by, Maiborodov found that his superiors were becoming increasingly concerned with bookkeeping. Circulars
and inspection reports from the land section focused more and more on
the formal correctness of his work while ignoring his actual relationships
with the peasants. Bureaucrats in the central offices did not care about
the peasants. All they wanted the captains to do was to make sure that
village and volost records were kept in proper order. Maiborodov
regarded himself as a man motivated by conscience, not the approval of
his superiors, and he had little respect for formalities. His concept of his
work was something like Pazukhin's original vision, and he struggled
against the descent into clerkdom. His chief method for retaining a measure of autonomy was to let volost and village offices discharge the many
petty duties piled onto him by uezd administrators (Maiborodov, folder
2, 127-28).

The day came, however, when the central government caught up
with Maiborodov. In 1909 Ia. Ia. Litvinov, who had succeeded Gurko as
head of the land section in 1906, made an inspection of Kherson gubernia and included Maiborodov's *uchastok* in his tour. The gallant
Maiborodov found this irritating. He had to devote a great deal of time
to putting his records in order before the inspecting party arrived, and
this made him ill disposed toward them from the start. When they began
to find fault with some of his decisions, he expressed his ill will openly,
so his memoirs say. In particular, he committed the indiscretion of
reminding them that they had no authority to pass on the legality of his

land reform projects. This was only the beginning. Litvinov and his staff had brought with them one of the first automobiles ever to be seen in the *uchastok*. They took Maiborodov out in it to make a tour of the volosts. It was May. The sun was hot and the roads were very dusty. The dignitaries from St. Petersburg had to manifest themselves to their people choking and blinking from underneath a thick, unmajestic coating of dirt and sweat. Worse, the automobile got stuck in a manure pile, and its passengers had to walk more than two miles before a coach came for them (pp. 112-17).

It is hard to tell exactly what kind of man Litvinov was. On the one hand, as Dubrovskii tells us, he was the sort who could say with a straight face, "Pressure from above can accomplish anything" (quoted in Dubrovskii, 1963: 169). One gets the impression from this remark that Litvinov was not exceptionally sensitive or given to reflective thinking about the nature of administration. On the other hand, he seems to have been energetic and single-minded. In any case, he was not the sort to forgive Maiborodov for his dusty roads, his manure pile, and his incorrigible inclination to engage in free-lance operation.

Maiborodov's version of the affair says that Litvinov was prejudiced against him from the beginning. During the long walk back from the manure pile, the head of the land section accused him point blank of spending all his time in the city of Odessa and leaving his *uchastok* without supervision. In this state of mind Litvinov was ready to seize upon any pretext to attack the defiant patriarch (Maiborodov, folder 2, 114-17). Not surprisingly, he singled out the only peasants in the *uchastok* who had any complaint against Maiborodov. This was a group in Bolshoi Buialik village who, Maiborodov says, constituted a minority of less than one-third of the heads of household in the village. They were being compelled to join in a village consolidation (see ch. 5, sec. A) by a better-than-two-thirds majority, and they were very unhappy. As we shall see in Chapters 6-9, village consolidation was becoming a key part of the Stolypin Land Reform in 1909, and it was quite legal for two-thirds of a village to impose this measure on all village land. Nevertheless, Litvinov took the part of the minority (p. 118).

First, he conferred with their representatives. Not content with this, he went to the village and listened to the assembled recalcitrants chant their opposition to land reform. Moved by this display, he foolishly assured the crowd that they would not be forced onto consolidated farms, though by so doing he was flatly rejecting a formal legal decision already made in favor of the majority. This Litvinov had no right to do, even if he was the director of the land section. Maiborodov tells us that work on the consolidation of Bolshoi Buialik continued in spite of Litvinov's disgraceful performance. Not for long, however—the disgruntled minority was now fully aroused. They joined the Union of Russian People (see Glossary), thereby obtaining the support of one Count Konovnitsin, the director of the Odessa branch of that notorious right-wing organization. Heartened and reinforced, the minority stepped up their complaints, and this began to alarm the would-be consolidators. Within a short time the MVD sent down orders to transfer Maiborodov to another *uchastok* in order to cool down the tension. Maiborodov was transferred in due course, and the consolidation never did go through (pp. 118-23).[21]

It happens that we also have some remarks from Litvinov concerning the affair of Bolshoi Buialik village. Parts of his report of the inspection were published in the land section's journal, and he mentioned a land captain whom he identified as "M."—without doubt, Maiborodov. Judging from the report, Maiborodov's impressions of Litvinov's bad mood were accurate. The director disapproved not only of the land captain M. but the whole administration of Kherson gubernia. The gubernia board was not watching its uezd congresses and land captains closely enough. Serious case backlogs existed in many of the congresses. The program to transfer peasants from communal to personal ownership was going satisfactorily and so was the collection of taxes, but this was in spite of the sloppy work of the MVD agencies, not because of it. As for village famine relief and village credit associations, they were in very bad condition, primarily as a result of the land captains' negligence. When it came to land reform, projects were being drawn up improperly and approved perfunctorily by land captains, uezd congresses, and uezd land settlement commissions (see Glossary) alike; consequently the surveyors were finding most of their assignments impossible to carry out. Things like this did not happen, said the disgusted Litvinov, in gubernias where boards were energetic and conscientious in supervising and leading the land captains (*IZO,* 1910: 128-30). It is in this connection that Litvinov first mentions the land captain M.

M. was one of several captains who were highly thought of by the gubernia board but whose negligence and incompetence proved on examination to be particularly striking. Indeed, M. seems to have been the worst of all. He allowed his volosts and villages to get so out of hand—especially "B-B village"—that he had to be transferred (p. 130).

Having disposed of the gubernia board, Litvinov went on to discuss specific uezd congresses and land captains. In case after case he found that captains were allowing projects for land reform to be drawn up carelessly. Instead of going to the fields and measuring them, surveyors were simply copying figures out of existing volost records or using peas-

---

[21] Maiborodov remained in his new *uchastok,* which was in the same uezd as his former one, until the Provisional Government eliminated the captains (folder 3, pp. 2, 16-17).

ant petitioners as sources of information. Local reform officials often
accepted peasant petitions for land rearrangement without checking to
see that they met government standards (e.g., 1910: 174-77). Interestingly, Litvinov did not accuse the captains of exerting undue pressure on
the peasants to consolidate their lands. The captains he described were
negligent, not overzealous. Their most common error was not to force
peasants to accept reform but to approve projects without checking
them, thus permitting injustices to be inflicted at random on this or that
group of peasants—sometimes would-be reformers, sometimes their opponents. The captains' chief motive, said Litvinov, was simply to avoid
trouble. They wanted to get projects for land reform accepted with a
minimum of effort; therefore, the side that threatened to make the most
trouble usually got their support. In short, administrators in Kherson did
not suffer from excessive zeal for reform except, perhaps, in uezd and
gubernia offices, where officials often approved sloppy reform projects
simply to impress the central government with their diligence (pp. 178,
181).[22]

As for the village of Bolshoi Buialik in particular, Litvinov tells us
that it was indeed scheduled for surveying in the summer of his visit.
Unlike many projects for village consolidation, it was going through all
right from a technical point of view. Legally, however, the issue was in
doubt, because a minority of villagers contended that the heads of
household in favor of the consolidation did not constitute the full two-
thirds majority required by law. Everyone agreed as to the number of
heads of household who supported consolidation—it was 570. The dispute centered on the total number of heads of household who had the
right to vote in the village assembly. According to one official count, the
legal total was 1,029; according to another, it was 610. The land captain
(Maiborodov) had selected the latter figure, which was more recent; the
minority insisted on the former. Thus in Maiborodov's view 570 constituted well over two-thirds of the village, whereas the minority considered
570 to be only slightly over half. Litvinov was unable to determine which
estimate of the village's population was valid. He did not care. No matter
which side turned out to be right, he still disapproved of Maiborodov's
project because, he said, it was being put into effect before the dispute
had been resolved. Here, however, Litvinov's account becomes cloudy.
He maintained that the dispute had not been resolved, yet he acknowl-

---

[22]S. M. Dubrovskii also read the above remarks of Litvinov, and he refers
to them in his monumental work on the Stolypin Reform. He ran across them in
the state archive in Leningrad, where, he says, they are listed as "secret correspondence" (1963: 179). This is one example of Dubrovskii's pretentiousness and
his unrestrained distortion of evidence. Litvinov's denunciations were not at all
secret, nor did they give any indication, as Dubrovskii claims, that the government was consciously forcing peasants into reform.

edged that the local authorities had already decided the matter. The law said that if the authorities had ruled on a dispute, then it was indeed resolved. It would seem that, despite Litvinov's prating about legality, he had no legal grounds for attacking Maiborodov. What he was really talking about was tact. Maiborodov was not a criminal, as Litvinov asserted, but had, at worst, neglected to explain the government's decision to the peasants. If, said Litvinov, the anticonsolidation minority were convinced that land reform was a gimmick the administrators were using in order to grab land away from the village, this in itself was clear evidence that Maiborodov had failed to do his job properly (*IZO,* 1910: 179-81).

Such was the substance of Litvinov's accusation against Maiborodov. Clearly the director of the land section was dissatisfied, but his report did not actually say what Maiborodov had done wrong. If he really meant to accuse Maiborodov of committing a crime, then he was implying that whenever a number of peasants protested against a reform project, however legal it was in the formal sense, the local captain was ipso facto guilty of criminal negligence.

On balance, Maiborodov's account of events in Bolshoi Buialik seems more convincing than Litvinov's. The director of the land section encountered a considerable number of cases in Kherson in which land reform projects were drawn up without securing the requisite majority of villagers in advance. Apparently the officials were hoping to bring the peasants around during the course of the surveying. In the summer of 1909, says Litvinov, this procedure was backfiring all over Kherson and in other gubernias as well. Surveyors were abandoning project after project as they encountered peasants whose expectations could not be met without violating government regulations (p. 181).[23] Obviously Litvinov was sensitive to this phenomenon when he arrived in Maiborodov's *uchastok,* and he was looking for trouble. In fact, however, Maiborodov did not start any projects without proper majorities, not even by Litvinov's own disjointed account. Moreover, the issue was not as Litvinov described it. According to the vice-governor of Kherson, who visited Bolshoi Buialik on 15 May, evidently to check on Litvinov's accusations, the minority had "persuaded" a fair number of the majority to change their vote. There had been 580 heads of household present in December 1908, when Maiborodov had persuaded the village assembly to undertake village consolidation. If it was true that 570 voted in favor, then Maiborodov certainly had solid support at the meeting. Later, however, the opposing minority obtained 425 signatures on a petition opposing the consolida-

[23]This point was made exhaustively by N. D. Chaplin, head of the survey section in the ministry of justice, in his inspection report of 1909 (TsGIAL, f. 1291, op. 120, 1910g., d. 19, ll. 15-16).

tion. According to the vice-governor, only 248 of the 425 were heads of household in Bolshoi Buialik, and most of these signed the petition after being threatened with violence if they did not. Litvinov did not refer to these allegations in his inspection report. Unless the vice-governor was utterly unreliable, then, the director of the land section was less than fair to his captain (TsGIAL, f. 1291, op. 120, 1909g., d. 43, ll. 73-74).

I have read through a number of Litvinov's accusations directed against all manner of local officials. They do seem to give undue attention to correct filekeeping, but they are not characteristically disjointed and unfair. His unconvincing description of Maiborodov's sins seems exceptional, which indicates that he may indeed have been in a bad mood. The most likely explanation for his anger, it seems to me, is not Maiborodov's sins but the would-be knight's belligerence. In the summer of 1909 Litvinov was in no mood to hear a land captain tell him, the director of all captains, to mind his own business.

Apparently Maiborodov did a thorough job of irritating his superiors. In June 1912, three years after the incident at Bolshoi Buialik, the land section submitted a proposal to the MVD council (see Glossary) that Maiborodov be brought to trial in the Odessa court for negligence and "the illegal deprivation of freedom of the heads of household of Bolshe-Buialik volost *[sic]*." According to its journal for August 1912, the council accepted the section's proposal, and the MVD issued an order to prosecute Maiborodov (f. 1291, op. 32, d. 19, l. 165).

Maiborodov's story illustrates a number of aspects in the land captain's descent to clerkdom in the post-1905 years. Obviously a descent was occurring. If Maiborodov is any indication, however, the captains were still inclined to resist it. Moreover, they still enjoyed some scope for their efforts to resist. The land section's control over its captains was still not much stronger than the captains' control over their villages; perhaps it was even weaker. Note that Litvinov, the Kherson gubernia board, and the MVD's council all had very different notions of what happened in Bolshoi Buialik, and one gets the impression that they were unaware of their differences. It is also of interest in this regard that although Maiborodov was transferred in 1909 as a result of the incident at Bolshoi Buialik, the order for his criminal prosecution, so laboriously decided upon in St. Petersburg, never came down to him. His detailed description of his service after 1909 gives no indication that he ever even heard of it. He remained on duty unprosecuted until after the February Revolution (Maiborodov, folder 3, 2). Apparently his friends in the gubernia offices still counted for something.

It must be added, however, that the inspection of 1909 was not without its effect on knighthood. Maiborodov tells us that many of the land captains in Kherson who served for "conscience" quit after suffering

Litvinov's insults. Most of them entered the service of the zemstvoes, whereupon the MVD replaced them with lesser men (folder 2, 112-13, 120).

Conclusions

One explanation for the rapid collapse of line-over-staff administration lay in the nature of tsarist organization. There was an implicit principle in Russian law, a principle so fundamental, so hallowed by long-established government practice, that it seems to have required no formal statement. This princple was as follows: anything an official in the imperial government is allowed to do, he is required to do. The phrase "He has the right" conveyed *in itself* the meaning "He must." This was not a written law but basically a collective habit of thought, solidly established between the lines, so to speak, of the government's formal legal system. In practice, an official who possessed powers (rights) never enjoyed the prerogative of choosing when he should exercise them. Anyone who believed that a land captain should exercise his powers in a given case could appeal against his refusal to exercise them, and such an appeal could result in criminal prosecution of the captain involved.

The operation of this principle may be observed in some of the central government's efforts to interpret the statute on land captains, especially its statements regarding articles 30 and 31 of the *Polozhenie*. Generally speaking, these articles granted a captain the "right" to disapprove of any decision of a village or volost assembly if he considered it to be illegal or harmful. Article 30 said he could check assembly decisions, and article 31 added that whenever he found one that violated the law *(zakon)*, or threatened to do the village serious harm *("klonitsia k iavnomu ushcherbu")*, or violated any person's legal *(zakonnye)* rights, he should prevent its execution and then submit it to the uezd congress along with his considerations. It was up to the congress to decide whether or not his allegation was correct. If the congress agreed with him, the assembly's decision would be revoked (*TPSZ*, 6196).

An MVD circular of 1 April 1891 explained what the captain's right meant. "According to the exact meaning of articles 30 and 31...," the circular said, "the land captain *must* submit illegal and harmful decisions to the congress" (*Sbornik*, 1901: I, 59). The Senate agreed wholeheartedly. In August 1893 it decided a case involving a complaint against a captain for refusing to find a village assembly's decision illegal. The plaintiff, a landholder of Kursk gubernia, was disputing the villagers' decision to allow a local peasant to build a mill. The Senate decided against the landholder because he had made his complaint improperly, but, as the Senate took pains to point out, this *type* of protest was quite legitimate. It was the captain's *duty* to submit assembly decisions of questionable legality to the uezd congress, and therefore every case wherein he did *not* deem a particular decision illegal was subject to protest. Whenever a captain failed or refused to submit an assembly decision to the congress, *anyone* could appeal this action (or inaction) to the gubernia board, whether or not he was involved in peasant administration (II, 464). Neither the circular of 1891 nor the Senate decision of 1893 bothered to state that when articles 30 and 31 granted a right, they were also imposing a duty. They merely affirmed without comment that these articles *explicitly* required the land captain to submit improper decisions to the uezd congress. Taken literally, articles 30 and 31 required nothing of the sort, but in the minds of tsarist officials, they did.[24]

In a sense, then, tsarist administration was prepared to see the captains as clerks even before they took office. If and when the government summoned the resolution to adopt consistent policies and issue coherent commands, the land captain would have to make some show of doing its bidding. This, ultimately, was what he was for. Pazukhin's line-over-staff administrator was sent out not to be a permanent institution but to prepare the way for effective, staff-run (bureaucratic) operation in the countryside. From the very beginning the captain's implied purpose was to eliminate the knightly independence that had ostensibly been conferred upon him.[25]

[24]Both the 1891 circular and the Senate decisions that supported it were revoked by another MVD circular, dated 8 Aug. 1900 (*Sbornik* 1901: I, 63-65), but this act had no bearing on the principle under discussion here. The August circular addressed itself primarily to the large number of cases involving captains who were accused of failing or refusing to find village assembly decisions illegal or harmful. These accusations were going directly to the gubernia boards for decision. As a result, the boards found themselves deciding cases the uezd congreses should have been deciding. Worse, whenever a gubernia board decided against a land captain, its decision had to take the form of an order to the captain telling him to submit the village's decision to the uezd congress. This meant that the congress was required to decide a matter the gubernia board had already decided. The congress's decision was final and not appealable; consequently cases could and did arise wherein two government agencies, the congress and the board, came to two different decisions without there being any procedure for resolving the difference. The 1900 circular untangled this snarl by requiring virtually all complaints against village decisions to be submitted to the uezd congress whether the land captain wished to submit them or not. Needless to say, none of this tangled development contradicted the principle that rights (powers) constituted duties.

[25]I am indebted to Mr. Brian Levin-Stankevich for pointing out to me that Russian legal scholars had recognized the principle that legal power conferred legal obligation by the end of the nineteenth century (e.g., Demchenko: 1903, 201; Vaskovskii, 1913: 115). These authors deal with judges, but they both assert that the principle applied to all types of formally vested powers. Before the end of the nineteenth century the cassation departments of the Senate were occasionally handing down rulings explicitly invoking the principle as a basis for their decisions (Demchenko, 1903: 227).

C. SIGNIFICANCE OF THE LAND CAPTAINS

The Captains' Role in Government-Peasant Interaction

By the standards of their contemporaries, the captains had to fail, but the historian has grounds for suggesting that they served for a time as a device for coping with the unresolvable contradictions of Russian government. If they did not bring legality to the countryside, they did at least take responsibility for its absence. More important, they called attention to its absence, and their activities helped sustain an intelligent discussion of its absence. When considered as executive measures, commands sent from ministries to captains were usually little more than exercises in wishful thinking, but they did involve the central offices more deeply in the countryside, and St. Petersburg's pretense at governing grew ever more elaborate. Equally significant for capital-city involvement in rural Russia was the struggle in both government and public opinion to replace the captains' despotic authority with more orderly institutions. We may say, then, that the captains' most vital role in government-peasant interaction was their assumption of responsibility for bureaucracy's foredoomed failure to be what it pretended and aspired to be. The captains *symbolized* the government's commitment to its bureaucratic pretenses and aspirations. If they did little to *satisfy* the urge to mobilize, they did a great deal to keep it alive.

As for the peasants, they felt the weight of the government's authority in the 1880-90s as never before, but they were beginning, thanks in part to the captains, to find new resources for coping with this weight in the government organization itself. They were beginning to learn ways and means for utilizing bureaucracy and even opposing it by using the bureaucracy's own terms. In short, the captains helped peasants to communicate with the government. Their cycle—like those of the *stanovye* and arbitrators before them—represents more than a failure.

A Case Study: The Captains' Role in Resettlement

When tsarist administrators spoke of resettlement *(pereselenie),* they usually had in mind the business of shifting peasants from overpopulated areas to other places within the empire where land was relatively abundant. The idea of regulating this process and encouraging it was by no means new in the 1880s, but it was Alexander III who first undertook to legislate a general system to govern resettlement. It happened that the resulting statement of resettlement policy passed through the State Council on 13 July 1889, only one day after the statute on land captains (*TPSZ*, 6198). Thus, the government's effort to manage resettlement developed into the massive exertions of Stolypin's day during the same formative period in which the land captains were falling into clerkdom. It may be instructive, therefore, to look briefly at the captains' role in resettlement to see what impact, if any, they had on this particular attempt to insert modern administration into peasant life.

Resettlement could refer to peasant colonization in any area, whether or not the government involved itself in the process. As Alexander III's government used the term, however, it was usually restricted to peasant movement onto state-held lands, especially those parts of Siberia susceptible to farming. The programs to be discussed below were aimed primarily at movement from European Russia to the lands beyond the Urals.

For our purposes, the most important provisions in the law of 13 July were as follows. First, no peasant could settle on state lands without permission from two ministries: the MVD and the ministry of state domains (after 1894, the ministry of agriculture and state domains). Second, once this permission was obtained, a would-be resettler could leave his home village *without* its permission. Third, when a resettling household departed, its land in the home village was turned over to the village along with the obligation to keep up tax and redemption debt payments on it.

The latter provision did not imply that settlers in Siberia suffered a net loss of land. If they lost their share of their home village's land, they made up for it by acquiring the land on which they settled without having to buy it. The government never did sell its Siberian acreage but instead granted settlers "permanent usage" *(postoiannoe polzovanie)* of their plots for an annual rental fee. In effect, resettlers were only replacing one set of payments to the government with another, and in Siberia they got more land for lower payments. Such was the arrangement until 1904, when the temporary rules of 6 June made the terms of resettlement even more attractive. From then on, home villages had to compensate departing resettlers for their shares of the land (*TPSZ*, 24701).

The law of 13 July represented an ambitious step. It would be two years or more before the MVD's new captains took up their duties in European Russia, and the government was already committing them—by implication—to managing one of the most radical reforms in village life it had ever introduced. To be sure, the captains would not have to install settlers in their new homes. This would be the business, primarily, of the ministry of state domains. It was the departure of the resettlers, especially the business of splitting them away from their communities, that would concern the captains. As we shall see, this would be trouble enough.

The first decade of resettlement under the law of 13 July offers us three contrasting periods: (1) 1889-92, prior to the captains' involvement; (2) 1892-94, gradual introduction of the captains to resettlement work;

and (3) 1894-99, the captains' work. Studying the evolution of resettlement through these three separate periods should give us some idea of the captains' contribution, if any, to a concrete interaction between government and peasantry.

A circular of 1890 suggests that during the first period—*before* the captains began operation—the MVD was extremely poorly informed regarding the realities of the countryside, both in Siberia and in European Russia. The circular set forth the following procedures. Resettlers had to get permission from *both* MVD and ministry of state domains. They had to send applications to St. Petersburg via uezd and gubernia offices, and these documents had to describe their own economic condition as well as that of their neighbors. The ministries had to be assured that the resettlers could make the trip and also that the villagers who stayed behind would not be left with more land than they could handle. If the remaining villagers seemed unable to keep up tax and redemption payments on their lands, not all the would-be migrants would be allowed to leave. Lots would have to be cast to decide who could go. After all this was settled—that is, after local officials had drawn up the proper documents in terminology acceptable to St. Petersburg clerkdom and sent them to the central offices, and after clerkdom's approval had at last descended back down to the petitioners—a two-month period began. During this time, and not before, the migrants had to sell their movable property, dwellings, and house lots and get on the road. If they did not get going in two months, the whole thing was called off (*Sbornik,* 1901: II, 16-18).

Assuming that a peasant head of household was fortunate enough to get through all the paperwork, he had then to face formidable practical difficulties. The two-month limit forced him to sell his belongings to his ex-neighbors under less than ideal bargaining conditions. When and if he did at last depart, he was told what routes to travel; when he arrived at his new lands, he had to take what the authorities provided. No provision was made for would-be resettlers to send advance parties to find good lands and mark them out for themselves. Indeed, the circulars strongly implied that peasant initiative was to play no part in the scheme. According to the MVD's notion in 1889 and the following two or three years, the migrating peasant's sole responsibility was to secure the necessary papers. His only hope of getting to Siberia and finding land rested with those unknown officials in Siberia to whom he would ultimately give his papers.

Only Franz Kafka could have dreamed up a more senseless arrangement. In the early 1890s there was no administration capable of performing the elaborate functions the government so blithely assigned to local officials. Any peasant who really wanted to make it to Siberia had a better chance if he went illegally.[26]

In Siberia a variety of circulars appeared calling for a massive drawing and registering of boundaries. Existing farms had to be marked off and new ones laid out. In fact, however, state domains' administrators were quite unable to make the necessary measurements. A memorandum of 1885 from the manager of state lands in western Siberia to the minister described the situation as follows:

> The job of assigning allotments is given to government surveyors, who are guided by general surveys of the territories in which they work. They are limited by the formal requirements of technical instructions; therefore, they set up allotments for whole volosts according to legal norms without taking into account the actual nature of the land and the economic conditions of agriculture in each locale.... The population, not perceiving any official concern for their material interests, or for legality, or even for proper technique in the operations of the surveyors, have no faith in them. The peasants are prepared to make any sacrifice in behalf of their belief in the freedom to utilize an unlimited expanse of land. The use of force against them in the name of official instructions regarding proper layout of the land...has only delayed the attainment of any final settlement. The surveys have not provided any data disproving the peasants' claims, and the work itself usually gives sound reason to doubt the competence and honesty of the officials. As a result land surveying has been for decades a matter of futile paper shuffling or no less futile land measuring, completely useless for the population and positively harmful to the government in that it has wasted money and resources. (*Ocherk,* 1900: 6)

This was the chaos into which legal resettlers would step after their long journey. The situation described above did not change appreciably in the following decades. A typical report from Irkutsk in 1897 indicated that incoming migrants were simply finding their own land and occupying it without any documents and without anyone bothering to measure off boundaries (*Dopolnitelnyi,* 1897: 263; see also *Ocherk,* 1900: 70, 102). Even in the years after 1906, when the government was spending more money on Siberian resettlement than on land reform in Eurpoean Russia, surveyors could not keep up with the demand for land measurement beyond the Urals (Skliarov, 1962: 320-25).

---

[26] In theory, benefits for *legal* resettlers were considerable. They could purchase railroad tickets at reduced rates (*Sbornik,* 1901: II, 22), and they enjoyed a number of benefits after their arrival at their new farm sites. (see *O rasprostranenii,* 8-9). However, these ameliorations were no help to a peasant trying to break away from his village against the wishes of his neighbors.

The scene in European Russia also presented difficulties. The 13 July statute required officials to measure each departing household's share of village land accurately and to determine its relation to the total acreage held by the village. Presumably this would form the basis for a calculation of the household's share of the village's debt and tax payments. But no such measure of peasant lands had ever been made before, and, as the government was to learn after 1906, making it would require decades of work by thousands of surveyors. Peasant landholding in European Russia was vague and confused. The investigations of the 1870s (ch. 2, sec. C) indicated that it was often harder to identify a household's allotment than to measure it, and the MVD's editing commission discovered this again in 1902-3 (*Svod...o nadelnykh zemliakh,* 1906: 36-47). Neither peasant custom, nor government legislation, nor Senate interpretation had ever identified peasant family holdings in any consistent, enforceable way; hence a would-be resettler's neighbors could utilize the exacting requirements of the 13 July statute to block his departure or at least render it very costly to him. If legal resettlement was to go forward, a large number of competent and zealous officials would be needed in European Russia, not only to help departing peasants cope with bureaucracy but also to protect them from their neighbors.[27]

At no time were there large numbers of competent and zealous officials in the countryside. Prior to 1892 there were none at all, and therefore it should not surprise us to learn that the law of 13 July quickly became inoperative. Illegal *(samovolnye)* migrants to Siberia far outnumbered legal ones in 1890-91, and an increasing number of these people, finding themselves poorly prepared for life in Siberia, were returning home much the worse for wear. Such was the administrative breakdown that an MVD circular dated 6 March 1892 ordered the governors in European Russia to prevent *all* peasants from departing for Siberia, whether they were legal migrants or not (*Tsirkuliary,* no. 22). This measure, however, only increased the flow of illegal resettlers, in part because the agencies for handling peasants in Siberia were gradually improving their methods (*Tsirkuliary,* "Zapiska...Tobolskogo Gubernatora," l. 10: 4-9, 13). It seems that in 1892 the MVD was forbidding peasants to depart from European Russia while the ministry of state domains was striving to help them once they got to Siberia.

Viewed as a system, the idea of preventing people from departing and then allowing them to arrive was absurd, but it made sense from an immediately practical point of view. Forcing a resettling family to return to its village in European Russia would only cost the government money and inflict some very poor and angry peasants on their old neighbor-

[27]Concerning the amorphousness of peasant landholding, see ch. 2, n. 15, and ch. 5, sec. B.

hoods, forcing whole villages to undergo once again the distinctly unpleasant process of redividing their land to accommodate the distinctly unwelcome prodigals (Coquin, 1969: 301-2). With the government's resettlement policy reaching its highest level of absurdity just as a major famine was driving unprecedented numbers of peasants to migrate, the wonder is not that legal migration declined in volume by 1892 but, rather, that there was any of it at all.

As we know (ch. 3, sec. A), 16 gubernias had captains by the end of 1890, and 12 more acquired them in July 1891. Allowing the knights a few months to accustom themselves to their new positions, we may hazard the estimate that they were in full operation in most gubernias of European Russia by 1892. This is about the time by which one may fairly expect them to have begun participating in the business of resettlement.

The earliest indication I have seen of this participation is an MVD circular of 20 July 1892, wherein the land section ordered its captains to stop annoying uezd treasurers with requests for financial aid for resettlers (*Tsirkuliary*, l. 25). In this matter, at least, the captains do not seem to have been oppressing peasants. On the contrary, this first reflection of the captains' work shows them hounding bureaucrats into doing something intelligent in the countryside. Some of the new line officers were actually undertaking to push the staff around, and they were succeeding well enough to annoy St. Petersburg. It is possible, even probable, that our knights were involved in the sharp increase of illegal migration during the period 1891-94.

The MVD's complaint of July 1892 did not reflect any serious opposition to resettlement per se. On the contrary, if Kaufman is correct, 1892 was the year when the government began to relax its rigid limits on peasant departure (1905: 42-43). More indicative of the land section's real views was its note of 15 November 1893 recommending that funds be provided to aid resettlers (*Tsirkuliary*, no. 30). A few months later the MVD circular of 2 July 1894 expressly commanded the captains to forget about earlier instructions and to get legal resettlement going again. They should make it a point to help migrants to depart. Among other things, they should encourage would-be settlers to send advance parties *(khodoki)* to find land in the new territory, thus assuring their families a place to live when they reached their destinations (no. 33). A circular of 18 November 1894 noted that gubernia-level administrators were not handling petitions for resettlement fast enough and curtly ordered them to speed up their operations (no. 35). A circular of 8 June 1895 ordered specific reductions in the required paperwork (*Sbornik*, 1901: II, 26).

According to the latter circular, the existing regulations imposed impossible burdens on departing peasants. After a would-be settler had received the ministries' permission to leave and had made all the necessary arrangements to travel, he still had to get his documents authenticated by the gubernia board and signed by the governor himself. While the papers were making their last weary trip via land captain to governor, the departing peasants had to live off their savings and whatever money they had received from the sale of their movable property and dwellings, thereby diminishing the resources that would be available to them in Siberia. The circular of 8 June introduced several shortcuts designed to allow peasants to leave sooner.

In sum, by 1894-95 the government had begun to free itself from the tangle created by its 1889 law on resettlement and was on the way to establishing a workable system. By simplifying legal resettlement and involving the captains in it, the above circulars made it more accessible to the peasants. Results, seemingly, were good. Kaufman notes that the percentage of migrants who went through Chelyabinsk bearing official permits rose from 22 in 1894 to 73 in 1895. During the period 1896-1903 this figure averaged about 60% (1905: 75). As for illegal resettlement, the government was still frowning upon it as late as 1894. The abovementioned circular of 2 July explicitly ordered captains to prevent would-be resettlers from setting out without proper approval. If they were caught en route, they were to be sent back home (*Tsirkuliary,* no. 33). By the end of 1894, then, the captains had taught the central government some lessons about smoothing out its administrative processes, but they had not yet persuaded their superiors to make radical changes in their policies. In particular, the central offices were still insisting that all resettlement be supervised.

If the captains were ever to produce an impact on resettlement, they should have done it by 1895-96. Appropriately, it was in 1895 that the government introduced fundamental changes in its resettlement policy. In March the Committee of the Trans-Siberian Railroad formally decided that hitherto illegal resettlers arriving in Siberia should be allowed to settle there (Kaufman, 1905: 46-47), and in the following year this principle achieved statutory expression in the laws of 15 April and 7 December 1896, allowing peasants to move to Siberia without any official permission (p. 64). Apparently the government was trying to improve its supervision of resettlement, thereby attracting peasants into its processes instead of forcing them. This made good practical sense, because peasant interest in resettlement was rising rapidly. In 1892-95 the average number of resettlers per year was about 100,000, whereas in 1896-99 it was 200,000 (pp. 42, 59, 66). Both government and peasants wanted resettlement on a larger scale than the government could properly administer, so the government administered what it could and dropped the pretense of administering what it could not.

One wonders if it was the captains who taught the government to take this line. I know of no way to prove such an assertion. On the other hand, I do not know where else the government might have picked up the idea of helping households to force their way out of their villages against the will of their all-powerful neighbors.

Certainly the idea did not come from the ministry of state domains and its agents in Siberia. Administrators in Siberia, hitherto anxious to bring in settlers, began in the mid-1890s to report shortages of arable land and to speak of their inability to handle the unprecedented flow of people. The MVD responded to the new Siberian attitude as early as July 1896 by sending out a confidential circular to the governors in European Russia that flatly contradicted the legislation of that year. It urged local officials to do what they could to discourage petitions for supervised resettlement and to stop migrants who went without official permission *(Konfidentsialno)*. A more elaborate circular to the same effect came out on 20 January 1897. It was published openly, so it did not contradict statutory law. It merely expressed the government's concern over the fact that the annual number of migrants to Siberia had almost doubled in the past year. Siberia, it seems, was filling up. Farmland near existing roads and settlements was already occupied as far as the Altai Mountains, and 12% of the would-be resettlers of 1896 had had to give up their search for good land and return to their original homes. The circular urged the captains in European Russia to spread this word. They should warn perspective settlers about the expenses and difficulties they would face *(Sbornik,* 1901: II, 26-33; Kaufman, 1905: 64-68). This refrain continued through subsequent circulars. That of 20 October 1897, for example, barred all advance parties from the sub-Altai region, where most resettlers wanted to go (Kaufman, 1905: 35).[28]

One gets the impression that the captains paid very little attention to these official cold winds from Siberia. In 1896 about 44% of the migrants going through Chelyabinsk lacked official permission, and in subsequent years this figure rarely fell below 40% (p. 75). Confidential circulars notwithstanding, the captains do not seem to have made much effort to confine would-be resettlers to their home villages.

So far as I know, there were no more secret instructions like that of July 1896, designed to impede legal resettlement by unofficially harassing

---

[28]The sub-Altai region was mostly grassland, requiring no clearing and enjoying heavier rainfall than the other grasslands to the west or east (Coquin, 1969: 303, 498). It was, therefore, the most heavily populated area in Siberia. In 1916 about 35% of Siberia's population lived there. (Zhidkov, 1972: 310).

It must be kept in mind that no one really knew how much arable land Siberia had. Kaufman made a thorough study of the matter, yet in 1905 he wrote that Siberia had no more empty farmland and that massive resettlement was a thing of the past (1905: 273-74)—this on the eve of Stolypin's resettlement campaign of 1906-12, the most intensive movement to Siberia that has ever occurred in Russian history (Coqin, 1969: 720).

those who tried to engage in it. True, the MVD circular of 20 January 1897 sought to discourage unsupervised movement, but its clauses regarding supervised movement were the most intelligent the government had yet produced. The captains would now be empowered to hand out passes directly to *khodoki,* entitling them to cut-rate railroad tickets (*Sbornik,* 1901: II, 31-32). In addition, the government would now help the *khodoki* communicate with the home folk. When a *khodok* found the land he wanted, he was to notify the local officials in the new territory, whereupon these worthies would determine whether or not the land was in fact adequate and available, and they would then communicate their verification directly to the officials of the home territory by telegraph! Then the land captain could begin setting up the migrants for their move. The circular of 20 January also simplified the procedures for getting resettlers on the road. There would be no more time limit on them for selling their dwellings and movable possessions, and any members of the party could change their minds and decide not to go without jeopardizing the departure of their erstwhile comrades. As for the gubernia boards, they were to give resettlement petitions priority over *all* other business in order to reduce the time required for paperwork to a minimum (p. 33).

Clearly, the circular of January 1897 does not reflect a desire to slow up resettlement. For some reason St. Petersburg was ignoring the cries of anguish from Siberia even while responding to them. The land section was officially warning the captains to discourage resettlement while giving them broad leeway to help would-be resettlers. Subsequent orders took a more unambiguously positive direction. The MVD circular of 16 February 1898 cut railroad fares for approved migrants even lower than before and offered yet sharper cuts to those who traveled longer distances eastward. On 18 April of the same year an MVD-MF circular extended cut-rate fares to all peasant resettlers, both those going to state lands in Siberia and those who were buying privately held lands or renting them on a long-term basis in European Russia (pp. 35-37). Finally, an MVD circular of 9 January 1899 informed captains that resettlement worked most smoothly when migrating families and/or groups made the trip a few members at a time rather than all going at once as they had been required to do in 1890 (pp. 38-39).

In sum, despite persistent irregularity and upheaval in the government's resettlement work during the period 1889-1906, certain trends may be observed in it. The law of 13 July 1889 proceeded from the uninstructed imaginations of St. Petersburg clerks, and it was so cumbersome as actually to impede resettlement. Within a few years, however, the government responded to pressure from its administrators in European Russia—chiefly the captains—by making unsupervised migration legal. The captains were urged to do what they could unofficially to discourage unsupervised movement, but the thrust of the government's efforts was to bring the procedures of supervision into line with peasant needs. One surmises that the captains acted as their superiors' eyes and taught them how to write more practical laws—as was their purpose.

Perhaps the old cycle from knight to clerk was not entirely a meaningless succession of failures. Indeed, if we conceive of the Russian state as essentially an agency for mobilizing human beings who have never wished to be mobilized, then the cycle takes on the appearance of an effective, or at least intelligible, administrative process. The whole purpose of the government's knight-servitors was to become clerks. This was the capital cities' way of communicating with their people and vice versa. The truly remarkable thing about the land captains was not that they became clerks but that they were *not* followed by yet another set of knights—not immediately, at any rate. What followed them, rather, was the Stolypin Land Reform, which brought with it a new approach to mobilization.

D. SUCCESSORS OF THE LAND CAPTAINS

At the same time the land captains were being enacted into law and sent out to work, other segments of tsarist organization were beginning to evolve into insturments of mobilization. By the 1900s two of them, the ministry of agriculture (MZ) and the peasant bank, would be prepared to compete with the captains as bearers of agrarian reform, or so the central government believed. As we shall see, the three would participate actively in the Stolypin Land Reform, opposing one another while also working jointly, and by 1911 the MZ would be well on its way to replacing the MVD's land section as the government's chief agency of mobilization in rural Russia. It will be helpful, therefore, to say a word here about the origins and early development of the MZ and the peasant bank.

The Ministry of Agriculture

The ministry of agriculture *(ministerstvo zemledeliia)* was established in 1894, but it did not get this name officially until the end of 1915. It was the ministry of agriculture and state domains from 1894 to 1905, and from then until 1915 it was the "chief administration of land settlement and agriculture" *(glavnoe upravlenie zemleustroistva i zemledeliia)*. Several structural changes were made in 1905 to correspond to the change in title. Chiefly, the mining administration was taken out and the MVD's resettlement organization was put in. In 1906 the department of state domains was expanded to enable it to manage the various changes in peasant landholding that made up what came to be called the Stolypin Land Reform. Hereinafter I shall disregard the ministry's formal names and refer to it uniformly as the ministry of agriculture or MZ.

Most MZ agents were specialists; that is, their *formal* roles derived solely from their practical knowledge of applied sciences—surveying, agronomy, agrarian economics, et al. Seemingly, this made them very different from the land captains, whose roles were defined primarily by their responsibilities. In theory, the specialist had only to dispense his knowledge, and that was that. Knowledge needed neither enforcement nor justification. It was conceivable that a specialist might dispense incorrect information or convey it ineffectively, but knowledge per se could not possibly produce harmful consequences. As long as the specialist stuck to his knowledge, therefore, he could do no wrong. If something went sour in the course of his work, technical processes and/or improvements in peasant agriculture could not possibly be part of the cause. Unlike the captain, the specialist did not have to solve social problems, or preserve order, or collect taxes. To put it another way, it was generally assumed that his knowledge served all these purposes by its own inherent quality, and this assumption was never questioned—except by an occasional peasant or captain, who thereby demonstrated his backwardness or narrowness of view. Thus the specialist needed neither authority nor virtue, nor did he need to commence his operations with an elaborate code of regulations setting forth his powers and limitations in relation to every official and institution he might conceivably encounter, nor could he be ordered to carry out policies and make reports by every agency in St. Petersburg. In short, he was much more independent in practice from other government agencies than the captains were. Other officials could impede his work, but they could not easily make him do their work or take responsibility for achieving their aims. He was also virtually independent of his own superiors. His "law" was his knowledge, and, generally speaking, no superior could command him to do anything but what knowledge dictated. Indeed, a low-echelon specialist might conceivably have more knowledge than his superior, and on this basis he might defy or even command higher echelons. As to the specialist's relationship with the peasants, his lack of authority to hear appeals or decide disputes made it unnecessary for anyone to bribe or attack him. His utter lack of formal responsibility for the peasants' welfare or development, or for anything except his science, left him free from both custom and authority.

To be sure, specialists disagreed profoundly among themselves regarding the nature of their "knowledge" and the manner of applying it. During the Stolypin Reform surveyors and agronomists often disapproved of each other, government agronomists clashed with zemstvo agronomists, general practitioners of agronomy came into conflict with specialists in its particular areas of study, and purveyors of "pure" science found themselves opposed to field agronomists who considered it their primary function to organize peasants and agitate among them. In short, "knowledge" was by no means a well-defined concept, and the independence it gave its possessors was ideal, not real. Moreover, as the specialists' organization took form, they manifested dissatisfaction with their pristine dedication to science and began to strive after more legal authority of the sort the captains enjoyed. During the Stolypin Reform they demanded full responsibility for rural welfare and development (ch. 9, sec. C), and in the course of World War I they at last succeeded in acquiring it (ch. 10, sec. D). Even so, the contrast between specialists and captains never disappeared. No matter how varied "knowledge" became or how much responsibility a specialist shouldered, he could still maintain a degree of independence—from superiors, colleagues, and peasants alike—by claiming to stand four square on science. The captains, as we have seen, had only their virtue to stand on; therefore they could be ordered to do almost anything by anyone, and they could be made to answer to just about anyone for just about anything they did.[29]

Since the MZ was staffed with specialists instead of knight-clerks or tax collectors, its organization differed from that of the MVD and MF (ministry of finance). Instead of operating through a chain of command, the MZ set up conferences and committees composed not only of its own agents but of all persons who were involved in furthering technical improvement. The purpose of these meetings was not merely to hand out orders and allow subordinates to ask questions about them. It was, rather, to exchange information and, when necessary, to secure agreement on this or that policy. In 1894, at the same time the ministry itself was established, the agricultural council *(selskokhoziaistvennyi sovet)* was set up alongside it to facilitate "the exchange of opinions between representatives of the government and agricultural enterprises." The council was required by law to meet at least once a year (*Otchet,* 1895: 3).

The idea of having a council attached to a ministry was not new in itself. All ministries had councils. In other ministries, however, the members were appointed from among the ministry's own staff by the minister. By contrast, the MZ's council was a congress. To be sure, its members were appointed by the minister, but they included men from outside the ministry and even from outside the government. D. N. Shipov, chairman of the Moscow zemstvo directorate, attended the first session (from 7 January to 15 February 1895), as did A. A. Bobrinskii, president of the Free Economic Society, and V. V. Dokuchaev, Russia's leading soil scientist (p. 12). Moreover, the council fostered the spread of local councils throughout European Russia with the explicit purpose of

---

[29]I have made more detailed comments on the differences between the ministries and their agencies elsewhere (Dec. 1964: 68-90). See also ch. 9, sec. C.

securing the cooperation and participation of farmers and zemstvo agricultural specialists in the ministry's work. Regional agricultural councils had been established as early as 1880-81. Alexander III had ordered their abolition in 1881, but from then on a significant number of farmers from all parts of European Russia—2,700 of them in 1882, increasing to well over 10,000 by 1907—had kept up a regular correspondence with the central offices, reporting on weather conditions, sown area, harvests, wages, plant and animal diseases, etc. and offering a multitude of descriptive reports on local practices and experiences. All this had been published by the department of agriculture in a quarterly journal that had been coming out since 1882 (pp. 3-5).[30] By 1894, then, a potential membership was already well established for local councils. More, the new ministry could use its rural correspondents as members for its own council in St. Petersburg and also draw on them for information and ideas (p. 13).[31]

One important advantage in the MZ's democracy of experts was that it allowed regulations to be drawn up and changed on an ad hoc basis in each locale. The specialists' rules were scientific, not legal; hence they had only to be practical and expedient. Local councils could enact and repeal them whenever experiments and experience dictated. So long as specialists kept to their professions, they could dispense with the inherent rigidity of legal-administrative system, with its massive codes, chains of command, incessant reporting, and steadily accumulating archives. In short, the MZ's organization enjoyed all the advantages of line-over-staff administration without suffering any of its disadvantages—always provided that it confined itself to technical processes and maintained the belief that technology made no impact on society except to enrich the members.

The MZ's "democracy" took a radical step forward in February 1901, when the government permitted the Imperial Moscow Agricultural Society to hold an all-Russian congress of agronomists. It was the first such meeting ever to be held in Russia. The participants were not gentry farmers but scientific experts in the employ of the government and zemstvoes—i.e., the notorious Third Element (see Glossary). Despite the cloud of suspicion under which these people operated in those days, their discussions ranged far beyond the business of agronomic science. Indeed, their final resolutions had almost nothing to do with agronomy. Most of

---

[30]The first issue of the journal that collated local information was entitled *1882 god v selskokhoziaistvennom otnosheniem po otvetam, poluchennym ot khoziaev.* Subsequent issues, which continued to appear through 1916, bore the same title except for the year.

[31]Proposals for this approach to agricultural work had been made earlier by former ministers of state domains, e.g., Valuev in the 1870s and Ostrovskii in 1892.

them dealt with the social and organizational problems a specialist faced when he undertook to introduce sound agricultural practices to peasant villages. It might even be said that the resolutions of 1901 comprised, in effect, a lengthy set of instructions to both government and zemstvo as to how peasant reform should be organized and conducted.[32]

The new approach to government did not come solely from the MZ. The 1880s and '90s saw a rapid acceleration in the growth of a population of native, trained, professional men, and all ministries were affected to some extent by the new blood.[33] Even the MVD began to show some interest in the new administrative techniques. In 1897 the governor of Saratov proposed to hold a congress of land captains in his gubernia in hopes of making them operate in more uniform fashion. He even wanted to let them submit questions in advance for discussion. He put this suggestion into his annual report to the tsar, and Nicholas II responded in the margin with a resounding "very useful" (*Svod vysochaishikh,* 1899: 79). I do not know if the Saratov congress was ever held, but on the whole the MVD does not seem to have been ready for such innovations. In 1900 the governor of Kaluga asked if it would be all right to hold a congress of land captains and tax inspectors in order to discuss their differences. The MVD pronounced this "premature" (TsGIAL, f. 1291, op. 32, d. 30, l. 10). After 1906, however, the MVD swiftly came around to the new way. In 1912 the land section's official history went into raptures about the wonderful achievements of the "unprecedented" Russia-wide congresses of gubernia board members and land settlement agencies in late 1907, early 1909, and early 1911 (Boianus, 1911: 11-14).

Still, the MVD lagged behind other ministries, and all ministries lagged behind the MZ. From its inception in 1894 the MZ manifested its eagerness to rely on any and all potential agencies of reform regardless of their official status. As we shall see, the Stolypin Land Reform involved the widespread adoption of this approach. After 1905 government by expert and quasi-democratic council extended itself very rapidly into the countryside, and it continued to play a vital role there until 1929. Much of the impetus behind this new, more penetrating variety of mobilization came from the MZ (ch. 9, sec. B).

There was tremendous potential for dynamic action in an organization of specialists, untrammeled by any responsibilities except those imposed by their professions. The tsars and their ministers had stumbled upon a discovery. The utilitarian doctrine not only gave individual men what John Stuart Mill was pleased to call liberty but also gave to

---

[32]See *Trudy* (1901). Each section in this opus is paged separately. The resolutions are in item 4 of the first part.

[33]Leikina-Svirskaia (1971) presents a detailed description of this development.

governments a far more powerful instrument of mobilization than any tsar, khan, sultan, or emperor had ever possessed before.[34]

The Peasant Bank

The peasant land bank was set up under the MF in 1882. Its original function was to lend money to peasants who bought land belonging to private estates, and until 1895 this was its only function. Its policies were conservative. It required large downpayments from its borrowers, and it allowed a maximum of 13 years for payment. Under these conditions the bank's achievements were modest. By 1895 it had helped the peasants of European Russia to buy about 6.2 million acres (Vdovin, 1959: 25-36, 97-98).

In 1895 a new law allowed the peasant bank to purchase estates on its own, thus making it possible for the bank to divide up large areas into lots suitable for peasant purchasers (*TPSZ*, 12195). The new law also extended the maximum period for repayment to over 50 years and allowed the bank's agents to demand downpayments as low as 10%. These changes cleared the way for the bank to accelerate its land distribution. In 1896-1905 it sold or aided in the sale of 15.4 million acres.[35]

The bank was a semi-autonomous organization. Until 1906 it got all its funds from the sale of its own bonds to private persons, and its local sections were managed by colleges made up of both elected and appointed officials. The administrative structure, which remained basically the same until 1917, deserves a few lines. General direction was in the hands of the MF. The central office of the bank was the bank council, consisting of a manager and six to twelve members, almost all of whom were appointed by the MF. Under the council were the sections, of which there were about 30 in 1905, or about one for every two gubernias in European Russia, Congress Poland, and the Baltic region.[36] Each section had a director, named by the MF, and two to four members. One or two members were appointed by the local governor, and the others were elected by the gubernia zemstvo assembly from among its members ("Banki," 927-28; "Krestianskii," 726).

[34]As the liberal journal *Vestnik Evropy* pointed out in an article of 1894 (Biriukovich, 1894: 791-92), the idea of a ministry for agronomic specialists was relatively new in all countries. Prussia had set up the first one in 1848, to be followed by Austria in 1866, France in 1881, Great Britain in 1888, and the United States in 1889. In the latter countries, the article said, the immediate motive was to bolster national agriculture in a time of falling prices on the world market. International depression was also of concern in Russia, but more pressing in 1894 was the major famine that had occurred two years before.

[35]Vdovin (1959: 90-91); "Krestianskii" (781); "Zemelnyi" (facing col. 448); Kofod (1914: 21-22).

[36]A section was set up in Transcaucasia in 1906 (Sanakoev, 1971).

Virtually all leading statesmen saw the peasant bank as an instrument of agrarian reform. It was obvious, after all, that the Russian countryside needed cheap credit if productive agriculture was to develop and prosper there. One had only to take a very small step to conclude from this that an organization dispensing credit could transform Russian agriculture, or at least relieve poverty.

As to the aim of the bank's would-be reform, this was much discussed on the higher levels of government from 1882 on. There were always some statesmen who thought the bank should help poor peasants, i.e, peasants who were short of land. The predominant view, however, was that the government should extend its aid primarily to individual peasants who wished to free themsevles from the constraints of paternalistic authority and become independent farmers apart from their villages. Nikolai Bunge, MF during the early 1880s and chief founder of the bank, thought its credit should release worthy individuals from forced association with lazy neighbors (Chernyshev, 1918: 220-21). In 1884 Alexander III wanted the bank to give special attention to peasants who moved physically out of their villages and settled on the land they bought (Vdovin, 1959: 27-28, 52-53). During the period 1889-94, the State Council went on record a number of times in favor of using the bank's money to support energetic, individual farmers rather than poor, communal, interstripped ones, and the law of 1895 supposedly reflected this view ("Krestianskii," 728; Pavlovsky, 1930: 151-52). As we shall see in Chapter 6, many of the would-be agrarian reformers of the early 1900s expressed the hope that the bank would support peasants who wished to get out of their villages.[37]

Until 1908, however, the work of the local bank sections did not justify the hopes placed in them. Only a tiny portion of the bank's loans went to individuals, while the vast majority went to villages. Official figures show them going to "partnerships" *(tovarishchestva),* especially after 1895, but in most cases the partnerships were simply villages or parts of villages buying land to be used along with the villages' own and divided into strips along with existing village fields ("Zemelnyi," facing col. 448; "Krestianskii," 728).[38] The law of November 1895 specifically discouraged loans to villages, but the bank sections did not wish to give up the practice. Worse, most recipients of loans appeared to be not prosperous and promising farmers but poor ones who lacked the wherewithal to introduce new methods even if they felt the inclination. Prior to 1895,

[37]Throughout the period 1880-1905 most leading statesmen believed that the communal village was an obstacle to good agriculture. See ch. 5, sec. B.

[38]In 1907 the leaders of the reform were convinced that partnership land was being held and farmed in the same way as allotment land. See, e.g., Stolypin's memorandum of 30 Aug. 1907, printed in Sidelnikov (1973: 161).

72% of the peasants receiving peasant bank loans had allotments of less than eight acres (Vdovin, 1959: 74-75).

Why did local bank sections go against the would-be reformers of St. Petersburg? For one thing, villages were better risks. In April 1908, at an interministerial conference on credit, a representative from the bank, one V. S. Koshko, stated this belief directly. The bank, he said, preferred to make its loans to villages and other stable groups because their members could be held collectively accountable (TsGIAL, f. 1291, op. 54, 1908g., d. 4, l. 21).[39] For another, the villages were not likely to tolerate the sale of land to anyone but themselves, because they were already renting most of the nonvillage arable land in Russia and had divided it in strips among their members. Of the arable state lands in 50 gubernias of European Russia, 86.8% were already rented out to peasants in 1904. On the arable crown lands, the figure was 89.2% (*Statisticheskie,* 1906: 46-47). Concerning private estates, figures are not so exact, but some Soviet scholars have recently suggested that in the early twentieth century much of the arable land on private estates was being farmed by sharecropping villagers (Anfimov, 1969: 48-94; Minarik, 1964: 704-6). Thus, whenever an individual peasant was daring enough to buy this land with the hope of farming it by himself, he had to force a whole village to give it up. Under these circumstances the former tenants were likely to make it very hard for the newcomer (Vdovin, 1959: 51-52). In September 1908 the governor of Penza warned his captains and police officials of the need to protect purchasers of peasant bank lands. "In most cases," he said, "they are surrounded by hostile natives" (Sidelnikov, 1973: 261-62). In August 1909 the governor of Poltava sent out a circular urging his officials to see to it that individual purchasers of peasant bank land insured their buildings, since their angry neighbors might burn them down (TsGIAL, f. 1291, op. 120, 1909g., d. 61, l. 69). This was the sort of consideration that made local peasant bank sections reluctant to make loans to individual buyers who had separated themselves from their villages.

The peasant bank was a bank, and its business, contrary to the lofty expectations of the government, was to make loans that would be repaid, thus allowing the bank's managers to pay their obligations in turn. The one abiding principle underlying the operation of the bank's local sections was that they had to stay solvent while lending money to a class of people who had always been considered hopelessly bad risks. This was in itself a very difficult task, and the bank managers could hardly be expected to add to their burdens by launching a crusade for social change. Even when an individual purchaser would not be in danger from his neighbors, the prospect of collecting mortgage payments from him

[39]I am grateful to Professor Anita Baker for calling my attention to Koshko's statement.

without the active cooperation of village and volost institutions (backed by land captains) must have appeared very dim. Much brighter was the possibility of lending money to villages. Villagers used primitive farming methods, but at least their members could bear risks collectively, and they were much less likely to fall behind in their payments than individual peasants.[40]

If we take these matters into account, the reason the bank sections appeared to have made their loans to poor, communal peasants becomes plain. Villages received the loans, and therefore the bank's records showed every one of the members getting a share. Since the villages included many landless and land-short members, the average holding of the officially designated loan recipients seemed very small. This, however, was all paper. It is hard to say who actually got the land the villages and partnerships bought—not even the bank knew—but it is doubtful that landless households got very much. In general, only a few families got shares of purchased land—those possessing the necessary stock and equipment and able to make their shares of the mortgage payments. In practice, then, the bank section probably did make their loans to prosperous peasants, though perhaps not progressive ones.[41]

As we shall see in Chapter 7 (sec. D), capital-city minds remained determinedly unaware that when enlightened peasants bought land from neighboring estates, they were taking over their fellow peasants' lands. Statesmen and scholars alike were entranced, indeed blinded, by the vision of progressive farmers breaking away from their backward villages and setting good examples, and they simply could not see that the backward neighbors, far from following the shining example of the heroes of progress, were quite likely to kick their enlightened heads in. Generally speaking, the government's pious discussions about the peasant bank's promise as a reform agency were more than usually fantastic, even for St. Petersburg minds. Statesmen could fill hundreds of pages with their memoranda without so much as mentioning the fact that the bank had to pay its own way. Scholarly discussions have generally followed

[40] By its own standards of fiscal responsibility, the bank was a success during the pre-reform years. Its bonds, which sold initially at 6½%, went down in the 1890s to 5½% and 4½%. See "Zemelnyi" (col. 450).

[41] At no time did local bank sections take seriously the idea of helping poor peasants, not even after 1907. In a profoundly typical case involving some defaulting peasants in Tambov gubernia, one of the local estate owners asked Stolypin to intervene with the bank and return some land it had repossessed. Apparently Stolypin asked Kokovtsov (the MF) about the case, for we have a long, documented reply from Kokovtsov, dated 30 Oct. 1909, in which he quoted at length from the bank section's report on the matter. The section members declared unequivocally that they were determined not to waste good land on worthless peasants. The bank wanted to sell only to those who were "really able to establish strong *(krepkie)* farms" (TsGIAL, f. 408, op. 1, 1909g., d. 119, l. 15).

this example. No scholar I know of has ever taken note of the peasant bank's mundane need to find good credit risks. No scholar has ever considered that it might have been difficult for a "local" bank section—with two gubernias to cover—to identify good risks and keep track of debtors among individual peasants.

We can easily see why local peasant bank sections were able to ignore the schemes and visions of the central government. The central offices could cherish any vision and send out any command, but they could not force a section to put its money into bad risks. Any minister who tried to order such actions in specific cases would soon have lost his job. The peasant bank was not only opposed to all attempts to involve it in social reform; unlike the MVD hierarchy, it was quite able to make its opposition felt. Only in 1908, after Stolypin had virtually torn it apart and put it together again (ch. 7, sec. D), did the peasant bank begin, reluctantly, to lend money to individuals rather than villages.

To sum up, when the tsarist government embarked on its agrarian reform in 1905, it had available not only land captains but also two other types of official: bankers and specialists. The question arose: which type should be the vehicle for reform? The captains may have prepared the way, but as long experience suggested, they were not well adapted to carry it out. Many statesmen and political leaders put their hopes in bankers, mainly because the extension of credit seemed to be a relatively mild way to change peasant society. Bankers, however, were not able to lead or transform anyone. This left only the specialists.

The specialist had certain intrinsic advantages over the banker as an agency of reform. As a professional he enjoyed the same sort of independence from his superiors as the banker. He was even more free to act as he chose, because he did not bear the deadening responsibility of getting a fair return. Imagine a progressive peasant establishing a new farm on land his neighbors had been farming. The peasant bank lends him the money, and the specialist sees to it that he uses the right tools, seeds, and fertilizers. The new settler raises a good crop, but his resentful neighbors drive their cattle through his standing grain and burn his house. At this point the banker is in trouble. The farmer will default on his payments, and the bank will have to repossess the land. No one will buy or rent the land except the village, so the local banker abandons reform and lets the village have the land. Indeed, the banker probably foresaw all this and so had to be driven to make the loan in the first place. The land captain also foresaw it, and he would have tried every way he could to block the loan, because his superiors would blame him for any violence in his *uchastok*. The specialist, then, was the only one of our three candidates for reform leadership who had any reason to want land reform. He too could foresee the disastrous result, and he certainly worried about it. When the grain was trampled, however, and the house burned, *his* record still showed a successful operation. He could shrug off the loss as a sacrifice (not his own) for the advance of science, he could blame the police for failing to protect his clients (cadres), and he could ask the bank for another loan.

The Stolypin Reform and the continuing efforts at land reform in the 1920s could be described as the triumph of the agronomist over the land captain. Certainly the agronomists saw it this way. In the past two chapters, however, I have been at pains to show that the captains did much to prepare the way for reform in both government and countryside. If they did not do all that the capital cities expected them to do, the knight-clerks at least sustained and nourished the expectations they embodied. If they did not bring legal system to the peasants, they did keep the capital city committed to the idea of peasant reform. It is, of course, difficult to prove such a statement, but in lieu of evidence I pose a question: what could the specialists have done if captains (and *stanovye*) had not been there in those ugly first years of reform to take responsibility for both order and violence off their shoulders? The reader will do well to keep the question in mind, for it comes up more than once during the period 1905-30.

CHAPTER 5

The Context of the
Stolypin Land Reform

The Russian peasant lives and has his being only in his village
community; the rest of the world exists for him only in so far as it
interferes with his village community.

Friedrich Engels

O troika, O birdlike troika! Who invented you? Only a people
full of life could have done so, a people that refuses to be daunted
by anything, a people whose land spreads out evenly across half
the world, so that you may race ahead full-speed and count the
milestones until they flash like spots before your eyes and you
grow dizzy.

Nikolai Gogol (1961: 277-78)

A. INTRODUCTION: THE OFFICIAL REFORM

Let us begin with a brief description of the Stolypin Land Reform as
its managers depicted it. This will not be a wholly accurate account of
what the government did, but official formulas and figures have the
virtue of simplicity if nothing else. They make a good introduction to a
discussion of the context within which the government had to act. The
following sections indicate in summary fashion the original aims of the
reform's enactors and its accomplishments along these lines until 1914,
when World War I brought it to a halt.

Official Aims

The main aim of the Stolypin Land Reform is commonly said to
have been the destruction of the peasant commune (Mosse, 1965: 257-74;
Atkinson, 1973: 773-87). In communes—or, to use the government's
term, communal villages *(obshchinnye selskie obshchestva)*—the peasants
held the cultivated land collectively. "Destruction" of a commune occurred when the heads of household in a communal village received their

families' shares of village land as their own personal property. The official term for this process was *ukreplenie*.[1]

Communal landholding was a widespread phenomenon in Russia. The government's figures for 1905 showed it predominating in all areas of European Russia inhabited by Great Russian peasants, which is to say in general that it flourished everywhere but in the Belorussian, Baltic, and Ukrainian gubernias and in the Don Cossack region (Sidelnikov, 1973: 13). Destruction of the commune, therefore, appears to have been a vast undertaking.

The grounds for assuming that the chief aim of the reform was to make an end of the commune are as follows: (1) most high-level officials, including the reform's authors, were fond of saying that the state would be stronger and the peasants more prosperous if the latter became private property owners; and (2) the reform laws provided that a head of household in a communal village could receive the lands his household was farming as his personal property if he so desired.

Actually, the Stolypin Land Reform aimed neither to abolish the commune nor to establish private property. If some of the reform's authors articulated their visions of an industrious yeomanry by using terms of this sort, the fact remains that abolishing communes and establishing private holdings amounted only to a lot of paper shuffling. A peasant with 40 separate strips of land was not going to change his attitude toward farming or law if he learned one day that his strips were his property rather than his share. A change of this sort would not produce the sturdy yeomen who peopled capital-city imaginations. At best, and even this was doubtful, it might pave the way for such a yeomen as might be found in the real countryside to proceed with land reform, and this happy ending was what the capital-city mind wanted. For the authors of the reform, and for capital-city minds in general, the main aim of peasant reform in 1905-14 was to *consolidate* Russia's fields into integral household lots and establish productive farms on them. A great many communal peasants did acquire their lands as personal property during the Stolypin era, but this was no *land* reform. Very often it was simply a peasant's first step prior to selling his strips and leaving his village for good, either to go to the city or resettle on some other land (Simonova, 1962: 398-458). Such departures must have produced a significant impact on village society, but they did not bring about reforms in peasant land utilization. The switch to personal ownership became part of a land reform—i.e., a change in the manner of land usage and possession—only when it was a first step toward the consolidation of strips.

---

[1]The verb *ukrepit* ordinarily means "to strengthen," but in the jargon of tsarist land law it signified "to acquire."

As we shall see, the authors of the reform were mistaken about the virtues of private property. State-directed land reform and agricultural improvement did not harmonize well with personal rights to land. Agrarian reform required *groups* of peasants to change the fields they were farming, and it was much harder to deal with groups of private property owners than it was to work through villages possessing the power to impose their collective decisions on individual members. Even when land reform was completed, the new "property owners" had to be prevented from using their rights of ownership to split up their farms into pieces too small for productive farming. When these facts of life became clear, the government quickly lost interest in private property. The capital cities did not see the matter clearly in 1905-6, but in fact the reform organization was setting out to mobilize peasant society, not to establish rights.

Official Land Settlement

The term the government employed to describe its activity in consolidating peasant land was *zemleustroistvo,* literally "land organization," or, as it is usually translated, "land settlement." In its ideal form land settlement created separate household farms, each one concentrated on a single plot of ground. However, it also included any change in land utilization or distribution that seemed to lead in this direction. Thus measures of *zemleustroistvo* were of two general types: individual land settlement *(edinolichnoe zemleustroistvo),* which produced fully consolidated farms with all land in one single lot; and group land settlement *(gruppovoe zemleustroistvo),* which involved measures of land rearrangement that fell short of full consolidation. Operations of the latter type were not supposed to be fundamentally different from the former but were intended, rather, to be steps *toward* consolidation.

Individual land settlement, the actual process of consolidation, resulted in the formation of *khutora* (separate, integral farms on which the owners resided) or *otruba* (separate, integral farms surrounding an area in which the owners of the farms resided in close proximity to each other, each on his own house lot). Figure 2 shows a village as it was prior to land settlement, and Figure 3 shows it after its consolidation into *khutora.* Figure 4 shows another village before land settlement, and Figure 5 represents its consolidation into *otruba.* Note that in Figures 2 and 3 the village dwelling area disappears, whereas in Figures 4 and 5 it remains. Both operations were examples of a particular type of individual land settlement in which all households in a village underwent consolidation at once. The government usually referred to this village-wide individual land settlement as a *razverstanie,* but this was also a traditional term for a thoroughgoing repartition *(peredel)* of a communal village's

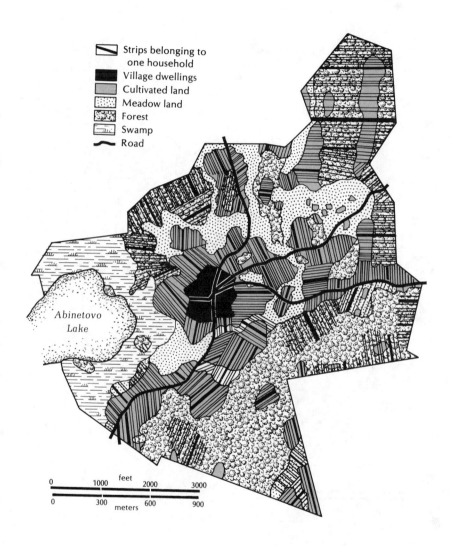

Figure 2. Novoselok village, Toropetskii uezd, Pskov gubernia, before the Reform.

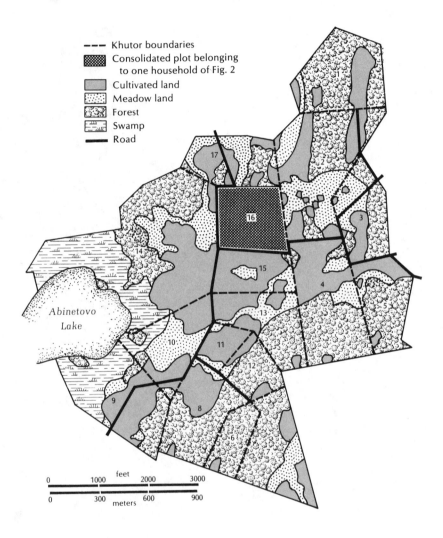

Figure 3. Novoselok village after the Reform.

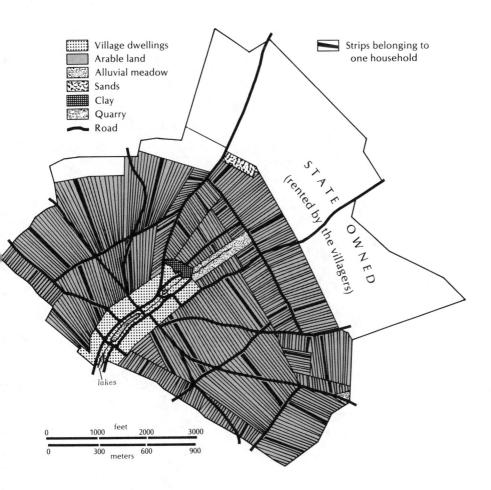

Figure 4. Khotynitsa village, Iamburgskii uezd, St. Petersburg gubernia, before the Reform.

Figure 5. Khotynitsa village after the Reform.

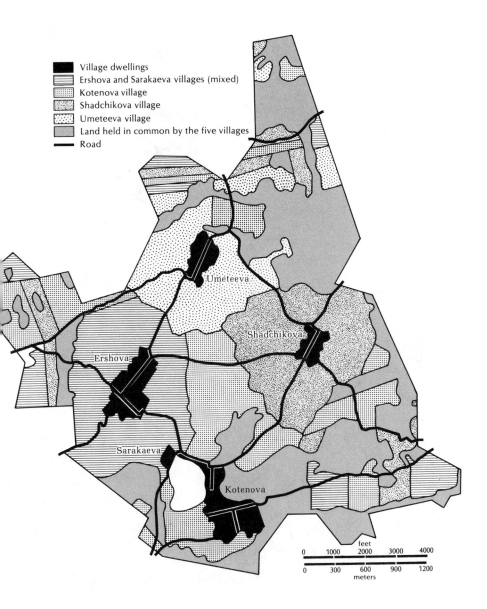

Figure 6. The villages Ershova, Sarakaeva, Kotenova, Umeteeva, and Shadchi-kova: Kozmodemianskii uezd, Kazan gubernia; before the Reform.

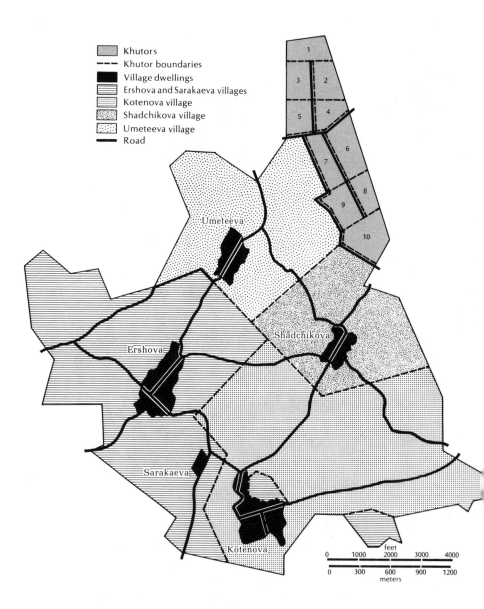

Figure 7. The villages Ershova, Sarakaeva, Kotenova, Umeteeva, and Shadchikova: after the Reform.

Figure 8. Lands of the villages Smedovaia and Klichino and of some private estate owners as they were before the Reform. They lie on the border between Kashirskii uezd, Tula gubernia, and Zaraiskii uezd, Riazan gubernia.

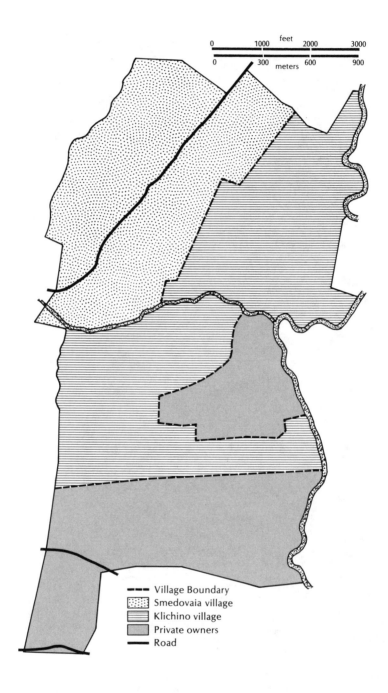

Figure 9. Villages Smedovaia and Klichino after the Reform.

land. A more precise term—and therefore the one I shall employ in this book—was village land settlement *(obshchestvennoe zemleustroistvo)* or, more simply, village consolidation.[2]

A second type of individual land settlement took place when a single head of household or small group of them consolidated his (their) strips while the rest of the villagers continued to divide their fields into strips. Most laws and instructions called this a *vydel,* but since this term could mean any kind of village land division in which a small group split away from a larger, even when no consolidation of individual households took place, I shall use the more exact "personal land settlement" *(lichnoe zemleustroistvo).* To repeat: village and personal land settlement were two different types of individual land settlement. Both produced khutors and otrubs.[3]

Group land settlement comprised any rearrangement of land that reduced the number of separate strips and/or fields belonging to households or villages but failed to set up otrub or khutor farms. The most important types were: (1) the breaking up of villages into separate settlements, each confined to an integral land area, (2) the disentangling of two or more villages (Figures 6 and 7), (3) the disentangling of peasant villages and private owners (Figures 8 and 9), and (4) any redistribution of land within a village which reduced the number of strips each household held. Group land settlement involved whole villages and, like village consolidation, required the approval of at least a majority of the heads of household.[4]

[2]Figures 2-9 are taken from a government publication—*Zemleustroistvo, 1907-1910gg.* (1911: *prilozheniia,* plans 9, 10, 15, 16, 31, 32, 39, and 40). The darkened strips in Figure 2 belonged to the household that settled on lot 16 in Figure 3. Figures 4 and 5 show how a village of 88 households consolidated its own land into 78 otrubs and purchased some adjoining state land it had long been renting in order to form 10 khutors and a common pasture. The dark strips in Figure 4 belonged to the household that received otrub lot 23 in Figure 5.

[3]The distinction between otrub and khutor is important insofar as we must deal in the following chapters with theoretical discussions regarding their respective advantages and disadvantages. In practice, however, the two terms were used interchangeably (Znosko-Borovskii, 1912: 4).

[4]Figures 6 and 7 show how five villages of Kazan gubernia were disentangled, three of them completely. In the course of the change ten households split away from the villages to form separate khutors. The two villages shown together under one color were interstripped on virtually all their fields, and they could only be partially separated.

Figures 8 and 9 show how two villages and ten private owners situated on the border between Tula and Riazan gubernias were completely disentangled.

The four categories of group land settlement described above were not all given equal recognition in statutory law. The first, second, and third were listed in article 1 of the statute of 29 May 1911 (Znosko-Borovskii, 1912: 1-2). The fourth, however, never achieved full legitimacy. It was authorized in a *nakaz* to the land settlement commissions of 19 Sept. 1906, and an MZ publication of

The distinctions between different kinds of land settlement were not precise. In village consolidations where full consolidation was not achieved for all households, the operation might be recorded as *obshchestvennoe* or *lichnoe,* depending on how the local agencies saw the matter. When some land was left under communal ownership, or the land of each peasant family still took up several plots, the result might be called either village consolidation or group land settlement. In a typical group land settlement project, a portion of a village's land could be consolidated into separate family farms as part of the operation (as in Figure 9).

It must be added that the reform did not cover the entire Russian Empire. The organization that was set up to carry it out ultimately extended only to 47 gubernias of European Russia. Elsewhere the reform was largely inapplicable, either because much of the land was already being farmed in consolidated plots, as in the Baltic gubernias, or because the population was not made up of peasant farmers whose lands needed consolidation, as in Central Asia. The settlement of peasants on integral farms was encouraged in Siberia and other areas where Russian settlers were moving in, but the reform organization did not take part in the process.[5]

Official Achievements

A summary of the reform's formal accomplishments unavoidably takes the form of statistical compilations, but the unfortunate fact is that no reliable ones are available. Students of the reform have not as yet studied materials from local reform agencies systematically but have contented themselves with reproducing the central government's claims. I shall perforce do the same here, and therefore the reader must keep in

---

1909 even went so far as to list traditional redistribution as one of the officially recognized types of group land settlement if it reduced the number of strips in a village (*Obzor...na 1 iiulia 1909,* 1909: 33). On the other hand, the MVD pronounced such redistributions both harmful and illegal—also in 1909 (*IZO,* 1909: 351). For further discussion of the definition of *zemleustroistvo,* see Martynov (1917) and also ch. 9, sec. A.

[5]The 47 reform gubernias were: Archangel, Astrakhan, Bessarabia, Chernigov, Don Oblast, Ekaterinoslav, Grodno, Iaroslavl, Kaluga, Kazan, Kharkov, Kherson, Kiev, Kostroma, Kovno, Kursk, Minsk, Mogilev, Moscow, Nizhnii Novgorod, Novgorod, Olonets (only from 1912 on), Orel, Penza, Perm, Podoliia, Poltava, Pskov, Riazan, St. Petersburg, Samara, Saratov, Simbirsk, Smolensk, Stavropol, Tambov, Tavrid, Tula, Tver, Ufa, Viatka, Vilna, Vitebsk, Vladimir, Vologda, Volyniia, and Voronezh. Only one uezd in Archangel came under the reform organization; two uezds in Vologda were not covered (Kofod, 1914: 114-19). The law of 23 June 1912 set up a separate organization to carry the reform to Congress Poland, and in Nov. 1914 commissions were set up, at least on paper, in three uezds of Orenburg gubernia (Dubrovskii, 1963: 239-40).

mind that the totals given in the following paragraphs (and throughout the book) do not record actual events. I present them only to indicate general trends.

Official figures varied widely. A work published by the MZ in 1911 claimed that by 1 January 1911 the government had already sold about 700,000 acres of state lands to peasants in the form of consolidated farms (*Zemleustroistvo,* 1911: 46-47); yet a government report of 1916 gave the amount of state lands sold this way during the entire period (1907-15) as slightly under 600,000 acres (Sidelnikov, 1973: 93). The later report is undoubtedly more accurate. Seemingly, the closer an official source was to the time it was reporting, the less reliable it was as a description of reality. In part, this was because reports from field operators exaggerated their achievements. The main reason, however, was that the processes of sale and consolidation were often long and complex. Completion could be reported at any one of several stages. At the end of a given year some farms were measured out but not yet physically occupied, while others were occupied and under cultivation but not yet measured out. Under these circumstances, yearly totals were always to some extent a matter of interpretation.

The figures given below are actually somewhat less than the reform's *total* achievements. The numbers of completed projects include only those finished by the end of 1913, and the number of petitions from the peasants go only to the end of 1914. The reform did not come to a full halt until 1917, but excluding the figures for the war years has the beneficial effect of eliminating the unusually gross inaccuracies, even by Russian standards, that entered into the statistics of land reform after World War I began. There are figures for completed projects during 1914 (see *Obzor,* 1915: *prilozheniia,* 10-13), but they reflect a time when field-work was being abruptly cut off, leaving many projects in suspension. Peasants on their way to join their battalions were having second thoughts about moving onto new fields, and a sizable part of the government's reform apparatus at all levels was whisked off to military service just as the reports on fieldwork were due in. Reported totals for 1914, therefore, are suspect. For 1915 and thereafter they are virtually useless. The actual number of land settlement projects completed in 1915 must have been well under 20% of planned performance, yet many scholars include the scheduled operations for that year in the total number of actually completed ones (e.g., Dubrovskii, 1963: 244, 582-84). On the other hand, it is relatively safe to use the number of petitions for land settlement during the year 1914, since the simple receipt of petitions required no action on the government's part except recording and filing.

By 1 January 1914 the reform organization had converted 22.5 million acres of allotment land to consolidated farms in either otrub or khutor form. The total area of allotment land in the 47 reform gubernias came to 321 million acres, so the consolidated portion (as of 1 January 1914) amounted to 7% (*Itogi,* 1912). About two-thirds of this area was consolidated by whole villages acting together, and one-third by individual households and groups of households breaking away from their villages (Pershin, 1922: 7, 10). During the same period the peasant bank sold 5.85 million acres of its lands to peasants as consolidated farms and helped peasants buy another 1.9 million with its loans (Dubrovskii, 1963: 252). Finally, the land settlement commissions sold about 575,000 acres of state lands to peasants in the form of consolidated farms (*Otchetnyia,* 1915: 22).[6] Thus the total area of land set up as individual consolidated farms in European Russia by the reform organization before 1914 came to about 31 million acres. Group land settlement was somewhat less extensive, covering about 12.4 million acres in all (Sidelnikov, 1973: 147), which brings the total area of land covered by the completed projects of the land settlement commissions before 1914 to 43.4 million acres.[7]

Approximately 1.75 million households were involved in these projects. Of these, 850,000 underwent individual land settlement on allotment lands (Sidelnikov, 1973: 147), 240,000 bought consolidated farms from the peasant bank or with its assistance (Dubrovskii, 1963: 252), and about 14,000 bought homesteads on state lands in European Russia (*Otchetnyia,* 1915: 22). In all, then, about 1.1 million of the land-settling households engaged in consolidation. The other 650,000 carried out some form of group land settlement. The total number of peasant households in the 47 reform gubernias was about 13 million in 1912 (Kofod, 1914: 120), so we may say that by 1914, 8.5% of the peasants had accomplished full consolidation, and another 5% had completed some form of group land settlement. By 1 January 1914, 13.5% of the peasants in 47 gubernias of European Russia had subjected about 11% of their land to some form of land settlement. This was what the reform organization achieved in just seven years.[8]

[6]This figure is a trifle large because it includes the year 1914, but the error cannot be more than 60,000 acres.

[7]This figure may be too high because it represents the simple addition of group and individual projects. According to A. A. Kofod, chief inspector of the reform organization, personal consolidations effected during the course of group land settlement were counted twice, as parts of group projects and as consolidations (1914: 112). Such consolidations made up 6.8% of the total area subject to *individual* land settlement (Dubrovskii, 1963: 591), so the figure given above for land settlement of all varieties could be as much as 2 million acres too high. I say "could be," because I am not as sure as Kofod was that the reporting procedures of the local commissions were uniform.

[8]I got the 11% figure by dividing the total area of peasant-owned lands, including both allotment land and land purchased after the Liberation (356 million acres—*Itogi,* 1912), into the 43.4 million acres that were consolidated or subjected to group land settlement.

The numbers of households submitting petitions for land settlement is of some interest, since it reflects popular interest in land settlement. By 1 January 1915 a total of 5.8 million households had petitioned for some form of land settlement on their own lands (*Otchetnyia*, 1915: 6). Of these, 2.5 million wished to consolidate their land, and 3.3 million wanted to participate in group land settlement. Considering that the peasant bank established about 240,000 households on consolidated farms before 1914, we may say that well over 6 million households requested some sort of land settlement before 1915, which comes close to one-half of the peasant population in the reform gubernias. It is important to note that 1.7 million, or 68%, of the households petitioning to consolidate their own land did so as whole villages (Karpov, 1925: 214-15). If this figure is added to the 3.3 million who petitioned for group land settlement, we see that 5 million, or 86% of the 5.8 million petitioning households, were operating collectively as villages, whereas 0.8 million, or 14%, were breaking away from villages. This fact should be kept in mind when considering the claim that the Stolypin Reform aimed primarily to "break up" the commune.

The above figures on petitions give a rough idea of the degree to which the reform organization succeeded in involving the peasants in land settlement. It must be added that the organization also engaged in simple land distribution. During the years 1907-14 the peasant bank sold about 9.7 million acres of its own land in the 47 reform gubernias and made loans to help peasants purchase 9.8 million acres directly from private owners (Sidelnikov, 1973: 174, 178). During the same period the land settlement commissions sold about 650,000 acres of state lands to the peasants (*Otchetnyia*, 1915: 22). It may be said, then, that the reform organization helped to turn over more than 20 million acres of non-peasant land to peasant farmers in European Russia.[9]

One final point regarding the reform's accomplishments: both the flow of peasant petitions for land settlement and the annual amount of

[9]This total includes not only the land sold as consolidated farms but all sales of nonpeasant lands to peasants in which the bank participated. As to the above figure for total sales of state lands, it represents only formally completed sales. Another 380,000 acres had been lined out and physically occupied by purchasers by 1915, but they had not yet negotiated their final sales agreements (*Otchetnyia*, 1915: 22).

Peasants in the 47 reform gubernias expanded their holdings in other ways. Not included in the above totals are allotment lands vacated by the several million peasants who left their villages, either to establish new farms in Siberia and other borderlands or to move into cities. Likewise, I have made no attempt to add in nonpeasant lands purchased by peasants without government aid of any kind. I suspect that the net result of these activities was *at least* 5 million additional acres made available to farming peasants in the reform gubernias during the period 1906-14.

fieldwork expanded in volume as the reform progressed. In 1907 about 220,000 households petitioned for land settlement on their allotment land; in 1913 the number reached 1.1 million. In 1907, 360,000 acres of village fields were subject to all types of land settlement; the corresponding figure for 1913 was slightly under 8 million (Sidelnikov, 1973: 147). Moreover, this expansion was accompanied by massive programs for agricultural improvement, and by 1914 central government and zemstvoes were working with unprecedented energy to distribute loans, subsidies, and expert advice to peasant farmers. It would serve no useful purpose to measure the government's achievements along these lines quantitatively, since much of the work was done by outside agencies. Suffice it to say that agricultural improvement not only expanded in volume as the reform progressed but also took many new directions. I shall take up agricultural improvement in detail in Chapter 9.

The only year in which the reform ran at full capacity was 1913, after the organization took form and before the war broke it up. It is interesting to consider that if the organization had merely kept up the rate it achieved in this year—that is, if the government had gone on completing land settlement projects on about 8 million acres per year—it would have taken until the 1950s to introduce some sort of land reform on all the allotment land in the reform gubernias. There is no reason to believe that the reform actually would have continued at the rate of 1913. It might have slowed down; more likely it would have gone faster, since, as we shall see, something very similar to it did in fact go faster under the Soviet regime during the 1920s (ch. 11, sec. B). I suggest this estimate of the time required to complete the reform for no other purpose than to indicate the enormity of the task land settlement embodied.

I cannot say conclusively whether the Stolypin Land Reform succeeded or failed. A word may be in order, however, on the manner in which scholars ordinarily assess the reform's achievements. Throughout the Stolypin era the atmosphere was filled with jabber concerning the relationship between land reform and peasant contentment. According to the capital cities' vision, the reform succeeded if the peasants were happy, or at least peaceful, and it failed if they were not. This sort of nonsense reached a crescendo in 1917, and it has re-echoed through scholarly literature ever since. Actually, successful land reform had no necessary relationship to peasant contentment or passivity. Peasants who did not want land settlement were obviously unhappy when they beheld its advance; peasants who wanted land settlement were also unhappy, partly because they had to wait too long and pay too much for it and partly because their success, when they achieved it, often plunged them into unforeseen risks and bitter feuds with their neighbors. If peasant satisfaction is the criterion for success, the reform certainly failed, as have all agrarian reforms and revolutions. If social "stability" is the criterion, the reform certainly failed, since its essential aim, notwithstanding the fantasies of its authors, was to upset the peasants' way of life.

If we dismiss these irrelevant criteria, we still cannot say with assurance that the reform succeeded. For one thing, there is no sure way to tell whether government action or the "natural" course of Russian development produced the peasants' acceptance of land settlement. A sizable number of scholars have favored the latter point of view.[10] For another, and this is the main point, the reform did not continue long enough for anyone to see what it was going to do. Full-scale implementation was interrupted only one year after it was attained, much too early to allow any intelligent prediction of the reform's ultimate direction or final evaluation of its accomplishment. All we can say with certainty about the government's success is that in 1906-14 the reform organization did take form and begin working. By 1914 it comprised about 7,000 surveyors, 700 "hydrographic" engineers, and 1,600 agronomists (*Otchetnyia,* 1915: 1; *Kratkii,* 1916: 47). When the war began, it was clear that the key programs of land reform in European Russia were village consolidation and group land settlement, with the latter becoming the more important of the two and with programs of agricultural improvement bidding fair to eclipse both of them (see ch. 9, sec. A). In short, the reform was not only expanding in 1914 but also undergoing rapid changes.

B. PROBLEMS OF REFORM

The Peasant Problem

Poverty and Backwardness

The Stolypin Reform was designed to cope with the peasant problem, which was, in a word, poverty. The peasantry as a whole grew wealthier throughout the period 1861-1917 (Simms, 1977; Benet, 1970: 61-73, 87-90, 120), but large numbers of them suffered from periodic famines and seemed to be unable to keep up payments on their debts and direct taxes. Many authorities on the peasant question both inside and outside the government blamed the peasants' difficulties on overly high taxes; others considered the growing shortage of farmland to be the basic problem. As we shall see in Chapter 6, however, the authors of the reform explicitly denied that any of these factors were *basic* causes of poverty. They claimed that the peasantry was suffering primarily from ineffective land use. The peasants were "backward," and therefore they were unwilling or unable to change their wasteful and unproductive

---

[10]E.g., voń Dietze (1920: 48, 76-77), Chernyshev (1912: xv), Pavlovsky (1930: 319-20), and Pershin (1928: 84-89).

methods of cultivation. This, said the enactors, was the essence of the peasant problem.

Peasant backwardness did not proceed from any general lack of interest in agricultural science in Russia. In fact, Russian agricultural science progressed rapidly during the decades prior to 1905, and by the 1880s the laboratories of Moscow and St. Petersburg had developed the most advanced soil science in the world. The very terms of modern soil classification are now mostly Russian words.[11]

Unfortunately, only the government and a few enlightened land-holders were able to benefit from capital-city science. The high level of Russian agronomy had very little effect on Russian farming, mainly because Russian soil was largely in the hands of peasants, and peasant society rejected science. Even in those small areas where agronomists came into direct contact with the peasantry, they were generally unable to persuade anyone to adopt new methods. A professor of agronomy appearing before Valuev's commission in 1873 testified that when an individual peasant received training in modern agriculture, he was generally unable to put his lessons into practice in his village even if he wished to (*Doklad,* 1873: V, Stebut, 1-2). In the 1880s and '90s A. P. Mertvago made some serious, sophisticated attempts to introduce intensive agricultural methods on an estate in Smolensk gubernia, but they failed, and Mertvago concluded that any such attempt had to fail until the day when all the potentially arable land in Russia had come under the peasants' wasteful plows. Only when the peasants were no longer able to resolve their problems by cultivating more land would they at last begin to improve their methods (Mertvago, 1900: 186-91). Things were so bad, said Mertvago, that in 1891 the most famous of the would-be transformers of peasant agriculture, A. I. Engelgardt, had to abandon his attempts at agronomic innovation. Unable any longer to support himself on his estate, this old populist, Mertvago's own model and teacher, crawled back to St. Petersburg to seek a government post (p. 201). The peasants were not only backward, it seemed, but determinedly so.[12]

---

[11]The leading Russian soil scientists were V. V. Dokuchaev (d. 1903) and his successor, K. D. Glinka (d. 1927). One of Dokuchaev's earlier works has recently appeared in English (1967). Glinka's work, *The Great Soil Groups of the World and Their Development,* was published in 1927 by the U.S. Department of Agriculture, which considered him the greatest soil scientist of his day. According to F. A. Shannon (1963: 6), American soil science dates only from the appearance of this work. James C. Malin (1961: 48-51) denies that the Russians' work was either original or relevant to the United States (unconvincingly, in my opinion), but even he acknowledges its impact on Western science.

[12]Abundant testimony to the difficulties of estate owners who tried during the 1860-70s to improve peasant agriculture on their lands is in *Doklad* (1873: VI). See also writings of N. A. Litoshenko and P. Zionovev in Barykov (1880: 215, 316-22).

This is not to say that capital-city images of poor and backward peasants necessarily had anything to do with reality. Many peasant farmers were neither poor nor backward, and it may be that some careful investigator of the future will find signs of a general uplift proceeding among them during the 1880s and '90s. Indeed, a few observers of that day argued that peasants were improving their agricultural methods, that sharecropping and labor rent on private estates often served as devices whereby enlightened estate owners were teaching peasants how to care for the soil properly (Meshcherskii, 1902: 5-7, 26-29, 33-35; Dmitriev, 1894: 46-47, 50-51, 89-91). Perhaps these minority views had some truth to them. In any case, the point here is not that Russian peasants *were* poor and/or backward, only that the reform's enactors—and most of capital-city society—assumed they were.

Peasant Tradition

Three elements in the traditional peasant socioeconomic order were taken to be the main obstacles to the introduction of good agricultural practice in the villages: three-field crop rotation, open-field land utilization, and communal landholding.[13]

The first of these was the most obvious. Most peasants in European Russia utilized their arable land according to a three-year cycle: fall planting in the first year, spring planting in the second, and fallow in the third. Each village divided its fields in three approximately equal parts, so that in a given year each part would be at a different point in the cycle. In this way the village had a spring and fall crop every year. Three-field rotation exploited the land too much and too little: too much, because the peasants rarely fertilized the soil or planted legumes and grasses that would restore nitrogen to it; too little, because the fallow period was much longer than necessary if modern methods of soil restoration had been used. The only possible defense of three-field agriculture was that it suited the needs of sedentary farmers who did not have regular access to markets. This was not such a bad defense in some cases. R. E. F. Smith's comment on peasant agriculture in the Muscovite period applies quite well to many peasants in the late nineteenth century: "The small size and low level of technology of the peasant unit contributed to its viability when disaster struck" (1977: 172). So long as survival

---

[13]On the general nature of these problems, see Pavlovsky (1930: 61-122) and Owen (1937: 305-17). K. Golovin (1896: 2-8) briefly describes the literary production of the 1890s concerning the peasant question. A more recent and much more elaborate description is Steven Grant's dissertation (1973). Recent Soviet scholarship also offers some discussion: see Busygin (1973); articles by A. L. Shapiro and V. M. Slobodin in *Ezhegodnik* (1964: 121-31, 158-66); and articles by Iu. M. Iurginis, N. A. Gorskaia, L. V. Milov, and V. G. Tiukavkin in *Ezhegodnik* (1966: 86-89, 173-92, 706-14).

in relative isolation was a village's main concern, and considerations of price and transport did not loom large, farmers were well advised to stick to methods they could sustain on their own. Nevertheless, literate Russians had already decided that three-field rotation was bad agriculture as early as Catherine II's reign, and at about that time the government commenced its attempts to root it out (Semevskii, 1903: II, 110-16, 144-56; Confino, 1969: 144-48).[14]

For all its patent disadvantages, three-field rotation seemed impossible to eliminate because it was woven inextricably into the peasant way of life. In particular, it was associated with "open-field" land utilization, which meant, in most villages, the extreme parcelization and dispersion of each family's land into tiny strips intermingled with one another in common fields (see Figures 2 and 4). Methods of interstripping varied widely from village to village. Generally speaking, the northern gubernias had smaller villages with too many tiny strips, whereas in the south, especially in the Ukraine, the villages were too large and a family's strips, though relatively few in number, were too far apart. A Ukrainian household usually held less than ten strips, but the distance from one to another would often be several miles (*Zemleustroistvo,* 1911: 41; Bochkov, 1956: 72).[15]

Interstripping did indeed place limits on each household's manner of farming. To be sure, everyone farmed his strips on his own, but all families who had strips in a single field had to follow a common schedule of crop rotation, mainly because the village cattle grazed on any unplowed fields, and there was no practical way to keep them out of a particular strip. One might argue that an individual household could improve its methods of cultivation even while following the village's cropping schedule. In practice, however, each household held so many different strips, so far apart from each other, that the use of intensive techniques seemed extremely burdensome even for the most enlightened of farmers. The subdivision of village land into intermingled strips not

[14]A few enlightened serfowners began trying to modernize peasant agriculture on their estates prior to Catherine's reign (Aleksandrov, 1976: 116). Apparently, however, most practicing farmers of the eighteenth and early nineteenth centuries paid little heed either to these shining examples or to the government (Confino, 1969: 54-55; 1963: 33; see also Augustine, 1970: 395-402). A. V. Chaianov has mapped out areas in Russia where three-field rotation still prevailed after 1900 (1966: 141).

It should be noted that planting techniques even less desirable than three-field agriculture were still widespread in Russia in the Stolypin era, chiefly in the far north and northeast, the southern and southeastern steppe, and Siberia, wherever land was still available in sufficient quantity to allow a farmer to move from field to field, exhausting the soil as he went.

[15]See Pershin (1928) for an exhaustive study of the varieties of interstripping that obtained in the various areas of European Russia.

only prevented any individual peasant from giving up or even improving three-field rotation but also made the physical tasks of farming enormously difficult. From Catherine II's time on, nearly everyone in Russia who had any book knowledge of agriculture was aware that the interstripping of fields locked the peasants into three-field crop rotation, and most reform-minded men believed this to be one of the chief elements in the "peasant problem" (Confino, 1963: 113-17, 124-30). When the Stolypin Land Reform was enacted and carried out, the assumption that interstripping was the main obstacle to good agriculture in Russia had already reached a very old age.[16]

It must be pointed out that the general disapproval of open-field agriculture had no basis in fact. It was a cultural phenomenon of eighteenth-century Europe, not a result of scientific observation. In the generation preceding the French Revolution, enthusiasts for the cause of scientific agronomy began a campaign all over Europe to transform the land surface of the earth into a checkerboard. Their mission, in essence, was to eliminate strips and fence off the land into separate squares, each to be farmed by an individual. Presumably, any peasant who lived on a square would conceive a desire for prosperity, take up the study of scientific agriculture, begin to keep books, and, in general, organize his family into an efficient production team. Note this presumption, for it was to be the heart and soul of all Russian agrarian reform—tsarist, populist, bolshevik, and what have you. Note that it arose in the imaginations of European agronomists at a time when they possessed virtually no empirical knowledge regarding peasant society or even agriculture.

What the agrarian crusaders of the eighteenth century did know was that certain of their contemporaries—statesmen, military commanders, and merchants, for example—strove to behave in businesslike fashion. They affected a purposeful attitude, as if trying to convince themselves and others that their behavior consisted of an orderly series of actions, calculated in advance to realize a consciously formulated intention. In a word, these paragons of enlightenment commanded one another's confidence by affecting to act in their own "interests." They strove to make their behavior conform to the image of a man who stood ready to rearrange his entire life and even his world-view at a moment's notice in order to put into effect the results of his calculations. Some of these men

[16]See the works cited in n. 13, especially Gorskaia and Milov. I have never come across a student of the peasant economy who suggested that open-field farming might have been a technique for pressuring the most indolent and irresponsible households in a village into performing the necessary tasks of cultivation. In a limited way, however, open-field farming might have made this positive contribution to a village's productivity. When a stripholder failed to plant his seed, or plow, or harvest, the whole village knew it immediately.

spoke of "duties" or "functions" rather than interests; the thought pattern was the same. They all regarded themselves as an elite with a mission to save the world, and the agrarian crusaders believed them.

Until the agrarian crusaders came along, this image of a man who organized himself around a scheme of means and ends had been to some extent a useful tool for explaining observed behavior, a hypothesis, if you will, that could be confirmed by an occasional observation. After all, one could see men who appeared to speak and act in this fashion. For the savior-agronomists, however, all connection between the image of a calculating man and the evidence of their senses disappeared. Peasants obviously did not calculate means and ends "rationally." This painful fact constantly impressed itself on eighteenth-century Europeans—those who kept their eyes open even when they disapproved of what they saw—and it forced the enlightened elite to make a painful choice between dismissing peasant farmers as subhuman or junking the belief that "natural" man calculated his interests before acting. The eighteenth century produced a number of bizarre resolutions to this dilemma, and one of them was the agrarian crusaders' checkerboard. Peasants were not subhuman, said the crusaders; they were merely imprisoned in their interstripped fields. Only free them by putting them on squares, and they would be as rational as any *philosophe.*

By the 1780s this idea had undergone some testing, and results were not impressive (except, of course, in England, where checkerboards were being imposed without any particular concept of humanity in mind). Arthur Young, one of the leaders in the agrarian crusade, was horrified to find in the late 1780s that many farmers on enclosed fields in France did not abandon three-field agriculture, despite the new squareness of their environment. They did not instantly renounce their customary ways in order to produce efficiently for the market. In other words, French peasants did not conform to the cardinal assumption of the agrarian crusade. But Young's faith in consolidation as the sine qua non of agricultural progress never wavered (1969: 295-303). Instead of renouncing the old image and looking for a new one that would conform to his observations, he and other prophets of science made it an article of dogma. They began to insist, *contrary* to the evidence of their senses, that peasants on squares would behave in accordance with accepted canons of economic thought, and their faith was to burn on in the hearts of their spiritual heirs without so much as flickering for well over a century. In Russia the government carried on a continual struggle against interstripping and three-field agriculture throughout the late eighteenth and early nineteenth centuries (Confino, 1969: 193-312; Druzhinin, 1946: I, 156-64), and after 1861, as we have seen, belief in the struggle still flourished in the capital cities, even though the government hesitated to act on it.

Nowhere in the world has any practical experience ever demonstrated that consolidated fields bring agricultural progress, and some present-day students of peasant agriculture actually deny that any such cause-effect relationship exists. Doreen Warriner, for example, suggests that although interstripping is indeed wasteful, it has not ever been absolutely necessary in any European country to consolidate strips before improving peasant agriculture (1965: 8-10). In some parts of East Asia peasant farmers still achieve a high level of productivity *per acre* on interstripped fields. Farmers in many "advanced" areas of Western Europe, especially France, were still dividing village fields into strips as late as the 1950s (Dovring, 1956: 42-54). Western Europe has seen massive efforts at consolidation since the 1940s, but open-field farming is still widespread today on some of the most productive farms. It is worth noting in this connection that the eminently practical Otto Schiller set up interstripped fields as a device for reorganizing Ukrainian collective farms during the German occupation in 1941-43 (1951: 1-15). In this case there can be no doubt that the primary aim was to maximize productivity. "The consolidated site," said Schiller, "is of managerial advantage only if it can be cultivated independently. This advantage disappears, however, as soon as the farmer depends on joint use of draft animals and machinery with his neighbor" (p. 5). Schiller offers the most convincing demonstration I have seen that there is no *necessary universal* relationship between land consolidation and agricultural modernization. This is not to say that the elimination of interstripping was futile. It seems, however, that any connection between it and advances in agricultural technique—as in Russia in 1905-30—has stemmed from cultural-historical circumstances, not from the validity of any theory regarding the impact of science on society.[17]

In pre-tractor days the need to wipe out interstripping was even less apparent. The Mennonites in Russia, whose consolidated farms served as models for Russian reformers (see, e.g., Druzhinin, 1958: II, 22), did not invariably organize themselves on consolidated household lots. At least a few of their settlements were communal villages with interstripped lots. Hard evidence is lacking, but it seems that enclosed and interstripped Mennonite farms were equally productive and that both kinds were as productive as any agricultural system in Russia prior to the advent of the tractor (Rempel, 1933: 103-11, 181-96, 257-59; Smith, 1927: 31-36, 194-97). Roughly the same may be said for other German settlements in the Ukraine and along the Volga. Those who interstripped their fields did

---

[17] For a more elaborate expression of Schiller's practical aims in the Ukraine, see his *Ziele* (1943). This is a directive to German agricultural managers, explaining, among other things, why and how interstripping seemed the best arrangement for utilizing the land under the circumstances of the German occupation.

not refrain from utilizing modern agricultural methods and producing for the market (Keller, 1968: I, 210, 276; Koch, 1977: 70-81).

Before taking up communal landholding, the third alleged obstacle to progress in Russian peasant farming, I must say something about the commune as an institution. This is not because I think it important to establish exactly what it was. Quite the contrary. I do not think a precise definition of "commune" has any value at all, except in a discussion of capital-city fantasies. I introduce the *concept* of the commune here only in order to bury it.

We have two Russian words that are commonly taken to mean peasant commune: *mir* and *obshchina. Mir* is a peasant word. Prior to 1930 most Great Russian peasants called their communities *miry,* following a tradition that went back a very long time—at least four or five hundred years, perhaps a thousand. Apparently it was exclusively a Great Russian term. Ukrainian and Belorussian peasants had other words for their communities. We may say, then, that since most Great Russian villages did receive their lands in the 1860s as collective owners, the word mir did in fact refer to a peasant community holding its land "communally." In this sense mir and commune meant the same thing. But the similarity is limited. When I say that the mir held its land communally, I am only making a descriptive generalization for the purpose of saying something coherent to nonpeasants about Great Russian peasants. My statement carries the same sort of meaning as a remark to the effect that Americans drove big cars in the 1970s. This does not mean that Americans considered it moral to drive big cars, or that they had an inherent tendency to drive big cars. Likewise, we should not infer, as capital-city society did in the late nineteenth century, that Great Russian peasants cherished strong feelings about communal landholding and considered it to be a fundamental element in their communities. As has been suggested in Chapter 2 (sec. C), peasants understood each other and their communities largely in terms of concrete personalities, not abstract schemes. To be sure, networks of personalities that made up peasant communities could be conceived of abstractly, but only outsiders felt compelled to erect abstract concepts into theoretical structures and then make society conform to them. The inhabitants of mirs generally favored or opposed communal redistribution, sale, or rental of land on a case-by-case basis, using or rejecting these processes in an infinite variety of ways as their situations changed. During the MVD's massive investigation of peasant villages in 1902-4, a report came in from a conference of local administrators and dignitaries in Vladimir gubernia stating the conference's unanimous opinion that peasants could not comprehend the MVD's abstract notions of land use and possession. Terms like "house lot" *(usadba),* cultivated field, communal ownership, etc. were used quite commonly in the villages, but their meanings varied. If the MVD enacted statutes in which these terms were precisely defined, said the Vladimir conference, peasant institutions would not be capable of enforcing them (*Svod...o nadelnykh zemliakh,* 1906: 76-79). As the reformers of the Stolypin era were to learn, the Vladimir conference's statement was not far from the truth. Mir, among other peasant terms, could not be attached to an abstract definition (Khauke, 1913: 8-77, 271-72, 285).

Obshchina, the other term for commune, had no concrete meaning at all. Peasants never used it except when conversing with outsiders. Capital-city intellectuals created it in about the 1840s and '50s out of models handed down by ill-informed German philosophers, and in the 1860s it came to embody a socialist utopian society taken largely from the imaginations of French intellectuals (Kimball, 1973: 491-514). Thanks, in part, to the pioneering sociological studies of Nikolai Chernyshevskii, it became a habit of thought in the capital cities to equate this profoundly un-Russian metaphor with the Great Russian peasants' mir. Ever since then, clarity has been going downhill. Scholars in the U.S. and USSR alike have been using *obshchina* for well over a half-century to refer to village communities in Great Russia, the Ukraine, and Belorussia, though villages in the latter two areas did not normally engage in land redistributions. In sum, the *obshchina*-mir-commune, as used by the capital cities in the nineteenth century and by scholars ever since, refers to nothing but capital-city fantasies. It is interesting to us only as a particularly flagrant illustration of the capital-city inclination to conceive of peasant society in abstract terms. This explains why two generations of MVD officials and senators, to say nothing of political activists, failed utterly to discover a usable legal definition of the peasant commune (Khauke, 1913: 8-77).

Having made this effort to sweep the rubbish of *obshchina*-mir-commune out of the way, we may now speak briefly of the peasant institutions with which the government had to deal when it embarked on the Stolypin Land Reform. These institutions first acquired legal validity in 1861 in the clauses of one of the codes in the Liberation statutes (*VPSZ*, 36657). There were three of them: the volost, the village *(selskoe obshchestvo),* and the mir. The village and the volost were clearly uppermost in the minds of the liberators. The statute of 1861 assigned them a large number of specific functions, while the mir got only one, the care of orphans (art. 23). Apparently, however, this did not signify the mir's unimportance. It meant, rather, that at the time of the Liberation the central offices of government conceived of the mir as being co-extensive with the village. Each village had only one mir; each mir was to be governed by only one village. So the liberators hoped, and they were sure enough that their statutes would produce this result that they mixed up mir and village. Article 17 said that the mir was to take charge of village *(obshchestvennye)* matters, while articles 31 and 177 ordered the village *(obshchestvo)* to handle *"mirskie"* funds and collect *"mirskie"* revenues. The authors of the Liberation statute would not have spoken in this fashion had they anticipated that mir and village might comprise different groups of peasants. As it happened, however, a fair number of villages did not coincide with mirs, and this unexpected outcome produced two results worthy of note: (1) scholars and would-be reformers found themselves unable to agree on any precise, consistent distinction between the *concepts* of mir and village, whereas (2) rural administrators had to confront actual mirs and villages that did not coincide. In effect, then, village and volost signified units the government could see, since they were on paper, whereas the term "mir" signified no particular entity but only suggested, by its official existence, that there was much in peasant institutions that was invisible to the government and perhaps should be left that way.

Clearly the official *selskoe obshchestvo* of the law books was not equivalent to a peasant community. By 1905 the "village" had undergone extensive juridical development, and doubtless it had become to some extent a part of peasant life, but it still bore the artificial, paper quality of its origin. Even so, it was much closer to peasant society than the various *obshchina*-mir fantasies of the capital cities, and it was also the closest thing there was to a general term referring to *all* peasant communities in European Russia. Perhaps more to the point, it was the only concept would-be practical reformers had to work with. Thus it will be useful to give some account here of the government's idea of it, especially the conviction that there were two types: communal *(obshchinnoe)*, wherein the village "held" all land in common except the dwelling lots, and "household" *(podvornoe)*, wherein each household "held" its own set of strips in the cultivated fields as well as its dwelling lot.

The intellectuals' term *obshchina* was never mentioned in any law regarding the peasants, but a number of clauses in the Liberation Statute (e.g., arts. 51 and 54 of *VPSZ*, 36657) referred to *obshchinnye* villages and made a distinction between them and the *podvornoe* type. By the 1900s this distinction had enjoyed a rich and full development in the government's thinking, but masses of reports, orders, and court decisions had not made it any clearer, mainly because neither peasants nor government had any consistent idea about what exactly it meant to "hold" peasant land.[18]

[18]It will bear emphasizing that an *obshchinnoe* village was not a commune. According to the law, it was not the mir that held the land but the village—i.e., the government's agency.

Certainly the peasants did not conceive of themselves as owners. In communal and noncommunal villages alike, they considered their collective function to be the management of land, not the mutual guarantee of individual rights. Even in a *podvornoe* village a head of household did not "own" anything. As a number of experts on peasant law began to point out during the Stolypin era, he was in essence an administrator. Peasant custom and much of the government's law described his position in terms of duties and responsibilities rather than rights (Meiendorf, 1909: 24-28; Khauke, 1913: 8-9, 186-219). A household head was replaceable at the village's discretion, he could be directed to use "his" lands as the village dictated, he could be deprived of "his" lands by the village's decision if he did not do as the village expected, and neither he nor the household members could choose his successor if the village actively opposed their choice. No scheme of *law* prevented a village—communal or noncommunal—from depriving its members of land or forcing them to take over land to make tax and debt payments on it (Meiendorf, 1909: 48-56). In practice, villages governed their households on much the same basis as the central administration governed villages. Ordinarily, village government allowed each household to arrange relationships among its members to suit itself, but only as long as the household as a whole fulfilled the obligations imposed upon it. If for any reason a village became dissatisfied with a household, it could send any or all of the members in exile. I have said elsewhere that the village's separateness from the government's law did not constitute autonomy in the modern sense of the word (1973: 232-5). Likewise, the peasant household's position in its village—communal or noncommunal—bore no visible relation to modern concepts of property right and corporate community. The village knew no line between private right and public duty (pp. 29-56). The main reason the government could not discover any clear line between communal and noncommunal ownership in the villages is that there was no idea of ownership there at all.

To return now to the subject at hand—the supposed effects of communal landholding on agricultural progress—there was no such broad agreement about them as there was about interstripping. From the 1870s on, advantages and disadvantages of communal landholding were hotly debated in the capital cities, and in 1905 the question remained open. On the one hand, it was argued that a communal village was better able to reduce interstripping and parcelization of land than a noncommunal village. In theory, the elder and assembly had much greater power over member households, since they could give out land to individuals and take it back at will. True, the law of 8 June 1893 (*TPSZ,* 9754) forbade a communal village to redistribute its land more often than once every 12 years and also reaffirmed the old prohibition against any redistribution not agreed to by at least two-thirds of the village assembly. This, however, was only formal law. In practice, communal peasants traded and rented their strips on a variety of bases: sometimes by a two-thirds majority, sometimes by some other ratio, sometimes by separate agreements involving only a few heads of household. This irregularity may have been frustrating to government officials, but it did give communal villages a certain flexibility, or so it seemed to their capital-city advocates. A village of separate owners, on the other hand, had no traditional basis for forcing its members to join in collective efforts at land rearrangement, and therefore the process of dividing and redividing land by inheritance could not be restrained, nor could the pernicious effects of this parcelization be corrected by collective action.[19]

From the state's point of view, however, communal landholding seemed unacceptable precisely because it tended to strengthen the traditional village. Even if it had been true that communal villages actually used their powers to improve agriculture and land use, the state would have seen them as obstacles. Land reform was an administrative process, and its purpose was to introduce conformity to a general system of law and economic relationships. Villages that somehow managed to operate successfully on their own would be even more likely to remain "backward" in their self-sufficiency than would desperately poor villages, for they would feel no *need* to reorganize themselves radically for the sake of being modern.

It was not that communal peasants consciously opposed the government's policies. Consistent, organized opposition in the name of some recognizable, collective sense of purpose would have been welcome to administrators. Had they experienced such opposition, they would have had something coherent to report to their superiors, and the government could then have formulated consistent policies. But nothing of this sort occurred before the Stolypin era. The problem was that the peasants did not organize themselves *consistently* around any common purpose at all (Uspenskii, 1969: 358-67). Common habits of thought they had in

[19]The basic work presenting the above view in the 1900s was considered to be K. R. Kachorovskii (1900), though it seems to me that his point was made more convincingly in an earlier work (Prugavin, 1888). P. Veniaminov (1908) used Kachorovskii's arguments against the Stolypin Reform. See Grant (1973) for a detailed description of pro-communal scholarship in the late nineteenth century. Techniques for redistributing land in specific villages are described in Barykov (1880). Some reports from Siberian gubernias in the 1890s indicated that communal landholding worked very well wherever land was abundant (e.g., *Dopolnitelnyi,* 1897: 77-78). The anti-communal view shines forth in all marxist literature but is most convincingly expressed in the works of government officials, chiefly Kofod (1905), Pestrzhetskii (1906), and Rittikh (1903).

abundance. The members of a village generally farmed their lands and tended their animals in roughly uniform fashion. Moreover, common purposes of an immediate sort were conceivable to most peasants. Neighbors might help to extinguish each other's fires, and large numbers occasionally joined in manifestations of collective discontent. Such occurrences, however, were noteworthy primarily for their brevity. Peasant rebellions in the decades after 1861 appeared to the enactors of the reform to have been hysterical reactions against alien intrusions, not conscious attempts to maintain some identifiable legal order or to pursue anything so abstract as a collective "class" interest. Many administrators, including the chief enactors of the reform, argued that the demands peasants made during their uprisings had no relation to their actual needs. MVD officials pointed to the fact that peasants who had plenty of land were at least as active in attacking gentry estates and grabbing land as poor peasants were. Rioting peasants, said the officials, were neither communal nor "class"-conscious; they were simply greedy and superstitious.[20]

As the enactors saw it, then, the main disadvantage of communal landholding was that it fortified the power of the traditional village over its members. This power would never be used to raise the peasants to a better way of life, nor had it anything to do with any common purpose. On the contrary, it stemmed from the peasants' persistent lack of awareness of common identity or common interest. The communal village, bolstered by its influence over all the details of each household's work, would keep its members bogged down in their primeval isolation no matter what influences the government or market brought to bear on it. It followed, said the enactors, that the communal village's "power" would have to be broken. There was no use training individual peasants to adopt new farming methods if they were not going to be able to put their lessons into practice, and there was no way for them to do this on lands constantly subject to seizure—i.e., redistributions—carried out in the name of tradition.[21]

[20]Stolypin did not consistently espouse this view (Karpov, 1925: 173), but the major enactors of the reform adhered to it firmly. V. I. Gurko noted that wealthier peasants were active participants in 1902 (1939: 172), and A. V. Krivoshein made the same point in late 1905, when he was already playing a major role in preparing the reform (Sidelnikov, 1973: 47-48). As we shall see (ch. 11), the bolsheviks adopted this interpretation of peasant violence shortly after Nov. 1917. The frequent failure of peasant revolts to live up to idealistic standards was at least one of the reasons for the Peasant Union's eschewal of violence in early Nov. 1905 (*Protokoly,* 1906: 9-10, 54-56, 61-62, 74).

[21]A. A. Rittikh, one of the leading authors of the Stolypin Reform, admitted in 1903 that communal villages could consolidate their lands more easily than noncommunal ones. A communal assembly needed a mere two-thirds vote, whereas its equivalent in a noncommunal village had to achieve unanimity. As he

The belief that communal landholding was an obstacle to land reform and, indeed, to all forms of technical progress was already very old by 1905. To be sure, many government officials had opposed administrative action to break the communal village in the past, but just about all of them had disapproved of it. At the conclusion of his massive investigation into Russian agriculture in 1872-73, Valuev had said: "Communal landholding and collective responsibility are flatly opposed to the development of prosperity in the villages.... Progress depends primarily on individuals who separate themselves from the mass" (*Doklad,* 1873: V, Valuev, 7). Almost all the witnesses his commission interviewed agreed with him (*Doklad,* 1873: *Zhurnaly,* 29).

In the ensuing decades this belief did not disappear. In May 1885 Polovtsov noted in his diary that *most* of his colleagues had once seen the commune as a utopia of sorts, but they were now unanimous in denouncing it (Polovtsov, 1966: I, 330). Polovtsov himself never veered from his conviction that the government should act to break down the commune (II, 221-22), and A. S. Ermolov was already speaking openly of the disadvantages of communal tenure before 1890 (Shipov, 1918: 10). Vorontsov-Dashkov, leading opponent of the statute on land captains and, until 1897, minister of the imperial court, believed throughout the 1880s that the commune had to be done away with, as did N. K. Bunge, MF from 1881 to 1886 (Chernyshev, 1918: 220-21, 232-37). Nicholas II went on record against the commune as early as 1896, when he underlined a recommendation from the governor of Tula that villages should be split into family-owned khutors. The governor's suggestion was primarily a fire prevention measure, to be adopted only in villages that had just burned down (*Svod vysochaishikh,* 1898: 222) but in the following year he grew bolder. He proposed that communal ownership be abolished in order to improve morality and welfare in the villages. Boldness called forth boldness. Nicholas underlined this recommendation with double lines and wrote in the margin: "I am FULLY convinced of this" (*Svod vysochaishikh,* 1899: 96).

Seemingly, opponents of the commune should have felt themselves to be a part of the mainstream of government opinion in the early 1900s. Strange to say, they felt exactly the opposite. They complained repeatedly of the government's reluctance to take any action that might weaken communal landholding (Gurko, 1939: 334; Rittikh, 1903: 98-99; Liubimov, 37-40). Obviously this was not a realistic appraisal of government

---

pointed out, however, no commune had in fact ever used its power to effect consolidation, whereas a fair number of noncommunal villages had consolidated their lands, even though the heads of household had had to agree unanimously (1903: 94-100).

opinion; yet there can be no doubt that would-be reformers believed themselves to be swimming against the current. One wonders why.

The reason, I think, is to be found in the peculiar policies of the MVD during the preceding decades. Generally speaking, the ministry took the "reactionary" view that existing village and volost institutions were the proper agencies for changing peasant society. The MVD assumed that farming was the peasants' basic means of support and that farmland was their major resource. Consequently it strove to preserve the peasants' hold on their land and to improve their ways of using it. According to the ministry's editing commission in 1902, the government had been attempting since 1861 "to strengthen authority and protect the economic security of the peasantry as a distinct estate on the basis of their inalienable possession of their allotment land" (*Trudy*, 1903-4: I, 4).

Note the editing commission's reference to the peasantry as a "distinct estate." It will be recalled that in the 1860s the MVD had not actually believed in this concept. The special arrangements for peasant government introduced at the time of the Liberation were designed to allow the peasants to merge with other estates. It was only in the following 20 years that the MVD found itself assuming stewardship over a "distinct estate" (ch. 3, sec. C). Otherwise, however, the above remark by the editing commission of 1902 represents a fair description of MVD policy. It points to the ministry's consistent belief that peasant allotment land had to be kept in peasant hands and its equally consistent fear that peasants with property rights would sell or mortgage their land irresponsibly, thereby dispossessing themselves. No one denied there were serious disadvantages to making peasant land inalienable; in particular, it rendered them unable to mortgage their land and thus deprived them of credit. Nevertheless, the MVD had had some negative experiences with the free sale of land by 1880, and these apparently outweighed the advantages of credit. The Bashkirs, for example, had gained the right to sell their land in 1869. Within ten years they had sold off about 5.4 million acres of it, and from 1874 on they erupted periodically into rebellions to get "their" land back (Bochkov, 1956: 84).

But this is not the place to justify or condemn the pre-1905 MVD's policies. All I wish to record here is that until the Stolypin Reform became law, the MVD strove above all to secure the peasants' *possession* of their land, and for this reason it accepted and fortified the peasants' own notions of possession whether it liked them or not. It was the prevailing practice for Great Russian villages to manage their land collectively; ergo, the MVD would act in Great Russian villages as if it were supporting communal landholding. It was never the MVD's intent to uphold communal landholding per se. What its leaders wanted to do, both before 1905 and after, was to change the peasants by working with them as they were rather than making laws requiring them to be something else. The MVD wished to strengthen the village—communal or noncommunal—so as to make it an institution capable of leading and/or protecting its members.

Another obvious reason for the MVD's reluctance to attack communal landholding before the early 1900s can be found in the results of its own investigations. Its inquiries of 1894-97 asked gubernia administrators whether communal peasants aspired to change over to household landholding. No, was the almost unanimous response (*Svod zakliuchenii,* 1897: III, 142-219). The reports offered a variety of evidence in support of this finding. Samara, for example, noted that although 1,000 households had paid off their share of the redemption debt, thereby acquiring the right to claim their lands as household property, 954 of them had not done so. Some Ukrainian settlers had come to Samara from Poltava gubernia and had set up villages with household tenure, but after a while even these had switched to a communal arrangement. Not surprisingly, Samara recommended that the government leave communal landholding alone (pp. 161-62, 186).

A practical objection to any attack on communal landholding was that it would have had no meaning in rural Russia. Mogilev's report of 1897 made this point. There were many formally noncommunal villages in Mogilev, but most peasants made no distinction between forms of ownership. Many villages could not tell whether they held their land communally or not, and so, said the report, a formal change from communal to noncommunal would not change peasant practice (pp. 152-53). The report from Ekaterinoslav agreed. It noted that since peasant lands had never been surveyed, the government had no way to identify plots of individual owners. Consequently the peasants' own manner of parceling the land, however crude, was the only basis available. "At present," said the Ekaterinoslav report, "peasants who have already taken over their land on the basis of household ownership do not have any documents showing their right to it except decisions of village assemblies and tax lists kept in the fiscal chamber. But these show only the quantity of land without identifying the boundaries" (p. 180). In other words, an officially communal village could become officially noncommunal, but "title" to the land would still derive from the pronouncements of village assemblies, and these decisions would be made without reference to any clearly defined law or measurement.

One or two reports hinted that a change from communal to household landholding would be not only pointless and contrary to the peasants' wishes but also harmful to the government's own aspiration to reform the countryside. Viatka gubernia remarked that whole villages did not switch from communal to household ownership at once; usually separate households did it one or two at a time. The result was to create villages with different types of ownership, and these, alas, often found themselves entangled in unresolvable disputes (pp. 146-48). Viatka did not mean to say that the peasants had shown any sign of trying to consolidate their lands, but if communal peasants ever did begin to stir in this direction, the presence of a few household owners in a village—each of whom would "own" a strip in every field—would make any collective decision to rearrange the land extremely difficult. Since everyone agreed that it would be a good thing to eliminate interstripping, and since most reports explicitly opposed any government action to achieve this end, it followed that nothing should be done to hinder peasants from acting on their own, should they ever feel the urge to do so. In the 1890s, then, many of the government's local agencies opposed piecemeal breaking up of communal fields in hopes that strong village institutions would ultimately eliminate communal landholding all at once. This resembled the populist view, except that populist writers generally spoke of communes eliminating interstripping, whereas the MVD spoke of villages eliminating both communal landholding and interstripping.[22]

We can now see why the authors of the Stolypin Land Reform felt they were swimming against the current in 1902-5. It was mainly because they were taking a new view of the peasant village. Hitherto the MVD had striven to reform peasant society by strengthening its institutions. From about 1902 on the ministry—and the government as a whole—gradually adopted the idea that peasant villages, communal and non-communal alike, were obstacles to reform and could never be instruments for mobilization. The authors spoke of eliminating communal landholding, but they meant, basically, the weakening of village institutions. This, in a nutshell, was the new view of the "peasant problem" that produced the reform legislation of 1906, and in 1902 it was indeed a minority opinion in the MVD.

To sum up our discussion of the "peasant problem," the reform's authors believed that many peasants suffered from unbearable poverty, caused basically by backward agriculture. To improve agriculture, they set out to allow individual peasants to escape interstripped fields. These were not new ideas in 1905. The novelty in the reform was the determination of its authors to undermine the village's authority over its members.

Some Obstacles to Administrative Action in Rural Russia

The intention to undermine peasant institutions implied either one of two attitudes toward the peasantry. Either the authors of the Stolypin

---

[22]Two very pragmatic populist reformers, Mertvago and Engelgardt, did not attach any importance to the commune. They both thought the legal form of landholding was a trivial matter, not worth either preserving or attacking (Mertvago, 1900: 51-52; Engelgardt, 1937: 281).

Reform were confident of the peasants' ability to organize themselves apart from traditional social structures, or they felt that the government was prepared to replace the institutions with its own agents. As we shall see in Chapter 6, however, no one was thinking quite this clearly during the process of drawing up the reform. Government leaders did intend to carry out land reform, whatever this might entail, but they did not think very deeply about practical problems. If they did, they kept it to themselves. Therefore, the following considerations about obstacles to administrative action in the villages do not necessarily reflect the government's thinking prior to the reform. Nevertheless, the obstacles were real enough, and they had their effect after 1906.

The Peasant Attitude toward System

In the early 1900s all concepts of land reform embodied an intention to divide land among peasant households in some equitable fashion. This required the measurement of land areas, but in fact it was impossible to use such measures to express the peasant's concept of "his" land. Most peasants knew where their strips of land were and roughly the fraction of each field they occupied at a given time. Apparently, however, most of them found it hard to translate their perceptions of separate fields into anything so abstract as the total area of a household's shares. As the vice-governor of Simbirsk said in a report of 1909, peasants could recognize variations in soil quality from one field to another, and they were aware of the practical advantages one location enjoyed over another, but they could not arrive at a single, composite value for each field, comparable to that of other fields. This was one of the main reasons they divided each field into shares instead of assigning a certain integral area to each household (TsGIAL, f. 1291, op. 120, 1908g., d. 25, ll. 164-65). N. D. Chaplin, head of the government's survey section, inspected the reform's local organs during the summer of 1910, and he concluded that existing peasant holdings should *not* be surveyed. The peasants could not tell who held what strips on the basis of their traditional legal order, and modern measuring techniques were introducing confusion and quarrels rather than order (1910g., d. 19, ll. 98-100).[23]

I know of only one authority on the peasants who attempted a serious investigation of their concept of area. This was P. P. Semenov, a renowned geographer and inveterate participant in peasant reforms. In the late 1870s Semenov contributed a study of Muraevskaia volost, Riazan gubernia, to Barykov's groundbreaking study of peasant life

[23]See also TsGIAL, f. 1291, op. 63, 1907g., d. 16, ll. 2-3; *Trudy* (1903-4: VI, 1-7); *Svod...po proektu pravil* (1906: 1-7); Anfimov (1969: 35-36); Dubrovskii (1963: 416); Nikolskii (1902: 174-76); and Kolobov (1913: 53).

(Barykov, 1880: 37-158). The inhabitants, all of them ex-serfs, had received their land at the time of the Liberation in the form of rectangular fields, each of which was measured out to a round number of *desiatiny* (one *desiatina* equals 2.7 acres). To divide these fields into appropriate shares for each family, a village had had only to mark off lengths along one side. Then, whenever the villagers conducted a redistribution, they could merely redivide this same side and make new marks. In other words, the peasants in Muraevskaia volost could identify their holdings and, had they wished, redistribute them without ever having to conceive of area. Indeed, the method of measurement set up for them by their former owners implied that they were unable or unwilling to deal in any such abstract entity as area.

Semenov himself rejected this extreme conclusion. He pointed out that in less than perfectly rectangular fields, where the side opposite the measuring line was not a straight line, the peasants sometimes adjusted their length measures along the baseline to compensate for variations in the distance to the other side of the field. Apparently, however, they made this sort of adjustment only in rare cases, and Semenov had to acknowledge that the few irregular fields, left over after the perfect rectangles had been lined out, were not divided according to area measures at all. Instead the peasants adjusted the width of each strip to correspond to the amount of grain harvested from each one (pp. 94-5, 108-14). Thus the fact emerges from Semenov's reluctant observations that the peasants of Muraevskaia volost had never divided their land by measuring lengths and widths and multiplying them to arrive at figures for area.

The peasants could count. They measured and compared lengths and quantities of grain, and they probably could have identified an area by the number of days it took to push a plow through it or the amount of seed required to sow it—as peasants often did in Russia and elsewhere. But area arrived at by multiplying length by width is an abstraction that can be separated altogether from the specific piece of land it identifies, and this sort of concept seems to have been meaningless to Semenov's peasants. "Modern" men can use abstract calculations of area to equate a long thin field with a square one, and they can do this without ever looking at the fields in question, but Semenov's peasants would not have ventured to compare such fields without first working them and arriving at some way to count their value directly. As H. Mendras has recently said of the French peasant's concept of space (in the late nineteenth century), "It is not conceived, any more than is time, as an abstract area infinitely divisible into universal units. It is always a real and particular expanse perceived through a repeated work experience" (1970: 62). Several other contributors to Barykov's volume expressed much the same view. They doubted the peasants' ability to measure their holdings in terms of area much more readily than Semenov did.[24]

Semenov pointed out that in rural Russia a *desiatina* was not simply a quantity of land in the same sense as the English acre. It was, rather, a specific rectangular shape with a length of 560 feet and a width of 210 feet. This is 2.7 acres. Another field 1,120 feet by 105 feet still contains 2.7 acres, but it is no longer a *desiatina*. Even the tsarist government, it seems, did not see fit to measure land in any way that might demand its holders to conceive of area abstractly. Add to this the consideration that each village used a *desiatina* of different size. Apparently the peasants in each set of fields had originally arrived at their respective *desiatiny* by such traditional measures as amount of seed, or weight of harvest, or time spent plowing (Barykov, 1880: 114, 336-37).

The point is not that peasants were *unable* to understand the concept of area. Doubtless, there were peasants who understood it quite well, and they all probably could have comprehended it if it had been explained to them. Peasants were not stupid or inept; they were simply indifferent to abstract concepts. If there is a fundamental difference between a nineteenth-century Russian peasant's concept of "his" land and that of, say, a modern American owner of private property, it comes down in the end to the simple fact that the peasant was inclined to *trust* the evidence of his senses and the "power" of individual persons, whereas a modern American will trust abstract reasoning more than either of these. A modern American might accept a triangular plot of land in exchange for a square one if he could determine by multiplication that the two plots were of equal area. A nineteenth-century Russian peasant would have been extremely hesitant to make such a trade.

I take the liberty of citing myself as an example of a modern American. If an investigator of American towns asks me where my land is and how much I have, I take him to my house and point at the fences, gardens, and sidewalks bordering my property. If he asks me the exact area of my lot or its dimensions, I will not be able to tell him without first burrowing through some records. I will have to admit that I have never troubled to locate the exact boundaries myself, not even at the time I bought the place. A survey was made, of course, but not in my presence, nor am I able to recall who made it. I cannot assure the investigator that the men who did make it were qualified to do the job. I *can* say to the investigator with perfect assurance that a driveway and certain hedges, gardens, and buildings are within my boundaries, but I

[24]See the articles by A. M. Mikhalenko (pp. 273-81), N. N. Zlatovratskii (p. 159), V. M. Borisov (p. 179-80), and P. Zinovev (pp. 303-5, 310) in Barykov (1880), and also Mendras (1970: 61-5).

find myself unable to tell him exactly where the boundaries are or how they might be located. Thus I might appear to the investigator to be fully as ignorant of area and other abstract concepts as a Russian peasant.

If, however, the investigator asked me how I and my neighbor would resolve a boundary dispute, he would begin to perceive a difference between my attitudes and those of a peasant. Suppose that he asks me what would happen if my neighbor laid claim to a tree that I had always assumed to be mine. I would answer approximately as follows. A qualified surveyor would come with his instruments and determine the exact distance of a corner of my land from a landmark whose exact location is registered in some official documents in the county office. I have never seen these documents; I have never been in the county office where I assume they are kept; indeed, I do not even know where the office is. I assume, however, that there is such an office and the documents in it do in fact represent the entire area of my community as a scheme of lots and sublots, all located with respect to landmarks, which are precisely located with respect to each other. The dispute would be resolved—and *should* be resolved—by the surveyor's measure and by a lawyer's expert knowledge of the official documents. If a surveyor, a lawyer, and, at last, a judge all determined that the boundary of my land did indeed exclude the tree, I would accept this as both fact and justice— unless, of course, I could find other surveyors, lawyers, and judges prepared to dispute this conclusion on the basis of alternative measures and documents.

My answer to the investigator suggests certain attitudes "residual" within me. For one, I believe (or act as if I believe) that I possess a "right" to my land solely beause there is an abstract scheme of law and measurement that proclaims this right by its own inherent correctness. I do not understand this scheme, but I can hire men who do. At least I believe I can. By persistent questioning, the investigator could get me to agree that my ability to "hold" land depends entirely on the place which this land occupies in an abstract scheme comprehended only by experts. I recognize this as a fact and when I do, I also proclaim it as good. Things *should* be this way. Even if the system deprives me of my tree, I continue to believe in its essential rightness. Even if I consider the decision in my case to have been unjust, I am likely to blame a judge or lawyer, not the system of laws, grids, and landmarks per se. Certainly I will not curse mathematics for my misfortunes. Nor would I protest that the tree was mine, despite all law and logic to the contrary, simply because I had cared for it all these years. Nor would I rally my friends in the neighborhood to vote the tree onto my land in defiance of precise measures and official documents. Nor would I be likely to request the richest man in my neighborhood to use his influence to make the judge change his decision.

Now we are prepared to speak of the difference between a modern American and a Russian peasant of Lev Tolstoi's day. Supposing that an occasional peasant had understood mathematics as well as I do, there would still be an important difference between his "residual" attitude toward his land and my attitude toward mine. If he had had to resolve a dispute with his neighbor over a land boundary, he would not have spoken of surveyors or lawyers. In most villages the matter would have been decided by his neighbors meeting in assembly, and they would have made their decision, justly or unjustly, entirely on the basis of empirical considerations: Who was actually working the land in question? What kind of men were on each side in the dispute? What families were involved and how powerful or popular were they? Who provided the vodka for this assembly? In the end, then, a peasant family, communal or noncommunal, "held" its land because the members visibly occupied it and, ultimately, because the village assembly said it could. The family's ability to "hold" land depended almost entirely on the place the family occupied in the village, not on a system of law and measurement that transcended immediate experience and social relationships. If a shrewd investigator had driven him to it, the peasant would have recognized this as a fact and proclaimed it as good. Things *should* be this way, he would have said. Even if the village deprived him of a strip of land he thought was his, he would probably have gone on believing in the village's essential rightness. Either this, or he would have had to give up the idea of holding a share of the village's land.

Thus, although this or that peasant may have known about measures of area, the peasantry as a whole was not prepared to recognize them as a foundation of identity. A village's land was not a thing apart, identified by a scheme understood only by alien experts. It was fully integrated into the village's myths. When anyone attempted to rearrange the land according to a scheme that went contrary to village custom, the reaction of the villagers was likely to be similar to that of a modern houseowner, were he to be compelled by his plumber to locate his toilet in his living room in order to make it flush more efficiently.

Speaking as a modern man, I may love my neighbors, or hate them, or ignore them; in any case I do not recognize them, not even implicitly, as the ultimate source of my rights. Nor do I believe it proper to bribe persons in order to protect what I consider to be my rights. When I want to know what my rights are, I consult experts who supposedly know the "truth" about them, and I expect everyone else to do the same. The peasant, on the other hand, consulted his fellows and/or men whom he believed to possess "power"; therefore, when he came in contact with administrators, he not only failed to understand their readiness to rely on abstract schemes but actually saw their schemes—when he did see them—as a threat to his way of life.

Not all Russian peasants of the late nineteenth and early twentieth centuries were "traditional." There were villagers who did not like the way things were, and by 1900 a growing number of peasants were inclined to welcome the "threat" of modern organization. On the whole, however, the government could find very little sign that the peasantry was discontented with the traditional village before 1905. Villages continued to treat surveyors and doctors as invaders, and very few villages displayed any spontaneous interest in land reform.

It should be kept in mind that peasants were not radically different from other social groups in rural Russia at the turn of the century. Gentry estates and local government agencies did not rely heavily on systematic measurement. The government initiated serious efforts to compel the gentry to consolidate their land in the 1830s, but in 1905 the process was still far from complete (Shidlovskii, 1904: 3-18, 116-35, 142-49). In the central black-earth region, east and south of the Oka River, it had hardly begun (Bochkov, 1956: 28, 76-78, 102). During the early 1900s the *Pravitelstvennyi Vestnik* occasionally carried full-page listings of bankrupt gentry estates being auctioned off by the government. Two areas were listed for each estate: one represented the figure on the original mortgage agreement; the other gave the bank's more recent measure. In one such announcement half the estates showed a discrepancy between the two figures. In about one-seventh of them the discrepancy was substantial (e.g., issue of 4 Jan. 1906: 7-8). Not surprisingly, the peasant bank had difficulties when it bought estates. Its circular of 1 December 1905 ordered local sections to establish an estate's boundaries, when necessary, by resorting to the age-old tsarist technique of getting all the neighbors to agree to where they were (TsGIAL, f. 1291, op. 119, 1906g., d. 67, ll. 91-92).

As for the government's own surveying, it is suggestive that before the reform organs in Moscow gubernia could embark upon their programs in 1907, they had first of all to redraw uezd and volost boundaries (Shlippe, 99). This proved a laborious task in just about all gubernias. As late as 1913, when surveyors were badly needed for land settlement work, almost 500 of them were engaged full time in redrawing governmental boundaries (*IGU*, 1913: 907). According to a study made by the land survey section (in the ministry of justice), the government employed very few surveyors in 1905, and the ones they did employ were less than first rate. Only 200 were available for fieldwork in 1906 (*Desiatiletie*, 1916: 6, 45). The MVD's editing commission of 1902-3 issued a forceful statement to the effect that both government and private surveyors were notoriously incompetent. The commission acknowledged pathetically that although everyone agreed on the need for a law requiring a survey to be made in every legal dispute over boundaries, no such law could be enforced. There were no uniform standards for surveyors to follow, nor was there any supervision to enforce such standards had they existed. Each area had its own practices (*Svod...po proektu pravil,* 1906: 70-74).[25]

In sum, rural Russia was ill prepared to organize itself into a modern system of land division in 1905. Existing agencies were unable either to measure the strips into which most land was divided or even to record such measures as were made. Even if they had been able to measure, they still faced the problem of establishing each peasant household's "just" share of land. They had to reckon with peasants (and not a few gentry) whose ideas of "justice" had very little to do with measurement.

Practical Problems of Land Settlement

The physical problems involved in doing a proper job of land settlement presented a formidable challenge even to the best of surveyors and the most advanced of peasants. Consider the process of village consolidation. The first step was to lay down a road network such that all proposed individual plots in the village would have access to a road and no road would cross any plot. The roads were not to have sharp bends in them (Kofod, 1907: 5). Natural barriers such as creeks and gullies were not to cross any of the new plots (Kofod, 1914: 82). Each peasant household had to get its fair share of land, but at the same time each consolidated plot had to comprise enough arable land to make it self-supporting. If there was not enough land in the village to make this possible, adjoining lands were to be purchased. Ideally the value of each plot was to be measured by both area and soil quality. Its shape had to be as close to a square as possible, and in no case was its length to be over five times its width or its corners to be less than 45-degree angles (pp. 65-66, 81-83). Moreover, each plot was to have a share of the common meadows and forests as well as plowland (Kofod, 1907: 37).[26]

But land settlement involved more than physical problems. It also gave rise to legal tangles of considerable complexity, mainly because the peasants possessed—or claimed to possess—a bewildering variety of rights to their land. It often happened, for example, that a few peasants formed a partnership *(tovarishchestvo)* to purchase nonpeasant lands. According to the government's law, such lands became private plots owned jointly by the partners on the same formal basis as if they were landed estates. Unfortunately for the coherence of government law, however, many partnership lands were not single plots but only strips in

[25]Concerning the inadequacies of private surveyors, see *Trudy* (1903-4: VI, 4); and Shidlovskii (1904: 162-63). An observer in Tambov gubernia described an instance in 1907-8 when private surveyors were no more effective than the government's (Dashkevich, 1909: 101-2).

[26]A full description of land settlement procedures is in *Instruktsiia* (1913: 1-8).

various fields, wherein peasant villages and former owners had been mutually entangled since before the Liberation. Worse, even partnerships that acquired integral plots tended to divide them into strips and then to exchange these strips indiscriminately with strips in allotment fields during village redistributions and/or divisions of household lots among heirs. When all partnership members lived in the same village, we might suppose that they could keep track of their exchanges. If they carried their disputes to the government's courts and/or reform agencies, however, they could find little satisfaction. It was much worse when peasants from *different* villages joined in a partnership. In such cases—which occurred with disturbing frequency—the peasants in these villages were unable either to uphold their various claims in court or even to identify their lands in accordance with custom. Prior to the enactment of the statute of 29 May 1911, neither law nor custom gave any indication as to what voice partnership members should have in sharing and/or reforming the lands in their respective villages. Any one of the partners could prevent any or all of the villages from engaging in land settlement by claiming that his strips were still private property, though in many cases these strips were not the same lots he and his partners had originally purchased. This was no small matter. Partnership purchases were by far the most common method by which peasants bought land right up until 1907.

The agents of the Stolypin Reform organization encountered many legal snarls of this sort. Each one had to be handled on an ad hoc basis by negotiations among the parties involved. In 1909 some experienced land settlement administrators noted that the government was often unable to deal with these snarls and therefore had to let the peasants carry out land settlement on their own (*Trudy,* 1909: 142). The statute of 29 May 1911 filled some of the gaps left by the sketchy decrees of 1905-6, but neither it nor any statutory law could overcome the fundamental problem of identifying "rights" in terms that would be meaningful to peasants (Martynov, 1917: x-xi, 38-47, 65-78; Boshko, 1917: 80-95). Whenever the government attempted to bridge the gap between legal-administrative system and peasant custom with statutes alone, the result was to muddle the statutes and render them fully as unclear as village tradition (Meiendorf, 1909: 84-85).

Finally, land settlement involved public relations problems. The worst of these arose in cases of personal consolidation. When a small minority in a village forced their neighbors to rearrange the village fields so as to extract from them a few separate consolidated plots, these few innovators became so unpopular that in many cases they had to be protected against physical violence. Village consolidation and group land settlement, where a clear majority favored reform, were not so bad. Even here, however, there could be difficulties, mainly because the majority had to be maintained so long. According to the initial reform laws, two-thirds of the heads of household in a village had to petition for any village-wide measure of land settlement before it could begin, and two-thirds had to go on approving the measure through all stages of its implementation. In the case of a village consolidation, this usually meant a year or two, assuming there were no serious legal tangles. Existing strips had to be identified and measured, and their relative value had to be assessed. Only when this delicate business was completed and each household's share established could the official in charge *(zemleustroitel)* draft a new village layout with separate integral farms corresponding in value to these shares. This layout had to be approved by both administrators and peasants, and only then could the new farms be measured off on the ground. If the two-thirds majority failed during any of these stages, the entire operation had to be canceled. Even a completed project, lacking only the signatures on the new deeds of ownership, could be thrown over by a small shift in the peasants' voting. Usually, therefore, a successful land settlement operation demanded a great deal of political maneuvering among the peasants, and this maneuvering could very easily fail.

The initial reform legislation of 1905-6 did not deal with obstacles to land settlement. It did not even mention the physical, legal, and public relations problems I have described above. The upshot was that these problems had to be resolved during the process of carrying out the reform, which meant that inadequately trained officials and a very confused peasantry had to puzzle their way through the reform pretty much on their own. The best the central offices could do was to stay out of the way.

Violence

Given the difficulties mentioned in the preceding sections, it is hard to imagine a land reform that would not provoke painful disputes among the peasants, profound distrust between peasantry and government, and outright hatred between local agents and institutions on the one hand and central ministries on the other. One expression of these tensions, and a problem in itself, was rural violence.

No description of the Stolypin Land Reform can ignore its close connection with violence. It was enacted and set going in the midst of widespread revolutionary disturbances by men who lived under the constant threat of assassination. Throughout its course its local agencies went about their work under a regime of martial law in the face of peasant opposition that could easily erupt into rioting. This is not to say that the reform necessarily caused violence. Violence, however, was certainly part of the context.

It is customary to measure the level of revolutionary violence by numbering incidents of it. This is unsatisfactory in many respects. In Russia the evidence regarding such incidents consists largely of official reports, and these are as much a reflection of police nerves as of peasant mood. It is extremely difficult, even for the shrewdest observer in the most orderly society, to distinguish among a group of pugnacious drunks who have just been locked out of the local tavern, warring gangs of horse thieves, and a gathering of people who are angry enough at what they consider to be an injustice to join together and throw rocks at someone. Moreover, incidents reported by officials do not necessarily bear much relation to the *level* of violence. An entire population may live in terror of violent attack without there being many actual attacks. Threats, insults, and deliberate invasions of private right are rarely reported to officials in any country, and Russians, especially rural Russians, have been notoriously reluctant to bring the government into their affairs. Indeed, it may happen that the incidence of reported violence falls as the degree to which people fear it rises. Reported incidents of violence, then, should not be taken too seriously as indicators of the importance of violence in rural life. Even Dubrovskii (1963: 515-16) and Anfimov (1962: 19) acknowledge that quantities of revolutionary outbreaks are very crude indicators at best. A yet more negative view of their relevance and/or validity may be found in Nifontov (1961: 181-88).

It should also be mentioned that the seemingly simple business of counting reported incidents of peasant violence allows much more room for error than is commonly assumed. One American student, who has checked into tsarist police archives for himself, has found glaring omissions and misinterpretations in Soviet compilations of documents relating to peasant violence during the Stolypin era (Vinogradoff, 1974: 4-13). Similarly, N. A. Maltseva, a Soviet scholar, has indicated the difficulties involved in simply counting rebellions and, incidentally, has demonstrated the unreliability of Dubrovskii's figures (1965: 126-31).

In the following paragraphs I shall present figures indicating two quasi-facts: (1) almost none of the reported peasant revolutionary outbreaks during the reform era had any direct relation to land settlement; and (2) the vast majority of land settlement projects were carried out without provoking any officially reported violence. Despite these "facts," I have the impression that the reform gave rise to a great deal of violence—or at least accentuated the general fear of violence—in the countryside. There can be no doubt that disputes over changes in land use often took violent forms—fights, the killing of animals, arson. Certainly the threat of active conflict was always real in any land settlement operation. Life could not have been easy for an individual who forced his fellow villagers to change their strips around in order to allow him to have all his land in one lot (e.g., Sidelnikov, 1973: 263-64). Likewise, new settlers who bought land formerly rented by local villagers frequently found their new neighbors very unfriendly (ch. 4, sec. D). When government officials ventured to persuade villagers to consolidate their lands, they must have found themselves involved, willy-nilly, in a very rough political arena.

Bearing this in mind, let us consider some figures. According to Dubrovskii, there were, in all of Russia, 3,228 large-scale peasant outbreaks in 1905, 2,600 in 1906, 1,337 in 1907, 855 in 1908, 819 in 1909, 928 in 1910, 507 in 1911, 307 in 1912, 128 in 1913, 178 in 1914, and 96 in 1915. These figures serve only one purpose: they allow us to trace the rise and fall of violence in rural Russia from one year to the next. About 1,220 outbreaks on a comparable scale occurred during the period 1890-1904, or an average of about 80 each year. In 1905-7, when the reform was being enacted and *before* it had actually produced any impact, the yearly average rose to about 2,400. In 1908-11, when land settlement projects were beginning to go forward on a relatively large scale and the reform agencies were still clumsily feeling their way, this average fell to about 780. In 1912-13, when the reform was operating under the direction of a more or less complete and stable organizational structure in accordance with a relatively consistent policy, the average fell sharply to 217. Thus, insofar as these quantities are indicative of anything, the level of rural violence declined during the reform but never fell nearly as low as it had been in the years before 1905 (Dubrovskii, 1963: 518).

Dubrovskii offers us yet another set of quantities, this one covering only European Russia, in which he includes not only large-scale outbreaks but also instances of arson and "several other" types of violence that he believes to have been politically motivated, i.e., "revolutionary." In effect, he is adding in both mass disturbances and individual acts. He cannot compile meaningful totals for the years 1905 and 1906, but in 1907 there were 2,477 such acts in European Russia; in 1908, 2,007; in 1909, 2,420; in 1910, 6,261; in 1911, 4,522; in 1912, 1,791; and in 1913, 646. In all, there were about 20,000 during the period 1907-13 (p. 530). This more exhaustive list shows a development in rural violence somewhat different from that which the quantity of large-scale outbreaks suggests. We see a sudden rise in the level of violence in 1910-11 and a falling off in 1912-14, rather than a gradual falling off throughout the post-1905 years. Both lists concur, however, in showing a marked decline after 1911. Dubrovskii insists that such a decline did indeed take place (pp. 516-29). If he is correct, and if we were to swallow whole the fatuous assumption that reported incidents of peasant violence reflect anything about the importance of violence or intensity of revolutionary sentiment in the countryside, then we *could* conclude that the successful spread of land settlement brought peace to the villages.[27]

But it is not my purpose to draw conclusions from street-pamphlet reasoning, only to suggest that scholars should use such reasoning with care. In this regard there is one other point to be made: most of the incidents reported by Dubrovskii and other champions of the peasant "movement" had nothing to do with the Stolypin Reform (except insofar as they sustained a pervasive fear in the countryside). Of the 20,000 incidents Dubrovskii says occurred during the period 1907-13, only 224 were reform-connected (pp. 551-52). The majority of peasant disturbances, before, during, and after the reform, had to do with peasants grabbing someone else's property or refusing to pay taxes or debts. Throughout the reform era the heaviest concentration of peasant disturbances took place in the right-bank Ukraine—Kiev, Podoliia, and Volyniia gubernias. Indeed, this generalization applies to the whole period 1861-1917, except for 1905-6, when apparently the Baltic gubernias saw the worst violence. In both these areas religious and national differences between gentry and peasantry probably played at least as large a role in the land-grabbing sort of violence as did economic considerations.[28]

It seems that the implementation of the reform caused virtually no reported incidents of peasant violence before 1908. In the hundreds of police reports, radical brochures, and peasant petitions printed in the three volumes of *Revoliutsii 1905-1907 gg. v. Rossii* that cover the period from October 1906 to July 1907, the reform is almost never mentioned, and there are no outbreaks at all in which the reform was a cause. As to the last half of 1907, A. V. Shapkarin's collection of reports on violence includes no documents having anything to do with the reform (1966: 42-98). Sidelnikov (1973: 273) claims to have found six instances of outbreaks connected with the reform in Shapkarin's volume for 1907; Dubrovskii says there were 20 (1963: 551). Even if these figures had any validity, they would demonstrate a very small amount of actual violence

[27]A. N. Anfimov disagrees with Dubrovskii. He insists that peasant rebelliousness increased in intensity throughout the Stolypin Reform even though the annual number of reported outbreaks did decrease in 1911-14 (1962: 80-84). Sidelnikov's figures, drawn from Shapkarin (1966) and Anfimov (1965), indicate that rebelliousness continued to increase in intensity until well into 1915 (1973: 273).

[28]Dubrovskii is unclear about the locus of violence. His figures indicate that the worst of it was in the central black-earth region, the Volga, and the Ukraine; yet he tells us that the peasant movement was at its strongest in the western gubernias and the Baltic (1956: 57-60). P. N. Durnovo, the MVD in late 1905 and early 1906, was quite sure that in Oct.-Dec. 1905 the worst overall violence—rural and urban—was in the Baltic area (Santoni, 1968: 84-97).

in connection with the reform prior to 1908. On the one hand, this may reflect the fact that very little reform was actually taking place in the villages. On the other hand, one would think that 1907 should have seen the worst reform-connected violence, for this was the year when the agents of the reform organization seem to have been making their worst blunders and doing peasants the most harm (see ch. 7, sec. E). In any case, land settlement caused very few reported incidents of violence even after 1907. Yearly reform-connected violence rose to its highest level—50 to 60 incidents in all European Russia—in 1911 and then fell again to the minimal level of 1907-8 in 1913 (Sidelnikov, 1973: 273).[29]

But the main purpose of this section is not to comment on the vagaries of Soviet scholarship or to number incidents of rural violence. I am speaking primarily of the extent to which the reform took place in a *context* of violence, and this context consisted of much more than peasant outbreaks. In 1905-6, when the reform was being enacted, urban riots, military mutinies, and warfare between national groups were all playing a role in the "Revolution." In the late summer and fall of 1905 the government's main challenge came from widespread strikes in industry and transportation. In October-December, when the first reform edicts began to appear, breakdowns in rail and telegraph communication were threatening to paralyze the entire national economy, and it was not certain that the army would be a reliable instrument for restoring order even if units could somehow be moved to areas where they were needed. Such was the disorder that the government closed all institutions of

[29]Sidelnikov claims a total of 368 reform-connected outbreaks for the period from June 1907 to June 1914, based on a chronicle of peasant outbreaks drawn up by Shapkarin (1966: 492-623). But this figure would be much too high for our purposes even if it were accurate, for it includes not only incidents arising from land settlement but also outbreaks connected with attempts to convert communal to personal property. As to the areas where Shapkarin's alleged reform-connected incidents occurred, by far the worst was the mid-Volga, which suffered over one-third of them. Other relatively bad areas were the central black-earth and central industrial regions and Malorossiia. Areas with only a negligible amount of reform-connected violence were the right-bank Ukraine, the Lithuanian gubernias, and the far north.

I must add that in a recent study of the Stolypin Reform Sidelnikov has written some additional prose about violent responses to land reform in the villages (1980: 273-87). Aside from a few descriptions of specific incidents, however, he offers no new observations on the subject. He is still content, by and large, to rely on Shapkarin (1966). Sidelnikov still feels compelled to stand by his old position that well under 400 instances of ostensibly reform-connected violence in 1907-14, most of them involving no more than setting fire to a hut, constitute prima facie evidence of massive peasant resistance to land reform (1980: 279, 282). Keeping in mind that Dubrovskii (1963: 551-52) came up with a total of about 20,000 peasant disturbances during this period (including arson), one wonders what Sidelnikov has in mind.

higher learning and kept them closed until the fall of 1906 (Oldenburg, 1939: I, 372).

In early 1906 most of the tsar's ministers believed urban revolution had passed its worst stages. Now, they believed, peasant violence would be the serious threat (Sidelnikov, 1973: 52-54; Santoni, 1968: 171, 180-81). The ministers were wrong. Violence of any kind had ceased to be a threat to government control. Sporadic outbreaks of rural and urban violence continued for some time, but they did not become massive again until 1917. Assassinations continued to be a real danger on all levels of the government. A. N. Naumov, then a gubernia gentry marshal, reports that armored vests were selling well in St. Petersburg in 1906—he bought one himself (1954: II, 102-3). Assassins almost killed Stolypin in August of that year. A bomb destroyed much of his home and office, narrowly missing him but permanently crippling one of his daughters and slaughtering a number of secretaries and petitioners (Gurko, 1939: 497-98). Nicholas II, of course, was the prime target. He was virtually a prisoner of his bodyguards throughout most of 1906. The first weeks of September present the anomalous picture of the emperor of Russia sailing about the Baltic Sea on his yacht, surrounded by a considerable portion of the Russian fleet, because no fortress or palace on Russian land was strong enough to ensure his safety (Bing, 1937: 217-18; Spiridovich, 1928: 114). All this was harassment, not revolution. Even so, my point is clear enough. The Stolypin Reform commenced during a time when virtually all people in Russia lived in fear of violence.

Riots and assassinations were only one side of the coin. It must be remembered that Stolypin's fame rests not only on his association with agrarian reform but also on the fact that he and his predecessor in the MVD presided over the execution of about 2,000 persons by military court-martial (Kucherov, 1957: 206; Oldenburg, 1939: II, 51). Actually the government killed off many more than this. The figure of 2,000 includes all segments of the population, not only peasants, but it is still too small to indicate the extent of the rural slaughter because it refers only to legally approved and recorded executions. There were also numerous unrecorded deaths. When police and soldiers fired into rioting crowds and burned rebellious villages, they took little time to count corpses. Even formal executions were not always recorded. About 1,100 of the executions by court-martial took place during the eight months between August 1906 and April 1907, when the law of 20 August 1906 was in effect. This law allowed a military commander engaged in stopping a riot to accuse, try, and execute rioters on the spot by decision of a court made up solely of his own officers (*TPSZ*, 28257). It was only during this period that arbitrary executions were likely to be reported (Polianskii, 1958: 30-31, 214-15). During the preceding year, when on-the-spot execution had been illegal, the government's efforts to suppress rural violence had been of a less formal nature. Military attacks on peasant villages reached their highest intensity when Petr N. Durnovo was MVD (from late October 1905 to 20 April 1906), and this was probably when most of the killing took place (Liubimov, 297-361; Santoni, 1968). Durnovo filled the air with pronouncements like: "It is useful to wipe the rebels' villages off the face of the earth and to annihilate them themselves without indulgence..." (Santoni, 1968: 252). No courts-martial here, and better yet, from the police point of view, no need for itemized reports. Such was the spirit of government-peasant relations when the Stolypin Reform came into being.[30]

The question arises: what effect did violence have on the enactment and implementation of the reform? The matter has been much studied, but no convincing answers have emerged. Clearly mobs and assassinations produced much excitement among statesmen and political leaders, but the effects of this excitement on actions and opinions seem to me endlessly diverse. Some men moved to the "right," some to the "left"; some worked faster, some slowed down; some left the government in disgust, some came back from retirement with a new sense of commitment; some felt isolated from the people, some felt at one with them. I have been able to recognize only one universal effect of violence on behavior in government circles: everyone was in the habit of claiming— and in most cases believing—that his proposals would reduce violence whereas opposing ideas were likely to intensify violence. In a time when the government itself was doing what it could to tear up peasant society, such claims were not only irrelevant but bogus as well. They do reflect, however, as Chapters 6-9 will indicate, a strong inclination in the central offices to avoid open disturbances. This did not mean that the central government was willing to abandon its reforms, but it did mean that local officials would be called to account if they aroused overt resistance among the peasants, and that the central government (staff) would be unusually (but not uniformly) receptive to innovations *after* they had been introduced by local line officials on their own initiative, provided that no violence had resulted.

C. CONFUSION OF MOTIVE AND ACTION IN THE REFORM

I have tried in this chapter to outline as simply as possible the principal aims the reform embodied, the problems it was intended to

---

[30]No peasant was executed by court-martial in any of the reform-connected incidents described in Shapkarin's collection. Indeed, Shapkarin reports no reform-connected incident in which troops were called in at all. However, the police killed a fair number of anti-reform rioters; see, e.g., a report of an attack

cope with, and some of the more obvious problems involved in imposing it on the countryside. I have called all these elements of the reform its "context," chiefly because they constitute the simplest part of the description of the reform. They form a more or less clear background, against which we may go on to discuss the relatively murky processes of enactment and implementation.

It will be seen in subsequent chapters that the background presented here is a little too clear, as are all generalizations regarding government-peasant interaction in Russia. What I have called the "aims" of the reform did not correspond to the intentions of its enactors and directors. Peasant poverty, communal landholding, and pacification were the main subjects of conversation among government officials and peasants when the reform was being enacted, but I doubt that any of these had much to do with *the* problem of agrarian reform or even the government's "real" aim. Government programs ostensibly inaugurated to cope with these rhetorical images ended by ignoring them. The "aims" of the reform proceeded from highly diverse political struggles among various government agencies and categories of peasants, clashes that raged both within government and peasantry respectively and also between these two persistently abstract entities. Some clashes were clear enough, some were not, but in no case that I know of were anyone's purposes either clear or consistent. In 1905-17 the ground was shifting too fast under everyone's feet for either statesmen or peasants to be sure what their aims were. Insofar as the background sketches I have presented here are clear, then, they are not quite true to life. The reader should not take this chapter on "context" as a final answer to the question, "what was the Stolypin Land Reform?" It is not an outline that subsequent chapters will fill in but only a framework within which we may consider meaningful questions about what the Russian government and peasantry did to each other in the last imperial years.

It is of the utmost importance to recognize from the start that government-peasant interaction was not a structure of ideas and motives that were wrong (unsuccessful) or right (successful). We have already seen in Chapter 2 that although the tsarist government desperately needed information about the countryside in order to act there, it had to disregard information in order to plan and carry out its actions. In Chapter 3 I noted that the government attempted in 1889 to extend bureaucracy into the countryside by empowering government agents to ignore the restraints of bureaucracy. These paradoxes were also a part of

on some personal consolidators in a village in Tambov gubernia (1966: 184-85). Formal punishment for anti-reform rioters was usually either a three-month jail term or, in the most serious cases, exile from the gubernia (pp. 182-86, 189-93).

the context of the reform—the unclear part—and they make it impossible to speak meaningfully of a single organization formulating a single policy and thereby producing results that can be evaluated in terms of the policy. No such simple pattern will fit any part of government-peasant interaction in 1861-1930, least of all the reform era.

We have, for example, the tsarist government's attitude toward the peasant village. I have said (sec. B) that before 1906 the MVD tried to strengthen the villages' authority, whereas in 1906 it undertook to undermine this same authority. But this only refers to conscious policy. The *implied* direction of the MVD's actions was more consistent. Both before and after 1906 the MVD and the government as a whole were striving to mobilize the peasants by subjecting them to bureaucratic management. Before 1906 the MVD tried to push *villages* into becoming instruments of a legal-administrative system; during 1906 and 1907 the government encouraged peasants to dismantle their old villages and join a new order of quasi-private property owners. These were only two different techniques directed to the same end. Paradoxically, the MVD's pre-1906 efforts to strengthen villages probably tended to make peasant authorities more rigid, thereby rendering them unable to remold themselves into organizations based on the common purposes of their members. On the other hand, the effort to break villages down during the early years of the reform actually seems to have strengthened peasant communities. Under the impetus of the government's attacks, the villages took up collective land settlement on a large scale (ch. 8 and 9), which meant that they were beginning to organize themselves to destroy their own traditions—much as the gentry had done in the 1850s and '60s. In effect, the villages did at last undertake to preserve themselves while coming to grips with the modern world. At the very time the MVD abandoned the principle of village growth and undertook to dismantle peasant government, peasants began to engage in consistent political action and at last came to a meeting of minds with the government. What, then, are we to say of the government's ideas and their results? If the government set out in 1906 to break the mir and ended by bringing on a more extreme form of land repartition than any mir had ever dreamed of, all in the course of a program designed to grant peasants the right to conduct their lives independently of the wishes of their neighbors, what can we say meaningfully about the success or failure of the government's operations?

Very little, it seems to me, which is why I should like to avoid talking overmuch about the government organization's success or failure and speak instead of the actions of men driven by an urge to mobilize themselves and the peasantry under the twin banners of necessity and salvation.

6

Enactment of the Reform

> ...only by being guilty of Folly does mortal man in many cases
> arrive at the perception of Sense. A thought which should forever
> free us from hasty imprecations upon our ever-recurring intervals
> of Folly; since though Folly be our teacher, Sense is the lesson
> she teaches; since if Folly wholly depart from us, Further Sense
> will be her companion in the flight, and we will be left standing
> midway in wisdom.
>
> Herman Melville (1963: 233)

A. PRELIMINARY INVESTIGATIONS, 1902-5

The enacting of the Stolypin Reform commenced on 23 January 1902, when Nicholas II appointed the "special conference on the needs of agriculture" under the chairmanship of Sergei Iu. Witte. The conference included some of the highest-ranking statesmen in domestic administration—Witte the MF, Sipiagin the MVD, and Ermolov the MZ, to name only the most illustrious. There were 19 members in all (Macey, 1976: 168-69). Later on, in 1904-5, the voting membership would expand (p. 347), but in its first years it was a relatively compact group of the tsar's highest servitors.

The calling of a conference on the peasant problem was not in itself a novelty. Witte's group, however, had one unique feature: its freedom of action. Its purpose was stated so broadly that it was able to venture far beyond the technical problems of farming into a sweeping investigation of peasant government and society (Gurko, 1939: 223). An order from the tsar in March authorized the conference "to discuss all questions relating to agriculture and all related areas of the people's work in order to propose measures to His Imperial Majesty concerning the most immediate needs, including the ways and means for their practical accomplishment, and to submit the opinions of the Conference and of its separate members to His Imperial Majesty on questions of a general administrative *(obshchegosudarstvennyi)* character where they have significance to the rural economy" (Savich, 1907: 1-2).[1]

There was an air of crisis in early 1902. In the countryside famine had become an abiding feature of the economy, a massive cancer, as it were, which demanded not only relief but a permanent cure. The exceptionally widespread famine of 1891 had called forth strenuous efforts at basic peasant reform, but, as we have seen, the government failed to come up with anything but superficial measures such as relief and resettlement. A major famine broke out in 1898, followed by an equally bad one in 1901 (Phillipot, 1953: 61; Ermolov, 1909: 204-61). Crisis was not confined to the villages. A Europe-wide stock market crash in 1899 had brought on a recession in Russia that posed a serious threat to economic development (Von Laue, 1963: 212-22). Student unrest reached a high point during the period 1899-1902 (Burch, 1972: 132-52; Oldenburg, 1939: I, 144-51). We may say, then, that Witte's conference began its work at a time when the government faced urgent necessities and was ready to take risks. Witte went so far as to say that the government had to place itself at the head of the coming "upheaval," and his fellow statesmen were not far from agreeing with him (Liubimov, 49-50).

Witte's procedures in conducting his investigation suggest a sense of urgency. To create a basis for the conference's deliberations in St. Petersburg, he set up committees in the gubernias and uezds to study their locales and report their findings. These local groups were not intended to act like subordinate agencies. Witte conceived of them as autonomous bodies that would, by and large, select their own members and raise their own questions. True, their autonomy was only administrative, not political. It was local *officials* who would have a certain freedom of action, not political leaders. Governors were appointed to preside over the gubernia committees, uezd gentry marshals were to manage the uezd level, and some of the membership was prescribed by orders from the central government. Within this framework, however, the appointed chairmen were to have free rein. They had the right to enroll anyone who might conceivably be helpful, and, like their parent conference in the capital, they could discuss virtually any problems and make any proposals they liked. This applied to both uezd and gubernia levels. Uezd reports went to the gubernia committees, but they were not amalgamated into one single

[1]The tsar had already established an interministerial body to study peasant poverty in Nov. 1901. This was the "commission for investigating the...welfare of peasants in the central agricultural gubernias." Its membership included more local zemstvo men than had any previous interministerial body, but its procedures did not depart significantly from previous investigations. In any case, it came under the aegis of Witte's conference in early 1902, and from then on it did little more than amass data (Simonova, 1971: 246-48).

document for each gubernia. Each gubernia committee conducted its own investigation apart from the uezds' work and then sent its report to St. Petersburg together with those from the uezds. This arrangement, Witte claimed, made the reports truly representative of local needs and desires (Witte, 1904: 4-6; 1960: II, 534-35). Perhaps he had a point. The émigré historian S. S. Oldenburg tells us that uezd committees were less vulnerable than their gubernia counterparts to pressure from the central government (1939: I, 182-83).

As a result of their wide-ranging autonomy, the local committees took a variety of forms, followed a variety of procedures, and produced a very wide variety of recommendations. In some areas local officials exercised censorship, and some committee reports were entirely suppressed (Prokopovich, 1904: 20-43). Pleve, MVD in 1902-4, dismissed the governors of Voronezh and Kursk when he saw the reports of their committees (Liubimov, 44). Even so, efforts at restraint were sporadic. The committee reports gave expression in one place or another to all but the most revolutionary trends of thought on rural problems. Most notably, 191 uezd committees and 37 gubernia committees ventured to suggest that the government should expropriate land from private estates in areas where peasants suffered from a shortage of land (Prokopovich, 1904: 207-9). In general, the government was so hungry for information and ideas in 1902 that it was asking virtually anyone to make virtually any proposal he wished (pp. 1-6).

Witte's committees conducted their discussions during 1902-3, and their reports began to come in to the central conference during January 1903. By 1 August they had all arrived. Abridged versions of them were published in 58 volumes (*Trudy*, 1903), and these volumes, in turn, were utilized by the conference as sources for a topically divided study of 23 volumes (*Svod*, 1905). Full sets of both reports and studies were subsequently distributed to central and local government offices and to all zemstvo directorates (Shidlovskii, 1905: 15-20). At last, in early 1905, the conference began a concerted effort to draft legislation. It made some progress, but the tsar disbanded it abruptly on 30 March.

In the end, Witte's conference produced no reform, but its work was not in vain. The mass of committee reports, analytical studies, and draft proposals came to be accepted by all nonrevolutionary parties and by the government as the main basis for discussing the peasant problem and, ultimately, writing the reform laws. In early 1906 the Council of Ministers (see Glossary) agreed that the conference's materials constituted the best single basis for legislation the government possessed (TsGIAL, f. 1276, op. 2, 1906g., d. 4, ll. 13-14), and in later years scholars continued to refer to them as valid indications of the needs and desires of rural society (e.g., Martynov, 1917:6-19). Even S. N. Prokopovich, a menshevik writer who did not value the conference's materials highly, conceded that they contained the best *available* collection of information and analyses on peasant reform (1904: 43-46).

While Witte's conference was at work, the MVD was not idle. It, too, commenced an investigation of peasant society in January 1902. I have already described its history in Chapter 4 (sec. B). Here it will be useful to suggest a few comparisons between its work and Witte's.

The MVD's investigation began very differently. Unlike Witte, who was trying (or affecting) to obtain an expression of rural public opinion before he put his central conference to work, internal affairs followed its customary method of forming an editing commission to draft proposed laws before it invited local administrators to make comments. Witte's local committees met during 1902 and 1903, before the central conference began its deliberations, whereas the MVD's editing commission set up conferences in the gubernias only in 1904. Ostensibly, then, Witte was hoping to derive information from a relatively free expression of opinion in the countryside, whereas the MVD was ordering bureaucrats to make reports on specific subjects.

Gurko, leading spirit of the MVD's editing commission, makes much of this ostensible difference in his memoirs. He affects to scorn Witte's disorderly methods and claims that Witte's local committees, unlike the MVD's gubernia conferences, failed to produce any valid information— i.e., information that could be compiled systematically (1939: 223). Witte, too, made much of the difference between the two investigations. He acknowledged the lack of supervision and direction in his committees, but he made a virtue of it. Lack of central control, he said, was what made them representative. Thus his interpretation of the difference between the two investigations agreed closely with Gurko's, even if his evaluation did not.

Recently M. S. Simonova, a Soviet scholar, has also laid great stress on the difference between the two investigations. Like Witte, she sees in them a contest between two ideologies: the MVD's reactionary, landlord feudalism vs. the MF's bourgeois liberalism. With regard to method, she suggests that the MVD's gubernia conferences, unlike Witte's committees, were under the governors' thumbs. The governors, in their turn, were closely watched by the central offices of the ministry. She cites an MVD instruction forbidding the governors to name anyone to the conferences who was not specifically prescribed in MVD orders (1965: 221-22, 226-29).

I have failed to perceive this sharp contrast. So far as I can tell, the MVD's gubernia conferences and their "subcommissions" were no more or less subject to the governors' domination than Witte's gubernia and uezd committees. Regarding the MVD instruction to which Simonova refers, I do not doubt it was indeed published, and this does suggest an attitude in the MVD's central offices in 1902 quite different from Witte's.

In fact, however, no more attention was paid to this order than was paid to Witte's attempts to grant autonomy to his local committees. In any case, an MVD memorandum of 1905 granted governors the right to appoint anyone they liked to the conferences and to bring in members from zemstvo assemblies by whatever procedure they thought best (*Svod...o nadelnykh zemliakh,* 1906: vii-viii), which reflects a change of attitude in the ministry that must have taken effect after Pleve's assassination in July 1904. In the end, then, the conferences' reports reflected the same absence of direction as Witte's committee reports. The MVD itself admitted this on numerous occasions (e.g., pp. 195-96; TsGIAL, f. 1278, op. 1, d. 310, ll. 22-23). In June 1906 the ministry (probably Gurko himself) publicly acknowledged in a note to the first Duma that most gubernia conferences had failed to discuss the issues raised by the editing commission's projects. The main principle embodied in the projects, said Gurko's note, was the idea that custom should be articulated into statutes. The majority of the conference reports had not commented on this at all, and a minority openly asserted that the principle was wrong: custom was too vague to be articulated (f. 1291, op. 122, 1906g., d. 12, ll. 207-8).

I think it would be a mistake to attribute the disorder in the MVD's materials solely to incompetence and organizational breakdown. Gurko's claims notwithstanding, it was the MVD's intention from the beginning to grant its conferences wide-ranging autonomy. The questions the editing commission posed to them allowed quite as much latitude for random discussion as Witte's vague directives to the committees. Many questions suggested, in effect, that the conferences should make any proposal they wished (e.g., *Svod...po proektu pravil,* 1906: 349). It seems that in 1902 the MVD was fully as anxious as Witte to extract ideas and information from the locales. Gurko probably trumped up his fulminations against Witte's disorderliness because he could not find any more convincing basis for claiming that the MVD's work was superior in quality.

The two investigations were similar in other ways. They both ended by discussing the same issues. The MVD set out originally to discuss peasant law, while Witte's conference was ordered to focus on agriculture, but in fact the two subjects intermingled in both investigations. Such is the implication of the MVD's memorandum to the Duma of 5 June 1906 (TsGIAL, f. 1291, op. 122, 1906g., d. 12, ll. 205-29). Many of Witte's local committees took up the discussion of peasant law from the outset, and the MVD's commission seems to have made a thorough study of their work. Indeed, the commission directly encouraged its local conferences to make use of Witte's materials by including a lengthy survey of them in volume VI of its own publication, the final annotated project that it sent to its local conferences to guide their labors (*Trudy,* 1903-4: VI, 251-380). The conferences seem to have responded positively to this encouragement, too positively to suit the commission. In December 1904 the MVD felt compelled to issue a circular urging the conferences not merely to echo Witte's committees but to consider the issues on their own (Savich, 1907: 10).

This urging was perhaps all the more necessary because the two investigations were carried out by approximately the same people. The MVD, especially Stishinskii and Gurko, participated actively in Witte's conference, and the MF was represented on the MVD's editing commission (Shidlovskii, 1905: 2-3; Simonova, 1965: 235-36; *Svod...o nadelnykh zemliakh,* 1906: 1022-25). Witte's committees consisted of one-fourth officials, more than one-half gentry, roughly one-third zemstvo delegates (in the zemstvo gubernias), and somewhat less than one-sixth peasants (Shidlovskii, 1905: 9-12). The MVD conferences included no peasants, but their composition was otherwise roughly comparable. Their membership was a little less than one-half officials, about one-third gentry, and a little less than one-fifth zemstvo delegates (*Svod...o nadelnykh zemliakh,* 1906: 1022-25). As to the peasant members of Witte's committees, Simonova points out that they were almost all servitors in volost and village administrations (1965: 225). According to Prokopovich, they were handpicked stooges, representing no one but the bureaucracy (1904: 13-19). In any case most of them got only as high as the uezd committees. Less than 2% of the gubernia committee members were peasants (Simonova, 1965: 225). On the whole, then, Witte's operation was more elaborate than the MVD's, but the differences between the groups responding to the two investigations were not substantial.

In sum, the same men conducted both investigations, they did their work under similar administrative arrangements, and they discussed much the same questions. The two investigations also came to the same bad ending. We have seen that the MVD's work was disrupted by war and revolution, and it produced no significant legislation (ch. 4, sec. B). Witte's conference fared no better. Witte's personal power, based entirely on the tsar's favor, began to decline in 1902 with the appointment of Pleve as MVD. He was dismissed from the MF in August 1903 and appointed chairman of the Committee of Ministers, formally a high position but lacking any administrative agencies of its own. Simonova tells us that Witte and his conference enjoyed a brief comeback after Pleve's assassination in July of 1904 and his replacement as MVD by the relatively "liberal" P. D. Sviatopolk-Mirskii. In early 1905 the conference was again working actively, trying to convert its mass of information into legislative proposals. With the outbreak of revolution in January, however, Witte's "liberal" inclinations fell rapidly into disfavor. On 30 March the tsar dissolved the conference and replaced it with another one under I. L. Goremykin, who had been MVD from 1895 to 1899 and was no friend of Witte (Witte, 1960: II, 536; see also Macey, 1976: 364-65).

Despite their common failure to produce meaningful legislation, Witte's conference and the MVD commission both arrived at some general ideas of rural reform. Alas, these ideas do not readily lend themselves to analysis and categorization.

The few ideas that seem to have commanded widespread support among Witte's committees were mostly general statements of purpose, unaccompanied by concrete proposals or practical recommendations for implementation. A clear majority of the committees believed in the abrupt elimination of custom as the basis for the peasants' legal order and its replacement by formal, written, codified laws (Witte, 1904: 72; Shidlovskii, 1905: 32-37). Some committees ventured to discuss the peasant legal-administrative order. Most of these expressed the opinion that elected peasant officials were generally corrupt and incompetent, while the land captains, regardless of their personal competence, were stifling local development by their very presence (Rittikh, *Krest. prav.*, 1904: 129-57, 293-300). A significant number recommended the establishment of all-class volost zemstvoes (Prokopovich, 1904: 134-38). These proposals, however, were only general expressions of desire, not programs of action. Likewise, the committees favoring compulsory expropriation of land for distribution to needy peasants said nothing about how this was to be achieved.

The committees' views on communal land tenure and interstripping warrant a separate paragraph. Only 160 of Witte's 618 committees discussed the communal village per se. Of these, 32 wanted to preserve communal landholding, 15 others thought it desirable but wanted to cut down the frequency of redistributions and eliminate interstripping, 14 wanted to "let things take their course," 3 wanted to investigate further, and 96 wanted to abolish communal landholding. Of these 96, only 10 explicitly envisioned land consolidation as a desirable result. The other 86 confined their reports to discussions of property rights (Shidlovskii, 1905: 25-26). All in all, these figures do not demonstrate anything conclusively. Certainly they do not point to any generally approved method of dealing with communal villages. They say nothing, for example, about the crucial problem of how to protect individual peasants who desired to escape their more patriarchal neighbors. This is not surprising. The questionnaires sent out by the conference to guide local committees did not include any questions directly relating to the peasants' legal order or system of land division. The only committees who discussed these questions did it on their own initiative, and they felt little compulsion to do any more than express opinions (Rittikh, *Krest. zem.*, 1904: 1).

A. A. Rittikh, director of the department of state domains in the MZ, active member of the special conference, and Witte's loyal supporter, gave the committees' diverse views on communal landholding a strange interpretation. He asserted that the majority believed in spreading indi-

vidual land ownership and consolidating peasant land without requiring
the villages' consent (*Krest, prav.,* 1904: 13; Macey, 1976: 187-88). From
then on many writers echoed his assertion, and it became common coin
in capital-city conversation (Oldenburg, 1939: I, 183-88). Even the MVD's
land section came to accept it, or so it said in its report to the second
Duma in 1907 (TsGIAL, f. 1291, op. 120, 1908g., d. 118, l. 54). In reality,
however, the committees gave the conference no clear mandate regarding
land reform. Witte's investigation, like Valuev's in the early 1870s, produced enough information and opinions to offer some comfort to just
about any idea of rural reform, but it did not clearly support any single
concept. One member of the conference, the venerable P. P. Semenov,
actually argued that the committee reports embodied a recommendation
to preserve communal landholding (Simonova, 1965: 231; Sidelnikov,
1980: 6).

The MVD's gubernia conferences likewise produced very little to
generalize about. Gurko explained this in his memoirs by referring to the
confusion of war, revolution, and constitutional reforms (ch. 4, sec. B),
and I have suggested that the MVD gave its conferences ample freedom
to produce a variety of conclusions. Perhaps more basic than either of
these explanations, however, is the fact that the editing commission's
draft laws (*Trudy,* 1903-4: V) affected to embody a consistent concept of
peasant society *as it was.* This did not clarify the thinking of the gubernia
conferences, as Gurko and others doubtless hoped. On the contrary, it
only drove the conferences into an elaborate effort to explain the failure
of the commission's would-be laws to encompass actual peasant practice.
Local groups could not arrive at a concept of what peasants needed or
what the government should do because they had to deal with six volumes of prose dedicated to the proposition that peasant practice could be
described in terms of a single scheme. This, it seems to me, is the main
reason the conferences came forth with such a bewildering plethora of
views (e.g., *Svod...o nadelnykh zemliakh,* 1906: 47-61, 161-70, 195-211)
that were not only mutually contradictory but frequently self-contradictory (e.g., pp. 195-96; Meiendorf, 1909: 29-56, 88-101).

Despite the similarity between the two investigations of 1902-5, some
of the statesmen involved in Witte's conference and the MVD's editing
commission were anxious to identify ideological differences. This, however, was largely a matter of dressing up political squabbles with high-
sounding phrases. The trumped-up differences stemmed primarily from
an interministerial struggle to seize control of agrarian reform and direct
it.[2]

---

[2]David Macey, who has studied the two investigations of 1902-5 more
intensively than anyone, has also observed that they produced essentially similar
results (1976: 244).

The closest thing I have seen to an actual ideological contrast between the MVD's commission and Witte's conference may be found in a statement issued by the MVD in its June memorandum to the first Duma (TsGIAL, f. 1291, op. 122, 1906g., d. 12, ll. 205-29). As said before, the author was probably Gurko. In many respects this statement made the two groups sound very similar. Both conference and commission, it said, endorsed the general proposition that private property should somehow replace communal landholding. They also agreed that no change should be forced on the peasants. Peasants should be *allowed* to participate in the transition to modern farms, not compelled. The difference between the conference and the commission, said the memorandum, lay in their respective concepts of legal reform. The MVD's editing commission wanted to maintain a measure of government supervision over the peasantry while encouraging the consolidation of peasant land. Land settlement, conducted within the framework of extant law (as codified by the MVD), would prepare the way for the elimination of the peasants' special legal status. Strips would be transformed into farms *on allotment land* under the direction of village and volost elders and land captains; then, and only then, modern forms of property would be introduced into the villages. Witte's conference, on the other hand, wished to eliminate the peasants' legal separateness as quickly as possible, retaining only those laws preventing the sale and mortgaging of allotment lands to nonpeasants. The majority of the conference thought consolidation desirable, but they did not want to achieve it by administrative programs carried out on allotment land. Instead, they wanted to sell new lands to those few peasants willing to leave their villages and to make of them the first modern farmers. The conference wanted to take away much of the villages' authority and help individual peasants carry out land reform on their own initiative. In short, the MVD's editing commission planned to make land reform the basis of legal reform; the special conference planned to do it the other way around.[3]

As oversimplifications go, the MVD's statement was not bad. It was far from true, as we shall see in subsequent sections, but it was much closer to real issues than the conventional metaphors of agrarian history. It reflected a controversy about programs of action, and this surely was closer to the real concerns of the government's agrarian reformers than the huffing and puffing over ideological preconceptions that characterizes most scholarly analyses of the Stolypin Reform.

No Soviet scholar would agree that the divergence between commission and conference could possibly have had any grounds other than ideological ones. They have rejoiced to find in the first-hand accounts of

---

[3]The above interpretation of the MVD's view is very close to the editing commission's own statement of its purposes in 1903 (*Trudy*, 1903-4: I, 19, 22-27).

Witte and other statesmen a ready-made struggle between two ideological camps, representing "classes," and they have proceeded to hang the whole story of the reform on it. In their well-established scenario a "reactionary-feudal" editing commission tilted with a "bourgeois-liberal" special conference. The only thing the Soviets have not yet settled is the question of which side won. Their biggest ongoing dispute regarding the projects of 1902-5 concerns the question of which one was the real basis for the Stolypin Reform.

Simonova has given a brief account of this debate and has come down on the side of Witte's conference (1965: 212-14). Actually, however, her own very valuable description of the conference and commission does not support any such ringing conclusion. Consider, for example, the peculiar position of Pleve, MVD from 1902 until his assassination in July 1904 and reputedly the all-time champion of "feudal reaction." He was opposed to land settlement on allotment land; that is, he rejected the basic aim embodied in the project of his own ministry's editing commission. Moreover, his approach to land settlement bore a marked resemblance to that of Witte's conference. Since the late 1890s he had been favoring the idea of helping enterprising peasants to leave their villages and settle on consolidated farms outside the purview of village and volost (pp. 215-17). Pleve, says Simonova, was the moving spirit behind the "temporary rules" of 6 June 1904 on Siberian resettlement (*TPSZ*, 24701), the first law since the 1860s to suggest that a communal village should compensate a departing household for the land it was leaving behind (Simonova, 1965: 216, 222-23). The "liberal" special conference found this product of the "reactionary" Pleve's work highly congenial and referred to it as a precedent for its own proposals to make it easy for individual peasants to break away from their villages (p. 237). Later on, in early 1906, the enactors of the reform also found the rules of 6 June to be a useful basis for their work (see TsGIAL, f. 1291, op. 122, 1906g., d. 35, l. 11). In fact, then, the views of those inveterate opponents, Witte and Pleve, were curiously commingled.[4]

Gurko, reputedly another MVD reactionary, strongly disapproved of Pleve's intent to sell land from private estates to peasants (Gurko, 1902: 56, 108-10), and in all likelihood it was he who kept this idea out of the editing commission's projects (1939: 132, 157-58). Do we conclude that Gurko was "feudal"? If we do, then how do we explain his determination to do away with traditional peasant institutions on peasant land more abruptly than either Pleve or Witte (see 1902: 177-81; 1939: 132, 167, 172)?

[4]Curiously, the peasant bank had the impression that in 1903 Pleve wanted to cut down on its work in order to protect gentry estates (TsGIAL, f. 592, op. 1, d. 239, l. 1).

As for the men who dominated Witte's conference and its local committees, their "liberalism" bore a remarkable resemblance to that of Valuev and his gentry-dominated commission of the 1870s. Whole pages from Valuev's investigation could easily be inserted into the conference's materials, and only an expert would be able to recognize them. Witte's so-called "liberals" were, on the whole, gentry landholders, and their chief concern, as always, was to protect themselves against what they saw as the real ills of rural Russia: the peasants' habitual thievery, stupidity, drunkenness, sloth, and general irresponsibility. Reform was necessary, they often said, because the peasants were grabbing the landholders' land illegally and ruining it with their wasteful methods. This was also Gurko's point of view, which suggests either that the views of Witte's conference were "reactionary" or that Gurko's attitude toward the peasantry was "liberal." But we cannot accept this suggestion, for we already know that Gurko's program of land settlement was opposed to the conference's.

The vision of a "feudal" MVD and a "liberal" conference is full of such ambiguities. This is why I doubt that there is any answer to the Soviet question: *which* of the investigations produced the Stolypin Reform? In fact, the investigations neither stemmed from any ideological commitment nor produced any clear program of reform.

In spite of their ambiguous results, the MVD's editing commission and Witte's special conference constituted the foundation from which the reform laws evolved. If the deliberations of 1902-5 did not predetermine the agrarian legislation of 1905-6, they at least set the stage for it. They produced information and ideas; more important, they sustained the government's commitment to reform. In 1905, when both investigations came to grief, the central ministries still found themselves on center stage, and they had to go on discussing reform projects and forming political combinations around them (see below, sec. D). Agrarian reform was as yet only a cloudy idea in 1905, but it had enough momentum behind it to set the ministries wrestling with each other to seize control of it.

I have striven to compare the two investigations rather than contrast them, as is usually done, in order to get away from the abiding assumption that enactment of the reform was an orderly procession of decisions, formulated in advance and then put into action in the course of a struggle between ideologically motivated factions. As will be seen, the enactment process evolved out of an interministerial conflict, not an ideological one. The main issue in the enactors' minds was not the nature of the reform but who was to control it. The most significant feature of the editing commission's projects was their clear implication that agrarian reform, whatever it turned out to be, would be in the hands of the MVD's land captains or some facsimile thereof (*Svod... o nadelnykh zemliakh,* 1906:

561-68, 638-52, 750, 845). The basic element in the conference's proposed reform was that it would go forward under the auspices of the MF's peasant bank.

B. THE ENACTORS

Introduction

If the Stolypin Reform emerged from a political struggle, it is proper to precede our discussion of the enactment process with brief descriptions of the leading contestants. If we are to understand the rapid shifting and veering that accompanied the creation and implementation of the reform, we should take as our basic units the men who did the shifting and veering, not the ideologies they sometimes employed as they steered their respective courses.

I shall not attempt to discuss all the administrators, courtiers, and grand dukes who exercised influence during the enactment process. Doubtless, D. F. Trepov, the court commandant after October 1905, and Baron Fredericks, minister of the imperial court, occasionally had an impact on events. Throughout the enactment process and the reform itself, the ministers had to give some attention to these men and, of course, to the tsar himself. Apollon V. Krivoshein, MZ from 1908 until 1915 and chief implementor of the reform, was especially adept at using court connections (Krivoshein, 1973: 63, 86, 230-82; Naumov, 1954: II, 146). But the tsar and his entourage did not commit themselves to programs or take over administrative organizations. The business of politicking, of becoming entangled in contradictions and confronting them, did not involve them directly. They dabbled in reform rather than enacting it. They were part of the enactment process, but a discussion of their activities would contribute very little to an explanation of how the government managed to come up with a reform.[5]

Nor shall I burden the reader with detailed descriptions of the work of lesser administrators. Several of these became heavily involved in drafting the laws, and they furnished many of the ideas that ultimately went into the reform. I should at least mention A. S. Lykoshin, member of the editing commission in 1902-5 and, from 1907 on, the MVD's

---

[5] Baron Fredericks had so little to do with the government that he was able to testify in 1917, probably quite truthfully, that he had no idea where the Council of Ministers met (*Padenie,* 1924: V, 33-34). As for Trepov, Simonova suggests that he brought up the idea of converting the MZ into the agency for carrying out the Stolypin Reform (1968: 201-2). This is conceivable, but I doubt it. The idea of a powerful MZ, controlling both Siberian resettlement and the peasant bank, had been in the air for many years. It was suggested as early as 1892 by V. G. Iarotskii (1892: 425-26).

leading implementor of land reform; A. A. Kofod, the first propagandist for land settlement on village land and ultimately chief inspector of the reform organization; Ia. Ia. Litvinov, Gurko's successor in 1906 as head of the land section; A. P. Nikolskii, MZ for a short time in 1906; and A. A. Rittikh, director of the MZ's department of state domains and thus the executive manager of the reform throughout its duration. Despite the importance of their contributions, however, it is safe to say that none of these men exercised sufficient influence to play a decisive role in the business of getting laws into effect. In this brief section I shall consider only the key contenders in the political struggle of 1905-6.[6]

The fewer the enactors, the simpler our task. It comes as a relief, therefore, to realize that Petr A. Stolypin played only a minor part in the enactment of the reform that bears his name. Of the three major reform laws, two were already in force when he first came to St. Petersburg in late April 1906, and the outlines of the law of 9 November 1906 had already gained general acceptance in the government. It is true that Stolypin's thinking before 1905 was in essential harmony with the initial reform legislation. Some men who knew him personally have testified that he was opposing communal tenure and favoring land consolidation as early as the 1880s (e.g., Meiendorf, "Brief": sec. 3, 2-5; Zenkovskii, 1956: 17). This may or may not be true, but it is quite certain that in early 1905 he was solidly, officially, and explicitly advocating government action against the communal village. He wrote a report to the tsar in March, recommending that the government gradually eliminate communal landholding by helping individual peasants to settle on khutors outside existing villages. Their example, he hoped, would bring the rest of the peasants to change their ways voluntarily (Stolypin, 1926: 83-87). This idea was identical with the one proposed by Witte's special conference (and by Pleve), and it did indeed become a part of the reform. But the simple fact remains: Stolypin was not in St. Petersburg when the government was drafting the Stolypin Reform.

Stolypin's separation from the central offices and his noninvolvement in policy making were probably his most appealing qualities in 1906. He

[6]Macey (1976: 202-9) stresses the importance of Rittikh's contribution, especially his book of 1903, *Zavisimost krestian ot obshchiny i mira*. In 1904-5 Rittikh seems to have been associated with Witte. He edited the conference's 23 volumes, and he is said to have written his books in Witte's service. To some extent, his rise in the government took place under Witte's patronage (Shlippe, 95). He generally took Witte's part in the special conference, and in the fall of 1905 he was closely involved in writing up the Witte-Kutler scheme of land expropriation (Veselovski, 1924: 4). The Witte-Kutler scheme is discussed in sec. D. Suffice it to say here that Rittikh's involvement in it must have put him at center stage during the last months of 1905. Nevertheless, important as Rittikh's work may have been in the formulation of the reform legislation, he functioned as an agent of other men, and his role cannot be said to have been decisive.

came to St. Petersburg in April as a sterling embodiment of that favorite of government myths, the champion-governor: the man fresh from the provinces who "knew" the countryside from experience and was free from the factions and intrigues of rotten St. Petersburg—a Pazukhin of sorts.[7]

From 1887 through 1902 Stolypin served as gentry marshal and governor in Kovno and Grodno gubernias. In 1905, when peasant disturbances reached their peak, he was governor of Saratov, where the peasants seem to have been more violent than in any other Great Russian gubernia. Apparently he acquitted himself well (Macey, 1976: 657-58). Delegates from Saratov to a conference of the All-Russian Peasant Union, held in November 1905, complained that peasant resistance was being crushed. Judging from their remarks, Stolypin had mounted a sustained and successful attack on peasant rebellion well before November, when the central government began at last to act decisively to stop rural disruption (*Protokoly*, 1906: 24-26; see also *Revoliutsiia*, 1955: I, 747-52).[8]

In the spring of 1906, then, Stolypin appeared to be a hero, an experienced administrator, and a reasonably intelligent man. In the eyes of St. Petersburg, however, his most important quality was his apartness. Convinced of its own inherent corruption, the capital-city mind tended to scorn established members of its own social milieu no matter what their achievements, especially in 1906, when general confusion had intensified factional squabbles and compelled almost all leading statesmen to take sides against one another. Stolypin's abilities were striking, but they would not have been enough to bring him suddenly to the highest post in the administration if they had not been lighted up by the vision of his innocence. Not only must we admit that Stolypin had no hand in enacting the reform; we may go on to assert that if he had been involved, he could not possibly have presided over its implementation. Thus we may safely exclude him from the story of the enactment. The main characters in our saga were Sergei Witte, Vladimir Gurko, and Apollon Krivoshein.[9]

    [7]I have referred to the champion-governor myth elsewhere (1973: 106). On Stolypin's arrival and first few months in St. Petersburg, see Gurko (1939: 461-64). Understandably, the old St. Petersburg hand dwells on Stolypin's ignorance and inexperience rather than his noninvolvement, making his new superior sound more like a hick than a hero. But even Gurko's cantankerous account conveys the freshness Stolypin brought—or was intended to bring—to the central offices. On Stolypin's background, see also Macey (1976: 649-61).
    [8]The Saratovians embarrassed the delegates from other gubernias by bragging of their manor burning (*Protokoly*, 1906: 23-26, 56-57, 62, 74). Saratov's rural violence, they boasted, had reached truly exceptional levels, and the other delegates agreed, though not with enthusiasm.
    [9]We may also exclude Petr N. Durnovo, despite his key position as MVD in late 1905 and early 1906. Santoni (1968: 164, 178) assures us that Durnovo

Witte

Sergei Iu. Witte, the first of our main actors, was MF from 1892 until August 1903 and chairman of the Committee of Ministers from then until October 1905. On 19 October he became the first chairman of the newly reorganized Council of Ministers. His dismissal from this position on 20 April 1906 ended his career as an active administrator.

Witte did not enter the government as a young man seeking a career. In 1886, when the tsar asked him to take a post as a department head in the MF and charged him with the financial management of the state railroads, he had already proven his abilities as an executive in private railway companies. He gave up a relatively high income presumably for the sake of the increased authority and scope of action of his new, lower-paying government job (Witte, 1960: I, 208). Thus it may be said of Witte that he entered the government to serve a particular purpose—the development of railroads—rather than the state as such. Witte's subsequent rise to positions of more general responsibility did not change this fundamental approach. His objectives broadened to include all aspects of industrialization, but he never ceased to see himself as a pursuer of objectives rather than as part of an existing order. For him government was more an instrument of change than a part of society.

Witte began his career in the government with one view of Russian society but then changed to another after a few years of service. Initially, in the early 1890s, he seems to have relied very heavily on images drawn from Lev Tolstoi's novels and K. P. Pobedonostsev's essays. He saw traditional society as a bastion within which lived innocent peasants and largely corrupt gentry landholders. The communal village was a repository of strength and good will, and it would protect the peasants during the difficult years of Russia's industrialization. As for the corrupt landholders, the government had to be persuaded to stop supporting them, whereupon they would either learn to work productively or lose their land (Von Laue, 1963: 50-56; Chernyshev, 1918: 247-58). In short, Witte began his reign with a set of convictions that allowed him to ignore rural Russia. It would not act on its own, but it would benefit and develop on its own as the national economy grew increasingly modern in form. If rural society did experience difficulties, one could always blame corruption.

Like most committed revolutionaries and bureaucrats, Witte changed easily from would-be benefactor to mobilizer. During the 1890s he gradually became conscious of an agrarian problem that would not resolve itself simply as a result of industrial development. Sometime in 1896-99 he began to see peasant society as an unsatisfactory arrangement that

focused all his energies on putting down revolutionary violence and took no interest whatever in agrarian reform.

would have to be altered so that villages would make more farm products available for urban and foreign markets and contribute more revenue to the government. In brief, the government would have to embark on agrarian reform in order to sustain industrial growth (Chernyshev, 1918: 259-67; McKay, 1970: 8-13; Von Laue, 1963; Sidelnikov, 1980: 28).

As to Witte's specific agrarian policies, they cannot be properly understood apart from his experience as MF. Before the late 1890s, in the days when his notions of peasant society still consisted only of Lev Tolstoi's sloppy fantasies, the only government action he foresaw in rural Russia was the settlement of smallholders on new lands. This meant speeding up the settlement of Siberia and extending credit to peasants who wished to buy land outside their villages (Von Laue, 1963: 114-17, 235-37). Witte did not see these measures as *land* reforms. His new settlers could go on living and farming in their accustomed ways. He was just trying to help those nice peasants get along while also increasing their production for the market and filling in the land around his railroads.

The conversion to a more active brand of reformism came primarily because Witte's efforts to speed up industrial development, especially his deepening involvement in international finance, brought him into bitter conflict with rural interests. With the low grain prices of the 1880s and '90s, overpopulation in the villages, and, of course, the famines, these "interests" considered themselves involved in a crisis, and they were looking for scapegoats. It was more or less natural for them to attack Witte. They denounced his revenue system, his budget, and his dependence on foreign bankers. They spoke of the unwholesomeness of factories and city slums and the sinister power of Jews. In particular, they claimed that high taxes were causing peasant poverty (pp. 276-88). Spokesmen for agriculture accused Witte of making farmers assume a heavy tax burden and pay high prices in order to finance industrial and urban development. Confronted with this growing opposition, Witte needed not only to advocate what he wanted to do but also to find elements in rural society that he could blame for its alleged economic ills. In the late 1890s the only vocal rural interests consisted of estate owners, zemstvoes, and the MVD's local agencies. The latter styled themselves spokesmen for the peasantry. These were the elements attacking Witte, and it was primarily in response to them that he developed new ideas on rural government and peasant society. He intensified his efforts to block the extension and expansion of the zemstvoes, which at that time appeared to be little more than agencies of the MVD and strongpoints of rural opposition to any policies that might favor the towns. As for the MVD itself, he picked out its weakest point, the arbitrariness of peasant administration, and struck at it with all the force and vituperation he could muster. This was how

Witte became a champion of peasant legal equality (Yaney, 1973: 305-17; 1964: 68-90).[10]

Once involved in rural reform, Witte could only plunge on. He could no longer choose his battleground solely on the basis of issues relevant to his own policies but had instead to seek allies wherever he could find them and to attack his enemies wherever they happened to be weak. In 1899 his old enemy Goremykin was driven from the MVD and replaced by D. S. Sipiagin, with whom Witte was on friendly terms (see Witte, 1926: 30-48). Mere personal contacts could not bring lasting peace between the two ministries, but there was a brief cessation in their war. It was in Sipiagin's time that Witte began to speak of the need for an all-government, interministerial conference to study the possibility of abandoning government support for communal landholding.

For a time, hope emerged that MVD and MF might cooperate in a general peasant reform. In 1901 Witte got a law passed giving him relatively secure control over zemstvo taxation, and on this basis he began in 1902 to shower blessings on these now promising organs of local management (Melnikov, 18). He became generous with subsidies to them, and as chairman of the special conference he provided them with an opportunity to express proposals for rural reform (Yaney, 1973: 353). This auspicious beginning of interministerial cooperation was interrupted in April 1902 by the assassination of Sipiagin and the appointment of Witte's archenemy Pleve as MVD. The alliance between Witte and some elements in the zemstvoes persisted (pp. 353-60), but the war between MF and MVD resumed. Our two investigations quickly came to represent mutually hostile factions, anxious to sharpen and exaggerate their differences rather than smooth them over. After all, the only acceptable weapons in this new kind of struggle were research reports, theories, and ideologies. It was very important, therefore, to stress the virtue in one's own theories and the evil in those of one's opponents. This was how it happened that at the very time the MVD and MF acquired approximately

---

[10]Witte particularly disapproved of the land captains (Veselovskii, 1924: 75; Witte, 1960: I, 298-300, 414). His hostility toward the zemstvoes (prior to 1901) is best portrayed in his own famous work, *Samoderzhavie i zemstvo,* which he wrote in 1899.

M. S. Simonova has written a useful, well-documented study of Witte's policies and politics during the 1890s (1963: 65-82). However, she ascribes the evolution of Witte's views on the peasantry after 1898 to his exaggerated view of the significance of law (p. 80). In so doing, she minimizes the essentially tactical origin of Witte's peasant policies. Witte had no regard for law, and he certainly never believed in the efficacy of purely legal reform. He only echoed the demand for it now and then because it made a good club in his war against the MVD. As Simonova herself attests, his real aim by 1905 was to do what he could to clear traditional peasant villages and households out of the way (1965: 226-28).

similar ideas of peasant reform, they found themselves engaged in an intense ideological controversy. The controversy was real enough; the ideology was largely a facade. Thus, when I speak of Witte's experience after 1902, I am not speaking of something that taught him more about agriculture or the peasants, thereby rendering him more deeply aware of the countryside's problems. Indeed, I doubt that Witte was learning anything that would pass for knowledge in the ordinary sense of the word. What he was doing, rather, was learning—or creating—a language that he and his fellow statesmen could use to make themselves intelligible to one another. The "ideas" he favored, like those of the other enactors, were designed to articulate a capital-city political struggle, not to make sense of the peasantry or of agriculture.

As we have seen, Witte and the special conference demanded the repeal of the "protective" laws under which the peasants lived. The peasants, said Witte, should not be jostled into freedom by benevolent administrators. Instead, the villagers should be left to confront the market on their own, while the government focused its attention on the few individuals who wished to leave. The government would not reform the villages; neither would it continue to support the villages' traditional power. All the government would *do,* as an active administrative organization, would be to help individual peasants to dispose of their strips and move out of their villages onto new lands.

The conference's notion of reform was designed to call forth in capital-city minds a series of stereotyped tableaux. First tableau: poor peasants, crowded together in their villages, suffering from hunger and disease, running into each other with their plows on their tiny strips. Second tableau: an agent, preferably one skilled in agronomy and surveying, leads a few progressive and enlightened peasants away to new lands, leaving the remaining households to spread out on their shares. Third tableau: the departing peasants, freed from the cloying constraints of interstripped fields, joyfully set up khutors on the new lands and eagerly adopt the latest agricultural methods. The ones who remain, freed from the traditional authority of the family and the village (and the MVD), plunge into a demand economy. They market their produce and raise their standard of living. All rejoice. Both the departing peasants and those who remain will now increase the gross national product, and they can look forward to greater prosperity for themselves. Proletarianization is avoided even in the shadow of industrial development.

Beautiful as Witte's tableaux were, they left many questions unanswered. Were the departing peasants poor and landless, or were they "advanced" and relatively well off? Witte, following the tradition of the peasant bank and the advocates of Siberian resettlement, answered this question out of both sides of his mouth. Sometimes he referred to his departers as poor peasants being saved from starvation; sometimes they were advanced, adventurous farmers whose successful use of modern methods on the new lands would inspire an interest in agronomy among the backward neighbors they left behind. Which version he gave depended on how the argument happened to be going at the time. The adroit use of both versions allowed Witte and his allies to proclaim the advance of agriculture and an end to poverty at the same time.

But agricultural advance and aid to the poor did not mix. If departers from a village were poor, how were they to pay the expenses of moving and settling and then set up model farms to inspire their old neighbors? If they were relatively well off, how was resettlement going to help the landless poor? It would surely not be the poor who bought up the departers' strips. They lacked the money, and no one would advance them any on a mortgage because allotment land could not be mortgaged.

The gap between advance and welfare had been recognized long before 1905. The peasant bank had already become familiar with it in the 1880s (ch. 4, sec. D), and marxist writers, chiefly R. E. Tsimmerman (pseud., Gvozdev), were discussing the problem in public by 1900. Disbursing aid and/or credit, said Tsimmerman in 1898, cannot ever be effective in eliminating poverty. It can only make the wealthy wealthier and widen the split between rich and poor (1898: 135-44). Tsimmerman's generalization is not an absolute truth, but as a rule of thumb it rests on the very solid fact that no competent, honest government official or sincere reformer is going to give or lend money to people who are not likely to put it to productive use. Decades of experience with the peasant bank (ch. 4, n. 41) and Siberian resettlement (Kaufman, 1905: 214-17) had shown repeatedly that it was not the poor who gained from government aid but the relatively well off, usually the so-called "middle" peasants. The *optimal* outcome of resettlement outside the bounds of village allotments was the concentration of both village and nonvillage land in the hands of competent farmers, who would either drive off the landless poor or use them for labor. Perhaps this was a grim prospect from a sentimental social reformer's point of view, but in the economist's eyes the undeniably beneficial result would be to raise agricultural productivity while providing a labor surplus to industry.[11]

This, however, was only a theoretical result. There was a distinct possibility that Witte's proposed reform would run into serious practical problems and come to a far less desirable end, mainly because the encour-

[11]Anita Baker tells us that the zemstvoes' various campaigns to develop credit cooperatives always began with the sentimental fantasy that cooperatives would simultaneously relieve poverty, foster individual independence, and advance agriculture. As Baker shows, however, it never took the saviors long to find out that aiding the poor did not advance agriculture or make anyone independent. Invariably, they either dropped the poor or went out of business (1973: 151-54, 168-69, 235-36, 313-19).

agement of extensive land buying would raise the market value of land. By 1900 much of Russia's farmland had already acquired a much higher price than its productive capacity justified. Peasants were often willing to buy or rent fields without considering whether or not they could get enough income from them to meet their payments. So long as they clung to the belief that it was better to extend cultivation to a large area than to improve methods on the area already available, land prices could go on rising without any change at all in land productivity. Thus Witte's reform could exacerbate an already bad situation. Even genuine farmers would find it more lucrative to rent or sell their land to backward peasants than to invest in agricultural improvement. Land speculation would become more attractive than land use. Enlightened landholders would mortgage or sell their croplands and use the capital to invest in nonagricultural ventures; peasants would use up their income paying high rents or keeping up high mortgage payments, and they would have nothing to spare for investment in agricultural improvement even if they developed an inclination for it. Primitive agriculture and poverty would continue to walk hand in hand in the countryside even as industry flourished in the cities. Of course, this is only another tableau, not a fact. It is no more valid than Witte's sunny visions. At the same time it is no less valid.[12]

As we have seen (ch. 5, sec. B), the problems of farming in actual peasant villages offered a measure of justification for the peasants' uncritical land hunger. Selling produce was all very well, and no one objected very strenuously to the purchaseable comforts of modern civilization—sugar, kerosene, matches, tea. At the turn of the century, however, villages still had to contend with more elemental phenomena such as famine, fire, and epidemics largely by themselves, and their reluctance to depend on outside social and economic networks, markets, and the like was more than a vestigial tradition. For purposes of survival the "primeval" community was a practical, going concern if it could somehow get enough land. Land hunger, then, was something more than a product of ignorance that could easily be swept away by enlightenment. It was an attitude that made sense in many areas and would go on making sense until the general situation changed in rural Russia.

So Witte's notion of agrarian reform was not without flaws. His proposed measures could not aid the poor while advancing agriculture. Worse, they might even have bound peasant farmers all the more tightly to primitive methods of cultivation by rendering advanced agriculture unprofitable. If we add to these considerations the simple fact that there

[12]Tsimmerman (1898: 35-44) and Mertvago (1900: 189-92, 216-32, 244-59) made this point in the 1890s from marxist and populist points of view respectively. For more recent discussions, see Anfimov (1969: 88-109, 179-88, 306), Malin (1961: 30-42), and Nötzold (1966: 68-69).

was very little "new" land in European Russia where enterprising peasants could go to get away from villages (ch. 4, sec. D), it becomes clear that the reform envisioned by the special conference could very well have done more harm than good to peasant society and rural economy alike.[13]

For the most part, Witte simply ignored the flaws in his program. I have already suggested the reason for this. Witte did not think about agrarian reform in order to develop workable ideas. All he wanted was effective slogans to accompany his moves to get control of the coming attack on rural society. Let me remind the reader that Witte entered government service with the purpose of building and organizing railroads. Initially he harbored some vague visions of peasant society, but they were only clichés, and in any case they had no logical relation to the concepts of agrarian reform he ultimately came to champion. He acquired his sense of social responsibility from the interministerial controversies in which he had to engage in order to build railroads. It is not at all surprising, therefore, that when he found himself compelled to make proposals for social reform, he failed to come forth with an orderly scheme based on the realities of peasant society.

Witte's role in the final stages of the enactment process was unique in the politics of tsarist administration. His special conference was dismissed in March 1905, and at this point the old railroad builder should have disappeared from the scene. He had lost his battle with the MVD, and the result should have been the burying of his program or its amalgamation into an MVD-dominated reform. As it turned out, however, events presented Witte with a few more cards to play.

At about the same time Witte's conference was being dismissed, the Russian army in Manchuria was suffering its last major defeat at Mukden, and it became apparent that the war with Japan could not be won. The army was far from beaten; indeed, it was rapidly growing stronger. It was the national economy that was weak in 1905. The government could no longer pay for its powerful two-front army because the bankers of Paris could not extend further credit until the war stopped. Peace had to be made, and it was Witte, with his considerable international prestige, who had to go abroad and do the job. He retained his largely honorary position as chairman of the Committee of Ministers, and in August he went to Portsmouth, where he succeeded in withdrawing Russia from its military debacle with something resembling honor. This achievement raised both his national and international reputation to new heights and made him indispensable to the tsar. It is no exaggeration to say that after

---

[13] Witte's hopes are discussed at greater length in sec. D. Stolypin's collision with peasant tenants on "nonpeasant" land is described in ch. 7, sec. D.

the peace of Portsmouth, Witte enjoyed a higher credit rating in Paris than the Russian government itself.

Witte was particularly necessary to the government when he returned to Russia in September because domestic violence, especially the revolutionary and anti-Jewish varieties, was now posing a more serious threat to Russian credit on the international market than war had. Foreign bankers, fearing for the large investments they had already made in the tsar's empire, would have been happy to extend the loan Russia needed so badly, but they could not sell Russian bonds to their customers at a time when the government seemed to be collapsing. Russia was on the brink of insolvency in late 1905, and her need for a foreign loan was her most pressing problem. No one in the higher levels of the tsarist government seems to have loved Witte, but domestic disruption was making him a very important man.

I cannot prove that Witte's credit abroad was the basis for his ascendancy in late 1905. Certainly Nicholas II made no explicit admission to this effect. The government's dependence on foreign bankers, many of them Jewish, was a delicate subject in St. Petersburg, and few statesmen were willing to acknowledge its importance by conversing about it, let alone putting their considerations in writing. Even in the absence of direct evidence, however, it seems obvious that the greatest danger to the government in those hectic days was financial. Witte was put at the head of the government in October 1905, during the darkest days of a general strike, primarily to make Russia presentable to Paris. So long as the loan was in doubt, he could continue to influence government policy, and it was on this basis that he re-entered the conflict over agrarian reform. Frenzied attempts to squelch violence and negotiate a loan in Paris accompanied each other from October 1905 to April 1906. On 18 April the loan agreement was signed, and Russia was saved on the very brink of financial collapse. Two days later Witte was dismissed and packed off to the State Council, whereupon his contribution to the Stolypin Reform came at last to an end. I shall return to these tumultuous months of Witte's last reign after introducing the other two enactors.[14]

[14]Witte's version of his dismissal suggests that he requested it himself on 14 Apr. (1960: III, 337-42), but I see no reason to believe this. Key documents regarding the loan negotiations are printed in Preobrazhenskii (1926: especially 242-301). See also Long (1968: 124-38).

Actually the loan agreement did not end the danger. The bankers still had to sell the bonds, and their failure to do so would ultimately have done almost as much harm to Russian credit as a refusal to make the loan in the first place. They had some hard going. The tsarist government's credit in Europe fell sharply during the months immediately following Witte's dismissal. The bonds went on sale at only 88 (i.e., 88% of their face value), of which the tsarist government received 83.5, but even this relatively low price was too high. The market value drifted downward in May-June 1906 and fell to a low of 68 shortly after 9 July, when

Gurko

Vladimir Gurko took over the MVD's land section in 1902 and managed it until December 1906, when he was accused of misappropriating funds and compelled to resign. His resignation marked an abrupt end to his career in government. The tsar pointedly refrained from appointing him to the State Council, and although he was subsequently elected to it, he was never to hold another administrative post. Before his sudden fall, however, he was at the heart of the government's efforts at land reform. From 1902 he served on just about all the conferences and commissions, both MVD and interministerial, that discussed the peasant question or drafted peasant legislation.

Unlike Witte, Gurko was born a member of the landed gentry, the product of a long line of government servitors, and he spent all his adult life occupying government posts. Before coming to the MVD in 1902, he served several years in the imperial chancellery, the hub of domestic administration. Gurko admits that the chancellery's central position put it quite out of touch with the Russian countryside, but he adds that his years in it gave him a profound understanding of the tsarist government as a whole—its traditional problems and roles as well as its more recent ones (1939: 35-42).

"Understanding" is too grand a word. It implies that Gurko had ideas which, if only they had been put into practice, would have set Russian government and society going in the "correct" direction. No one in pre-revolutionary Russia knew this much, least of all Gurko, whose ventures into theory produced little more than superficial social darwinism combined with raw Great Russian chauvinism. One of his "ideas" was that Witte's policies were allowing Jews and foreigners to dominate Russian trade and industry (Gurko, 1902: 199). Another was his objection to massive resettlement in Siberia on the grounds that migrants departing from western Russia would leave land vacant near the German border, thus allowing German settlers to flood in and push the cultural boundary between German and Slav further eastward (p. 56). As to peasant reform, he seems to have given very little thought to it before he took over the land section. His book of 1902 on Russian agricultural development devoted only 12 pages out of about 200 to peasant farming (pp. 171-82).

Nevertheless, Gurko did appreciate the immense range of problems the government faced in the countryside. Perhaps he did not possess

Nicholas dissolved the first Duma (Long, 1968: 238). On 28 July, however, a cheerful dispatch came to V. N. Kokovtsov, then the MF, from one of the leading negotiators of the loan, informing him that the bonds' market value was rising and that all storms were past for the time being (Preobrazhenskii, 1926: 323-25). This prediction proved to be accurate, though the government had to go on buying its own bonds from time to time until 1908 (Kokovtsov, 1935: 189-90).

much concrete information about the practical consequences of his policies in the villages, but he did realize better than most men of St. Petersburg that policies had consequences. He generally refused to consider reform proposals apart from their implied effects as well as their expected ones. Gurko was one of those rare men who never forgot that the most he could claim for any reform proposal, including his own, was that it was not as bad as the existing situation nor as harmful as the alternatives.

Like Witte, Gurko exercised considerable influence on the government's decision making but still did not get things his way. His ideas resembled Witte's in that they stemmed primarily from what he took to be the practical necessities of the Russian state, but here the resemblance ended. Necessity for Gurko demanded that Russian government and culture be maintained on historical foundations, whereas Witte acted as if he believed that the government's basic need was to do away with these foundations. To put it in terms of economic theory, Gurko believed—or acted as if he believed—that a nation's wealth lay within its borders, whereas Witte believed—or acted as if he believed—that a nation got its wealth by functioning in the world market. Gurko opposed the gold standard; Witte was willing to make any sacrifice to keep Russia on it (Gurko, 1939: 519; Von Laue, 1963: 276-83). To put the contrast in terms of specific policy making, Gurko's reform plans made it a point to identify the elite who would carry them out, whereas Witte focused his attention on the plans per se. Gurko was inclined to trust in proven ability; Witte put his faith in paper.

As to the substance of their respective programs, Gurko accepted Witte's emphasis on raising agricultural productivity by getting land and capital into the hands of competent farmers. Unlike Witte, he thought that the way to do this was to keep nonpeasant soil out of wasteful, destructive peasant hands. Private landholders were generally more advanced than the peasants, he argued. Therefore it would be foolish to encourage them to sell their land to peasants, let alone force them to sell it (1902: 56). However popular any program to distribute additional land to peasants might be, it would be disastrous to the development of agriculture. If the government wanted competent farming, it should make credit available to improve agriculture on existing farms, not to facilitate massive land buying, with its potentially disastrous effects, and certainly not to extend shoddy methods to an even greater area (pp. 108-10). Gurko contended that the modernization of private farms would benefit even poor peasants. They could earn far more money as hired laborers on modern farms than they were getting from their own pathetic strips (pp. 49-51; Simonova, 1971: 255).

Gurko was not a "reactionary nobleman," as Soviet scholars insist on calling him. He was, if anything, a proto-fascist. The private ownership he advocated so passionately was not, in his mind, a device for old families to maintain their privileges but a "stimulus" to productive land cultivation (Gurko, 1902: 58). His elite were not blood lines or even holders of large estates, of whom he generally disapproved, but effective farmers who could organize themselves to grow and sell their produce at a profit while strengthening the economic sinews of the Russian state. In Gurko's mind farmers held their land to serve and advance the state, not to sustain (or recapture) an old order (Simonova, 1968: 213-14).

Gurko's views on peasant agriculture proceeded from the same basic attitude. Despite his low regard for peasant farming, he still took an interest in reforming it, and in his eyes the problem on village lands was essentially the same as on private estates: to make credit available for introducing modern methods. The difference was that credit could not be extended to village farmers until their farms consisted of mortgageable lots, and therefore a thoroughgoing land reform would have to precede agricultural improvement. Thus, when he took over the land section, Gurko set out to reform village land. When he wrote his book of 1902, he was content merely to recommend that individual peasants be allowed to claim their strips as private property and convert them to khutors (pp. 177-81). In his memoirs, written long after the Revolution, he recalls having much more radical intentions in mind. He says his purpose in joining the MVD's editing commission was nothing less than to destroy the commune (1939: 132). He wanted to sweep away all the government's "protective" limitations on peasants and let them sink or swim on their own (p. 167). "Left to themselves, the weak elements might perhaps perish, but their demise would have little significance for human progress and for the vital strength of a people and its government; in fact, their removal might prove even beneficial" (p. 172). Thus spoke the head of the land section, ostensibly the protector-in-chief of the Russian peasant: commander over all land captains, peasant captains, commissars for peasant affairs, and arbitrators in the Russian Empire.

Curious that a man of Gurko's views should have been set over the land captains. It was even more curious that he got himself onto Stishinskii's editing commission and managed to become its leading spirit. The explanation offered in his memoirs is simple: he concealed his more extreme views and worked to further his purposes while using terms deceptively acceptable to his colleagues. He outwardly accepted the commission's guiding principle: that the peasants' legal status, especially the communal villages' right to hold their land, must not be infringed. Gurko's projects faithfully reflected the commission's official purpose to introduce a measure of consistency into peasant administration and to codify peasant law. Most of the provisions in them were designed to define rights and duties with systematic, unpeasantlike clarity, but they reflected an intention to conform to village tradition (*Svod...o nadelnykh zemliakh,* 1906: 47-61, 161-70, 195-211).

Some of the commission's members may have believed that the new clarity would strengthen villages and families. Gurko, however, seems to have believed exactly the opposite. Since the essence of peasant law was obscurity, he reasoned, clarification would hasten its destruction. Given the archaic, personal nature of peasant legal order, the insertion into it of abstractly defined individual rights—any rights—would effectively deprive villages and families of their authority over individual adults. In his own words Gurko was working to introduce "a rational system of land tenure ...under which a transference to private ownership would become indispensable but would not constitute the declared aim of the reform" (1939: 158). His memoirs do not tell us exactly what he means by "rational system of land tenure." In his book of 1902, however, he expressed the conviction that peasants should settle on khutors (1902: 181). Witte felt the same way, but Gurko differed with Witte (and Pleve) in that he did *not* want to set up the new farms on nonpeasant land. What Gurko wanted, then, was to entangle village and volost authorities in a snarl of unworkable laws and then to persuade at least a few peasants to break away from customary modes of land use. These few khutor-formers would reduce custom to inapplicable incoherence and place all peasants in a position whence their only escape would be the acceptance of private property.

But how did Gurko plan to beguile peasants into accepting land reform? His idea, according to his memoirs, was to undertake relatively modest village reforms that would be acceptable to the peasants, such as the breakup of large villages into small ones. Then, in the course of these general disentanglements, government agents could step in to encourage a few individual peasants to exchange their strips for khutor lots. Such peasants would always be available, for there would always be some who would be dissatisfied with the shares they got in the village-wide reform. Presumably these malcontents could be persuaded to form khutors, and khutors would constitute private property de facto without any immediate need for a formal legal statement to this effect. So Gurko said. Ultimately, he assumed, this process would erode the communal village. The peasants would do the natural thing: change over to private ownership en masse. Then the whole apparatus of guardianship would disappear of its own accord (1939: 132, 157-58).

Former statesmen engaged in writing their memoirs are inclined to construe the past as if they had made it happen, and Gurko is no exception. His image of himself as a mastermind in 1902-5 is suspect. The seeming slyness of his alleged scheme, his acting as if he were shoring up tradition when in reality he was trying to wipe it out, is particularly hard to swallow. Nevertheless, it is not farfetched to suggest that the land section's efforts to "control" peasant villages ever since the 1860s embodied a general concept of legal "reform" that resembled Gurko's scheme. As I have suggested, the section never intended to strengthen peasant institutions for their own sake but only to forge instruments for modernizing peasant society. I cannot prove it, but I strongly suspect that the only thing false in Gurko's alleged scheme is the claim that it was his own. It sounds very much like an approach he picked up more or less unwittingly from veteran officials in the land section. He was not fooling his colleagues in the MVD, as his memoirs suggest, but was working within the framework of their views and attitudes (ch. 3, sec. D; ch. 4, sec. B).

Some clauses in the editing commission's projects do in fact embody the sort of attack on communal landholding that Gurko claims to have had in mind. Take, for example, articles 115-29 in the project on peasant landholding. In effect, they rendered all villages, communal and noncommunal alike, incapable of resisting any attack on them by small minorities among their own members (*Svod...o nadelnykh zemliakh,* 1906: 515-68). Articles 115 and 116 allowed a mere one-fifth of the heads of household in a village to claim an integral area of the village's land and form a new village on it. The editing commission put this forth as a measure to reduce the size of overly large villages, but in fact it applied to villages of as few as 40 households. Indeed, a similar provision allowed this operation in villages with 20 to 39 households, except that the separating group had to include at least two-fifths of the households (p. 524). Article 126 strongly suggests that reduction in village size was not the real purpose of these measures. It required that in all cases of village division in which more than ten households broke away, the departing families would be compelled to divide their new area into consolidated farms held individually, not communally, by the respective households (p. 558). This drastic provision aroused considerable opposition in the gubernia conferences. Only 13 of them approved it unanimously and four more by majority vote; 20 rejected it (pp. 558-61). This, however, was the only anti-village article that aroused serious opposition in the gubernias. Other clauses—requiring village consolidation in both communal and noncommunal villages if two-thirds of the villagers approved, requiring communal peasants who switched to household ownership to consolidate their fields into otrubs, et al.—were approved by a clear majority of the conferences (pp. 573-91). These measures, taken together, were actually *more* drastic than the reform legislation of 1905-6. Thus the editing commission's projects bear out Gurko's explanations of the land section's tactics. As early as 1902 the MVD was indeed preparing an attack on peasant society and, perhaps, trying to conceal the fact. What is most interesting is that a majority in the Committee of Ministers voted against sending the commission's project to the governors, whereupon

Nicholas II overturned their vote and personally approved the continuation of the MVD's investigation (Sidelnikov, 1980: 45).[15]

To return to Gurko, I might add in passing that he did not hold consistently to his alleged slyness. On at least three occasions in 1905 he supported radical proposals to change communal landholding abruptly into personal property by legislative fiat. In the spring he tried (but failed) to persuade Witte's conference to adopt a recommendation that all communal villages that had not redistributed their land during the preceding 24 years should be declared noncommunal (Simonova, 1965: 235-36; Sidelnikov, 1980: 54; Macey, 1976: 336). Apparently he was speaking as the official representative of his ministry. In June he tried the same thing again (Macey, 1976: 371), and in October he joined Witte to propose that *all* communal land be directly converted to personal property by order of the tsar (Simonova, 1968: 215). Needless to say, Gurko's memoirs do not mention these frenzied departures from his self-styled subtlety.

Gurko's views on reform embroiled him in contradictions fully as perplexing as those emanating from Witte's notions. Just as Witte had to base his proposed programs on the instruments at hand—chiefly the peasant bank and the zemstvoes—so too had Gurko to fit his plans into the context of his organization. For him the chief instrument was the land captains. It is certainly understandable that Gurko should have wished to transform his outmoded patriarchs into agencies of reform, but this purpose introduced a fundamental contradiction into his program. On the one hand, Gurko's plan to codify peasant law sought to limit the land captain's authority and strengthen peasant institutions. On the other, the editing commission's project allowed small groups of peasants to attack their villages, and this required the villages and captains to make decisions not governed by traditional law. Peasant law knew no grounds for deciding disputes between would-be private farmers and traditional village institutions. It followed that someone outside the framework of peasant institutions would have to do the deciding: in particular, the land captains; so said the projects of 1902-3. In effect, then, the editing commission's measures to attack the villages did not limit the captain's

[15]Only one of the above measures was enacted in 1906: the provision for village consolidation by two-thirds vote in both communal and noncommunal villages. Dubrovskii incorrectly states that the reform decree of 9 Nov. 1906 contained the one-fifth rule (1963: 175). In fact, this provision, somewhat altered from the projects of 1902-3, only got into law in the statute of 14 June 1910 (*TPSZ*, 33743, art. 34). A vague suggestion of this provision did appear in the "Witte-Nikolskii bases" of Apr. 1906 (see sec. D) and in a reform proposal brought before the first Duma in June 1906 by the MZ (Stishinskii, 20).

authority. On the contrary, they gave him (by implication) much greater power than he had ever enjoyed before. Simply by deciding individual disputes, he could arbitrarily and continually disrupt the village's basic scheme of land division.

The prospects for the MVD's scheme were dubious at best. On the one hand, the government was initiating a process by which the peasant was supposed to become economically responsible for himself; on the other, the MVD and its land captains were in fact assuming responsibility for the peasant's success. If and when any "reformed" peasants failed to produce and prosper, the MVD would blame the captains, and the captains, proceeding on this assumption from the outset, would not be likely to rely heavily on individual peasants to look after themselves. Had the MVD projects of 1902-3 been enacted, it is doubtful that peasants would actually have been left to sink or swim on their own, in accordance with the intention Gurko claims he had (1939: 167). Real land captains would not have allowed either sinking or swimming. Weighted down by the clerk-like responsibilities Gurko was eagerly piling upon them, they would either have kept the peasants out of the water entirely or dragged them through it at the end of a rope. Ostensibly Gurko was proposing to create a free economy; in fact he was proposing to set in motion a crude engine for administering mobilization.

Gurko saw many of his ideas buried during the enactment process of 1905-6. Contrary to his wishes, the reform laws assigned a major role in agrarian reform to the peasant bank. Gentry and state lands were sold to the peasants in unprecedented volume after 1905, and by 1917 nonpeasant agriculture seemed well on the way to disappearing. Gurko's general *aim* survived, however, and it ultimately turned out to be a basic element in the reform. This was the rationalization of peasant land use by reforms carried out directly on allotment land. As we have seen, Gurko's initial plan was to encourage the division of large villages into smaller ones, hoping that a few peasants would form khutors in the accompanying redistribution of the village's lands (1939: 132, 157-58). He wanted, in other words, to move *toward* consolidation through a series of radical redistributions of village land. In the end, this was what the Stolypin Reform did (see ch. 9, sec. A).

The outcome, however, was not altogether positive. There was an implicit contradiction in gradual land reform in the villages, unforeseen, apparently, by Gurko and everyone else. Gurko and his editing commission assumed that when a village embarked on land settlement, one measure would lead to another, bringing the members step by step to full consolidation. In practice, however, a move *toward* consolidation could produce effects that discouraged any further moves. A partial reform either satisfied the villagers, in which case no further change was likely to be desired, or it displeased them and rendered them mutually hostile, in which case they would have difficulty reaching new agreements.[16]

Even supposing that the peasants did not react in this fashion and somehow continued to press for new reforms, continual rearranging of their lands would defeat the purpose of the reform, which was not merely consolidation but also security of tenure. Continual moves *toward* consolidation would create a situation in which farmers had continually to face the loss of their fields in the course of new reforms, and such cultivators were no more likely to invest in soil improvement than communal peasants had been under the old regime of redistribution.

The editing commission gave only one indication that it recognized the contradiction between repeated land reforms and security of tenure. This was article 168 in its project on peasant landholding, which provided for the elimination of interstripping between villages (*Svod...o nadelnykh zemliakh,* 1906: 772). The impact of this operation on the participating villages resembled that of a personal consolidation in that all the land in each village had to be reshuffled in order to carry it out. According to other clauses in the MVD's project, such general reshufflings could be imposed on a village, communal or noncommunal, by two-thirds of its household heads as often as seemed desirable (pp. 573-91). Seemingly, therefore, many villages would have had to face the possibility of undergoing successive projects of what the Stolypin Reform would later call "group land settlement" (see ch. 5, sec. A). This would have posed a serious threat to security of tenure had it not been for article 168, which expressly protected security of tenure by providing that any such reform could only be imposed on a village by a two-thirds majority once every 30 years. For 30 years after the carrying out of a group project, a village could not go through another such project except by unanimous agreement among its assembly members. It may be said, then, that article 168 indicated at least a fleeting realization in the editing commission of the contradiction between moving *toward* consolidation and the completion of consolidation. Seemingly, it even resolved the contradiction, though in doing so it implied that land reform would be a very lengthy process. Actually, no article in the editing commission's project established real security of tenure because the project failed to set any limit on the frequency with which small groups of villagers could demand to consolidate their strips against the will of the majority (pp. 515-68). Taking the commission's project as a whole, then, it did not recognize or cope with the contradiction between security of tenure and land reform. Article 168 was a freak.

[16]Witte seems to have glimpsed this potential dilemma in 1904, but he only mentioned it in passing in order to attack the MVD's programs (1904: 91-92).

The alternative to moving gradually *toward* consolidation was to go all the way to khutors in one giant step. This was indeed what a number of the leading reformers came to favor after 1906. In many areas, however, abrupt change posed formidable physical difficulties, and it represented a much more drastic disruption in the peasant way of life than many peasants were willing to accept. Certainly Gurko never advocated such a measure, for it would have undermined his fantasies about peasants engaging in land reform and commercial agriculture out of their natural inclination to take responsibility for themselves. But, then, Gurko would have had no reason to propose such an alternative, since he did not perceive the contradiction in his project to begin with. In any case, Gurko's projects of 1902-3 embodied contradictions fully as sharp as the ones in Witte's proposed reform.

Not surprisingly, many of the contradictions in both schemes found their way into the reform laws enacted in 1905-6 and thence into the reform itself. Land captains and peasant bank carried their traditional modes of operation directly into the government's attack on villages, in spite of the manifest unsuitability of both these institutions as agencies of social change.

Krivoshein

Apollon Krivoshein was certainly one of the principal enactors of the Stolypin Reform. He produced the law of 4 March 1906, setting up the reform organization, and he played a major role in blocking Witte's attempts to secure control over the reform for the MF. More, he was the only one of the three major enactors who remained in the government after 1906. Thus Krivoshein was both enactor and implementor. If any one man could be called the creator of the "Stolypin" Reform, it would be he.

Scholars have taken no interest in Krivoshein. There are archives in his name in the USSR, but until very recently no one has used them. No book, no article, not even a dissertation was devoted to his career until 1973, when his son at last produced a biography (Krivoshein, 1973). He left no memoirs, and prior to 1906 he seems to have kept his associates in the dark as to what he was thinking. Consequently we know very little about his views on the peasant question prior to 1906.

We do know that Krivoshein's career before 1905 was spent mostly in the MVD. His son tells us that he worked for the land section from 1887 to 1896, when he became vice-director of the department in charge of peasant resettlement in Siberia. In 1902 he became director (pp. 11-14); in 1905, when his department was transferred to the MZ, he went along with it, rising at the same time to the rank of deputy minister. He spent the month of February 1906 as acting MZ but was then dropped again to deputy status (see below, sec. D). In October he switched ministries again, going into the MF as a deputy minister to head the peasant and gentry land banks. There he remained until his return to the MZ in May 1908 as minister and director of the reform.

Krivoshein's rise to high position was unusually abrupt. When he at last became the MZ in 1908, he was still only an actual state councilor—that is, he held only the fourth rank *(chin)* in the government service—although two of his deputy ministers were third-ranking privy councilors (*IGU*, 1908: 409).

Krivoshein's associates tell us that he espoused no theoretical views on agrarian reform before 1905. Gurko and Witte both say he was an opportunist who adapted his views to the political climate (Gurko, 1939: 153, 194-97; Witte, 1960: II, 536; III: 204-5). Witte considered Krivoshein a scoundrel. In February 1906 he brought all his influence to bear to prevent Krivoshein's appointment as permanent MZ, even threatening to resign if Nicholas carried through his intention to appoint him (Witte, 1960: III, 204-5, 210-14).

If Krivoshein was indeed an opportunist without theories, then he stands as a perfect symbol of the reform in its last stages of enactment, when theoretical positions lost their importance and individuals took stands only in order to fit them to the demands of their respective organizations. We have seen how Witte and Gurko skipped from one position to another in order to keep themselves at the head of the "movement." Almost everyone involved in the reform had to do this sort of thing to some extent. B. A. Vasilchikov, MZ and director of the reform from July 1906 until May 1908, objected bitterly to the key reform law of 9 November 1906, yet he presided over its energetic execution for almost two years (Dubrovskii, 1963: 122-23). In those heady days organizations had wills of their own, and the opinions of the men "in charge" had often to be sacrificed for the sake of operation. Even if Krivoshein had had firm convictions, they probably would not have changed the process of enactment or even his role in it.

One item of information about Krivoshein's activities before 1905 is of more than passing interest. It concerns his work as head of the department of Siberian resettlement. In June 1900 peasant captains in Siberia received an order to "encourage" peasants in their areas to convert to personal holdings and form khutor farms. Shortly thereafter, according to Kaufman's account, a flood of petitions came in from peasants requesting government officials to help them break with their villages and consolidate their fields. Apparently, however, the petitions were bogus—the captains had trumped them up. Almost no khutors were actually formed, and in 1904 the officials indicated their reluctance to do any more "artificial" land settlement work until they had more information on the state of affairs in the villages (Kaufman, 1905: 99-101, 148). The temporary rules of 6 June 1904 indicated a new moderation in the government's efforts. There was to be no more "encouragement." The rules allowed very vaguely and offhandedly for the forming of khutors and otrubs in Siberia, but land reform would be permitted only when it did not produce any detrimental effects on neighboring peasants. If all this was Krivoshein's doing, which is likely, then it is no wonder he was hesitant to express his views on the peasant question before 1906. In 1904-5 he could not very well have opposed reform, but in the light of his experience what kind of reform could he have favored? We may say of Krivoshein that although he lacked a theory, he certainly had more experience at dealing with the ups and downs of peasant reform than either of his fellow enactors.

Krivoshein brought to the endless conferences and committees of 1905-6 a distinctive attitude toward reform that was missing in both Witte and Gurko. Witte spoke very little of administrative action, preferring instead to make assertions about how peasants would respond to his proposed laws. Gurko spoke often of administrative action, but what he usually had in mind were the statutory laws under which the presumed administrators would work. Krivoshein, on the other hand, spoke very little about laws and predictions of peasant behavior. Siberia seems to have taught him not to put much stock in writing laws or planning what peasants would do.

We have his note to the tsar of early February 1906 (Veselovskii, 1924: 105-10), suggesting that no matter what the government did, peasant reform would take a long time. There was no point in talking of immediate measures other than outright relief to the hungry, because there were no immediate measures. All conceivable reforms would necessarily be long range. Moreover, all reform measures were to some degree unpredictable in their effects. The central offices did not know what the peasants needed, nor were they going to know until agents went to the villages and began to work. What the government had to do, therefore, was to set up collegial commissions in the gubernias and uezds without further delay and let them find out about the peasants' problems as they operated. Then, when the central offices had learned from their experience, the government might be able to write laws. For now, let the commissions begin work and adopt measures of their own as their various locales required. Some would make mistakes, some would even do harm, but on the whole the commissions would improve the situation. In Krivoshein's own words: "The government must leave off proclaiming promises and begin at last to act. It must begin to carry out its laboriously prepared, exhaustively studied, but until now very little implemented measures to improve peasant conditions. The important thing is to act, to begin the reform, and let action itself show us the best means to accomplish our aims" (p. 109). As we shall see, this manner of proceeding became the modus operandi of the reform organization.[17]

Krivoshein's concept of reform suffered from contradictions fully as serious as those which plagued Witte's and Gurko's schemes. He was calling for an organization very similar in spirit to Pazukhin's line-over-staff visions. Indeed, Krivoshein's projected agents would perhaps be much less constrained by the forms of law and bureaucracy than Pazukhin's would-be patriarchs, for their explicit purpose was to subvert peasant institutions. What had been an unspoken implication in 1889 now emerged as a crusading passion, and crusades, it seems, are much more likely than implications to get out of hand. To be sure, Krivoshein was proposing to set up colleges of officials, not knights of virtue, but such groups could conceivably break away from the central government's control even more easily than the isolated land captains. The force of their established positions might give them a certain weight against the center—always assuming they did not break up into warring factions—as long as the center was unable to formulate precise instructions. Thus the government's commitment to action threatened to deprive the central offices of control over their agents.

Not that centralized control was necessarily an ideal characteristic for the reform organization. Supposing that St. Petersburg did retain close control over the local commissions, and supposing further that the central offices did change the reform's aims during the course of its implementation, as Krivoshein predicted they would, rapid reverses in policy would descend upon the reform's field agents and throw them into confusion. Land rearrangements and legal disputes begun under one set of directives would have to be interrupted and started over whenever a new set of rules came out. Such was the foreseeable outcome if the reform organization turned out to be the usual centralized hierarchy. However Krivoshein's vision turned out, decentralized-uncontrolled or centralized-chaotic, his refusal to commit himself to exact plans and programs did not free him from dilemmas.

Conclusion

By 1905, if not earlier, all three of our major enactors were acting in accordance with Krivoshein's philosophy. Witte and Gurko pretended to advocate coherent ideas of reform, but this was primarily because they

[17]Sidelnikov (1973: 305) says that Krivoshein wrote this note in Nov. 1905. Krivoshein's son says that his father wrote it only in late Jan. 1906 (1973: 52). In any case, Nicholas did not read the note until early Feb. 1906 (Sidelnikov, 1976: 129).

represented two competing organizational networks. Both MVD and MF felt compelled to articulate opposing arguments because they did in fact oppose one another, not because anyone had made a deep study of peasant society and developed serious convictions. Neither Witte nor Gurko knew much about peasant society, and if they had, their knowledge would not have produced an acceptable program of land reform. Krivoshein was right: action would have to show the way. Krivoshein could say this openly not only because he had the wit to perceive the reality of the government's position but also because he had no organization to uphold. As we have seen, he had been an MVD man before 1905, but in 1905-6 he found himself in the MZ, a ministry of secondary importance. The idea that the MZ might run the reform not only fostered but actually demanded Krivoshein's venturesome approach, for this relatively new office possessed no organization or ideology for peasant reform in 1905, and it would have to start from scratch to formulate them. Thus it could not have been difficult for Krivoshein to point to the weaknesses in the programs set forth under the auspices of the established ministries and to stress the advantages of an agrarian reform unburdened by preconceptions.

C. THE GOVERNMENT COMMITS ITSELF TO PEASANT REFORM, 1903-5

In the years prior to 1905, when the ministries were still assembling their ideas for peasant reform, the government as a whole was already beginning to act upon the villages, and the tsar was committing himself publicly to introduce major changes in the rural economy. The manifesto of 26 February 1903 was the first of a series of public statements declaring Nicholas's intention to take positive action to cope with the inadequacies of peasant institutions. According to this first proclamation, the coming reforms were to be based on the "inviolability" of communal ownership, but they would provide means whereby individual peasants could "depart from the village." (Savich, 1907: 3-5). Public opinion gave the February manifesto little attention; nevertheless the government's *public* stance changed sharply. Like Alexander II's rescript of 20 November 1857 (promising to free the serfs), the 1903 manifesto meant that there could be no turning back.

But there could be delay. The only immediate result of Nicholas's manifesto was the decree of 12 March 1903, which abolished much of the communal village's collective responsibility for tax paying (*TPSZ*, 22629— collective responsibility had already been abolished in noncommunal villages in 1899). As we have seen in Chapter 2 (sec. E), this measure, taken by itself, created more problems than it solved. It did not change village administration but only threw it into confusion, leaving local officials without any viable legal basis for assessing taxes or collecting them. It was not a reform but a deepening of the government's commitment to reform.

The decree of 12 December 1904 went one step further. The tsar's chief concern, it said, was "to combine peasant institutions with the general legal system of the Empire" (Savich, 1907: 6). This was rather a bald statement in the light of the tsar's assurances about the commune in his manifesto of February 1903. One would think Nicholas might have added on some small reassurance about leaving communal peasants alone, but he did not. The government was not yet prepared to speak explicitly of breaking down its guardianship over peasant tradition, but this was the first time a statement from the throne failed to speak of maintaining it. All the ministers approved (Witte, 1963: II, 331-35).[18]

The tsar's rescript of 30 March 1905 to I. L. Goremykin, ordering this old MVD hand to consider reforms in peasant landholding, went yet further. It suggested that "peasant land organization" *(zemelnyi stroi)* was the "foundation of national welfare" and that it had to be "strengthened." Measures had to be taken "to develop methods of land use for the peasants that correspond to changing economic conditions" *(IGU, 1905: 279)*. Thus in 1903 the tsar promised to allow individual peasants to leave their villages; at the end of 1904 he abandoned his pose as guarantor of village prerogatives; in March 1905 he was proposing, albeit vaguely, to attack the villages.

Gurko's memoirs suggest that March-April 1905 marked a profound shift not only in the government's public policy but also in the thinking of the government's leading officials. He tells us that in 1903-4 most government officials still believed that the communal village, for all its disadvantages, was an indispensable element in rural administration. Only a very few favored any government action to weaken the villages' power over their members, and these few were keeping silent (1939: 334). As we have seen (ch. 5, sec. B), Gurko's assumption was common among tsarist officials in the early 1900s, but it was erroneous. Most statesmen, from the tsar on down, had already come to believe that communal landholding was harmful. Moreover, Witte's committees of 1902-3, involving almost all the central government's agents in the gubernias and uezds, expressed a widespread desire to weaken the villages' traditional power, and the MF was openly encouraging them to express this desire. Likewise, the MVD's editing commission was drafting a number of provisions whose practical effect was to destroy traditional villages, both communal and noncommunal. The major change that took place in the government

---

[18]Witte claims that he drafted the decree. S. E. Kryzhanovskii, a high-ranking official in the MVD, also claims to have drafted it (1938: 19).

during 1903-4 was not in its attitude but in its publicly expressed intentions.

One of the clearest expressions of the change in the central government's public posture in early 1905 was the reception it gave to the writings of D. I. Pestrzhetskii, official in the land section and expert on peasant law. In September 1904 Pestrzhetskii gave a public lecture in which he argued that communal landholding was the chief obstacle to progress and prosperity in rural Russia. The MVD published the lecture. It went to press on 16 December 1904 and appeared in the first days of 1905 (Pestrzhetskii, 1905). In late 1905 Pestrzhetskii published a serialized article on the same theme in the *Vestnik Finansov,* a journal of the MF. This article was reviewed favorably in some detail in the *Izvestiia* of the MZ (*IGU,* 1906: 23-24), and an expanded version was then published in book form under the auspices of the MVD (Pestrzhetskii, 1906). This book was advertised enthusiastically in the January 1906 issue of the land section's *Izvestiia* (*IZO,* 1906: 42-44).

Pestrzhetskii's book of 1906 set forth a plan of peasant reform that went approximately as follows:

1) The government should strive to establish individual land ownership and eliminate interstripping (pp. 134, 142).

2) Right now, communal peasants should be granted the right to claim their strips as private property. In villages where there have been no redistributions for a long time, the government should simply declare each household to be the owner of the strips it is farming (pp. 138-40).

3) Consolidation of peasant land, however, will require much more time. "If we insist that consolidation of the land accompany its separation into personal ownership, we shall set back the transfer of the peasants to personal ownership not for decades but for centuries" (p. 141).

4) As a basis for consolidation, the government should strive to separate each *village* into a single integral lot (p. 136).

5) The best way to bring about consolidation is to encourage the gradual formation of khutors and/or otrubs by a few individuals, *either within or outside of the villages.* Their example will gradually show the way to the remainder. These few should be encouraged, but on the whole, consolidation must go forward only very slowly (pp. 144-46).

Pestrzhetskii's ideas were certainly not unique. They were in essence an amalgam of Witte's and Gurko's proposals for positive action. They are significant to us because at the end of 1905 at the latest the MF, MVD, and MZ all found them acceptable. It bears mentioning that in early 1906 Pestrzhetskii was promoted to the fourth rank *(chin)* in the civil service. This was, said the promotion order, a result of his "special projects in the land section" *(IZO,* 1906: 200). Promotion to the fourth rank, be it noted, was not merely a matter of seniority but was only awarded by the tsar for meritorious service (Lazarevskii, 1910: II, 119).

We may say that in 1905 Pestrzhetskii managed to set off sympathetic vibrations throughout the domestic administration, and this suggests that the government as a whole was convinced of the need to change the villages and was publicly committed to this enterprise. Moreover, the high-ranking servitors were generally agreed as to what the change would be. Only one question remained unanswered after March 1905: *who* would carry out the reform?

D. THE ENACTMENT PROCESS

The Goremykin Conference

The drafting of the reform began on 30 March 1905 with the calling of Goremykin's conference. According to its initial instructions, this new interministerial gathering was to articulate principles on which the forthcoming peasant reform was to be based. Actually it did do some work along these lines and came up with some compromise proposals. Unlike Pestrzhetskii's ideas, however, most of them were so moderate as to be practically meaningless. As in all the reform projects of the day, individual peasants were to be allowed to leave their villages, but Goremykin's proposals offered them no practical way to acquire land. The peasant bank was to expand its programs of land buying and selling, but only in order to make it easier for *villages* to buy land they were already renting. What this meant, in essence, was that there would be no *land* reform at all—not on peasant land, or even on nonpeasant land. Had the ideas of Goremykin's conference prevailed, the peasants might have expanded their holdings and gotten some tax relief, but the government would have withdrawn from its commitment to act upon the villages and to reform land use (Simonova, 1968: 204-7).

Witte's return to power in October 1905 made it certain that these ideas would not prevail. Goremykin's conference dragged on until January 1906, but its proposals were either ignored or co-opted by new political combinations (p. 214). It did produce one significant result, however. It devised a crude compromise plan for a reform organization and got it enacted into law. This was the decree of 6 May 1905 (Savich, 1907: 35-37).

The 6 May law did two things: (1) it set up the interministerial Committee on Land Problems to draw up legislation on the basis of the conference's forthcoming statements of principle; and (2) it reorganized the MZ with the explicit intention of making it the administrative organ for the reform. The reorganization of the MZ involved two important changes in its structure: the mining department was transferred out to the MF (and thence to the newly formed ministry of commerce and industry in October), and Krivoshein's Siberian resettlement department was transferred in from the MVD. This was far from a complete organizational scheme for a reform, and it was by no means a final, irrevocable decision; nevertheless, the 6 May law did signify that the government was seeking to effect a compromise between the MF and MVD. Ultimately it did serve as the basis on which the reform organization was established.

Many agencies having to do with peasant administration remained outside the newly reorganized ministry: chiefly the land section in the MVD, the peasant bank in the MF, and the land survey section *(mezhevaia chast)* in the ministry of justice. The MZ never did take over all the agencies concerned with peasant life, and the reform would eventually involve all the above ministries jointly. In May 1905, however, none of this was clear. Proposals were afoot to get all these agencies together. Goremykin rejected a distinctly anti-MF suggestion to transfer the peasant bank into the MZ. On the other hand, he sought (without success) to switch the MVD's land section, together with its captains, into the new ministry to serve as its executive agency (Simonova, 1968: 202). As for the survey section, the editing commission's projects of 1902-3 had insisted emphatically on transferring it from justice to the MVD *(Svod...po proektu pravil,* 1906: 100-108), but in 1905 no one seems to have wanted to offend the minister of justice by trying to take away his section. The section's place in the administrative structure and its role in the reform were finally determined only in October 1908 *(Desiatiletie,* 1916: 3-4, 13).

In sum, Goremykin's conference failed to produce any measures of agrarian reform, but it did set up two elements of a reform organization. Only one proved to be significant. The new MZ enjoyed a relatively long life and played a vital role in the reform. The other, the Committee on Land Problems never really came into existence; I have found no indication that it ever met. It was formally abolished by Krivoshein's decree of 4 March 1906 (see below).

It is of more than passing interest that the new MZ actually ceased to be formally a ministry. The decree of 6 May made it a "chief administration" *(glavnoe upravlenie),* and until late 1915 the letter of the law continued to regard the "minister" as a mere "chief administrator." "Chief administration" was an ambiguous term. Usually it referred to a section *within* a ministry, but sometimes, on rare occasions, chief administrations came into existence whose heads possessed the prerogatives of ministers. The chief administration for land settlement and agriculture was one of these.

Despite its ambiguous title, the new chief administration became the most powerful "ministry" in the government, and for this reason the act of reducing its formal status has generally been passed off as a mere shuffling of papers. More than one "insider" has stated confidently that the only purpose was to compel the incumbent minister, A. S. Ermolov, an old Witte ally, to resign, thereby allowing Goremykin to appoint a man of his choice (Witte, 1960: III, 207).

I think, however, that the intent behind the 6 May law went deeper. Judging from the efforts of Goremykin's supporters to shift the land section into the MZ, their overall purpose was to render the new reform organization dependent on the MVD. In the MVD's view, the MZ was not trustworthy. With its "Third Element" agronomists and its quasi-democratic local societies, it could hardly be expected to mount an invasion of the villages or even participate in one; yet the reform would demand agronomists. Goremykin probably considered it politic to leave these potentially rebellious experts under a superficially separate organization while making sure that the land section and its captains would be able to direct the organization's operations. The MVD could appear to compromise with the MF by surrendering direct control over the reform to the MZ, but at the same time, by reducing the MZ to a lower-level body, the old-time peasant "guardians" could guide its work to suit themselves. In a word, the new MZ was to be a device, not the leading authority over the coming reform. Ostensibly the fruit of self-effacing compromise between the two leading ministries, the new chief administration was actually designed to be an instrument for whichever one could appoint his own man to head it. This, doubtless, is the main reason why the position of "chief administrator" shifted so rapidly during the ensuing year.

The Legislation of November 1905

Beginning in September 1905, when Witte returned in triumph from Portsmouth, the major development in the enactment process appears to have been his campaign to regain the initiative in the struggle over the reform organization. He became chairman of the newly powerful Council of Ministers on 19 October, the day of its establishment, and in the ensuing months two of the three key reform laws were formulated and published. We shall not be very far from the truth if we say they were products of Witte's campaign.[19]

[19]The reformed Council of Ministers is described in Szeftel (1963: 488-92).

On 3 November, two weeks after Witte took over the council, the tsar issued two decrees, both approved by the council. The first ordered that the peasants' redemption payments be lowered by one-half in 1906 and canceled altogether as of 1 January 1907 (*TPSZ*, 26872). The second liberalized the terms on which the peasant bank made its loans (*TPSZ*, 26873).

Canceling the redemption debt was not simply an act of benevolence. In a substantial number of villages—those which had once been the property of serfowners—it wiped out much of the legal authority of the village institutions. Since the Liberation, the redemption debt had been the only *legal* basis for compelling former serfs to remain in their village communities and accept the authority of village custom over their lands. The statute of 14 December 1893 (*TPSZ*, 10151) had given villages the power to prevent a member from paying his share of the debt ahead of his neighbors, but no law had explicitly revoked the right of a member to depart from the village without the village's consent if and when his share of the debt was paid. On 1 January 1907, with the debt canceled, it would become theoretically possible for former serfs to separate themselves from their villages whenever they wished and, in communal villages, to claim their shares of land as their own.[20]

But this reasoning had no real validity, owing to the persistent obscurity of peasant legislation since 1861. A number of laws and Senate decisions gave force to the principle that a peasant separating from a communal village had no claim to compensation for his strips of land. And even if this problem were ignored and the terms of the Liberation statute taken to be the actual law of the land, many of these terms applied only to ex-serfs. In particular, the famous article 165 of the statute on redemption (*VPSZ*, 36659)—the key provision that allowed an

---

[20]It should be emphasized that the cancellation of redemption debts was in fact benevolent, for Soviet scholars have distorted the matter with an unusual lack of restraint. Dubrovskii asserts that since the 3 Nov. law did not mention arrears, the peasants had to go on paying them until 1917 (1963: 90). He seems unaware that all arrears in redemption payments had been canceled by the decree of 11 Aug. 1904 (*IZO*, 1904: 3), which announced the birth of Nicholas's son Aleksei. The only arrears left to be paid after 1906 were those which accumulated during the period 11 Aug. 1904–1 Jan. 1907. On 1 Jan. 1909 these amounted to 35.5 million rubles, and a year later they came to 28.8 million (*IZO*, 1910: 169). If this was a typical year, the burden of arrears payments during the reform era came to 6.7 million rubles annually. Anfimov tells us that actual payments amounted to 14 million rubles in 1910, 10 million in 1911, and 8.8 million in 1912 (1962: 258), but even if he is correct, it was hardly a crushing burden. Compare these figures with the 886 million rubles spent on *legal* vodka during 1913. In 1913 even this token collection came to an end. Neither Dubrovskii nor Anfimov troubles to mention it, but the decree of 21 Feb. 1913 canceled all redemption arrears (*IZO*, 1913: 57).

ex-serf who paid off his share of the communal debt to claim his strips as personal property and even to consolidate them—had never been extended to cover peasants on state and crown lands. In short, the legislation in force in November 1905 gave no clear indication whether or not a debt-free member of a communal village actually had the right to depart or to demand compensation for his share of the village land in the event of his departure. The first of the 3 November decrees did not "liberate" the peasantry from their villages but only hinted at their liberation.[21]

The statutes of the reform never escaped from the vagaries of nineteenth-century legislation. The law of 9 November 1906 brought former peasants of the state and crown lands into the same category as ex-serfs (Sidelnikov, 1980: 97), and for over two years the reform organization operated on the assumption that *all* lands received by peasants during the process of carrying out the Liberation were indeed allotment lands. But then two Senate decisions—those of 18 February 1909 and 22 February 1910—noted that the 9 November law did not apply to former serf households whose forebears of the 1860s had avoided redemption payments by agreeing to accept small (one-quarter) allotments of land (*IZO*, 1912: 106). What a shock the Senate's discovery must have been to the unfortunate peasants and administrators who had already converted such lands to personal property in 1907-8 or, worse yet, had actually consolidated them.[22]

It seemed that the more elaborate reform laws of 14 June 1910 and 29 May 1911 (see ch. 9, sec. B) would at last take care of the irregularities in pre-1905 statutes regarding peasant land rights, but even these relatively detailed enactments did not provide for all varieties of peasant village. For example, the MVD found itself unable to decide whether or not the June 1910 law applied to villages of "free plowmen," i.e., those

---

[21]Chernyshev notes that Stishinskii was the only leading statesman involved in the reform who was aware of these legal difficulties in 1905-6 (1918: 358). In Mar. 1906 the united departments of the State Council decided by a vote of 23 to 17 that no special legislation was needed prior to 1 Jan. 1907 to assure communal peasants of the right to claim their lands as private property. According to the majority, the redemption statute of 1861 already provided for this (TsGIAL, f. 1291, op. 122, 1906g., d. 12, l. 196). According to the eminent legal scholar Khauke, however, Stishinskii was right and the majority were wrong (1913: 65-66). Article 12 in the "general regulations on peasants" in the Russian "code" of laws *(Svod Zakonov)* did extend article 165 of the redemption statute to all peasants (Sidelnikov, 1980: 95), but the *Svod* by itself lacked legal force.

[22]The 9 Nov. law is discussed more fully in ch. 7, sec. A. The MVD really did apply this law to one-quarter allotments during the early years of the reform. See, e.g., an MVD explanation of 1907 (*IZO*, 1907: 303); some decisions of the Saratov gubernia board and the land section in 1907-8 (TsGIAL, f. 1291, op. 120, 1908g., d. 106, ll. 76-77, 80-81); and a land section memo as late as 31 Mar. 1910 (f. 408, op. 1, 1909g., d. 129, ll. 129-31).

peasants who had been released from serf status prior to 1861. The legislation of the nineteenth century failed to establish whether or not their land constituted "allotment land," and in 1910 the government still found itself unable to decide the matter (TsGIAL, f. 1291, op. 120, 1909g., d. 102, ll. 15-16, 122-23).

More important, the new reform laws of 1910 and 1911 also failed to deal with the problem of households in communal villages whose members had abandoned their shares of village land and taken up residence elsewhere. According to existing statutes, these expatriates, some of whom had long since abandoned farming, retained the right to demand a share of village land whenever the village held a redistribution. After 1906 they had excellent practical reasons for exercising this right. Village land no longer required redemption payments; better yet, it could be converted to personal property and then sold or rented. A "proletarian" whose father had abandoned his debt-burdened strips 30 or 40 years before suddenly found himself entitled to a share of some very profitable real estate (see, e.g., op. 63, 1907g., d. 17, l. 39; Shapkarin, 1966: 283-85).

Obviously these homecoming proletarians constituted a threat to communal villages, but they interest us even more because their existence jeopardized the privateness of the "property" received by resident members who took advantage of the reform to separate from their villages. The 9 November law provided that a separating household was entitled to either the strips it was using at the time it separated or, under some circumstances, the strips it had received at the last official redistribution. This provision was the statutory basis for a separator's right to his land. But this right was not clear. If the village held another redistribution at some time after the separator had claimed his strips, and a long-absent homecomer from the city turned up to demand a share, then *all* households had to surrender portions of their land in order that the returning proletarian could acquire his just portion. Given this state of affairs, was it just that peasants who had claimed their strips as personal property should now be free of any obligation to surrender their share to the homecomer? In 1907 a fair number of communal peasants were already raising this question when they voiced their protests against their "progressive" neighbors' attempts to claim shares of communal land as personal property. If some households did this, the protestors said, then the remaining villagers would have to bear the full burden of providing shares to any would-be homecomers (TsGIAL, f. 1291, op. 63, 1907g., d. 10, ll. 22-24; d. 14, l. 43).

The land section manifested impatience with these protests. The peasants, it said, were mistaken. The new personal property holders would indeed have to assume their share of the burden imposed by homecomers. The best way to manage this, suggested the section officials, was to satisfy the homecomers' claims with cash instead of land. Then the village would have only to bill the separators for their share, and both "private" owners and communal holders would be satisfied (d. 10, ll. 22-24). Technically, this reassurance from St. Petersburg proved to be correct, and it was ultimately upheld by the Senate (*IZO*, 1913: 208-9). The rights of peasants who remained in communes were protected, assuming that they had sufficient capital to buy out homecomers and that local officials were aware of their superiors' views on this subject. For progressive farmers and zealots for reform, however, the government's concern for communal peasants' rights marked a severe setback. The tsarist government was admitting that villagers who converted their land to personal property *and went on to consolidate it* would still be bound by communal obligations. The laws of 1910 and 1911 did nothing to alter this sticky state of affairs. We may say, therefore, that they still did not provide their beneficiaries with "private property."

In practice, the government's agents could make it difficult for returning proletarians to take advantage of their erstwhile fellow-villagers. Each redistribution had to have the approval of the uezd congress, and the records of congress actions toward the end of the reform indicate that petitions to redistribute did not go through easily (see, e.g., op. 121, 1915g., d. 6). Generally speaking, only a redistribution petition with a village's unanimous support stood a chance of getting government approval. The legal procedure for forcing a village to provide land to a homecomer was certainly no clearer than legal guarantees of "personal property." Moreover, the resident villagers had effective ways to make life unpleasant for outsiders. The fact remains, however, that *law* never did evolve to the point where it guaranteed new property rights against traditional claims (Khauke, 1913: 115-17).

I refer to these examples of the erratic nature of tsarist law making to emphasize the point that the theoretical implications of the November decrees had no force in themselves. In an orderly legal system the removal of legal barriers to an action may constitute permission to take the action, but this could not be assumed to be true in tsarist law. On 1 January 1907, when peasants began to claim their ancient right to separate from their villages, there would be no procedure by which they could exercise this right nor any law to define their new relationships with their neighbors and the government. Administrators would not know what to do with would-be separators; judges would have no basis for resolving civil disputes. The peasants would have no rights, only the government's promise to extend rights to them. The 3 November decrees, like all the legislation of peasant reform since 1903, did not yet set a reform in motion but only deepened the government's commitment to enact one. In effect the government was giving itself 14 months to bring its laws up to date with the new situation its own decrees had created.

It is probable that the decrees of 3 November reflected Witte's notions of land reform at that time. I cannot say, however, whether he actually initiated them. The decree on redemption payments was fobbed off as a "liberal" measure; consequently Witte claims in his memoirs that he was responsible for enacting it and, indeed, had been trying to enact such a measure for years (1960: II, 497). This is a flat lie. He and his "liberal" assistant, N. N. Kutler, had strenuously opposed a recommendation to cancel the redemption debt in 1902-3 (Simonova, 1971: 262). Nevertheless, Witte did support the cancellation in November. On the MVD side, Gurko had spoken in favor of cancellation in the summer of 1905, and Goremykin had been assuming as early as April that the debt would be canceled in the near future (Simonova, 1968: 203, 212). By the fall of 1905, then, just about everyone favored cancellation of the redemption debt. It seems fruitless to seek a particular faction or person in the government who was responsible for the decrees of 3 November.[23]

The next step, however, was all Witte. On 16 November 1905 the MF published an "appeal" to uezd zemstvoes to come to the aid of the peasant bank. It was an unofficial appeal, entitled simply "From the Ministry of Finance," but it was official enough to appear in the government's own daily paper, the *Pravitelstvennyi Vestnik* (p. 2). Of course Witte was not the MF in November 1905; he was chairman of the Council of Ministers. Apparently, however, he was able to manipulate the incumbent minister, I. L. Shipov, an old friend and trusted subordinate. Shipov had accompanied Witte to Portsmouth in the summer of 1905 and had then been promoted to MF at his old chief's insistence. It was Shipov's cooperation that allowed Witte to issue the ministry's appeal of 16 November.[24]

The appeal requested zemstvoes to set up local (uezd) committees for the purpose of smoothing relations between the peasant bank and the peasants. Only with the uezd zemstvoes' help, said the appeal, could the bank expand its operations quickly enough to respond to the peasants' needs. Witte's underlying purpose here is obvious. He believed that if the peasant bank and the zemstvoes could work together on a large scale to buy and distribute land to promising peasant farmers, the MF would be

[23] A. F. Meiendorf, who was an experienced servitor in the MVD's land section, an expert on peasant law, a first cousin and intimate advisor to Stolypin, and, in general, a man who knew what he was talking about, maintains that it was Goremykin who initiated the proposal to cancel the redemption debt (Meiendorf, "Brief," p. 10).

[24] On Witte's relationship with Shipov, see Kokovtsov (1935: 84). In one section of his memoirs Witte explicitly denies that Shipov was "his man" (1960: III, 346). In another, however, he suggests that Shipov was a pliable tool for his superiors (I, 365-66).

able to conduct an agrarian reform without having to rely on MVD
agencies or to involve itself directly in the intricacies of village land
arrangements. If Witte could get such a reform in motion without having
to risk the pitfalls of the government's formal legislative process, then his
fellow statesmen would find it very hard to stop him. Witte had been
none too friendly with the zemstvoes in the past, but since 1901 relations
had been much more cordial. Now the local assemblies appeared to be
highly desirable allies. They had some contact with the rural populace,
their lack of financial resources made them responsive to purse strings,
and they possessed technical staffs. Most important, they shared Witte's
distrust of the MVD. By adroit use of subsidies, Witte could expand the
zemstvoes' operations and strengthen their position vis-á-vis other ministerial agencies while tightening his own control over them. This was
approximately the reasoning that made him into a champion of "autonomous institutions" in 1904-5 and moved him to send out his appeal on
16 November.

The appeal was accompanied by a much quieter campaign to marshal the MF's tax inspectors as agencies of the peasant bank. On 26
November, only ten days after the appeal went out to the zemstvoes, the
head of the peasant bank asked the gubernia fiscal chambers to make
inspectors available immediately to help buy up estate land as fast as
possible. The idea, said the note, was to get some land into peasant
hands in time to stave off rural violence during the following year
(TsGIAL, f. 592, op. 1, d. 216, ll. 2-3). It seems, then, that Witte had
more on his mind in November 1905 than expanding zemstvo participation in government. As it turned out, the tax inspectors did not play as
major a role in the buying and selling of estates as the bank hoped in
November 1905 (see, e.g., ll. 14-15), but the effort to involve them continued at least until the end of 1907 (ll. 54-60).

Taken together, the three measures of November 1905 embodied an
embryonic reform. Each *attempted* to solve one of the three main problems arising from the individual peasant's liberation from his village:
freeing him from its constraints, providing the resources to set him up on
a farm of his own, and establishing an organization to supervise the
operation. The canceling of redemption payments was a long step toward
getting him out; the liberalizing of the peasant bank's terms helped him
to buy land; and the zemstvoes, Witte hoped, would form the requisite
organization. As will be seen, all the laws enacted in the following year
were conceived to deal with one or more of these general problems,
though they did not accord with Witte's plan.

The Kutler Proposal

At the same time Witte was turning to the zemstvoes, he installed
one of his loyal subordinates as MZ. Here he was following in Goremy-

kin's footsteps. Goremykin had not only reorganized the MZ in May 1905 but also installed his ally, P. Kh. Shvanebakh, at its head. Shvanebakh, one of Witte's bitterest enemies, was abruptly replaced in October by Nikolai N. Kutler, who had been Witte's right-hand man for dealing with peasants ever since the 1890s.[25]

Spurred on by Witte, Kutler drafted a scheme for agrarian reform and brought it before the Council of Ministers in late December 1905 (Dubrovskii, 1963: 90-93). The council debated the plan, but on 10 January 1906 Witte wrote a report to the tsar in which he admitted that his ministers could not agree. Under the circumstances, he said rather lamely, the whole matter of agrarian reform might best be left for the Duma to decide (Sidelnikov, 1973: 55-57; Veselovskii, 1924: 12). Thus perished Kutler's scheme. Nicholas treated the hapless MZ with unusual harshness. He drove Kutler not only from his post but completely out of government service, denying him even the conventional dignity of an appointment to the State Council. But if Kutler's scheme lost all practical significance for the administrative politicians of early 1906, it is still of crucial importance to the historian. It tells us far more clearly than any of Witte's own words what Witte was up to during his last few months of power.[26]

Kutler's proposal (Veselovskii, 1924: 27-41) included two elements: an organization and a set of functions for the organization to perform. The field agencies of the organization were to be land settlement commissions, which were to be set up on the uezd and gubernia levels under the central direction of an interministerial land settlement committee. The latter would be chaired by the MZ. The commissions were to be chaired by salaried agents of the MZ, but they would be made up mostly of elected representatives from the zemstvoes. They were *not* to include those old bastions of MVD power, the governors, gentry marshals, and chairmen of zemstvo directorates. The central committee would be half administrators appointed by the tsar and half Duma representatives elected by the Duma (pp. 38-39).

Kutler added an explanatory note to his project (pp. 42-63) in which he set forth the ends he hoped his organization would achieve. They were twofold, including both long-term operations designed to raise peasant productivity and short-term measures to alleviate land shortage (p. 42). Kutler did not say anything specific in his note about peasant produc-

[25]Shvanebakh was also an old MF hand, but he hated Witte and all his works (Shvanebakh, 1918: 115; Von Laue, 1963: 279-83).

[26]Witte denies that he had anything to do with Kutler's proposals (1960: III, 199-202), but his contemporaries are unanimous in assigning him a significant role in their conception (e.g., Gurko, 1939: 325; Shidlovskii, 1923: I, 88-89; Kokovtsov, 1935: 100; Kryzhanovskii, 1938: 62; Liubimov, 259). See also Simonova (1968: 210-11, 215) and Sidelnikov (1980: 57-58).

tivity, but his earlier writings suggest that he had in mind Witte's general aim of turning some peasants into modern farmers while driving others into factories (p. 42; Simonova, 1971: 253-54). Obviously this would take a very long time, Kutler admitted, so the commissions should occupy themselves at first with the more readily realizable goal of relieving land shortage. The commissions' first task would be to find peasants who needed land and to help the peasant bank buy up nonpeasant land to sell to them. The simplest and most rapid way to begin this enterprise was to find peasants who were already renting land and sell them that land (Veselovskii, 1924: 29-32, 47). This was so urgent a measure that the commissions were empowered in many cases to *force* owners of rented land to sell it at a price established by the government (pp. 29-32).

Kutler's (and Witte's) insistence on the distribution of nonpeasant land to peasants attracted more attention than any other part of the plan. It is also the part that interests us here. What did Witte have in mind? Did he wish to bring relief to the poor? He said he did in late 1905, but if this was true, then he was going directly against everything he had done since he entered the government. Did he think expropriation would appease peasant wrath and head off revolution? He said he did, but if he meant it, he was far more ignorant of the realities of the countryside than even his worst enemies believed. Kutler does not appear to have been ignorant of these realities, and it comes as no surprise, therefore, to discover that in previous years he had not considered land shortage to be a major problem (Simonova, 1971: 253-54). In other words, barring some sort of religious conversion in 1905, Kutler did not really care about handing out land to poor peasants. He wanted to get his hands on a fair amount of land in order to carry out a land reform. It is my contention that neither Witte nor Kutler actually believed in soothing angry peasants. What they both wanted was to impose agrarian reform on the peasantry without having to rely on the MVD's agencies. They wanted to rely solely on the peasant bank and zemstvoes to break down communal landholding, encourage the consolidation of land, weaken the villages' authority over their members, and, in general, convert peasants into citizens (see Veselovskii, 1924: 42-45; Simonova, 1968: 208-9).

Two points must be made with regard to Kutler's program for land expropriation. It was not likely to alleviate poverty, and even if it had somehow produced this effect, it would not have appeased peasant wrath, for it was not in fact a short-term operation.

To take up the first point, Kutler's project required peasants to pay for their new land, and their new mortgage installments would have to be at least as much as the rent they were already paying. Perhaps they would be much more. Kutler called upon the MZ's commissions and the peasant bank to determine the price peasants would have to pay for the expropriated land, and they were to make their calculations without regard for the price the government had paid to the original owners. This may have had a reassuring sound to it. Local autonomous institutions, equated in many capital-city minds with virtue and wisdom, would protect the peasants from scheming speculators and all the eccentricities of the market. In fact, however, the government had only limited financial resources, and it could not afford to cut too much off the price it paid to the landlords. It would pay a high price because Kutler's plan gave the landlord-dominated uezd zemstvoes a predominant influence in the new commissions. Thus Kutler did not seriously contemplate cutting peasant payments very far below existing rents. It followed that the financial burden on the peasants would not have been relieved by Kutler's expropriations. Very likely, it would have grown heavier.

Probably as a result of such considerations, Kutler offered no justification for the forced sale of land to the peasants except some urgent remarks to the effect that the government needed to do something *immediately* to stave off revolutionary violence. Forced sales, he insisted, were the only measure of reform that could be carried out quickly (Veselovskii, 1924: 42). But Kutler's own note indicated that the government could complete the necessary distribution of estate lands in one year only if it had about 4,000 surveyors (assuming that one surveyor could measure off at least 270 acres each day). With 1,300 surveyors, Kutler added, it would take three years (p. 61). In fact, the government had only about 200 surveyors available for fieldwork in 1906, and it would take until 1908 to raise this figure to over 1,300 (*Desiatiletie,* 1916: 17). At best, Kutler's "immediate" program would take at least until 1910 to complete. So much for the idea of distributing land to head off revolutionary violence. Understandably the tsar rejected Kutler's project and with it Kutler himself. Witte had overreached himself.

I am not suggesting that Kutler and Witte were dishonest or foolish. The point is that they had something in mind other than peasant welfare and fear of revolution. Had Kutler's project been approved, his MZ-led commissions would have been able to wield considerable power in their uezds. They and the MF's peasant bank would have been in a position to decide which lands were to be expropriated, the price owners would receive, and the price peasants would pay (Veselovskii, 1924: 32-34). These commissions would have carried weight, and they could, conceivably, have used their weight to achieve any number of purposes.

The following rules were to govern the MZ commissions' operations. Land having special economic value—e.g., orchards, land under garden crops, fields on which modern agricultural methods were being used— was not to be subject to expropriation at all. Land being used by its owner but not possessing special value could be expropriated, but no more than one-half of a very large estate could be taken, one-third of a medium-sized estate, or one-fifth of a small estate. Unused fields or fields rented out to tenants were all subject to expropriation. No estates were to be expropriated in a locale unless the peasants who lived there actually needed land. No peasant receiving expropriated land could possess a total area above a certain prescribed amount. The owner of an estate marked for expropriation was to have six months warning before a commission could take his land, so that he would have an opportunity to sell his land to the peasant bank on his own. When a commission actually came to the point of taking land, it was, if possible, to take the outer portions of an estate and leave the inner part to the estate owner (pp. 29-32).

These were vague rules. They would allow local commissions wide latitude to decide who would get land or lose it and at what price. With the backing of a united central bureaucracy, a commission could easily use the land it acquired to encourage land reform by individual farmers and undermine villages. Thus, if Kutler's project held forth little promise as a device to stop violence, it was still, potentially, an effective basis for imposing an agrarian reform without the participation of the MVD.

Witte vs. Krivoshein: Enacting the Law of 4 March 1906

Toward the end of January it began to appear as if Witte would lose everything as a result of Kutler's political demise. Not only was Kutler to be ousted, said the irate Nicholas, but the hated Krivoshein was to be raised up from deputy minister to take his place. This was the time when Krivoshein had the wisdom or good luck to get his note (sec. B) before Nicholas, demanding peasant reform and committing himself at last to an opinion on what the reform should be. As might be expected, he was strongly opposed to the Witte-Kutler proposal. Krivoshein pointed out, among other things, that both rich and poor peasants were rioting, and he concluded from this that bringing relief to the poor would not stop riots. In any case, the government's purpose should be to extend the regime of private property and its incentives, not to destroy it by arbitrary confiscation. These Gurkoesque remarks, which came at the beginning of Krivoshein's note, must have helped very much to attract the tsar's favorable attention. On 3 February Nicholas sent the note along to the Council of Ministers with approving comments in the margins. Kutler's formal dismissal came the following day.

But Witte fought back. When Nicholas first revealed his intention to make Krivoshein MZ, the hard-pressed industrializer of Russia threatened to resign. The big loan was still in jeopardy, so the hard-pressed tsar reluctantly agreed to make Krivoshein only the acting minister until Witte found a suitable replacement. Witte had made a mistake, but he still carried weight. He obligingly denied that he had had anything to do with Kutler's plan and hastily found a replacement for his disgraced former colleague. This was A. P. Nikolskii, who became MZ on 27 February. Poor Krivoshein found himself once again a deputy minister.[27]

Apparently Witte was back in the saddle by early March, but the month of February had been Krivoshein's. Before the latter's abrupt demotion he managed to twist Kutler's proposed organization around a bit and to get a new version of it enacted into law. This was the decree of 4 March (Savich, 1907: 38-41), representing in essence a meeting of the minds between Krivoshein and Gurko and, more generally, an effective compromise between MVD and MZ. Needless to say, the new organization was not pleasing to Witte.

The provisions of the 4 March decree will be discussed more fully in Chapter 7 (sec. A). A few general points will suffice here. Kutler's uezd and gubernia commissions were changed to include governors, gentry marshals, and chairmen of zemstvo directorates. There would still be elected men on both uezd and gubernia commissions but not as many as Kutler had wanted. The central committee was to be reconstituted as the chief committee for land settlement, and *all* its members would be bureaucrats appointed, ex officio, by the tsar. Finally, Krivoshein's law referred briefly to the local, zemstvo-elected commissions for which Witte had "appealed" back in November. It ordered them—wherever they might exist—to "cooperate" with the new commissions, i.e., to do what they were told or else get out of the way (pp. 38-39).[28]

Like Kutler's commissions, Krivoshein's were ordered to give first priority to helping the peasant bank sell nonpeasant land to peasants; encouraging gradual land settlement in the villages was still considered to be of secondary importance. One wonders if Krivoshein had changed his mind about the proper course of land reform. His law gave the peasant bank's operations the highest priority, whereas his earlier note to the tsar had said that helping the bank with land sales should never be anything but a small matter. Here and there a peasant or two could use some assistance in buying land, the note had said, but in the main the new commissions should get to work directly on village lands (Veselovskii, 1924: 107-8). The fact is, Krivoshein had not changed his mind. The 4 March decree's emphasis on land distribution was only a facade. Krivoshein did want his new commissions to work closely with the peasant

---

[27]Nikolskii was an old protégé of Witte's who had written a book in 1902 strongly disapproving of communal landholding. He had also pointed out the futility of any attempt to codify peasant law and recommended instead the abrupt introduction of civil rights into the villages, a measure which he carefully (and naively) distinguished from the compulsory abolition of communal landholding (1902: 18-21, 69-93, 181-95).

[28]The considerations of the Council of Ministers regarding the 4 Mar. law prescribed that the zemstvo-elected bodies should "combine" *(slitsia)* with the new commissions (Savich, 1907: 41).

bank, but the primary purpose of their work was to be the reform of village land, not the selling of nonpeasant land to the poor. Krivoshein had merely taken a new tack in the interministerial battle. He and Gurko were trying hard throughout the month of February to get the peasant bank out of the MF and into the MZ, with the apparent intention of diverting its resources to village reform. Their basic idea was to compel the bank to divert its resources from nonpeasant land to the villages; that is, they intended to make it accept allotment land as collateral for its loans—something the bank had never done before (see Sidelnikov, 1980: 68).

Witte managed to stop Krivoshein's move to kidnap the peasant bank. In the conference that drafted the 4 March decree, only Gurko supported Krivoshein's more ambitious organizational designs (Veselovskii, 1924: 104). The majority of the members approved the 4 March decree but voted to leave the bank in the MF, and the Council of Ministers backed the majority, saying that the union of the bank with the MZ would be "untimely" (pp. 122-23). At the end of Krivoshein's February offensive, then, the MF still had the bank, and Witte had suffered nothing more than the embarrassment of having to order the MF to alter the bank's procedures to meet the new demand to sell land to individuals in consolidated lots (p. 123). Witte was smarting, but he would still have something to work with when he began to rebuild his shattered organization in March.[29]

The February concord between Gurko and Krivoshein seems to have emerged from the general frenzy in the Council of Ministers to agree on something before the State Duma met. Ever since the Duma's establishment in August of the previous year, the ministers had been working under pressure to unite themselves behind a program of peasant reform. By February 1906 time was running out. The Duma was scheduled to convene on 22 April. Under the circumstances, compromise seems to have come a little easier than usual. Gurko and Krivoshein found it especially easy to come to terms. Their views had never been very far apart, and they both had reason to oppose Witte. At the council meeting of 24 January the ministers were able to agree to strip the land captain of his judicial prerogatives and make him give way before new, all-class local institutions. Also, the peasants were somehow to be freed from the bonds of communal ownership (TsGIAL, f. 1276, op. 2, 1906g., d. 4, ll. 12-16).

[29] An expression of the MF's bitter reaction to the 4 Mar. decree (as approved on 17 Feb.) may be found in a note of 28 Feb. 1906, written by A. Putilov, director of the peasant bank. Putilov denounced Krivoshein's new organization on the grounds that the zemstvoes would not cooperate with it (Veselovskii, 1924: 146-47).

The cementing of the Gurko-Krivoshein alliance seems to have taken place sometime after 10 February. In its meeting of that day the Council of Ministers was still unfriendly to the upstart Krivoshein. Many ministers doubted that the MZ could handle an agrarian reform. Its personnel were technicians, and the council thought that a social reform required experienced leaders. True, Goremykin's conference had reorganized the MZ to carry out the reform back in May 1905, but perhaps after all it would be wiser to put the MVD in charge. So said the "memoria" from the council (Veselovskii, 1924: 120-22). But Krivoshein attached a note of his own to this document, presenting his view that the MZ would have to be in charge of land settlement (p. 123). The tsar read Krivoshein's argument and noted in the margin that he agreed (p. 122). Armed with Nicholas's support, Krivoshein brought Gurko around. On 17 February the council approved the project that was to become the 4 March decree, thereby establishing once and for all that the MZ, whatever it was, would run the reform.

Witte's Last Gasp: The Nikolskii Commission

After 27 February, with Krivoshein out of the council and Nikolskii in, Witte found himself in a position to make one more effort to salvage his schemes. The thorny question of expropriation had been laid to rest by the tsar, and some of the differences between MF and MVD had been resolved by the compromises in the 4 March decree. It now appeared that the Council of Ministers might agree on a reform program. A memorandum from the council meeting of 5 March proclaimed the ministers' intention to do just this as speedily as possible. If the Duma had to cope with government-sponsored programs, the council hoped, then its members would be less likely to waste time on idle controversies. The projects were to be drafted by an interministerial commission under the chairmanship of the new MZ, Nikolskii (TsGIAL, f. 1291, op. 122, 1906g., d. 35, ll. 4-6).

But Witte and his council wanted to do more than draft programs for the Duma to consider; they also wanted to get some kind of immediate reform measures underway before the Duma met, measures ostensibly designed to relieve land shortage and at the same time to make some provision for the change in peasant status that was to occur on 1 January 1907. On this both MF and MVD were agreed. An interministerial conference under Gurko had already agreed on a draft explicitly allowing individual peasants in communal villages to claim their strips as personal property, and on 10 March the Council of Ministers voted to send it to the State Council for approval (d. 12, ll. 41, 49-51).

On 18 March the united departments of the State Council rejected Gurko's measures. The main reason, said the majority of the members:

such important legislative acts should have the forthcoming Duma's sanction (ll. 196-200; Gerbe, 1911: 117). But even if the ministers failed to get their immediate measures through, it is still significant that they could agree in early March on a concrete piece of legislation specifically requiring villages to adhere to the government's legal system. To be sure, substantive disagreements among the ministers had never been very sharp, but organizational rivalry between MF and MVD had hitherto prevented the enactment of any substantial change in village law. Now, in March 1906, the Council of Ministers' agreement on this matter suggested that Witte, Gurko, and Krivoshein had resolved their differences, at least momentarily. The need for action had at last driven the MF and MVD to compromise.[30]

Once united on the reform's substantive provisions, the ministers moved with unprecedented rapidity. Urged on by Witte and his newly united council, Nikolskii's commission (which included Gurko and Krivoshein among its members) held its first meeting on 10 March and decided, not surprisingly, that its general aim was to bring peasants into a common legal framework with the rest of society. The members agreed as to which ministries should write up which law projects, but, fearing that the drafting of legislative acts might stir up new interministerial controversies, they also decided to ask the Council of Ministers whether each minister should write up a full-scale project to bring before the Duma or merely submit a general statement of purpose (TsGIAL, f. 1291, op. 122, 1906g., d. 35, ll. 8-13). The ministries had already written up some projects and were to write a few more in the ensuing months, but the council decided not to present any of these to the Duma at once. Instead, the commission was instructed to greet the Duma with a list of general "bases" for discussion.

Forty "bases" were duly drawn up and submitted to the council, whence Witte brought them to the tsar (f. 1276, op. 2, 1906g., d. 4, ll. 209-14). One of them proposed to eliminate the land captains and the entire administrative apparatus for governing peasant villages (basis 4). Others called for all-class institutions of government in villages, volosts, and *uchastki* to supplement the existing zemstvoes (bases 8-18). Others provided for land settlement on peasant lands (bases 19-27) and for land sales to the peasants (bases 28-32, 34-40). And of course the peasants were to have the benefits of modern law, which meant, among other

[30]The Gurko conference's proposals were ultimately incorporated, with a few changes, into the 9 Nov. 1906 decree, and Dubrovskii has concluded that they were the basis for this decree (1963: 98-100). Gurko (1939: 499-500) makes the same claim. As will be seen, however, there was too much reshuffling of proposals between March and November to make the similarity between the earlier project and the final decree any more than coincidental.

things, the adoption of the old Witte-Gurko-Pestrzhetskii proposal that communal villages without redistributions for a long time were to be transformed abruptly into villages of personal property holders (basis 2).

Ostensibly the fundamental assumption underlying these bases was that the government was not going to *force* peasants into reform. A peasant village of the traditional sort—now renamed a *zemelnoe obshchestvo,* per the MVD's project of 1902-3—would still be able to maintain its separate customary order if its members so desired. Custom, however, was no longer to have any *legal* force. *Zemelnye obshchestva* were to be free societies whose members could resign whenever they liked. Had the Nikolskii bases been enacted into law, traditional villages, communal and noncommunal alike, would have lost their official label, *selskoe obshchestvo,* and with it their official status in law. *Selskoe obshchestvo* and volost, hitherto the official terms for traditional peasant institutions of government, would now be applied to new, all-class bodies that would exercise legal authority over all inhabitants in their respective territories regardless of class, and they would operate under a single legal system common to all citizens. When a peasant appealed to these new institutions against his *zemelnoe obshchestvo,* they could intervene on his behalf whenever it appeared to them that his "rights" were being denied him. In other words, the ostensible assumption underlying the "bases" was a fiction. In fact, traditional peasant villages were to be deprived of all their legal prerogatives. They would be able to maintain their customary ways only so long as they had the unanimous support of their members. The Nikolskii bases *did* call for the destruction of traditional villages (ll. 206-8).

Here, seemingly, Witte scored his most telling victory. Had he failed to put the reform squarely in the hands of the zemstvoes? Had he been forced to accept the participation of MVD agencies such as governors and gentry marshals, together with a potentially hostile MZ? No matter. Instead of merely keeping MVD agencies out of the reform, as he had originally set out to do, he would now go one step further. He would ban the MVD's police from the villages and eliminate the land captains entirely. The MVD would remain in the countryside, but its legs were to be cut off. With the dependable Nikolskii as MZ, Witte now had at least as solid a basis for controlling the reform as Kutler's scheme had offered. Even if the MZ should fall into hostile hands, its agents extended only as far down as the uezd level, and they would be dependent on the new volosts. Even if the new land settlement commissions should prove to be susceptible to MVD pressure through the governors and gentry marshals, they would still be outside the main lines of Witte's organization of MF-subsidized zemstvoes. The new "all-class" villages and volosts would rule unchallenged in the countryside, and they would be able to thumb their noses at MZ and MVD alike. As for the peasants, their traditional institutions would have no defense (except violence) against any one of their members who found it convenient to disrupt them.

So Witte found himself momentarily on top in April 1906. On the 18th, however, the big loan was signed in Paris, and on the 20th he was dismissed. Worse, his old enemy Goremykin replaced him as chairman of the Council of Ministers. Within the next few days Witte's whole council followed him out of the government. Nikolskii was replaced as MZ by none other than Stishinskii, last living founder of the land captains and perhaps the only remaining upholder of traditional peasant institutions in the government. Durnovo was replaced as MVD by Stolypin, new champion from the provinces, utterly unfamiliar with the central government and its ways, and unable for a while to act decisively. Shipov, Witte's MF, was replaced by Kokovtsov, whom Witte had deposed in October 1905. Shvanebakh, perhaps Witte's most dedicated enemy, came into the government as state controller. Witte had at last brought his ministers into line only to see them replaced by his worst foes.

Enter Stolypin: The Legislation of Late 1906

Goremykin barely had time to form his ministry before the Duma convened on 27 April. His new ministers, as yet unfamiliar with their positions, were unable to initiate any meaningful dialogue with the representatives of the people. They had had no time to digest the Witte-Nikolskii bases left behind by their predecessors, and they were certainly not prepared to set forth projects of their own. They confronted the new legislature in a confused silence, made all the more awkward by the simple fact that they had never contemplated such a body before. According to Gurko's description of the encounter, no one on either side knew what to do. There was no protocol to follow, and no one was in a position to draw one up. It was never established, for example, whether the chairman of the Council of Ministers should visit the president of the Duma or vice versa; consequently they did not visit one another (Gurko, 1939: 468-74). Probably any group of ministers would have had similar difficulties. The preparations made by Witte's group during the months prior to the Duma's opening were all designed for a body of men, similar to the old State Council, who would consider it their primary duty to support the ministries when and if they could agree among themselves. Such a body the first Duma was not. Had Witte's ministers remained in office, they would at least have brought their "bases" before the newly elected legislators—as Goremykin apparently did not—but it is extremely doubtful that the delegates would have given them serious attention in any case. As Witte said later in a speech of 1909 before the land commission of the State Council, the Nikolskii bases went "to the archives to rest quietly and be forgotten" (Gerbe, 1911: 118).

Thus the first Duma had to get along without any direction at all from the government, and so, not surprisingly, the members began to bring forward agrarian reforms of their own. Much to the government's dismay, many of them included proposals to expropriate private estates. To this open challenge the government had somehow to respond. In early June, despite what must have been Goremykin's and Stishinskii's revulsion, the MZ and MVD submitted concrete proposals for peasant reform to the legislators that conformed, at least approximately, to the Witte-Nikolskii bases of April. And since they did conform to the old bases, the new projects also embodied the old absurdities.[31]

The MVD brought its project before the Duma on 6 June; the MZ followed on the 10th. The MVD's project (TsGIAL, f. 1278, op. 1, d. 310, ll. 2-19) did not include the Nikolskii commission's idea to eliminate land captains and form all-class villages and volosts; these matters the commission had assigned to the ministry of justice. But the MVD's explanation of its project did contain a general announcement that all special laws and governing institutions for the peasants were to be eliminated. It also assured the Duma that no government institutions, either central or local, were to be empowered to act outside the limits of law and bureaucracy. In particular, no agency of the government would be authorized to intervene in the peasants' civil affairs except at the peasants' own request (ll. 24-26). On the other hand, the project allowed individuals and small groups of peasants the right to separate themselves from their nongovernmental *zemelnye obshchestva* by acquiring their land as private property. They could also consolidate their lands, and although this latter right was to be limited in order to protect the rights of neighbors (ll. 2-19, arts. 106, 125-44), it conveyed the same implication as the Nikolskii bases had. The theoretically nonintervening government would need only one dissident peasant in a *zemelnoe obshchestvo* as sufficient pretext for charging in and dismantling the whole customary order. It should be added that the MVD's project also included Witte-Gurko's drastic provision automatically eliminating communal landholding in villages that had not redistributed their land for a long time. As to the MZ's project, it was persistently vague, but it did provide that land settlement would go forward under the direction of the MZ's land settlement commissions in accordance with peasant requests (Stishinskii, 79).

The government's projects went nowhere. The president of the Duma acknowledged their receipt, but the members neither discussed them nor submitted them to their land commission (*Gosudarstvennaia,* 1906: II,

---

[31]Ultimately, the government managed to thrust a fairly wide variety of reform projects before the first Duma (Savich, 1907: 145-46; *Gosudarstvennaia,* 1907: 244-49).

1086-87, 1213). Instead, the first Duma devoted its efforts to devising laws for the forcible seizure of nonpeasant landed estates. On 9 July, a month after the ministries submitted their projects on agrarian reform, Nicholas proclaimed the first Duma's dissolution (*Pravitselstvennyi*, 11 July 1906: 1). He also reshuffled his cabinet. He dismissed Goremykin and Stishinskii and raised Stolypin—still largely an unknown but obviously a supporter of the Witte-Nikolskii peasant-bank approach to land reform—to be chairman of the Council of Ministers. The new chairman retained his post as MVD, which made him the first chairman of the newly reorganized council to be a minister as well. B. A. Vasilchikov, yet another champion-governor from the provinces, replaced Stishinskii as MZ.[32]

The post-July government was something like a clean slate. Krivoshein and Gurko retained their posts and continued to play active roles in formulating the oncoming agrarian reform, but their positions were distinctly subordinate. New men would have to assemble the pieces constructed during the previous years into a workable reform, and they had just about six months to do it. By 1 January 1907 a certain minimal amount of legislation would be needed if judges and administrators were to deal with the newly debt-free peasants.

Stolypin adopted the same overall strategy Witte had used in March: he undertook to get a few temporary rules enacted in a hurry, leaving all broad questions regarding the nature of agrarian reform to be resolved later. In August the Council of Ministers set up a commission under Gurko to draw up another set of immediate measures, and it produced the decrees of 5 October and 9 November, the latter of which was the third and last of the major laws that set the Stolypin Reform in motion (Dubrovskii, 1963: 121-26; Gurko, 1939: 499-502; Macey, 1976: 670-71).

If we view the 9 November decree as primarily a housekeeping measure, designed to clarify the peasants' rights in their new status, then its most important contribution was to set forth a statement of these rights that supposedly applied to all categories of peasant alike: former serfs, former state and crown peasants, etc. As said before, the statement was far from adequate, but it represented a significant improvement on existing statutes. Not surprisingly, it was similar to the projects of January-March 1906. In some ways, however, it was quite different. The November decree did *not* provide for any abrupt, large-scale conversion of communal land to personal property, nor did it empower a small minority in a village to consolidate their strips without their neighbors' consent. The only drastic land settlement measure it carried over from

[32]Vasilchikov had been a gentry marshal until 1900 and a governor from then until 1903. During the Russo-Japanese War he was a leading organizer of the Red Cross ("Vasilchikov").

the earlier projects was a clause providing that a village, communal or noncommunal, could redivide all its lands into integral household farms in a single operation if two-thirds of the heads of household voted to do it. This provision came originally from the MVD's old projects of 1902-3, and it had reappeared, slightly modified, in the MZ's proposal to the first Duma (Stishinskii, 26). As we shall see in Chapter 7 (sec. A), it proved to be the single most important statement in the reform legislation of 1905-6, but the point I am stressing here is not the radical effect the November decree did in fact ultimately produce but its mildness in relation to the "liberal" proposals of the preceding months. It must be acknowledged that the implementors of the reform ultimately twisted the wording of the November decree to allow minorities and individuals to consolidate without the approval of their fellow villagers (ch. 7, sec. C). Even so, the enactors of the decree took a big step backward from the relatively extreme mobilizations proposed in early 1906.

Stolypin enacted other measures of peasant reform in late 1906. Most of them were designed to further the Witte-Pleve notion of selling nonpeasant land to peasants and extending more credit on more generous terms to the purchasers. The decree of 12 August made arable crown lands available to the peasant bank for sale to peasants (Sidelnikov, 1973: 90-91). On 27 August arable state lands were made over to the chief committee for land settlement for distribution according to the same rules that governed the peasant bank. State lands, however, were not to be sold via the bank. The land settlement organization would handle them entirely on its own (pp. 91-93). The reason for leaving state land sales wholly to the disposition of land settlement commissions was that the MZ's department of state domains was already managing this land, and the commissions worked under this same department. Thus there was no apparent need to involve the peasant bank.

Several months later, on 14 October 1906, a decree came out drastically liberalizing the terms on which the bank's loans were granted. It lowered interest rates on outstanding loans from the bank and on all future loans as well. On 13-year loans the rate went down to about 4.3%; on 18-year loans, to 3.4%; on 28-year loans, to 3.7%; on 41-year and 55½-year loans, to 4.0%.[33]

[33]In the words of the 14 Oct. decree: "We order: 1. That beginning with the second half of 1906 the annual payments (per hundred rubles) of past and future borrowers from the Peasant Land Bank be lowered—for 55½ year loans, from 5.25 and 5.75 to 4.5 rubles without changing the number of payments; for 41-year loans, from 5.75 and 6.2 to 4.95 rubles; for 28-year loans, from 6.75, 7.10, and 7.15 to 5.8 rubles; for 18-year loans, from 8.75, 8.9, and 9 to 7.5 rubles; and for 13-year loans, from 10.75, 11, and 11.1 to 9.25 rubles" (Savich, 1907: 231-32). I am indebted to Bruce Reinhart and the late Aaron Strauss of the Department of Mathematics, University of Maryland, for their indispensable assistance in translating the tsarist government's schedules of payments into annual interest rates.

As a result of the 14 October decree, the peasant bank found itself
paying a higher rate of interest on its bonds than it charged on its loans.
Henceforth it would have to be sustained by government subsidies. By
the end of the regime these would total 144 million rubles (Bilimovich,
1930: 319).[34]

The last of the initial reform laws was the decree of 15 November
1906, which made it possible (in theory) for peasants to mortgage not
only their purchased, nonvillage lands to the peasant bank but also their
allotment lands. Moreover, they could use bank loans not only to buy
new land but also to improve their methods of cultivation on the land
they had (Savich, 1907: 234). This was precisely the measure Krivoshein
and Gurko had been trying to force upon Witte and the MF ever since
February 1906, and it was passed at last in the teeth of MF Kokovtsov's
determined opposition (Dubrovskii, 1963: 122-26). Stolypin seems to have
had high hopes for it, which is probably one of the reasons he shifted
Krivoshein into the MF to take over the peasant bank personally. If all
went well, the bank would at long last transfer some of its resources
away from buying nonpeasant land and apply them to improving and
rearranging village land. Peasants consolidating their own village lands
would be able to cover some of their expenses—e.g., the costs of road
building, well digging, drainage—with long-term loans.

The 15 November law was unique in the legislation of 1906 because
it offered material incentives to peasants who consolidated their land. A
peasant buying allotment land could normally mortgage it up to 60% of
its cost, so said the new law, but if the land being bought was an integral
farm, he could borrow up to 90%. If a peasant was improving his farming methods on his existing allotment, he could mortgage it up to 40% of
its value, but if he consolidated his allotment, he could get up to 60% of
its value for agricultural improvement measures (Savich, 1907: 234, art.
B).

The above laws indicate that Stolypin still retained his original
Witte-like belief in "liberating" progressive peasants from their villages
and setting them up on new farms (sec. B). He also seems to have shared
Witte's indifference to the effects of this liberation on peasant institutions.
Not only did he accept with apparent equanimity the villages' loss of
control over their lands but he also managed to enact his famous law on
civil rights. This was the decree of 5 October (*TPSZ*, 28392), which
Gurko (of all people) drafted with the purpose of guaranteeing certain
rights to individual peasants and setting limits to the authority of villages
and land captains over them. Peasants could now belong to more than

[34]After 1905 the peasant bank's bonds were of two types: one paid 4½%, the
other 5%. It must be added that the government had been subsidizing the gentry
land bank in this fashion (though not to this extent) since 1889.

one village. Moreover, they could change their social status, obtain an education, and enter government service on the same basis as anyone else. They could even be land captains. This was a popular law among capital-city liberals, and it was very helpful to peasants who wished to leave their villages. Of greater importance to land reform, however, was its impact on the villages themselves. Chiefly, it weakened a village's legal means of defending itself against its individual members. A single household now had the option of selling its strips to any peasant from outside the village, thereby automatically admitting the outsider into the village. As has been said (ch. 3, n. 7), the law of 5 October did not produce any immediate practical effects; even so, it established the principle that peasants who wished to sustain their old ways and institutions no longer possessed any *legal* power to do so. It also meant that land reform would be easier to impose against the peasants' will.

By 1 January 1907 the outline of Witte's general scheme of November 1905 had been to some extent filled in. The government had published rules, albeit vague ones, to provide dissatisfied peasants with a way to get out of their villages, and it had seriously weakened the villages' legal means to coerce their members. There were programs to set peasants up on new lands, and there was an organization, on paper at least, to manage these programs. Stolypin had set aside complex and controversial issues, such as all-class villages and volosts, the land captains' judicial powers, and legal relationships *within* peasant households. These, he thought, could wait for more elaborate discussions involving the Duma and State Council. This is not to say that Stolypin deemed such matters unimportant. He fully shared the ancient conviction of tsarist bureaucrats that peasant reform required massive changes in the law. Beginning promptly in January 1907, he undertook serious attempts to introduce such changes, and he sustained his efforts until the day he died (Diakin, 1972: 238-74; Kryzhanovskii, 1938: 105-48, 217-19). In 1906, however, Stolypin was in a hurry. Instead of legislating basic changes in local administration and peasant society, he had to content himself with forcing his administration to move.

In the end, this was all the Stolypin Reform amounted to. All the elaborate schemes for a rural legal order that were drafted and half-drafted between 1902 and 1914 were buried. Only fragments got into law. Witte's and Stolypin's attempts to legislate a new order and the MVD's long struggle to codify the old one both perished together, victims of the same simple yet eternally surprising fact that it is impossible to *legislate* a social order. By and large the only meaningful laws the government could write were those which ordered its administrators to move, enabled them to move, and, most important, committed them to move. Whenever the government tried to tell its organizations *how* to move, its efforts at legislation broke down.

Conclusions

I have been at pains to show that the enactment process consisted primarily of a battle between ministerial organizations. All these organizations agreed on the need for agrarian reform and its basic nature, but they made it a point to disagree on what an agrarian reform should do, because it served their tactical purposes. On the whole, the substance of their arguments—the so-called basic issues—never really interested them.

No one ever won the battle. The three warring ministries managed to reconcile their differences and to create a reform that closely involved all of them. Their compromises were invariably vague and disorderly; the reform laws simply dumped a number of mutually contradictory proposals together and let the reform agencies find their own way.

Constant interministerial struggling had the apparent disadvantage of making the reform a blundering and misdirected affair from the beginning. As I have suggested, however, the disadvantage was only apparent. Social reform is inherently and unavoidably a blundering affair. Organizational disorder was more than offset, both before and after 1906, by the commitment to action that organizational conflict fostered. Each law the government passed, by its very failure to accomplish its purpose or even to make its meaning clear, served to deepen the government's commitment to act, thereby forcing each ministry to give the appearance of acting. Each law not only resolved conflicts but also created new ones, thus assuring that each of the ministries would go on striving to involve itself in a common effort to meet the government's ever-expanding commitment. This was the dynamic of the reform, or its dialectic, if you wish. It was the basic element in the government's operation, and it was one of the basic elements in the development of a national political consciousness in the countryside—at least as important, in my opinion, as revolutionary conflict between state and people or class conflict between rich and poor.

Of course, if one insists that an enactment process be a clear progression from general principles to detailed statutory provisions, the enactment of the reform was a botch from beginning to end. If one insists that the reform laws should have been neat structures of ends and means, the enactment process did far more harm than good. But if we see the Stolypin Reform as essentially a movement, undertaken in the face of seemingly insurmountable obstacles and sustained in spite of uninterrupted disenchantment, then we may begin to appreciate the frenzied efforts of the enactors as something much more significant than rivalries between ignorant men mouthing irrelevant ideologies in order to further their own "selfish" ends.

CHAPTER 7

The Reform Begins

...all the world does never gregariously advance to Truth, but only here and there some of its individuals do; and by advancing, leave the rest behind; cutting themselves forever adrift from their sympathy, and making themselves always liable to be regarded with distrust, dislike, and often...fear and hate. What wonder, then, that those advanced minds, which in spite of advance, happen still to remain, for the time, ill-regulated, should now and then be goaded into turning round in acts of wanton aggression upon sentiments and opinions now forever left in their rear.

Herman Melville (1963: 232)

A. THE INITIAL REFORM LAWS

As we have seen, three laws constituted the formal basis for the Stolypin Land Reform: the decrees of 3 November 1905, 4 March 1906, and 9 November 1906. The first ordered that the annual redemption payment be lowered by one-half in 1906 and canceled thereafter. This implied that the government would no longer prevent a peasant from breaking with his village but did not yet provide positive assurance that the village would have to let him go. The second established the reform organization per se. The third was designed primarily to provide some of the assurance that was lacking in the 3 November law. I have discussed the first of these laws in Chapter 6 (sec. D). The second and third, however, still await our scrutiny.

The Law of 4 March 1906

The organization envisioned in the 4 March law was in essence a hierarchy of interministerial colleges. At its head was the Committee for Land Settlement Affairs, and in each gubernia and uezd was a land settlement commission.

To begin from the bottom, the uezd land settlement commission was to have 12 members: the uezd gentry marshal (who served as chairman), the chairman of the uezd zemstvo directorate, the "permanent member" (appointed by the MZ as full-time manager of the commission's activities), the uezd member of the regional *(okruzhnyi)* court, a tax inspector, a land captain, three elected representatives from the uezd zemstvo assembly, and three peasant representatives selected from among candidates nominated by the volost assemblies in the uezd. This made an equal number of elected and ex officio members. Two of the latter— the gentry marshal and the chairman of the zemstvo directorate—were elected officials de jure, but they were more like functionaries than representatives in practice. There were several land captains and tax inspectors in each uezd, but ordinarily only one from each group was to be in attendance at any particular time; so the law implied. The only new official was the permanent member, who had no other job but to oversee the functioning of the commission. He was the only member who drew his salary from the MZ.[1]

The gubernia commission had 14 members: the governor (who served as chairman), the gubernia gentry marshal, the chairman of the gubernia zemstvo directorate, the permanent member, the fiscal administrator, the chairman of the local section of the peasant bank, a member of the regional court, one of the permanent members of the gubernia board, and six representatives elected by the gubernia zemstvo assembly, of which three had to be peasants who held allotment land. The representative element in the gubernia commission was slightly weaker than in the uezd: six elected members out of 14 in all. As in the uezd commission, only the permanent member was supposed to spend all his official time doing the commission's work.[2]

The central organ of the reform organization, the Committee for Land Settlement Affairs, was to be under the chairmanship of the MZ, who was also the executive head of the reform organization. Its other members were a deputy minister of agriculture, the director of the peas-

---

[1]In uezds where there were no zemstvoes the government appointed "representatives" from the local populace and substituted a local bureaucrat for the chairman of the zemstvo directorate. In uezds without gentry institutions the gentry marshal was also replaced by a bureaucrat. The manner of choosing these substitute representatives was left up to the MZ in accordance with a tsar-approved decision of the Council of Ministers, dated 9 Jan. 1907 (TsGIAL, f. 408, op. 1, 1906g., d. 1, ll. 52-54). In uezds with lands belonging to the imperial family a representative from the administration over these lands was added to the commission. In the southwestern gubernias—Kiev, Podoliia, and Volyniia—an arbitrator replaced the land captain, and the chairman of the congress of the justices of the peace replaced the uezd member of the regional court.

[2]In gubernias with lands belonging to the imperial family a representative from the administration over these lands was added to the gubernia commission. In gubernias without zemstvoes or gentry institutions arrangements similar to those mentioned in n. 1 had to be made.

ant bank, and representatives from six ministries: finance, internal affairs, imperial court, justice, agriculture, and state control. The committee had no elected members.[3]

The foregoing was all the 4 March decree had to say about the organizational structure for the reform. It offered no description of the commissions' manner of operating, nor did it estimate their cost. It said nothing concrete about the commissions' relationships with other government agencies. The MZ was simply directed to request credits for setting up the first commissions, hiring necessary surveyors and technicians, and providing loans and subsidies to peasants who would be moving to new lands during the months remaining in 1906.

The primary purpose of the new organization, said the decree, was to help the peasant bank purchase land and sell it to peasants who were suffering from a shortage of it (Savich, 1907: 38). The uezd commission was charged to help determine the usefulness and value of the land the bank was buying, help the bank divide up its land for sale, and identify the neediest peasants. If peasants asked for help in negotiating their purchases, the commission was to render it. These were the commissions' *primary* functions (pp. 39-40). None of them, be it noted, had anything to do with land reform on peasant land.

On occasion, if a commission had time on its hands after helping the peasant bank to sell land, the law allowed it to perform other services. For one thing, it could further land distribution on its own by assisting peasants to rent or buy available state-owned lands. For another, it could fulfill its secondary purpose, i.e., helping peasants "to improve their manner of holding land and using it" (p. 40). Finally, the commissions could help villages whose fields were intermingled with those of private landowners to rearrange their holdings into separate integral lots. The latter two services were indeed measures of land reform on peasant land, but the enactors of the 4 March law stressed their secondary importance. The Council of Ministers explicitly warned against burdening the commissions with too many tasks all at once. The uezd commissions "may" be assigned such tasks, said the council in its considerations regarding the 4 March law, "but only...on the basis of a petition from the governor of zemstvo assembly that has been approved by the central government" (p. 42). This de-emphasis of land reform on village fields marks the extent to which Krivoshein had to forsake (or conceal) his own beliefs in order to get the 4 March decree enacted over

---

[3] As time by, the committee acquired more members. The head of the survey section in the ministry of justice was added in July 1906, and a little later another deputy minister from the MZ came in. Individual members were added now and then by special orders from the tsar. A. A. Kofod, for example, became a member in this way in 1912 (*Kratkii*, 1916: 7).

Witte's opposition. As noted above, he considered the reform of allotment land to be a far more urgent task than land distribution (ch. 6, secs.
B and D).

The Law of 9 November 1906

The third law did three things. One was to assure that a peasant
head of household in a communal village could claim his strips as personal property if he desired. The central government would not merely
refrain from denying a head of household the right to transfer his strips
from communal to personal ownership but would positively guarantee
this right. As the introductory section of the law said: "The actual fulfillment of this right (to leave the commune)...meets practical obstacles in
the majority of rural communities.... Therefore...it is necessary now to
eliminate obstacles in the existing laws to the actual fulfillment of the
peasants' right to their allotment land" (Sidelnikov, 1973: 100). Strictly
speaking the transfer to personal ownership was not in itself a measure of
land reform, inasmuch as land was not actually rearranged (ch. 5, sec.
A), and the reform organization had no official connection with it. When
some land settlement commissions did try to involve themselves in trans-
fers of ownership, the Committee on Land Settlement Affairs ordered
them to refrain (*IZO,* 1907: 322-23). The relevance of these paper trans-
fers to agrarian reform arose solely from the assumption embodied in the
9 November law that a peasant would have to become the personal
owner of his strips in order to consolidate them.

The second contribution of the 9 November law to the reform was
that it granted to a communal peasant who claimed his strips as personal
property the right to demand that the village accept his strips of land in
exchange for an equivalent area consolidated into one single plot. This
was the operation that I identified in Chapter 5 (sec. A) as personal
consolidation. Personal consolidation was a much more complex affair
than a mere change in legal title, and the government could not guarantee it quite as unequivocally. True, it would be a simple matter if the
village called for a general redistribution. In this case, any peasant in a
communal village who had become a personal owner had the right to
claim his strips in one integral plot whether the other villagers liked it or
not (art. 14, sec. I; Sidelnikov, 1973: 102). Conversely, the village had the
right to demand that he accept consolidation of his strips whether he
liked it or not. If the village held no redistribution, however, the best the
government could promise any would-be consolidator was that he could
ask for an otrub (art. 12, sec. I), and the government would approve his
request only if his consolidation would not be "difficult or impossible"
for the village as a whole (art. 13, sec. I). If the government deemed a
proposed personal consolidation "difficult," the village could be required

to buy the strips in question at a price to be decided by the government. According to the 9 November decree, then, a would-be otrub-former's neighbors could block his claim if (1) they could persuade the government that the forming of an otrub on village land would be difficult, and (2) they could get up the price the government required them to pay for his strips.[4]

Certainly these safeguards for the village were not unreasonable. If individual members were free to consolidate their strips at their pleasure, a village could be forced into continual redistributions of its fields (ch. 6, sec. B). But the safeguards in the decree of 9 November were not strong. There were no specific guidelines to tell judges and administrators what constituted "difficulty" for a village. The decree only identified the officials who would do the deciding (in the event that the peasants disagreed among themselves). Article 15 provided that disputes arising from individual attempts to consolidate were to be decided by the uezd congress of land captains. By implication, the congress would also handle complaints arising from village consolidations—an implication that was later made explicit (*IZO*, 1909: 213). In this respect the 9 November decree was a model product of the enactment process described in Chapter 6. After four years of intensive study no one in St. Petersburg had come up with a way to separate individuals from their villages. The only important issue the November decree decided was *who* would do the job. Until 1910, when the law of 14 June (*TPSZ*, 33743, arts. 33 and 37) transferred the resolution of disputes over consolidation from the uezd congress to the MZ's uezd land settlement commission, the agencies of the MVD would be in charge.[5]

---

[4]Actually the 9 Nov. decree did not make it crystal clear that the "government" would establish the price the village would have to pay for the strips. On the one hand, article 13 said unequivocally that the volost court would do it; that is, a peasant institution would decide how much compensation a would-be personal consolidator received in the event of a decision that his consolidation was too "difficult." The court's decision, so article 13 implied, would be final. On the other hand, article 15 prescribed that *all* disputes arising over personal consolidations were to be settled according to the *primechaniia* (supplementary clauses) to article 12 of the general regulations on the peasantry, and one of these clauses ordered that disagreements over the valuation of a peasant's strips be decided by the uezd congress (Sidelnikov, 1973: 307). The wording of the 9 Nov. decree, then, was ambiguous, probably the result of a compromise such as committees are wont to make in order to get a formal decision made.

[5]The government took one intervening step in 1908. The law of 4 Dec. ordered that the permanent member of the uezd land settlement commission be included in the uezd congress with voting power whenever cases involving peasant land arrangements were under discussion (*IZO*, 1909: 11, 310).

Actually, the land settlement commissions had never been excluded from the process of personal consolidation; on the contrary, they did the bulk of the work from the beginning. What they lacked before 1910 was the *authority* to

I have already referred in Chapter 6 to the third important contribution of the 9 November law: a brief clause providing for village consolidation. Both communal and noncommunal villages could redivide all their land into integral household farms if two-thirds of the heads of household eligible to vote in the village assembly gave their assent. Note that it had to be two-thirds of *all* the household heads, not just those who came to the meetings. Anyone desiring to effect a village consolidation had not only to persuade the assembled peasants to accept it but actually to assemble them.

As said before, village consolidation turned out to be the basic aim of all land settlement operations. In 1906, however, it did not fit well. With one hand the enactors of the reform were taking pains to guarantee individual heads of household the right to acquire personal ownership of their strips; with the other they blithely gave two-thirds of a village the right to seize *all* land within the village's boundaries, no matter how it was owned. Personal owners, household owners, and communal owners alike could be compelled to give up their strips and accept an integral field in exchange. This one brief clause in the 9 November law threw all peasant landholding—that is, all interstripped holdings—into jeopardy. It not only made possible the violation of ownership by village consolidations but implied that any land settlement operation, group or individual, could be grounds for the seizure of *personal* property by a village.

It is impossible to say definitely what Gurko and his colleagues in the MVD had in mind when they introduced the clause on village consolidation into their initial draft proposals back in 1902-3 and then kept it alive until its final enactment in the 9 November decree. Whatever they intended, I have the impression that their understanding of this radical idea was very murky. Perhaps they recognized the absurdity of granting property rights to strips and allowing villages to seize these strips, all in one piece of legislation. Perhaps the would-be reformers of the MVD consciously accepted this absurdity in the interests of interministerial compromise. But this view of the matter implies a degree of clear-headed perception among the peasant experts of St. Petersburg that I find unconvincing. More impressive to me is their ignorance not only of peasant custom but of the government's own law—either ignorance of statutory provisions or disregard for legality; it is impossible to say which. The authors of the 9 November decree stated publicly at the time of its enactment that consolidation of a noncommunal village's land by a two-

---

decide disputes between villages and would-be consolidators. The committee's circular of 30 June 1907 provided that either side in a dispute over a consolidation could request the commission to mediate (1907: 322-23). Once such a request was made, the dispute could not be referred to the land captain and/or uezd congress until the commission had failed to resolve it to the satisfaction of both parties.

thirds vote had hitherto been impossible (Savich, 1907: 214). In September 1906 the Committee for Land Settlement Affairs had made a similar avowal (*IZO*, 1906: 339). In fact, however, a Senate decision of 20 December 1903 had affirmed the right of a two-thirds majority to consolidate noncommunal land in a case involving a Grodno village. Further, this decision had appeared in an official journal published by the MVD for the express purpose of guiding local government officials in the proper application of the laws regarding the peasants (*IZO*, 1904: 20-22). One is compelled to think that the legislators of 1906 had a very hazy idea of the laws they were presuming to reform.

The Purpose of the Initial Reform Laws

One thing is clear: the government wanted the two-thirds rule very badly. In 1902-3, when the MVD's editing commisison had proposed an earlier version of it, all but six of the gubernia conferences had approved (*Svod...o nadelnykh zemliakh,* 1906: 752-59). In 1906 the reformers seem to have believed that household lands in a noncommunal village were traditionally protected by law from village interference, yet they were quite willing to sweep this protection away and, incidentally, to subvert their own aim to establish and stabilize individual land tenure.

Historians commonly say that the enactors of the 9 November decree intended to allow peasants to become private *(chastnye)* property owners (ch. 5, sec. A). Judging from the above account, however, there are serious objections to the very use of the term "private property" to describe what a communal peasant got when he made a formal break with his village. The type of ownership expressly granted by the 9 November decree was personal *(lichnaia)* ownership. The decree extended it automatically to all heads of household in noncommunal villages, all members of a communal village who claimed their strips as individual owners, and all dwelling areas *(usadby)* belonging to peasants who were still members of communal villages (art. 1, sec. III; Sidelnikov, 1973: 104). But what exactly was personal ownership? The 9 November decree did not say, but the 5 October law had already provided that a personal owner had the right to sell or mortgage his strips to other peasants, whether they were fellow villagers or not. Subsequently the decree of 15 November extended his possible sources of credit by allowing him to mortgage his strips to the peasant bank.

These were the rights that made "personal property" resemble the modern concept of private property, but this was the only resemblance. Personal property was still far from private right. A personal owner of land strips was no more free from the constraints of open-field division than his communal neighbors were. He could not build fences around his strips, and if the village assembly permitted other peasants to walk across his land or let their animals graze on it, he could not prevent them. In a way his land rights were even weaker than those of communal holders. If his neighbors called for a general redistribution of the village land, communal holders had only to take new strips in the same fields, whereas a personal holder could be forced to accept a consolidated plot whether he wanted it or not. In January 1909 an MVD-sponsored congress of gubernia officials approved, with charming directness, a statement to the effect that although this requirement constituted an anomaly and a flat violation of private right, it was necessary in order to make the 9 November law's provisions on personal consolidation workable (*Trudy*, 1909: 129-31). Presumably the same "necessity" was behind the rule allowing a two-thirds majority in a village to force consolidation on all households alike, including personal "owners." No wonder that B. S. Martynov, a legal expert of the Stolypin era, said in 1917 that there were still no generally accepted legal formulae to define private property on peasant land (1917: 206-15, 266-85). In Martynov's own words, "it is impossible to conceive of land settlement on the basis of subjective, private rights of ownership" (p. 284). The MVD was more direct. An "explanation" of 24 July 1912 stated flatly that communal land formally converted to personal property was not actually personal property (*IZO*, 1912: 402-3).

The government's inability—or lack of desire—to establish private property on peasant land is only one instance of the reform law's discrepancies. There was also the matter of land distribution. Every one of the laws of 1905-6 stated or inferred that the reform's most urgent purpose was to facilitate the sale of land by the peasant bank to individual peasants. Even the law of 9 November treated the consolidation of village land as a secondary matter. The law's main purpose, according to the MVD's considerations at the time of its enactment, was to ensure "that land-poor peasants be able to complete their move without delay to the lands they have acquired with the help of the Peasant Bank" (Savich, 1907: 207).

It is safe to assume that the government's paper emphasis on land distribution in 1905-6 was primarily a result of two considerations: a desire to placate liberal opinion, and a sincere belief among many of the leading administrators (including Witte, Stolypin, and Pestrzhetskii, but excluding Krivoshein and Gurko) that land settlement would have to be carried forward on nonpeasant land before there could be any hope of developing it in the villages.

The first of these factors may or may not have been important. It may explain why the government spoke so much of helping land-poor peasants despite the fact that no leading administrator believed seriously and consistently in expending scarce resources to sell land to people who would probably be unable to work it profitably. As noted in Chapter 6 (secs. B and C), Stolypin and Pestrzhetskii clearly intended resettlement to be a stimulus to the enterprising. Witte sometimes affected to believe that land distribution would relieve poverty, but he never meant it. The government's talk of uplifting the poor by moving them out of villages onto new lands was essentially a mixture of facade, self-delusion, and sloppy thinking, vaguely attributable to the influence of liberal opinion.

On the other hand, the idea that land reform should begin on non-peasant land had solid support in the government. This notion proved to be as illusory as the elimination of poverty (ch. 4, sec. D); nevertheless, as this chapter will show, land distribution was indeed to be the government's main program of land reform for over a year after the reform laws were enacted.

In sum, the authors of the earliest reform laws had three purposes: (1) to make a show of using land reform to relieve poverty, (2) to allow individual peasants to get out of their villages and establish separate, consolidated farms, and (3) in the long run, to break down traditional peasant institutions, thus converting Russia's arable land into commercial farms and Russia's peasants into citizens.

B. INITIAL ESTABLISHMENT OF THE REFORM ORGANIZATION

Administrative Provisions

Following its conception on 4 March 1906, the reform organization may be said to have been born on 26 April, when a decree granted the Committee for Land Settlement Affairs 1.8 million rubles to cover its expenses during the remainder of the year. One million rubles of this were for operating costs; the remaining 800,000 rubles were for loans and aid to be disbursed directly by the commissions to peasants who were moving to new lands. Operating costs consisted primarily of salaries to permanent members of uezd land settlement commissions and their secretaries (*IGU*, 1906: 390).[6]

The first thing the new organization had to do was find surveyors. The decree of 4 March had suggested that the Committee for Land Settlement Affairs should obtain them, but it did not say how. This question was decided by Stishinskii, MZ from late April until early July 1906. On 27 May he asked the director of the land survey section in the ministry of justice to provide surveyors for the reform (*Desiatiletie*, 1916: 4). One wonders why. In 1903 Stishinskii's own editing commission had asserted

---

[6]The old State Council had rejected this measure by a vote of 46 to 39, one of its last acts before going out of existence. Nicholas accepted the minority, and the measure became law (Macey, 1976: 473-75). One of the last contributions of the old autocracy was to allow the Stolypin Reform to begin.

that justice's surveyors were hopelessly incompetent (*Svod...po proektu pravil*, 1906: 100-108). The answer seems to lie in the government's fear of sending specialists of any kind out among the peasantry. Surveyors were associated in some minds with the notorious "Third Element," and Stishinskii probably felt that if he could not avoid the use of specialists altogether, he could at least make sure that the central government would have its own, thereby reducing its reliance on zemstvoes and private agencies. This was how Stolypin felt (Verpakhovskaia, 1911: I, 4). Justice's surveyors could be kept under close supervision by the gubernia surveyor's office. "Undesirables" could be quickly discharged and their names kept on file in St. Petersburg (*Desiatiletie*, 1916: 4). Then, too, justice's surveyors do not seem to have been noticeably less competent than other varieties (ch. 5, n. 25).

On 1 June the minister of justice hastened to accept Stishinskii's invitation. This meant that a total of about 200 ill-trained uezd surveyors would be made available to assist such land settlement commissions as might be established. They were to work under the technical supervision of the gubernia surveyors, in whose offices reposed all existing records of land surveys previously made in their respective gubernias. Gubernia surveyors were experienced men. In 1906 they had an average of 35 years in service. Only half of them had had formal training, but presumably they knew what a proper survey looked like (*Desiatiletie*, 1916: 6; *IZO*, 1906: 304-6).

Finished for the moment with the problem of surveying, the government next focused its attention on the uezd land settlement commissions. On 14 June 1906 a circular went out from the MZ and MVD to the governors containing a few general instructions concerning the nature of the comissions' work. The commissions' main purpose, the circular said, would be to arrange for the sale of the peasant bank's land to the neediest peasants. Interstripped fields on allotment land were detrimental to the progress of agriculture, and it would be a good thing to aid any peasants who wanted to eliminate them. Nevertheless, only a few commissions would be able to involve themselves in land settlement directly, owing to the shortage of funds and surveyors. These few commissions should be identified as soon as possible so that available resources could be allotted them, but in general the reform organization should stick to the main problem: land shortage (*IGU*, 1906: 427-29).

An MZ circular of 30 June was more specific (*IZO*,1906: 304-6). Uezd commissions were to be set up in 33 gubernias during 1906, no more than six in each. There were to be no gubernia commissions for the time being. Theoretically the existing staff of uezd surveyors was big enough to give one to each of the new commissions, but since only one-third of them were capable of working independently, they should work in teams of three: a qualified man and two apprentices in each.

Thus only about one-third of the uezd commissions, or two in each of 33 gubernias, were to have surveyors attached to them during 1906. According to the 30 June circular, uezd commissions with surveyors could be expected to do a little work on the consolidation of allotment land, but the rest could do no more than aid the peasant bank to find and identify deserving recipients of loans, help families move to new lands, and rent out state lands to land-poor peasants.

Only a week after the 30 June circular came out, the tsar dissolved the Duma and raised Stolypin to be chairmen of the Council of Ministers. It had been four months since Krivoshein's 4 March decree, and no new legislation on agrarian reform had come out. We may say, however, that the MZ's new administration was already on its way. Judging from the disposition of surveyors and funds called for in Stishinskii's 30 June circular, signs were already beginning to appear that the reform organization was putting its muscle behind intravillage land reform rather then peasant bank sales. Despite all rhetoric to the contrary, commissions that engaged in land reform were to get more surveyors and funds than commissions that only helped the peasant bank.

The most important order concerning the management of the reform in its early stages was the committee's instruction *(nakaz)* of 19 September 1906, which came out after the first uezd commissions had already been set up *(IZO, 1906: 333-42)*. It was by far the most detailed body of regulations on the land settlement commissions' activities to be written during the entire year. The *nakaz* repeated what preceding circulars had emphasized: the primary task of the commissions, at least for the present, was to aid the poorest peasants to acquire land. The commissions were to collect statistics in their uezds in order to determine what a barely sufficient allotment of land was, and then they could concentrate their energies on peasants who owned less than this figure (pp. 333-34). They had to measure off state lands into farms for sale or rental to the needy (pp. 336-38), help the peasant bank do likewise on its lands (pp. 334-36), and help peasants who wanted to resettle in Siberia (pp. 338-39).

Generally speaking, the *nakaz* made all transactions of the peasant bank matters of concern for the land settlement commissions, and there was more than a hint that the bank was to become a mere auxiliary for the reform organization (pp. 334-36). Whenever a commission thought a purchase or sale of land by the bank did not serve the purpose of land settlement, it could halt negotiations (arts. 15 and 46). Disagreements between local bank sections and land settlement commissions could be appealed to the central bank council, but if the MZ's representative on the council did not agree with the council's decision, it had ultimately to go to the Council of Ministers (art. 19). As to actual field operations, the *nakaz* prescribed that all sales by the bank were to be in the form of single, consolidated plots if possible (arts. 22 and 24). Land-poor peasants already renting the land had the first option to buy; second in priority were land-poor peasants whose fields were intermingled with the land for sale; third, any peasants, land-poor or not, trying to consolidate their own strips; and fourth, any peasants who agreed to possess and farm the land they bought as otrubs (art. 25). Land was not to be sold to a village unless it actually practiced periodic redistributions (art. 31). But these rules were not so important in themselves. What is important is that the commissions were responsible for imposing them upon the bank (art. 46).

Note that the *nakaz*'s provisions regarding the peasant bank, like Kutler's proposal to expropriate land, reflected the assumption that land rented by peasants and divided into strips could be redivided into consolidated farms without arousing peasant resistance. It also contained the scarcely veiled threat, later fully unveiled by Stolypin (see below, sec. D), that if local peasants did not come forth to buy consolidated lots on the land their villages were renting, outsiders could be brought in to occupy them (arts. 41 and 42).

The *nakaz* also spoke of land settlement on the peasants' own land. Indeed, it had a great deal to say on this subject, despite its ostensibly secondary importance. The *nakaz* ordered the new commissions to "familiarize" peasants with land settlement (art. 2). In particular, they were to enlighten peasants as to the advantages of individually owned integral plots (art. 68) and extend "any kind of help" to individuals and groups desiring to improve their land usage and farming methods (arts. 70 and 79). The *nakaz* did not say just how the commissions were to go about "familiarizing" the peasants, but article 75 suggested that the land captains would be closely involved. In any case, once a group of peasants had been persuaded to agree to a land settlement measure, the *nakaz* offered detailed instructions on how to proceed.

The would-be innovating peasants were to begin by requesting the land settlement commission for help. Upon receiving a request from the necessary majority of peasants (see arts. 69-73), the commission was to send a land settler *(zemleustroitel)* to the village (art. 75). If *zemleustroitel* and reformer-peasants agreed on a project, the former would take responsibility for seeing it through to its completion. The *nakaz* implied that the *zemleustroitel* would ordinarily be a member of the commission, but any surveyor, local official, or citizen who was willing to undertake the task could try his hand. The local captain could do it if he chose, although the only function the *nakaz* specifically required of him (and his uezd congress) was to check each peasant request for land settlement to ensure that its proposed measures did not violate the law (arts. 68-86, pp. 339-40).[7]

[7] As it turned out, the *zemleustroitel* for most land settlement projects was

Once a project was pronounced legal, the *zemleustroitel* drew up his plan for rearranging fields and then made his survey. Finally, he marked the new boundaries and drew up a final agreement for the peasants' signatures. He had, of course, to secure the reforming peasants' acceptance for his scheme, and, if possible, he was also to get the consent of all other peasants whose lands were involved. When and if he got his plan approved by the requisite number of household heads and, of course, by the land captain, it went to the uezd land settlement commission for approval (arts. 81-83). When the commission had given its final approval and the document was at last filed in the office of the gubernia surveyor, the new division of land became legally binding (arts. 84-85).

It is important to note that the *nakaz* left would-be consolidators free to change their minds right up to the signing of the final "deed." Admittedly it never said just how a land settlement project could be stopped. Supposing, for example, that a bare two-thirds majority of a village voted to initiate a village consolidation—by a vote, say, of 68 to 32—and then three heads of household changed their minds. Did the project stop then and there? The *nakaz* did not say, nor did the central government ever say, so far as I know. Take another hypothetical case: in a communal village of 80 households, a group of 20 claim their strips as personal property and then petition to consolidate. More than 40 of the other 60 heads of household—i.e., a majority of the village assembly— refuse to grant the petition, but the uezd congress then decides that the 20 can consolidate wihtout causing the 60 undue damage. A project is begun, and after two years of work a final plan is drawn up. At this point, 5 of the 20 consolidators change their minds and decide to keep their strips. In order to allow their withdrawal from the project, the entire plan must be thrown out and redone. Question: did the 5 actually have the right to withdraw? Was the government obliged to draw up another plan to gratify the 15? If 5 out of 20 had the right to cause this much confusion, delay, and expense to both government and village, did one single household have a similar right? If the 5 did not, did 11? Or 15? No law or instruction ever answered these questions, nor have I been able to perceive any uniform pattern of action among reform administra-

either a surveyor or a permanent member of an uezd land settlement commission. In 1913, a typical year in this respect, the *zemleustroitel* in 41% of the land settlement projects was a permanent member, and in another 41% a surveyor played this role. Hard evidence is lacking, but in most cases where a permanent member was formally designated as *zemleustroitel*, a surveyor probably directed the actual field work. So the head of the survey section claimed in 1910 (TsGIAL, f. 1291, op. 120, 1910g., d. 19, ll. 86-87). As for the land captains, they acted formally as *zemleustroiteli* in only 12% of the projects of 1913 (*IGU,* 1913: 908).

tors when these questions came up—as they often did. As we shall see (below, sec. E), each separate combination of village factions and administrators had to answer them for itself. Having said all this, however, I must still make the point that the *nakaz* of 19 September did establish the *principle* that consolidating peasants could back out of a project at any time up to its completion. The new commissions were to function solely as service units, without any legal power to coerce. The *nakaz* stated repeatedly that harmony among peasants and between officials and peasants was a primary consideration in all land settlement work.

The *nakaz* briefly mentioned communal peasants who claimed their strips as personal property (arts. 68-69). If some peasants asked a commission for help in making a claim, the commission should indeed help them. Change of tenure was only a paper transaction, not a land reform measure, but the 9 November decree had not yet been enacted, and the *nakaz* had somehow to prepare the committee's agencies for situations in which peasants had to separate from their communes in order to buy new lands. There being as yet no positive guides for the legal steps necessary to separate from the commune, the instruction simply allowed commission members to assist would-be land purchasers to find their way through the local offices. This idea did not remain in effect very long. As said before, the 9 November decree ordered land captains to take over the business of transferring peasants to personal ownership, and in mid-1907 an MZ circular expressly ordered commissions to stay clear of such matters (*IZO,* 1907: 322-23).

Speaking generally, the 19 September *nakaz* and 9 November decree implied a partial shift of responsibility for reform from land settlement commissions to land captains. The *nakaz* was vague about the captains' role, but it certainly gave them entry into all measures of land settlement. It spoke more of them than had the 4 March decree or any of the circulars and proposed laws that had come out prior to the first Duma's dissolution (not surprisingly, since Witte's ministry had agreed to get rid of the captains—ch. 6, sec. D). And what the *nakaz* did vaguely, the 9 November decree did specifically. Persuasion by advisors from the commissions was to be considerably augmented by the authority of the captains, who, in theory at least, could still use their combined judicial and executive authority to good effect if they had reason to believe that the government would stand behind them. Commissions could act only when the peasants requested their aid, and the only power they had was to withdraw their support from any project they did not like. A captain, on the other hand, could stop a project or delay it not only on legal grounds but also, in personal consolidations, out of consideration for what he believed to be a village's welfare.

This post-July shift suggests that the government's attitude toward agrarian reform underwent a change after the dissolution of the first

Duma. Unfortunately, the sources I have seen provide no clear indication as to where the change took place, or how, or why. We can be certain of only one thing: in the fall of 1906 the government decided that land reform would involve not only the committee's own commissions and the peasant bank but also the MVD's land captains. Kokovtsov and Vasilchikov, respectively the MF and MZ in late 1906, opposed the decree of 9 November and also that of 15 November (allowing peasants to mortgage allotment land to the peasant bank). Apparently they objected to the MVD's resurgence (see Dubrovskii, 1963: 122-26).

One matter the *nakaz* of 19 September failed to clear up was how the commissions were to distribute loans and grants to land-settling peasants. Eight hundred thousand rubles had been budgeted for them in April, but in September the central offices had not yet made any statement regarding procedures for disbursing them or terms of repayment. Aside from some vague remarks to the effect that amounts up to 165 rubles could be lent or given to peasants who engaged in land settlement, either on their own fields or on newly bought ones (arts. 52, 53, 68; *IZO,* 1906: 338), the *nakaz* said nothing about financial aid. I leave it to a more perceptive student of the reform than myself to imagine how uezd commissions actually went about disbursing loans and grants without knowing the terms of repayment. The fact is, a few commissions did make such disbursals. Procedures for drawing and disbursing money were at last established in February 1907. Terms of repayment were only published a month later (*IGU,* 1907: 163-64, 280-81).

The documents setting forth these procedures were the MZ circulars of 27 February and 17 March. Since Vasilchikov was the MZ in early 1907, I assume they were his handiwork. In essence they embodied the following principle: every single loan and subsidy had to be approved separately in St. Petersburg by the central committee in full assembly on the basis of exhaustive information about the economic condition of the recipient and the purpose for which he intended to use the money. One would have to go back to Dmitrii Tolstoi's law of 1889 on resettlement in Siberia to find a more awkward, unworkable approach to peasant administration (ch. 4, sec. C). Judging from appearances, Vasilchikov wished to make it virtually impossible to issue loans and subsidies to support land reform, and it became apparent in late 1907 (if not earlier) that his obtuse policies were achieving this aim. As of 1 October 1907 the uezd commissions reported total disbursals since the beginning of the reform of only 134,000 rubles in loans and another 50,000 in subsidies (*IGU,* 1908: 184-85). Even these low figures may have been exaggerated. According to Dubrovskii, land-settling peasants received only 76,000 rubles in government aid of this sort up to the end of 1907 (1963: 266). Nevertheless, Vasilchikov kept to his obfuscating course until the very end of his stay in office (see *IGU,* 1908: 273-74).

Having all but prevented the disbursal of loans and subsidies, Vasilchikov was willing to be quite lenient about demanding repayment. The circular of 17 March 1907 allowed recipients to pay nothing back at all for five years and then repay the principal—interest-free—in ten annual installments (1907: 280-81). This measure turned out to be a significant contribution, for in May 1908 Krivoshein replaced Vasilchikov as MZ, and one of the new minister's first acts was to eliminate his predecessor's obstacles to loan distribution. From then on, loans and aid began to flow somewhat more easily from government to land-settling peasants. On the other hand, Krivoshein left his predecessor's generous arrangements for repayment intact. The circular of 17 March remained in effect until the end of the reform.

So much for the early stirrings of the reform organization. It should be added that it took time to set up the local agencies. By December 1906 only about 140 uezd commissions were in being, and as yet they had evoked very little interest in land settlement. Over 9,000 petitions had come in asking help in acquiring land and resettling outside the villages, whereas less than 600 had to do with land settlement on allotment land (*Rossiia,* 1 Feb. 1907: 3).

If progress was slow, it was sure. Approximately 200 more commissions were set up in 1907, bringing the reform organization close to its full strength on the uezd level (Sidelnikov, 1973: 131). The first gubernia commissions came into being in the spring and summer of 1907, wherever the extent of land settlement activity seemed to call for them (*IZO,* 1907: 65). Thirty-two opened in 1907, four in 1908, three in 1909, none in 1910, and seven in 1911—a total of 46 in all (Sidelnikov, 1973: 131). At first many gubernia permanent members were appointed on a part-time basis from the existing gubernia administration, and for a time their new "posts" constituted only an additional duty. The job became a full-time one in most gubernias by 1909, but it was only in 1912 that the position achieved formal recognition in the budget (*Kratkii,* 1916: 12). The uezd commissions, on the other hand, had official, full-time permanent members almost from the beginning.[8]

Achievements

Judging from figures for 1906 and 1907, the government's overall accomplishment in *land* reform was not impressive during its first year or two of operation. No land settlement projects were completed on village

[8]Olonets was the 47th reform gubernia. I have not been able to ascertain whether or not it ever acquired a gubernia commission. Government-sponsored land settlement began there only in 1911 (*Kratkii,* 1916; 11), and it never went very far in that subarctic region (Pershin, 1928: 331).

land during 1906. This was understandable, since the commissions only began to take form in this year, and most projects required at least two years to compete. In 1907, according to the most conservative official estimate I have seen, about 8,300 households were completely consolidated; in 1908, 42,000. Most of these must have been in process since 1906 or early 1907. About three-fifths of them were carried out in the western gubernias and the left-bank Ukraine. Great Russia proper saw almost none, except in the steppe gubernias (Kofod, 1914: 114-20). Group land settlement seems to have gone even slower during these years, though it was clearly more popular among the peasants (*IGU,* 1908: 47-48).

By contrast, the peasant bank was moving at a brisk pace in 1906-7. In 1906, with or despite the commissions' help, the bank sold 106,000 acres of its own land and financed the sale of 1.3 million acres directly from owners to peasants. In 1907 it worked much harder, selling 490,000 acres of its own land and financing the sale of 2 million acres directly (Dubrovskii, 1963: 325). The bank's purchases went even more rapidly. In 1906 it accumulated 3.1 million acres, which was a half-million more than it had purchased during all the preceding 11 years since it had started to purchase land. In 1907 it bought another 4.1 million (pp. 319-20). At the time the MZ took pride in all this. It put out a propaganda tract in 1908 that devoted 15 pages to the peasant bank's "successes" and only four to land settlement (*Aperçu,* 1908).[9]

But the bank's work had little to do with land reform. Only a small fraction of the land sold by the bank in 1906-7 went to individual peasants: 3.2% in 1906 and 2.5% in 1907 (Pavlovsky, 1930: 159). Not all of this took the form of consolidated lots, but even if it had, the contribution to land reform would still have been minuscule. As for the commissions' efforts to sell state lands, they were pathetic at best. In 1906 they sold no state land at all; in 1907 a mere 26,000 acres was turned over, of which only 58% was in the form of consolidated farms (*Zemleustroistvo,* 1911: 47).

While land reform crept forward at a snail's pace, resettlement in Siberia was turning into something of an avalanche. About 69,000 households flooded eastward in 1907, 105,000 more followed in 1908, and another 97,000 in 1909 (Sidelnikov, 1973: 218). Unfortunately, St. Petersburg had not foreseen this outcome of its attack on the village. In October 1906 the minister of finance had recommended that funds for Siberian resettlement be cut back, on the grounds that the sale of state and crown

[9]The above figures for sales and purchases of bank land cover only the 47 reform gubernias. Figures for land purchased directly from owners with the bank's help cover all gubernias where the bank operated. In addition to the lands acquired by purchase, the bank took over 3.3 million acres of crown lands from the ministry of the imperial court in accordance with the decree of 12 Aug. 1906 (ch. 6, sec. D).

lands in European Russia would be adequate to satisfy the peasants' demand for land (pp. 186-87). This seems to have been the prevailing opinion in the capital, for in April 1907 the minister of communications (who directed the railroads) was complaining that no one had warned him of the impending deluge. His trains were unable to accommodate the masses pouring into his stations (pp. 191-92). Even the Siberian governors were demanding a halt, especially those whose territories touched on the Kirghiz steppe, where resettlers were encroaching on native pastures (p. 196). But there could be no halt. Peasants already en route could not reside indefinitely in railroad stations, and the new laws made it impossible to prevent fresh waves of colonists from setting out. In a report to the Council of Ministers in July 1907, Vasilchikov noted that the government had promised free resettlement in 1904-6, and it could not simply withdraw its offer. Somehow the government had to slow down the inundation, said the distraught MZ (pp. 193-97), but he could not say how.[10]

In sum, the government's situation in 1907 was not an enviable one. In the western gubernias land settlement was at least beginning, but in most of European Russia the commissions seemed to be doing nothing at all. The government had sailed into the reform, bravely making believe that poor peasants with heavy mortgages would become model farmers once they were set up on land their neighbors had been renting. The peasant bank, however, was having no part of such fantasies. It was simply selling land to villages and leaving it in strips as if nothing had happened in 1905-6 (*IZO,* 1909: 286; 1910: 29-34; see also Iaroshevich, 1911: 116). Not even with Krivoshein at its head could the bank persuade its local sections to cooperate with the MZ's agencies. Given the pressures and disappointments of the reform's first year, it is hardly surprising that so many peasants ignored the government and moved to Siberia, but this route of escape quickly clogged up and threatened to become physically impassable. Stolypin's administrators were inextricably involved in rural reform, but they could not control their local agencies, and they were beginning to realize that they did not know what they were doing.

C. FAMILIARIZATION

The First Petitions for Land Settlement

The picture was not altogether dark. If we set aside the sort of blissful expectations that had made Kutler, for example, dream of producing

[10]The flood abated after 1909. Only about 35,000 households went to Siberia annually from then until the outbreak of World War I.

4,000 surveyors overnight (ch. 6, sec. D), 1907 was a successful year for land settlement. The government was having a hard time getting in motion, but the peasants, on their part, were showing a surprising interest in its promises. As said before, less than 600 petitions for land settlement on village land came in during 1906, but in 1907 reform agencies received about 220,000 of them, of which 81,000 contemplated full consolidation into otrubs and khutors. In 1908 the total jumped to 386,000 (*Zemleustroistvo,* 1911: 32, 34), and even the MVD began to notice that land settlement was enjoying an unanticipated popularity (TsGIAL, f. 1291, op. 119, 1906g., d. 67, ll. 26-27). Interest in it was spreading rapidly through much of the European Russian countryside, and in the end this interest proved far more significant than the blunders and setbacks of the reform's first year.

Peasant desire for land settlement in 1907 is not easy to explain, for before that year they had shown very little interest in changing their land arrangements. A. A. Kofod, a Danish agronomist working for the Russian government, spent several years looking through all of European Russia for consolidated farms and for any indications of active peasant desire for them. He found very few, almost all of them in western Russia (Kofod, 1905). As we have seen in Chapter 5 (sec. B), the MVD investigation of 1894-97 noticed the same absence of peasant interest in land reform (*Svod Zakliuchenii,* 1897: III, 175-239). Even in Siberia there was no sign of a desire for personal, consolidated holdings prior to 1905 (Kaufman, 1905: 99-101, 148). How, then, do we account for the petitions of 1907-8?

One answer to this question lies in the government's efforts in 1906 and thereafter to "familiarize" peasants with land settlement. It would be foolish to suggest that government activity was the *sole* cause of the peasants' growing interest in land settlement on allotment land. For one thing, many commissions did their work crudely at first. Some of the earliest land-settling peasants were not models inspiring emulation but victims of botched surveys and a confused administrative organization (Kofod, 1914: 66, 84-85; *Desiatiletie,* 1916: 6-8, 10-11, 16-17; *IZO,* 1910: 29-35). According to one zemstvo-sponsored study, the land settlement commissions did characteristically shoddy work in Kiev gubernia during 1906-8, although in neighboring Volyniia gubernia consolidation projects went relatively smoothly (Iaroshevich, 1911: 115-16). Nevertheless, whether or not the government's early efforts at familiarization actually furthered the spread of land settlement, at least we may say that they coincided with a striking change in peasant attitudes toward land reform.

The question before us is: what did the government do that might have produced this change? What government activities may have contributed to the flow of petitions for land settlement?

Publicizing the Reform

For one thing, the government advertised. So far as I know, the idea of publicizing the reform came up for the first time in the *nakaz* of 19 September 1906, which directed the new commissions "to take measures to familiarize the population with the tasks of land settlement" (*IZO*, 1906: 33). In the following months the commissions made efforts to proclaim the advantages of consolidated farms. They distributed pamphlets, and commission members went about making speeches to village assemblies wherever one or more peasants seemed interested.[11]

The idea of setting up model khutors to advertise the reform emerged very early. At a meeting of land settlement officials in the southwestern gubernias in March 1907, some of the participants proposed from the floor that khutors on peasant-bank land should be used as models for other peasants to observe. More, the commissions should provide transportation to and from these farms for peasants who came from far away. In this way, the officials suggested, at least a few leading men in each village could see the new way of life for themselves (*Rossiia*, 25 Mar. 1907: 2). Model khutors did in fact become the commissions' most widely employed method of advertisement. So enthusiastic was the Committee for Land Settlement Affairs about the possibilities of model farms that it

[11]Partial lists of these pamphlets are in *Selskokhoziaistvennoe* (1914: Appendix, 47-50) and *Sistematicheskii* (1912). The earliest indication I have found of the actual distribution of a pamphlet is in the 29 Apr. 1907 issue of *Rossiia* (p. 3).

Also contributing to familiarization was the deluge of periodicals on agricultural improvement that poured down on the countryside. Most of them began to come out during the reform era. Not all were government publications, nor were they all devoted exclusively to peasant agriculture. So far as I have seen, however, the authors who wrote in them were either government or zemstvo specialists, and none of them neglected peasant agriculture. All were proponents of peasant land reform of some sort, though not necessarily the government's measures. The following titles are illustrative of the journals with a Russia-wide circulation: *Derevnia* (Village—monthly), *Krestianskoe khoziaistvo* (Peasant Economy), *Vestnik selskogo khoziaistva* (Agricultural Messenger—weekly), *Selskoe khoziaistvo i lesovodstvo* (Agriculture and Forestry). The last of these was the MZ's publication, but the others came from private groups. There were also many local journals, such as *Iugo-vostochnyi khoziain* (monthly—published by the Don Oblast agricultural society), *Iuzhno-russkaia selsko-khoziaistvennaia gazeta* (weekly—Kharkov agricultural society), *Khoziaistvo* (weekly), *Khutorianin* (weekly—Poltava agricultural society), *Khutorskoe khoziaistvo* (monthly). By 1913 dozens of these publications were circulating, though there had been no more than 20 in early 1906 (*Khutor*, no. 1, 1906: 4). On the whole, they were devoted to practical farming, not politics; therefore historians have ignored them. One gets the impression, however, that they had considerable impact as propaganda for land reform. I suspect they far outweighed the anti-reform propaganda from right and left political parties.

transported peasants from all over European Russia to the western gubernias, where the first successful models appeared (Kofod, 1914: 108).[12]

It is impossible to estimate how successfully the reform was advertised. An inspection made in 1909 came upon a significant number of villages in Penza, Voronezh, Riazan, and Tambov gubernias whose rural inhabitants had never even heard of the 9 November law, to say nothing of receiving instruction on it (TsGIAL, f. 1291, op. 120, 1910g., d. 19, l. 10). At least we may be certain that the success of the government's and zemstvoes' publicity was far from absolute.

Familiarization and Village Consolidation

Familiarization meant more than advertising. In a sense the entire program of land distribution was nothing more than a gimmick to familiarize peasants with land settlement. An individual who moved out of his village to settle on a consolidated farm was intended to be a beacon light for his backward neighbors, compelling them to change merely by the force of his example. But in many cases these forward-looking land purchasers would be more than examples. As we have seen, many of the lands the peasant bank acquired from private estates were already being farmed by villages and were divided into the customary strips (ch. 4, sec. D). A peasant who established an otrub lot or khutor farmstead on them was not merely lighting the way. Like the would-be personal consolidator, he was demanding that his neighbors clear themselves and "their" land out of his way. This was familiarization in spades.

If we are to grasp the significance of the government's attempt to familiarize peasants with land reform by allowing a few of them to buy consolidated farms, we must consider the peasants' perception of the matter. There were many fearful ones who did not focus upon models of self-improvement but instead contemplated the alarming possibility that a household head in their village might buy some of the land they were farming and force them to give up their strips. The more strenuously the government proclaimed this possibility, the more fearful these village "conservatives" became. Probably some of them directed their fear and anger at the government, but the most obvious object of their distrust was within the village. The new rights granted by the government gave every villager who had cause to wish his neighbors ill a mighty weapon against them. If he could get one of the peasant bank's easy loans to buy

---

[12] By 1910 at least a few model khutors had been established in almost every reform gubernia. In January, therefore, the committee ceased transporting peasants long distances at its own expense, and left the matter of display to the local commissions (*IGU*, 1910: 134-35).

land the village was renting, he could take a piece of land from every household in the village, and his neighbors would have no legal means to stop him. This state of affairs could not help but affect the village social order. Whether or not a village actually suffered invasion, every villager had now to live with the possibility that one of his neighbors would betray him and seize part of "his" land. The possibility was only on paper, and it pertained only to certain rights, but, insofar as the government's efforts at familiarization were effective, there was no village dispute in any category of social relations that was not affected by it.

The situation was equally dangerous in communal villages without rented land. Any household head could petition to consolidate his strips in the village's own fields. To be sure, a personal consolidator did not threaten to diminish the total area of village farmland. If he had his way, however, he abandoned a strip in every village field, thus necessitating a general reapportionment in every corner of the village. Worse, personal consolidations could come often. The law of 9 November threatened communal villages with the possibility of a general redistribution or something very like it every year, if only one villager would petition for personal consolidation each year, and if the local authorities chose to honor all these petitions. Obviously, such a turn of events would render farming much more difficult and unrewarding than it already was. Villages with rented lands were utterly helpless before the whim of any member who qualified for a peasant-bank loan. Communal villages were potentially subject to the whims of their separate households if the local land captains proved willing to decide that each request for personal consolidation was neither "difficult" nor "impossible" for the remaining villagers. This situation—as well as model farms and agronomic principles—was what peasants became "familiar" with when the government familiarized them with the reform.

It is necessary to ask how the land captains used their new powers in the early years of the reform. Did they compel villages to get their strips out of the way regardless of consequences, or did they protect the villages against dissident members? The answer is neither simple nor conclusive. Indeed, it is so ambiguous that we shall do well to put off discussing the matter to a later section (sec. E). Here it will suffice to say that the central offices of government wanted the captains to stand firmly, if tactfully, on the side of would-be consolidators.

If the reader will accept this summary statement for the moment, then we can continue our discussion of the peasants' reaction to the 9 November decree. As I have suggested, when peasants became familiar with the decree's provisions and listened to government officials speaking of otrubs, khutors, and civil rights, many of them heard threats against the relationships that sustained mutual trust within village society. Only a very harmonious and stable village could resist the oncoming paranoia.

But the reform era was *not* a time characterized by stable, harmonious villages. Not only the perils of land reform but the whole course of government policy was breaking down such traditional bonds as may have existed in earlier decades. Households were breaking away at an unprecedented rate—resettling in Siberia or moving to the cities—and with each departure the remaining villagers had to get up the money to buy the strips left vacant. If villagers did not buy the departers' land, outsiders could come in and occupy it, thus becoming members of the village whether the residents liked it or not. Speaking generally, every private right granted to the peasants in the name of liberalism, or progress, or state necessity intensified the nagging fear among them that a neighbor might use his new power to strike at them.[13]

Probably this state of affairs had much to do with the flood of petitions for village consolidation in 1907-8. As familiarization proceeded and villages began to become aware of the threat or actuality of disruption at the hands of their own members, they could perceive a clear advantage for themselves in getting the whole business of land reform over with in one relatively concise operation. A village that consolidated all its land stood some chance of being left alone. True, this would be a radical change, but it would not be substantially more disruptive than repeated partial consolidations by minority groups. For many villages it was the only permanently effective way to resist the awful alliance between government agencies and their own recalcitrant minorities.

It is hard to say when the government became fully aware of the connection between the threat of personal consolidation and peasant acceptance of village consolidation. Certainly recognition had come by 1910. The committee's rules for implementing the law of 14 June 1910

[13] A peasant going to Siberia retained possession of his strips and the right to convert them to personal property until he occupied his new land. Having converted his old strips to personal property, he could then take all the time he wanted before selling them. In other words, he was not under pressure to sell, and he could dispose of his share of his old village at his convenience (*IZO,* 1909: 240-41). One assumes that peasants departing for the towns or for bank land enjoyed the same privileges.

In theory, the law of 15 Nov. 1906 (authorizing peasant-bank loans secured by allotment land) provided relief to villages in need of capital to buy up the strips of departing members. A few St. Petersburg administrators had actually advocated that the bank perform this function, notably Gurko and his conference of Jan. 1906 (TsGIAL, f. 1291, op. 122, 1906g., d. 12, ll. 51, 74-82), together with a fair number of members in the old State Council (ll. 193-94). But sometime during the course of 1906 pro-reform statesmen seem to have forgotten about the villages' need for capital. The 15 Nov. law was indeed used primarily to satisfy this need, but very little money was actually lent out (Sidelnikov, 1980: 209-10). As the bank's representative on Gurko's conference had said, there was no practical way to use allotment land as collateral (TsGIAL, f. 1291, op. 122, 1906g., d. 12, ll. 44, 82-83).

stated plainly that the only purpose in carrying out personal consolidations was to bring on village consolidations (*IZO,* 1910: 236-37). In April 1910 the land section indicated its awareness of the situation in its own quaint way by sending a memorandum to the governor of Samara suggesting that he would do well to carry out just a few personal consolidations in villages where majorities were opposed to it. Village consolidation had been going so well in Samara that the local land settlement organization had decided not to do any personal consolidations except in cases where villages agreed to them. It was nice, said the land section, to hear of Samara's success with village consolidation, but a few personal consolidations *against* village opposition would show everyone that each peasant did indeed have the right to consolidate. More surveyors would be sent to take on the extra work involved (TsGIAL, f. 1291, op. 120, 1910g., d. 19, ll. 29-31).

Herein lies a paradox. The government's efforts to separate forward-looking, "free" individuals from "backward" masses tended to unify the outmoded, collapsing villages in a common desperation. The reform's enactors had persuaded themselves that they were liberators, and they had all denied any intention to force consolidation on peasants; therefore none of them had ever considered the possibility that granting freedom to individual households might plunge villages into continual, forced redistributions. Because the enactors wrote self-contradictory laws in 1905-6 in their haste to seize control of the reform organization, the villagers of 1908-14 were able to unite themselves to stave off the government's "liberating" attack, and the upshot was that the reform organization found itself directing villages into a rapid transformation.

Historians of the reform have missed this strange turn of events, mainly because they have been unable to conceive of the destructive effects of "liberal" innovations in traditional societies. N. V. Oganovskii, an articulate and well-informed populist writer of the Stolypin era, was still, in 1921, condemning government-managed land settlement for forcing peasants into agrarian reform, while in the same breath he expressed his approval of measures that allowed individual peasants to defy village authority. In particular, Oganovskii approved the rule that allowed village minorities of one-fifth or larger to demand consolidation of their land (1921; 80-84). Like the enactors of the reform in 1905-6, Oganovskii simply could not imagine that peasants might use "progress" and "freedom" to victimize each other. This, I think, is the sort of thinking that prevented anyone from anticipating the flood of petitions for village consolidation that began to come in during 1907. The government had believed it was setting up separate, competitive, self-reliant individuals in accordance with the canons of Western mythology. Instead, it inadvertently drove many peasants to join together in revolutionary, though peaceful, collective actions. In short, the villagers modernized themselves by resisting captial-city society's muddled attempts to modernize them. The reform worked despite itself.

D. THE PEASANT BANK AND THE REFORM IN 1907

In the foregoing section I have discussed very briefly the villages' initial reaction to the reform. It is time now to turn to the government's concrete activities. In 1907, it will be recalled, the reform organization was devoting most of its energy to getting peasants out of villages and setting them up on consolidated farms on new lands. The peasant bank was buying unprecedented quantities of land, ostensibly to be sold in integral household lots to peasants who were departing from their villages. As I have said, however, the local bank sections were not in fact selling their land in the form of integral farms. The vast majority of their sales in 1906-7 went to villages and partnerships (sec. B).

In June 1908 Stolypin inaugurated a determined campaign to force the peasant bank to take up land settlement. Apparently Krivoshein could not do the job himself, though he had formal charge of the bank. Stolypin had to intervene and to impose a fundamental reorganization on the bank's agencies.[14] His method was to order Krivoshein to send out three "temporary agencies" *(otdeleniia)* to guide the work of the local bank sections in critical areas. They covered 22 gubernias, about seven apiece. The new agencies had one purpose: to stop the sections from selling their land to villages and partnerships and make them divide the land they purchased into integral household farms (Sidelnikov, 1973: 161). The temporary agencies were to divide up the bank's land among the various offices involved in the reform and hold each one responsible for selling its share. These offices included land settlement commissions, bank sections, and specially appointed "liquidators." Within one month these local agencies were to survey their assigned lands, divide them into farm-sized lots, and decide what to charge would-be purchasers for them—truly a program reminiscent of the old Kutler-Witte optimism.

On 30 August, after the month was up, Stolypin wrote a secret memorandum (see n. 14) in which he expressed qualified satisfaction with the achievements of two of his bulldozing "temporary agenices," the first and third, though he complained that most of their work had thus far been done only on paper, not on the ground. The second he found totally unsatisfactory, and he fired its members (pp. 158, 163). Meanwhile, he kept up a flurry of conferences and circulars, and on 3 October he was ready to bring some lengthy proposals before the Council of Min-

[14]The following account is taken largely from Stolypin's secret memorandum of 30 Aug. 1907 (Sidelnikov, 1973: 157-69).

isters. Several tsar-approved edicts followed, the most important a circular from the Committee for Land Settlement Affairs dated 19 February
1908, which contained an elaborate set of rules governing the sale of
bank land. Such are the bare outlines of Stolypin's struggle with the
peasant bank in 1907.[15]

The attack on the bank seems to have substantially augmented the
confusion that accompanied the reform's beginnings. By way of illustration, we have the observations of one L. V. Dashkevich regarding some
events that transpired in Kirsanov uezd, Tambov gubernia (1909: 92-
112). As Dashkevich described it, the uezd land settlement commission in
Kirsanov assumed formal responsibility for selling the bank's land in late
1906. During its first few months of existence it did very little, but in the
early summer of 1907 it received orders to get all the bank's land measured and distributed by early August, when "three temporary sections of
the bank council" were going to sweep through the area and confirm the
final sales (p. 94). "Three temporary sections" doubtless referred to one
of the agencies Stolypin set up to reorganize the bank. Two weeks later
new instructions came down from St. Petersburg: now the land settlement commission was to stay out of the bank's affairs and let the visitors—
the temporary section—handle the crash program to sell the land all by
themselves. As it turned out, the temporary section came twice, once in
July and once in August. The first time they decided to sell to partnerships and villages; the second time they favored individuals. Either way,
practical results were the same. No one could cut up all the bank's land
into viable farms and sell it in just one season, so in fact the land came
under the use of such villages and partnerships as could readily avail
themselves of it (pp. 95-99).[16]

A few weeks after the second group of visitors had come and gone,
the Council of Ministers canceled the actions of both groups and ordered
the land settlement commission once again to take charge of selling the
bank's lands. This time there would be no compromise. Only khutor lots
were to be set up, no otrubs. Again the Kirsanov commission met to
draw up a crash program. It gave itself until fall—that is, two or three
weeks at most—to divide 54,000 acres of bank land into khutors of 27 to
54 acres apiece. Since there were no surveyors in Kirsanov, a private
Jewish firm was called in from Smolensk. These visiting experts helped
very little. They worked well into the winter months, but all they could
do in so short a time was simply to measure off the requisite lots without
considering whether the land on each one could actually sustain a farm.

---

[15]See Sidelnikov's notes (1973: 321-22). The rules of 19 Feb. 1908 are printed
in *Sbornik* (1908: 661-81).

[16]The second group of visitors was the same temporary section that had
come through before, but with new members. Stolypin had fired the first ones.

Many were on meadowland that no one had ever cultivated; many had no water supply (pp. 99-102).

Not surprisingly, the peasant of Kirsanov uezd did not want many of the new khutor lots. Even when the government threatened to sell them to settlers from Poltava gubernia—good Ukrainian stock, reputedly more capable of independent farming than Great Russians—the locals did not budge.[17]

In the end, the government gave way. On 19 February 1908 the surveys of late 1907 came to the same abrupt termination as their predecessors. The new circular (n. 15) established yet another set of procedures for selling bank land: a somewhat more relaxed arrangement calling for more careful surveying and allowing otrubs to be formed wherever khutors would not work. Once again plans had to be remade and ground resurveyed. In 1909, when Dashkevich wrote his account, much of the bank land still remained unsold (pp. 101-5).

Dashkevich's quasi-eyewitness description is not accurate in detail. The government never insisted that only khutor farms be set up on bank lands. The committee's circular of 12 June 1907 simply called for *"otrubnye"* farms in general (TsGIAL, f. 592, op. 1, d. 170, ll. 44-52). This was indeed a stronger statement than the bank's earlier instructions, which had not insisted on consolidation at all (ll. 4-5), but there was never any push to sell bank land exclusively to khutor-formers. On the whole, Dashkevich's acquaintance with the administrative apparatus of the Stolypin Reform was less than intimate, and his bias narrowed his vision. He had been hostile to the reform from its outset (just as he had opposed the land captains ever since their introduction in 1889) because it furthered the interference of bureaucracy in the countryside. All his work rings with the farmer's hatred of central administration. The reckless "adventuring" of the government, he said, had brought on the Russo-Japanese War and the Revolution of 1905. Now the "revolutionary" Stolypin Reform was violating the peasants' rights and destroying their

[17]Dashkevich did not refer explicitly to Ukrainians, but most peasants from Poltava were in fact Ukrainians, and Stolypin did specify *"khokhly"*—i.e., left-bank Ukrainians—in his memorandum of 30 Aug. 1907. *Khokhly,* said the irate prime minister, were to be brought in and settled wherever local peasants did not buy the bank's land (Sidelnikov, 1973: 162). In 1908 the MZ gave out similar instructions regarding new bank lands being opened up in Samara and Saratov gubernias. If locals did not buy the land during 1908, outsiders were to be brought in, preferably émigrés from Kiev, Podoliia, Volyniia, and Poltava—all Ukrainian gubernias (*IGU,* 1908: 515). Ukrainians were not the only pioneers available to the MVD. In early 1909 the bank sought and received deputy-MVD Lykoshin's help in arranging for the migration of Latvian peasant to Kaluga gubernia to take up residence on land the locals had not purchased (TsGIAL, f. 1291, op. 120, 1909g., d. 16, ll. 1-4). Such were the exigencies of selling khutors to individual peasants.

sense of legality. The bureaucrats had blundered into the reform without knowing what they were doing, and now they were desperately trying to cover their mistakes with a flood of ministerial circulars that had no clear relation either to statutory law or to each other. In essence the reform was a series of "experiments" conducted by ignoramuses, in which peasants were being used as guinea pigs. But they were not even experiments, since there was no way of recording results systematically and therefore no way of coming to meaningful conclusions. How could the government "administer" a reform of peasant land, Dashkevich asked, when it had not even been able to complete the general survey it had begun in the time of Catherine II (1909: 9-50, 124-27)?

Obviously Dashkevich was not a man striving to present a balanced account of the problems of administrative action. On the other hand, his impressions of government action in Kirasanov uezd, though they mix rumor with fact, probably reflect the general character of the reform organization's work in 1907. Tambov was among those gubernias that came under the second of the three temporary agencies, whose work was indeed unsatisfactory to Stolypin and whose members he fired, presumably in August 1907. Reverses in the government's program did occur in Tambov in the order presented by Dashkevich, though they may not have been as extreme as he suggested.[18]

Stolypin seems to have been experiencing an Armageddon in his agrarian policies in 1907, no less unnerving than the one he had just been through in his dealings with the second Duma.[19] In late 1907 he was still clinging to his utterly mistaken belief that the life or death of the reform—and of the government itself—depended on the successful sale of bank lands. He was by no means averse to pressuring his subordinates to sustain his failing policies. He was quite prepared to import Ukrainians into the central black-earth region, although it would have taken a considerable portion of the army to protect them from the natives, and even with the army's protection the Ukrainians would have been hard put to support themselves on waterless meadowlands. Obviously Stolypin did not comprehend his own reform very well in 1907, and it cannot be denied that some of his hysterical commands created confusion in the countryside.

It should be added, however, that the peasants themselves do not seem to have suffered undue pressure to form otrubs on bank land dur-

[18]Another account from a local eyewitness in Tambov testifies to the disorder and dismay produced by the government's early efforts at reform. See Benckendorff (1954: 144-47), who was an uezd gentry marshal at the time.

[19]Stolypin had not only had to dismiss the second Duma in June 1907 but also to change the electoral law so as to ensure that the third Duma would be more cooperative. His action had been openly illegal, and many historians have termed it, justly, a coup d'état.

ing 1907. If we can believe the MZ's own account, the settling of outsiders did not take place anywhere in European Russia in 1907, Stolypin's threats notwithstanding. An official statement of early 1908 tells us that over 97% of the bank land sold prior to 1 October went to natives of the uezds where the land was located (*IGU*, 1908: 312).

Bank officials, on the other hand, were under extreme pressure. The bank had never held so much land, and the local sections had no staff to manage it, i.e., assign rental payments and collect them. The only way the bank could realize any income on its colossal investment was to sell, and the bank organization was straining to do this as rapidly as possible (TsGIAL, f. 592, op. 1, d. 218, ll. 105-7). But pressure on local officials to sell land at a rapid rate seems to have produced the opposite of oppression in the villages. Reports of inspections made in 1908-9 indicate that the most widespread practice on bank lands in 1907 was to give way to the peasants' demands. In a report of his inspection of Penza gubernia in 1909, A. S. Lykoshin noted that bank lands were being sold in strips, not only in Penza but "almost everywhere." Lykoshin had to conclude that no significant land reform was taking place, but, he hastened to add with evident satisfaction, the reform was proceeding peacefully (*IZO*, 1910: 29-31). Land reform was not a howling success in 1907, but Stolypin's antics, however undignified, were not *forcing* peasants to do anything.

In one respect, Stolypin's attack on the peasant bank succeeded. Bank sales to individuals rose sharply in 1908 while sales to villages dropped, and this trend persisted until the end of the reform (TsGIAL, f. 1291, op. 120, 1908g., d. 33). In 1910, when the bank sold more land than in any other year, 2% (40,000 acres) of its sales went to communal villages, 5% (90,000 acres) to partnerships, and 93% (1.9 million acres) to individuals. From then on the ratio increased slightly in favor of individuals (Sidelnikov, 1973: 173-74). During the whole period 1907-14, 94% of the land sold to individuals went to consolidated farms. In 1916 the MZ reported that of all the land the bank sold during these years, both to individuals and groups, 79% went to individual consolidated farms (*Kratkii*, 1916: 37).

But the prime minister's successs was far from complete. In the summer of 1907 he was anticipating that the bank's massive land purchases would continue indefinitely. As soon as he imposed his regulations, however, the bank began to slow its rate of purchase drastically. In 1908 it bought only 1.5 million acres, and in 1909, 0.4 million. Thereafter the bank's land buying remained at a relatively low level (Sidelnikov, 1973: 172). On the other hand, the bank continued to finance peasant purchases of land directly from private owners on a large scale. It financed the transfer of 1.9 million acres in this way in 1907, and this figure dropped only slightly, to 1.6 million, by 1909. It rose again to slightly under 1.9 million in 1910 and then began gradually to decrease. In 1913, the last prewar year, the bank financed the direct purchase of 1.1 million acres (p. 178). Since this operation was not so susceptible to control by Stolypin's decrees, relatively little of the land was sold as integral farms. The portion of land sold with the bank's help that went to individuals increased from 1.5% in 1907 to 30% in 1911, 32% in 1912, and 34% in 1913 (p. 178), not nearly the sort of transformation that took place on the bank's own land. These percentages are even less impressive when we take into consideration the fact that not all land sold directly to individuals took the form of otrubs and khutors. It seems, then, that the bank was able to go on using a substantial portion of its funds to support villages rather than individuals right up until 1914.

I have already indicated several possible explanations for the bank's behavior during the reform era. At this point it will be helpful to summarize them briefly. For one thing, the bank had a traditional policy of lending to land-poor peasants; better to say, it was accustomed to making its loans to groups of peasants, thus making its records show the bulk of its loans going to land-poor peasants (ch. 4, sec. D). In 1905-7, with statesmen and capital-city rhetoricians clamoring more loudly than ever for aid to the poor, with a mass of laws and orders from St. Petersburg piously prescribing that the land-poor should indeed get more land, it was hardly a time for the bank to give up its facade. Not surprisingly, most bank directives of the years 1905-6 reflect a seemingly serious intention to make loans to land-poor peasants (see, e.g., a circular of 26 Nov. 1905, TsGIAL, f. 1291, op. 119, 1906g., d. 67, ll. 95-99; also a letter to the zemstvoes of 9 Dec. 1905, ll. 87-90). But if the local sections made loans directly to individuals, they would have to give up their philanthropical pose. No individual would be able to repay a loan unless he possessed animals and equipment and had the ability to manage a farm effectively—which is to say that needy peasants were not usually ideal prospects for loans. Even a deluge of well-meaning directives was not enough to make a local section extend loans to peasants who lacked the resources to keep up mortgage payments. In short, land settlement required the bank to publicize its indifference to welfare.

This was not the only obstacle to the sale of integral farms to individuals. When a bank section did reluctantly decide to give up its facade of welfare agency and begin extending loans to reliable individuals, it still faced the problem of peasant sabotage. Even the most credit-worthy individual borrowers were very poor risks if they had to live in the immediate vicinity of hostile neighbors, former tenants who had been evicted to make way for the new khutors. Finally, and probably most important, it was sound financial practice for the bank to sell its lands as rapidly as possible simply to keep its capital moving, and the most straightforward way to do this was to turn the land over unsurveyed to the villages that were already farming it.

On balance, the bank won its struggle with Stolypin. The prime minister's limited success in making the bank sell khutor lots drastically slowed the business of selling to peasants, and the local sections responded after 1907 by cutting down drastically on land purchasing. To be sure, other factors contributed to this trend. Land prices rose so steeply after 1906 that even wealthy peasants could not justify the investment required. Then, too, the gradual pacification of the countryside probably encouraged some estate owners to hold on to their land and farm it. Finally, the growing popularity of village consolidation among the peasantry caused the MZ to lose interest in the business of selling bank lands. After 1908 the reform organization became increasingly reluctant to allow its much-needed surveyors to spend their time on anything but land reform on allotment land (ch. 8, sec. A). Doubtless, all these factors played their part, but the fact remains that the bank could not afford to hold too much land for too long a time without deriving an income from it. The bank won its struggle primarily in the sense that it insisted on operating like a bank and refused to make believe it was an agency of land reform.

Sometime in 1908 the government began to realize that the peasant bank was not going to be the main instrument of land settlement. Nevertheless, land settlement continued. As the bank's programs faded into the background, significant numbers of villages were petitioning to consolidate collectively. Perhaps this was why Krivoshein left the peasant bank in May 1908 and transferred to the MZ to replace Vasilchikov. Certainly, as we shall see in Chapter 8 (sec. A), the new MZ's actions indicated an intention to push for village consolidation and let the bank's programs hang.

In fairness to Stolypin, it must be said that his mistaken emphasis on the bank's work was far from unique. Most capital-city minds shared his faith in the use of nonpeasant land to bring about the reform of peasant land. Not only Witte and Kutler but just about all the liberal and radical parties in St. Petersburg based their policies on this same cornerstone. Even old Engelgardt, justly famed for his practical wisdom and his concern for peasant welfare, had believed that consolidating rented land was the best means to start up the consolidation of allotment land (1937: 298-99). The only essential difference between Stolypin and other capital-city experts on the peasantry was that Stolypin could not simply propose ideas; he had also to confront their practical consequences *and assume responsibility for them.* When the inherent absurdities of his initial program gradually became manifest, he could not simply shrug his shoulders and blame everything on oppressive land captains. The government had committed itself to a land reform, and somehow it had to carry one out.

E. THE LAND CAPTAINS AT THE BEGINNING OF THE REFORM: THE QUESTION OF COERCION

The preceding sections have described the main lines of government operation during the reform's first year or two. In essence, the central offices were blundering into one program while the peasants embarked on another. I have stressed this point not because I think Stolypin and his administrators were peculiar but because the virtually random nature of the reform's beginning furnishes us with an excellent example of how agrarian reforms work.

There is one difficulty. My effort to depict the reform's origin as an exploration runs contrary to a solidly established convention of scholarship to the effect that land settlement was forced upon the peasants. This notion carries with it a cliché-image of an administration whose agents were striving toward a single goal and who all knew what this goal was. Since this image of monolithic purpose is an unshakeable element in scholarly scenarios, I must pause here to discuss it, especially the passionately held conviction that the peasants' petitions for land settlement were squeezed out of helpless village assemblies by despotic, brutal administrators.

The Situation of the Land Captains

The first question that comes to mind involves the identity of these despots. Who, precisely, forced peasants to petition for land settlement projects?

Obviously it was not the uzed land settlement commission or its permanent member. A body of men on the uezd level could not give the continuous attention to each village that coercion or even mere familiarization would demand. Each permanent member had some hundreds of thousands of people to deal with, and in 1907 he was devoting most of his time to wrestling matches with the peasant bank. Thus we cannot imagine the MZ's land settlement organization playing a vital role in carrying the reform to the people. In general, commission members could only deal with villages where some heads of household were already interested in land reform and prepared to initiate a project. One observer tells us that a commission member would visit a village only after ten or more households formally invited the commission to help them with land settlement measures (Preyer, 1914: 276-77).

Who, then, was to introduce peasants to land settlement, forcibly or otherwise? Ideally it would be local figures, men who were known to the peasants and who commanded their respect. Throughout the reform era a multitude of decrees and circulars repeatedly called on all members of the commissions, not only the permanent members, to go out and do land reforms (see, e.g., *IGU,* 1912: 146), and it seems that many commission members did promote the reform on their own. A medal established in late 1912 "for distinction in land settlement work" was awarded during 1913 to 130 uezd gentry marshals, 28 gubernia gentry marshals, 39 chairmen of zemstvo directorates (both uezd and gubernia), 41 zemstvo-elected commission members, and 42 peasant-elected members (*Izvestiia Kantseliarii,* 1913: 65-66, 106-7, 274). In theory any educated man could introduce a village or two to the idea of land settlement. This will not do, however, as an explanation for the flow of petitions that came in during 1907-8. *If* any outside agent entered villages and whipped them into signing petitions against their will, it had to be either a land captain or zemstvo official. No other body of men had access to villages or knowledge of them. As we shall see in the following chapters, zemstvo administrators came to play a much more vital role in land reform as the years went by, but at the outset, when petitions for village consolidation first came flooding in, they were still operating on a small scale. Moreover, they were not generally inclined to use illegal methods to compel peasants to accept dictates from St. Petersburg. By and large, the land captains were the only government agencies in a position to "familiarize" in 1907-8.

Several questions confront us. Did the captains in fact undertake to familiarize the peasants with the reform laws? If so, how did the government get them to do it and what was it they did? What impact, if any, did their efforts produce? I know of no direct, reliable evidence that will provide us with answers to any of these questions. Reports of what the captains actually did are contradictory. Here and there captains were reported to have been active[20] or passive, [21] corrupt[22] or honest,[23] educated[24] or uneducated,[25] doctrinnaire[26] or practical,[27] indifferently formalistic[28] or sincerely devoted to what they imagined to be their duty,[29]

[20] *IZO* (1909: 51).
[21] *IZO* (1908: 126; 1909: 25, 93-94).
[22] Dubrovskii (1963: 167-68).
[23] *IZO* (1909: 93).
[24] Semenov (1915: 280-81).
[25] *IZO* (1909: 55); Maiborodov (folder 2, 120).
[26] *IZO* (1909: 52); Maiborodov (folder 2, 124).
[27] *IZO* (1909: 50-51); Maiborodov (folder 2, 94).
[28] *IZO* (1907: 59-60; 1908: 187; 1909: 51, 54).
[29] *IZO* (1909: 93); Kisel-Zagorianskii (152).

ignorant[30] or informed[31] regarding peasant society, for[32] or against[33] the reform, friendly[34] or unfriendly[35] toward local zemstvoes, submissive[36] or defiant[37] toward the local gentry, willing to sacrifice peasant interests to further their own careers[38] or determined to protect "their people" against a blind bureaucracy.[39]

I know of no sure way to determine which of the above characterizations, if any, hold true for land captainry in general. Eyewitness evidence on specific captains is unreliable, since virtually all of it comes from individuals and institutions who had reasons for praising or blaming quite apart from the evidence of their senses. We have a substantial number of letters and petitions ostensibly written by peasants about land captains and other reform agencies. Some complained of atrocities; some testified to a government agent's kindness and competence. Soviet scholars have published many of the former; contemporary pro-government newspapers published many of the latter. I have never seen a single one of either sort that sounds like an authentic peasant statement. Generally speaking, peasants expressed themselves in terms of general issues only when they thought it would bring them some advantage in their local conflicts. Whether or not the local captain was saint or devil depended entirely on which side he took in his "people's" squabbles. I have seen only one account of a captain's work during the reform written by a peasant that rises above the level of local politics. This is S. T. Semenov's autobiography, *Dvadtsat piat let* (which will be discussed in some detail below).

The newspapers deserve a paragraph or two. Russia rejoiced in something approaching freedom of the press during the Stolypin era— also known as the era of yellow journalism—and one would expect that an institution so inimical to civil rights as the land captains would have received considerable attention from reporters. Such was the case. Local

[30] Maiborodov (folder 2, 20). Maiborodov speaks here of a captain who had jurisdiction over a village of Germans but did not himself speak German. Maiborodov himself had German, Bulgarian, and French villages under his jurisdiction during the course of his service, but he spoke none of these languages. Nor did he see anything wrong with this (pp. 21-23, 40, 124). He notes, as a rarity, one land captain in Bessarabia who spoke the languages of the local peasants (p. 51).

[31] Kisel-Zagorianskii (54-55); *IZO* (1909: 50-51).

[32] *IZO* (1909: 53); Maiborodov (folder 2, 97-100).

[33] *IZO* (1909: 54-55, 92-93; 1907: 135). See also TsGIAL, f. 1291, op. 63, 1907g., d. 9, l. 19; d. 10, ll. 117-21; d. 17, ll. 40, 42, 63.

[34] Kisel-Zagorianskii (94); Novikov (1902: 26-28).

[35] Maiborodov (folder 2, 33).

[36] Dubrovskii (1963: 164).

[37] Maiborodov (folder 2, 74-85).

[38] Dubrovskii (1963: 168-69).

[39] Naumov (1954: I, 187-95); Maiborodov (folder 2, 108-20).

and national papers—far left, far right, and liberal alike—produced an enormous supply of anecdotes concerning the activities of reform agencies in the countryside, most of them denouncing government officials for a variety of crimes and excesses. A reasonably industrious historian can find all the material of this sort he can possibly use. Much of it rests conveniently at hand in tsarist government archives, where each product of the free press is kept neatly together with a corresponding demand for explanations sent by a central office to a local agency and a reply or two from the agency.

In general, the quality of newspaper accounts was not high. One St. Petersburg paper ran pictures of starving peasants in Tavrid gubernia. The paper said they were khutor farmers, but a highly indignant permanent member of the uezd land settlement commission reported that they were shots he himself had taken of some communal peasants (TsGIAL, f. 1291, op. 120, 1910g., d. 14, ll. 268-69). In another, more involved case, the *Novoe Vremia,* a relatively reputable St. Petersburg daily, reprinted a story one of its reporters found in an Odessa newspaper. According to this report, some rich peasants in a Kherson village managed in May 1910 to get permission for a personal consolidation that awarded them far more land than they had coming to them. A crowd of their fellow villagers, justly enraged, stopped a surveyor from marking out new fields. The police dispersed them, arresting eight of the most unruly. Now the surveyor was continuing his evil work. A Moscow paper *(Russkoe Slovo)* caught the same story, but instead of merely reprinting it, as *Novoe Vremia* had done, it sent its own correspondent to look into the matter. In the Moscow version, rich, would-be consolidators bought up land from some poor neighbors and then applied for consolidation. "Our correspondent" did not say exactly how the poor neighbors were able to sell their shares of communal land. Perhaps they did it by claiming them as personal property. In any case, the kulaks got their fists on the land and commenced their consolidation. When the surveyor came, a crowd of women descended upon him. The "khutor-formers" were beaten up and the surveyor chased away. The area was in upheaval for three days, until a force of cossacks, led by the governor himself, restored order by arresting up to 200 people. Now the surveyor was once again inexorably at his work (ll. 178-79). The land section, its clerks alert to every unfavorable sound, collected these press releases and sent an inquiry about them to the governor of Kherson. On 28 May the governor sent in the following story. The village in question had agreed to allow a small number of its members to carry out a personal consolidation. then the villagers had changed their minds and voted 339 to 7 to carry out a full village consolidation. A few "rich" peasants, who had been among the original personal consolidators, then began to agitate *against* village consolidation. They submitted petitions with false signatures, and then, when

peaceful methods failed, they attacked the surveyors. Local agencies subdued this outbreak, and as of 28 May the village consolidation was again
proceeding with full support from the vast majority of villagers (1. 181).

I cannot say with certainty which of these stories is true, if any.
What does seem certain is that press stories were not entirely reliable as
records of events in the countryside. Doubtless, newspaper editors were
as hard put as the government to find trained people willing to work in
villages. We confront the fact, then, that we really know very little about
what the land captains were doing in 1906-7.

The shortage of hard evidence notwithstanding, a few generalizations may be advanced concerning the *situation* of the land captains. As
we know from Chapter 3, the capital cities had been disapproving of
them and expecting everything from them since the time of their inception. As we know from Chapter 6, many of the leading enactors of the
reform wanted to do away with the captains altogether and very nearly
achieved this aim in 1906. Even the captains' own superiors were dissatisfied with them and had been since the late 1890s, when the land section's
efforts to reform them had commenced.

We have seen that most of the land captains' formal duties were
already ludicrously burdensome before the reform began and therefore
were very little performed in fact. In theory, since the captains were absolutely resonsbile for whatever happened in the villages, they lived in per-
petual danger of being blamed and attacked for events entirely beyond
their knowledge, to say nothing of their control. Actually their peril did
not loom large before 1907-8 because their superiors had no systematic
way of checking up on them. The rural knights had generally operated in
the absence of either law or supervision, and no one, they least of all, had
had any meaningful, commonly accepted standard by which to measure
their failure or success. An inspection of five gubernia administrations in
1907-8 (Chernigov, Saratov, Voronezh, Tambov, Poltava) revealed a total
absence of anything like a standard set of comprehensive regulations for
uezd administrations, land captains, or peasant volosts. Only two (Voronezh and Tambov) had troubled to set up record-keeping requirements
on paper (*IZO,* 1908: 306). On the whole, it is not far-fetched to surmise
that a pre-reform captain who wished to survive in his job had above all
to avoid trouble. He had to get along with his fellow captains and stay
on the good side of the uezd's gentry marshal. More important, he had
to rely heavily on the volost and village elders in his *uchastok* to keep
things quiet and provide him with materials for his reports. A wise captain left his village alone except when it was necessary to lend support to
traditional authorities. By 1906 respect for tradition had become the
lore—though not invariably the practice—of the trade.

The reform laws put the captain in a difficult position. Before 1906
he had symbolized the unity of statutory law and tradition (ch. 3, sec. D).

In practice, he had played this role by ignoring statutes and orders, and this was how he had been able to survive and make himself acceptable to the peasants in his *uchastok*. The reform laws, however, were much more violently at odds with "tradition" than any previous enactments, and in 1906 it suddenly became much harder for a mere symbol to obscure the opposition between state and village. A captain confronted by a peasant petitioning for the "acquisition" of his strips or personal consolidation had to make a sharp choice between continuing in his old role or suddenly adopting a new one. If he took the former path, he would contrive ways to deny the petition, or at least delay or discourage it. In other words, he would violate statutes and orders in order to protect traditional peasants from their "progressive" neighbors.

A captain who chose the other path—i.e., strove to spread the reform as actively as he could—would at least act on the petitions he received and perhaps even proselytize for land settlement. In this case he would be upsetting tradition in order to "liberate" any peasants who could be persuaded to demand their freedom. This course was almost invariably the more difficult of the two. It involved the captain in a village squabble in which he had to uphold the weaker side, though in fact he lacked the physical means to do this effectively. Worse, his involvement as an advocate of rebellious minorities endangered what little actual influence he had. His original purpose, it will be recalled, was to protect the peasantry from the bombardments of bureaucracy. To the extent that he had done this, he had taken his stand on the power of village and volost oligarchies. As soon as he tried to support individual peasants against these oligarchies in the very radical manner envisioned in the reform laws, he deprived himself of his own foundation. Suddenly the statutes and orders from St. Petersburg became the only support he had, and since he had never come close to enforcing and/or carrying them out, he became, in effect, fair game for any village or volost elder who wished to accuse him of failing to act in accordance with statutes. Before the reform, of course, peasant oligarchs had had little reason to resort to such tactics, but when a captain ventured to support disruptive minorities who were undertaking to destroy village society, the old "kulaks" had excellent reason to take advantage of his vulnerability.

Imagine a hypothetical captain presenting himself to one of his villages as a "familiarizer" in 1907. First he has some announcements to make to the peasants. "Forget the redemption payments," he says. "Forgive me, all you who have heard me speak so often about how necessary and moral it was to keep them up. Those of you who have been making them since the 1860s and have almost finished paying for your land, you get nothing back, even though you have paid much more than the state peasants and those ex-serfs who only commenced their payments in the 1880s. Tough luck."

With this jarring message off his chest, our captain gets down to the main issues. "For 15 years I have commanded sons to obey their fathers and fathers to be responsible for their sons. I have commanded you to obey your village elders and I have made the elders responsible for your welfare and good behavior. I have not only managed things this way, I have often told you that it was godly and righteous to manage things this way. I have steadfastly supported your elders when they punished you for going against their authority. Now all this has changed. I want heads of household to become sole owners of the family strips, and I want them to exploit their sons' labor more efficiently. If you petition to 'acquire' your strips and the elder tries to discourage you, I want you to disobey him. He is backward. If your neighbors object, defy them. I will support you. You will not only be a better farmer, you will be behaving righteously. I realize that I have been calling your elders and your conservative neighbors righteous ever since I came here, but this is no longer true. Forgive me for having misled you all these years." And as our captain speaks, he realizes that if the peasants do not respond to his words with enthusiasm, he will be blamed for failing to "familiarize" them adequately.

Of course, no actual land captain ever said anything like this. The above speech is simply a construction designed to show what the peasants were likely to hear when *and if* a captain went out to "familiarize" them with the reform. Real land captains did not go out to make speeches of any kind. In 1905-6, in the midst of rapidly changing orders from the center, any declaration on the captains' part was very likely to be countermanded within the following weeks. The more often they spoke on behalf of government policy, the more likely they were to make fools of themselves.

To sum up, the reform changed the land captain's position radically. It was no longer safe simply to rely on the oligarchies of peasant society and hope for the best. On the other hand, the reform laws offered no alternative manner of acting. They urged captains to "familiarize," but they also held them responsible for any trouble their familiarizing produced. Thus we may imagine that in 1907 reliance on tradition was still a very realistic guide for the cautious captain who wished to survive, and the violence of 1905-6 must have made a great many captains cautious. As the reform commenced, many of them were just crawling out of their hiding places or creeping back from the refuges to which they had fled. In Saratov, the most violent Great Russian gubernia, they had fled the countryside "almost without exception" in 1905—so said a report from Governor Stolypin in early 1906 (Karpov, 1925: 174)—and this seems to have been fairly common in all gubernias. An MVD circular of 4 January 1906 said, in part: "Many uezd gentry marshals have absented themselves from their uezds without good reason, and land captains have abandoned their *uchastki* without authorization" (*IZO*, 1906: 22). Such was the impact of violence on the captains that a goodly number of them simply did not return to their posts in 1907. For the captain who did return, the old peasant institutions still offered him the best support he could find. It seems, then, that when a captain undertook to "familiarize" peasants with the promise of land settlement, no matter how gently, he was taking serious risks and making enormous difficulties for himself— unless, of course, the peasants in a village actually desired his help. It is hard to imagine large numbers of these harassed and overburdened clerks attempting to force peasants into radical rearrangements of their land by cracking whips at them. As we shall see, our meager evidence indicates that they did nothing of the sort.[40]

The Role of Coercion in Land Settlement

Dubrovskii's View

Dubrovskii believes that peasant petitions for land settlement were squeezed out of their signers by naked force. Most historians agree with him (e.g., Robinson, 1932: 264; Sidelnikov, 1980: 179). I center my atten- tion on Dubrovskii, however, because he has made a greater effort to compile evidence in support of his belief than anyone else.

Dubrovskii's effort fails. In the 1963 edition of his magnum opus on the reform, he willfully distorts his evidence in order to suggest not only that local agents of the reform organization forced communal peasants to break from their villages but also that the central government *wanted* its agencies to use force. His evidence: government reports condemning the use of force by local agents and actions taken by the central offices to prevent their subordinates from pressuring peasants (1963: 167-82). He presents only one instance in which a nongovernmental soucre testified to the reform organization's use of illegal pressure. This was a protest against the reform written by a member of the "black hundreds." Dubrovskii says it was a "hysterical" protest, yet he devotes three pages to it, and he suggests that we take it seriously as prima facie evidence regarding the actions of government agencies in the countryside (pp. 182-85). He is quite aware that the black hundreds and a great many conservative gen-

---

[40] A report on five gubernias showed that between one-third and one-half of the land captains were replaced in 1906-7 (*IZO*, 1908: 281). This rapid turnover was not due solely to the reform laws. Santoni's account (1968: 165-69) indicates that the October Manifesto was the rudest shock rural officialdom had to suffer from the central offices. Witte published it in the newspapers before issuing it to the government's administrators via regular channels. Several memoirs by offi- cials of that day agree with Santoni in emphasizing this open expression of impe- rial scorn for the government's agents outside St. Petersburg (see, e.g., Kurlov, 1923: 31-40; Martynov, 1972: 59).

try were violently opposed to the reform and were working actively to undermine it. He knows very well that their statements about the reform were no more reliable than their denunciations of Jewry. This is why I say that he distorts evidence willfully. What his evidence actually shows is that the central government strove to prevent its agencies from pressuring peasants into land reform.

But there is another side to Dubrovskii. Later on in his book he points out that land settlement benefited many peasants and that in many cases peasants adopted khutors and otrubs willingly. In this connection he flatly denies that government coercion was the basic cause for the spread of consolidation. The cause, he says, was the general development of capitalism in Russia (pp. 187-88, 231-34). Government agents did use coercion to further land settlement, but this was only because they were irredeemably clumsy, cruel, and ineffective. The primary effect of their actions was to slow down the natural spread of land reform, mainly because the government's clumsy measures exacerbated conflicts among the peasants (pp. 553-61).

These observations are not without ambiguity, but they are immensely useful in laying to rest the outworn and grossly inaccurate image of a peasantry utterly without its own interest in land reform. Dubrovskii's own concepts force him to the essentially correct conclusion that the reform was most likely to go well when arbitrary coercion was kept at a minimum and when officials refrained even from entirely legal action whenever it adversely affected the overall welfare of peasant communities. Attempts to compel peasants to act collectively against their will actually served no one's interests, not even those of parasitic landlords, who, by Dubrovskii's account, masterminded the government's policies and programs.[41]

Thus, even if we assume that coercion did take place on a large scale in connection with the reform—though there is surprisingly little evidence of this—we have little reason to believe that force was a *major* stimulus to land reform. As I have suggested (sec. C), many peasants feared that government agencies would act to protect the rights of individual peasants, and this fear may have brought many communal peasants to petition for village consolidation. But if this was the case, then we are speaking of a struggle among peasants, not between peasants and government.

---

[41] In one of his more lyrical passages Dubrovskii asserts that 30,000 *pomeshchiki* (landholders) ran the whole government (1963: 164). Here he repeats a slogan widely used in leftist pamphlets of the reform era and recently recirculated by some American scholars (Haimson, 1979). Thirty thousand is a poetic approximation of the 27,000 landholders who owned 1,350 acres or more as of 1905 (Shestakov, 1927: 73-74).

The Central Offices' Attitude toward Coercion

It is a fact that the MVD-police hierarchy set out to exert pressure on land captains to arouse the peasants' interest in the law of 9 November 1906. Although the captains never received formal commands to force peasants into reform against their wills, the MVD's central offices did take a number of measures to encourage their rural agents to proselytize for the government's programs and to assist peasants who expressed an interest in them. It was possible for captains to interpret such measures as de facto orders to find ways to force reform in the villages. One illustration of the sort of pressure the captains felt may be found in a report of an inspection of MVD offices in Novgorod gubernia in late 1907 (*IZO*, 1908: 185-91). The inspecting official, N. N. Kupreianov of the land section, noted sharp variations from one *uchastok* to another in the number of petitions coming in from heads of household requesting personal ownership of their strips. It did not occur to Kupreianov that conditions might have varied from one *uchastok* to another. His report ventures only one explanation: some land captains had not been as active as others in familiarizing peasants with the provisions of the decree of 9 November 1906. His inspections of specific land captains confirmed his opinion, which was not simply reported to his superiors but published in the land sections' journal, along with explicit accusations against several "inadequate" land captains, that is, land captains whose *uchastki* had not produced many petitions for "acquisition."

As we have seen, the land section's practice of singling out particular captains for public condemnation had begun in 1904 (ch. 4, sec. B). Land captain Maiborodov suffered a vicious attack by Ia. Ia. Litvinov after the latter's inspection of Kherson gubernia in 1909, and he came close to being prosecuted as a criminal (ch. 4, sec. B). Not only captains were pilloried in this fashion but also their superiors on the uezd and gubernia levels. MVD circulars spoke endlessly of the collective responsibility all officials in each area had to bear for the success of the reform. Each administrator had not only to act but also to coordinate effectively with other agencies, and if any of them did not, the local governor was to straighten him out. So the MVD commanded. Everyone in the MVD hierarchy, from governors on down, was held to account for the rate at which petitions flowed in, and woe unto those areas where the flow was slower than elsewhere.[42]

There were also rewards for high scores. The land captain who satisfied his superiors' thirst for petitions received generous travel and per diem allowances and in some cases bonuses and even promotions. A

[42]A typical MVD circular to this effect is in *IGU* (1908: 142-43). See also two of Stolypin's circulars to governors in June 1910 in Verpakhovskaia (1911: I, 171-75).

captain who turned out an impressive number of petitions could receive unofficial bonuses in the form of extra clerical allowances. According to the late Dr. Vladimir Gsovski, all these benefits were common in Moscow gubernia, where he served as an assistant land captain during the reform era.[43]

Promotions were an especially lucrative prospect in 1907, when the reform organization was expanding rapidly and every uezd had to have a permanent member for its land settlement commission. Obviously only a very limited number of the 2,500-odd land captains in service could actually be promoted to the 300-odd new posts, but the captains were certainly prime candidates and promotion was certainly attractive. A permanent member's annual salary was 2,000 rubles, as opposed to a top salary for the captains of 1,800. Add to this the generous travel and per diem allowances the permanent members enjoyed, not to mention the advantages of residence in the uezd capital city. Then, too, the captains' pay had to support the cost of their clerical help, whereas the permanent members' clerks came to them in addition to their salaries. In short, a captain whose peasants petitioned for reforms in relatively large numbers had reason to hope for a rapid improvement in his situation (Gsovski interview).

To see governmental pressure for petitions in its crudest form, consider a circular from the governor of Riazan to his land captains in August 1908 (Sidelnikov, 1973: 133-34). The circular comes too late to be called evidence for what the captains were doing in 1907, but it affords an excellent illustration of the sort of thing that *could* occur in the course of land reform.

What the governor wanted, he said, was to carry out the provisions of the 9 November decree. The fact that very few Riazan peasants had petitioned to transfer their strips to personal property "showed that the population had not been familiarized" with the advantages of personal landholding. Pamphlets had been distributed, but this was not enough. From now on the captains' service performance would be judged "on the basis of monthly figures showing how many peasants were separating from the communes." Beginning in September, a low figure could bring a formal accusation of negligence and a high figure could win a bonus. If the captains knew what was good for them, they would set aside certain days for going out to converse with peasants. The best time to strike was when a village was undergoing redistribution. Certain households stood to gain land while others would lose, and the potential losers would be

---

[43] I interviewed Dr. Gsovski in 1960, when he was chief of the Foreign Law Division, Library of Congress. On the benefits showered upon captains who served the reform well, see also Maiborodov (folder 2, 108), Kisel-Zagorianskii (52), and Dubrovskii (1963: 168-69, 172).

likely to find *ukreplenie* very appealing. It behooved an alert captain to know about every redistribution in advance so that he could get in touch with the inevitable malcontents and play on their desire to keep their shares of land intact. The machiavellian governor not only advised his captains to adopt this tactic, he commanded them. His circular explicitly directed them to play village politics in order to lure a few individuals into reform, thereby threatening to break up their village. The captains would have until mid-October to submit lists of villages in their *uchastki* where redistributions were likely to be forthcoming.

Clearly the governor of Riazan was pressing his captains hard. He was not the only one. The governor of Saratov sent out roughly the same sort of orders to his captains in January 1909 (*IZO*, 1909: 90). At least one other governor pressed even harder. In a circular of 21 January 1909 the MVD told its governors in a tone of marked disapproval that one of their number—unnamed in the circular—had ordered his captains to push their peasant-elected subordinates (chiefly the volost and village elders) into converting their own strips to personal holdings and consolidating them. Any elders who refused were to be driven out of office. This order, warned the circular, was wholly illegal (TsGIAL, f. 1291, op. 119, 1906g., d. 67, l. 30).

We have, then, several instances of governors pressuring land captains in crude, even illegal fashion to solicit petitions from the peasants. I refer to the methods used in the above cases as "crude" pressure because in each case a higher official gave his subordinate land captains to understand that quantity of petitions would be the main criterion for judging the quality of their work. *If this pressure for quantity of petitions had been typical of the government's attitude, it would certainly be true that the MVD organization was willing to use force to drive the peasants into reform.*

However, I do not believe that this sort of pressure characterized either the central government's attitude or even the MVD's attitude toward coercion. I have taken pains to recite the above instances because they are the only ones I have seen (in addition to one other, to be discussed below) that indicate "crude" pressure. Doubtless, other such incidents occurred during the Stolypin era, but I have not discovered them.

To be sure, an abundance of circulars and instructions flowed out of St. Petersburg, designed to stir sluggish captains into action and compel them to perform their tasks properly. Captains were repeatedly ordered to respond swiftly to peasant petitions for reform measures and do all the necessary work of investigating and recording properly. Take, for example, a memorandum from Litvinov to the governor of Voronezh, dated 21 June 1907. The head of the land section was writing, he said, because he was dissatisfied with the progress of *ukreplenie* in Voronezh. Only a small number of petitions was coming in, and this probably indicated that many captains were not doing their jobs. But Litvinov was no Kupreianov. He did not care very much about mere numbers of petitions. What really disturbed him was that captains were not acting on the petitions they did receive. Of 932 heads of household who had thus far petitioned to acquire their share of village land in Voronezh, only 97 had actually completed thier acquisitions. Moreover, only 54 of the 97 had acted with the consent of their villages. Obviously, said Litvinov, the captains of Voronezh did not recognize the importance of the 9 November decree, and they were failing to persuade the peasants of the advantages it brought them. The captains were not seeing to it that village and volost authorities carried out *ukrepleniia* with dispatch, and they were not troubling to win the cooperation of the broad masses (op. 63, 1907g., d. 4, 1. 24).[44]

Litvinov's memorandum to Voronezh does not reflect a desire to hound peasants. As we have seen in Chapter 4 (sec. B), the old land-section hand was much more inclined to hound captains. His memorandum reflected an approach to rural administration that the land section had been taking since the late 1890s: to implement all policies simply by ordering captains to carry them out and then to blame the captains if anything went wrong. Nothing in Litvinov's message suggested a desire to dragoon peasants into reform. On the contrary, he was telling captains that anyone who drummed up petitions by force or chicane would face the extremely embarrassing necessity of having to respond to them and carry out the operations they called for. There would be no rewards for large numbers of petitions unless actual reforms took place. Indeed, if large numbers of petitions failed to produce positive results, punishment would very likely follow.[45]

An inspection report of early 1908 made this state of affairs explicit. The author, a land-section official, explicitly and repeatedly approved of captains who *prevented* peasants from petitioning for *ukreplenie* or consolidation unless they were fully prepared to carry out all the necessary operations and bear the necessary expenses. The small number of peti-

[44]Similar messages abound in other collections of materials for 1907: see, e.g., TsGIAL, f. 1291, op. 63, 1907g., d. 5 (Kiev), d. 8 (Tver), d. 9 (Kazan), d. 10 (Ekaterinoslav), d. 11 (Kaluga), d. 13 (Vologda), d. 14 (Tavrid), and d. 17 (Stavropol).

[45]Admittedly Litvinov sometimes came close to crude pressuring during the early years of the reform. In a report on his inspection of Ekaterinoslav gubernia in spring 1908, he pronounced the program for *ukreplenie* there a "success." Of 17,000 petitions received, 13,600 had been carried through, though only 12% had had village approval (*IZO*, 1909: 320). Villages in the Ekaterinoslav flats had relatively few strips and were much simpler to survey than they were in other areas. Even so, the 13,600 *ukrepleniia* reportedly carried out by May 1908 must have been very hasty affairs. Litvinov's approval of them was not typical of him.

tions coming forth in their areas reflected the captains' diligence and ability, not their sloth (*IZO,* 1910: 76, 78, 81). On the whole, this was the attitude expressed in MVD directives throughout the reform.

It will bear mentioning that neither the MVD's land section nor the Committee for Land Settlement Affairs had the final word in any of their decisions regarding land reform. They could be and often were overruled when their decisions violated the law or produced inequities. A sizeable number of complaints against captains and other reform agencies made their way to the Senate, which now and then overturned decisions that it deemed illegal or inappropriate.[46] The tsar himself intervened periodically in the reform's processes via the old technique of marginal notes on annual reports from governors. For example, the report from St. Petersburg gubernia for 1908 asserted that quality was more important than quantity in land reform projects, and Nicholas scribbled his approval. In the following year the governor proclaimed his joy at having imperial support, and he pressed his point further. He *boasted* that the number of land settlement projects undertaken in his gubernia in 1909 was far less than it had been in 1908, because this showed that the quality of the work was improving (TsGIAL, f. 1291, op. 120, 1911g., d. 70, ll. 2-3). It is hard to see in all this a desire in the central government to force peasants to petition for agrarian reform.

Even if we imagine a central government conspiring to dragoon communal peasants into "acquiring" their strips as property, this would hardly explain the peasants' growing inclination to petition for village consolidation. In 1907 all the central government wanted within the villages was *ukreplenie,* not consolidation, and *ukreplenie* was the issue in all the examples cited above. Instances of crude pressure *to consolidate* may be found in the records but not before 1908 (see ch. 5, sec. B). Thus, if an occasional captain did trick or force small groups of peasants into petitioning for personal consolidation in 1907, he was not doing it because of encouragement from his superiors. Moreover, he did it without stirring up any protests or attracting any attention from the free press. In short, it is highly unlikely that the captains exerted undue pressure for land settlement at all. The flow of petitions for village consolidation in 1907-8 cannot be explained by conscious machinations on any level of the government's administration.

Coercion and the Land Captains in 1907

I have suggested that the captains had good reason to steer clear of any reform petition that threatened to disrupt a village, and the land section's efforts to drive them into action convey an impression that

[46]See, e.g., some Senate decisions compiled in TsGIAL, f. 1291, op. 120, 1912g., dd. 24 and 25.

many of our rural knights were indeed reluctant to "familiarize" peasants with the radical possibilities in the legislation of 1905-6. One imagines that if captains had been eager to persuade peasants to embark on land reform, the governors of Riazan and Saratov would never have felt a need to issue their machiavellian circulars in 1908-9. In fact, reports from the MVD's local agencies imply overwhelmingly that the typical captain did not work very hard at familiarization during the reform's early years (see, e.g., TsGIAL, f. 1291, op. 120, 1909g., d. 69). Governors generally tried to make their captains appear more active than they were. In 1909, for example, many of them falsely reported large numbers of captains acting as *zemleustroiteli,* managing separate projects of consolidation on their own (ll. 367-68). According to the bulk of the MVD's own evidence, however, the captains did not push the reform. Here and there they actually tried to oppose peasant petitions for *ukreplenie* and consolidation. In 1908 one inspecting officer traveling through Smolensk gubernia came upon a whole uezd-full of captains striving to block the reform.[47] In Kaluga gubernia in 1907 not only captains but the vice-governor were acting in this fashion (op. 63, 1907g., d. 11, l. 22). As late as 1909, Chernigov gubernia reported an uezd gentry marshal who was still doing everything he could to oppose all varieties of land settlement (op. 120, 1909g., d. 72, ll. 1-10). Back in 1907 the governor himself had opposed the reform actively. The MVD had been able to get rid of him, but alas, said the new governor in 1909, the administration could not touch a marshal (ll. 34-35).

But officials who opposed the reform were no more typical than those who pushed it. The best policy for a captain in 1907 was either to avoid reform altogether or to follow the example of the peasant bank's local sections, that is, to cooperate with peasants in carrying out reforms in a mutually satisfactory way while reporting results as if they conformed to government specifications (see *IZO,* 1909: 21-26, 50-56). The head of the survey section noted in his inspection report of 1910 that an ambitious official who wished to turn out *quantities* of projects to please his superiors could usually achieve this by allowing peasants to do pretty much as they liked and then reporting what they did as if it were part of the government's programs (TsGIAL, f. 1291, op. 120, 1910g., d. 19, ll. 96-97).

Consider the following description of the evolution of a land settlement project, taken from the pages of S. T. Semenov's memoirs. Admittedly it is defective in several ways as an illustration of my remarks about 1907. It depicts events in 1908-10, and the project was for personal con-

---

[47]*IZO* (1909: 54-55). Other reports, less extreme but similar, may be found in 1907: 135; 1909: 92-93; and TsGIAL, f. 1291, op. 63, 1907g., d. 9 (l. 19), d. 10 (ll. 117-21), and d. 17 (ll. 40, 42, 63).

solidation, not *ukreplenie*. Moreover, Semenov's village was in Moscow gubernia, atypically close to urban influence. Nevertheless, Semenov's account is the most detailed description of a land settlement project I have seen, and it possesses the additional advantage of having been composed by a peasant. Better yet, Semenov was a professional writer, faithful only to the evidence of his senses, and he consistently held himself above the tiresome sloganizing that filled most "peasant" petitions and appeals. He held no particular ideology. On the one hand, tsarist authorities punished him for revolutionary activities in 1905, and Soviet writers have treated him as a hero. On the other, he became, in 1908-10, the leader of a consolidating minority in his village. He was, in short, one of those rare, interesting characters who make a serious effort to see things as they are. Not surprisingly, he was murdered. Surprisingly, he was not murdered until 1922.[48]

Semenov spent two years in exile in Europe following the Revolution of 1905. What he saw there convinced him of Russia's need for land reform. He did not wholly approve of the 9 November decree, but it was close to what he wanted, and when he returned to his village he began to speak in favor of consolidation (1915: 238-41, 245-51). At first he tried to interest his neighbors in a village consolidation, or at least a redistribution of the traditional sort that would cut down on the number of strips belonging to each household (pp. 245-67). This failing, he and a few sympathizers began to push for otrub lots for themselves. A long, highly irregular conflict began in which two minority groups opposed each other more or less steadfastly while the rest of the villagers fluctuated back and forth between them. One minority, which included the village elder, opposed any kind of change in land division. The other, made up largely of "enlightened" peasants who had been politically active in 1905, tried to separate from the rest and form otrub and khutor lots (pp. 267-367).

At an early stage Semenov took his case to the local land captain. It must have been difficult for him, for he hated land captains. He portrays them as an unmitigated evil throughout their existence (pp. 86-92, 186-88). His own local captain, however, happened to be an exception. He was progressive, liberal, competent, and he had attended a university. Semenov did not like everything the captain did, but his account suggests that without the captain's support the small band of otrubists would not have had a chance against their opponents (pp. 280-90, 311-12).

It would take too long to recount the years of legalistic stalling and dodging that followed Semenov's appeal to the captain. To summarize,

---

[48] For a Soviet version of Semenov's biography, see K. Lonunov's introduction to a recent edition of Semenov's stories (Semenov, 1962: 3-15). Naturally Lonunov does not mention Semenov's involvement in the Stolypin Reform.

the captain was sympathetic, but with volost and village authorities against reform, he had to proceed slowly. The village persuaded a peasant to bring suit against Semenov to reclaim some land from him, and so long as this case was dragging through officialdom, Semenov was unable even to change his strips to a personal holding, much less consolidate them. Meanwhile, the opposition tried to drive Semenov out of the village assembly, on the grounds that his aged father, not he, was the legitimate head of his household. These were only maneuvers, but each one meant months of delay and repeated trips to the uezd capital for hearings. The matter was further complicated by politics in the uezd congress, where the gentry marshal and a number of land captains were doing everything they could to block the reform. To Semenov it seemed that they allowed the law's delays to last as long as possible. As for the local captain, he had very little power. When the village opposition shouted and threatened, no matter how groundlessly, he did not dare oppose them directly but always sought to pacify them with this or that maneuver. Meanwhile, Semenov and his accomplices struggled on, wondering whether consolidation was such a good idea after all. Semenov experienced no overt violence from his neighbors, but they threatened him. He was afraid they would burn his house (pp. 326-30). His children were ostracized and occasionally beaten up by former friends. His wife frequently suffered insults. The peasants never stayed angry very long, comments Semenov, but he and his fellow otrub-formers suffered much harassment (p. 326).

When at last the permanent member of the uezd land settlement commission came to the village bringing surveyors, Semenov had just eight allies left. The rest of the villagers were so hostile that they refused to talk to the surveyors at all. Consequently the new lots were measured out with only a minimum of argument, though the opposition could easily have delayed the matter at this point (pp. 339-48). Instead, when it became clear that the survey was actually being completed, Semenov gained a few allies, some of whom had formerly been among his strongest opposers. There was yet another year's delay after the survey as a result of Semenov's own personal lawsuits. Ultimately, however, the otrubs became a reality and, said Semenov in 1915, they were a success. Many villagers who had stuck with communal tenure began to express an interest in following the example of the progressive minority (pp. 352-67).

As I have said, Semenov's story proves nothing by itself. It does indicate, however, how difficult it was in any village, no matter how backward, for a captain to *initiate* petitions or reforms by simply grabbing peasants and forcing them to do his will. Nor was there any discernible reason for a captain to wish to do anything of this sort.

Let us imagine one of Dubrovskii's imaginary brutal land captains, working under a historically impossible governor who was already, in 1907, pressing his administrators hard to encourage land settlement. Despite all the risks involved, our "satrap," to use a Dubrovskii cliché, tries to avoid punishments, secure bonuses, and perhaps even earn promotion by getting peasants to claim their strips as personal property and, in some cases, persuading them to petition for the consolidation of their land. Let us say that he does the most arbitrary thing any land captain was ever accused convincingly of doing; that is, he encourages separators and consolidators by awarding them somewhat larger shares of land than the remaining villagers think fair. So far as the majority of villagers are concerned, this is coercion. Perhaps, in order to protect his protégés from retaliation by angry neighbors, our enterprising captain goes further. He threatens to use his authority in other spheres of peasant life to the detriment of any would-be opposers. Let us say, for example, that he resorts to the simple device of leaving all the villagers' petitions and statements without action for months at a time. Sidelnikov has printed a petition of 1911 from some peasants in Ekaterinoslav gubernia, alleging that local officials were forcing a personal consolidation by preventing an entire village from farming its land (1973: 138-41). Or perhaps the captain persuades the land settlement commission to use its funds for loans and aid as bribes to influence voting in village assemblies. A circular of 7 July 1912 from the Committee for Land Settlement Affairs explicitly encouraged the use of grants to gain the support of individual peasants when it seemed necessary (*IGU,* 1912: 712). Thus, although the petition printed by Sidelnikov was palpably fantastic and neither it nor the above circular bore any relation to the captains' activities in 1907, we may say that an ambitious captain might conceivably have resorted to such techniques in 1907 had there been a governor in existence who wanted his captains to do this.

What is not conceivable, however, is this imaginary captain forcing or cajoling separators to petition for consolidation against their wishes *and then getting the consolidation carried out.* No rearrangement of the land could have been accomplished against the opposition of a whole village. Sooner or later a surveyor had to draw up a plan, the uezd commission had to approve it, and one or more peasant families had to occupy their new fields. If the project broke down at any of these stages— and it did whenever would-be otrub-formers proved unwilling to fight long and hard for it—then all the officials involved, including the land captain who had scared up the petition, had a costly failure to explain, quite possible a bloody one as well. Recall Maiborodov's experience in Kherson gubernia (ch. 4, sec. B). Captains who employed coercion to incite peasants to petition for *ukreplenie* or consolidation could not possibly carry their projects to completion. *The only practical reason any official had for coercing peasants was to support or protect one group against another.* Coercion was not and could not have been a means to force the peasantry to do something none of them wished to do.

Conclusions

The above argument is not meant to imply that land captains played no role in familiarization. Not only Soviet scholarly works but also an abundance of tsarist government publications testify to the vital importance of the captains in introducing the reform (see, e.g., Dubrovskii, 1963: 163-64, 237-38; *Travaux,* 1912: 19). It seems, however, that the essence of their contribution to land reform was not in their active support of it. Few captains were as diligent and capable as Semenov's. Their primary importance lay in their presence. Whatever a particular captain may have done or failed to do, he was there in his *uchastok,* symbolizing the authority that inspired hope in reform-minded minorities and fear in village conservatives. His presence made it possible for peasants here and there to conceive of stirring against their villages when at long last the reform laws opened a way. Had the captains not made themselves known in the countryside during the decade preceding the reform as authorities above peasant institutions, it is doubtful that venturesome minorites could have disturbed the peace of mind of their conservative neighbors. Had Kakhanov installed his volost zemstvoes in 1885, they might have secured a dominant role for local gentry in peasant politics, but one wonders if their presence would have led reforming minorities in the villages to hope for outside support. If in 1889 the central government had withdrawn from the countryside instead of putting agents in the *uchastki,* would autonomous local parliaments have mustered sufficient resolution on their own to threaten the villages? More to the point, would anti-village minorities have believed in the power of these parliaments and tried to use them as a lever against tradition-minded, entrenched majorities? I think not. The captains had been conceived as patriarchs but born as line-over-staff agents. Designed to uphold peasant tradition with naked power, they could also be used to attack it. Ineffective as they may have been in *promoting* land settlement, their presence in the countryside gave comfort to any peasant, like Semenov, who dared to rebel against the traditional power of his neighbors.

CHAPTER 8

Evolution of the Reform Organization

The basis of a state's true power, no matter what its form of government, lies in the human personality, educated and conditioned to self-reliance. Only the habit of self-government can develop a people's capacity for organization and self-assertion. By emphasizing bureaucracy and governmental guardianship we create nothing but depersonalized and disunited mobs of people, mere human dust.

Ivan L. Goremykin (1898)[1]

I have already described the formal structure of the reform organization as it was in 1906 (see ch. 7, sec. B). The purpose of this chapter is to show how the organization functioned, that is, to identify the actual arrangements and connections through which it worked and kept informed of the results of its work. "Functioned" is perhaps not the right word, since the initial reform laws and the organization's early experience did not clearly indicate the tasks it needed to perform. The organization had not only to complete projects but also to embark on a quest, as it were, to discover what its purpose was, and this quest, which continued throughout the reform era, was an important element in the "functioning" of the organization.

To develop, the organization had above all to be flexible. The center had to direct and coordinate its local agencies, but at the same time it had to respond to their experience. On the whole, this was what the reform organization did during the period 1906-14. Indeed, as Chapters 10 and 11 will show, its essential elements continued to function in this way until 1929. To be sure, one can point to instances of rigid fixation upon this or that policy, as in Stolypin's raid on the peasant bank in 1907. The fact remains: the organization did impose radical changes upon itself in response to its experience. Principally, it developed from a

[1]Quoted in Von Laue (1963: 157-58).

program to establish private property into an instrument of mobilization. The question we are asking here, then, is: what sort of organization was it that could give the appearance of directing its affairs while allowing itself to be directed by its experience?

A. THE COMMITTEE FOR LAND SETTLEMENT AFFAIRS

Purpose

The Committee for Land Settlement Affairs was the first element in the reform organization to begin work. The law of 4 March 1906 gave it a number of responsibilities, among them the drafting of further reforms, but its most important role, as it turned out, was to coordinate the reform. Coordination of the reform at the center was of two types: between the reform organization and the departments of the MZ, and between the MZ and other ministries. The minister could take care of the first type by himself. As MZ he could, by his own authority, do such things as coordinate Siberian resettlement with land settlement in European Russia. For example, in December 1909 he provided that families moving to Siberia could travel free of charge if their departure had produced khutors in their home villages (Sidelnikov, 1973: 208). This sort of cooperation—between sections within the MZ—could be attained without resorting to an interministerial committee. When it came to the second type, however, the MZ had to act through interministerial colleges such as the Committee for Land Settlement Affairs.

Aside from its MZ-chairman, the committee's most important members were the heads of the key organizations involved in land settlement: the MZ's department of state domains, the ministry of justice's land survey section, the MVD's land section, and the MF's peasant bank. If the reform was to be conducted in reasonably coherent fashion, these key officials had to be kept in substantial, continual agreement. Mere formal agreement would not be enough. Each member of the committee had to be sufficiently convinced of the wisdom or necessity of the committee's decisions that he would work actively to enforce them upon his own subordinates. He would have to hand out rewards for contributing to the committee's work and inflict punishments for obstructing it. Each land settlement project required the participation of agents from all or most of these separate organizations, and if any one of them did not participate actively, the peasants would find it extremely difficult to get their land free from traditional restraints. Most peasants did not have the leisure or the means to make repeated visits to uezd offices. If a group with a petition for land reform found themselves shunted from one official to another, forced to devote weeks and months to learning and then satisfying the formal requirements of each branch of government, very little land reform would take place. It was absolutely vital that land settlement projects be carried out in each locale on an assembly-line basis, with each official doing his part on schedule, and this meant that any one official could easily frustrate the efforts of all the rest. Somehow the committee's members had to compel their subordinates to cooperate systematically.

Cooperation among the Subordinate Departments

A number of practical considerations inclined most ministries involved in the reform to be mutually cooperative. The MVD joined the effort, at least at first, because much of the reform had been enacted in its land section. Admittedly the land section's *agents* did not cooperate as enthusiastically with land settlement as their superiors wished (ch. 7, sec. E). The attitude in the central offices, however, was fairly clear. For most of the leading officials of the land section, the reform represented an opportunity to impose administrative regularity and central direction on the land captains. The section had been trying to reduce its captains to clerks since the mid-1890s, and the reform presented an excellent opportunity to complete this process. The leading men in the section during the 1900s—Gurko, Litvinov, and Pestrzhetskii, to name only a few—had staked their careers and reputations on the introduction of active measures to bring "law" to the countryside, and they had tied themselves, one and all, to the belief that the reform constituted such measures. So had Stolypin himself, and he was not only MVD but also, from July 1906 until September 1911, chairman of the Council of Ministers. The full weight of his influence and that of his leading subordinates offered a measure of assurance that the organs over which they exercised direct control—i.e., the police hierarchy—would at least find it difficult to oppose or delay land settlement. The MVD might still compete with other ministries, but it could only do so by taking over the "movement" of bureaucracy into the countryside, not by opposing it.

The land survey section, formally part of the ministry of justice, did its work on land settlement directly under the orders of the MZ. As I said in the preceding chapter (sec. B), this arrangement originated in an informal agreement between the two ministers in the spring of 1906 and blossomed, after about 18 months of apparently harmonious cooperation, into the rules of 14 October (*Desiatiletie,* 1916: 4-13). Harmony produces little evidence; consequently it is not readily explicable. We may surmise that the main reason for it lay in the very considerable advantages the reform brought to the survey section and its agents. In 1906 the ministry of justice was considered in govenment circles to be a half-moribund institution in which pay was low, promotions rare, and inefficacy proverbial. The courts had a reputation for slowness and inefficiency that more than one tsar had noted with scorn, and the survey section shared it (ch. 5, sec. B; ch. 6, sec. A; ch. 7, sec. D). After 1906, however, the section underwent a stunning transfiguration. The reform raised the gubernia surveyors into high positions of authority in a busy and booming organization, comprising, by 1913, over 6,000 practicing surveyors and a network of training schools (*Desiatiletie,* 1916: 25). All surveyors' income rose sharply. A senior surveyor's annual salary went up to 1,500 rubles plus allowances, and in addition to this guaranteed minimum he earned a fee for each verst of boundary measured, each marker placed, and each *desiatina* mapped. Bonus rates were paid when a land settlement project actually went into effect (*IGU,* 1909: 349-50; *Desiatiletie,* 1916: 50-52). With rewards like these, the survey section was happy to have the MZ's supervision.

To be sure, the survey section was not without aspirations. Its direc-tor, N. D. Chaplin, often claimed that surveyors were the only men qual-ified to carry out land settlement projects. MZ administrators, he was fond of saying, should stay out of the surveyors' way. Moreover, survey-ors should extend the sphere of their work. They should be trained in agronomy so that they might manage agricultural improvement as well as land reform. This was interministerial imperialism with a vengeance. Even so, Chaplin was significantly less agressive than his more influential rivals in the MVD and MZ. He was careful to express his dreams of glory only in positive form; that is, he only praised his own surveyors. Unlike the relatively unrestrained MVD officials and MZ agronomists, he did not say right out that agents of other ministries were incompetent and corrupt (see, e.g., his inspection reports of 1909 and 1910—TsGIAL, f. 1291, op. 120, 1910g., d. 19, ll. 12-19, 82-83, 86-87, 90-95, 112-14).

The position of the peasant bank was very different from that of the MZ or survey section. In 1906 the bank had already been at work for over 20 years, and its agents had their own ideas and procedures regard-ing peasant "reform." Only the land section could boast a longer expe-rience. The legislation of 1905-6 provided for the bank's rapid expansion while leaving the MVD's captains weakened and demoralized. Moreover, the bank got into action months before the MZ's land settlement organi-zation came into being, and its concept of reform differed sharply from that which the land settlement comissions came to embody. The bank wanted merely to sell land to peasant villages as rapidly as possible; the commissions wanted to make peasants over into commercial farmers. Thus the bank was neither dependent on the committee nor in sympathy with it. The committee had to face a conflict between the newly rede-signed MZ and the bank's superior organization, the hitherto very power-ful MF.

The reform's changes in direction after 1906 added fuel to the con-flict. According to the original plan, bank sections and commissions were to perform two separate functions in cooperation with each other: one would provide credit, and the other would distribute it. This, however, was not what they did. As they went into actual operation, they evolved very quickly into two separate organizations for distributing credit, and they had very different ideas about how to distribute it. Under these circumstances they found themselves competing for funds from the government treasury. Prior to 1906 the bank had paid for its operations out of its own resources, but, as noted above, the law of 14 October 1906 lowered interest rates on bank loans far below the percentage it had to pay its investors (ch. 6, sec. D). As a result, the bank became dependent on government subsidies to support its loans at the same time the MZ was beginning to expand its own rural credit programs. The battle over land-selling methods escalated into a contest for scarce resources, chiefly funds and surveyors.

It must be emphasized that the struggle between bank and committee did not take place solely in St. Petersburg. Had it been possible for central offices to impose directives on their subordinates simply by publishing them, the committee would have had no difficulty in bringing the bank into line. But, in fact, the struggle raged on all administrative levels, and the central offices seem to have had very little control over it—as Krivoshein's attempt to direct the peasant bank indicates.

Consider, for example, the matter of financing land settlement on village lands. The decree of 15 November 1906 (and its later substitute, the law of 5 July 1912) authorized the peasant bank to make loans secured by allotment land. These loans could be made for a number of purposes, some having little connection with land settlement. A village could borrow to pay for village land left behind by its departing members, and an individual buying new land could supplement the regular loan (secured by the new land) by taking out yet another loan secured by his allotment land. Another purpose, somewhat more closely related to land settlement, was *ukreplenie,* the conversion of strips in a communal village to individual ownership. The 15 November law allowed a household head who converted his strips to personal property to borrow money from the bank and to use his newly acquired strips as collateral. Loans made for the above purposes did not further land reform on allotment land, nor did they bear any necessary relation to agricultural improvement of any kind. From the committee's point of view, therefore, they had little importance. The only significant provisions in the 15 November law were those authorizing bank loans to peasants who undertook land settlement measures on village land or introduced some sort of improvement in their methods of cultivation (Sidelnikov, 1973: 153-57, 321-22).

In the event, the peasant bank proved unwilling to make loans on allotment land for any purpose whatsoever. During the period 1907-14 it lent 433 million rubles to purchasers of its own lands and another 487 million to peasants who purchased private lands directly. During this same period it lent less than 11 million rubles on the peasants' own allotment lands, of which only 2 million went for the support of land settlement and agricultural improvement. Two million out of about 930 million—somewhat less than one-fourth of 1% of all bank loans made during the reform years—went to improve the peasants' use of their own land (pp. 170-71, 174, 178). One gets the distinct impression from these figures that the local bank sections struggled at least as hard against the committee's commissions as the MF did against the MZ.[2]

In April 1908, at an interministerial conference devoted specifically to the question of rural credit, a peasant bank representative, V. S. Koshko, explained the local sections' actions. Koshko stated flatly that the bank was not capable of making loans for agricultural improvement. It was true, Koshko acknowledged, that if a loan was to support agricultural improvement *effectively,* it would have to be big, so big that it would require collateral. The only collateral peasants could offer was land; therefore, if new methods and equipment were to be introduced on peasant land, they would have to be secured by mortgages on *allotment* land—as the 15 November law provided. The trouble was, said Koshko, the bank had no way to determine the value of an individual household's share of allotment land, not even if the household head owned it. Only local, volost-level agencies could conceivably lend money to an individual villager on the security of his land, because only such agencies could possibly have any idea of its market value, and since no such agencies existed, neither the bank nor any other government agency could accept this land as collateral. In effect, the bank did not want to have anything to do with the MZ's push for agricultural improvement and land settlement on allotment land (TsGIAL, f. 1291, op. 54, 1908g., d. 4, l. 20; ch. 4, sec. D). So the bank's representative said, at precisely the time when Krivoshein was giving up his position as bank director. After about 18 months in office, while Krivoshein had enjoyed the full support of both prime minister and tsar, he had not been able to persuade or compel the local sections to lend money on allotment land. Nor was he able to do it in the ensuing years. In January 1909 the new director of the bank announced to a conference of land settlement workers that intravillage land settlement was none of the bank's business (*Trudy,* 1909: *prilozheniia,*

---

[2]The bank's principal method was not to reject applications for agricultural improvement loans but to ignore them. From 1906 until 1 July 1909 about 4,300 requests were submitted. Of these, only 1,800 got any response; about 1,100 were approved (*IZO,* 1909: 317).

90-95). The MZ never did overcome the bank's recalcitrance (see, e.g., *IGU*, 1911: 593-95).[3]

St. Petersburg had somewhat better luck in compelling the local bank sections to sell their land to individuals in the form of integral lots. In the preceding chapter (sec. D) we saw that Stolypin failed to achieve this goal in 1907. In subsequent years, however, he persisted, and at last he did produce an impact.

Consider for a moment the lengths to which Stolypin had to go to win even this limited victory over the gubernia level. It will be recalled that he began his campaign in 1907 by sending out "temporary agencies" to whip the local sections into line. As it turned out, these agencies were not at all temporary. They became a permanent part of the bank's organization and continued to supervise the sale of bank lands in their respective territories (*IGU*, 1908: 310-13). Along with these less than all-powerful organs of central direction, Stolypin established a network of "liquidation sections." The rules of 19 February 1908 set up a special liquidation section in St. Petersburg to operate next to the bank council. Its function was to take away from the council all affairs related to the sale of the bank's lands. The new section was much the same kind of body as the council; it even had the same chairman—the bank director—and it included three members from the council. It was quite different from the council, however, in that none of its members—except the chairman—were from the MF. Its three members consisted of the representatives on the bank council from the MZ, MVD, and state control.[4] On the gubernia level, each bank section also acquired its own companion liquidation section. It was a college modeled after the St. Petersburg original. Its chairman was the director of the bank section, and the members included the permanent member of the gubernia land settlement commission (MZ), the gubernia surveyor (justice), and two MF-appointed members of the local bank section. According to the February rules, the new sections handled all sales of bank lands, and the bank section no longer exercised jurisdiction. Disagreements among the members of a local liquidation section were to be resolved by the "temporary agency" within whose territory the section was located (*Sbornik*, 1908: 661-62, 672). Thus Stolypin's efforts of 1907-8 deprived the bank's organization of virtually all control over its own land. The result, it will be recalled, was that much of the

---

[3]Interestingly, 1914 was by far the biggest year for bank loans secured by allotment land. In this single year about a half-million rubles were disbursed—about one-fourth of all such loans during the entire reform era (Sidelnikov, 1973: 171). If this represented a trend, it signified the triumph of the committee over the bank.

[4]The state control *(gosudarstvennyi kontrol)* was a ministry in all but name. Its function was to audit the government's accounts.

land was indeed sold in the form of integral farms, but sales went slowly and the bank cut down on its purchases. When we speak of the reform organization on the gubernia level, we shall see (below, sec. C) that in the years after 1907 the bank sections were gradually cut out of land reform and deprived of almost all their surveyors.

Hostilities between bank and committee took yet one more unpleasant form. Beginning in 1908, Krivoshein mounted a campaign to take over the bank by shifting it into the MZ. The first step, it seems, took place in the fall, when a group of 32 Duma representatives brought forward a bill providing for the transfer (TsGIAL, f. 1291, op. 120, 1908g., d. 53, ll. 1-2). This went nowhere, largely because Stolypin opposed the idea, but two years later, in the fall of 1910, Krivoshein brought forth his own recommendation in the Council of Ministers. He failed again. He could not even persuade his fellow ministers to let the MZ set up a separate bank of its own, and at last he had to settle for getting his agents a voice in decisions regarding peasant applications for loans secured by allotment land (f. 592, op. 1, d. 221, ll. 3-16, 143-47).[5]

This concludes our investigation of the major conflict among the committee's members. Clearly it posed serious problems for the reform organization, and the committee was not overwhelmingly successful in resolving them. But it would distort reality to speak only of conflicts between the MZ and the peasant bank. What is of greater importance is that the Committee for Land Settlement Affairs somehow allowed the bank to maintain its integrity throughout the reform era, yet prevented the bank's disagreements with the reform organization from breaking down land reform itself. We should not marvel at the discord between bank and MZ; instead, we should contemplate the committee's unprecedented success in keeping these discords from taking destructive, paralyzing forms. The Committee for Land Settlement Affairs is significant not because of its difficulties, which were quite usual in the tsarist government, but because a modus vivendi emerged under its collegial direction within which the ministries could keep the reform moving. In the period 1902-15, in the midst of intense interministerial conflicts, the Russian government decided to act upon rural society and was able to coordinate its action and resolve its conflicts under a single administrative system. It was the first time.

The Basis for Interministerial Cooperation

It is not enough simply to say that collegial direction worked. The tsarist government had been trying to coordinate ministries under colle-

[5]See also *IGU,* (1910: 448; 1911. 593), Kokovtsov (1935: 250-51, 265-70), Zenkovskii (1956: 59-60), and Oldenburg (1939: II, 77-78) regarding the MZ-MF fight for possession of the bank.

gial direction ever since the reign of Nicholas I, when each ministry had begun to form its own separate quasi-bureaucracy; on the whole, interministerial councils had not worked very well. Collegial direction did not coordinate ministerial agencies into effective administrative organizations during the nineteenth century—not in rural Russia, at any rate—because the only force compelling gubernia and uezd agents to coordinate their efforts was the authority of the separate ministers over their own respective agencies. One might think that ministers would find it easy enough to compel their subordinates to cooperate with one another, but in fact it was extremely difficult. When a minister urged his gubernia agents to work in conjunction with those of other ministries, he was, in effect, urging them to set aside the policies and regulations he himself had established for them, thereby carving up his own organization into 80-odd separate groups, with each one operating in its own gubernia in accordance with its own unique modus vivendi (Yaney, 1973: 376-80). Thus the Committee for Land Settlement Affairs was not, as such, a very promising basis for administering a land reform. If collegial direction did at last work during the reform era, something or somebody had to make it work, something or somebody that had not been there before.

Generally speaking, the most important unifying element in the committee was the *commitment* to land reform that the government had taken upon itself during the interministerial controversy of 1902-6. As we have seen in Chapter 6 (sec. C), the squabble between Witte's special conference and the MVD's editing commission had been a *public* controversy, by far the most widely and thoroughly publicized debate between separate segments of the tsarist government that had ever taken place in Russia up to that time. The tsar had publicly committed his government to peasant reform in 1902-3; from then on the ministers vied for control over agrarian reform, and their struggle drove them to advocate unworkable aims in public while maneuvering behind the scenes to secure key roles for their local agencies in the organization-to-be. As the debate proceeded and "information" from the countryside began to pile up in the chancelleries, it became increasingly difficult to speak of practical problems, even had anyone desired to do so, and ministerial rhetoric gradually confined itself entirely to superficial descriptions of unattainable results: e.g., the "release" of individual peasants from communal villages, the granting of loans to poor peasants who were also progressive farmers, the sale of state lands in the form of consolidated farms. When in 1905-6 the ministers at last faced the necessity of resolving their conflicts and enacting legislation, their public declarations, especially the legislation itself, spoke of nothing but these promised results.

Since the enactors' promises were public, retreat would be extremely difficult, if not impossible. The ministers *had* to produce an acceptable reform in rural Russia, which meant that their primary need was not to enforce the statutes of 1905-6 but to find out which provisions stood any chance of working. Their situation was very similar to that of Alexander II in 1861 (Yaney, 1973: 185-89), except that in 1906 it was not only the tsar himself who was committed to act but ministerial organizations. The tsar-liberator had felt no need to coordinate his ministers in order to act. Nicholas II could not operate in any other way (p. 383).

The government's commitment to capital-city visions of agrarian reform also committed the peasantry. To put it another way, the government's visions, publicized in the course of a very noisy debate, compelled ministerial bureaucracy to break down peasant society. All the enactors had spoken of letting peasants go along "at their own pace," yet as soon as the reform began, all such notions immediately became outdated. The government's action abruptly deprived the peasants' social order of its legitimacy and, in effect, invited individual households to go to war with each other. Since traditional peasant society was already in the process of breaking down, many individual households did indeed go to war. When they did, the government agents participated. They *had* to participate. Most importantly, they had to participate under the aegis of bureaucratic formulae. The government was establishing rights and duties, not just keeping savages quiet, and there is no way to identify rights and duties except in the form of general statements applicable to everyone alike. In particular, the land would at last have to be surveyed so that it could be identified and owned in accordance with a general scheme of law and measurement.

The government's new commitment abruptly eliminated all the hitherto excellent reasons for not trying to extend legal-administrative system into the countryside by administrative means. Now system would have to extend itself or die. The "bureaucracy" was out in the open now, and it could no longer hide from its own inadequacies by refraining from action. If the reform failed to find a function and perform it, it would mean the end of the central government's influence not only in the countryside but in all aspects of the national economy. Bureaucracy, having irrevocably proclaimed itself to the populace as an instrument of salvation, would have to contemplate its own inability to function and, consequently, its futility—for bureaucracy's only legitimacy, even in its own eyes, is its ability to function. This was the main reason why neither government nor peasantry could stop or even slow down in 1907 and thereafter. This was, I think, the underlying reason that so many political leaders and statesmen in the third Duma and State Council felt compelled to accept the law of 9 November 1906 as an irrevocable fact, despite their horror at the clumsiness of the reform organization in 1907.[6] There was an element

[6]For some typical remarks to this effect in the Duma and State Council, see Chernyshev (1918: 352, 360), Sidelnikov (1973: 253, 256-59, 285-86), and *Zakon* (1914: 349).

of truth in Stolypin's speech to the State Council on 15 March 1910, when he asserted that the law of 9 November 1906 had been "verified" by four years of "life itself" (*IZO*, 1910: 171). In part, of course, it was the continuing threat of revolution that forced conservatives and moderates in the legislature to unite behind the government during the reform era, but the only way they could cooperate effectively was to accept as their own the government's commitment to the unconservative, immoderate, unforgiving movement of system into the countryside. The pressure of this commitment was the primary basis for whatever coordination was achieved among the ministers under the aegis of the Committee for Land Settlement Affairs.

The Committee's Sources of Information

To direct the reform and, perforce, to allow it to direct itself, the committee had above all to keep itself informed of the progress of its agencies in the countryside. We must ask, therefore, how it did so.

The committee's local agencies, the land settlement commissions, were collegial in form; that is, their official decisions had to be approved by a group of men. When it came to reporting information and exercising authority, however, the reform organization was esentially a bureaucracy. At its head was the department of state domains in the MZ. In the earliest days of the reform, when there were no gubernia commissions, the permanent members of the uezd land settlement commissions were directly under this department. In 1907 permanent members of gubernia commissions began to appear, and the formal structure of the committee's organization evolved into a chain of command extending from department, to gubernia permanent members, to uezd permanent members, to surveyors in the field. Here we shall consider the portion of the chain that stretched from St. Petersburg to the gubernias, on which the committee depended most directly for meaningful information.

Information on the progress of the reform came to the committee from a large number of sources outside the chain described above. For one, ministries other than the MZ checked on the work their own agencies did in connection with the reform. The land section inspected its captains more frequently with every passing year, and it regularly published excerpts from the inspection reports about conditions in various areas and the performance of its officials (ch. 4, sec. B). Other ministries also generated data, though not nearly so generously as the MVD. The peasant bank council published exhaustive statistical reports, but it did little or no inspecting of its local sections. Likewise, the land survey section made relatively little effort to keep track of its gubernia agencies systematically. Aside from maintaining a blacklist of surveyors whose morality was in doubt, all it contributed were the yearly inspection reports of its chief (*Desiatiletie,* 1916: 29-30, 58; TsGIAL, f. 1291, op. 120, 1910g., d. 19, ll. 2-25, 79-117). These reports were useful as far as they went, though they only covered five or six gubernias each year. The committee also tapped many sources of information outside the government: newspapers and journals of every persuasion, zemstvoes, political parties, and various private persons who, for one reason or another, took an interest in the reform.[7]

Valuable as all this information was, it is not what I am discussing here. What I want to take up in the following paragraphs is the committee's own administrative techniques for gathering information.

The department of state domains could not hope to inform itself in detail about every land settlement project. Its main concern was the gathering and evaluation of general information on what the local organizations were doing, what their problems were, and how well the aims of the reform were being achieved. Systematic information on the basis of which the department could answer these questions came from the gubernia land settlement organizations, primarily from their annual field-work schedules. We shall discuss these schedules in section C, when I take up the workings of the gubernia organization. Here I wish to focus on the department's supplementary sources of information, its methods of learning *about* its machinery rather than *from* it.

One such method was to call conferences *(sezdy)* of local officials connected with the reform. Selected surveyors, land captains, permanent members of land settlement commissions, and permanent members of gubernia boards would meet under the leadership of St. Petersburg administrators to discuss their problems and consider questions put to them by their superiors. Conferences might meet at any time, but most of them were held when the committee was preparing to write a new instruction. For example, in May 1911 the permanent members of the gubernia land settlement commissions met with an assortment of uezd permanent members, gubernia surveyors, et al., about 120 participants in all. The purpose was to discuss problems arising from the impending law of 29 May 1911. Recommendations made by participants found expression in the instruction of 19 June 1911, which expanded upon the provisions of the May law (*IGU,* 1911: 527-30, 547-50).

Conferences were somewhat formal affairs. One imagines that a fair number of participants strove to impress their superiors rather than inform them. Yet the proceedings were much more than mere parades. Local officials described their activities, and if nothing else their remarks

---

[7] Concerning agricultural journals, see ch. 7, n. 11. The committee and its member ministries made extensive use of newspaper attacks on its agencies. See, e.g., TsGIAL, f. 1291, op. 120, 1910g., d. 14, one of many collections devoted to the government's reactions to hostile press reports on the reform.

revealed how varied their practices were, especially when they disagreed with each other and with the central offices. Moreover, the participants could and did make suggestions about the reform organization's policies.

Consider, for example, the conference of land settlement workers from the southwestern gubernias and Bessarabia, held in Kiev in early 1907. It was probably the first intergubernia meeting dealing with land settlement, and its primary purpose seems to have been to gather information. This presumably is the reason it was restricted to the area where a significant amount of intravillage land settlement was taking place. Had the conference been merely a gimmick for handing down commands or working up enthusiasm, the committee would have held it elsewhere.

The committee learned, for one thing, that local practice varied widely. Some commissions were encouraging prospective purchasers of peasant-bank land by renting out khutor lots to them and allowing them to work the new land without committing themselves to buy it. Other commissions were getting the land sold as fast as they could and not troubling with rentals. Amounts of downpayment demanded from peasant purchasers varied sharply from one uezd to another (*Rossiia*, 18 Mar. 1907: 2).

The committee also learned something about views current in its local agencies. Judging from recommendations made at the conference, most local land settlement workers wanted to weaken the villages' legal power to resist consolidation. Some participants went so far as to suggest that personal consolidations should be carried out whenever one or more households demanded them *in communal and noncommunal villages alike.* All agreed that village consolidations should require only a simple majority (25 Mar. 1907: 2). These relatively radical ideas produced no immediate impact on the central offices, but some of the conference's proposals were actually adopted. I have already noted that the idea of setting up model khutor farms came up here (ch. 7, sec. C). The participants also approved the committee's policy of paying incentive bonuses to surveyors in addition to their annual salaries (27 Mar. 1907: 2).

More influential than the southwestern meeting was a Russia-wide conference of permanent members of gubernia boards held in October 1907. This was an MVD-sponsored affair, the first one in its history, and the ministry was so impressed with the wisdom of the participants' resolutions that it authorized governors to implement them immediately (*Trudy*, 1908: 1, 5-8, 12). In January 1909, a little over a year later, the MVD sponsored a combined conference of MZ and MVD officials, also the first of its kind (*Trudy*, 1909: i-iii). Conferences of MVD agents within each gubernia also became fashionable in 1909.[8]

[8]See, e.g., a description of a gubernia-level assembly of land captains in Feb. 1910 (*IZO*, 1910: 122). Poltava gubernia held a conference as early as Feb. 1909,

MVD-sponsored affairs generally gave more time to whipping up spirit and formulating projects than to information gathering; even so, the participants engaged in something approaching a frank interchange of ideas. Especially noteworthy was a discussion in the intergubernia conference of January 1909 concerning the degree to which land settlement officials should sacrifice technical perfection in their projects for the sake of satisfying peasant demands. Should the commission refuse peasant requests for reform that did not conform to the government's concept of proper land settlement, or should they carry out any measure the peasants could be persuaded to accept? For example, if a peasant wished to convert his strips into three separate otrub lots instead of one, should the land settlement commission refuse its help even if the village acquiesced? No, was the conference's answer. The participants unanimously rejected a policy of forced technical perfection, maintaining that since the variety of existing land arrangements posed many different problems, peasants should not merely be allowed but encouraged to cope with these problems as they saw fit. But the point here is not that the participants opted for flexibility. What interests us is that they argued openly from various angles and even opposed their superiors (*Trudy*, 1909: 143-59). As we shall see in Chapter 9 (sec. A), the MVD's central offices were turning against this sort of flexibility at the time of the January conference, and they made this clear enough at the sessions. Nevertheless, the participants stuck to their guns. One supposes that the superiors encouraged their subordinates' recalcitrance and heard their arguments with interest. We may say, then, that intergubernia conferences did bring out honest expressions of opinion from the locales, and that these opinions constituted relatively valid reflections of local conditions.

But conferences were infrequent affairs, and they were still, for all their frankness, products of local agencies. They did not offer the central offices a basis for directing subordinate organs that was independent of the organs themselves. After all, local officials were not unprejudiced sources of information, and not all the ideas they put forth were necessarily good ones. For example, a substantial minority at a conference of 1911 wanted to force peasants who had begun a land settlement project to accept it upon its completion *even if they no longer wanted it.* Krivoshein rejected this proposal out of hand. The reform, he said in a speech of May 1911, had to be voluntary (*IZO*, 1911: 221-23). Obviously the committee could not rely wholly on its local officials for direction, not even when they appeared in conferences. If the central offices were to

---

which included gentry marshals, permanent members of land settlement commissions, and land captains (p. 406).

comprehend events in the gubernias, they had to possess independent sources of information.

One such source was the special investigation. Occasionally the committee sent out investigators to study small areas in depth in order to witness more directly the shape land reform was taking. The biggest single operation of this sort went forward in 1912-13, when 12 investigators, working in accordance with a more or less uniform plan, conducted studies of the reform's results in selected uezds scattered through 12 gubernias.[9]

For a more consistent autonomous source of information, the department of state domains depended on its inspection section, which was managed throughout the reform by A. A. Kofod. Kofod's organization was divided into three parts, each covering about one-third of European Russia, or about 15 gubernias. Each had its own inspector. In theory, the inspector could play any number of roles. He could participate actively in gubernia matters, virtually supervising the commissions, or, alternatively, he could confine himself to compiling information sent in from gubernia offices. Judging from the absence of regulations and correspondence regarding the inspectors, we are justified in presuming that they did not do much decision making either in the gubernia offices or in St. Petersburg—though it is worth noting that they were paid more than gubernia permanent members. As of 1914 their annual salary was 4,000 rubles, whereas gubernia permanent members got only 3,500.[10]

It might be argued that Kofod used his position as chief inspector to change the course of the reform. After all, he was the only man in St. Petersburg who had believed in village consolidation as early as 1905, and the reform organization did in fact begin to emphasize village consolidation in 1908, contrary to the original intentions of the other leading enactors and administrators. Anyone who takes the view that administrators have the "power" to direct their administrations will surely be tempted to account for the reform's change of direction by suggesting that Kofod imposed his "will" on the gubernia commissions and convinced his superiors of the wisdom of his ideas.

But the correspondence between Kofod's opinions and the evolution of the reform is not so easily explained. On the one hand, gubernia and

[9]Their findings were published in separate volumes in 1914-18. Two of these were Mozzhukhin's study of an uezd in Tula (1917) and Pershin's parallel work on a Perm uezd (1918). A statistical compilation of all 12 reports was presented in *Obsledovanie* (1915). Other investigations are cited in Pershin's monumental study of 1928 (pp. 142-44, 275-77, 397-99).

[10]*IGU,* 1914: 749. The law of 1 July 1914 added two more inspectors, thus decreasing the area each one had to cover. I doubt, however, that the new inspectors ever went to work.

uezd commissions did not follow all Kofod's precepts. The Danish propagandist never ceased to believe that his commissions should avoid otrubs
and press for khutors wherever the latter were not physically impossible
(Kofod, 1914: 66-68), but the commissions paid little heed to his many
instructions to this effect. Throughout the reform era consolidations went
forward at a ratio of about four to one, otrubs to khutors (Pershin, 1922:
20-21). Furthermore, a substantial majority of the khutors were in western Russia, where past experience had shown they were relatively acceptable to the peasants. Kofod also opposed group land settlement, but in
1914 this type of work was displacing village consolidation as the main
activity of the committee's organization. Here again, technical rigor gave
way to peasant demand, and Kofod was powerless to prevent it. On the
whole, there is little reason to believe that Kofod's instructions carried
any weight simply because they were his. His main role in the committee's organization was to keep the committee informed.[11]

To sum up, the committee had access to a number of official and
unofficial sources of information besides the usual flow of routine reports
from its operating agencies. Private periodicals expanded in number and
circulation during the reform era, and their comments on the activities of
reform agencies, however distorted, served the central offices as an instrument to force subordinates to send in detailed descriptions of their
experience. The government also employed a number of devices within
its organization to obtain information about local developments: conferences of officials, periodic inspections, and a regular inspectorate. All
these sources were new to tsarist experience in the 1900s, and, one
presumes, they had much to do with the committee's unprecedented
freedom from the rigidity that characterized nineteenth-century rural administration. St. Petersburg's commitment to agrarian reform would have
had little effect had there not been practical devices for rendering central
offices sensitive to the experience of their agents.

A Case Study

Having offered some generalizations about the committee's efforts
to respond to local experience, it will be useful to present a concrete
example of policy development. The evolution of the committee's loan-
and-subsidy program is particularly suitable for this purpose, because it
not only shows the committee changing direction but also reflects a characteristic of the reform's development.

[11]Peasant petitions for group land settlement had always been more numerous than those for consolidation, but numbers of projects undertaken and completed did not begin to reflect this preference until the latter years of the reform
(*IGU*, 1908: 47-48; 1909: 438).

It will be recalled that 800,000 rubles were credited to the department of state domains in April 1906 for disbursal to land-settling peasants (ch. 7, sec. B). This amount was intended to suffice for the remainder of the year. Distribution of actual loans and grants was left to the uezd commissions. As said before, almost none of this amount was disbursed, owing partly to the peasant bank's opposition to land settlement on its lands and partly to Vasilchikov's rigid notions of accountability. The bank's opposition was particularly important in 1906-7 because the *nakaz* of 19 September 1906 ordered the committee's loans and subsidies to be used primarily to smooth the sale of land to individual, consolidating peasants, and, as we know, very few sales of this sort were made before 1908 (ch. 7, sec. D).[12]

As to Vasilchikov's passionate concern for keeping tight control over loan distribution, there was a modicum of justification for it. He was correct in the short run about the local agencies' inability to distribute funds. Even in 1908, when, under Krivoshein, central regulation could not have been very burdensome, the commissions handed out only a little over 800,000 rubles. Whatever justification there may have been for Vasilchikov's centralizing inclinations, however, they reflected an obscurantist, peasant-bank approach to rural reform. His disappearance from the scene in April 1908 brought a sudden reversal in the MZ's policy on loans and subsidies to land-settling peasants.

The reversal received official expression in October, when the committee sent a circular to the governors restoring decision-making power on loans and grants of less than 150 rubles to uezd commissions (*IGU,* 1908: 818). Individual applications would no longer have to go all the way to St. Petersburg for approval. Decisions were to be reviewed on a higher level only in cases where a commission did not agree unanimously or a would-be recipient made a complaint. The gubernias would still have to request the money they needed each month, but they would not have to send supporting documents along with each request. The only reports the committee would require would be monthly records of loans issued. The circular promised that new rules to govern the distribution of loans and subsidies would be issued shortly, and they would be very general. The committee preferred "not to give the commissions any definite instructions but to allow them to establish their own systems, depending on circumstances" (p. 820). The commissions could even distribute loans and subsidies via zemstvo administrators if they liked. Indeed, the committee itself would channel part of its funds for land settlement loans and subsidies directly to the zemstvoes (p. 819). The committee did venture a few timid suggestions. Each loan should be given out in one lump

12The relevant articles in the *nakaz* are 52, 53, and 68 (*IZO,* 1906: 337, 339).

sum, not in small installments. The peasants were likely to use small installments to cover daily expenses instead of putting the money into land settlement. Loans should be given only to peasants in need, not to those who could afford their own improvements. Finally, the committee's funds should be used only for land settlement purposes. But suggestions like these were too general to be called limiting norms. The gist of the October circular was that the uezd commissions were to make their own policies.[13]

Krivoshein was never to depart from his freewheeling approach. To be sure, he occasionally disapproved of his commissions' actions. In 1910, for example, he took exception to their inclination to be overly generous. According to an article in the MZ journal in September, uezd commissions were giving out too much money to land settlers for such items as seed, fertilizer, and machinery—items that did not fall into the category of "costs of land settlement." Worse, the commissions were handing out much too much money in the form of subsidies rather than loans. The article cautioned the commissions to use land settlement funds only to cover expenses involved in land settlement itself. If they handed out money indiscriminantly to new consolidators, simply to help them along, they would be giving land settlement artificial support, thereby endangering the very foundation of the reform: the creation of farms that would be self-sustaining enterprises. This was doubly true in the case of nonreturnable subsidies. The commissions were not to support consolidators, only to make it possible for them to support themselves. Such was the MZ's sermon to the uezds in 1910. Krivoshein might have carried the matter further. He might have demanded, MVD fasion, that reports be made, records kept, and procedures followed. This, however, was not what the article proposed. It simply asked the commissions, together with the zemstvoes, to avoid giving out subsidies and to recommend more flexible rules to govern the repayment of land settlement loans (*IGU,* 1910: 854-56).

As to Krivoshein's manner of dealing with zemstvoes, it was much criticized by its beneficiaries, but on the whole he supervised them even less carefully than his commissions. The circular of October 1908 marked his first major move to use zemstvoes as MZ agencies for agricultural improvement in the villages. Relatively large-scale handouts to zemstvoes for agronomic aid to peasants commenced in 1909, and in the late summer of that year "agronomic conferences" met in a few uezds and gubernias to discuss, among other things, zemstvo use of MZ funds. The sorest point was the government's insistence that the amount of agronomic aid

---

[13]An article in the following issue of the MZ's journal defined "land settlement purposes" very broadly as any kind of improvement in land use (IGU, 1908: 842-44).

going to an area correspond to the amount of land settlement taking place there. In some locales—Poltava gubernia, for example—specialists expressed their willingness to concentrate their efforts at agricultural improvement on consolidated farms (TsGIAL, f. 1291, op. 120, 1909g., d. 61, ll. 70-74); in others—e.g., Riazan—zemstvo specialists insisted on their right and duty to extend agronomic aid without regard for the recipients' mode of land use (ll. 76-78).[14]

As time went by, resistance by zemstvo specialists became more vocal. A committee circular of 18 December 1909 ventured to criticize zemstvoes for distributing funds earmarked for land settlers to peasants who kept their old strips (*IGU*, 1910: 3-4), and from then on zemstvo agronomists never ceased to complain of the oppression under which they labored. In the end, Krivoshein gave way. His more or less final word on the subject came out in an MZ circular of 24 April 1910 (TsGIAL, f. 1291, op. 120, 1909g., d. 61, ll. 290-92). In this document the ministry retreated from its demand that zemstvoes use its funds to support land settlers. It invited zemstvoes to request funds for distribution to any and all peasants who might require agronomic aid, with the understanding that each recipient zemstvo would match the MZ's subsidy with funds of its own. The MZ's central offices would check each zemstvo request but only in order to apportion funds among the locales in accordance with their levels of achievement in the reform, not to dictate what zemstvoes would do with the money they got. The circular said explicitly that zemstvoes did not have to use their grants to support land settlers. So far as I know, this continued to be the MZ's operating principle with regard to agronomic loans earmarked for the support of land settlement. The government would lecture the zemstvoes occasionally on the virtues of land settlement, but local specialists never suffered any *procedural* check on their activities.

Krivoshein and Stolypin not only stated a belief in zemstvo autonomy, they acted on it. Typical of their attitude was their response to a note to Stolypin from the governor of Kherson in January 1910, protesting against the enormous, unregulated power being thrust upon zemstvoes in the form of MZ subsidies (ll. 184-86). Stolypin responded with a note to Krivoshein, disagreeing sharply with the governor and asking for an explanation of his conduct. Upon receiving Krivoshein's assurance that the governor's little fight with his zemstvoes was over (ll. 187-88), the MVD-prime minister did not treat his subordinate in Kherson with undue severity. It sufficed to send a formal reply to the governor's note telling him, in effect, that it was his *duty* to get along harmoniously with the

[14]A land section memo summarizing zemstvo attitudes in the fall of 1909 is in TsGIAL, f. 1291, op. 120, 1909g., d. 61, ll. 315-17.

zemstvoes. Above all, he should not get in their way while they spent the MZ's money (ll. 231-35). Generally speaking, this was the reform administration's characteristic mode of administration. The MZ directed its "subordinate" agencies to find their own way in the countryside and report periodically on what they found. So long as they did not stir up violent opposition or attract unfavorable publicity St. Petersburg imposed very few limits on their work. Not surprisingly, the MZ's distribution of loans and subsidies "in support of land settlement" accelerated rapidly. In 1913, 6.5 million rubles were disbursed (*Kratkii,* 1916: 43).

The evolution of the committee's policy regarding loans and subsidies to land settlers suggests that the committee did indeed inform itself about developments in the countryside and also responded to this information. Generally speaking, the committee's approach to administration closely resembled that of the MZ. As we have seen, the MZ envisioned itself as a *purposive* organization rather than a *normative* one. Implicit in its mode of operation was its concept of itself as an instrument to *move* society, not to establish a new framework for it (ch. 4, sec. D). In the same spirit the Committee for Land Settlement Affairs strove primarily to enable its local agencies to act and did not worry overmuch about regulating their action.

B. THE UEZD COMMISSIONS

Formal Changes after the March Law

The uezd land settlement commissions underwent very little change in formal organization after their initial establishment in March 1906. The instruction of 19 September 1906 made them sound more business-like by identifying a quorum. To do business, at least five of the 12-odd members had to be present, and the five had to include: (1) the gentry marshal, *or* chairman of the zemstvo directorate, *or* permanent member; (2) at least one zemstvo representative; and (3) at least one peasant representative (arts. 101-2, *IZO,* 1906: 342). This minimal number probably identifies the working commission better than the full complement of members set forth in the law of 4 March 1906. We may also be certain that it was generally the permanent member who presided, not the marshal or zemstvo director.[15]

The only other significant change in uezd-level organization came in

[15]Inspection reports throughout the reform era complained repeatedly about the marshals' absenteeism (e.g., *IZO,* 1909: 409-10; 1911: 412). Shlippe (103) tells us of a gubernia marshal, A. D. Samarin, who worked very hard at his job but who expressed his unwavering disapproval of the reform by never attending meetings of his land settlement commission.

the law of 14 June 1910, which required that disputes arising from consolidations be heard *and decided* by uezd land settlement commissions rather than the uezd congresses of land captains. Appeals against uezd-level resolutions were to go to gubernia land settlement commissions, whose decisions would be final. The Senate's first department could hear appeals against a gubernia commission's actions, but only on the grounds of illegality (arts. 37-38, *TPSZ,* 33743). The effect of these provisions was to transfer the whole business of land settlement from the MVD's land captains to the MZ's permanent members. From 1910 on uezd land settlement commissions would no longer be merely advisory boards; they would be deciding who was to own what land, and their decisions would have the force of law.

Relations within the Commissions

The most striking feature of the uezd commissions was their unity of purpose. One finds evidence here and there of opposition to the reform outside the commissions among peasants, zemstvoes, and government officials. In 1906, for example, 15 uezd zemstvoes refused to put up candidates to be peasant representatives on the commissions (*Zemleustroistvo,* 1911: 22). This sort of resistance soon died out, but other forms persisted. We have already noted the large number of land captains who resigned their positions in 1906-7. Some of these, doubtless, were motivated at least in part by opposition to the reform, and many local officials who continued to hold their posts did not support land settlement projects (ch. 7, sec. E). There were, then, many kinds of opposition to the reform in the uezds. At no time during the reform era, however, was there any sign of opposition *within* the uezd land settlement commissions—none, at any rate, that I have encountered.

There must have been disagreements in uezd commission meetings. Debates in intergubernia conferences of land settlement workers reveal many grounds for argument among men engaged in carrying out projects (see above, sec. A). Nevertheless, I have run across only one concrete instance of a debate in an uezd land settlement commission. I bring it up here not as a typical illustration but as the only available one.

It is in Maiborodov's memoir. In about 1907-8, when Maiborodov was a land captain in Kherson gubernia, a case came up in his uezd commission involving the sale of some peasant-bank land on which Jewish tenants were residing. Apparently the Jewish farmers had lived on the land for several generations. The law did not allow them to buy land; therefore, when the bank bought it from their landlord and offered it up for sale, they stood to be dispossessed. Seemingly, long-established farmers were to be driven abruptly from their homes and left without any

possibility of acquiring new land. Worse, the Russian or Ukrainian purchasers would probably use the land much less effectively than the original tenants had. The permanent member opined that under the circumstances it would be both unjust and impractical from all points of view to
sell the land. He stood alone. It was not a time for being kind to Jews.
All other members of the commission, with Maiborodov leading the
pack, voted the other way. But it all ended happily. Maiborodov reas-
sured the Jews that they would not be dispossessed. In the future, they
would simply pay rent to peasant landlords (folder 2, 103-7).

Here was a case of strong disagreement within an uezd commission,
yet it implied no opposition to land settlement as such. If one illustration
shows anything, this one suggests that membership on the commissions
was restricted to believers, and their disagreements were essentially tactical. The commissions, it seems, had nothing to discuss except *how* to
implement the reform. This being the case, anyone who opposed land
settlement had nothing to say as a member of a commission and nothing
to gain from serving on it. Government officials on the commission
wanted the permanent member's work to succeed because their own
respective superiors were hounding them to achieve *his* success. In turn,
unity among the government officials on the commission rendered opposition from elected members fruitless. True, one or more elected members
could appeal a decision to the gubernia land settlement commission, but
this too served the organization's purposes by giving the gubernia permanent member an additional check on work in the uezds. If he thought
it served the interests of the reform, he accepted the appeal; if not, he
rejected it. So long as the reform organization as a whole was determined
to move, then, the uezd commission was no place to oppose it.

The Commissions' Relations with Other Administrative Organs

The uezd commissions did not begin as autonomous functional mechanisms with reasonably well-defined purposes. At first they had to enlist
the aid of other government agencies: land captains, peasant bank sections, gubernia surveyors, and the gubernia offices of the MZ. The reform
had overall purposes—intravillage land settlement, intervillage land settlement, land sales, et al.—but it was by no means clear in 1906-7 which
would have priority. The first commissions into the field had somehow to
achieve them all, and they had, therefore, to secure just about everyone's
cooperation.

As time went by, the reform organization began to relieve uezd officials of their wide-ranging responsibilities. In part, this was done by limiting their scope of action strictly to land settlement projects. The MZ
circular of 30 June 1907 took the committee and its subordinate organs
out of cases involving the transfer of land from communal to personal

tenure (ch. 7, sec. B), and the committee's instruction of 19 May 1912 shifted responsibility for the sale of state lands to the regular gubernia agencies of the MZ.[16]

But the most important organizational development for the uezd commissions was not the narrowing of their functions. It was, rather, the emergence of the gubernia organization. From 1907 on, the gubernia level gradually assumed responsibility for coordinating the minsterial agencies involved in land settlement, and this made it possible for uezd permanent members to concentrate on land settlement projects per se. By accepting the gubernia's system, the uezd agencies "freed" themselves to do their fieldwork without having to negotiate every project with other officials. The reform organization did not merely narrow the uezd commissions' scope of action; it put them on a schedule and made them—or rather their permanent members—into purely operating units.

The evolving relationship between uezd commission and peasant bank section reflects this process. The instruction of 19 September 1906 vaguely directed the uezd commission to do such things as "take part" in the bank's negotiations to buy land, "present its conclusions" to the bank concerning the price it should pay for its land, "take part" in breaking up land into salable plots, and "assist" in the sale of these plots (arts. 11-33, *IZO*, 1906: 334-36). Commissions also had to approve loans to peasants who were buying direct from landowners (arts. 34-36). This arrangement explains much of the friction that developed between the reform organization and the bank, and it helps to account for the general inefficacy of the government's efforts at land distribution in 1906-7. During much of 1907, 300-odd uezd commissions were attempting to deal as equals with 30 bank sections, each of which covered one or two gubernias. More disastrous than this lopsided arrangement was the crude combining of two collegial bodies in a single enterprise without any clear indication of which one was to do what. The purpose of uniting them, of course, was to allow the commissions to impose their schemes on the sections. As it worked out, however, the clash between two colleges, espousing widely different aims, effectively eliminated the decision-making power of both. Neither could force the other to act; they could only block each other. Under the circumstances, it is remarkable that the commissions and sections sold any land at all in 1906-7.

As we have seen (sec. A), the committee issued elaborate regulations in February 1908 to govern the sale of bank lands. In their own modest way they were workable. They left the peasant bank securely in the MF's hands but also provided a framework within which MZ and MF agents could do their jobs without having to fight each other. Most important

---

[16]The instruction is printed in *IGU* (8 July 1912) as a separately paged section. The above-mentioned provision is on p. I, sec. I, art. 4.

for our purposes, the new rules relieved the uezd commission of responsibility for dealing with the bank sections. The commission continued to take part in the bank's sales as before, but now all it had to do was report its findings to the new "liquidation section" on the gubernia level. The 300-odd uezd commissions no longer had to negotiate with the 30 bank sections. Instead, the permanent member of the gubernia commission could do the negotiating directly from his position as member of the liquidation section.

The relationship between uezd commission and gubernia surveyor followed a similar course. The initial arrangements, established in June 1906, were revoked as soon as gubernia commissions began to form. The June 1906 circular had attached available surveyors directly to uezd commissions (see ch. 7, sec. B). This, however, proved to be a mistake. Some surveyors were remaining idle in uezds where peasants did not petition for land settlement, while in many other uezds the peasants wanted land settlement work done but could not find surveyors to do it. As petitions for consolidation increased in number, the shortage of surveyors became critical, and it became vitally important that every one be utilized to his maximum capacity. This was why the circular of 16 May 1907 transferred the business of allocating surveyors to the gubernia level (*IZO*, 1907: 247-48). From then on the uezd commissions had no surveyors of their own. Each year they had to tell the permanent member of the gubernia land settlement commission how many projects they were ready to carry out, and surveyors were then assigned to them specifically for these projects.

In 1906-7 the uezd commissions' relationship with the gubernia office of the department of state domains manifested the same anomalies as we have observed in its arrangements with the bank section. Despite the fact that the uezd permanent member and the gubernia manager of state lands worked for the same department in St. Petersburg, the initial contacts between new reform leader in the uezd and established official in the gubernia capital produced conflict. The instruction of 19 September 1906 was a little harsh with managers. It put uezd commissions in charge of selling state lands and ordered the hapless managers to "cooperate" (arts. 37-54, *IZO*, 1906: 336-37). The MZ circular of 12 February 1907 went even further. It ordered managers to do the commissions' technical work for them if they so requested, and it added pointedly that any manager who failed to help a commission would have to explain himself to the MZ (*IZO*, 1907: 89-90). It is not hard to imagine the managers' sentiments when they received these orders. It is very hard to imagine them welcoming requests for "cooperation" from the new uezd agencies. Not surprisingly, the sale of state lands proceeded slowly (ch. 7, sec. B). After a few years the MZ underwent a change of heart. In 1912 the MZ's gubernia office assumed a leading role in the sale of state lands, and the land settlement commissions ceased to interfere (n. 16).

It would be well to review the development of the uezd commission's role in the reform before passing on to the more complex gubernia organization. Initially it had to work all by itself to help the peasants get more land and/or improve the land they had. In 1906-7 the government set out to achieve these aims by trying to make the uezd commission influential enough to command the cooperation of other agencies of peasant reform. It quickly became apparent that uezd commissions could not dictate to other agencies, especially those on the gubernia level. The business of coordination, therefore, was shifted to the gubernias. The uezd commission's tasks were narrowed and simplified, thus allowing the permanent member greater freedom from administrative reponsibilities and enabling him to devote himself to his operational tasks. The commissions became, in short, simple operating units. As for peasant bank sections, gubernia surveyors, and local offices of the MZ, they no longer had to deal with swarms of uezd officials. Instead, as we shall see in the following section, they found themselves compelled to join a gubernia-level organization.

When uezd commissions ceased to be responsible for directing other agencies and instead concentrated all their attention on fieldwork, their mode of operation changed. The legislation of 1906 envisioned a group of ardent enthusiasts going off among the peasants to spread the word about land reform and carry out projects. In practice, however, the vast majority of *zemleustroiteli* who actually directed fieldwork turned out to be surveyors (ch. 7, n. 7). It was they who interacted with the peasantry and formulated the experience on the basis of which the reform organization developed its policies and purposes. All the commissions had to do was to approve or disapprove the completed documents the *zemleustroiteli* laid before them: petitions, plans for land settlement projects, and at last the completed projects themselves. Since the permanent member checked these documents before they came to the commission, the commission as a body had little more to do than assure that the permanent member was not doing anything the gubernia would disapprove of. In short, the uezd commission became passive, unable to obstruct the reform, able at best only to keep the permanent member within the loose limits set for him by the central offices.

The account in the preceding pages omits what was perhaps the most important relationship the uezd commission had with other government agencies: namely, its connections and conflicts with the land captains. This is a relatively elusive subject, with more implications than can conveniently be discussed in a description of administrative organization. It will receive separate treatment in Chapter 9 (sec. C). Suffice it to say here that trends of separation and compartmentalization may also be observed in the initially intimate relations between commissions and erstwhile knights.

C. THE GUBERNIA LEVEL

The Nature of the Gubernia-Level Organization for Land Settlement

Gubernia land settlement commissions began to take form in March 1907 (*IZO*, 1907: 64-65). Since they only came into existence where uezd commissions were already at work, they never did any actual fieldwork. From the outset they devoted themselves entirely to administration and coordination. Initially, in the summer and fall of 1907, the department of state domains seems to have used its new gubernia agencies as crude instruments of centralization. The edicts of 1906 had assigned money and surveyors directly to the uezd commissions and, as it were, unleashed them upon the countryside. Now, in 1907, the department felt a need to assert some sort of control over the power it had so freely disbursed. It did this by barraging the gubernias with orders urging governors and/or land settlement commissions to keep both money and surveyors in the gubernia capitals and send them out only when uezd commissions sent in requests based on well-documented projects.[17]

Had this tendency toward crude centralization continued, the uezd permanent members would have quickly followed the land captains into clerkdom, and land settlement would have progressed much more slowly than it did. Beginning in late 1907, however, gubernia organizations began to work in more sophisticated fashion.

An MZ circular of 19 December 1907 called upon the gubernia commissions to draw up fieldwork schedules (*IGU*, 1908: 2-4), and from then on the main function of the gubernia organization was to compose these schedules and supervise their execution. The business of drawing up fieldwork schedules was first described in a committee circular of 15 February 1908 (*IGU*, 1908: 157). According to this document, schedules were to be compiled each winter on the basis of land settlement projects that had already been formulated by individual *zemleustroiteli*, accepted provisionally by the peasants involved, declared "possible" (i.e., not illegal) by the uezd congress of land captains, and approved by the uezd commission. By the time a project was ready to be put on the fieldwork schedule the way was clear for actual surveying.

[17]Two MZ circulars of Feb. 1907 (*IZO*, 1907: 85-89) illustrate the department's passionate concern to centralize control over uezd expenditure. The earliest circular I have seen requiring uezd commissions to request surveyors from the gubernias for each separate project was dated 16 May 1907 (pp. 247-48).

Theoretically, fieldwork schedules served two purposes: (1) in the countryside they allowed resources to be utilized effectively and enabled land-settling peasants to plan their farmwork while projects were underway; (2) in St. Petersburg they provided the committee with its basic source of information regarding the progress of the reform. I say the schedules served these purposes "theoretically." It seems to me that they also did it actually to some extent, else the government would not have relied on them so heavily. It must be kept in mind, however, that they were crude devices. An MZ report on the year 1914 noted with satisfaction that, despite the war, 60% of the scheduled projects had been completed. This was not so bad, said the report: "under normal conditions" only 65% were completed (*Obzor,* 1915: ii). The schedules, then, were not accurate predictors. Neither peasants nor government could rely on them in the way one relies on a train schedule. The *zemleustroiteli* frequently failed to make up their projects intelligently, and the surveyors were unable to complete the work on time. If the schedule was to be maintained, surveyors had to abandon each uncompleted project so as to get to the next one on time. At best, then, fieldwork schedules could only guarantee that surveyors arrived at their jobs promptly. Actual completion of projects depended on a number of factors, not all of which could be measured (TsGIAL, f. 1291, op. 120, 1910g., d. 19, ll. 15-17, 83-85, 88-89). What the schedules did accomplish, however, was to introduce *some* order into the reform organization's operations—enough, at least, to allow both central offices and peasants to estimate how inaccurate a given schedule would be during a particular year.[18]

Work on the schedules began in February, when uezd permanent members presented themselves in the gubernia capitals, armed with estimates of their needs for the coming year. These estimates called for a specific number of surveyors and other technical personnel, and they included a detailed list of the necessary equipment. Mere figures, however, were not enough. The uezd permanent members had to bring along the projects themselves, accompanied by the necessary authorizations and approvals. More, they had to estimate the time required for each project and for traveling between projects. Finally, all projects in each uezd had to be listed in order of their priority.

The assembled uezd permanent members and surveyors had about two weeks to convert their several estimates into a gubernia-wide schedule. Within this time they had to assign specific projects to each survey-

[18]In the reform's early years some gubernias compounded the problem by overlapping each surveyor's projects. A *zemleustroitel* would be allotted four days on one project and nine on the next, but the two periods would overlap on the schedule, thereby requiring him either to finish each project ahead of schedule or else cover two projects during the same days. See, e.g., the schedule for 1910 for Tver gubernia (TsGIAL, f. 1291, op. 120, 1910g., d. 14, ll. 102-31).

ing team and specify exact dates for beginning and completing them. The schedule also provided for expenses, equipment needs, and travel plans. Ideally, every surveyor now knew where he would be during the entire fieldwork period, which extended from 1 April until mid-autumn.

When the schedule was ready—ideally by early March—it went to the gubernia land settlement commission for formal approval, which was granted by a big gathering, including regular commission members and all uezd permanent members in the gubernia. Approval had to be fast, because the governor had to use the schedule as a basis for issuing orders to surveyors and disbursing requisite funds. He had to finish this quickly enough to allow all personnel to be on location at their first projects, bearing appropriate equipment and documents, by 1 April.

It was also in April, *when the schedules were already going into effect,* that the committee received copies of them in St. Petersburg and began compiling them, dispatching extra surveyors where needed, and giving final approval. When the schedules reached St. Petersburg, they came first to the chancellery of the MZ, where they were checked by representatives from the survey section and the department of state domains. The former undertook to cut down schedules that called for more surveyors than the government could provide. The latter made sure that the projects conformed to the best principles of land settlement and that the department's budget would cover them. Ultimately the committee had to give its final approval.

But all this checking and rechecking in St. Petersburg had little effect on actual fieldwork. By the time the central offices completed their deliberations, the projects were already well underway. All St. Petersburg was doing was compiling information in order to concoct instructions for the following year. The central offices were not directing their agencies, only keeping up with them.

As fieldwork began, monthly progress reorts came in from the gubernias to the department of state domains, where they could be checked against the schedules. This completed the system. Progress reports provided the central offices with a measure of the schedule's intrinsic validity and also allowed them to keep track of real accomplishments on the operating level. Managing the reform became at this stage a matter of bookkeeping. Ideally, the central offices knew what every surveyor *should* be doing in every uezd at any particular time, and by the end of each year they would know what had actually been done. Discrepancies could be noted; explanations could be demanded; suitable rewards and punishments could be dispensed.

This marvel of regularity, however, was only attained in St. Petersburg. The situation in the gubernias was quite different. A gubernia permanent member was not dealing with mere slips of paper. When he received information, he had to do more than simply record it; he had to cope with it on the spot. When surveyors ran into unforeseen complications on their projects, he had somehow to alter the schedule and send out new orders. This was no simple task. The gubernia permanent member had overall responsibility for keeping reform agencies at work, but no official had the authority to change a schedule on his own. The gubernia surveyor always had to be consulted, and quite often, when it came to taking surveyors from one uezd to help out in another, the gubernia permanent member found himself confronting gentry marshals, zemstvo boards, and permanent members of the gubernia board—to say nothing of his own uezd subordinates. Even the bank section could become involved. In short, the permanent member of the gubernia land settlement commission did not simply follow rules and orders mechanically. Unlike the uezd permanent members, whose *administrative* relationships became increasingly routinized after 1907, gubernia permanent members had to make organizational adjustments on the basis of their own judgment in interaction with a potpourri of local administrators. To be sure, the uezd member's fieldwork was hardly cut and dried. When it came to adminstrative problems, however, he had very little to do except to tell the gubernia permanent member about them. But whom was a gubernia member to tell about his problems? Practically speaking, there was no one. This was the essential quality of his position. Theoretically he could carry disputes to St. Petersburg or complain to his governor, but these procedures were too slow to help keep fieldworkers on schedule.

Under these circumstances it is understandable that the gubernia reform organization tended to concentrate authority in the hands of functional officials and to minimize the role of the gubernia land settlement commission as a collegial body. One sign of the commission's withdrawal from active administration was the quorum established for it in the circular of 15 February 1908, when preparations for the first fieldwork schedule were already underway. It was only to be three men (as opposed to the uezd commission's five). One had to be the permanent member, and one had to be an elected member. There were no other requirements, not even for the big gathering that approved the fieldwork schedule. From 1908 on, a permanent member could transact his commission's official business merely by finding two other members—out of 13—to meet with him.

This tiny quorum spelled the end of the gubernia land settlement commission's active role in the management of the reform. After 1908 it followed essentially the same path as its uezd counterpart; that is, it became a passive, semijudicial body, not making decisions but only, at most, checking on them to see that they conformed to rules imposed by the next higher echelon. But the gubernia level evolved this way for a different reason. The uezd commission lost its active role because its operations were in the hands of fieldworkers in interaction with peasants;

the gubernia commission faded away, so to speak, because the permanent member had to work on an ad hoc basis to secure the cooperation of other officials.

It is true, of course, that members of the gubernia land settlement commission could still influence the reform's operation. This was especially true of the governor, whose wide-ranging authority made him a force to be reckoned with, even if it did not enable him to coordinate the administrative agencies in his territory (see Yaney, 1973: 105-9, 323, 345). Many orders from the committee were addressed directly to governors rather than commissions. But we are not attempting to discuss comprehensively all the vital factors which made the reform possible, without any one of which the reform might well have failed. We are discussing here a much narrower question: what made the reform organization operate? Clearly it was neither the governor nor the gubernia commission. In practice, commission members could neither direct the permanent member nor even help him very much. Most important, they could not obstruct him effectively. Like the members of the uezd commission, they only served the reform organization as a check, albeit an important one, on its own agents. If we ask what made the reform operate on the gubernia level, the answer lies not in any formal authority, individual or collegial, but simply in the coordination the gubernia permanent member was able to achieve with other key officials who were involved in the reform.

The Evolution of the Fieldwork Schedule

Who were the "other key officials"? In 1907 there were two of them: the head of the local peasant bank section and the gubernia surveyor. The MZ circular of 19 December 1907, which described the procedures for drawing up the first fieldwork schedule, called upon these two, together with the permanent member of the gubernia land settlement commission, to form a conference _(soveshchanie)_ to compile uezd estimates into a gubernia-wide schedule. The conference was to be collectively responsible for submitting a completed schedule to the gubernia land settlement commission for approval, and its members were to supervise the fieldwork itself to see that it followed the schedule. Other administrators and technical experts could be called in whenever their official functions were necessary to carry out the schedule, but responsibility rested with the three core members. No one of the three was given supreme authority. Whichever was senior in rank was to preside at their meetings _(IGU,_ 1908: 3).[19]

[19] In gubernias where there was no bank section, the head of the section in the nearest gubernia sent one of his section members.

On 19 February 1908, exactly two months later, the committee's statement on the peasant bank came out. As noted above, this new document made the same three officials into a formal body—the local liquidation section—in which the head of the peasant bank section (or his delegate) presided (*Sbornik,* 1908: 661-62, 672). It seems, then, that the reform was still a joint operation in early 1908. The committee still considered it vitally important that peasant bank sections and land settlement commissions work in harmony.

The gubernia *soveshchanie* was a novelty in tsarist administration. It was distinctly not a college but a loosely organized staff of technical experts and administrators. We study it here as described in commands from St. Petersburg, but I have seen no indication that it originated there—especially since it contradicted the principle of collegial operation that governed St. Petersburg's concept of gubernia administration. The following account of its evolution strongly suggests that the *soveshchanie* evolved from the experience of gubernia and uezd administrators.

It began as a small, informal group. According to the circular of 19 December 1907, its chief function was to assign surveyors to uezds in accordance with the projects the uezds submitted. Highest priority was assigned to individual land settlement. Consolidation, the circular said, was the most desirable sort of land reform regardless of whether it was personal or village, or even if it was simply the formation of khutors and otrubs on land purchased from the peasant bank. Group land settlement— projects that merely reduced the number of strips belonging to each household, or split up a village into smaller units—had only the lowest priority. As we know (n. 11), more petitions for group land settlement came in during 1907-8 than for any other kind of *land* reform. The government, however, was not yet persuaded of their importance. Nor was the government yet persuaded of the peasant bank's unimportance. The circular made it a point to order that the bank could not under any circumstances be denied its share of surveyors. If, perchance, there were a great many projects for intravillage consolidation in a particular area, its high priority was to be disregarded to the extent that at least one-half of the surveyors in the area had to be assigned to the peasant bank (*IGU,* 1908: 3).

A year later, on 8 December 1908, the committee issued another circular on fieldwork schedules, setting forth procedures to be followed in 1909. The system was basically the same as the one for the previous year, but there were a few significant changes. The *soveshchanie* gained some additional members. The governor himself was now to be chairman, and the three members of the previous year were to be joined by one of the permanent members of the gubernia board and the head of the MZ's gubernia agency (p. 952). The circular of 31 January 1909 added a "hydrotechnical" engineer (*IZO,* 1909: 46).

The new members did not change the nature of the *soveshchanie* or its role in the reform. It remained in essence an informal group. Judging from the absence of rules governing votes and quorums, its meetings were still places for transacting business rather than arriving at formal decisions. The governor's official presence suggests the importance of the group rather than any increased formality in its procedure. He did not have to attend meetings. When he was absent, the senior man presided. Probably he only put in an appearance at the first planning session and then chaired the last one, when the *soveshchanie* approved the schedule prior to its submission to the land settlement commission. It is doubtful in any case that there were many formal meetings. Most likely the members came in individually to consult with the gubernia surveyor and the permanent member of the land settlement commission whenever they had specific demands to make or information to contribute. This manner of operating was not substantially different from what had gone on the year before.

The most important new feature in the *soveshchanie* of 1909 was the distinctly lower status of the head of the local bank section. He was now just one of several members, all of whom were clearly peripheral to the two key officials, the gubernia surveyor and the permanent member. The clearest indication of the bank's diminished status may be found in the new assignment of priorities in the fieldwork schedules. According to the circular of December 1908, highest priority was reserved for projects left over from the schedule of the previous year; second in line were new projects for intravillage land settlement, either individual or group; third were sales of bank lands; fourth, the division into integral lots of private lands purchased directly with the bank's help; and fifth, the sale of state lands. This sounds similar to the arrangement of the previous year, but the 1909 priority list had some new features. In the 1908 schedule the only intravillage projects that had gotten high priority were consolidations. Projects for group land settlement were at the bottom of the list. The new circular, by contrast, gave all intravillage projects—both individual and group—priority over the forming of khutors and otrubs on nonpeasant lands. Nor was this the only slight the bank had to suffer. It was no longer to have at least half the surveyors. If surveyors turned out to be in short supply, said the circular of December 1908, the bank was to get only as many as it had used in the previous year. In effect, this marked a sharp cutback in bank operations. The total number of surveyors available for work in 1909 was about double the number for 1908; thus the peasant bank was not likely to get more than one-fourth of them (*Desiatiletie,* 1916: 21-25). Moreover, the circular implied that this relatively small allotment might be restricted entirely to the bank's own land (which was controlled by the liquidation section). Projects of the fourth and fifth priority—direct sales of private estates and state lands to peasants—could be left off the fieldwork schedule entirely if necessary. In short, land sales to peasants were no longer vital operations in December 1908. The head of the peasant bank section was still formally connected with the *soveshchanie*, but his active cooperation was no longer necessary to the conduct of fieldwork.

In the course of 1909 the fading away of land sales proceeded apace. A circular of 12 December 1909 announced yet another set of rules for making up fieldwork schedules (*IGU*, 1909: 1173-76). They were basically similar to the arrangements described above, but there were a few new twists. The identity of the key officials was at last formally established. The *Soveshchanie*, now capitalized, consisted of the governor, the permanent member of the gubernia commission, the gubernia surveyor, a member of the gubernia board, and the local "hydrotechnical" engineer. As before, other officials could participate when their functions were involved. Among these "others" were the bank section head and the chief of the MZ's gubernia agency. The auxiliary status of the bank was now made explicit. As for surveyor allocation, it was taken care of before scheduling began by assigning the bank's central liquidation section a total of 300 surveyors and 100 assistant surveyors to cover all bank lands in the empire. By this time there were 3,350 surveyors in the field (*Desiatiletie*, 1916: 25), so the bank's share for 1910 was not much more than one-tenth of the total number. The sale of state lands suffered an even sharper downgrading. Projects for such sales were to be scheduled only when they were necessary to the completion of reforms on peasant land.[20]

The circular of December 1909 also introduced some fundamental changes in priorities for land settlement on allotment land. It will be recalled that the original priority list of December 1907 had distinguished consolidation from group land settlement and given the former preference over the latter. In the fieldwork of 1910 first priority (after unfinished projects from the previous year) went to "collective" consolidations, which included consolidations of whole villages and personal consolidations that involved sizable groups of peasants within villages. Various types of group land settlement took second place, and only then, after all other types of land settlement on village lands, came personal consolidations of separate households. All consolidations had to follow the rules of good land settlement if they were to have high priority. If a collective consolidation departed from the rules—for example, if the participants assigned more than one lot per otrub or allowed the otrub lots to be long and thin—they fell to a lower level, along with or below group land settlement projects.

[20]The number of surveyors assigned to the bank continued to decrease after 1910. In 1911 only 270 surveyors went to bank projects (TsGIAL, f. 592, op. 1, d. 158, l. 3), and in 1913 only 164 (*IGU*, 1913: 907).

The evolution of the fieldwork schedules suggests that the process of land settlement developed the organization that carried it out. In a sense the schedules were a tune played by the surveyors and permanent members of uezd and gubernia commissions, and the entire formal organization for land settlement danced to it. There was no point during the schedule-making process when any collegial body had sufficient time even to examine the proposed schedule, let alone make significant changes in it. As the head of the survey section pointed out in 1910, the gubernia commission had to take what the *soveshchanie* presented (TsGIAL, f. 1291, op. 120, 1910g., d. 19, l. 83). As for the committee and the central offices in St. Petersburg, they did not even begin their inquiries until the schedule had gone into effect. Far from opposing this devolution of operational direction, the committee did what it could to hasten its development. With each passing year the gubernia *soveshchanie* gained an increasing measure of functional autonomy and was expressly encouraged to pursue land settlement aims that contradicted capital-city notions of agrarian reform, such as Kofod's insistence on complete consolidations.

I do not mean to imply that the gubernia permanent member became all-powerful. In practice, the *soveshchanie* had to base its work on projects submitted by uezd permanent members, and *all* officials of the reform organization had ultimately to serve the needs of surveyors, the lowest echelon of all. And the surveyors? Were they "powerful"? Only insofar as they functioned effectively. Their greatest practical need was to be assigned to projects that would bring them the best piecework pay, the fattest bonuses, and, of course, the greatest professional satisfaction; therefore they were largely dependent on their ability to secure the cooperation of peasants. Doubtless they made every effort to avoid villages where they might encounter opposition, and they certainly did not seek opportunities to play the tyrant. In sum, the fieldwork schedules rendered all officials autonomous but bound them securely to the demands of their assigned functions. An official could do as he liked if he performed, but performance meant securing the cooperation of those with whom he worked, especially those who worked *for* him. In the end, it was the peasants who directed the reform, and the achievement of the gubernia organization was to provide them with a mechanism for this purpose.

D. THE EVOLUTION OF AN ORGANIZATION FOR IMPROVING PEASANT AGRICULTURE

Importance

By 1913 land settlement on peasant lands had become the central objective of the Stolypin Land Reform, but it was by no means the only one. Indeed, if the reform had persisted a few years more, consolidation might well have gone the way of land distribution and been shunted off to the side. The government was already shifting its resources to support agricltural improvement, and it seemed quite likely when World War I broke out that this tendency would continue.

Agricultural improvement never became sufficiently organized to lend itself to orderly description. I have found no sure information about what the fast-growing regiments of zemstvo and government agronomists were actually doing in the countryside during the latter years of the reform or how they were spending the money allotted to them. I have not even been able to determine with precision how much money the central government allotted to them. One thing is clear, however: agricultural improvement was a vital part of the reform, and we must at least glance at the organization that grew up around it.

First a word about its significance. Certainly the MZ attached great importance to it. In 1913 the budget for the department of state domains— i.e., the executive organ for land settlement—amounted to about 27 million rubles. Its asking budget for 1914 was 28 million, of which 24.4 million went to land settlement (*IGU,* 1913: 970-71, 1080). This was the smallest increase the MZ requested for any of its departments for 1914. The biggest requests were for the departments of forestry and agriculture, and the latter was the main organization for granting loans and subsidies to foster agricultural improvement. Agriculture's budget had risen from a mere 3.9 million in 1906 to 29 million in 1913, and since most of this department's money went into matching grants to zemstvoes, it generated much more expenditure on agricultural improvement than the budget indicated. According to a government publication, zemstvo expenditures on agriculture rose from 6.9 million rubles in 1909 to 16 million in 1913 (*Itogi,* 1914: 7). It must be admitted that these funds did not go exclusively to peasants; hence the above figures are only *indicators* of the trend toward agricultural improvement on peasant lands, not measurements.

Other MZ departments involved in agricultural improvement were also flourishing. The section of rural economy and agricultural statistics was tiny by comparison with the department of agriculture, but its asking budget for 1914 gave it the biggest *percentage* increase of any MZ department: from 3.7 million in 1913 to 6.2 million in 1914 (*IGU,* 1913: 1018). The section for land improvement projected a slightly slower expansion, from about 10 to 13.5 million (p. 1017; and also *Otdel,* 1914: 8-14). Both these sections were involved to some extent in land settlement; the section for land improvement provided "hydrotechnical" engineers. Most of their work, however, was devoted to agricultural improvement.

The tsar himself proclaimed his concern for agricultural improvement in 1913. One of his measures to celebrate the Romanov tricentennial consisted of setting aside all the peasant bank's income from the sale of crown lands for the MZ to use in the improvement of peasant agriculture (*IGU,* 1913: 223-24). The peasant bank had long resisted the MZ's persistent attempts to get at its treasury (sec. A). Now Nicholas II was intervening on the MZ's side. His tricentennial decree was only the beginning of an attack on the MF's tight-fisted attitude. In January 1914 he secured Kodovtsov's resignation as minister and as chairman of the Council of Ministers, replacing him, as minister only, with one P. L. Bark, a lowly actual state councilor.[21] As this relatively obscure official took his post, he received a stern rescript saying pointedly that the tsar would not tolerate the enrichment of the government at the expense of the people. Nicholas wanted a "transformation." In particular, he wanted to "introduce basic changes into the direction of state finances," his main purpose being "to unite our concern to increase the productive strength of the state with our concern to serve the needs of the people" (*Izvestiia Kantseliarii,* 1914: 26).[22]

It was to be expected that land settlement would give way to agricultural improvement. If the reform organization had gone on indefinitely doing nothing but extending checkerboard fields across European Russia, it would have reached—perhaps actually was reaching—a point of diminishing returns. By and large, land settlement was going forward most rapidly on relatively productive land. As the most fertile fields were consolidated, the remaining interstripped land would offer an ever-decreasing return on the cost of rearranging it. As the organization for land settlement approached this point, it became practical for the government to divert increasing amounts of its resources to programs for improving farming methods on existing consolidated farms. True, there was considerable pressure within and without the government to go on consolidating peasant land until every last interstripped field was swept away. With the passage of time, however, the obvious need to exploit existing khutors and otrubs was creating stiff counterpressures. Never mind the swampy potato patches of Vologda gubernia, the agricultural specialists were saying, let us put our resources into improving the new farms we already have. After all, the purpose of agrarian reform is to make Russian agriculture prosperous and productive. Let us not waste the state's resources and delay our attainment of this laudable goal by

[21]Actual state councilor was the fourth-highest *chin* (rank) in the imperial bureaucracy. Ministers usually held the second or third ranks.

[22]Nicholas had been calling for agricultural improvement in strident tones since the early years of his reign (see, e.g., *Otdel,* 1914: 12). Now, in 1913-14, he was putting some muscle behind his vocal efforts. Needless to say, no Soviet scholar has ever mentioned the tsar's actions on behalf of agricultural improvement.

rigidly pursuing land settlement far past the Arctic Circle and out into the deserts of Turkestan.

Land in the northern gubernias lay under a heavy forest cover, and much of it was swampy. More people occupied themselves with industry than agriculture. As an MVD inspection report of 1909 said, the peasants of Kostroma and Iaroslavl gubernias generally cared very little about their land, and it would not be easy to persuade them to exert themselves to improve it. To make matters worse, their interstripping was formidably complex. Often scores of villages were intermingled in a single set of fields, thereby making the consolidation of separate households almost impossible (*IZO*, 1910: 80-82). Worse yet were the sheer physical problems involved in establishing and maintaining separate farmsteads in the north. More often than not, land had to be cleared and drained and considerable time and money invested in intensive cultivation. Even the best farmers suffered frequent crop failures when the frost ended too late in the spring or came too early in the fall, and a single household was ill prepared to keep the relatively large population of bears and wolves out of its fields (see, e.g., Bogoraz, 1924: 47-50). Finally, surveyors were reluctant to work in the north. It was hard to measure boundaries through trees and thickets, and markers could not be firmly anchored in the mud. An order of 1910 raised piece rates for surveying swampy forest land, but even this did not attract enough surveyors to the northern gubernias (*IZO*, 1910: 75-78, 80-82). It is understandable, then, that very little land settlement took place north of the Volga except in the vicinity of cities and railroads. Agricultural specialists were reluctant to work for less pay while achieving less results against exceptionally formidable legal and geographical obstacles. Understandably, they preferred the relatively rich soils to the south, where the new consolidated farms were at last making modern methods practicable. Sooner or later, then, the Stolypin Reform was very likely to shift over from land settlement to agricultural improvement, if, indeed, it was not already doing so in 1914.[23]

Description

Government-sponsored agricultural improvement was largely a matter of encouraging peasant farmers to use better equipment and methods

[23]Litvinov, head of the MVD's land section, seems to have believed in switching the reform's emphasis to agricultural improvement as early as 1909. The formation of khutors and otrubs was going so well, he said, that local agencies should now devote more attention to extending agronomic assistance to existing farms. He noted approvingly that some zemstvoes were already active in this matter. They were using credit cooperatives as intermediaries to distribute the government's loans and subsidies to deserving farmers (*IZO*, 1910: 182-83).

on their lands by extending credit to them and sending out experts to advise them. The basic idea was to work directly with individual farmers, and therefore the basic administrative problem for agricultural improvers was to find out what individual farmers were doing and what they needed. Lacking agencies of its own for this sort of thing, the MZ chose to rely on zemstvo-employed agricultural specialists to distribute loans and materials to farms where they would do the most good. In 1906-7, however, zemstvo specialists were few in number, and they had very little direct contact with peasants. In order to operate, they in turn had to find agencies close to the villages, and for this purpose they associated themselves with rural credit cooperatives. Thus agricultural improvement brought with it a radically new form of government organization. Autonomous economic associations, lacking clear administrative or legal definition, began to work under the informal direction of agronomists, whose connection with the central government was also highly informal.

The tsarist government made a distinction between agricultural improvement and land settlement. For administrative purposes the former did not include the establishing of farms but only their actual exploitation. Surveying boundaries, digging wells, draining and irrigating fields, and building roads were all parts of land settlement, so the tsarist government said. These were things one should do for peasants at the time they formed their consolidated farms. Taken together, they constituted land reform, and the government treated them differently from measures of agricultural improvement. Surveying was done at government expense, and the other above-listed measures were supported by "land settlement" loans and subsidies, which were distributed under the loose supervision of the department of state domains. Agricultural improvement, on the other hand, came under the direction of other offices and took a variety of forms, though in many cases it was directed to the same peasants. Most of this "agronomic help" went to pay agronomists' salaries. Smaller amounts were paid out to: (1) set up stations for renting out farm machinery and selling high-quality seed, (2) provide loans to buy machinery and seed, (3) establish demonstration farms and fields, and (4) provide loans to help peasants improve their stock raising and diversify their crops (*Kratkii*, 1916: 47-49).

As the men involved in agricultural improvement saw it, their work extended much further than the above categories. Anything peasants might need was a legimate subject for an agronomist's concern—fire insurance, school curricula, public health, etc. Agronomists did not take official responsibility for all these matters, since this would have brought them into conflict with other ministries. In principle, however, the agricultural specialists of the reform era were not averse to playing the role of ombudsman, and they did in fact move into fields of operation that bore little relation to agronomy. For example, both central government and local institutions considered the construction and fireproofing of houses and barns to be a part of "agricultural" improvement. Loans for this purpose involved substantial amounts of money, which increased rapidly during the reform's latter years—from 2 million rubles in 1911 (Dubrovskii, 1963: 269) to 4 million in 1913 (*IGU*, 1912: 1039). In 1914 the land settlement commissions turned this part of their operation over to a new department in the MZ, the section for rural construction (*Izvestiia Kantseliarii*, 1914: 155-56). The war seems to have halted further progress along these lines, but it is of interest that the MZ requested approximately 6.2 million rubles for its new section for the year 1915 (*IGU*, 1914: 1005).

It is not especially difficult to comprehend the variety of official functions that accumulated under the "organization" for agricultural improvement. Despite their breadth and diversity, they were associated with observable fiscal appropriations and bureaucratic offices in St. Petersburg. These offices worked in much the same way and faced similar problems. What is difficult to see is the local agencies through which the St. Petersburg departments worked.

As said before, most departments worked through rural credit cooperatives. In essence, these were little banks in which the people in one or more villages deposited their savings and from which these same people could borrow. There were two types: (1) MVD-dominated *obshchestvennye-soslovnye* associations, managed within the framework of traditional village and volost institutions; and (2) credit cooperatives (before 1905, *ssudo-sberegatelnye tovarishchestva;* after 1905, *kreditnye tovarishchestva*). The latter received financial support from the state bank and therefore operated more or less independently from the MVD. In the early years of the reform most cooperative institutions were still of the former type. As of early 1908 there were, on paper at least, 4,620 village "associations" and only 2,877 bank-supported "cooperatives" in the 47 reform gubernias. The 4,620 "associations" supposedly possessed almost seven times as much capital as the relatively small "cooperatives" (*Trudy,* 1909: *prilozheniia,* 24-27). In fact, however, the MVD associations were not prospering, probably because they were not eligible for government loans (Baker, 1973: 163-64, 197-98). By 1914 they had dropped to 4,375 in number, while the number of credit cooperatives had increased substantially (p. 412). Indeed, the former may already have been much weaker in 1908 than they appeared on paper. An inspection of Samara gubernia in 1909 found 200 MVD associations still in existence, exactly the number that had been reported in 1908, but, according to the inspectors, most of them were "not functioning" (*IZO,* 1910: 127). We are justified, then, in leaving the *soslovnye* associations out of account. Doubtless a few of them helped the cause of agricultural improvement, but they were clearly not in the mainstream.[24]

Bank-supported cooperatives were a different matter. Though they came under the MF's jurisdiction rather than the MZ's, agrarian administrators and specialists considered them vital to agricultural improvement, and apparently it was these men, rather than the MF, who contributed the most to their evolution (Baker, 1973: 66-83, 109, 115-23, 268-82; see also ch. 9, sec. C).

It would be erroneous to insist that credit cooperatives were the only instruments for extending agronomic aid to peasants. A variety of cooperative organizations were flourishing in rural Russia during the Stolypin era—combinations of producers and consumers, machine-buying groups, etc.—and they were quite willing to borrow the government's money. It seems, however, that credit cooperatives were the most important links between government programs and *individual* farmers. A typical article by a government agronomist, published in 1911, proclaimed that credit cooperatives *had* to be the major channel from government to peasantry. Credit and agronomic help had become one and the same thing, he said, and therefore credit cooperatives had to expand into all kinds of agricultural activity. The government should not spread its funds around to all kinds of cooperatives; instead, credit cooperatives should undertake to do all kinds of things (Zavadskii, 1911: 42-53).[25]

We need not seek any very complex explanations for the key role of credit cooperatives in agricultural improvement. They were, by the very nature of their work, better informed than other groups regarding the reliability and promise of individual peasants in each locale. Other kinds of cooperatives played a vital role in agricultural improvement, but ordinarily they did not want to be bothered with the annoying responsibilities of estimating the personal assets of their members and collecting payments from them. Credit cooperatives did this sort of thing as a matter of course, a fact of life that made them the most promising agencies for distributing government loans and aid and also bringing agronomists into direct contact with farmers (Baker, 1977: 139-60).

Now that I have described some of the parts that made up the "organization" for agricultural improvement, we are prepared to discuss it as a unit. I am envisioning it, be it remembered, as a part of the reform organization, which implies that I am conceiving of the reform organiza-

[24]After 1905 MVD associations could become eligible for government loans by agreeing to accept the supervision of the state bank. Presumably this acceptance allowed them to shake off the tutelage of village and volost institutions. In fact, not many associations took advantage of the new privilege (*IZO,* 1913: 137).

[25]One credit cooperative that branched out into other functions, per the agronomists' ideal, is described in Alekseev (1923: 53-59).

tion as if it had been made up of two separate segments: one, an administration for scheduling fieldwork; the other, a process of dispensing credit and guidance to individual farmers. The former consisted of surveyor teams operating out of the gubernia capitals under the loose, overall supervision of the department of state domains; the latter consisted essentially of a flow of money to zemstvoes and cooperatives under the far looser supervision of several other MZ departments, chiefly that of agriculture. We must remember, however, that the two segments were only different from one another, not separate. The government's willingness to change its attitude toward specialists as radically as it did during the Stolypin era did not emerge from a vacuum. It sprang, rather, from the central offices' commitment to land reform. If agricultural improvement called for a radically different organizational structure, even so, the government's recognition of a need for this departure stemmed from the interaction with peasants into which its land reform had carried it.

As I have suggested, the essential feature of the "organization" for agricultural improvement was an interaction between government agencies, zemstvoes, and credit cooperatives in which the agencies turned money over to zemstvoes and cooperatives for distribution to individual peasants in the form of loans and aid. This was by no means a coherent structure in itself. The only feature that gave it at least a semblance of structure was the fact that it was staffed by specialists. Specialists engaged in agricultural improvement, unlike those in land settlement, felt no need *initially* for an elaborate administrative framework (although they began clamoring for one soon enough, as we shall see). They were not concerned to identify their responsibilities, thereby fitting themselves into any existing administration. They wished, rather, to keep themselves entirely apart from administration. They acted and thought very much like schoolteachers. Like teachers who set out to "educate," the specialists set out to "improve," despite the fact that no one, least of all their supervisors, had any concrete, generally accepted idea of what the process of improvement entailed. As in modern education, the only thing that gave a semblance of coherence to the whole operation was a tacit agreement among all concerned that the would-be improvers were "qualified specialists" and could, for this reason alone, be assumed to know what they were doing. Thus, when an administrator undertook to describe agricultural improvement, he had only to say how many specialists were at work and where. There was no need to say *what* they were doing except in the most general terms.

As of 1914, five government departments and programs of significant size operated according to this principle: the department of state domains, the department of agriculture, the section for rural economy and agricultural statistics, the section for rural construction, and the chief administration for small credit. The latter agency was in the MF;

the others were in the MZ. Each had a loan program, but none had sufficient agents to distribute loans directly to individual peasants. The department of state domains, with its land settlement commissions, had by far the most extensive organization, yet it too had to leave much of its loan distribution work to zemstvoes.[26]

The MF's chief administration for small credit and the MZ's department of agriculture had very few agencies outside St. Petersburg. In structure, both their "organizations" resembled the land settlement administration. Each was headed by a central committee dominated by the parent ministry but including representatives from other ministries. Both had collegial organs on the gubernia level that included the leading gubernia-level officials who were involved in rural affairs. Here the resemblance with land settlement ends. These gubernia-level colleges included the chairmen of the gubernia zemstvo directorates as voting members, but neither of them included elected representatives. Nor did either college have subordinate organs in the uezds or separate offices of their own in the gubernia capitals. In the case of the department of agriculture, gubernia-level officials in charge of improving peasant agriculture were mere staff members in the MZ's gubernia offices. As of 1913 there were still only 26 such officials in all European Russia, and therefore most of them had to cover two gubernias.[27] After 1910 they acquired 97 "administrative agronomists" to help them keep track of the flow of funds and the horde of specialists they were officially supposed to be supervising, but even these assistants had no clear position in the administrative hierarchy (*Obzor*, 1914: *prilozhenie; Agronomicheskaia*, 1914: 134-40). The MF's inspectors of small credit were in even worse condition. They operated out of St. Petersburg and did not have any sort of permanent gubernia offices (Baker, 1973: 172, 195-97). The other agencies mentioned above had no organization whatever outside St. Petersburg and had to transact their business through the department of agriculture's 26 men. We may say, then, that for the most part the government had very little formal administration for distributing agricultural improvement loans to peas-

---

[26]In theory, the department of state domains was not involved in agricultural improvement. Nevertheless, many land settlement commissions distributed their land settlement loans and aid in this fashion, so I take the liberty of lumping the department together with the agencies for agricultural improvement. Varying methods of distribution used by the commissions are described in *Obzor* (1914: 53-55).

[27]The department of agriculture appointed its first officials to distribute loans and subsidies to peasants in 1900 (*TPSZ*, 18695). Initially they were called *upolnomochennye* (agents), but the law of 12 June 1902 (*TPSZ*, 21694) added *inspektory* (inspectors), and from then on both terms were used more or less interchangeably to describe the department's 26 gubernia loan disbursers.

ants, *and the directors of the reform showed very little interest in creating one.*

Our brief discussion of loans and subsidies for land settlement (sec. A) indicated that purse strings by themselves were not an entirely satisfactory means of control in rural Russia, not even when they were administered. Tight control meant red tape. If a central office wanted to impose a policy on the recipients of its funds, it had to receive and check all loan applications in its own offices. The alternative was to let the local agencies disburse loans according to their own lights. This, it seems, was what the five agencies of agricultural improvement did. They did not do it willingly, or wholeheartedly, or without keeping up a pretense of "sound" fiscal practice, but they did it.

The result is hard to determine. We have a voluminous literature of complaints from zemstvo specialists that their efforts were frustrated by government bureaucrats (see, e.g., Polner, 1930). On the other hand, ministerial journals kept up a flow of critical remarks about zemstvo irregularities (see, e.g., *IGU,* 1910: 3-4). For better or worse, however, zemstvoes and ministries were cooperating more intensively during the reform era than ever before.

On the whole, loans to zemstvoes for agronomic purposes—swamp drainage, irrigation, machine distribution centers, etc.—were supervised very little. The memoirs of A. D. Golitsyn provide an illustration. In 1908 or so, when Golitsyn was a Duma representative from Kharkov, he was asked by his uezd zemstvo to secure a subsidy for a land improvement project. He was a man of influence and had no trouble getting the money. All he had to do was visit his friend the director of the department of agriculture. The director told him there was money available for zemstvoes, but they had made no attempt to agree on a system for distributing it. Consequently the government just handed out its funds on a first-come, first-serve basis. As long as the gubernia zemstvoes made no move to regulate distribution, commented the director, the money would simply continue to go to the first uezd zemstvoes that petitioned for it (Golitsyn, 181-82). Such was the arrangement for loan distribution in the early years of the reform. There being no formal system, distribution depended to a considerable extent on the abilities and/or whims of individuals. According to F. V. Shlippe, vice-director of the department of agriculture in 1912-13, things were still pretty much the same during his term of office (Shlippe, 116). He says that he took positive steps to work out a distribution system. He called a meeting of some chairmen of zemstvo directorates and presented them with a series of proposals. The chairmen accepted them in principle and so did Shlippe's superiors, including Krivoshein himself. Nevertheless, these arrangements never became official, and although Shlippe claims they improved the situation, he admits that loan distribution continued to be an ad hoc affair (pp. 116-19).

Perhaps Shlippe's remarks reflect St. Petersburg's lack of information rather than actual conditions in the gubernias. In 1908, when Golitsyn got his friendly loan, agricultural specialists in a few gubernias were already beginning to hold occasional congresses to coordinate their work, and permanent consultative bodies—*agronomicheskie soveshchaniia*—were being set up to handle the distribution of government funds. Both zemstvoes and central government participated in these congresses and consultative bodies, and it is difficult to imagine them not exercising some directing force (*Agronomicheskaia,* 1914: 142-43, 155-62).[28]

In any case, it is certain that in 1913-14 agricultural improvement began to undergo rapid expansion, and it was at this time that the demand for systematization grew much stronger at all levels of the "organization." In 1913, as Nicholas II was beginning to express his determination to improve the peasants' lot (n. 22), the MZ began issuing appeals to zemstvoes and agricultural societies to organize their agronomists so as to facilitate the ministry's disbursal of funds. In 1914 a Russia-wide conference of MZ inspectors and agronomists agreed to make the regularization of local agronomic work one of their primary aims (*IGU,* 1914: 487, 1073-74). Meanwhile, during the three-year period 1911-13, zemstvo institutions were extended to 13 new gubernias, which meant that all reform gubernias except Archangel and the Don Oblast now had them.

In view of all the zemstvo literature about stifling bureaucracy and overcentralization that has come down to us, it will bear emphasizing that *none* of the developments described above constituted an attempted "takeover" of agricultural improvement by St. Petersburg. On the contrary, the law of 16 June 1912 went in the opposite direction by *formally* assigning full responsibility for the distribution of land settlement loans and subsidies to zemstvoes (1912: 710-11). Admittedly. Krivoshein aspired to impose watchdogs on zemstvo fiscal systems (see, e.g., *Deiatelnosti,* 1911: I, 14), but this is much less than prima facie evidence that he sought "power" over zemstvo specialists.

The specialists themselves wanted formal regulation and centralization at least as badly as Krivoshein. Whenever an opportunity presented itself, they fulminated loudly against the lack of uniformity in zemstvo agricultural activity from one uezd to the next. Not many specialists desired supervision for themselves, but they certainly wanted a regulated structure of loan distribution (see, e.g., IGU, 1911: 1017-19;

---

[28]The department of agriculture called a Russia-wide conference of its inspectors and agronomist-administrators in 1910 (*IGU,* 1910: 268-71, 334-40). It also sponsored numerous regional conferences (1911: 1016-20, 1038-41, 1074-76) and conferences of different categories of specialist (1912: 57, 78-86).

1912: 80, 82-83, 86). In 1914 Vladimir Trutovskii, an unrestrained advocate of government by zemstvo specialists, voiced his hope that zemstvoes would now transform themselves into a single, unified directorate over "social production" (1914: 141). He meant zemstvo specialists and their "organization," not the elected zemstvo assemblies, which is to say that he did not approve of democratic restraints on bureaucratic organizations, so long as the organizations were staffed by "scientists." Also in 1914 V. Brunst of the Moscow Agricultural Society was counseling local cooperatives and uezd zemstvoes to submit their petitions for government loans through gubernia zemstvo offices, thus allowing staffs of scientist-bureaucrats to compile the petitions before presenting them to the department of agriculture. Otherwise, cautioned Brunst, cooperatives and zemstvoes would compete with each other and allow government offices to manipulate them (1914: 7-8). The MZ, then, was not the only party interested in regulation in 1914. Its proposals for reorganization were essentially a response to zemstvo needs, not an attempt to dominate the network of zemstvoes and cooperatives that Krivoshein himself had worked so hard to create.

To sum up, we may say that the government's programs of agricultural improvement and land settlement constituted not only administrative activities but basic changes in rural political order. In 1914 the MVD hierarchy was clearly on the way to being confined to police work, and the peasantry was being left to the mercies of a corps of specialists whom neither zemstvo assemblies nor central administration could control. This was the organizational heritage that the Stolypin Land Reform left to Russia.

E. CONCLUSIONS

It must be emphasized that the formal organization of the reform was only one of many elements in its operation. As many scholars have noted, the ground for its development had been well prepared by economic growth during the previous half-century. It will not do, then, to visualize the reform as a product of some statesman's brain. It was something new, but it was not a new theory or scheme of organization imposed upon the countryside according to a plan. The purposes and organizational structure of the reform developed *after* the government had blundered into largely unsuccessful attempts to implement its "theories."

The Committee for Land Settlement Affairs did not *direct* the organization for land settlement; its central offices devoted themselves primarily to coordination, communication, and compilation. Had it wished, the committee could have interfered in local decision making on a grand scale. It could have insisted that fieldwork be held up while the department of state domains checked every land settlement project, thus forcing the organization to remain within the boundaries of its regulations while ignoring the broad purpose of social change to which it was committed. But the committee did not attempt to control its organization from St. Petersburg. Local fieldworkers enjoyed considerable freedom to adapt themselves to local conditions. If the committee had not allowed its local organs to operate in this ad hoc fashion, the reform would probably have undergone the same dwindling development as the peasant bank and land captains. Land settlement progressed as it did primarily because the committee members realized that they did not know what "proper" work constituted and therefore consciously left each commission free to find it out in each area in interaction with the inhabitants.

This is not to say that the reform organization was decentralized. The committee as a whole allowed local commissions to find their own ways, but, unlike the land captains and all other predecessors in rural administration, local land settlement agencies *measured* much of what they did, and this not only compelled them to coordinate with each other in each gubernia but also tied them to a Russia-wide system that became more "centralized" as it developed—centralized in the sense that it embodied a uniformity of purpose that could impose itself on official behavior in the countryside. To be sure, it was the local scheme of coordination that "controlled" local action, and St. Petersburg could not interfere in this without seriously impeding the work. But it was only by working as a system that local agencies were capable of inflicting their achievements and methods on the central offices, and as system developed it enmeshed the agencies in a machinery that made demands of its own. By 1910 or so, an apparent decentralization was growing up under the committee's tutelage into a centralized bureaucracy. Thus it serves no purpose to speak of centralization or decentralization in the reform organization. It seems to me that we would do well to give up these terms and to speak instead of a relationship between *committed* superiors and subordinates who cooperated with each other on the basis of measurable achievements.

Finally, the government did more than simply step out of the way of progress in 1906-14. If statesmen did not plan agrarian reform, they did make it possible for plans to unfold; this in itself was an unprecedented, indeed spectacular, accomplishment. If the reform organization per se did not coordinate government agencies, it did clear the way for specialists in the countryside to form the relatively precise machinery of the land settlement organization. As for the "failure" to organize agricultural improvement, this too was an achievement, for it allowed agrarian reform to expand relatively rapidly and, perhaps most important, it kept the reporting of information relatively honest. In a sense, the rapid changes in rural administration from 1889 to 1914 represented a series of blunders, but successful government-imposed social reform is essentially a series of such blunders. The reform evolved amidst a continual conflict of interests among men who were struggling for power, but at every step of the way these same men repeatedly showed themselves willing to set aside their interests, jettison their plans, and accept defeat in their personal struggles in order to get an agrarian reform in motion. This explains, at least in part, how it was that by 1914 the tsarist government had put itself in the hands of agricultural specialists: the same men it had distrusted so profoundly less than a decade before.

CHAPTER 9

The Reform Becomes a Movement

Until now the government and its organs have appeared to be the organizational and even the cultural basis of our society. At present, however, the professional-economic organization of the people themselves...is growing up alongside it.

Land ownership is in chaos because in recent years there has been an uninterrupted flow of radical, ill-prepared, mutually contradictory agrarian laws.

N. V. Oganovskii (1917: 6, 7)

A. THE SPREAD OF LAND SETTLEMENT

In 1913 government investigators studied the results of land settlement in 12 uezds, each in a different section of European Russia (ch. 8, n. 9). Figures from 11 of the 12 reports were compiled into a single statement, which came out in 1915. Judging from this compilation, a substantial number of consolidated farms did indeed exist. By the end of 1911, 14,600 heads of household in the 11 uezds had acquired their own khutor or otrub farms. Of these, almost 2,300 had sold all or part of their lots by 1913, when the study was made, which left more than 12,000 still in the hands of their original owners (*Obsledovanie,* 1915: 89, 104). Not all the new farms were fully consolidated into one single lot. The vast majority, however, had three fields or less (Pershin, 1922: 14). Not all khutors and otrubs were being worked in progressive fashion. About 3,000 were still practicing three-field crop rotation, and about 4,300 did not use fertilizer (*Obsledovanie,* 1915: 94, 97). Only 6,300 of the new owners were members of cooperatives (p. 99). On the whole, however, the 11-uezd investigation suggests that, despite limitations, consolidation was certainly going forward by 1913.[1]

[1] More than 1,300 of the consolidating farmers were renting out some or all of their lands, but the investigators could not be sure of the amount (*Obsledovanie,* 1915: 99). It is impossible to judge what general significance, if any, the renting of farmland had.

Dubrovskii insists that the investigation of the 12 uezds was rigged to exaggerate the progress of consolidation (1963: 270-71), and Pershin (who made one of the investigations) seems to have thought the project as a whole was an uneven production. But Pershin never went so far as to call the investigation false or to deny the spread of land settlement: not before 1930, at any rate. In his major work of 1928 Pershin stated that he considered the studies made in Orel, Tula, and Pskov gubernias to have been reliable and useful, whereas the reports from Tambov and Moscow were faulty (1928: 89, 143, 276-77, 398). I gather that Pershin's major complaint against the investigation as a whole was its failure to compare agricultural and social progress on khutor and otrub farms with what was happening at the same time in unconsolidated villages. Pershin's descriptions of land settlement operations are the best I have seen (see especially 1918: 207-36), and I wish to emphasize that I am not venturing to disagree with him in this matter. I am not claiming that consolidated farmers were per se more progressive or prosperous than other kinds. What I am claiming, and with this the pre-Stalin Pershin agreed, is that consolidation did go forward. More important, other programs evolved as the government strove to extend consolidation. The reform organization had to change its direction sharply simply to arrive at consolidation and then, after 1909, it continued to change. As we have seen in Chapter 8, the government took up new activities, chiefly group land settlement and agricultural improvement, and it is this change of direction in the reform, not the mere achievement of planned goals, that is of primary interest in the following pages.

The Advance of Consolidation

The consolidation of allotment land first began to go forward on a large scale in the western gubernias in 1907-8; then it spread, in 1908-9, to the southern steppe and Samara gubernia, whence it gradually extended into Great Russia and Malorossiia. There are some historical-geographical explanations for the different rates at which consolidation progressed in different areas. According to Kofod, it first began on a large scale in the western gubernias because the villages were almost all noncommunal by tradition, and they had before them the example of a few integral farms that had already been set up well before 1905. Consolidation then spread rapidly in the southern steppe and Samara, because, Kofod surmised, the land there was relatively uniform in quality and the peasants, who had settled there relatively recently, still used it in uniformly backward fashion. It may seem paradoxical, but it was easier to modernize land usage in areas where agricultural practice was still primitive. Peasants who had not yet invested much effort in their land were less reluctant to redivide it and to adopt new practices (Kofod, 1914: 66-67, 112-33; see also Martynov, 1917: 133; Pershin, 1922: 27).

As for the areas where consolidation got off to a late start, each had problems peculiar to itself. In the southeastern steppe the water supply was critically low. Stavropol gubernia, for example, had large areas of excellent soil and a high average rainfall, but almost all the surface water was unfit to drink (Dinnik, 1900: 391). In the central black-earth gubernias, where even private estates were often interstripped with each other, many villages were divided into several separate lots, with estate lands and the lands of other villages sandwiched in between. Consolidation often depended on exchanges of land with private owners, and these could not be forced to make trades by the government's administrative agencies until after the law of 29 May 1911 went into effect (Pershin, 1928: 172-207, 229-34). In the upper Volga and central industrial gubernias, especially to the north and east, villages were often interstripped with each other. In Kazan gubernia, for example, 40 or 50 villages could be tied together in this way across a whole uezd. Until the law of 29 May 1911 went into effect, these villages could only be separated into integral territories if two-thirds majorities in every one of the assemblies agreed. Without unanimity among villages the government could not impose a separation unless the tsar issued a special command (*IZO,* 1909: 357; 1910: 75-76). The area to the north of Kazan and the Volga we have already discussed in Chapter 8 (sec. D). The terrain made surveying difficult, and the soil was not very fertile. Many peasants had long since lost interest in farming and taken up other trades; others, chiefly those who lived near cities and railroads, had made considerable progress in intensifying their agriculture. Both types, indifferent and progressive, were reluctant to accept radical changes in landholding (*IZO,* 1910: 77-78).[2]

Despite these difficulties, peasants in problem gubernias did begin taking up consolidation in about 1910, and they kept it up at a moderate rate until the war. In some late-starting gubernias, notably Kazan and Voronezh, land settlement spread rapidly in 1913-14, though most fieldwork was devoted to group projects rather than consolidation. Voronezh produced a large number of *petitions* for land settlement in 1914; Kazan was high in completed projects (*Obzor,* 1915: 1-3; Dubrovskii, 1963: 582-84). Only in the north, beyond the Volga, did land settlement fail to take hold.

But geographical and cultural generalizations regarding the spread of the reform should not be taken too seriously. Consolidation sometimes developed along entirely different lines in uezds and *uchastki* that were geographically and historically similar. The main reason for this persistent inconsistency seems to have been the enormous and enduring influence

[2]On the peculiar problems of land settlement in Astrakhan and its disastrous failure there in 1907-8, see Kofod (1914: 124-25). The same source describes the difficulties in the Don Oblast (pp. 128-29).

of local experience, especially the success (or failure) of individual projects and the presence (or absence) of capable administrators (see, e.g., *IZO,* 1909: 51-52). Government officials engaged in carrying out the reform spoke often of the primary importance of good examples in the spread of land settlement. A successful consolidation was likely to incline peasants in neighboring villages to try it themselves. It also made the task of carrying out new projects immensely easier, since successful consolidators constituted a local corps of experts, so to speak, who could advise their neighbors. One gets the impression that consolidation had its most dramatic and lasting success in areas where German colonists were the first ones to undertake it. As said before, many German villages held their land communally and divided their fields into strips much as Russian villages did (ch. 5, sec. B). According to a few reports, the initial success of consolidation in Volyniia and Samara gubernias may be attributed primarily to its introduction via these German villages. The Germans, said one report, took great care to measure and divide the land accurately and fairly when they consolidated, and this set a standard for their Russian (and/or Ukrainian) neighbors to follow (*IZO,* 1910: 84-86; see also Kofod, 1907: 6-7; Iaroshevich, 1911: 159-61). I am not suggesting that German villages were the main inspiration from which consolidation evolved, but their impact in a few locales does illustrate the powerful effect of concrete examples on the progress of land settlement in each area.[3]

The effects of unsuccessful attempts at land settlement could do at least as much harm as the successful ones did good. When a land settlement project got bogged down in lawsuits, or proved too costly to the land settlers, or led to violent encounters between neighbors, peasant resistance to land settlement was likely to grow stronger for miles around.

---

[3]Apparently some of the local leaders in the Samara consolidations were immigrants (or visitors) from German communities in the United States.

Much of Samara's successful consolidation took place in Novouzenskii uezd, and this was where German influence allegedly had its effect. I should add that other factors were operating. Kofod ascribed the rapid spread of land settlement in Novouzenskii to a particularly effective official, not to German villages (1914: 110). A land section memo of 5 Mar. 1910 stressed the contribution of Samara gubernia's zemstvo to land reform. As of early 1910 it had extended 380,000 rubles in agronomic aid to land-settling peasants, far more than any other gubernia. Kursk, the second highest, had lent only 90,000; Kostroma, the third, only 12,000 (TsGIAL, f. 1291, op. 120, 1909g., d. 61, l. 323). This is all very well, but German inspiration was obviously a vital factor. The government's reluctance to acknowledge this is understandable. Russians do not like to see themselves either encouraging German influence or responding to it. It would have been especially tactless for Kofod, a Dane, to mention the German role. It is worth noting in this regard that both MF and MVD had consistently forbidden the peasant bank to make loans to German villages—see, e.g., a memorandum from the Saratov peasant bank section dated 8 Nov. 1902 (f. 592, op. 1, d. 154, ll. 9-10).

Similarly, a project marred by technical and legal flaws was likely to establish a neighborhood tradition for sloppy work that might last for years. In Simbirsk and Saratov gubernias, which adjoined Samara and had large areas that were similar to the Samara countryside, the earliest models of consolidation were on peasant-bank land. According to one report, the carelessness and incompleteness of these early projects established a precedent for subsequent work that affected both land settlement commissions and peasants, and it required considerable effort to introduce what the government regarded as correct consolidation procedures (*IZO*, 1910: 29-31, 33-34). This was probably the main cause of the relatively slow spread of land settlement in these gubernias in comparison with Samara (1909: 286; see also Iaroshevich, 1911: 116).

The Rise of Group Land Settlement

Group land settlement was at all times more popular among peasants than consolidation (ch. 8, n. 11). In 1907, the first year of the reform, 93,000 households petitioned for group projects, whereas only 76,000 asked for help with individual land settlement, including both village and personal consolidations (*IZO*, 1908: 47). Thereafter, requests for both types increased sharply in volume, but group land settlement more than sustained its lead. Nevertheless, the land settlement commissions carried out far more consolidations than group projects during the course of the reform (ch. 5, sec. A). On the face of it, the government seems to have resisted peasant demands and imposed land reform according to its own rigidly held doctrines.

But, as we have seen, the government's attitude toward group land settlement changed after the reform began. At first the central offices gave priority to consolidation. Administrators pushed for group land settlement only in problem gubernias, where they considered it necessary to prepare the ground for consolidation (*IZO*, 1910: 75-76). Gradually, however, the reform organization gave in to peasant demand. Each year the fieldwork schedules gave higher priority to group land settlement (ch. 8, sec. C), and the law of 29 May 1911 explicitly encouraged it (see below, sec. B). During the reform's final years more households participated in group projects than in consolidations (ch. 8, n. 11). The MZ's survey of its activities during 1913 claimed explicitly and proudly that its commissions had come to recognize the importance of group land settlement and had been giving many group projects priority over consolidations (*Obzor*, 1914: 4). Thus, if we view the reform as a development rather than a mechanical operation, it looks like a process in which the government gradually modified its policies in response to its interaction with peasants.

It is impossible to say definitively what the spread of group land settlement signified. It is not far-fetched, however, to see in it an implication that the government organization was responding flexibly to its experience. It is important to point out this implication because most scholars who study the reform ignore group land settlement entirely, and they are fond of insisting that the land settlement organization was characteristically rigid.

Most recently, P. N. Zyrianov (1973: 193-94) has argued that the rise of group land settlement signified the approaching collapse of the reform. He supports this assertion by referring to Dubrovskii's figures (Dubrovskii, 1963: 245), which show that about three-fourths of the land undergoing group work was only being subjected to a simple division between two or more villages. Zyrianov's reasoning is both groundless and irrelevant. Dividing intermixed villages into separate, integral areas was seldom a simple affair. Moreover, simplicity is beside the point. What is significant about all forms of group land settlement, whether simple or complex, is that they were desired by groups of peasants and they also furthered the purposes of the government's land reform. Zyrianov makes yet another groundless assertion in support of his argument for collapse. He attributes the rise of group land settlement to a widespread movement among land captains to sabotage land reform. This notion is at least relevant to the realities of Stolypin's day, since many captains did actually oppose the reform (ch. 7, sec. E). Nevertheless it is quite wrong. By the time the government began to support group land settlement actively, the captains had been effectively removed from the reform organization (see below, sec. B). Zyrianov is exceptional among scholars in that he acknowledges the existence of group land settlement, but in his treatment of it he cannot see beyond the old radical-liberal assumption that the tsarist government never brought benefits to its people except out of weakness.

Even Pershin, whose work of 1928 still stands as the best study of the Stolypin Reform, does not rise above this assumption. Like Zyrianov, he is atypically aware that group land settlement took place, but he claims that the reform organization made very few concessions to peasant needs. In Pershin's view the government's unyielding insistence on full consolidation and personal land ownership widened the gap between itself and the peasants as the reform went on. Land reform took place, he says, but the government impeded the process rather than helping it along (see, e.g., 1928: 84-89, 326).

Let us consider Pershin's account, since it raises questions that are important to our understanding of the reform's development. He is at his worst when he lets forth his postrevolutionary diatribes against the tsarist MZ. In a number of places he distorts the meaning of the land settlement laws themselves to make them sound rigid. For example, he alleges that the law of 29 May 1911 would not allow a village to divide into several separate villages unless the farms in each one were consolidated. Group land settlement, in other words, would not be allowed unless it was accompanied by individual land settlement (p. 81). This is patently false. The 1911 statute explicitly allowed separate groups of peasants whose lands became involved in land settlement to maintain communal ownership and, if they desired, to divide their fields into strips (arts. 27, 42, and 50, *TPSZ*, 35370). Pershin also asserts that the 1911 statute excluded all mention of improved land arrangements that were not accompanied by formal changes in legal status (1928: 86-87). This is true in a sense, but Pershin's inference that the statute "forbade" such reforms is nonsense. As we shall see (sec. B), the 1911 law opened the way for improvements in land arrangement not specifically mentioned in its clauses.

Pershin makes a point of distinguishing "spontaneous," peasant-initiated land reforms from official, government-approved projects. The former were illegal, he says; the latter were legal. The former did not produce private property, whereas the government insisted that all its projects lead toward the establishment of individual ownership. The peasants had to initiate reforms on their own because oppressive bureaucracy, insisting rigidly on private property, tried to stop them. Thus the very existence of "spontaneous" reform demonstrates ipso facto that the reform organization was heavy-handed and ineffective.

According to Pershin, peasant-initiated land settlement generally introduced "multi-field" crop rotation and/or "wide-strip" farms to communal villages without altering the form of land ownership. A communal assembly, operating within its traditional patriarchal framework, could agree to reduce the number of strips belonging to each farm and simultaneously widen each one into a usable field, all this without changing the legal form of ownership or going through the tangled formalities of an accurate survey. In effect, "spontaneous" land settlement was a redistribution carried out to improve farming techniques rather than to equalize holdings. When this was done without official approval, it was an illegal redistribution. Pershin claims that illegal redistributions occurred with growing frequency as the reform proceeded despite the government's efforts to discourage them (pp. 73-77, 322-29). Until 1912, he says, the government barely tolerated land settlement by the traditional means of redistribution; thereafter, the administration forbade it altogether. In the central industrial region 110 villages petitioned for land settlement via redistribution before 1912, and only 12 were able to complete their projects. This was bad enough, but in 1912 the government clamped down even harder. The cutoff was so sharp that even projects already in process were terminated. The result, Pershin alleges, was that peasants in the central industrial region increasingly had to carry out their land-settling redistributions illegally (pp. 87, 324-29; see also Stepanov, 1925).

Before going on to discuss Pershin's remarks, I must point out that redistribution was not only a village affair but also a category in government administration. The law said that redistributions were the concern of land captains and their uezd congresses. No redistribution could be legal until these authorities approved it. It followed that when peasants called what they were doing a redistribution, they found themselves entirely under the MVD's direction. If the MVD had been the only source of authority in the countryside, and if redistribution had been the only official category of land reform, the peasants would indeed have been unable to conduct land settlement on their own terms. Pershin would have been correct. But he was not correct. As he well knew, redistribution was *not* the only means available to villages for rearranging their lands. There was also group land settlement, and from 1911 on peasants could adopt changes under this sobriquet without having to deal directly with MVD officials. Pershin should not have said that the "government" prohibited land rearrangements initiated by peasants; he should have said the MVD prohibited them, and he should have pointed out that the MZ followed policies quite different from the MVD's, especially during the reform's latter years. But he did not point this out. In his discussions of peasant-initiated reforms Pershin simply ignored the fact that if the peasants in a village called what they were doing group land settlement, they could do anything a redistribution could do without being at the mercy of the MVD.

I see no reason to dispute Pershin's assertion that land-settling redistributions became more popular during the reform's latter years. A number of field studies reflected this development. O. Khauke, a distinguished student of peasant society, referred in 1913 to an investigation of two uezds in Iaroslavl gubernia that showed "qualitative" *(kachestvennye)* redistributions—i.e., land-settling redistributions—going forward on a large scale. He also noted that many *noncommunal* villages in the western gubernias were carrying out qualitative redistributions. Indeed, Khauke believed that qualitative redistributions were on the upswing all over European Russia (1913: 98-99, 105-6, 150).[4] But it does not follow that these redistributions were all carried out against the government's opposition. Nor does it follow that the government was attempting to squelch spontaneous land settlement. Nor does it follow that the government became more rigid as the reform wore on.

[4]Two postrevolutionary studies of individual villages in Moscow gubernia show that both introduced qualitative redistributions during the reform's later years (Dyskii, 1923: 23-24; Alekseev, 1923: 8).

For one thing, it is highly probable that many qualitative redistributions were actually group land settlement projects, or redistributions carried out in response to personal consolidations. The MZ harbored a number of sticklers for strictly correct land settlement—Kofod, most notably (1914: 64-69, 80-84, 154-62)—but by and large its officials were inclined to allow the broadest latitude in projects of group land settlement. This was especially true of its loosely controlled agronomists in the locales, but the central offices were also favorable on the whole. The *nakaz* of 19 September 1906 had given its blessing to *any* land rearrangement that permitted improved agriculture, regardless of its formal nature (ch. 7, sec. B), and no official act had ever abrogated this provision. Certainly the law of 29 May 1911 did not, and the law of 14 June 1910 went the other way by explicitly authorizing a redistribution—without waiting for the legal 12-year interval—whenever a village suffered a personal consolidation (arts. 34-36, *TPSZ*, 33473). As Pershin himself tells us, redistributions of this sort frequently reduced the number of strips in a village and widened them (1928: 74). Not only did the MZ *not* discourage its commissions from helping with qualitative redistribution, but its publications periodically affirmed the principle that all varieties of land rearrangement for the sake of good agricultural practice merited the government's help. As we have seen, Krivoshein's circular of 23 October 1908 on loans and subsidies explicitly permitted their disbursal to support *any* measure of land reform that would improve land use (ch. 8, n. 13). In short, peasants who carried out qualitative redistributions during the reform years did not lack for friends in power.

Then, too, it made little difference in the villages if the MVD began to frown upon qualitative redistributions in 1911-12, for, as said before, the laws of 1910 and 1911 virtually took the captains and their congresses out of the land settlement process. Furthermore, the idea that the MVD was characteristically rigid and heavy-handed demands some looking into. Pershin never tells us precisely what government order or orders brought about the sharp cutoff of redistributions that the MVD allegedly imposed in 1911-12. I have never found any. It is quite likely that the developments he described in the central industrial region were the result of actions taken at the gubernia level. On the other hand, I have found evidence indicating that the MVD's central offices took a firm stand regarding qualitative redistributions in January 1909. I am not sure that even this event can be properly described as fossilization or oppression, as Pershin would have us believe. Let us consider the MVD's view of the matter.

Before 1909 the ministry's attitude toward qualitative redistribution was not well defined. In late 1907 P. P. Zubovskii, then a high-level land section official, made an inspection of the MVD's rural agencies in Smolensk gubernia, during which he observed many cases of qualitative redistributions *"po chetvertiam"* or *"na chetverti"*—by quarters (*IZO*, 1909: 50-53). "By quarters" referred to a rule of thumb according to which no single strip was to be smaller than one-fourth of a *desiatina* (about two-thirds of an acre). A number of land captains reported to Zubovskii that they were permitting these redistributions and even encouraging them. When a "qualitative" violated the law of 8 June 1893, which restricted the number of redistributions to one every 12 years, these tolerant captains simply turned their backs and took no official notice. According to one "tolerant," whom Zubovskii considered to be one of the most capable captains he had ever met, widespread use of "qualitatives" was the main explanation for the small number of requests coming in from Smolensk to convert communal land to personal ownership. Conversion, said the captain, was not a necessary step toward land reform if villages could bring about improved land use through their traditional institutions. If anything, *ukreplenie* would jam the works. Not all captains in Smolensk took this view. Zubovskii found some who were going strictly by the book, forbidding any redistribution that was not legal. Administrative policy, and therefore the law itself, varied sharply from one *uchastok* to another. Zubovskii neither condemned nor approved of "qualitatives" explicitly, though I think his remarks had an approving tone. He did believe that it was necessary for the government to adopt a uniform policy, so that all redistributions would be recorded and all captains would be enforcing the same law.[5]

The issue came to a head in January 1909, when the ministry held a congress of selected permanent members of gubernia boards and land settlement officials. On this occasion administrators from St. Petersburg proposed to their assembled local agents that peasants should be forbidden by law to carry out land settlement on their own. The reason, said the administrators, was that any rearrangement of the land not covered by law would set peasant holders outside both custom and law. A peasant with "wide fields" on communal land would no longer find an adequate remedy in village custom if a neighbor infringed upon "his" land. Custom did not recognize wide fields. If our protestor turned to the government's courts, he would find no satisfaction there because he would lack proper documents based on surveys. Redistributions were recognized in law as legally binding acts, but the substantive decisions embodied in them had no legal validity except insofar as they conformed to custom. When a villager made an official complaint against his village's decisions during the course of a redistribution, the uezd congress judged the matter,

[5]Smolensk's lack of uniformity was not an isolated phenomenon. In Feb. 1909 the gubernia board of Voronezh was appalled to discover a captain who approved redistributions regardless of legality and permitted his villages to conduct them without supervision (TsGIAL, f. 1291, op. 120, 1909g., d. 102, ll. 6-10).

but it was required by law to make its judgment conform to custom. In short, the MVD proposed in early 1909 to treat redistributions as entirely distinct from all processes having to do with private property, the simplest of which—conversion of allotment land to personal ownership—demanded documents giving the area and dimensions of each strip. The MVD did not wish to mix up the administrative categories of land settlement and redistribution, simply because it wished to avoid confusion between the legal categories of village and private property. If these categories got mixed up, the MVD said, no one would have any basis for deciding disputes over land (*Trudy*, 1909: 143-45). This was the reasoning of the ministry's central administrators when they told the January conference that qualitative redistribution was an inappropriate device for establishing secure land tenure in the countryside.[6]

It is probably true that the MVD's position was less than realistic in the middle of a sweeping land reform, but it was not "rigid," nor was it any more "oppressive" than shotgun rearrangements imposed by "spontaneous" village assemblies on their members. The MVD noted that unregulated monkeying with village lands would leave the inhabitants in a tangle. If they were unable to work their way out of it, the MVD would be blamed.

The central offices' reasoning failed to impress the participants in the 1909 conference. They unanimously rejected the idea of prohibiting land-settling redistributions. A majority went so far as to recommend that peasants be actively encouraged to do their own land reforming; the minority simply accepted the fact that prohibitions against spontaneous land reform would be pointless, for peasants would do their own land settlement if they wished, law or no law (pp. 143-59). So much for the weight of bureaucracy.

The central administrators chose to disregard their local agents. They did not change the law, but an MVD circular of 19 March 1909 called for closer attention to technical propriety in land settlement work (*IZO*, 1909: 212-16). Reports on land section inspections in the following summer and thereafter consistently expressed strong disapproval of local officials who allowed land-settling peasants to set up farms that did not meet government standards (e.g., 1910: 29-35, 75-83, 213-19, 324-27). An

---

[6]The MVD may also have had in mind the threat of returning urban cousins demanding their shares of village land in a redistribution. If there was no legal distinction between allotment land still held by a village and land newly converted to private plots, it became all the easier for proletarian land speculators to throw villages and individual farmers alike into confusion (see ch. 6, sec. D).

This is not to suggest, however, that the MVD was altogether consistent. As the reader may recall, Gurko and some of his colleagues on the MVD's editing commission had favored (in effect) qualitative redistributions in 1902-4 (ch. 6, n. 3).

"explanation" from the land section, dated 4 November 1909, strictly forbade villages to redistribute more frequently than the 1893 law allowed, and it ordered captains to discourage any kind of redistribution, regardless of its aim. Redistribution, said the "explanation" in distinctly Stolypinesque tones, might strengthen the commune (1909: 351).[7]

All this took place in 1909, two or three years earlier than Pershin's alleged fossilization in government policy. It transpired in the MVD, not the land settlement organization. It is, however, the closest approximation I have ever found to the abrupt change in the government's policy to which Pershin referred in his works of the 1920s.

Dubrovskii suggests that the government crushed peasant-initiated land settlement (1963: 193-94). Pershin tells us that the government tried to crush it but did not succeed. Pershin is closer to the truth of the matter, but he ascribes a monolithic character to the government that simply was not there. If there was a coherent development in government policy toward peasant spontaneity, it was from the MVD's sporadic and uncontrolled regime toward the MZ's purposive but very loosely directed organization. At first land-settling peasants had to work with their local captains, and their fortunes varied according to the proclivities of each captain. As the reform progressed, the MVD tried harder to encourage local officials to stop land-settling redistributions, but at the same time its officials lost much of their influence on peasant landholding. Peasants found it increasingly easy to achieve land settlement purposes without involving themselves in the administrative category of redistribution. The evidence suggests that the rise of group land settlement signified the triumphant entry of peasant initiative into the reform.

Pershin's views, I think, were colored by two factors. First, he was an agricultural specialist in tsarist times, and he had in common with his fellow specialists a habit of blaming all ills on "bureaucracy." By bureaucracy he meant any organization other than his own and any administrator in his own organization whose functioning impeded his own. Second, he did his best writing while working for the people's commissariat of agriculture (NKZ) during the 1920s, and he had to persuade his new chiefs that land settlement, though initiated by the tsarist regime, was a good thing. He therefore took pains to assure his readers that there had been two sorts of land reform prior to the Revolution: good land settlement proceeding from peasant wishes, and bad land settlement imposed by the tsarist government. Given the facts of Pershin's life, he *had* to downplay the rise of group land settlement.

---

[7]Some MVD inspection reports published in Feb. 1910 assured the reader that although the reform organization had initially made concessions to peasant demands, it no longer did this (*IZO*, 1910: 78, 82).

Summary

        I have described the spread of land settlement with as much precision as is meaningful at the present state of our knowledge. I hope I have indicated that land reform generally came earliest and spread most quickly where peasants found it easier to accept and where specialists found it easier and more profitable to carry out. In each area, however, it followed its own separate paths and developed its own special variations, depending largely on the vagaries of reform officials' experiences in interaction with peasants. Peasant initiative played a role in the reform's development, both as a part of the government's own evolution and as a phenomenon in itself, but we have no way of knowing how much land reform took place outside the government's purview. We can be fairly certain that peasants had less need to resort to illegal redistributions after 1911, as the MZ improved its methods of group land settlement and *zemleustroiteli* gained experience working with villages. Even if illegal land reform did continue in the later years of the reform, this would not necessarily indicate that the government was rigid, as Pershin asserts. It would indicate, rather, that official surveyors could not keep up with peasant demand for land settlement, that the pressure of government measures to break down villages was uniting them into effective groups of citizens capable of articulating their collective interests, and that the reform organization felt itself bound by a commitment not only to improve agriculture but somehow to establish a systematic legal order in the countryside.

B. THE SPECIALISTS TAKE OVER

        Most of the changes that took place during the implementation of the reform we have already discussed. The facade (or self-delusion) of helping the poor was dropped almost immediately. Within a year the peasant bank ceased to be the chief means for introducing the peasantry to consolidation. More gradually, from 1909 on, programs to achieve land reform by breaking up villages—the conversion of communal to personal property, and the consolidation of single farms and groups of farms apart from their villages—gave way to village consolidation and group land settlement, both of which demanded village unity.

        Village consolidation and group land settlement seem to have emerged from a combination of peasant demand and the interests of local officials. We have seen that the threat of continual personal consolidations probably inclined villages to accept village-wide reform (ch. 7, sec. C). On the other hand, officials engaged in land settlement stood to gain in a direct, material way if they consolidated whole villages at once.

Village consolidation produced far more squares for far less work than successive personal consolidations, and this was important to surveyors, for they received a substantial portion of their pay on a piecework basis (Kofod, 1914: 135). Obviously the performance figures of land captains and uezd permanent members also showed up better when their work was devoted to village operations. Two things are clear in any case: the decision to emphasize village consolidation did not originate in the central offices, and the rise of group land settlement came about against the central government's original wishes.

The Captains Fade Away

The unintentional character of the reform's evolution was closely tied to its other features, not the least important of which was the continual conflict among the agencies and institutions that were carrying out the reform. These conflicts were not always simple affairs in which one clearly indentifiable side fought another on the basis of sharp differences of opinion or clashes of interest. I have referred a number of times to the running feud between the peasant bank and the MZ. Obviously this was an important conflict, but it was a relatively simple one, and therefore I think it was atypical. Most conflicts surrounding the reform were more complex. There were often more than two sides, the participants were sometimes ignorant of the issues involved, and the issues themselves could change with bewildering rapidity. Officials, specialists, and peasants collided with one another, but since the colliding parties did not always know who they were hitting or what they themselves wanted, they were often at a loss to articulate their sentiments or to know where their interests lay. What they did, more often than not, was to employ stereotyped ideological phrases that had little to do with their own purposes or those of their opponents. One can find abundant support in these phrases for such abstract issues as zemstvo vs. government, land captains vs. specialists, or tradition-minded peasants vs. would-be reformers. Aside from this massive sputtering, however, there is little indication that easily identifiable, general conflicts of this sort were really taking place.

It may be enlightening, as an illustration of the government's agony, to describe a somewhat more complex (and more typical) development than the peasant bank's. Let us call it, for want of a better term, the phasing out of the land captains.

There were at least three parties to this particular conflict, if conflict be a proper word for what occurred. First, there were the intellectuals in the central offices of the land section, who had been striving to tame the captains into obedient, predictable agents ever since the late 1890s (ch. 4, sec. B). Second, we have the land captains themselves, ignoring or resisting the central government's pressure because, by and large, they had no other course open to them (ch. 7, sec. E). Third were the agricultural specialists, at least a few of whom were themselves ex-captains but who considered themselves to be hostile to everything the captains stood for (Dubrovskii, 1963: 269-70).

Two statements may be made regarding this three-way interaction that have sufficient support in the evidence to be called at least quasi-facts. One is that the land section did *not* want its captains to be phased out of land settlement. Almost every issue of the section's journal rang with denunciations of captains who did not work actively in the villages to lead peasants into land reform while protecting them from all adversity. The archives hold a good deal of unpublished correspondence that conveys much the same message. The other "fact" is that the captains were indeed phased out of land settlement in spite of all the land section's urging. In 1913 many captains were no longer troubling to attend village meetings where land settlement projects were being discussed, nor were they doing much to speed projects on their way once villages had approved them. So said the director of the department of state domains to Litvinov in a message of 7 January 1913 (TsGIAL, f. 1291, op. 120, 1913g., d. 2, ll. 1-2). In 1915 the MVD was still making feeble efforts to whip its captains into action, but by this time it was reduced to asking the governors what had gone wrong (op. 121, 1914g., d. 11, II, l. 7). Let us pause to look at some evidence regarding these two "facts" before attempting to explain them.

Land section officials began as early as 1907 to speak in shrill tones about the important role captains were to play in land settlement. At the conclusion of the October congress of permanent members of gubernia boards (the captains' direct superiors), deputy minister Lykoshin deplored the captains' shattered morale, remarking acerbicly that "the majority" of them were shiftless and ignorant. He went on, however, to proclaim his belief in the captains. Their work was even more important now, in this time of great changes, when the government had an even greater need than before for "cadres" of experienced men in the countryside. There was to be no talk of eliminating the captains (*Trudy,* 1908: 7-8).

The congress had to recognize that the government was about to submit a project to the third Duma—ultimately to become the law of 14 June 1910—proposing to switch authority for deciding disputes over personal consolidations from uezd congresses to land settlement commissions (p. 29). This, however, did not discourage the participants. Having noted their coming ejection, they dismissed the matter and embarked on a lengthy discussion about a new set of rules *to govern the captains' work in carrying out personal consolidations.* Officials from the land section spoke enthusiastically and at length about how uezd congress decisions were going to guide peasants into proper land settlement (pp. 30-39).

The peculiarities of the congress of October 1907 become intelligible if we recall that the reform leaders were running into serious difficulties. The peasant bank was blatantly ignoring land settlement, and Stolypin was in the midst of his all-out attack on the local sections. Conversion to private property in the communal villages was still going at a snail's pace—so the land section believed—and the main reason seemed to be that captains were not responding to peasant petitions for it. As we have seen, the captains were suffering a crisis. The threat of rural violence still hung over them; the new agrarian legislation of 1906 had profoundly altered their roles (ch. 7, sec. E); the government had been on the point of eliminating them in 1906 (ch. 6, sec. D) and was now preparing to get them out of land settlement. Worst of all, Stolypin, their own chief, was trying to negotiate institutional reforms that would extend zemstvoes and law courts down to the volosts, thereby, it would seem, eliminating the captains altogether (ch. 6, sec. D). From the captains' point of view, their mission to the countryside was coming to a rather undignified end. Morale was low in 1907 and would remain low thereafter.

Consider a speech given on 1 February 1910 by the governor of Moscow, V. F. Dzhunkovskii, to the land captains and gentry marshals of his gubernia. They had assembled to celebrate the twentieth anniversary of the day when captains first took up their duties in Moscow gubernia. As one would expect, the governor commented on the important services land captainry had rendered to the nation. He went on, however, to make some candid remarks about the present. "News of the approaching reform," he noted, was producing among captains "a growing indifference *[okhlazhdenie]* toward their work." Dzhunkovskii did not try to deny the news or minimize its significance. All he could do was console the captains with the prospect that the new organizations coming into the countryside would have great need of experienced officials. Thus, although the land captains of old would soon cease to exist, there would be ample opportunity for men who had been captains to move into new jobs and work in new capacities (*IZO,* 1910: 74-75). This was, I suppose, as much as Dzhunkovskii could say and still retain credibility. Still, his words sound a little strange for an anniversary celebration designed to inspire its participants. He was saying, in effect: "Work on, captains. You may not be doing anything important, but if you carry out your duties well, I may be able to promote you into more significant jobs when the new laws come out."

Such was the depth to which the captains had sunk by 1910. Compared to Dzhunkovskii's somber realism, the speeches at the congress of October 1907 were brightly optimistic, but if the optimism was a trifle shrill, we should not be overly critical. The October congress, the first of its kind in the MVD's history, was called primarily to inspire the battered captains to new efforts in the face of staggering adversity. Obviously the land section did not wish to disband its agents; it still needed instruments in the countryside. Somehow, therefore, the captains had to be encouraged to go on working, despite the fact that no one could tell them anything meaningful about what they were supposed to be accomplishing.

The congress of January 1909, held a little over a year after the 1907 affair, had the same morale-building purpose as the latter. Now, however, the land section had some new messages to deliver. The most important theme was the captains' *cooperation* with land settlement commissions. It was doubtless in order to dramatize its new brotherhood with the MZ that the MVD invited permanent members of land settlement commissions to attend (*Trudy,* 1909: i-iii).

Lykoshin spoke again, this time at the beginning of the session, directly after Stolypin's speech of welcome. He told the assembled local administrators that the reform was changing direction and that they were to change with it. Until now, the government's major aim had been to convert communal property into personal property. This was no longer true. Henceforth consolidation and the expansion of institutions of small-scale credit would be the basis for agrarian reform (p. xiv).

One of the main issues discussed at the 1909 congress was the efficiency of peasant administration, especially the uezd congresses of land captains. It was pointed out that if the MVD-dominated organization was to play a role in consolidation, uezd congresses had somehow to deal with their cases more speedily. Large backlogs had accumulated in many areas. Congresses in Poltava, Orel, Grodno, Voronezh, Kovno, Kharkov, Simbirsk, Kherson, and Penza gubernias were especially bad (p. 78). Several reasons were given: many gentry marshals did not attend meetings, captains were lazy, etc. (pp. 83-86). But no participants at the January meeting brought up the basic reason: the captains had far too much to do. Their burdens from pre-reform legislation were already overwhelming (ch. 4, sec. B), and they simply did not have time to go into every village in their *uchastki* and drum up support for land reform. As always, the land section was unwilling to acknowledge the captains' burdens. In January 1909 it was still intent on getting them into land settlement, and it was still following its old principle of the 1890s that all problems could be solved by sending out new orders.

The section's frenzied attempts to involve its captains in land settlement did not stop with the January congress. Confronted with the upcoming law of 14 June 1910, which would minimize the captains' official role in land settlement, the section took up a campaign to make them act individually to take over and direct land settlement projects as *zemleustroiteli.* From early 1909 until the very end of the reform, the section never ceased to assert that "mere" surveyors should not have charge of projects. Instead, the MVD's virtuous captains were to involve themselves directly in reforming villages and lead the "advanced" forward against the "backward."

Apparently the section cherished hopes that the new image of the land captain as *zemleustroitel* would become a reality immediately, during the field period of 1909. The committee's circular of 8 December 1908—issued only a month before the January congress—ordered governors to urge their captains into action. In October 1909 Stolypin commanded his governors to submit reports by 15 November describing their captains' work on land settlement projects during the 1909 fieldwork period (TsGIAL, f. 1291, op. 120, 1909g., d. 69, l. 2). One wonders what Stolypin had in mind. It took considerable effort to get a land settlement project ready for inclusion on the fieldwork schedule, and in December 1908, when the original circular had gone out, it had already been too late for anyone to start up a project and get the necessary approvals prior to the February deadline, even assuming that a willing village had been ready at hand. But, then, we have seen these manifestations of the capital-city mind before.

Reports on the captains' efforts to be *zemleustroiteli* did come in in due course (ll. 23-217). So far as I can see, they gave the MVD very little to go by. Gubernia practices varied widely, and there was no indication of what the variations signified. In a few gubernias—e.g., Kovno (l. 51) and Kharkov (l. 201)—no captains even pretended to act as *zemleustroiteli* in 1909. In some other gubernias a substantial number of captains directed projects while still performing all their regular duties. In Novgorod 44 of them were assigned projects, and 31 allegedly finished at least some of them (ll. 94-100). In Penza the corresponding figures were 34 and 30 (ll. 111-17), in Kaluga 24 and 18 (ll. 66-71), in Smolensk 26 and 20. More revealing than these figures was some additional information in Smolensk's report that had been left out of the others. Of 50,000 acres of allotment land consolidated in Smolensk during 1909, land captains had done only 3,500 (ll. 169-79).

There were a few gubernias where a small number of captains were freed from their regular duties in order to work full time as *zemleustroiteli*. Results were uneven at best. In Ekaterinoslav, to take one example, five captains were released from all other responsibilities. Of the five, one completed no projects at all, and two others covered only an insignificant area, whereas a few captains who had *not* been released from their duties consolidated a substantial amount of land (ll. 52-58). In Samara two captains were released from all other duties, and they accomplished a great deal (ll. 149-63). A report from Grodno proclaimed that four captains had been released from their duties to do land settlement work, but apparently the governor had not understood the land section's intent. The four "captains" to whom he referred had actually resigned their positions upon being appointed permanent members of uezd land settlement commissions. Only one authentic captain in all of Grodno had undertaken any projects, and this solitary hero had not yet finished any (ll. 48-50).

Occasionally the governors' reports referred to specific projects and, here and there, offered explanations for failures. Poor Maiborodov once again came under official scrutiny (see ch. 4, sec. B). The report from Kherson mentioned that his attempted consolidation of Bolshoi Buialik, covering about 48,000 acres, had failed because he had started it "incorrectly" and carried it out "carelessly" (ll. 204-5). Doubtless this was a sop to Litvinov's wrath. The governor of Perm reported that one captain's project had been rejected because it had been drawn up according to peasant desires rather than the government's technical requirements. Another captain had started a project but then gone on leave and left it to a surveyor to finish (ll. 120-21).

The reports cited above do not offer a solid basis for assessing the "success" of the captains as *zemleustroiteli* in 1909. The MVD attempted to compile the information in them and quantify it (see ll. 220-27, 364-71), but according to one office memorandum these calculations were of no value because the reports, by and large, were false to begin with (ll. 367-68).

But if the information in the reports is less than accurate, it does offer us illustrations of the way in which the land section and its captains were communicating with each other. In December 1908 the section desperately wanted its captains to run out into the snow and whip up some projects. Apparently some captains actually tried to do this, but the results were not altogether fortunate. We have already contemplated Litvinov's rage in the summer of 1909 as he drove through Kherson gubernia, discovering captains who had started village consolidations without securing the necessary two-thirds majorities (ch. 4, sec. B). When he returned to St. Petersburg, he learned that many of these projects were turning out to be unworkable. But Litvinov did not relent. In December 1909 he demanded and got a set of reports on the amount of per diem allowances issued to the captains during the previous year. Presumably he was looking for a correlation between the number of projects undertaken by captains and the amount of travel pay they received (ll. 7, 228-312). The reports did not please him, and in February he ordered some of the governors to explain why the two figures did not correspond. Replies came in during early March 1910; the gubernia offices were nothing if not prompt (ll. 313-61). They said, in effect, that uezd land settlement commissions had charge of handing out per diem allowances and that therefore the governors knew nothing about the matter (see, e.g., l. 327). At this point, I suppose, Litvinov could only chew his fingernails.

We, however, have no cause to chew ours. Unlike Litvinov and his officefuls of would-be quantifiers, we do not need to know in detail what was happening in each gubernia. We have only to note the fact that the frustrated chief of the land section really did want his captains to play a major role in the reform. He really did want to find a way to keep the MVD on an equal footing with the MZ in the countryside.

The MVD's fight for its presence in the villages continued in subsequent years. In 1910 the land section started giving captains special courses in surveying and agronomy. This, the section hoped, would prepare them to be *zemleustroiteli* (*IZO*, 1910: 441-42). Stolypin may have shared the section's hopes, despite his efforts to drive the captains from their positions. On 28 October 1910 he sent out a command urging captains not only to initiate projects but to take them over and complete them (TsGIAL, f. 1291, op. 120, 1909g., d. 69, ll. 383-84). In May 1911 he rebuked the governor of Orel for ordering captains to devote their time to encouraging peasants into land settlement and not to involve themselves in actual projects (1910g., d. 27, ll. 17-18). And Stolypin's successors kept up the struggle. MVD circulars to the governors went on complaining until well after the war began that captains were not directing enough projects. Most governors continued to take the usual measure: i.e., to demand reports from the captains on all their activities. In 1914 one unusually enthusiastic governor (Kherson) boldly ordered that captains be named *zemleustroiteli* in all projects not directed personally by permanent members of uezd land settlement commissions (op. 121, 1914g., d. 11, I, l. 154). At about the same time, however, another governor (Perm) seems to have acknowledged a basic reality by ordering his captains to put themselves under the command of the uezd permanent members and cooperate with them (II, ll. 24-25).

In the end, the MVD's campaign failed. It will be recalled that in 1913 permanent members were directing about 45% of the projects, surveyors about 43%, and captains about 12% (ch. 7, n. 7). These were official figures. Probably surveyors managed a much bigger share of the projects in practice. In any case, the captains did little of the work. To be sure, the number of captains who directed projects increased each year. Of the approximately 2,500 in service during the reform era, about 100 acted as *zemleustroiteli* in 1907, 119 in 1908, 535 in 1909, 995 in 1910, and 1,216 in 1911. In 1914 about three-fourths of them directed projects. At the end of the reform, then, very many land captains were at least affecting to direct projects, but the reform outstripped their efforts. Their projects formed only a small part of the government's annual land settlement campaigns (Dubrovski, 1963: 237-38; Sidelnikov, 1973: 320).

But we are not discussing the land captains' participation. I am only indicating that the land section did wish for them to participate in and, if possible, to dominate land settlement. If the specialists took over the reform, it was not because the land section wanted them to. It must be kept in mind that this "fact" relates only to the land section, not its agencies. From the evidence presented here, it seems doubtful that the captains themselves, or even the governors, shared the section's wish to play a key role in land settlement.

We come now to the second of our "facts": that the captains actually were phased out of land settlement. At this point it seems unnecessary to gather further support for this "fact." It will be useful, however, to explain it. Fortunately, the explanation is simple: the specialists of the MZ neither needed nor wanted the captains to participate actively in agrarian reform.

I have found three reports to this effect from governors, i.e., from the MVD's own officials. The first came from Samara in May 1910. It was an unusually frank retort to Litvinov's blustering demands that land captains spend more of their time acting as *zemleustroiteli.* Only two captains had done this in 1909, said the governor, and they had both failed to complete their projects. The governor did not intend to prevent his captains from taking up projects in the future, but he hoped they would not. They were not qualified to do technical work; moreover, they should be spending more of their time helping peasants make up proposals for projects (TsGIAL, f. 1291, op. 120, 1910g., d. 19, ll. 66-67a). The second report, dated 29 March 1914, came from Kazan. The governor predicted that captains would not be participating in land settlement on a large scale in future years, mainly because the commissions were building up their own "cadres" of specialists under the aegis of the MZ. The specialists, unlike the captains, had nothing but land settlement work to do, and therefore they were able to concentrate on it and develop skill at it. Most uezd commissions had "assistant permanent members" now, and with their growing staffs and experience, they had no need for the relatively inexpert captains (op. 121, 1914g., d. 11, I, l. 33). The third report, from Grodno, was not nearly so complacent as the first two about the captains' declining role in the reform. The governor resented the MZ agencies' "selfish aspirations" *(vedomstvennye stremleniia)* to monopolize the reform. His conclusion, however, was similar to Kazan's. Surveyors and agronomists did not put much faith in captains when it came to carrying out projects (l. 28).

It is appropriate to recall at this point that as the captains were giving up land settlement, they were also failing to expand village credit associations (ch. 8, sec. D). Here, too, the MZ's experts did not feel any need for active help from MVD agencies.

It must be emphasized that I am not speaking here of the captains' contribution to land settlement, only the degree to which they dominated and shaped the reform's development. Judging from the rapidity of the reform's spread, it is hard to imagine the captains not making a significant contribution, but, as Maiborodov pointed out, their activities went unrecorded in St. Petersburg. If a captain introduced the idea of land settlement to a village and helped the villagers carry out their projects, he got no official credit for his work (folder 2, 98-100, 148-49). Occasionally one finds a reference in the land section's records to a captain's unsung achievements. An irate permanent member of the Vilna gubernia board wrote a "special opinion" on the subject in the journal of the board's meeting of 31 March 1914. Sometimes, he said, captains who completed projects did not get credit for them (TsGIAL, f. 1291, op. 121, 1914g., d. 11, I, l. 14). In Chernigov's report on the captains' role in fieldwork in 1909, special mention was made of a captain who had directed no projects officially but whose "modest and sincere" preparatory work had been instrumental in bringing about the first personal consolidation in the gubernia (op. 120, 1909g., d. 69, l. 212).

But the captains' active contribution to land reform is not at issue here. I only refer to the matter in order to separate it as clearly as possible from our topic, the captains' phasing out. To return now to this topic, I have one more point to make: the process does not seem to have involved any basic conflict between the land section and the MZ. There were, of course, disagreements and instances of hostility between the two organizations during the reform's evolution, but conflict does not seem to have been an essential feature of their relationship. Alongside the many fights between them we have instances when the land section and its agents took actions that could be legitimately described as bowing gracefully out of their roles in land settlement.

Consider an MVD circular of 11 August 1910 regarding small-scale credit (*IZO*, 1910: 397-98). Like the section's previous edicts, it encouraged the captains to develop village credit associations—i.e., the ones that were directly under the captains' own supervision. Unlike previous edicts, however, it also said that cooperatives were just as good as village associations, and it urged the captains to help them wherever they came into existence. Credit cooperatives, it will be recalled, were under the protection of the MF, and they enjoyed relative freedom from the captains (ch. 8, sec. D). Unfortunately, said the circular, some captains had the mistaken idea that the MVD wanted them to reinvigorate village credit associations in order to drive out other kinds. This, said the MVD, was not true. One should not put too much stress on one circular, but the instructions in the August 1910 document do sound a distinctly pacific note. In this instance, at least, the land section showed signs of *joining* other elements of the reform organization instead of trying to be the main instrument of the reform.

Consider also the land section's response to a note of December 1912 from a permanent member of an uezd land settlement commission in Perm gubernia to the permanent member of his gubernia commission. The note contained a request that surveyors engaged in land settlement projects be permitted to call meetings of village assemblies without having to get permission from the land captain. It often happened that in the course of a day's measuring a surveyor would need a formal decision from the peasants regarding a proposed change or correction in their project. According to the statute on land captains, village assemblies could not meet without the captain's permission; thus the surveyor could not proceed with his work until someone made a trip of up to 30 miles by horseback to the captain's office. If the captain happened to be at his desk when the messenger arrived, the delay might be as little as one day; otherwise it could be much longer. This, said the uezd permanent member, constituted a serious obstacle to land settlement work (TsGIAL, f. 1291, op. 120, 1913g., d. 13, l. 1). The land section got wind of the uezd permanent member's note, and it was not long in expressing its interest. Instead of upholding its captains' prerogatives, it asked the governor if there was any unpleasantness in the relationships between MZ and MVD agencies in the gubernia. The governor's reply assured the land section that there was no interoffice hostility in Perm. After a friendly exchange of opinions, said the governor, officials in the gubernia capital had resolved the matter by empowering surveyors to call village assembly meetings without advance notice. They had only to inform captains after the meetings had taken place (l. 4). Judging from the cessation of correspondence, this answer satisfied the land section. There were occasions, then, when the MVD showed itself willing to let its captains withdraw from their prerogatives for the sake of expediency. It is worth repeating in this regard that the land section frequently sent out orders to the effect that captains should cooperate closely with commissions (see, e.g., d. 2, ll. 10-11, 23-24).

An even more convincing indication of the absence of any consistent, all-pervading conflict between land section and MZ is reflected in the MVD's attitude toward the extension of the land settlement organization into Orenburg gubernia. Orenburg was the only place in the empire where land captains were operating and commissions were not. If the MVD had considered itself to be locked in mortal combat with the MZ and its specialists, Orenburg was the one place where it could conceivably use captains to push land reform on its own terms. Here, if anywhere, was the MVD's opportunity to take over and operate the reform if it really did desire such an opportunity. But the evidence suggests that the MVD had no such desire, at least not in 1914. When in this year the government decided to introduce land settlement commissions into some uezds of Orenburg gubernia, it was at the MVD's request.

The story, in brief, is as follows. The gubernia board decided once in 1906 and again in 1910 that Orenburg did not need land settlement commissions (1912g., d. 78, ll. 14-15). The laws of 9 November 1906 and 14 June 1910 allowed captains and uezd congresses to take care of land settlement wherever commissions were lacking, and in these early years the board seems to have thought that MVD agencies could indeed handle the reform on their own. It was not hard to do, since no land settlement took place in Orenburg prior to 1914, either within villages or on peasant-bank land (Dubrovskii, 1963: 580-86).

In 1912, however, the board underwent a change of heart. The major cause for this, according to the board's statement of 1914, was the law of 29 May 1911, which extended the commissions' consolidating powers to cover all land, not merely allotment land, thereby making consolidation a practical possibility (TsGIAL, f. 1291, op. 120, 1912g., d. 78, l. 10). Probably the fact that Orenburg got zemstvo institutions in 1912 also had something to do with the change, though the board did not say so. In any case, the governor of Orenburg wrote to the MZ in December 1912 to request that land settlement commissions be extended to his gubernia. The land captains, said the note, could not do the job (l. 3). Later, in his note of 1914, the governor added that no local MVD agencies felt qualified to carry out land settlement (l. 10). Many Russian peasants and even some Bashkirs were ready for consolidation, so most captains said, and it was time to introduce the MZ's organization (l. 14).

Apparently the land section was less than enthusiastic. In a memorandum of 25 April 1914 it said that the only kind of land settlement Orenburg had seen was an occasional personal consolidation for an individual peasant. The section had already denied the governor's earlier requests for commissions, and there was nothing new in this one. So why should the section change its policy (ll. 8-9)? But, in fact, the section did change. The MZ was preparing to introduce a few uezd commissions when the war broke out, and the MVD went along (*IGU,* 1914: 1099). If the land section and its agents did want to contend with the MZ, they certainly did not want to do it in Orenburg.

To sum up, a general conflict between land section and MZ was a distinct possibility during the entire course of the reform, yet no conflict occurred. Squabbles and misunderstandings arose from time to time, but none was big enough to make cooperation between the two organizations impossible. *On the whole* their interaction called forth cooperation, flexibility, and mutual self-sacrifice.

Cooperation, however, is no more adequate a term than conflict to describe what was going on in the reform organization. If conflict did not take the form of an open battle between organizations after 1905, it still raged. Hostility among administrators actually seems to have grown more intense as they found themselves working in closer harness than ever before. As system advanced, however, the nature of the hostility changed. The old tension between patriarchs and scientists became more diffuse.

As captains and specialists struggled to assume each others' roles, they began to experience the old mutual hostility between them as inner tensions within each individual and within each organization. They continued to speak of a war between arbitrary knights and disciplined specialists, but in practice the two sides could no longer be separated into a clear battle, for the specialists were becoming knights and the MVD was trying to train its knights to act and think like specialists.

Here, roughly, is what transpired during the phasing out of the land captains. The land section began in the late 1890s to try to make professional administrators out of its captains. This was impossible, because in order for the captains to be professionals their responsibilities had to be identified, and the process of identification only made it increasingly clear that no one man could discharge so many responsibilities. Instead of limiting and defining the captains' functions, the section merely piled more functions on them as the need arose. The effect of this peculiar "modernization" was to reduce the captains to complete dependence on the volost and village administrations they were supposed to be governing. Only with peasant cooperation could the captains hope to maintain a facade of orderly administration. After 1906, as the land section began to observe its captains systematically, it reacted to its discoveries of their "failures" by putting on more pressure. The effect was quite different from what the section wanted. Greater pressure to accomplish the impossible only served to render the captains more dependent on their peasant "subordinates" than before at the very same time they were being ordered to help disrupt and undermine these "subordinates."

The land section did not create this situation intentionally. It blundered into a blind alley, so to speak, in its frenzied efforts to wrestle with a population of more than 100 million peasants who were rapidly (and inadvertently) destroying their own traditions under the powerful, incomprehensible impact of markets, cities, railroads, and other gifts of modern organization. The land section, in short, was doing what it could with what it had. Alas, its efforts to modernize its agents only destroyed them. Captains simply could not inflict land reform on the very peasants on whom they were forced to depend. They had not been able to do the job as patriarchs; they could not do it any better as overburdened clerks. In spite of all their knightly rhetoric, therefore, the captains and governors *welcomed* their old enemies the specialists. By taking over one of the roles the captain was supposed to be playing, the specialist awakened his hostility, but on the whole it must have been a relief to the old knight to slip out of his self-contradictory position and make believe he was a patriarch again. In short, the "conflict" between captains and specialists was not the sort that produces dramatic victories and defeats. There was much gnashing of teeth, but sides did not crystalize. Men did not organize around the organizational ideologies they professed to follow.

Perhaps the best way to conceive of conflict and cooperation in the reform is to abandon the image of machines running into each other and tying each other up. Imagine instead the explosion of a cartridge case full of gunpowder grains. Each grain sets off those around it, and each seems to run afoul of the other, but the overall effect of these encounters is to build up a single force, united and strengthened by the very conflicts among its components. The tsarist government operated in much the same way during the reform. It was undergoing drastic rearrangements, but it continued to operate as a unit because its commitment to system forced it to follow a common direction. It was burning, so to speak, but the heat no longer dissipated in random fashion. The very disorder among the ministries compelled them to move together, for movement had become their only means of self-preservation.

A dialectic of sorts was taking place. In the 1880s the MVD, itself an instrument of bureaucracy, had clashed with bureaucratizing elements in the government, and this conflict had produced, among other things, the land captains. This synthesis in turn created its antithesis—the bureaucratizers who came to dominate the land section by 1900—thereby giving rise to yet another synthesis: the MZ and its specialists. The struggle between captains and their St. Petersburg directors prepared the soil from which the agronomists could grow into the semigoverning role they were playing in rural Russia in 1914. Throughout the period, then, organizational structure reasserted itself more or less continually as it continued to break down and assume new forms.[8]

The Commissions Gain New Powers, 1910-11

Land settlement came to full flower with the laws of 14 June 1910 and 29 May 1911. I have already referred to the 1910 law in various places. It expanded the powers of land settlement commissions at the captains' expense (TPSZ, 33743, arts. 33 and 37), provided for village consolidation in noncommunal villages if only a simple majority of the villagers wanted it (arts. 45 and 46), allowed minority groups of villagers in communal villages to consolidate their strips almost at will (art. 34), declared communal villages that had never held a general redistribution to be noncommunal (arts. 1-8), and set limits to the amount of allotment land a peasant could acquire as property (arts. 56 and 57).

---

[8]The dramatizing function of conflict—or contest, to use Huizinga's term—has been little studied. Historians are generally so anxious to identify sides and then decide which was "right" or "successful" that they rarely consider how internal conflict in an organization (or culture) may strengthen and reflect cohesion by dramatizing interdependence among the members. Among the few authors who have recognized the unifying impetus of conflict are Thurman Arnold (1935), Rudolf von Ihering (1879), and Johan Huizinga (1955).

Many of these rules were neither wise nor workable. Limiting the amount of allotment land a peasant could *ukrepit* and/or purchase was a gesture in favor of that persistent capital-city dream of a countryside divided into squares, each one occupied by a sturdy, smallholding yeoman farmer. The idea was that owning his square would make the yeoman sturdy, but articles 56 and 57 indicated that owners had to be carefully supervised, lest the checkerboard be disrupted and some yeomen acquire so much land that they hired others as laborers. So ownership was not the essence of the capital-city dream. Like many would-be reformers in the bureaucracy, the Duma and State Council legislators stood prepared to cut down on property rights for the sake of their precious checkerboard. Like most fantasies embodied in the 1910 law, however, the checkerboard could not be enforced. Peasants with the wherewithal to buy land beyond their limit were able to buy it (Sidelnikov, 1980: 117).

Somewhat more harmful was article 34 of the 1910 law. It provided that as few as one-fifth of the households in a village could demand consolidation of their strips and force their neighbors into a redistribution without regard for the impact of this measure on the village as a whole. This provision had originated as articles 115 and 116 in the project drawn up by the MVD's editing commission in 1902-3 (*Svod...o nadelnykh zemliakh,* 1906: 524). As I said in Chapter 6 (sec. B), this was a drastic village-breaking measure. It rendered communal villages, together with any personal owners of strips who resided within their bounds, legally helpless before repeated demands for personal consolidation by recalcitrant minorities. It seems to me that the inclusion of this outdated and unnecessary provision in the 1910 law reflected the inertia of capital-city minds, especially those which inhabited the Duma and State Council in 1908-10. By the time the law took effect, gubernia fieldwork schedules had already made clear that the reform organization was focusing its efforts on village consolidation and group land settlement—measures requiring village solidarity (see ch. 8, sec. C).

But there was some virtue in article 34 after all. Regardless of the legislators' intentions, the introduction of (legally) unrestrained personal consolidation had the practical effect of eliminating the significance of personal ownership. It was not only communal villages that would now be helpless before personal consolidators but personal owners as well. Once a personal consolidator secured a commission's approval for his project, a peasant who "owned" his strips through an earlier *ukreplenie* had to suffer redistribution right along with his communal neighbors. Thus the "rights" acquired by the *ukreplenie* of communal strips lost what little significance they had had.

Apparently the legislators had no intention of producing this effect, for, as said above, articles 1-8 of the 1910 law called for a drastic acceleration of *ukreplenie.* Indeed, these clauses, especially article 1, constitute the quintessential illustration of the distance between St. Petersburg legislators and rural reality. Article 1 ordered all communal villages that had not redistributed their land during the previous 24 years to be reclassified as noncommunal. All household heads in these villages automatically became personal property holders, and that was that.

Article 1 was another of the radical proposals that had circulated through the various reform projects of 1905-6. Gurko had supported it on numerous occasions (ch. 6, sec. B), but it had first come to life in Witte's conference. Obviously the legislators of 1908-10 intended it to further the insertion of private right into the villages, but the only real effect of this unusually inane provision was to render the status of all communally held land unclear. So said Stolypin in a speech before a subcommittee of the State Council (Gerbe, 1911: 90-91). No generally accepted procedure existed for determining whether or not a redistribution had actually occurred in a village. This being the case, all attempts to invoke article 1 in actual villages simply started arguments that neither peasants nor government agents could resolve. Ordinarily, silly laws of this sort caused no trouble, since the villages ignored them and the government forgot about them as soon as they had been filed away. In the case of the 1910 law, however, the confusion it caused gave aid and comfort to everyone in the countryside who wanted to oppose land settlement. In theory, village consolidation in a village of personal property holders would be easier, since the 1910 law also declared that a noncommunal village needed only a simple majority of votes in order to carry it out. In fact, article 1 made it possible for any villager to block any alteration in land ownership in his village simply by requiring a court of law to determine whether or not there had been an authentic redistribution in the last 24 years. In practice, no court could make such a determination very easily; thus it became much easier than before to tie up village land in legal disputes. So long as the disputes lasted, no reformer could touch the land nor could the peasants. Land settlement commissions could not carry out reform, and villages could not carry out redistributions. It is not surprising, therefore, that before the year 1910 was out, the MVD began telling its agents *not* to apply article 1 (e.g., *IZO,* 1910: 518-19).

Interestingly, these details of village life did not make much impression on the empire's political leaders. The subcommittee of the State Council paid no attention to Stolypin's objections to article 1. Instead, its members followed the Duma's example by engaging in an interminable and irrelevant debate about the principles of law involved in it (Gerbe, 1911: 134-205). Only one member showed any sign of grasping the practical problem, the historian V. I. Sergeevich (pp. 200-202).

We may say, then, that if the law of 1910 produced any useful result in the countryside, it was not because the legislators of the Duma and

State Council knew what they were doing. Nevertheless, it did produce useful results. Chiefly, it strengthened the reform organization and rendered it more flexible. The MZ's uezd commissions acquired the MVD's uezd congresses' power to approve or reject projects for land settlement and also the wholly new prerogative of *altering* projects to which surveyors and peasants had already agreed (*IZO,* 1910: 240). Along with their new powers, the commissions gained legal sanction for the switch from village breakup to united village action that had been manifesting itself in gubernia fieldwork schedules. Henceforth a noncommunal village could be consolidated at the behest of a simple majority of its members.

In conclusion, the 1910 law did much to speed the Stolypin Reform on its way, even though the members of the Duma and State Council had no conception of the Russian countryside as it was and could only hash over some of the stale formulas the bureaucracy had found interesting back in 1902-5. Not surprisingly, there were some highly important things the law of 1910 did *not* do. It did not define the processes of land settlement, nor did it extend the jurisdiction of the commissions beyond allotment land. These two matters were taken up in the law of 29 May 1911 (*TPSZ,* 35370).

The 1911 law broadened the commissions' authority so far that it actually represented an abrupt departure from the old dream, common to liberal and MVD alike, of establishing a uniform system of property rights (Martynov, 1917: 38-49, 65-78). Article 18 forbade appeals to the courts against the commissions' substantive rulings on boundaries. More important, the courts could no longer rule on commission decisions as to which lands were subject to their jurisdiction. Judges could still hear complaints against illegal procedures and violations of law, but protests against the commissions' substantive rulings on land—any land—went only to higher echelons of the reform organization (see Znosko-Borovskii, 1912: 60-66). The committee itself became the final court of appeal. Only when its members could not agree on a case did it go to the Senate. Articles 9 and 48 increased the variety of measures a commission could take to deal with unwilling parties to consolidations. In particular, these articles made it easier to settle disagreements among consolidating peasants by awarding money compensation to those who did not get the fields they wanted (see pp. 46, 140-44). A number of articles made it possible—for the first time—to consolidate mortgaged land and land rented out to tenants on long-term leases. It was no longer necessary to secure the consent of mortgage holders or tenants (Martynov, 1917: 273-83). Finally, and most important, articles 50 and 54 explicitly extended the commissions' jurisdiction beyond allotment land. They could now impose consolidation on interstripped *private* lands if only a simple majority of the owners favored it (Znosko-Borovskii, 1912: 152-58). In cases where a village's land was interstripped with a private estate, either party could impose consolidation on the other (pp. 162-65). Article 23 authorized the compulsory separation of interstripped villages if only one of them petitioned for it.

The above articles were vitally necessary to the progress of land settlement. At the same time, however, they weakened the effect of other articles in the 1911 law that attempted to identify land *not* subject to seizure and exchange without the consent of the owner, i.e., articles that protected private rights. There were several such provisions. Articles 7, 46, and 52 expressly provided that houselots and khutors (but not otrubs) could only be pulled into land settlement with the consent of their owners. This applied even to village consolidations (see pp. 30-42, 134-37, 158). If a household separated from its village and formed a khutor and the village subsequently decided to consolidate en masse, the new redivision could not touch the khutor already in existence unless the owner consented. Article 2 limited the application of the reform to private holdings not exceeding a certain area, thus giving some protection to large estates. Finally, article 43 allowed a villager who held both private land and allotment land to decide for himself whether to subject his private holding to a village consolidation.

Articles 50 and 54 seriously weakened these guarantees by subjecting *any* holding that was even slightly subdivided or interstripped to compulsory land settlement. According to these articles, the largest estate in Russia could be compelled to give up some of its land in exchange for other areas if its neighbors so desired and if a land settlement commission ruled that it was indeed interstripped with its neighbors. I repeat: the commission made the ruling, and its ruling could not be appealed to the courts (pp. 16-17, 25, 130-31). In short, land settlement, as set forth in the law of 29 May, began to look like a very sweeping phenomenon. It purported to establish private property on peasant land, but in fact it posed a serious threat to all property rights.

The 1911 law also gave commissions considerable latitude in deciding which land settlement projects would be acceptable. Technical perfection was still clearly desirable, but it was not required. A number of articles provided for halfway measures. Articles 42 and 50 introduced the idea that an opposing minority in a village consolidation could maintain the old order of communal strips in their own integral area (pp. 122-30, 153-58). More generally, article 30 allowed an ostensibly consolidating village to leave some of its lands under common ownership or simply reduce the number of strips in its fields without attaining fully integral farms (Martynov, 1917: 125-35).

Finally, the 1911 law made it quite clear that village consolidation was the primary aim of land settlement. Article 21, for example, warned that personal consolidations had to be carried out so as not to impede further land settlement among the remaining villagers (Znosko-Borovskii,

1912: 77). On the other hand, however, commissions were not to rush into village consolidations. Peasants still retained the right to withdraw from a project at any point before their final vote to accept the surveyed lots (pp. 34-35).

What all this comes down to is that the 1911 law virtually restored the broad definition of land settlement that had been set forth in the original *nakaz* of 19 September 1906 (ch. 7, sec. B) and also granted peasants definite rights to engage in land settlement. I have seen no indication that the loosening of technical requirements and jeopardizing of property rights caused any fundamental change in the commissions' actual practice. Nevertheless, it is significant that the laws of 1910 and 1911 allowed the commissions sufficient power to balance local peasant needs against capital-city aims and standards. The commissions gained so much flexibility that they were able, in many instances, to set aside legal rights for the sake of agrarian reform.

The Price of Flexibility

Flexibility had two sides. On the one, the commissions would now be better able to respond to local needs; on the other, they would have more power to impose unwanted reforms. The reader will recognize the contradiction between these possibilities as a very old one in tsarist government. In the reform era flexibility was still needed in order to deal with an inchoate peasantry, and this need still had somehow to be squared with the equally vital need to confine authority within a systematic legal framework. If land captains and courts were now out of the reform organization's way, the problems and contradictions they had embodied were not. Villages and volosts still had to be managed, and the process of land settlement still had to transplant peasants from one legal order into another. Along with their new powers, then, the specialists began to acquire problems, problems they had hitherto been able to dismiss by blaming other officials.

The question of how individual specialists dealt with their new powers is no easier to answer than it was in the case of the land captains. We can say a few words, however, about the situation of the MZ's officials during the last years of the reform. The laws of 1910 and 1911 gave rise to an impressive quantity of legal studies, and these offer us some insight into the direction in which the regime of agricultural specialists was moving prior to 1914. It will be recalled that the reform was originally enacted on the basic assumption that Russian agriculture would improve if peasants' rights to their land were guaranteed by legal system. Private right and agricultural improvement were assumed to be mutually supportive. Only in the latter years of the reform did legal scholars begin to notice that the two purposes were at odds with each other. The law of

1911 made unmistakably clear what had previously been only an implication: measures taken to achieve agrarian reform tended to erode private rights; private rights were obstacles to agrarian reform.

Poniatie zemleustroistva (The Concept of Land Settlement), a book published in September 1917 by B. S. Martynov, a legal scholar at St. Petersburg University, represented one of several attempts to find a way to conceive of the 1911 law *within* a system of private property rights. By 1917, of course, the 1911 law had become ancient history, but, Martynov insisted, the problem of private right remained, and he still cherished the hope that his considerations would be useful to future reformers. As it turned out, events were unkind to Martynov, but if his book failed to attract widespread attention in his own day, it is still of some interest to the historian of agrarian reform (see especially pp. 166-273).

Martynov says that by implication the 1911 law superseded and replaced virtually all previous legislation on landholding in European Russia. It contained no codification of existing property rights, nor did it offer any new set of rights, but it did identify land by the prerogatives the government could exercise upon it, and it prescribed a series of actions that had to be carried out by the government on a piece of land before the plot could be termed "property." The 1911 law did not say what rights this "property" would ultimately entail, excepting only that when the government completed its required processes on a given plot, it would formally abandon its prerogative to impose further reforms on this plot. Other statutes presumably would give fuller definition to the new rights. Land settlement, Martynov concluded, was strictly a state action. It neither protected rights nor granted them. There were no rights in the villages to begin with and even if a scholar could be found to construe village custom so as to discover rights in it, these rights would not find much support in the 1911 law. As to the granting of new rights, commissions could assign plots to individual holders, but they did so as a duty to the state in obedience to its regulations, not out of respect for anyone's claim. If a peasant involved in a land settlement project did not get what he wanted, he could not appeal to the courts on the basis of a right. He could only complain to the reform organization that its agent had not done his duty properly. Nor did peasants have a right to land settlement itself. They could reject a project, but they could not legally compel a *zemleustroitel* to carry it out to suit them. In practice, of course, a particular agent might respond favorably to a peasant petition or complaint, but this would be because he considered it expedient and technically correct to do so, not because the complaint possessed legal validity. According to a Senate decision of February 1912, the law required commissions to approve projects only in conformance with the "demands of land settlement." Complaints against projects could have no other grounds than their technical unsuitability (TsGIAL, f. 1291, op. 120,

1912g., d. 25, l. 2). Thus Martynov was quite right when he said that the only time a *right* to land came fully and permanently into existence was after the completion of land settlement. According to the 1911 law, this completion was attained only when the land was held in the form of a khutor.[9]

There is some doubt that the government's power to manipulate land was going to wither away even after the completion of consolidation. After all, khutors still needed agricultural improvement, and programs to achieve this were in the hands of agricultural specialists, men who insisted on seeing the land as a resource to be used in accordance with science rather than a patchwork of private possessions to be used according to the holders' pleasure. Throughout the reform era the MZ's journal rang with proposals for new laws to keep up Russia's agronomic advance. As early as January 1905 a typical article suggested that the government should have power to impose land improvement measures on private holders, whether or not they were interstripped (*IGU*, 1905: 83). In August of the same year another enthusiast called for an extension of forest preservation and anti-erosion laws in order to "regulate" *(normirovat)* land use wherever the "owner's" practices were "endangering the rural economy." It would not do to achieve this by writing rules, said the MZ's journal. Local conditions varied too widely. Instead, local commissions of specialists should have the power to decide on proper usage in each case and to impose punishments for violations of their decisions

[9]We should not conclude that the 29 May law disrupted a pre-existing system of private landholding on nonpeasant land. Even the "owners" of landed estates lacked full legal powers over their domains. Scholars like Martynov had been pointing out for some time prior to 1917 that there never had been an effective system of private property in Russia.

Take the business of surveying, for example. Just before the Revolution the Duma was in the process of enacting a law that would allow an "owner" to survey the boundaries of his land and have a law court record the result. No owner, regardless of social status, had ever had such a right in law, for the statutes had always required a landholder to obtain the consent of all neighbors who held or owned adjoining lands. This was true of consolidated and interstripped holdings alike. At least one surveyor considered the projected law inadequate. That is, he did not believe it would actually guarantee owners the right to survey their land. He noted ironically that the government had been quite willing to empower land settlement commissions to make official surveys, but it seemed to be afraid to do the same for law courts (Meznev, 1916: 4-12).

Martynov might have argued, then, that newly constructed khutors and otrubs could *never* be held by right. Only government prerogatives, sustained by permanent land reform agencies, could have guaranteed a farmer's tenure on his land. This was no trifling matter of legal technicalities. As noted above (n. 6), land that had once been held by villages under the provisions of the Liberation was still subject to claims based on village "custom." Some basis for opposing these claims really was necessary.

(pp. 678-82). Surely an organization staffed by such crusaders would not be content to leave even the squarest family farm to the whim of its holder. We have seen that the law of 1910 affected to prevent new khutors from growing too large. In August 1913 the MZ announced that it was discussing a project that would prevent them from being divided up (1913: 879-87), and in October 1914 it brought this project before the Duma (*Obzor*, 1915: iii, 9-12). The MZ was not going to let the right of inheritance interfere with good agriculture.

MZ agents were not the only specialists to show small concern for private rights. In 1909-10 the director of the survey section was already recommending that peasant land disputes be somehow removed from the jurisdiction of law courts and that the power of land settlement commissions be expanded. This renegade minion of the minister of justice was too tactful to say it openly, but he meant that existing peasant property rights, such as they were, had to be eliminated to allow land reform to go forward (TsGIAL., f. 1291, op. 120, 1910g., d. 19, ll. 5-7, 10-11, 98-100).

Governmental concern for land use did not diminish with time. As agricultural improvement programs gained momentum, the inclination to ignore individual rights grew steadily stronger. It is neither surprising nor exceptional that in May 1911 a substantial number of land settlement officials should have asked for the power to compel peasants who had embarked on land settlement projects to complete them (*IZO*, 1911: 221-23). Indeed, officials occasionally acted as if they already possessed this power. In 1912, 38 members of a very large village in Kursk gubernia (15,000 people of both sexes) petitioned for personal consolidation. In July 1912 the land captain came before the village assembly to announce the uezd congress's approval of the petition. The crowd responded with open hostility and shouted threats at the captain. After the meeting several petitioners, obviously terrified by the crowd, told the captain that they wanted to back out, *whereupon the captain replied that they could not*. As if this were not bad enough, the local *prokuror* saw nothing wrong in the captain's action (Shapkarin, 1966: 341-44). Finally, to take the specialists' view of law to its conclusion, it is appropriate to note here that in 1922 a group of the nation's leading agronomists expressed their apparently unanimous conviction that land settlement had to go forward entirely on an agronomic-economic basis. "Juridical" considerations were of no importance (Chaianov, 1922: 4-5). This was flexibility with a vengeance.

C. THE SPECIALISTS AS ORGANIZERS

The most far-reaching change that occurred in prewar rural administration was the virtual takeover of the reform organization by agricultural specialists, chiefly surveyors, agronomists, and statisticians. Perhaps "takeover" is too strong a word. After all, most surveyors and agronomists began their work at the government's invitation and got most of their pay from the state treasury. If there was a takeover, then, it was not something the specialists did all by themselves but something that developed as a result of government-peasant interaction (ch. 8, sec. D).

I have already made some general remarks regarding the agricultural specialists' approach to rural administration in Chapter 4 (sec. D). Let me review them briefly. Theoretically, specialists had no responsibility except to their science. They had a law of sorts to follow, but, unlike the land captains, they did not have to *enforce* rules on anyone, nor did they have to assume responsibility for everything that happened around them while they worked. Moreover, the rules that governed their functioning were limited to their science. New ones could not readily be imposed upon them (except, of course, by scientific discovery). Ideally, therefore, the specialist held no authority himself, and he could not readily be used as an instrument of someone else's.

All this was only theory. In fact, few specialists were content to be without responsibility for rural society in general, and they were not so reluctant to assume or use authority as they sometimes affected to be. Nevertheless, they clung to the autonomy science promised them. As a group, they never allowed any *concept* of authority to mar their ultimate faith in science; which is to say that they rarely thought about authority at all and only mentioned it in specific instances, either to claim it for themselves or denounce someone who was venturing to impose it upon them.

The relationship between Russia's agricultural specialists and their science was a complex one. In the 1900s field agronomists in Russia were still insisting that their knowledge raised them above other men, allowing them to ignore "mere" administrators while bringing truth to peasants. Many of them, however, were also denouncing this knowledge. In particular they denounced Russia's schools of agronomy, which operated on the "scholastic" presumption that their main purpose was to develop and teach their subject as a coherent system, without regard for its practical utility. S. P. Fridolin complained in his memoirs that Russia's higher schools of agronomy were immersed in "scholasticism" in the 1900s, when he began his career as an agronomist (1925: 92). A. Fortunatov, one of the leading populist agronomists of the prewar decades, recalled in 1917 that in the 1870s, when he received his training, his professors did their work in laboratories and experimental farms, and they expected their students to do the same (1917: 140-74). He was too cultivated a man to denounce his old teachers, but by 1901 he had come to believe that field agronomists had much more to do than acquire and develop scientific knowledge. In that year he told a congress of agronomists that he no longer considered university-level training to be necessary for fieldworkers. It was enough for agronomists to complete secondary school, he said. Experience working with peasants was more important than higher education for men who were to conduct actual reforms (*Trudy,* 1901).[10] Fortunatov was a sort of intellectual father to the populist-agronomists of 1900-1930 (Chaianov, 1967: IV, 13). Their views regarding their work were too varied to allow us to say that they all agreed with him, but it is certain that scorn for "pure" science was as widespread among them as their veneration for it.[11]

Chaianov

One of the specialists' leading spokesmen during and after the reform era was A. V. Chaianov (Fridolin, 1925: 91; *Trudy,* 1930: I, 165-68). It would be something of a distortion to pronounce his opinions typical, but his general attitude toward administration and reform was widespread among the *"agronom-organizatory,"* as he called them (Chaianov, 1967: IV, 19). This attitude consisted of two sets of self-contradictory notions: one having to do with the specialists' role in administration, the other having to do with their relationship to peasants.[12]

Take administration first. Chaianov insisted that agrarian reform could not proceed from theories, plans, or goals drafted in advance. Any attempt to predict or legislate reform would unduly hamper the specialists who were to carry it out (III, 15-20, 60; IV, 20). The constructing of an organization would have to be left to the specialists themselves, working in their *uchastki* in direct contact with the inhabitants and identifying the practical problems of agricultural improvement peculiar to their respective areas. As Chaianov visualized it, each agronomist would go out to his area on his own, armed only with his science. First he would study

[10]Items in this volume are paged separately. Fortunatov's speech is the first item in the second series in pt. 1, and the above statement is on pp. 3-6 of his speech.

[11]The career of A. A. Izmailskii (1851-1914) presents an early instance of the war between "pure" agronomic science and the practical business of agricultural improvement. Izmailskii attended Russia's best schools of agronomy and wrote several studies of soil structure. From 1888 on he worked closely with V. V. Dokuchaev, Russia's greatest soil scientist of the day. Yet Izmailskii did not approve of Dokuchaev's emphasis on research. He never accepted the academic degrees he earned, and he spent most of his time working "in the field" as an estate manager and zemstvo teacher (Kompaneets, 1971: I, 87-97).

[12]The following paragraphs are drawn from three of Chaianov's works: "Chto takoe agrarnyi vopros?" (1967: III, 7-70), "Metody bezdenezhnogo ucheta khoziaistvennykh predpriatii" (III, 163-72), and "Osnovye idei i metody raboty Obshchestvennoi Agronomii" (IV, 12-110). The first of these was originally published in 1917, the second in 1920, the third in 1918.

local geology, geography, history, flora, fauna, people, markets, agricultural practices, etc. Then, on the basis of his findings, he would be able to perceive the discrepancies in peasant agriculture. This, at last, would be the basis on which he would formulate criteria to guide his work. It followed that specialists had to operate autonomously. Interference by remote superiors, however enlightened, would only hamper them (IV, 29-36; III, 20-21).

But if Chaianov wanted his specialists to be independent and spontaneous, he also wanted them to coordinate with each other as if they were parts of one big clock mechanism. Land settlement, he said in 1917, would have to be centrally planned. "All sides of agrarian reform," he said, "must be worked out and set going at once" (III, 45). In the early 1920s he manifested even greater enthusiasm for centralization and, in general, the imposition of theory on action. As a leading member in the High Seminar of Agricultural Economics and Politics at the Petrov Agricultural Academy, he formulated more than his share of abstract, "scholastical" rules to guide reformers in the field. In an article devoted to calculating the optimal size of a farm he set forth the following rule for determining the value of a farmer's labor as a function of the distance between his house and the field in which he worked (1922: 37):

$$Y = x[A.K_1 + B.K_2 + C.K_3] + \frac{1}{1 + 3xa}(SR + S_1P) + \frac{1}{1 + 2xa}(TR + T_1P)$$

I do not know what practical use this rule might have had, but Chaianov's dedicated efforts to articulate it certainly suggest that he believed it possible to impose it on field agronomists. In another work he went so far as to recommend that the entire national economy be "subordinated to a single economic system run by a single managing will" (1967: III, 163). This system was to be formulated on the basis of pre-established goals, and all activities were to be aimed at these goals. Productive enterprises would be identified solely by planned inputs and outputs, which would be the basis for allocating labor and equipment to them. Needless to say, there would be no profit or market (III, 163-72). Thus Chaianov's concept of administration embraced two elements: a lone specialist and a machine-like organization.

The second part of Chaianov's vision—the specialists' relations with the local population—is on the same level as the first. An agronomist had to work on the *uchastok* level, "close" to the people, associating himself with their needs and interests, immersing himself in their culture. Cultural immersion was what made him autonomous. The essence of agronomy, said Chaianov, lay not in theories but in their practical application. Science, as the agrarian reformer saw it, was not a structure that directed and controlled him but a pile of tools and materials that he used to suit the demands of each territory. For any would-be authority who ventured to order a specialist about, Chaianov had a standard answer: no one knows how our science should work in a particular village except the man who is immersed in the society of that village (IV, 25-29, 47).

But no. This was not yet the heart of Chaianov's message. A social agronomist should not simply do what peasants wanted. He should never obey the dictates of any elected body if it conflicted with the "general agricultural development of his country." The specialist understood this development better than the local people, said Chaianov, because agricultural development was his life work (IV, 43-44). Indeed, the agronomist, armed and sanctified with his science, was the true representative of the people, for science knew better than any assembly what the people needed. This flawless harmonization of science and democracy led Chaianov to recommend explicitly that specialists associate themselves with the "advanced" minority among the peasants in his area. The *agronom-organizator* should find the "most active and conscious" farmers and use them as a "cadre" to set an example for their backward neighbors (IV, 22-23, 77-80).

It is difficult to imagine Chaianov writing this balderdash in 1918, as if forgetting that this sort of cadre-forming had been tearing villages apart since 1907, forgetting also that science had not been prospering in the countryside since the summer of 1917, when "advanced" peasants had been deprived of government protection. The luckless cadres of Stolypin's day had been left to the mercies of their less advanced neighbors, while Chaianov's erstwhile scientist-leaders were making themselves scarce. As we shall see in Chapter 10 (sec. A), the year 1918 was a bad time for advancing, and Chaianov knew it. His imaginary specialist, "free" from administrative constraint, would have to carry a gun and go about in the company of an armed gang if he seriously undertook to form cadres of "active and conscious" farmers. But, then, Chaianov was not overly concerned with practical obstacles. To do him justice, he was trying to say something meaningful to himself and his fellow specialists in a dark hour, and it would have done very little good simply to say that it was dark.

Chaianov's talk about immersion was closely related to a refrain that had become very common among his fellow specialists during the 1890s and 1900s. For years they had been writing and speaking of the peasants' inability to change their agricultural practices within the context of traditional Russian rural society, but they invariably tied on solemn warnings against any interference in the villages that might disturb the peasants' "natural" course of development (see, e.g., Popov, 1899: 105-28, 131-33; Fridolin, 1925: 57-68). Then, having delivered their warnings, they concluded with ringing assertions about their own responsibility to "lead" pesants forward (e.g., Vonzblein, 1914: 13-15; Trutovski, 1914: 38-53, 114-15). One might summarize their concept of agrarian reform as follows: the peasants' situation was hopeless, and therefore the specialists should lead them forward by doing nothing. This, however, was not how specialists saw the matter. They resolved the absurdity of their position by coming up with a procedure and an administrative structure. The procedure was the *beseda,* or conversation. The peasant could not be forced into change or lectured to, nor would models of good agriculture do much by themselves to bring him to change his ways. The only way to produce lasting effects in a village was for a specialist to maintain a dialogue with the villagers, face to face (Vonzblein, 1914: 13-14; Brunst, 1910: 3-23).

Ultimately the patient efforts of agronom-conversationalists would produce a network of rural cooperatives. While specialists were conversing, peasants would go out and organize themselves into credit unions and then use them as a basis for expanding into other forms of collective enterprise. At this point another element had to be added to the *beseda.* As each group of inspired peasants went forth from their conversations to modernize, they were to be further encouraged by funds distributed to them via local zemstvo agronomists (Vonzblein, 1914: 14-15; Fridolin, 1925: 68-84). The specialists were very strict about giving funds only to cooperatives. No individual peasant, however gifted at conversation, should receive loans directly, for this would put him in competition with the cooperatives and also set off competition between cooperatives and zemstvoes. In short, zemstvoes and cooperatives had to organize themselves into a unified (but democratic) system (M-ov, 1914: 31-33). From about 1900 on, then, conversations, cooperatives, and subsidies became the keys to rural reform as agricultural specialists saw it. Immersed agronomists who used these devices with skill could get villages moving without actually having to move them. So agronomists had been believing for some years before Chaianov offered them his vision, and in the light of these beliefs, his call to action was quite intelligible, even in the maelstrom of 1917-21.[13]

Chaianov wanted to include everyone in his unified system of autonomous democratic assemblies, not just specialists. All local assemblies were to be autonomous governing bodies, free from interference by the central government. Yet he insisted that these assemblies join themselves to a general machinery. This, too, was a fantasy he shared with most of his fellow specialists.[14] Alas, it fit very poorly with his concept of auton-

---

[13]See the resolutions adopted by the all-Russian agronomists' congress in 1901 (*Trudy,* 1901: pt. 1, first series, item 4, 1-22) and also those adopted by the agronomists' congress of 1913 (*Trudy,* n.d.: I, 3-20; II, 34-41). There was much discussion of the role of conversational agronomists at the latter congress. A variety of views were expressed, but all assumed that conversations, cooperatives, and credit would change peasant society.

[14]See *Trudy* (1901: pt. 1, first series, item 4, 1-5); and *Trudy* (n.d.: I, 14-16).

omous agronomists conducting agrarian reform in the name of science. Free, autonomous peasants would be very likely to obstruct free, autonomous agronomists. Chaianov was well aware of this. Therefore he (and most of his colleagues) explicitly disapproved of peasants. In 1917-21 he showed much concern, understandably, about their inclination to seize private estates, and he insisted that these seizures be stopped, or at least regulated. He did not care so much about the land peasants were already renting, but many gentry estates and "kulak" farms were employing intensive agricultural methods. These productive enterprises were setting the tone for the whole neighborhood. Simply by existing they carried a message to local inhabitants that good agricultural methods brought advantages to those who employed them. They were worth far more to the cause of reform, Chaianov believed, than police battalions, bonuses, loans, and speeches. The government, whatever form it took, should preserve them, which meant that it should keep peasants off them. Peasants on the whole were "dark masses" (Chaianov, 1967: IV, 109) and *"malokulturnye"* (III, 37), and they would ruin productive farms if left to themselves. Their barbaric misuse of equipment, animals, and soil would convey a message throughout the countryside that was precisely the opposite of Chaianov's. It would tell all peasants everywhere that investing money and effort in agriculture was not only a waste of time but a useless hazard. Anyone foolish enough to achieve lasting success with his land was only inviting hostility and invasion. If dark masses were allowed to take over productive land, the population would learn once again the old lesson from Mongol (and pre-Mongol) days: those who produce are the first to be robbed. In short, Chaianov in the summer of 1917, like Alexander III in the 1880s and Lenin a few months later, wanted to impose laws on the peasantry that went contrary to their will. Unlike his predecessor and successor, however, he refrained from cluttering up his high-sounding ideas about autonomous democratic assemblies with considerations as to how such laws might be enforced.

Chaianov's desires to control peasants went yet further than the protection of existing farms. He wanted also to bar dark masses from forests and arable land not yet in use. In the southeastern steppe, for example, virgin soil still lay unplowed, and Chaianov wanted to make it available to peasants from crowded areas, chiefly the Ukrainian gubernias of Kiev, Podoliia, and Poltava. If local peasants took the land, it would only prolong and extend their persistently wasteful methods and ruin more soil, while the relatively advanced farmers of the Ukraine would be left, as before, with too little land on which to employ their skills (III, 36-37, 59-63).

Stolypin's *khokhly* again (see ch. 7, sec. D)—but this time local peasants were not being forced by a "reactionary" minister to consolidate their rented land. Instead, liberal, scientific spokesmen for autonomy would be conversing with them about "advancement." To Chaianov, I suppose, this was an important difference. Yet it is hard to imagine him believing that he could rely on local assemblies and cooperatives to keep their own members off productive lands and invite Ukrainians in to take over. But I repeat: he was issuing a call to action, not writing an objective study. In 1917 local assemblies were all the specialists had to work with. The best Chaianov could do was tell his colleagues what to strive for and wish them luck. As I have said more than once (e.g., ch. 3, sec. A), this consciously fantastic approach to administration worked better in Russia than scholars generally wish to admit.[15]

Chaianov and Pazukhin

Chaianov did occasionally recognize contradictions in his concepts of organization. Sometimes he went so far as to acknowledge that his messianic specialists might encounter opposition among the peasantry. He offered two ways of dealing with this: (1) "propagandizing" and "inspiring" backward peasants (1967: III, 60; IV, 36-37, 50-76), and (2) recognizing that it would require "decades of stubborn, molecular work" (IV, 105) to convert European Russia into consolidated, productive fields (III, 60-61; IV, 54). In other words, all the defects in Chaianov's schemes were to be resolved by political and conversational skills of the specialists themselves and by time.

Certain implications may be discovered in Chaianov's vision. Our study of rural administration during the nineteenth century (ch. 3, sec. C) tells us that if the specialists' conversations were going to go on molecularly for decades, they would have not only to reform society but to join

[15]Not all specialists shared Chaianov's fears of dark masses. A commission of them met in July and Aug. 1917 to prepare a land reform to submit to the forthcoming constituent assembly, and they expressed a wide variety of opinions on the role peasant assemblies should play in distributing landed estates. Most of them avoided the contradiction between democracy and agricultural improvement by simply calling for both, as if there were no contradiction. It deserves mention, however, that one participant, N. Makarov, *consistently* supported village autonomy; that is, he advocated village initiative in taking over estates and also refrained from listing rules for the government to impose. He actually believed villages would be able to manage even the most modern estates on their own (*Trudy,* 1917: vypusk 2, 4-21). But, then, Makarov's relatively consistent rejection of central authority proceeded from an indifference to productivity and even to the marvels of agronomic science. Peasant villages constituted the *only* starting point of his reasoning, and his concept of reform made them ends in themselves. He explicitly accepted the principle that they were not productive units, and with this in mind he was still willing to leave "reform" entirely in their hands. In other words, he made an unusually unequivocal return to the thinking of the MVD prior to 1904-5. See his 1917 report to the Agrarian League (*Osnovye,* 1917: 15-18).

it and become institutions. Moreover, their willingness to transcend science and assume responsibility for social reform implied that they would have to grapple with all the problems social reform might encounter. This would be all right if, as Chaianov assumed, these problems could be resolved by conversation. Supposing, however, that conversation did not always suffice, then authority might be necessary. Chaianov never went so far as to admit this, and his failure to do so reveals an implicit, never-stated assumption underlying his "reasoning": someone other than the *agronom-organizatory* would have to provide funds and keep order while the heroes of science went about doing their stubborn molecular work. If violence broke out during their conversations, someone else would have to handle it and also take the blame for it. Someone else would impose Russia-wide schedules and budgets upon their work. If we insert these assumptions into Chaianov's scheme, it ceases to be preposterous and begins to make sense. Indeed, it accurately describes the situation of the specialists in the period 1907-16 and again in 1921-29. Prior to 1917 the police and land captains were alive and well in the countryside, ready to employ the provisions of martial law to sweep away any dark masses who attacked surveyors and burned the houses of progressive cadres. In St. Petersburg the MZ's bureaucrats were there, ready to impose the plans and ideas formulated by local specialists *and also to take the blame when these plans went wrong.* The specialists found it easy to conceive of themselves as missionaries, operating entirely without force or conflict on no other basis than the invincible truth of science and their own winning ways, because for many years they were in fact able to leave the dirty work to others. Thus Chaianov's notions of organizing testify in a backhanded way to the land captains' contribution to agrarian reform. The presence of captains, to say nothing of police and soldiers, fortified the agronomists' belief that peaceful benefactors could do it all by themselves and, perhaps more important, gave them the impregnable assurance of intrinsic righteousness that drove them to their mission.[16]

It seems to me that Chaianov's image of the *agronom-organizator* bears a close resemblance to Pazukhin's rural knight (see ch. 3, sec. D). Chaianov's specialists were to be persuaders, not law enforcers, but, like Pazukhin's dream captains, they were to be free of law and administra-

[16]The specialists had not only land captains to use as scapegoats but also each other. In the years after 1905 zemstvo agronomists whipped themselves into a passionate hatred for their counterparts in the MZ (Fridolin, 1925: 89-90). One perceptive participant in the agronomists' congress of 1913 observed that it was a good thing the zemstvoes had not taken over the Stolypin Reform in 1905. Had they done so, the agronomists of 1913 would be attacking them instead of the MZ. He concluded that the MZ was doing agronomists a real service by drawing their hostility onto itself (*Trudy,* n.d.: II, 65).

tion. Chaianov's specialists were to *learn* their areas by studying them, whereas Pazukhin's knights were supposed to *know* them simply by having lived in them, but both types of hero demanded freedom from bureaucratic interference on the grounds of their familiarity with the local scene. Both knights and *organizatory* were to formulate laws, policies, and procedures out of their own experience in direct, untrammeled interaction with peasants. Chaianov's specialists wanted to get peasants onto wide fields and organize them into cooperatives, whereas Pazukhin spoke of keeping order; as we have already seen, however, the latter actually had progress in mind, and the specialists, on their part, were very anxious to protect peasants from anything that might mar their "natural" development. Then, too, Chaianov and Pazukhin were equally willing to use government authority to prevent such eminently "natural" developments as the concentration of land and wealth in the hands of a few and, in general, the victimization of the weak by the strong. Chaianov's family farms enjoyed a legal status similar to that of Pazukhin's villages. They were not to be bought, sold, or broken up, and they were to be taken over by the government if they were badly run—that is, if the farmers failed to participate enthusiastically in their local cooperatives (Chaianov, 1967: III, 25-35, 60-61). If Chaianov's farms were different from Pazukhin's villages, then, the difference did not lie in the degree of freedom peasants would enjoy from outside interference. Chaianov and Pazukhin were also in full agreement about the nature of the peasantry. They both considered peasants to be dark masses, and they both believed it would take decades to prepare them for citizenship. Finally, it is worth adding that knights and *organizatory* had similar problems with education. In capital-city pipedreams both captains and specialists were well educated; in reality they were not. By 1905 most land captains did not meet any particular educational standards (ch. 4, sec. A). As for the specialists, Trutovskii admitted in 1914 that 57% had not finished secondary school (1914: 115). On the whole, then, Chaianov's reformers and Pazukhin's guardians were very much the same sort of people.

The basic similarity between captain and specialist was that they were both mobilizers. Chaianov's and Pazukhin's dark masses had above all to be awakened and developed, not merely utilized, and it was the task of guardians and "social agronomists" alike to change them, i.e., to harness them to a vast machinery of production and distribution. We have already discussed Pazukhin's implicit mobilizing tendencies (ch. 3, sec. D). Chaianov was much more explicit. The problem was not to introduce agronomy per se, he said. Scientific agriculture would flourish by itself once society was prepared for it. The *agronom-organizator* was on the front lines, as it were, of a profound psycho-spiritual transformation in which people who were living only to produce and receive their proper share of a limited range of locally available goods were to become *willing* instruments of an infinitely greater productive system. The agronomist was not himself a farmer. His basic task, rather, was to "advise and influence" farmers: to be the "yeast," as Chaianov put it, that would cause peasant society to ferment. His mission was to "replace old ideas in the heads of the people with new ones" (1967: IV, 21). "Social agronomy" was "a system of social measures" (p. 13). The agronomist "was creating a new human culture, a new popular consciousness, and he was allowing this new culture itself to create a new agriculture" (p. 20).[17]

Like most mobilizers, Chaianov told his colleagues that their purpose was to make peasants free. He added, however, that freedom *(volia)* had a specific meaning: it was not only political liberation from the arbitrariness of the old regime but also "the free structuring *(svobodnoe stroitelstvo)* of a democratic state and a democratic zemstvo, the harmonious working together of all the living and cultural forces of our country to produce public education and health, and the developing of our people's spiritual and economic life" (III, 38). The agronomist was not merely to turn land over to peasants. He was "to give it to them in organized form and also to reorganize the land they already possessed" (p. 40). Freedom, then, depended on the completion of the Stolypin Land Reform, though Chaianov would not have put it this way. In Stolypin's day specialists generally preferred to see themselves rescuing peasants from the government's harsh mobilizing efforts, and it would not have pleased them to hear the suggestion that they were themselves the willing agents of a mobilization much more extreme than anything the creators of the land captains or the enactors of the reform had contemplated.

D. THE OFFICIAL END OF THE STOLYPIN REFORM

Officially, the reform ended several times. The last paper termination came with the Provisional Government's decree of 23 August 1917, explicitly ordering a halt to land settlement (Owens, 1937: 210). But the reform organization should already have ceased operating as of 3 May 1917, when a decree came out formally abolishing the land settlement commissions. The same decree also set up "land commissions," whose primary job would be to redistribute land, not to improve its use. Anfimov sets the end of land settlement somewhat earlier, with the law of 29 November 1916 (1962: 335). Dubrovskii claims that the law of 10 June 1915 marked the end (1963: 307).

[17]The concept of a messianic social agronomist was much discussed in the congresses of 1901 and 1913 (see, e.g., *Trudy,* 1901: pt. 1, second series, item 1, 4-7; *Trudy,* n.d.: I, 3).

Practically speaking, it was war that brought on the cessation of land settlement, not decrees. In August 1914 men working in the reform organization were called to the colors as indiscriminately as everyone else. About one-fourth of the *zemleustroiteli* and agricultural specialists went into the army immediately (*Otchetnyia*, 1915: 1). Governors' reports indicate that about one-third of the land captains were gone by the summer of 1915 (TsGIAL, f. 1291, op. 121, 1914g., d. 11, II, ll. 8-40), and the official history of the reform reports that about 40% of the surveyors had gone to war by 1916 (*Kratkii*, 1916: 61). Village and volost elders also departed in great numbers (see, e.g., Anfimov, 1965: 117). Many personnel in rural administration who were not drafted as soldiers were nevertheless compelled to give up agricultural improvement to do war work. The hydrotechnical engineers, for example, were hauled off en masse to ply their trade with the army as soon as mobilization began. Worst of all, many of the specialists and administrators who remained with the MZ could no longer go on working at their old tasks of land settlement and agricultural improvement. On 1 August 1914 (O.S.) the ministry took official responsibility for supplying food to the army (*Obzor*, 1916: 1), and it immediately diverted many of its personnel to work on the construction of grain elevators (*Ocherednye*, 1916: 3-4). The business of food collection and distribution quickly grew to be the old reform organization's chief preoccupation. As we shall see in the following chapter, procuring grain would not only take up the specialists' time during the years following but also compel them to give up their roles as benefactors.

Not surprisingly, the reform organization cut back sharply on land settlement as soon as the war began. An MZ circular of 29 July 1914 (O.S.) instructed its agencies not to replace men called to the army. The fieldwork schedule should be fulfilled if possible; projects already begun should be completed if nothing else. Whatever the commissions might accomplish, however, they would have to operate on a much lower budget than the one originally approved for 1914. Credits authorized up to 1 November would have to last until the end of the year (*IGU*, 1914: 750-53).

Fieldwork schedules continued to be drawn up. Despite all difficulties, an MZ circular of December 1915 ordered the commissions to prepare one for 1916 (*Kratkii*, 1916: 28-29), and the Provisional Government's MZ was still contemplating further fieldwork as late as March 1917.[18] At best, however, the work went half-heartedly. In addition to the severe shortage of personnel, there was also the government's growing reluctance to undertake changes in land use while so many villagers were

[18] MZ circular of 14 Mar. 1917, *Izvestiia po prodovolstvennomu* (May 1917: *ofitsialnyi otdel*, 34).

away. Even if the soldiers from a village had approved a consolidation prior to their departure, implementation of it while they were gone could not help but disturb their peace of mind and sharpen their inclination to return home. For the most part, therefore, the only work done during the war was the completion of projects already begun and unanimously approved by the participants. This was the way the reform ended: not with a bang but a whimper.[19]

But, as the title of this chapter suggests, the reform had become a movement. The suspension of land settlement and agricultural improvement proved to be temporary. The tsarist government's programs survived the tsar and, indeed, revolution, invasion, and a very long, devastating civil war.

Let us recall that in the early summer of 1914 the Stolypin Land Reform was flourishing. Land settlement commissions were working far more efficiently than in their early years, and they were responding to peasant needs with a much finer sensitivity. The movement for agricultural improvement was growing rapidly; specialists were intensifying their work where they were already established, and they were extending new agencies to every corner of the empire. Courts of law and the MVD's police-like administration were being edged aside, along with the annoying niceties of private property, and the way seemed clear for the specialists to proceed with the full-scale modernization of Russian agriculture.

Seven years later, in the summer of 1921, the Russian countryside had changed in many ways. Much of the urban population had disappeared into it and the transportation system was in disarray. Grain markets were in confusion, and many peasant villages had ventured to take charge of land distribution. Nevertheless, prospects for agrarian reform were not altogether unlike what they had been in 1914. Land settlement was once again underway, with the group variety predominating even more than it had in 1914. Private property had ceased to exist altogether. The Soviet government was giving all the support it could to agricultural improvement and, in particular, to the specialists, who had once again taken over the management of agrarian reform. In February

---

[19]Anfimov expresses a bizarre belief that the reform organization pushed land settlement harder than ever in 1914-16 but was at last forced to give up its efforts in late 1916 by the "peasant movement" (1962: 330-35). Soviet scholars have devoted much effort to seeking out such a movement during the war years, but they have found very little. In all the Russian Empire, Anfimov managed to drag up only 149 instances of serious peasant disruption—including rebellions of nomadic tribes in Central Asia—from the war's beginning up to the February Revolution (1965: 18-28, 513-14). Considering the exigencies of recruiting, forced labor, horse requisitioning, and the growing threat of grain requisitioning, this strikes me as small potatoes. The government had excellent reasons for not pushing land reform without having to be afraid of the peasants.

Lenin had told his party to stop talking twaddle about unifying the national economy under a properly marxist proletarian dictatorship and to listen, in quiet humility, to the advice of specialists (*Polnoe,* XL, 339-47). Despite the years of disintegration, then, the agricultural specialists were still out in force, and they were still crusading with all their old fervor. The reform had disappeared from view and Stolypin's name was no longer in favor, but the end of the reform, like its beginning, had been largely a figment of the capital-city imagination.

E. SUMMARY

As I noted in Chapter 5, the Stolypin Reform did not last long enough to give historians a reliable basis for judging its nature or its significance. We have seen, however, that land settlement did spread into the far corners of European Russia, producing dramatic changes in both villages and government offices. Innumerable conflicts broke out among the administration's agencies, but instead of polarizing into battles they provided much of the energy that drove the government into new programs. Government and peasantry both manifested considerable flexibility and responsiveness in their interaction; precisely because of this, their interaction showed little sign of creating a system of private rights in the countryside. The exigencies of consolidation jeopardized ownership on all interstripped fields; efforts to prevent the misuse of consolidated lands gave impetus to new legislation that would probably have set severe limits to property rights on all farmland, interstripped and consolidated alike. Despite all protestations to the contrary, specialists, like the captains before them, wanted mainly to *move* peasants, not to establish or protect them.

CHAPTER 10

Disintegration, Part One, 1914-1917: Agrarian Reform During World War I

Mankind has been interwoven half consciously and half uncon-
sciously to form under compulsion a single organization. . . . Upon
the spiritual strength of the members of the community will it
depend, whether they are subordinated to the obscure will of the
mechanism or master its compulsion.

Walter Rathenau (1921: 25, 28)

A. INTRODUCTION: THE NATURE OF DISINTEGRATION

This chapter and the one following undertake to explain how it was
that both government system and agrarian reform weathered their apparent terminations during the war years and were prepared in 1921 to
resume operations. The basic explanation lies in the nature of the disintegration that took place after 1914. It was not a simple process. Bourgeois economy and tsarist regime did not run steadily downhill from one
unavoidable catastrophe to another, nor did revolutionary masses steadily gather themselves to rise against their masters. To be sure, networks
of production and distribution did break asunder, as did political combinations and administrative organizations, but these phenomena unfolded
in the midst of a continual struggle to mobilize that generated new structures and relationships even as old ones lost their meanings. Disintegration and mobilization are likely to mean much the same thing at any
time in Russian history, but in 1914-21 these treacherous terms dissolved
into each other almost completely. Ministries and regiments, law courts
and budgets, transportation networks and industrial enterprises: all these
modern entities ceased to operate as part of a system, but the centuries-
long effort to integrate them did not abate. On the contrary, an unprecedented number of the empire's inhabitants joined the movement to systematize Russia, and, as always, their struggle for system intensified their

urge to mobilize their fellow countrymen. The organization of the Stolypin Reform was typical in this respect. It ceased to operate for a time, but the *agronom-organizatory* and their peasant protégés did not become insensitive to calls for mobilization. We cannot comprehend the disintegration of 1914-21 apart from a persistent urge to mobilize.

I shall have much to say in the present chapter about the tsarist government's military mobilization. Indeed, one might think I should describe it in detail, since it affected the peasantry at least as powerfully as the Stolypin Land Reform, to which I have devoted five chapters. Consider only that on 17 July 1914, the day of the first call to arms, 3.1 million men were ordered to active duty. A few days later the decree of 21 July called up an additional 800,000 (Golovine, 1931: 45-46).[1] By 1917 over 15 million officers and men, the vast majority of them peasants, had been wrenched out of civilian life. This figure does not yet include the uncountable men drafted for "labor" in the front-line zones, nor does it take into account the extensive requisitions of horses and carts that struck almost every village and landed estate in the empire (pp. 47-49). According to the MZ's account, requisitioning of draft animals took about 20% of the total number in Russia by December 1916.[2] Surely this must have been a memorable experience for the peasantry. Significant as it was, however, war mobilization was not designed expressly for the purpose of attacking and changing peasant society. Its importance to us lies only in its impact, not in the processes of thought and action from which it came. We shall not see the army in this study but only glimpse it now and then as it impinged on agrarian reform.

War did not introduce the urge to mobilize to peasant society. We have seen in Chapters 7-9 that villages were already learning to organize themselves during the later years of the Stolypin Reform. We can say, however, that in the years of war and revolution the urge continued to spread among the peasants, outliving the symbols of legal-administrative system, feeding on itself with unusual intensity by destroying the very systems it threw up, goading ever greater numbers of men into collective action. To be sure, many peasants acted in conscious opposition to the mobilizing symbols of patriotism and ideology and sought only to defend their families against a hostile world, but this was only another way for the urge to mobilize to extend itself. Men cannot oppose or escape mobilization collectively except by mobilizing.

Unfortunately, we shall see very little of this turmoil of mobilization and disintegration within the villages, for meaningful evidence is in short

[1]Soviet estimates of the number of men mobilized during July-August are somewhat lower (see, e.g., Berkevich, 1947: 12-13) but still go well over 3 million.
[2]*Ocheredyne* (1916: 21). See also Anfimov (1962: 113-15); Pogrebinskii (1950: 38-39, 44).

supply. Our main topic is the work of the erstwhile agrarian reformers during the period 1914-17 and the political-administrative context within which they engaged in this work.

To describe the agricultural specialists' experience in one sentence, agrarian reform underwent a sharp change in direction during World War I. On 1 August 1914 Nicholas II commanded Krivoshein and his ministry to assume responsibility for supplying the armed forces with food (*Obzor*, 1916: 1). The only organization he had available was the embryonic government-zemstvo alliance of agricultural specialists and "advanced" peasants that had been engaged in land settlement and agricultural improvement. Thus, during the first year of war, large numbers of surveyors, agronomists, statisticians, and other forms of agricultural improvers followed their leaders in the MZ and local zemstvo administrations into the business of buying grain. In this way agrarian reformers continued to operate in the countryside even as the reform organization dwindled away. This is where disintegration became a very complex affair for the specialists. As we shall see, their efforts to serve the armed forces by procuring food did much to disrupt the agriculture they were supposed to be improving. This seeming paradox should have weakened their position in the villages and put an end to agrarian reform under their tutelage, but apparently it did not. Disintegration did not impede the general push toward peasant mobilization; on the contrary, it may actually have accelerated the processes of agrarian reform. The main purpose of this chapter and the two that follow is to make this point and to explain it.

B. THE MZ VENTURES INTO MILITARY FOOD SUPPLY, 1914-15

Initially the MZ's new responsibility meant very little. The governors already possessed emergency powers to cope with speculation and price inflation, and existing law required them to exercise these powers under the MVD's supervision. How Krivoshein and his reform organization were to fit themselves into this scheme of things was not immediately clear, and for a time the army looked after its own provisioning while each governor did as he thought best (Zaitsev, 1930: 37-38). Within a month or so the MZ appointed a purchasing commissioner in each gubernia to obtain food for the army, but this did not establish a new organization. The commissioners were not new agents occupying separate positions but regular officials taking on new duties. Even so, the MZ was trying to introduce drastic organizational changes as speedily as he could. In particular, Krivoshein was trying to push the MVD out of food supply. Most of the first commissioners he appointed were chairmen of zemstvo directorates, i.e., men who would not readily cooperate with the MVD (TsGIAL, f. 456, op. 1, d. 564, ll. 23-24).

On paper the new commissioners were powerful men. The law of 17 February 1915 authorized them to block the transport of vital items of supply outside their respective gubernias, to fix maximum prices on army purchases, and to command sellers of grain to make their goods available to the armed forces at these prices. If any grain supplier refused a purchasing commissioner's command to sell, the commissioner was authorized to seize the grain at 15% less than the army's maximum price for that area (Zaitsev, 1930: 7). In short, the new commissioners had unlimited power to buy whenever and wherever they pleased. Unfortunately their responsibility was not in the least unlimited, not at first. They had no orders to keep grain prices stable or to make bread available to any consumers except the military. Their job was to raid the market, not to sustain it.

One wonders exactly what led the government to put this business in the hands of the MZ. Ever since the founding of ministerial administration in 1802, food supply had been the concern of the MVD. Indeed, the MVD continued to administer a relief program of sorts throughout the war. More precisely, an interministerial conference (MVD, MF, and state control), established in 1905 to receive petitions for famine relief via the MVD's organization, met periodically to consider petitions and respond to them. This conference had no program nor did it ever try to formulate one. Most of its loans were small in scale. For example, it approved several in February 1917 amounting to only 40 rubles apiece (TsGIAL, f. 457, op. 1, d. 1267, ll. 62-65). To be sure, it handled a few large loans of the same sort the MZ's organization was issuing (see below, sec. C). In December 1915 it lent 500,000 rubles to the Iaroslavl gubernia zemstvo to buy food (*Izvestiia osobogo*, 15 Mar. 1916: 35), and in January 1916 it decided to make a number of large loans to Nizhnii Novgorod gubernia to help the administration build up a grain reserve (TsGIAL, f. 457, op. 1, d. 1267, ll. 60-61). On balance, however, the conference's activities were petty. The MVD never did play a significant role in the government's efforts to build a food supply system (see the materials in f. 1291, op. 32, d. 28).

The decision to entrust military food procurement to the MZ was far from automatic or even permanent. The MVD did not give way gracefully. On at least one occasion, in late 1915, it tried to set the MZ's organization aside and recapture its old monopoly on food supply administration.[3] By this time the MZ had already made some compromises, indicating a certain sensitivity to the MVD's irritation. Krivoshein had

[3]Letter of 11 Dec. 1915 from A. Khvostov, then the MVD, to I. Goremykin, chairman of the Council of Ministers (TsGIAL, f. 457, op. 1, d. 209, ll. 1-5).

started out in August 1914 by appointing only one governor to be a commissioner of army supply; by December 1915 almost two-thirds of the commissioners were governors and governors-general (f. 457, op. 1, d. 209, l. 2).[4] One gathers that the MZ had to struggle for its new responsibilities.

I have seen no official explanation for the MZ's assignment to food supply in 1914, but it is reasonably safe to assume that it was primarily a result of the ministry's development during the Stolypin Reform. By 1914 the MZ, together with its network of zemstvo specialists and cooperatives, had been edging the MVD out of government-peasant interaction for several years. As war began, the government found itself heavily dependent on the peasantry, and it must have seemed practical to utilize agencies that had gained the peasants' trust. It was also more or less natural for the MZ and its "agencies" to want to be involved in the management of grain distribution. What better way to extend their influence yet further into the villages than by peddling the villages' grain?

In the end the MZ's new responsibility committed its zemstvo-cooperative network to an entirely new kind of interaction with the peasantry. Within three years the benevolent conversationalists of the Stolypin years would begin to receive orders to extort grain from peasants by force, and for this task they were very poorly equipped. But who could have known in 1914 that the relatively simple process of buying grain to feed 3 or 4 million soldiers and sailors would grow rapidly into a life-or-death struggle to maintain the very existence of urban civilization in Russia by forcibly dragging grain out of a hostile countryside? Certainly the MZ had not known. In August 1914 it gallantly promised to feed not only the Russian army but Serbia, Montenegro, and France as well (*Ocherednye,* 1916: 3). As the MZ undertook its new task, then, it seems to have envisioned grain distribution as a way to *benefit* farmers by drawing off excess production and resuming grain export. Only later did the ministry's responsibility for getting grain begin to cause it embarrassment.[5]

[4] By late 1916 another reversal had taken place. In September no governors in European Russia were serving as purchasing commissioners (TsGIAL, f. 456, op. 1, d. 166, ll. 17-20).

[5] The MZ's promise to export grain to Russia's allies was quite serious. France received 310,000 tons of grain from Russia during the course of the war (Augé-Laribé, 1927: 189-90). Shipments from Archangel, which came to about half the total amount going to France, were still being made as late as Jan. 1916 (TsGIAL, f. 456, op. 1, d. 961, l. 115). No reliable totals are available for grain shipped to Serbia and Montenegro. As of Apr. 1915 Russia had dispatched 18,000 tons in their direction via the Danube and/or Rumania (d. 954, ll. 145, 326-27), and the MZ was still planning to send an additional 120,000 tons (l. 128). Grain export began to go out of style in the fall of 1915, and it seems to have ceased after Jan. 1916. See, e.g., a protest against further grain shipments

One immediate practical reason for assigning military food supply to the MZ was that its zemstvoes and cooperatives could locate sources of food and predict harvests. Within a few months, however, it became obvious that the procurement and distribution of grain would demand much more than information. The government would also have to concern itself with the supervision of railroads and river boats, to say nothing of marketing and finance. In early 1915, to everyone's surprise, the army found itself running short of just about all types of materials, and the generals seem to have decided that they had no time to wait for the MZ to gather information. On 19 May the tsar abruptly transferred food supply to the ministry of commerce and industry (Zaitsev, 1930: 9).

But the reign of the minister of commerce was shortlived. The Duma met in June 1915 and quickly passed legislation setting up an interministerial directorate, formally termed the "Special Conference for the Discussion and Unification of Food Supply Measures," with the MZ as chairman. The minister's new powers were similar in nature to those he had enjoyed as purchaser of food for the armed forces. His purposes and responsibilities, however, were now much broader. In theory, at least, the special conference was not merely to *utilize* food producers, markets, and transport but also to *manage* them, and it would be responsible for feeding not only the army but the whole population. The food supply conference was not the only such general economic directorate. There were to be three others: defense, transport, and fuel supply. Defense was to possess supreme power. The tsar signed this massively new arrangement into law on 17 August (*Obzor,* 1916: 9; *prilozheniia,* 5-10).

In theory, the MZ's new position tremendously extended his influence. The 24 members of his conference were drawn not only from other ministries but from all major institutions of government and economic organization. There were seven Duma representatives, seven from the State Council, one each from the unions of zemstvoes and towns, and only eight, or one-third, from the various ministries. This awesome array did not actually direct food supply. Unlike the Committee for Land Settlement Affairs, the conference was only an advisory body. The MZ was bound to consult the members on important questions, but he was not

---

from the chief of staff of the southwestern front in Oct. 1915 (ll. 324-25) and a report from a Black Sea port in Jan. 1916, suggesting that grain accumulated there for shipment to France be milled and distributed to the Russian army (d. 165, l. 3). It deserves mention, however, that the ministries of finance and foreign affairs never gave up advocating grain export. Italy asked Russia to send her some grain in Nov. 1916, and Russia's minister of foreign affairs sent a note to the MZ recommending that he accede to this request from a loyal ally. The note was dated 26 Nov. just three days before the MZ introduced Russia's first forced procurement campaign (d. 995, l. 22). Some segments of the tsarist government took a long time to convince themselves that food might be in short supply.

obliged to abide by their decision. Thus the August law broadened the area in which the MZ exercised paper influence without imposing any formal limits on his paper power to make decisions and act on them (Zaitsev, 1930: 9-13; Pogrebinskii, 1950: 51-52).

It made sense for the government to try to establish central control over national production and distribution. A year of war had demonstrated that the army would require far more support for a far longer period of time than the private economy could provide on its own. Worse, the army was in imminent danger of losing the war altogether. By May 1915 it had run short of both weapons and ammunition, and the generals had had no choice but to order a retreat back across Congress Poland into western Russia. Collapse was avoided only at great sacrifice of men and material. The German army advanced into Russia at its pleasure, and in August virtually nothing was preventing it from going farther but its own logistical problems. Clearly there was a need to marshal Russia's resources.[6]

But if the government's aim was practical, it was not necessarily practicable. The administration was profoundly unprepared to manage the national economy, and the actual work of the special conferences had an air of unreality about it from the beginning. The Special Conference on Food Supply, for example, was supposed to transform villages into machines for producing and delivering supplies, but, as we shall see, it could only struggle on a day-to-day basis with the desperate confusion that had called it into being.

C. THE DIFFICULTIES OF FOOD DISTRIBUTION IN WARTIME RUSSIA

Having brought the MZ and its network of specialists and cooperatives through their first year of war, let us pause to consider the disintegration that was taking place around them as they expanded their efforts to mobilize the countryside. We need to discuss three matters in particular: the general obsession with food shortage, the army's techniques of food procurement during the year before the MZ's special conference came into being, and the powerlessness of the ministers. These seem to have been the difficulties the MZ's special conference had to face most directly. The purpose of discussing them here is to present a more con-

[6] According to a recent study, the Russian army was much stronger by Sept. 1915, and the Germans would have failed to advance much farther if they had tried (Stone, 1975: 186-90, 211-12). Even if this be true, the fact remains that Russia's military commanders were unaware of their favorable situation. So far as they knew, it was sheer chance that the Germans stopped in the fall of 1915 (Falls, 1959: 121-25).

crete vision of the position the MZ's specialists occupied between government and peasant during the months prior to the Revolution.

Famine Hysteria

It is not easy for a historian to perceive, or even conceive of, what our would-be agrarian reformers actually did during the disintegration of 1914-17. We do know that they dominated the wartime organization of zemstvoes and towns (Gleason, 1972: 31-32; Fridolin, 1925: 104-6), and in the countryside their procurement work deepened their already heavy involvement in rural government. Alas for the specialists, food procurement did more than anything else to split Russian society. The struggle between producers and consumers of food mangled what had been a reasonably good relationship between government and peasant, abruptly weakening the government's ability to influence peasant behavior while rendering government power odious to a substantial number of rural inhabitants. The most decisive element in the specialists' wartime experience was their plunge into the middle of this rupture. In 1917 Chaianov's hero-benefactors, hitherto St. Petersburg's missionaries of progress to the villages, were forced to choose sides for or against the villages.

The rupture between food producers and consumers took its purest and clearest form in rural areas in the food-producing regions: the Ukraine, the Volga below Kazan, the region south of the Oka, the plains north of the Caucasus Mountains, and western Siberia. In these regions— in the countryside—it was a simple matter of state vs. society. The villages had an ample supply of grain and meat and needed virtually nothing the government had to offer them; the rest of Russia lacked grain, and the government faced the unequivocal necessity of attacking food-producing villages in order to get it. There could be no compromise; there was no room to maneuver. Government collectors and village hoarders could only communicate by fighting.

Scholars do not generally accept the fight between food producers and consumers as a serious part of history. It lacks ideological merit. Historians in the Soviet Union prefer to see poor peasants struggling against wealthy landholders; elsewhere, scholarship is pleased to see oppressed masses rebelling against arbitrary despotism. Next to these edifying panoramas, the vision of two frightened dogs fighting over a bone lacks grandeur, and for this reason it has not attracted much attention. It is too early in the chapter to argue the matter. Suffice it here to make one relatively simple point: *there can be no doubt that the black-earth gubernias produced more than enough grain to feed the empire throughout the period 1914-17.*

No figures on grain production and surplus during the war are reliable, but those of the government's central statistical committee are more conservative than most. According to a committee report dated mid-1917, grain reserves in Russia had risen from about 8 million tons at the outset of the war to 16.4 million in mid-1916. They fell to 12.7 million by mid-1917 and, the committee estimated, they would fall another 5.5 million by mid-1918—assuming that consumption continued at the level of 1915-16 (*Izvestiia po prodovolstvennomu,* Sep.-Oct. 1917: 12-17). In short, grain reserves remained much higher through 1917 than they had during peacetime. But the most telling evidence for bountiful harvests and ample grain supply in 1914-16 is not in official figures. It is to be found, rather, in the department of agriculture's collections of informal reports on local conditions (see ch. 4, sec. D), the last one of which came out at the end of 1916. These collections offered detailed information indicating that harvests remained high throughout the prerevolutionary period. Further, the sown area continued at prewar levels up through the sowing of winter grain in 1916, except in a few areas, chiefly the southeastern steppe. Official figures, such as they are, suggest that harvests did not fall off enough even in 1917 to cause any real grain shortage at the end of the year. Gordeev (1925: 89) estimated that sown area in 1917 reached 91.5% of what it had been in 1913. Orlov (1918: 284) claimed that the 1917 crop for all Russia was only 10.6% less than the mean harvest during 1909-13. As far as we know, then, Russia possessed an abundance of grain through 1917. By the end of this period many Russians were living in fear of hunger, but farmers in the black-soil gubernias possessed more than enough food (see Volobuev, 1962: 383-87). This is why the state came down upon them.

Outside the grain-producing regions the struggle between producers and consumers was more complex. In towns everywhere, in the countryside north of Oka, in eastern Siberia, and in much of central Asia, grain was generally in short supply. In these areas, therefore, the roles of procurer and hoarder did not correspond exactly to state and society. Grain shortage could either strengthen or weaken the state. A man in need of grain could oppose the state because it failed to supply him with enough food, but he could also join the state in a campaign to get food. A government—or revolutionary party—could attract followers by appealing to the general suspicion against "hoarders and speculators," and it could organize people on a grand scale by calling upon them to attack grain-producing regions. On the other hand, suspicion was a continuing source of weakness in any organization. Who could be sure that a procurer was not hoarding on the side? Among grain consumers, then, the threat of food shortage gave strength to any organization capable of dealing with pervasive mistrust among its followers and mobilizing them for decisive action.

We shall not understand the state's relationship to famine or the specialists' role in food procurement if we insist—as specialists usually did—on visualizing famine as a physical problem, to be solved by finding grain and delivering it to hungry people. Famine was a state of mind or, if you wish, a type of mass hysteria. It resembled a stock market panic, except that in the latter everyone fears falling prices, whereas in the Russian "famines" of 1915-10 everyone anticipated rising prices. In stereotypical economic panics people try to sell, thereby depressing prices and making their fears come true. In famine hysteria people and institutions try to hoard grain, thereby actualizing the shortages they fear and/or the price rises they anticipate. An individual might hoard grain to prepare himself and family for approaching dearth or simply to make speculative profits; a town, or regiment, or factory might "store" grain to assure its members of a supply; the result in all cases is the same. Grain disappears from markets, and the demand for it rises far beyond the mere physical need to eat.

Famine hysteria permeated the empire from 1914 on. It is not so surprising that grain-*consuming* areas would report threatening food shortages. What is remarkable is that in 1915, a year of more than ample harvests, the vast majority of cities and rural areas in the grain-*producing* gubernias reported critical shortages of grain. Samara and Saratov gubernias, for example, claimed that *all* their uezds—as well as their towns—were short of food. Kursk was the only grain-producing gubernia in which most uezds did *not* report shortages in early 1915, but even in this bastion of honesty 40% of the uezds reported a grain shortage (*Obzor,* 1916: 25-27). And when it came to sugar, Kursk sank to the normal practice. Kursk was one of Russia's sugar-producing centers, but it claimed to be running out in 1915 (*Svedeniia,* 1 Jan. 1916: 24).

It is hard to imagine experienced officials taking these whoppers seriously—calling conferences to discuss them, sending out inquiries to get more information. As later reports were to show, the appeals of 1915 reflected not scarcity but fear and, in part, a rapid expansion in consumption. People were not only storing grain and sugar, they were actually eating more than they ever had before. A report from Saratov gubernia in 1916 said that workers were consuming more sugar than in peacetime because they had more money to spend and, with the outlawing of vodka, less to spend it on (*Izvestiia osobogo,* 15 Mar. 1916: 29). On more than one occasion the government observed with dismay that meat consumption was rising rapidly throughout Russia for much the same reason (1 Apr. 1916: 15). Obviously a great deal of grain was going to feed livestock, not only in 1915 but in subsequent years. A. Khriashcheva tells us that despite "shortages," requisitions by the military, and all other difficulties, there were more cattle, sheep, and pigs in Tula gubernia in 1917 than before the war (1921: 31). Tea drinking also rose sharply. In 1915-16, when Vladivostok was already beginning to lose its struggle to handle the piles of war material coming across its docks, it was importing *and shipping* more tea than ever before (*Izvestiia po prodovolstvennomu*, May 1917: 51).

Facts notwithstanding, the central government viewed the appeals it received in 1915 with sympathy. The governing body of the MZ's newly formed food supply organization began to discuss the idea of handing out loans to "needy" cities and locales as early as June 1915 (TsGIAL, f. 457, op. 1, d. 980, ll. 4-5). At a meeting of 12 September 1915 it decided to make loans to help towns accumulate grain reserves with the purpose of enabling municipal governments to sell grain whenever prices threatened to go up (d. 262, l. 4). In other words, the government proposed to keep grain prices low by buying up large quantities of grain.

This may have been a silly idea, but it proved to be very popular. A great flood of loans from the central administration to zemstvoes and city dumas went out in the last months of 1915. Apparently there was little supervision. A single October meeting of the subcommission charged with receiving petitions for loans dispatched over a million rubles with virtually no discussion (d. 978, ll. 1-2). Only in February 1916 did the subcommission venture to complain of unwarranted petitions. Zemstvoes and towns had sometimes applied separately for loans to cover the same territories. Others had applied to more than one government agency for the same loan (l. 25).[7]

In September 1915, with nonsensical reports of grain shortage in black-earth villages streaming in and loans streaming out, the MZ's new food supply organization began to amass "information," and it decided to use as its sources these same hysteria-prone local authorities who had started the "famine" (*Obzor*, 1916: 43-45). The MZ was quite sincere when he said in December 1915 that the government's duty was to help *agriculture* recover from its "very serious upheaval" (p. 122). He really did intend to go on putting out large amounts of money so that grain could be stored *in food-producing areas*. At this point various government offices quietly began establishing their own hoards. The peasant bank, for example, set up among its own staff members a commission whose purpose it would be to purchase food—using the bank's funds—to assure the bank's employees a steady supply (TsGIAL, f. 592, op. 1, d. 127, l. 78).

Zemstvoes and town dumas began receiving their loans in early 1916, and, as might be expected, they set out to spend them on grain. They appeared in the markets as competitors. Each one sent out its own agents to buy wherever they could as quickly as they could, and as they

[7]From late 1915 on, government loans to "starving" cities to help them buy up grain and store it were regularly listed in the journals of the food supply organization, *Svedeniia* and *Izvestiia osobogo*. Total amounts of these loans through the spring of 1916 are given in *Obzor* (1916: *dopolnenie*, 4).

crowded into the market, prices rose even faster than the demand for reserves warranted. As a result, some of the more public-spirited zemstvo-town men—in the food-*consuming* gubernias, where the threat of shortage was closer to being real—suggested in early 1916 that the central government not only issue loans to local institutions but also hand out food to them, taking it from the army's reserves (*Obzor*, 1916: *dopolnenie*, 5). The government hastened to comply with this suggestion. By spring 1916 the food supply organization was issuing the army's grain to a variety of "needy" towns and institutions (pp. 10-11), and the MZ was pressing his army supply agents very hard to expand their purchases so as to allow yet more handouts.[8] Not surprisingly, food prices continued to rise and "shortages" grew more critical.

It seems, then, that we have no need to speak of traders and peasants selfishly hiding their grain to get more money for it (or, later, to escape government requisitions). No need either, at this point, to discuss breakdowns in transport, shortages of manufactured goods, and other "rational" explanations for famine in wartime Russia. If we wish to comprehend the onset of a critical shortage of food during 1915-16, two years of abundant harvests, we need only consider the tsarist government's well-intended actions to prevent famine. They illustrate perfectly the compulsive fear of food shortage that began to seize imaginations and rule minds in Russia in 1914-15.

The picture was not all dark. Apparently a considerable number of men began striving in 1916 to make a Russia-wide distribution system work, and the quality of the government's information showed a distinct improvement. A survey of grain reserves completed in January 1916 found *three* times more than the government had hitherto believed to be available (*Izvestiia osobogo*, 15 Mar. 1916: 58). Kursk somehow acquired an adequate supply of sugar (1 Mar. 1916: 53), and the MZ's commissioner in Saratov sent in a refreshingly honest revelation that per capita sugar consumption had risen far above prewar levels. Some memos of late 1916 suggest that the food supply organization was able to estimate how much grain Moscow and Petrograd should have received and to announce that the capital cities had received *more* than their quotas (TsGIAL, f. 457, op. 1, d. 941, ll. 8-15). Ufa gubernia went so far as to protest, in a unique spirit of self-denial, that government loans and purchases were one of the principal causes of the price rise they were intended to combat. Admittedly Ufa's upsetting remarks did not go far. The central office asked other gubernias what they thought of them, and *all* responses agreed that Ufa was wrong (*Izvestiia osobogo*, 1 Mar. 1916: 33-34). The government should continue its spending. Even so, Ufa's

[8]See, e.g., the MZ's orders of 4 Apr. (*Izvestiia osobogo*, 1 June 1916: 19-20).

admission suggests a certain relaxation. One supposes that the central government's generosity assured someone in Ufa that it would not be necessary to falsify reports in order to get the government's money.

In the end, however, trust and self-denial did not prevail. Prices continued to rise in 1916, and the towns continued to experience sporadic shortages. To make matters worse, everyone knew that harvests had been good in 1914-15, and this made shortages suspicious. Reports of grain disappearing into the hands of "speculators" continued to flood in, and statesmen and administrators began to believe them.[9] Thus people not only believed themselves to be threatened by shortages but now began to suspect everyone else of cheating them. Petrograd suspected Moscow of taking more than her share off the trains en route to the Gulf of Finland; city dwellers suspected farmers; gubernia zemstvoes suspected one another; the central government suspected local institutions; soldiers suspected civilians; and everyone suspected merchants and "corrupt" officials. Most of the suspicions were probably justified. Most individuals and institutions seem to have hoarded grain, either on their own behalf or in the public interest. By 1917, therefore, many people were indeed facing starvation. Hysteria had created a fact.[10]

[9]See, e.g., *Obzor* (1916: 61-62, 135-36; *dopolnenie,* 4); *Svedeniia* (15 Jan. 1916: 23); *Izvestiia osobogo* (15 Oct. 1916: 73-74); *Izvestiia po prodovolstvennomu* (Sept.-Oct. 1917: 5-6).

[10]As early as 8 Aug. 1914 the government had a report that people in Finland were hoarding large quantities of grain (TsGIAL, f. 456, op. 1, d. 283—*listy* are unnumbered in this *delo*). Finland received the bulk of her grain from quotas assigned to Petrograd, and we may well imagine that such reports inclined Petrograd officials to filch grain from cars bound for Helsinki. On a smaller scale, a typical letter of early 1917 from a factory in Murom complained that it was receiving too little food and was therefore losing its workers to other factories, where food was mysteriously abundant (f. 457, op. 1, d. 603, l. 7).

One report on Petrograd's and Moscow's destructive competition for food was printed in *Svedeniia* (27 Nov. 1915: 43). This, however, was still in 1915, before the central government began to take measures. By mid-1916 the two capital cities seem to have reached a working agreement. One sign of this was a memorandum on sugar from the MZ's organization, dated 15 June 1916, which said that sugar would be distributed according to a general plan based on the theory that rural dwellers "needed" five-sixths of a pound per month, whereas city dwellers had to have one and one-third. The inhabitants of Petrograd and Moscow were in a special category of their own. They required two and one-half pounds per month. Apparently this measure helped to build trust between the capital cities for a while, but it inspired little sympathy in the rest of the empire, especially the rural areas (see *Izvestiia po prodovolstvennomu,* June-July 1917: 39). On their part, the cities were not inclined to worry over food shortages in rural Russia. Government journals repeatedly complained of peasants using up grain to make illegal vodka (see, e.g., *Prodovolstvie,* 1 Sept. 1917: 5).

Military Procurement during the First Months of War

In theory, the MZ had charge of military food supply from August 1914 on, but, as I have said, this was only a paper arrangement at first. There were no agencies capable of meeting the army's needs, and when the MZ's special conference came into being in the fall of 1915, it could only impose itself on administrative arrangements and relationships already in being. We must now ask what these were, for they played no small role in bringing on the famine hysteria described in the preceding section.

The Russian army mobilized much more rapidly than its generals had anticipated. This was probably the reason it had to feed itself in an essentially random way during the first months of the war. Officers on all echelons bought or commandeered buildings, supplies, horses, civilian laborers, and trains as they needed them, often without consulting civil administrators or even their own superiors. Sometimes the officers spent too much for what they bought, competing with each other like bidders at an auction; sometimes they took goods and compelled the owners to accept a low price; now and then an officer would simply take. As Zaitsev tells us, in eminently moderate terms, "The military authorities were inclined to underestimate the importance of the rear as compared with the front....They had no compunction in ruthlessly cutting the most vital economic threads and connections, injecting into the delicate and complicated task of supply their military simplicity and finality, and greatly exaggerating the importance of orders and prohibitions in the economic field" (1930: 8; see also pp. 15-16, and Golovine, 1931: 162-71).

Krivoshein put the matter less moderately in a statement of 18 August 1915, the day after he became chairman of his new special conference: "The requisitioning of the population of Russia for re-enforcement of garrisons which are doing nothing in the rear has complicated the problem of agricultural labor to the point that the harvest could become a catastrophe" (Cherniavsky, 1967: 132). As late as December 1915 Krivoshein's successor, A. N. Naumov, was still complaining about separate army units making purchases on their own, contrary to orders from their own superiors (*Obzor*, 1916: 20).

The business of meat supply showed up the worst features of army administration. According to Golovine's account, the army began its meat gathering with a high-level decision as to how much each soldier should receive each day. It was then easy to determine how many men were to receive this ration and, by simple multiplication, to arrive at a total amount of meat to be purchased. This done, orders were sent out to purchase the meat, and apparently they were carried out vigorously all over European Russia and Siberia. Great quantities of animals, some slaughtered and some still on the hoof, were accumulated and sent to the front. At this point, however, it was discovered that live animals had to be fed and dead ones either canned or refrigerated. Unfortunately fodder was hard to accumulate in a hurry and facilities for canning and refrigerating were extremely limited. The army's bookkeeping had been impeccable, but much of its meat spoiled and many of its animals starved. The army's forays into the Russian meat market had upset prices and supply arrangements, to say nothing of the transport system, but they had not put much meat into the soldiers' stomachs (Golovine, 1931: 164-66, 170). In other branches of operation results were not so immediately disastrous. Grain and sugar did not spoil as readily as meat. The method, however, was everywhere the same. In early September 1915 the MVD, then N. B. Shcherbatov, described many similar instances of wasteful highhandedness in acquiring supplies of all sorts during the preceding year (Cherniavsky, 1967: 231; see also pp. 100-101, 120, 123).

A typical expression of the army's ad hoc approach to procurement was the decree of 17 February 1915, which outlawed grain shipments between the various sectors of European Russia. The intent was to enable military officials in each sector to buy their quotas without having to look very far or confront complications. Best of all, they would not have to coordinate with each other (Pogrebinskii, 1950: 50-51). Procurement in separate territories would minimize conflict between units and administrative departments, reduce the central commanders' administrative burdens, and please the front-line units by reducing their dependence on external agencies. It was, of course, grossly unfair and wasteful to allow each unit simply to grab for itself in its own locale, but in the short run this crudely self-reliant procedure must have appealed to combat troops.

Labor drafts for the army were handled in this same catch-as-catch-can fashion throughout the war. In February 1916, a few months after the front had settled down, the governor of Podoliia gubernia wrote to the commander of the southwestern front, reminding him that all labor done for the army in Podoliia had been performed by peasants whose villages were within the gubernia boundaries. The governor ventured to suggest that local peasants were bearing a disproportionate share of the war's burdens (*Ekonomicheskoe*, III, 34-36). In July the tsar attempted to correct this imbalance by calling for labor drafts from the interior gubernias, especially from the nomads of Central Asia, who had not been required to provide soldiers. Results were discouraging. Civil administrators and local institutions in the interior gubernias of European Russia did not show any enthusiasm for grabbing yet more peasants beyond the number already taken as soldiers (pp. 48-50). In Central Asia the Kirghiz and other tribes went into hiding or migrated when local officials spoke of calling them up to work on roads in western Russia (pp. 44-45). An MZ report of late 1916 had to acknowledge that labor drafts for the army were still coming entirely from six gubernias, all of them near the front lines: Kherson, Bessarabia, Podoliia, Kiev, Poltava, and Chernigov (*Ocherednye,* 1916: 9-12).

Apparently the army interfered as freely in politics as it did in the economy. The MVD complained in July 1915 that the Duma was holding his ministry responsible for administration in the frontal zone, but in fact "everything" there was managed by the military authorities, "who are armored by the terrifying words—'military necessity'" (Cherniavsky, 1967: 27). The MVD was not exaggerating the central government's helplessness. By the end of 1915 governors in western Russia had developed the habit of corresponding directly with local military commanders, as if the generals had become their administrative superiors (*Ekonomicheskoe,* III, 34-36). The MZ's military supply commissioners behaved in the same fashion.[11] P. G. Kurlov, who was the director of the army's "civil" administration in the Baltic area, recalls in his memoirs that the army's agents—including himself—threw the regular civil administration into confusion from the very beginning of the war by their arbitrary interference (1923: 200-204). No wonder that in 1915 the Council of Ministers referred repeatedly to the division of Russia into the army's *oprichnina* and the civil government's *zemshchina* (e.g., Cherniavsky, 1967: 233).

Oprichnina and *zemshchina* seem inadequate to describe the army's depredations, for in fact they knew no territorial limits. The MVD declared "categorically" at a meeting of the Council of Ministers in July 1915 that as a result of the army's meddling he could no longer take responsibility for order in the city of Moscow. "There is no real power and authority there now," he said; "there is no accord between civil and military authorities" (p. 33). It was the army, said the angry minister at the council meeting of 2 September, that had allowed the unions of zemstvoes and towns to expand their organization throughout European Russia, encroaching without restraint upon prerogatives properly belonging to the government. "All this is done by usurpation, under the protection of the military authorities," added the MVD (p. 237). Earlier, at a meeting in July, the minister of the navy had "cheered" his colleagues by telling them that the commander of the Black Sea naval forces had decided to let private shipowners in his area have their ships back. The commander had not asked the ministers if this was all right, any more than he had asked their permission to take the ships in the first place. He simply informed them of his decision. The ministers were grateful to him for taking the trouble to inform them (pp. 34-35). Apparently the army and navy could do as they wished whenever they wished. Military officers did not undertake to govern anyone or assume any recognizable

[11]This fact emerges from a reading of the telegrams sent to the MZ by his military purchasing commissioners (see, e.g., the materials in TsGIAL, f. 456, op. 1, d. 843).

authority. All they had was power, and all they did with it was to suit themselves.

The army's raids on the economy were not solely the doing of its own officers. Civil authorities, especially specialists working in zemstvo and municipal administrations, were more than willing to utilize the army's arbitrary actions for their own purposes (see, e.g., Anfimov, 1962: 194, 244). Indeed, local institutions greeted military mobilization as a bonanza. Freewheeling supply officers were big spenders, after all, and there is nothing like the promise of profit to bring patriotism to a boil, especially in view of the panic that had struck farmers at the war's outset, when it seemed that the abrupt cutting off of grain export and prohibition of vodka manufacturing would create a grain surplus and plunge agriculture into a depression. How relieved were the cooperatives, zemstvoes, and merchants to see gallant supply officers thrusting aside all regulation as they placed their orders, clanking their swords at anyone who ventured to impede deliveries and jingling their abundant purses at anyone who could provide what they needed in a hurry (Golovine, 1931: 155-57; Zagorsky, 1928: 82-83, 88, 92-93; Polner, 1930: 71, 78, 185-87, 241-47). The Special Conference on Food Supply published a booklet on this subject in late 1915. It said that towns and zemstvoes had been regulating and manipulating markets on their own authority since the outbreak of the war. These local institutions had no legal power to operate in this fashion, so in fact they were legislating for themselves as they went along (*Sovremennoe,* 1915: 5). In a word, they were engaging in line-over-staff administration. In September 1915 Georgii Lvov, head of the union of zemstvoes, recalled the zemstvoes' operations during the war's early days with glowing pride. "We actually combined with the army," he chanted exultantly to a large gathering of his fellow zemstvo administrators (*Sobranie,* 1916: 6).[12]

Of course, more than greed was involved. The zemstvoes and towns were genuinely, enthusiastically patriotic, and their hatred for Germans and Germany was unfeigned (see Rosenberg, 1974: 20-24; Wolters, 1969: 148-53; Diakin, 1967: 45-50). Equally sincere was their hatred for the central government's regulatory agencies and their delight at seeing "bureaucrats" upset. Momentarily, at least, the army's disorderly grabbing brought together in a single, patriotic, antigovernment enterprise the conservative landholders of the zemstvo assemblies and the "liberal" professionals who dominated their administrations.

[12]As the "bourgeois" authority V. I. Grinevetskii put it, private business organized itself to meet the army's needs before the ministries realized they had to act fast (1922: 16). The same phenomenon occurred in other countries, both belligerent and neutral. Private enterprise has always been swifter to comprehend the possibilities of war than "rigid" bureaucrats (see Redlich, 1929: 122-29; Feldman, 1966: 47-48, 157-63).

Ministrial bureaucracy took a very different view of the army's mobilization. The army-zemstvo-town combination of 1914-15 adopted line-over-staff methods not only because army officers wanted to shuffle off the constraints of staff but also, and principally, because sizable elements of the civil government's staff in the locales found these methods to their taste. Thus, as local institutions and administrative agencies reponded to the army's raids with enthusiasm, ministers found their organizations eroding away and along with them the basic principles on which ministerial government had been striving to operate ever since its founding in 1802. In 1903-5 the government offices in St. Petersburg had committed themselves to a massive and painful effort to subordinate government and society to law, and by 1914 it had gone too far to be able to switch all its gears overnight, no matter how "necessary" it might be. The army's depredations struck the ministers as a radical, irresponsible renunciation of everything they stood for. The generals seemed to be talking and acting like revolutionaries. They were posing as leaders of the "people in arms," said Ivan Goremykin, chairman of the Council of Ministers (Cherniavsky, 1967: 205). They were strengthening their own popularity by allowing the press to attack the civil administration (pp. 223-25). In June 1915 the general staff went so far as to promise free land to winners of combat medals, demonstrating thereby a dismaying inclination to usurp legality and government authority, not to mention the rights of landholders. Their action let loose rumors throughout the countryside that *all* soldiers would get land at the the end of the war. The ministers were horrified (pp. 22-26). At the end of the summer of 1915 they were telling Nicholas in no uncertain terms that if he wanted to go on letting the army run free, he should find new ministers.[13]

The Russian army's manner of supporting itself during the first year of war was unique among the great powers. In France the army acquired the legal power to do the same sort of thing, but officers never used it to disrupt the national economy, mainly because there was no time when even the most frenzied French general saw any need to do so. The French economy could mobilize itself; therefore the army found it expedient to depend on civilian organizations (Renouvin, 1927: 28-33). In Germany the war sparked major reorganizations in industry, but private enterprise and civil administration did their own mobilizing. Military units did not feel compelled to make random attacks on the economy in order to sustain themselves (Feldman, 1966: 41-5, 101-4). Only in late 1916 did planned reorganization begin to break down in Germany, bring-

---

[13]Rumors about a general distribution of land among war veterans really did circulate widely in the villages in 1915. So said a report from the governor of Riazan to the tsar dated 29 July 1915 (Anfimov, 1965: 117; see also pp. 70 and 219).

ing on the sort of sporadic and haphazard mustering of resources with which the Russian army had commenced the war (pp. 149-54, 253-66; see also Mendelssohn-Bartholdy, 1937: 76-84, 106-13).

As for the Austrian government's wartime mobilization, it was quite as arbitrary as the Russian from a legal point of view. The Austrian army disregarded private rights at least as freely as its Russian counterpart (Redlich, 1929: 82-84, 96-97), and in the realm of politics Francis Joseph's regime was even more arbitrary than that of Nicholas II. The Austrian parliament, unlike the Russian, was not called into session when the war began or, indeed, at any time during the first two years of war (pp. 77, 138-40). When it came to civil administration, however, the Austrian army behaved in far more orderly fashion than the Russian. From the beginning the generals showed themselves quite willing to abide by the civil bureaucracy's system. The military did not shove civil administration aside but instead utilized it as an instrument (pp. 95-100), 110-29). As Josef Redlich says, "The actual instruments of the regime were the civil servants in the ministries concerned, with their subordinate provincial, district, and local authorities, supplemented by officials from other departments and by business men, experts, engineers, chemists, technicians, industrialists, and merchants of all sorts, called in to render war service. The real organizers, however, were technicians, business men, and industrialists, nominally called up as reserve or militia officers" (p. 128). Austrian civil administration did not show signs of losing its coherence—i.e., breaking down into separate territorial units—until 1917 (p. 171).

Among all the major warring armies of Europe, only the Russians *began* their work by raiding their own government and population indiscriminantly. Only Russia began its fight under a line-over-staff organization. Those who consider "revolution" to be a meaningful term might say that the Russian officer corps initiated the Russian Revolution. To use my terms, the tsarist government was the only European regime to destroy itself for the sake of military mobilization in World War I.[14]

The Great Retreat and Its Impact on Civil Government

Most accounts of Russian's wartime food supply organization describe a partial restoration of order in the national economy after the first months of war. New civil institutions began to coordinate with each other to regulate production and distribution systematically, and the

---

[14]The Ottoman Empire mobilized in much the same way as Russia and suffered much the same result, though its "revolutionaries" employed different ideological labels (Emin, 1930: 107-9, 153-54).

army gradually learned to cease its raiding. Staff reasserted a measure of influence over line.

This scenario suffers from a number of defects. Staff did not actually begin to assert itself in Russia's military mobilization until the fall of 1915, a full year after the war began. By this time, the tsarist government had departed so far from its normal routines that it was unable to restore the pre-1914 legal-administrative structure of ministerial government. The special conferences could only preside over local offices, not manage them; thus the assertion of staff over line was at best a very limited affair. Russian government administration was not to recover from the "revolution" of 1914-15 until 1921.

I shall argue in the next few pages that the basic reason for the extraordinarily long endurance of line-over-staff organization in Russia during World War I and the ensuing civil war is to be found in a non-event of the year 1915: the great retreat. It will be recalled that the Russian army spent the spring and summer withdrawing hastily from Congress Poland and much of western Russia. In August it appeared that nothing could stop the Germans from advancing as far as they liked (n. 6), and the Russian army command was preparing itself for a massive, earth-scorching evacuation. The plan was to devastate the land and uproot the population all the way eastward to a line extending north and south through Tula and Tver (Cherniavsky, 1967: 120-23, 228-30). Great cities had to be stripped of their industrial equipment; tens of millions of people were to be left to the mercies of the enemy without adequate food or fuel, or else driven eastward to starve and freeze under native supervision.

As it happened, the plan never had to be put into effect. The great retreat never took place. Unlike Napoleon's great horde of 1812, the German army of 1915 stopped its advance well short of Smolensk and did not venture further. Non-events, however, can be fully as important as events. It was primarily the prospect of the great retreat that caused Nicholas II to prolong the use of line-over-staff methods of military procurement and to render his ministers permanently helpless by assuming command of the army.

Nicholas had been undermining the ministries' control over their organizations ever since the war began. The specialists of the zemstvo and town organizations fancied that it was they who had pushed the bureaucrats aside. As they saw it in the summer of 1915, their heroic efforts were sustaining the armed forces while the senile clerks of Petrograd only stumbled about and got in the way. They believed the central government was unable to direct its agencies effectively because it was "autocratic," whereas the hirelings of zemstvoes and towns were working well because they were somehow "democratic." Democracy was triumphing because of its intrinsic merits; autocracy was caving in because of its intrinsic defects. But, in fact, democracy had nothing to do with the demise of the Petrograd staff. It was Tsar Nicholas II, not his people, who ensured that his army would be able to deal directly with local organization. In 1914 the autocrat was the only surviving nonbureaucratic element in the government, and it was he, Nicholas, not the specialists, who brought on the "revolution" of 1914-15 by throwing his full support to the generals.

Nicholas did not undermine his civil administration in 1914-15 because he wanted to. He had labored since the beginning of his reign to strengthen government bureaucracy, and though he loathed it more passionately and consistently than any mouth-revolutionary in Russia, he believed it was necessary for his country. As war began, however, he observed that the regular machinery of government was incapable of meeting the army's needs. This was the reason he let the generals act on their own.

But Nicholas did not merely set the generals loose at the beginning of the war. He continued to let them operate beyond the restraints of Petrograd's staff for a year or more. Line-over-staff organization continued to flourish in the business of military supply at least until the end of 1915. Even the relatively manageable area of munitions supply retained its spontaneous quality as late as November, when purchasing agents from the unions of zemstvoes and towns were still simply listing orders for munitions without attempting to coordinate transportation or allocate raw materials or labor. There was no talk of policy or plan. Local offices of the unions simply made separate contracts with each factory and workshop for each order. The factory received a certain price; the office got its shells by a certain date. Judging from the records of the unions' local managing committees, no other matters were discussed at their meetings.[15] Only on 6 July 1916 did the "chief committee for army supply of the unions of zemstvoes and towns" *propose* to the minister of war that war industries be coordinated and scheduled (TsGIAL, f. 1090, op. 1, d. 19).

By the summer of 1915 unrestrained mobilizing had produced a growing demand for systematization. The specialists who ran the unions of zemstvoes and towns were clamoring for a centralized, all-Russian staff—meaning, of course, a staff dominated by specialists. The question was: were the new institutions and relationships in the locales now capable of supplying the army through an empire-wide systematic organization? Could the specialists of the zemstvo-towns take over the ministries in Petrograd and use them effectively to manage Russia's resources? In August 1915 there was only one man outside the army who answered this

[15]See, for example, the journal of the Petrograd oblast committee for a meeting on 26 Nov. 1915 (TsGIAL, f. 1090, op. 1, d. 19—the materials in this *delo* are not paged; this is the second journal in it).

question in the negative: Nicholas II. Instead of presiding over his new government of special conferences, the incorrigible autocrat-revolutionary assumed command of his army and went to supreme headquarters in Mogilev to join his troops. System might or might not prevail under the special conferences; in either case it would not be centralized under Petrograd ministers. From now on the tsar would govern Russia through his generals.

I do not pretend to know all the ideas Nicholas had in his mind in the fall of 1915. He was a man accustomed to being misunderstood, so he was not in the habit of articulating his thoughts to anyone, his busy-body wife included. Perhaps it is true, as most of his contemporaries believed, that he had no serious idea in this head and simply blundered from one random deed to another. One can say, however, that his actions in August-September 1915 conformed closely to those of a military leader who sensed that his army was about to retreat across Russia. His generals were telling him that they would have no chance of keeping their regiments together unless the most drastic measures were taken. Officers constrained by regulations could not handle the unprecedented upheavals their great retreat would provoke. They could not wait for preliminary investigations and sober considerations. No staff would be able to direct the army as it struggled to dismember more than half of European Russia's economy. The very existence of a staff-over-line organization, with its inevitable studies, reports, and analyses, would only render the government's difficulties more obvious and erode what little confidence men still had in it. So the generals said.

Nicholas agreed. If the German offensive continued, he would have to make an extremely unpleasant choice: either resist by retreating far into Russia and scorching the earth, as his generals advised, or withdraw from the war on Germany's terms.

If Nicholas did contemplate this choice, he was quite alone. Both ministers and zemstvo-town specialists evaded the issue. The ministers had already disapproved very strongly of the army's relatively mild scorching in Congress Poland. In September 1915 they were vigorously denying that any further scorching would be necessary (Cherniavsky, 1967, 120-23, 228-30). Generally speaking, they recognized the drastic consequences of a retreat but refused to believe that it might be necessary. The leaders of the zemstvo-town organizations did exactly the opposite. They were convinced that the devastation already wrought in Poland had been a spontaneous act of cooperation between population and army, and they chose to regard the refugees as noble volunteers in Russia's cause, inspiring examples whom the inhabitants of western Russia should be encouraged to emulate. As of September 1915 these administrator-specialists were enthusiastically planning the evacuation of large numbers of refugees to new emergency centers far behind the front (Polner, 1930: 160-61; *Sobranie,* 1916: 6). Surely this vision did not lack grandeur, but the zemstvo-town specialists never showed any signs of grasping the extreme implications of a scorched earth extending through western and central Russia. They sincerely intended to do their best for all involved, but the best they could have done was far from adequate to meet the challenge they were affecting to face. Actually, they were not facing it. In early September an assembly of the zemstvo union's gubernia directors conducted a spirited discussion of the efforts they were going to make on behalf of refugees and retreating soldiers. The only topic was *how* resources were to be utilized (*Sobranie,* 1916: 19-21, 38-51, 70-72). Only one participant asked *whether* the available resources could possibly meet the needs of an actual evacuation. One I. P. Pozdniakov remarked that massive evacuation and devastation in western Russia would be a calamity that no one could plan and from which the nation would not recover. He stood alone. The other speakers ignored his unique and doubtless irritating eruption (pp. 217-18). When Pozdniakov insisted on repeating his point, chairman Lvov flatly told him he was out of order (pp. 227-28). From then on the assembly heard no more from Pozdniakov.

This is not the place to judge the wisdom or foolishness of scorched-earth retreating. For my purposes, the tsar's policies are only part of the scenery, not the main action, and I need only make the point that his fatal decision to assume direct command of the army served the specialists' cause. In September 1915, when Nicholas moved to army headquarters in Mogilev, he left his ministers virtually without authority and, in effect, turned the whole problem of economic management over to the specialist-dominated institutions that had arisen during the previous year.

Obviously the tsar was not leaving administration in the hands of specialists because he believed in their superior abilities. He never did let them get their hands on the ministries. As the experience of 1917 was to show, specialists were incapable of *imposing* anything on their constituents or their subordinate organizations, least of all devastation (see below, sec. D). If Nicholas had made them ministers and the German offensive had continued, they would have come into conflict with the army. Confronted with the reality that underlay their persistently empty oratory, they would have striven to prevent the general staff from carrying out its "evacuation." Any civil administration in Russia in 1915 would have gone on assuring itself that rhetoric would stop the German tide without anyone having to make unpleasant decisions. If Nicholas wanted to make such decisions, he would have to do it himself; or so it seemed. He went to the army to put moral support and the symbols of authority where they were needed to fight the war (and, if necessary, destroy the country). What he wanted, it seems, was simply to sustain his generals' line-over-

staff authority, and therefore it would not do to have anyone in control
of the ministries, not even the war-loving, ready-for-anything specialists.

I cannot refrain from making a suggestion—admittedly tentative—
regarding the importance of food supply in the tsar's and generals' thinking. First, an obvious fact: Russian political leaders remained convinced
throughout the war that Germany was on the verge of collapse as a result
of her critical food shortage. Scholarly works replete with statistics and
logic were already proving in 1914 that Germany was on the verge of
famine and collapse. One of many such works, by a recognized expert in
commerce and economics, was M. V. Kechedzhi-Shapovalov's *Voina i
khoziaistvo Germanii* (War and the German Economy), which came out
before the end of 1914. In 1917 the flow of print about starving Germany
was still coming. It will not do to dismiss this effort at victory through
statistical analysis just because it proved to be erroneous. If economic
calculations have any value at all, Germany should indeed have collapsed. Her ability to live with a critical shortage of raw materials until
late 1918 was an astounding, unprecedented achievement in mobilization,
and no one, including the Germans themselves, could have predicted it.
It was precisely the unexpectedness of Germany's survival that caused
would-be planners the world over to take her as a model for centralized
economic organization. Certainly the Russians did. The journal of the
MZ's special conference repeatedly, explicitly, and publicly recommended
that Russian food administrators seek to emulate their German counterparts (see, e.g., *Izvestiia osobogo*, 1 Sept. 1916: p. 105-7), and it accompanied its recommendations with detailed studies of the German food
supply organization (see, e.g., 1 Apr. 1916: 93-116; 15 Oct. 1916: 99-112;
also *Svedeniia*, 1 Jan. 1916: 62-74; *Izvestiia po prodovolstvennomu*, May
1917: 135-41).

Despite Germany's long-lasting success, however, Russian statesmen
and generals certainly had good reason to go on believing that food shortage would bring her down. A secret report of 1917, written by one V.
Gefding under the close and sympathetic supervision of Petr Struve,
pointed out the bases for this belief. Germany had somehow continued
to feed herself in 1915, but as 1916 dawned one could still hope that
Italy's entry into the war, sealing off the flow of imports from the south,
would bring her down (TsGIAL, f. 1090, op. 1, d. 180, Struve, 3). Then,
when Italy failed to produce the desired famine, new causes for cheer
emerged. In 1916 the German potato crop failed and Rumania joined the
allies, bringing with her a substantial quantity of grain theretofore available to Germany (d. 180, Gefding, 4, 36). True, the Germans occupied
Rumania shortly after she entered the war, but this would still not provide enough grain to fill German stomachs in 1917. So Struve and Gefding
believed, and because many highly placed economists had shared their

belief throughout the war, Russia's leaders did have some grounds for considering it imperative to keep grain out of German hands. No sacrifice was too great if it would keep the German army out of Russia's food-producing gubernias. Failing this, the German generals had to be convinced that an attack to the east would gain them only burned fields and a starving population. Presumably this would make them less likely to make the effort. But if they did make the effort, it would be necessary to carry out the threat and actually scorch the earth.

It may have been incorrect for the tsar and the zemstvo-town liberals to think in these terms. It may have been evil. But it was not stupid.

As said before, however, the tsar's move to Mogilev proved unnecessary. The German offensive did not continue, and the Russian army got a breathing space during which a quasi-systematic organization of the national economy actually began to operate. It worked rather well on the whole. It may be that the tsar's peculiar situation in supreme headquarters and the concomitant helplessness of his ministers was a significant impediment to good management, for it is a fact that the government of special conferences ultimately failed to make the Russian economy supply the army and cities with the necessities of life. On the other hand, the arrangement had some advantages. The largely specialist members of the special conferences could at least compile information and suggest guidelines to their ostensibly subordinate agencies. To be sure, the central offices of civil administration never acquired sufficient authority to enforce commands in any systematic way, but the ministers were still of use. Since their helplessness was not a matter of public knowledge, they could be blamed for all failures, defeats, and disappointed expectations. Periodically, individual ministers could be dismissed and replaced in ritualistic fashion, thus sustaining a general belief that the government really could organize the national economy if and when the proper leaders were discovered.[16] This arrangement held together as long as the economy continued to run on its own. In late 1916, however, the transportation network proved unable to carry enough supplies, and shortly thereafter, in February 1917, authority collapsed in Petrograd. Under the circumstances, it no longer sufficed to blame ministers. A higher form of scapegoat had to be sacrificed. This Nicholas was able to provide.

It is customary to speak of Nicholas's "failure" in 1914-17 and to find fault with everything he did. To accept this interpretation, however, one must assume that it was actually possible to organize the Russian economy by bureaucratic methods. If we were to drop this assumption, we would contemplate the possibility that Nicholas simply performed his

[16]Eroshkin (1960: 310) has made a diagram showing the rapid succession of ministers during the period Sept. 1915-Feb. 1917.

proper function: to take the blame for what his government did. It is even conceivable that he was much more keenly aware of what was going on than the specialists, most of whom never ceased complaining of him the whole time he was putting Russia in their charge.

But if Nicholas's actions in 1915-17 were congenial to the zemstvoes and towns, they benefited the army most of all. The generals lost most of their battles and threw the Russian economy into irredeemable confusion, yet they were able from the very beginning to deflect all public criticism to the civil administration. This was an intellectually shoddy *coup de paroles,* but it was quite understandable and even statesmanlike. It was not statesmanlike, however, for the generals to believe their own propaganda. By 1917 they had forgotten that their success had been entirely due to the tsar's support, and in March they found it remarkably easy to recommend to Nicholas that he step aside and let the city of Petrograd undertake to manage the Russian economy. They gave no indication that they knew they were throwing away their only protection.

The preceding sections have described some of the difficulties imposed by circumstances upon those who involved themselves in the collection and distribution of food in Russia during World War I. Chiefly, they were the army's persistent use of line-over-staff methods in its procurement, the tsar's deliberate emasculation of the central offices of civil administration, and the spread of famine hysteria. Historically, these difficulties emerged from the extreme haste with which the army mobilized at the war's outset and the widespread belief in 1915 that the Germans would drive much further into Russia than they did.

In the late summer of 1915, when the MZ took charge of Russia's food supply in toto, its *agronom-organizatory* and village cooperatives had suddenly to confront these difficulties. Famine hysteria, disorderly military procurement, and the beheading of ministerial bureaucracy marked the disintegration of systematic organization in Russia, but they also gave rise to the specialists' frenzied efforts to organize Russian society more tightly than ever before. From 1915 until the collapse of the tsarist regime the specialists would legitimize their rapidly evolving organization on the basis of the army's needs, and the army in turn would find its legitimacy in the tsar's personal authority. Such were the relationships under which the special conferences would do their work. In particular, the Special Conference on Food Supply would have to arrange things so that food producers (and/or hoarders) would distribute their possessions to food consumers. Note that I refer to difficulties, not problems. The reason is that they were not susceptible to anything like a solution. They were to be lived with, not overcome, by any person or persons who undertook to collect grain in Russia after 1914.

D. THE MZ VENTURES TO SUPPLY THE NATION, AUGUST 1915–OCTOBER 1917

Tsarist Food Administration

When the MZ became chairman of the Special Conference of Food Supply, he set up a new batch of local plenipotentiary agents called, appropriately, commissioners of the chairman of the Special Conference on Food Supply. Sixty-one of them were assigned to gubernia-size territories, while eight others took charge of large cities. On paper, the new commissioners of the special conference were separate from the military purchasing commissioners who had been working for the MZ since 1914. They were explicitly ordered *not* to concern themselves with supplying the army. In fact, however, many of them were the same old purchasing commissioners with an additional title. In almost all cases both titles were assigned to officials already in position: governors or chairmen of zemstvo directorates (Zaitsev, 1930: 14; TsGIAL, f. 456, op. 1, d. 137, l. 4). Be this as it may, the new offices did embody distinctly new duties. The instruction of 25 October 1915 ordered them to consider the whole problem of food distribution throughout the empire and develop ways to cope with it (*Obzor, 1916: prilozheniia,* 212-15). To do this, they were supposed to form conferences of political leaders and officials in their respective gubernias (or cities).

Like the chairman of the special conference in Petrograd, gubernia commissioners did not have to act as their conferences of political leaders suggested. A commissioner had only to consult with his conference, and then he could do as he wished. He did not have to form any conferences below the gubernia level, and the law only prescribed part of the membership in his own gubernia conference. He could bring in additional members at his pleasure (Zaitsev, 1930: 11-14; *Obzor,* 1916: 214). On paper, the new commissioner's powers were much broader than those of earlier plenipotentiaries. He could "require" the cooperation of all authorities, military and civil, and all local institutions. He could commandeer storage facilities, and he could collect food "by any means and on any condition." Finally, he could regulate trade and dictate prices in the markets in his territory as he saw fit (*Obzor,* 1916: *prilozheniia,* 5-16; Zaitsev, 1930: 11-12, 41-44).

Practically speaking, the new commissioners' powers were nebulous at best. Their functions and prerogatives were never defined in relation to those of the military purchasing commissioners and the MVD's governors, who also possessed the paper power to order almost anyone to do almost anything. Nor were the MZ's all-powerful agents ever told specifically what relationship they would have, if any, with the commanders of military districts, each of whom ruled over several gubernias and exercised powers—on paper—quite as despotic as those the old governors-general had enjoyed. Nor was it clear how MZ agents, governors, and military district commanders related to the coordinators of rail transport, who worked for the ministry of communications and were also all-powerful on paper. Each locale had to work out its own ground rules to keep the growing population of plenipotentiaries in order, but these rules must have lost much of whatever stability they had in the face of occasional raids by temporary plenipotentiaries, such as the all-powerful food collectors sent out by the MZ in December 1916 (see below).

One wonders what effects this plethora of agents actually produced on administration in the countryside. My impression is that they were no more than spoons, stuck into a very murky soup in the absurd hope that their stirring would make the soup crystalize into a structure. The only result Petrograd could see was that the spoons either dissolved or splashed. They either did nothing or they fought each other. In practice, individual plenipotentiaries must have done a great deal to keep the economy in motion, but Petrograd had no systematic way of knowing this.

The general confusion and conflict between army commanders and civil authorities were doubtless reduced by the tsar's decree of 23 November 1915, which explicitly confined the army's power in civil matters to the front-line gubernias (Zaitsev, 1930: 15-16). The government also strove for unity by setting up interconference conferences to take care of matters that concerned the agencies of more than one conference (*Obzor,* 1916: 20-23). All this, however, had more symbolic significance than practical utility. The regime of special conferences never became much more than a continuing attempt to *look* like an administrative organization. The men at the top spoke constantly of unified plans and codifications. Typically, Georgii Lvov proclaimed in 1915 that "all Russia must be welded into one military organization" (quoted in Zagorsky, 1928: 84). Commissions and subcommissions endlessly gathered information and formulated projects, while the halls of government resounded with speeches about the shameful lack of regularity in existing arrangements.[17] Meanwhile, out in the provinces, plenipotentiaries went on reacting to events as they took place—no small accomplishment after all—and did what they could to keep the pieces left over from the old administration from colliding with the rapidly expanding zemstvo-town-cooperative organizations. The Special Conference on Food Supply managed to keep in touch with its agencies but only by pushing off the discussion of general plans into separate commissions while devoting its own meetings almost entirely to the consideration of specific reports and requests from the locales.

[17]E.g., *Obzor* (1916: *dopolnenie,* 3); *Izvestiia osobogo* (15 Mar. 1916: 5-12); *Sobranie* (1916: 14-15, 73, 81-90).

As we have seen (sec. C), much of the conference's early work consisted of handing out loans to towns and zemstvoes: sometimes at their own request, sometimes at the request of the chairman's own plenipotentiaries. In the first months of 1916 it began distributing grain directly out of reserves accumulated by the purchasing commissioners for the armed forces, and this management by generosity became for a while the prevailing modus vivendi in food supply. Generosity had its bad features, but it did give the conference a lever of sorts: much the same kind of lever as the MZ had used for the development of agricultural improvement prior to the war. As noted in Chapter 8 (sec. D), a benefactor cannot manipulate his beneficiaries with precision, but at least his presence becomes a fact in their lives. Moreover, the MZ's handouts seem to have reduced famine hysteria from its 1915 level. Ultimately it helped to produce ungovernable inflation, but in the short run, until late 1916, it did inspire enough confidence among its uncontrollable local agencies to call forth relatively accurate information about food prices and reserves.

At the same time it was handing out loans, the conference began attempting to regulate markets. Lacking an apparatus for active management, it played a passive role at first. On rare occasions it ventured to reject a local regulation or resolve a dispute, but on the whole it did little more than record reports from its commissioners and from local institutions as to the regulations they were imposing on markets and transport facilities in each area (see, e.g., *Izvestiia osobogo,* 15 Mar. 1916: 12-16). The locales made their own policies, and the center confined itself to keeping track of them.

In early 1916 local agencies were taking the view that inflation and price fluctuation were the greatest threats to proper food distribution. Their most common policy was to impose price ceilings on scarce items. But local ceilings called forth additional problems, mainly because they varied from one place to another (*Obzor,* 1916: 74-75). With different price regulations in each town, grain and other "necessities" tended to flow toward markets with the highest ceilings (or no ceilings), thereby forcing other towns either to raise their own ceilings or suffer scarcity. To make matters worse, ceilings were imposed on different food products in each area. Straw and hay, for example, were only regulated in some areas (pp. 80-81), as were fish and sugar (pp. 104-19). Some uezds and gubernias handled the problem of competing marketplaces by forbidding the "export" of goods outside their boundaries—as many army commanders had done in 1914-15—but since the ultimate result of trade barriers would have been to isolate each region and destroy the Russia-wide market entirely, there arose a general demand for effective *central* regulation of prices. It was ostensibly central government agents who had been doing the "local" regulating; therefore the special conference found itself becoming increasingly committed by its "own" agents to the establishment of a uniform price schedule for all Russia. It was expected to exercise power, but only through organs accustomed to making policy for themselves.

The conference responded by enacting the rules of 12 February 1916. These were modest enough. They did not venture to set up a uniform grain price scale for the whole empire but only imposed a standard *procedure* for local agencies to follow when they set ceilings in their respective locales. The rules did not attempt to regulate all grain transport but only applied to railroads (Zaitsev, 1930: 51-52; Struve, 1930: xvii).

Modest rules corresponded to the administration's actual capability, but they were inappropriate to the situation they were designed to correct. In July 1916 the conference took a more drastic step. It commenced a study of the costs of food transport, and in September it used the results as a basis for establishing a unified Russia-wide price schedule. Alas for careful calculation, the Special Conference of Defense objected to the conference's proposed prices. Spokesmen for military (and urban) interests believed that food supply's specialists were helping farmers to cheat soldiers and workers. Defense had supreme authority, so lower price ceilings went into effect in the fall of 1916.[18] Subsequently grain began disappearing from the market (Struve, 1930: xvii-xviii). The MZ's conference came to believe that a food crisis was imminent, and in November 1916 it formally proclaimed one.

At this point the conference began to act more aggressively but at the same time more disjointedly. In October the MZ and his fellow conferees were coming to realize that farmers would not voluntarily bring grain to markets unless prices were raised. The grain-consuming population would either have to pay higher prices or starve. Certainly this realization did not fit well with the idea of broadening the farmers' role in grain collection, but the conference bravely ventured into one last experiment with representative institutions. A decree went out on 10 October ordering that subconferences be formally established in uezds and volosts to work under the commissioners' gubernia conferences. These new bodies resembled the old land settlement commissions in that they combined agents from the various ministries with elected men. The volost body bore a vague resemblance to the volost zemstvoes so dear to Kakhanov in 1884 and Witte's committees in 1903; that is, it was set up to be dominated by the gentry. Indeed, A. A. Bobrinskii, MZ at the time, went out of his way to pack local subcommittees with gentry farmers wherever they were available (pp. 19-22). The new local bodies were to have power

[18]The "unified" firm prices were set forth in a series of enactments that came out during September and October. They were assembled in *Izvestiia osobogo* (Nov. 1916: 13-27).

of their own, independent from their hitherto plenipotentiary commissioners. By the same token, the commissioners lost their independence.
They could no longer act without first getting their conferences' approval. If a majority of a conference disapproved of a commissioner's proposal, the matter had to go to the chairman of the special conference in
Petrograd (i.e., the MZ) to be resolved (pp. 18-21). This was still less
than autonomy, to be sure, but the food supply organization certainly
took on a more representative appearance. Doubtless such arrangements
already existed de facto in many gubernias (see *Izvestiia osobogo,* 1 Sept.
1916: 80-91), but before October it had been left up to individual
commissioners to decide whom they would consult and when. Now they
were told.

But the idea of giving power to local conferences did not get far. In
fact, the new local bodies were never set up. Having decided in November
that there was a bread crisis, the conference authorized the new MZ—
none other than Rittikh, ex-manager of land settlement—to take emergency measures, and these were issued forthwith in the law of 29
November (*Sobranie uzakonenii,* 1916: no. 338, art. 2696, pp. 3716-18).
This fresh product of the capital-city imagination empowered the conference to impose quotas for grain delivery on each gubernia and ordered
gubernia zemstvo directorates (no conferences or assemblies were mentioned) to impose quotas on the uezds. Uezd zemstvo directorates were
to impose quotas on their volosts and villages. Ultimately each village
and estate was to be required to sell a certain amount of grain to the
government at a price no higher than the maximum established in October. On 7 December Rittikh published a new order (TsGIAL, f. 456, op.
1, d. 110, l. 64) dispatching new plenipotentiaries to the gubernias and
uezds to supervise the new collection, and all officials were ordered to
cooperate with them. In particular, all permanent members of land settlement commissions and surveyors were ordered to devote their full
attention to grain collecting under the new agents' authority.

There was very little trace of local autonomy in Rittikh's initial legislation. Quotas and deadlines were imposed from the center, and the only
decision left to local agents was how to apportion the burden. If an area
failed to bring in its share, said the 29 November law, the army would go
out and get it (Zaitsev, 1930: 22). Anfimov (1962: 301) refers to this law
as the beginning of forced grain procurement in Russia.

In the event, Rittikh's collection did not demand much. According
to his initial decree, 16.1 million tons of grain were to be collected by 6
January 1917 (TsGIAL, f. 456, op. 1, d. 110, l. 79). Allegedly the special
conference arrived at this figure by using zemstvo estimates of harvests
for 1916 and figures for average, per capita grain consumption in each
area for the years 1909-13. Consumption figures for each gubernia were
subtracted from harvests, and the resulting figure, if positive, provided a

basis for calculating the gubernia's contribution to the collection (ll. 72-74).

Responses from gubernia zemstvoes were almost entirely devoted to protests.[19] None questioned the calculations the MZ had used to arrive at the quotas, but they all found reasons not to meet them. Many—e.g., Tavrid—complained that their grain had already been sold and carried off to other gubernias (d. 137, l. 57); some—e.g., Ufa—reported that their peasants had refrained from threshing their grain, thus making collection difficult and time-consuming (l. 86); and one gubernia—Kherson—claimed that widespread rural disorders made collection impossible (d. 134, l. 20). Not satisfied with mere protesting, most gubernia directorates reduced their quotas when they apportioned them to their subordinate uezds. Uezd zemstvo directorates followed suit, demanding yet less from their volosts. The orders that actually came to the peasant volosts and landed estates asked the recipients to sell only 63% as much grain to the commissioners as the central government had demanded initially, and the volosts cut the amount even further, as did the villages (*Izvestiia po prodovolstvennomu,* May 1917: 10-11).[20]

Rittikh sent out many harsh answers to the flood of protests. Typically, he sent a telegram to his commissioner in Tavrid gubernia ordering him to use force if necessary to make his quota (TsGIAL, f. 456, d. 137, l. 32). In practice, however, he was extremely tolerant. He extended the time allowed for collection twice, and the second extension allowed the gubernias until the end of June 1917 to get their grain in (d. 111, ll. 44-47). He also set up a variety of incentives for prompt delivery, allowing, in effect, higher prices than the legal maximums.

Rittikh's attempted reversion to crude Muscovite tribute-collecting methods was understandable, given the growing desperation in Petrograd. His de facto softness was equally understandable, given his dependence on local institutions dominated by freewheeling specialist-benefactors. Zemstvo organizations and cooperatives in food-producing gubernias were all but refusing point-blank to provide grain for food consumers. Note, in this regard, that Rittikh felt compelled to publish and republish a guarantee that his collection was to benefit *only* the army. Ninety percent was for soldiers, he said, and only 10% for workers in vital war industries, and he repeatedly urged his governors to convey this message to peasants (see, e.g., *Izvestiia osobogo,* Jan. 1917: 17). He must have been

[19]E.g., Kostroma (TsGIAL, f. 456, op. 1, d. 121, l. 10), Bessarabia (d. 113, l. 19), Simbirsk (d. 129, ll. 11-14), Stavropol (d. 130, ll. 3-4).

[20]Village assessments were estimated to have been less than 60% of the amounts assessed by the uezds. Rittikh's office gave a much cheerier picture of gubernia and uezd apportionments (TsGIAL, f. 456, op. 1, d. 111, l. 116), but the above report, which came from the Provisional Government's MZ, is probably closer to the truth.

convinced that people in the countryside did not want to contribute to civilian welfare outside their own immediate areas, for in fact he was lying grandiosely. According to the central statistical committee's figures, the army per se only consumed 9 million tons of grain annually (*Izvestiia po prodovolstvennomu,* Sep.-Oct. 1917: 12-18), and this amount is considerably less than 90% of 16.1 million. Moreover, the MZ's original (unpublished) explanation of its assessment stated that over a third of the collection would be used to cover civilian needs (TsGIAL, f. 456, op. 1, d. 110, l. 79). Apparently Rittikh discovered sometime in early December 1916 that his tribute collection was setting off a civil war between grain producers and the rest of the population, and he decided to go softly.

Being understandable, however, did not make Rittikh's new methods effective. How much he actually collected will never be known, but the results could not have been heartening. By the end of February 1917 grain reserves in the cities were rapidly aproaching exhaustion (Volobuev, 1962: 391). The army and cities were not starving, but they were very much afraid of starving. This was the status of the imperial food supply when the tsar fell.[21]

The Provisional Government's Food Administration

In late February 1917 the troops in and around Petrograd mutinied against their officers and joined the crowds of striking workers and frustrated food shoppers in the streets. Popular disorder in the city swelled to unmanageable proportions. The front-line generals reacted by cutting their ties with the old ministers and entering into more or less regular communications with the leaders of the major political parties in the Duma, who had persuaded themselves that they constituted the only possible basis for restoring order. Petrograd was a major supply center for a considerable portion of the army; therefore the generals were quite willing to have anyone take over there who could keep trains running. Armed with the generals' support, some Duma leaders formed a ministry and "ordered" the crowd to arrest the incumbent ministers. Meanwhile, the tsar thoughtfully agreed to abdicate. Thus began the Provisional Government (Hasegawa, 1969: 19-20, 291-400; Feldman, 1967: 5-67).

In order to dress their rule with some shred of legitimacy, the new ministers affected to represent the populus. The Petrograd crowd had

---

[21] A number of authors have offered estimates of the amount of grain Rittikh actually collected (e.g., Gordeev, 1925: 83), but they have all been derived from paper quotas, not from records of actual collections. No one has studied Rittikh's campaign seriously, and all judgments of its success or failure remain suspect. A. Shingarev, the Provisional Government's first MZ, made a speech highly critical of his predecessor in May 1917, but he did acknowledge that the flow of grain to the cities speeded up during Dec. 1916-Jan. 1917 (*Sezd,* 1917: 1-2).

thrust forward some leaders of its own, and these formed councils—"soviets"—in the various sectors and institutions of the city, including factories, army regiments, and naval ships. Each soviet sent delegates to a central council—the Petrograd Soviet—which met, over a thousand strong, in the same building where the Duma leaders were engaged in setting up their administration. Presumably the Soviet *was* the people, so it took upon itself the task of watching over the ministers to make sure they lived up to their affectation to be representatives of the common good. An assembly of one thousand was too unwieldy and indeterminate to do anything but acclaim and denounce. In order to hammer out policies and commands that might give expression to its will, the Soviet elected an executive committee, which was made up mostly of leaders from radical parties. This committee remained in permanent session so that the people's will might have continuing expression. It made decisions and issued commands, but it never undertook to administer anything directly. The Duma ministers were happy to have the Petrograd Soviet and its executive committee because the support of these bodies gave them legitimacy. On the other hand, officials of the Provisional Government on all levels had to suffer frequent interference from soviets and from people who affected to act in their name.

The new government's constitutional structure was both national and local. Soviets in the Petrograd area anointed the executive committee of the Petrograd Soviet with authority, and the committee in turn anointed the soviets to be its authorized agents. Similarly, but in this case tacitly, the executive committee of Petrograd blessed the new ministers with authority to manage the government of all Russia, with the proviso that the ministers should not violate the committee's pronouncements regarding what it took to be the popular will.

It would not do, of course, for the Petrograd Soviet to continue very long to speak for all toilers in the empire. In early April, about a month after the February Revolution, a would-be congress of deputies from local soviets all over Russia gathered in Petrograd with the purpose of forming a more truly representative body. Only about 400 delegates showed up. Since they represented only about 80 cities and a few army units, they modestly decided not to call themselves a congress but only a preliminary conference. They confined themselves to forming an all-Russian executive committee that would be empowered to express the will of the masses until a real congress could be assembled. This executive committee, which was to serve as the voice of all toilers in Russia until June, consisted of the executive committee of the Petrograd Soviet plus 16 new members elected by the conference. In other words, a slightly augmented municipal council became in form as well as in fact a national governing body (Gronsky, 1930: 62-71). Rather incongruous by Western standards, but this was probably the only possible arrangement. After all, civil administration in Russia had been effectively decentralized since August 1914, and Petrograd could do no more than cling to the facade it had inherited from the tsarist ministers. For this purpose the Petrograd Soviet was quite adequate.

The resemblance between the soviets' political role in 1917 and that of the zemstvo-town administrations in 1914-17 is striking. Both were able to do as they pleased and talk the most extravagant nonsense for quite a while without suffering the slightest doubt that they were the people incarnate. Both had available to them a government organization whose services they could command and on whom they could blame everything that went wrong or threatened to go wrong. Both made the mistake of joining themselves to the structure they were milking and gradually taking it over; that is, they both came to believe their own rhetoric and charged forward to assume responsibility on their own, thereby exposing their own helplessness. Both were easily swept away. Outside the field of politics there was a considerable difference between the two "movements." The zemstvo-towns engaged in practical work and did much to organize the economy. The soviets did no practical work to speak of, and their gyrations helped to accelerate the destruction of the national economy.

The hasty agreements between Petrograd Soviet and Duma leaders at the time of the February Revolution served as a constitution of sorts. They sprang from the imaginations of politicians and journalists who had had no experience with either mobs or administration, and they were arrived at in ad hoc fashion in the midst of a shouting, well-armed mob. Historians have always studied the men who made these agreements with the question in mind: why did they fail? Or: why did they last only eight months? Consequently *all* our histories of the Provisional Government are discussions of its weaknesses.

They are all beside the point. It was a striking achievement for a clutter of ill-trained, inexperienced pamphleteers and parliamentarians to restore order and set trains in motion not only in Petrograd but throughout the empire. That a series of mutually contradictory pamphlets scribbled out by exhausted men who were always on the verge of hysteria could have sustained a regime for eight months under the circumstances of 1917 constitutes one of the most remarkable accomplishments in the history of Russian government and the history of liberal movements in general. Clearly the government and soviet leaders were men of stature and courage, fully as tough and capable as any tsar or commissar has ever been. Yet they are remembered as fools even by those who affect to espouse their cause. Historians dislike losers.

From an administrator's point of view, the February Revolution represented a temporary resolution of the conflict between bureaucracy and line-over-staff organization. By agreeing to throw the tsar to the crowd, the generals relinquished legitimate authority to the new ministers in Petrograd. The regime of special conferences that had begun its work in August 1915 assumed formal control over government administration, military and civil alike. The initially spontaneous unions of zemstvoes and town completed their pilgrimage to centralized system. In short, line surrendered itself wholly into the hands of Petrograd's moribund staff, now inflated with a new set of ideological pretensions. But centralization came too late to give Petrograd any real chance of imposing its will on Russia. Despite their new paper power, the Provisional Government's ministers were unable to exercise any more control outside the city limits than their predecessors had.

The new ministers made very few changes in their organizations. Only the MVD underwent any significant turnover in personnel or structural change. Land captains and governors were abolished; police were subordinated to zemstvo directorates. As for the other ministries, the top posts changed hands even more rapidly than they had under Nicholas, but they generally kept their organizational structures and personnel intact. In mid-May the MZ still had a deputy minister and a department head left over from the tsarist regime.[22] To be sure, the rhetoric of ministerial leapfrog changed after February. The Provisional Government's ministers—unlike their tsarist predecessors—resigned and were appointed on ideological grounds, and their differences of opinion were aired in public. When they lost their posts, their ideologies departed with them. Ideologies, rather than persons, were the scapegoats of 1917.

In some ways fortune favored the Provisional Government. Thanks primarily to the armies of the British Empire, the Germans had their hands full on the western front throughout most of 1917, and they were little inclined to do anything major in the east (Falls, 1959: 279-81, 306, 310). Even more fortunate was the fact that the government took "power" when spring was not far off. Winter had been one of the chief factors in bringing on the crisis in transport. The onset of warm weather temporarily eased the fuel shortage and simplified the vital processes of repairing and operating trains. When the ice broke up on the rivers and spring floods abated, transport by wagon and waterway once more began to supplement and support the railroads. In February 1917 breakdowns of transport (together with Rittikh's procurement campaign) had caused large amounts of grain to accumulate in railroad depots in the grain-producing areas. These stores, together with the harvest of winter grain, sustained the cities until well into the summer (Volobuev, 1962: 213, 442; see also Browder, 1961: II, 633-34). All this helped to restore at least a

---

[22]*IGU* (12 May 1917). N. Grudistov was the deputy minister, N. Chernavskii the department head. The editor of the MZ's journal continued in office until the end of the Provisional Government.

minimal circulation of goods and supplies, and in the summer of 1917 the cities were eating more or less regularly again. The Provisional Government would have a relatively easy time of it as long as warm weather and German inaction lasted.

In the fall, however, time ran out. Fear of famine had brought out the crowds in February, and when the newly bureaucratized specialists could not come up with grain, the crowds turned on them. Of course, the Provisional Government had never had a chance of success at getting food to the cities and army. It rested very self-consciously on the whole people, an entity that included not only hungry crowds but also food-producing peasants who were profoundly unwilling to sell their produce cheaply for the benefit of food consumers. The Provisional Government and its attached soviets contemplated a population divided into two distinct groups, one of which would starve unless it could prey upon the other. No bureaucracy or any law or institution could represent or govern both at once. The best anyone in Russia could do was either to lead consumers against farmers or organize farmers to defend themselves, and anyone who chose the latter alternative was undertaking, willy-nilly, to destroy Russian civilization, Petrograd first of all. Anyone who aspired to govern Petrograd—and Russia—had to pursue the former course, as Lenin very quickly perceived after his rise to what he believed to be power.

As we have seen, however, specialists were attached to the deliberate, staff-over-line procedures of bureaucracy. They could not have brought themselves to act drastically even if they had been willing to shuck off their superficial pretense at being democratic. Thus the controlled collapse of the spring and summer quickly went out of control. Industrial production fell off. Not only finished products but also raw materials, such as coal, oil, and metals, became ever more difficult to obtain (Volobuev, 1962: 289-92). Such was the shortage of fuel even as early as June that representatives from industry on the Special Conference for National Defense accused the railroads of appropriating some of the fuel they were supposed to be delivering.[23] But the railroads needed more than fuel. During 1917 the number of cars and locomotives in service decreased steadily, even as the number in existence increased, simply because railway managers could not keep them in repair (pp. 206-9; *Ekonomicheskoe,* II, 219). The fuel shortage was real enough in 1917, but the disorganization of transport was the cause of it, not the result. As factories and mines closed down for lack of fuel, materials of all sorts became unavailable, and yet more factories closed down. Urban unemployment rose sharply despite a desperate labor shortage (*Ekonomicheskoe,* II, 294-97). Profits and gross income of private companies fell off drasti-

[23]Journal of the meeting of 10 June (*Ekonomicheskoe,* II, 237-38).

cally throughout the year, although the Provisional Government paid out money for defense at twice the highest rate its tsarist predecessor had reached (pp. 282-83, 308, 337-38).[24] Moreover, the government's unprecedented rate of expenditure helped to cause a sharp increase in the rate of currency inflation. The Provisional Government printed money four times as fast as the tsarist government had, and its inclination to adopt this technique of financing sharpened rapidly during its last months. Between 1 July and 1 September the government covered about 78% of its expenditures with paper and ink (pp. 355-58; see also Michelson, 1928: 378-443).

Dislocation in commerce and industry were severe enough, but they appeared relatively mild compared to the impact of peasant withdrawal from the market. After June 1917 the amount of grain brought in by government agencies from the countryside fell to a lower level than ever before. Worse, the peasants no longer contented themselves with refraining from the sale of grain. Significant numbers of them ceased paying taxes and rents, renounced their debts, and rejected all modern notions of civil rights, especially private property. Peasant soldiers began to abandon the army on a large scale. Most frightening of all, this massive backturning took place in the presence of a relatively large urban society, including an army of about 10 million, that could not survive without grain from the countryside.

The Provisional Government did not give up the struggle for grain without a fight. The new MZ, A. S. Shingarev, closely following in the esentially aimless footsteps of preceding administrations, strove to reorganize his ministry to render it simultaneously more democratic and more dictatorial. One of his first moves was to get his fellow ministers to issue the law of 9 March 1917 (Browder, 1961: II, 615), changing the Special Conference on Food Supply into the State Committee on Food Supply (usually referred to as the State Food Committee). The new committee was more representative and also more powerful—on paper— than the special conference had been. It included 37 members, 10 of them from the soviets, and its role was not merely consultative. Its decisions were binding on the MZ. On 25 March there followed a more elaborate act, establishing the committee's local organs and empowering them to take direct control of all grain, from the time of its planting up to its sale to the consumer. All grain in storage, plus all that was yet to be har-

---

[24]Volobuev only admits that profits fell off after he has engaged in lengthy denunciations against private companies for making high profits (1962: 218-40, 262-78). He suggests, weakly, that the decline in 1917 was not real but only proceeded from fraudulent bookkeeping (pp. 282-83). Such are the exigencies of Soviet scholarship.

vested during the remainder of 1917, became the *property* of the government (*Izvestiia po prodovolstvennomu,* May 1917: *ofitsialnyi otdel,* 4-21). Shortly thereafter, Shingarev perceived that his local organs might have trouble transporting the grain he had just appropriated on paper. On 17 April he issued an order on his own authority, without consulting the State Food Committee, empowering local food supply committees to draft men, carts, and horses whenever they deemed it necessary (pp. 23-24, 55). The law of 11 April went yet further than any of the above. It attempted to deal with the possibility that a farmer might refuse to *grow* grain. If a farmer refused to sow his land, the local food supply committee was to take it over and rent it out to someone who would. Rent would be paid to the original owner according to rates established by the local food supply committee (p. 29). Taken together, these laws reflected the same schizophrenic combination of harshness and leniency as Rittikh's proclamations prior to the February Revolution. For example, the law of 25 March said that anyone refusing to yield his grain would suffer confiscation; yet an additional instruction required confiscators to pay the maximum price for everything they took (pp. 22-23).

On 5 May the government shifted this hastily erected pasticcio of autonomous institutions and drastic prerogatives into a new ministry, called, appropriately, the ministry of food supply. This organization was authorized to concern itself not only with bringing food to cities but also with the distribution of manufactured goods, especially agricultural tools, to farmers (June-July 1917: *ofitsialnyi otdel,* 1-7). Shingarev continued to direct his creation for another month or so until early June, when A. V. Peshekhonov became the first officially designated minister of food supply (Zaitsev, 1930: 23).

On paper, the new food supply apparatus embodied all the agricultural specialists' dreams. It was directed by an assembly of "experts," i.e., the State Food Committee. The minister was no longer a leader in his own right but merely an agent of the committee, which he did not chair and in which he did not vote. He and other government officials participated in the meetings, but no administrator could vote. There were about 30 voting members, drawn from the "temporary" committee of the Duma, soviets, unions of zemstvoes and towns, cooperatives, and a few other institutions involved in the national economy. Local food supply committees were set up in gubernias, uezds, and volosts. Like the central body, their voting membership was made up entirely of elected representatives, and on each level the committee was the decision maker. The elected membership on the gubernia committee came to about 30, drawn from zemstvoes, town dumas, soviets, cooperatives, peasant union, and other, like institutions. Uezd and volost committees were somewhat smaller but similar in makeup. The volost committee was made up mostly of peasants, but it included a considerable number of nonpeasant members, including three landholders elected by the uezd zemstvo assembly.[25]

Obviously the local committees were too large to do business from day to day; hence they were authorized to elect boards from among their members to act as executive bodies. The gubernia committees were designed to be centers of operations. They could overrule uezd and volost levels at will, but they themselves could *not* be overruled by the State Food Committee except on those occasions when their decisions were appealed. Even then, the central committee could only overrule a gubernia committee's decision if it violated a law or ministerial order (pp. 26-27).

So far as I know, no study has been made to determine how much of this vast structure of committees actually came into being. Certainly the State Food Committee accumulated a very large staff in Petrograd (pp. 24-25), and Shingarev ordered all available surveyors and permanent members from the land settlement organization to subordinate themselves to his new agents (order of 14 Mar., *Izvestiia po prodovolstvennomu*, May 1917: *ofitsialnyi otdel*, 34). At least some local committees must have taken form. E. A. Lutskii describes the work of two actual uezd committees in Tambov gubernia (1948: 51), and several other committees proved their existence during the late summer by provoking violent resistance from local inhabitants (*Krestianskoe*, 1927: 158, 165, 167, 215-16, 219, 263-64). S. N. Prokopovich, minister of food supply during the last weeks of the Provisional Government's reign, made a speech in October expressing his satisfaction with the good work they were doing (Browder, 1961: II, 647-52). Moreover, it cannot be doubted that some committees were still functioning when the bolsheviks took over. The bolshevik people's commissar of food supply was striving to subjugate them in early 1918, and some were still functioning during the following summer (Orlov, 1918: 18-35, 57-58, 88; see also Chebaevskii, 1957: 227, 243, 245, 247).

Even so, I find it hard to imagine the new committees actually functioning as parts of an administration. There was not time after July 1917 for elections to be held, committees to meet and elect their executive boards, agents to be sent out to accumulate information, and uniform instructions to be issued to these agents to get them working together in harmony. We have observed that it took more than three years to set up the land settlement commissions, and this had been an exceptionally hasty, disorderly operation. Recall, for example, the antics of the "temporary" peasant bank sections in Tambov gubernia in 1907 (ch. 7, sec. D). If it took a relatively effective central organization several years to

---

[25]Zaitsev (1930: 23-24); *Izvestiia po prodovolstvennomu* (May 1917:) *ofitsialnyi otdel*, 16-21).

get moving during peacetime, we are permitted to doubt that Shingarev's food committees turned the whole rural economy upside down in one summer. In fact, many reports came in during the late summer citing volosts and uezds where committees did not exist at all or existed only nominally (e.g., *Izvestiia po prodovolstvennomu,* Sept.-Oct. 1917: 2-9; *Prodovolstvie,* 1 Sept. 1917: 10-13, 22). To put it briefly, the Provisional Government's food supply agencies either did not exist at all in the provinces, or, where they did exist, they were too decentralized to be termed parts of an organization. The only solution the Provisional Government could find to its food supply problem was to rely on food-producing peasants to bring in their grain voluntarily. Not surprisingly, the first issue of the food ministry's popular journal, dated 15 July 1917, stressed its reliance on peasant support. A characteristic article by one M. Minin assured peasants that it would be their own elected committees taking their grain from them and that this made procurement a good thing (*Prodovolstvie,* 15 July 1917: 7-8).

But rhetoric was not enough to make a random pile of local colleges into a tribute-collecting organization. The erstwhile liberal Shingarev and his erstwhile radical successors seem to have recognized this, for they began striving to eliminate the democratic, decentralized elements in their organization immediately after establishing them. Taking a cue from his predecessor Bobrinskii and from Nikolai Miliutin's trick with arbitrators in 1861 (ch. 3, sec. C), Shingarev did what he could at the outset to pack local committees with the right kind of people. His years as a physician in rural Voronezh had engendered in him a profound sympathy for the aspirations of agricultural specialists, so he favored these as well as estate owners (Zaitsev, 1930: 28-29; Pershin, 1948: 71). But this slight amendment to the principles of democracy was hardly enough. On 29 April an edict from the State Food Committee announced the forthcoming appointment of "emissaries," who would go out from Petrograd to "help" local committees get going (*Izvestiia po prodovolstvennomu,* May 1917: *ofitsialnyi otdel,* 35). In July the committee sent out "instructors" to establish "closer and livelier contact" with the locales (June-July 1917: *ofitsialnyi otdel,* 9-10). In practice, both emissaries and instructors acted as inspectors (Sept.-Oct. 1917: 54-56; see also Zaitsev, 1930: 28-29). In late August the Provisional Government authorized the minister of food supply, *not the State Food Committee,* to suspend the activity of any local committee whose work displeased him (*Izvestiia po prodovolstvennomu,* Sept.-Oct. 1917: *ofitsialnyi otdel,* 26-27). From this time on the government bypassed the State Food Committee freely. The law of 27 August, doubling maximum grain prices, was addressed to the minister of food supply alone. It extended powers to him without mentioning any of the committees, central or local, that had been set up in the spring (p. 30). In a circular of 20 August Minister Peshekhonov called upon his agencies to take "exceptional measures" to get grain, including the use of armed force. He wanted his collectors to form "warrior bands" *(voinskie druzhiny)*. He even said that if they failed to employ such measures when necessary, he would put them on trial for criminal negligence.[26] During September and October the ministry's journal repeatedly called for centralized control. The minister openly declared that the democratic nature of his organization was a "vice," and reports from his agents were expressing much the same view (*Prodovolstvie,* 15 Oct. 1917: 7-8, 15).

It was the same old pattern, intensified a hundred times. A new central office sends out agents to the countryside, or else has them elected there, and gives them orders to move the world. Then it attacks them when they "fail." The history of the would-be democratic food supply committees of 1917 bore a marked resemblance to that of the *stanovye,* arbitrators, and land captains of the previous century. Ideology, it seems, had very little impact on administrative practice and the realities of government-peasant interaction. Zaitsev sums up the Provisional Government's food supply measures as follows: "The revolutionary authority of the provisional government...differed from the historical authority of the Russian state precisely in the fact that all its measures bore the marks of their absolutely illusory character" (1930: 97). He is right about the Provisional Government but wrong, it seems to me, in seeing the Duma-Soviet ministers as fundamentally different from their predecessors (or successors). The only real difference between the law mongerers of the empire and those of the Provisional Government lay in the fact that the latter had very little time.

E. THE EXPERIENCE OF THE AGRICULTURAL SPECIALISTS

War Fever

The preceding sections may have given the impression that the *agronom-organizatory* were dragged unwillingly into food supply by their bureaucratic superiors. One might suppose that they resented the war, since military mobilization interrupted their programs of agricultural improvement and brought on a revival of the old, hated practices of arbitrary authority. Farms had now to be exploited to serve the whims of generals. Surveyors and agronomists who continued to function in rural Russia had to abandon their quest to transform the countryside through conversation.

---

[26]*Izvestiia po prodovolstvennomu* (Sept.-Oct. 1917: *ofitsialnyi otdel,* 38). Grain-grabbing gangs were already operating out of various urban centers when Peshekhonov called for them. According to Raimov (1950: 49-50), they were already at work in Ufa and Orenburg gubernias. Regarding other areas, see *1917 god v Saratovskoi* (1961: 259-60, 269, 333); *Prodovolstvie* (15 Oct. 1917: 19).

It certainly would have made sense for the specialists to hate war, but they did not. They found it exhilarating. They rushed into food supply work with real enthusiasm, spurred on by a consuming desire to serve the nation. Most of them associated themselves with political parties that radiated hatred for Germans and made it a point to hurl accusations of treason at anyone whose ardor for victory was less than feverish (Rosenberg, 1974: 20-24; Wolters, 1969: 148-53; Diakin, 1967: 45-50). This is not to say that specialists loved blood and cannon per se. However, it did please them when Russia's military leaders encouraged them to overlook the niceties of law and administrative regularity while coping with urgent necessities and undertaking mighty labors.

Intellectual enthusiasm for World War I was a trans-European phenomenon in 1914. The war offered to all its participants an unprecedented opportunity to devote themselves wholly to a sacred cause— national mobilization—and no group showed greater fervor in this cause than professionals. "The War threw confusion into our ranks," said Romain Rolland of the European intelligentsia in a statement of 1919. "Most intellectuals put their science, art and reason in the service of their governments." What had happened was a "near-complete abdication of the world's intelligence and its voluntary enslavement to unchained forces." This was a terrible thing, Rolland said. War was a terrible thing, and it became all the more terrible when conducted by specialists (quoted in Mayer, 1967: 887).[27]

Rolland's views on the awfulness of war need not detain us. More interesting are the hints he gives us about the specialists' urge to mobilize. His phrase, "voluntary enslavement to unchained forces," is an excellent description of behavior dominated by this urge. What Rolland failed to perceive, however, was that the urge was *characteristic* of specialists, not a fall from grace. Military mobilization was not a breaking away from specialist ideals but a fulfillment of them. Rolland declared accusingly that intellectuals had "transformed thought into the instrument of passion" in 1914, as if he considered thought to be one thing and passion another. When specialists served "the selfish interests of some political or social caste, of some state, nation, or class," this was passion and voluntary enslavement. On the other hand, voluntary enslavement and passion were distinctly not involved when intellectuals mobilized in some higher cause. The following remarks, for example, did *not* express passion in Rolland's view: "We are the servants of the Mind! We recognize no other master. We exist to carry and defend its light, to rally around it all

---

[27]Rolland called his statement "The Declaration of Intellectual Independence," and he went around getting other European intellectuals to sign it. Among those who did were Benedetto Croce, Hermann Hesse, Bertrand Russell, and Albert Einstein.

misguided men." Nor was Rolland voluntarily enslaving himself when he called upon his fellow intellectuals not to "recognize" different peoples but to "know only *the* People." "People" in Rolland's mind were an entity that "forever marches forward on the rough road drenched with its sweat and blood." Apparently these "People" did not belong to any caste, state, nation, or class except when they allowed passion to carry them away. We may infer, then, that Rolland considered "Mind" and "People" to be aspects of "thought." Anyone who did anything for any other reason was indulging in passion and, probably, enslaving himself. By this deft shuffling of concepts, Rolland separated the "voluntary enslavement" of 1914 from what he imagined to be the specialists' true calling, and by making this separation he blinded himself to the specialists' *inherent* inclination to mobilize. His equating of "Mind" and "People" with thought allowed him to stop far short of admitting that specialists were *in essence* creatures of passion, eager to subject not only themselves but everyone else to their curious image of social order. It never occurred to Rolland that his Mind-Truth-Humanity might embody a far more monumental (and devasting) urge to mobilize than any mere nation or class or state; nor, needless to say, did it ever occur to him that specialists were of all people the *most* prone to mobilize, not the least. Rolland's wordplay is, of course, the same sort as Chaianov customarily employed when he demanded "freedom" for *agronom-organizatory* while denouncing "arbitrary" land captains.

Specialists throughout the European subcontinent had excellent reason to find war rewarding in 1914. Suddenly men with technical and administrative skills were vitally needed. Indeed, they were looked upon as saviors. New jobs opened up, salaries rose, and, better yet, specialists now had the opportunity to enjoy the unrestrained fervor of a crusade without having to risk their necks or take responsibility for any but the most immediate consequences of their actions. Best of all, the leaders of their countries had not foreseen the need for thoroughgoing national mobilization, and there was no readymade organization for it, not even so much as a concept of an organization. Specialists would now enjoy the heady excitement of improvising new systems from scratch. For a time, at least, they could do their work in a continual spirit of adventure, without having to submit to the exacting and tiresome requirements of their own plans and programs. They did not have to apologize for the ad hoc nature of their work, for it was *necessary*. Better yet, it was necessary because of other people's sins. Best of all, the guilty parties were bureaucrats, aristocrats, generals, and politicians—all those vermin who had for so long been standing in the way of the specialists' earnest struggle to shower the benefits of science upon humanity.

One of the best illustrations I have seen of a specialist frustrated by the disciplines and burdens imposed upon him by his own passion to mobilize is in the memoirs of S. P. Fridolin. Fridolin began working as an uezd zemstvo agronomist in 1904, with the idea that he would get close to peasants and lead them "forward." At the very beginning, however, he ran into opposition. The administrators in his zemstvo directorate did not want him so close to peasants. They preferred that he work in his office in the uezd capital (1925: 44-45, 54-55). Fridolin was annoyed at this, but he managed to satisfy his superiors' demands and still pursue village projects on his own time. He began to write about his work in agricultural journals, but here too he aroused hostility, this time from "scholastical" agronomists who believed that his ad hoc work was not methodical and therefore not properly scientific. If he did not make science the basis of his work, declared his capital-city colleagues, he would not achieve practical results nor would his efforts contribute anything to science (pp. 65, 80-81). Finally, after five years of struggle against zemstvo administrators and scholarly agronomists, Fridolin experienced the ultimate frustration: he realized that his work was actually harming the peasants. Instead of learning what local conditions were and *then* making agricultural practice fit these conditions better, he had been trying to "improve" local practice so that it would conform to abstract standards (pp. 57-68, 70-71). He decided that if he was to cope effectively with local conditions, he would have to give up being a general practitioner and center his attention on one type of agricultural activity. He selected stock raising as his specialty, and this at last gave him a basis for working closely and effectively with peasants (pp. 74-78).

Alas, his achievement was short-lived. The Stolypin Reform was now well underway and zemstvoes were setting up agronomists on the *uchastok* level. *Uchastok* agronomists had their own ideas about working with peasants, and they did not include Fridolin's very modest, specialized aims. They wanted primarily to organize peasants into cooperatives and *lead* them, and this took so much time that they could not give much attention to agriculture per se. Moreover, these peasant leaders—*starosty,* to use Fridolin's sardonic term—were suspicious of an "instructor" like Fridolin. Each *starosta*-agronomist wanted to keep "his" people to himself. Fridolin was told not to come out of the uezd capital unless a *starosta* called him in as a consultant. Thus, by 1914, Fridolin found himself once again confined to an office. On the eve of war he had gone through more than ten years of struggle to make some kind of meaningful contact with peasants, and all he had achieved was to entangle himself in "bureaucracy" (pp. 93-96, 102-3). Worse, this bureaucracy was the agronomists' own product. Its red tape had not come down from "bureaucrats" on high but had grown up out of the agronomists' own struggle to break away from red tape. Not surprisingly, war came as a relief to Fridolin. He resigned his position and went off positively rejoicing to work as a meat supplier for the southwestern front (pp. 104-6).

Fridolin's straightforward account speaks more directly of the specialists' state of mind than Rolland's Beethovenish bombast. One can begin to perceive a connection between the specialists' holy work for Mind-People and their sinful rejoicing over war. There is even a hint that their sin proceeded directly from their holiness rather than contradicting it. In Fridolin we have at least one example of a pious reformer turning into a drum-thumping nationalist overnight *precisely* because he was pious. The point suggests itself that for Russia's agricultural specialists agricultural improvement and World War I were much the same sort of operation. Both demanded peasant mobilization and justified the destruction of traditional peasant society. Both made the invasion of peasant villages look like salvation.

This is not the sort of point one can prove. Russian materials offer little in the way of explanation or proof of any urge to mobilize in the hearts of specialists. As Chaianov's writings suggest, specialists do not easily admit even to themselves that their science is useful to them because it gives them both cause and license to govern arbitrarily. They are not ordinarily inclined to ponder the association between the pursuit of their professional callings and something as murky as an urge to impose system on the world and mobilization on its inhabitants. Not many specialists in any country accepted Rolland's confession of sin in 1919, but they all shared his assumption that devotion to the cause of Mind-People has nothing to do with passion or voluntary enslavement. Therefore, it is not easy to find evidence that will give concrete form to my suggestion about a connection between agrarian reform and total war. Lvov's outlandish speeches about the "great retreat" (sec. C) and Chaianov's preposterous fantasies about saintly *agronom-organizatory* (ch. 9, sec. C) only suggest the element of passion in specialist attitudes; they do not reveal its workings. Fridolin's unusually personal account is the closest approach I have seen in Russian materials to the explanation I am seeking.

It is of the utmost importance, however, to gain some insight into the agricultural specialists' *mentalité*, even though they themselves were unwilling or unable to discuss their attitudes straightforwardly. For this reason I hope the reader will tolerate a brief excursion away from the area of Russian agricultural reform. One must take one's evidence as it comes, and it happens that the most thoroughgoing and convincing expression I have ever seen of the specialists' world-view before and during World War I comes from German industry rather than Russian agriculture. Admittedly it is hazardous to identify a phenomenon in one country and then draw inferences about another. In this instance one must accept Rolland's suggestion that a specialist *mentalité* did indeed extend across Europe and produce similar effects on behavior in all countries, though this is far from being the whole truth. Yet, for my purposes, it is at least useful to describe a German model, and it is even intellectually defensible to do so if only the reader keeps in mind that I am not venturing to characterize the Russian specialist mind but only to present an extreme expression of a tendency recognizable in Russian specialist thought and action.

Specialist war fever seems to have reached its greatest intensity in Germany; or, let us say that it produced its most spectacular results there. Such was the success of German war mobilization that by 1917 its organizations and techniques had become models for all other nations, foes as well as allies (Redlich, 1929: 119). As noted above, the central offices of Russia's food supply organization repeatedly pointed to the German achievement as something their own country should follow (sec. C). In July 1917 the first issue of the ministry of food supply's "popular" journal proclaimed its intention to direct the national economy the way the German government was doing. At the beginning of the war, said the journal, we Russians assumed that we would enjoy abundance while Germany starved. Now, however, the situation has reversed itself. As a result of German organization and our lack of it, Germany is managing to survive and Russia is threatened with famine (*Prodovolstvie*, 15, July 1917: 3-5). Indeed, Germany leads all Europe in the effectiveness of its measures to mobilize her economy and prevent speculation (pp. 28-29). A speaker at a food supply congress in the summer of 1917 sounded the same note. The Germans have already been rationing food for two years, and now we Russians will have to accept similar restraints (1 Sept. 1917: 31). One of the most unrestrained admirers of German "state capitalism" was Lenin. Of course, he disapproved ideologically, but in 1917 he held up Germany's mobilizing organization for both Provisional and Soviet governments to emulate. He even suggested that socialist *agitators* could learn much from the German government's methods (*Polnoe*, XXXIV, 175-76, 191, 309; XXX, 279; see also Buchanan, 1972: 28-33, 52-53). In short, Germany's achievements at economic mobilization were impressive, and if such achievements were associated with the German specialists' urge to mobilize, then we might expect to find in Germany, if anywhere, the most extreme and also the most sophisticated expressions of this urge.

If any one man could be said to have created Germany's wartime mobilization system, that man was Walter Rathenau. Rathenau worked with industry, not food supply, but his leadership in industrial mobilization provided both framework and inspiration for the organization of agriculture. Rathenau stood forth as a culmination of the specialists' dream. Educated as a physical scientist (Kessler, 1969: 21), he was, during the decade before the war, one of Germany's leading business executives (pp. 55-175). When war began, his accomplishments and abilities carried him into a key position in the war ministry's office for supplying industry with raw materials (pp. 176-82; Feldman, 1966: 45-48; Redlich, 1944:

315-17). His experience before and during the war carried him the whole length of the ideological road from capitalist entrepreneur to state socialist (Kessler, 1969: 183-231), while he traversed the professional spectrum from specialist-administrator to statesman. His last position was foreign minister of the Weimar Republic, and his last major act before being murdered by proto-Nazi thugs in 1922 was to participate—unwillingly—in the negotiations leading up to the Treaty of Rapallo with the Soviet Union (Joll, 1960: 122-23). His diverse and highly original achievements made him a living embodiment of the worldwide "technocratic" notion that specialists should run the world.

Rathenau's practical achievements need not be described here. After all, he was not Russian, nor was he involved in agriculture. What does interest the student of Russian agrarian reform is the breadth of his experience as a specialist and, most important, the depth of his own insight into it. He was a highly articulate student of his own accomplishment and a profoundly analytical observer of the unfolding of his own personality as it became immersed in his accomplishment. I know of no man in any country who became as deeply involved in the mobilizing specialist's experience and who faced his own frenzies and dilemmas as unflinchingly as Rathenau did.

Speaking generally, the Russian specialists' wartime syndrome was to greet the opening of hostilities with joy, plunge into military mobilization with whole heart, and then turn away bitterly from the great cause in disillusionment, blaming a variety of sins and authorities for the "catastrophe." Rathenau's response was infinitely more complex. To describe it in brief, he perceived this same syndrome in himself but did not indulge in it unreservedly. For example, he expressed enthusiasm for the war by throwing himself wholeheartedly into the work of mobilization and shouting about "this great time, when everything in us is renewed and clarified" (1918: V, 15). Yet he disapproved strongly of German policy from the beginning (1927: I, 156-57, 171-72; Kessler, 1969: 176-78). Unlike other specialist-intellectuals, he did not seek release from his frustrations by blaming statesmen and generals. He avoided pretentious rhetoric about the loftiness of his own aims as compared with the unworthy purposes of others. Throughout the war he continued to perceive that the pursuit of general aims—any general aims—brought on unforeseeable consequences. "We have availed ourselves of mechanisation for the sake of its integrating powers," he said in 1916. "We have now to call it to account concerning its secret tendencies to promote disintegration" (1921: 30).

Rathenau devoted much intellectual effort to comprehending his father, Emil, a successful industrialist who had played a leading role during the 1880s and '90s in founding and developing the electric power industry in Germany. There was nothing personal in Walter's study. He was not examining his father as part of a family but as an element in a much broader history. What fascinated Walter was the impact of electric power on industrial organization, and he wanted to comprehend his father as a part of this impact. Walter took an unusual approach to his study: he viewed industrial development as a socio-psychological phenomenon. In his eyes, Emil was not merely a participant; he himself was the phenomenon. Emil's own urgings and experiences not only arose from industrialization but also gave rise to industrialization.

Walter saw the electric power industry as a very special type. The building of power stations and the distribution of electricity allowed men to transcend geography. Current required no trains or wagons or boats to carry it. Only run a few wires across the countryside, and one could turn lights on in Rome with coal burned in Silesia. With power thus freed from time and space, it became an independent variable, the favorite dream of statisticians and social scientists everywhere. Electricity was eminently calculable, plannable, and predictable; indeed, its use demanded calculation, planning, and prediction. If one used coal for power, one built one's factory near a coal mine, and that was that. The coal itself told industrialists where to locate their plants. Electric power gave no such direction. Its users had to calculate plant location in accordance with other factors. And if a few industrialists began to think this way, it would not be long before all of them were demanding that all factories be located in accordance with a general plan based on a common aim to *use* power efficiently. Not only plant location had to be planned but also the production process and even the future demand for one's products, which implied that society itself would have to be planned or at least predicted. An entrepreneur who wished to harness, transmit, and use electric power on a large scale would very likely want to make himself part of an extensive technical apparatus that would coordinate all industrial production and distribution. Electrically powered industry would never be a random conglomeration of enterprises, each taking random profits and losses as prices rose and fell. Maximum profit (efficiency) could be attained only by a single vast array of interrelated machinery organized primarily to *utilize* available power in the most efficient way. New resources, new inventions, and new sources of capital had to be plugged in where they would best serve the needs of a single system of production. This was the way Emil Rathenau thought (Kessler, 1969: 11-16). "He thought in terms of things," said his son, "not concepts and values" (Rathenau, 1927: II, 197). Apparently Walter also looked forward to an economic system organized around production rather than consumption (I, 52-56).[28]

[28] By 1921 Lenin had grasped this vision and accepted it as his own without reservation. Electrification, he frequently said, would bring about social transformation. Indeed, he believed that the Soviet government could not possibly

Emil did not own the industries he built. He was an industrial manager who used other men's money and made profits for them, as if personal wealth were of relatively small importance to him. According to Walter, Emil wanted to create a system that could carry power to all mankind, simply because it pleased him (Kessler, 1969: 15-16). This was why Walter believed his father to be more than a mere instrument for introducing electricity to the world. If profit did not move Emil Rathenau to do his work, then one could consider his personality as a force in itself. If one wished to understand the electric power industry, one had not only to speak of turbines and transformers but also to reflect upon the urges that drove Emil Rathenau to build them and plug the world into them. So Walter Rathenau believed.

Walter saw his father as a man possessed by a vision. Emil was at his best when he was laying plans for some new development or expansion. These were his periods of optimism. When it came to carrying out plans, however, he became pessimistic and self-critical (pp. 7-9). Walter concluded early in life that this syndrome originated in a kind of entrapment. Each time his father undertook to create a new power system, he liberated himself and his fellow men. As soon as he involved himself in the actual building and sustaining of his system, however, he became its slave. He ceased to believe in his work and continued to function only because necessity drove him to it. His only escape was to start a new system and enslave himself once again. In a word, Emil operated under an inescapable curse. His planning liberated him from reality momentarily but then tied him to it more tightly than ever. This continual cycle of damnation and redemption was the basic force that built the electrical industry and kept it working (pp. 15-19).

As a youth, Walter felt a passionate longing to stay clear of the whole affair. Even stronger than this longing, however, was his fascination with electric power and the seemingly limitless liberation that its systems offered to the human race. According to his biographer, Walter was torn by the conflict between these two feelings throughout his life (pp. 17-21). This was probably the reason he began his career in science and industry, then veered sharply into literature, and thence, after two or three years, switched abruptly into corporation management (pp. 21-22, 43, 58-59). In 1903 the wandering son virtually took over the management of his father's far-flung industrial conglomerate and began to work closely with him.

At this point Walter felt more positively about the planning-implementation process than he usually did. Instead of emphasizing the liberation-slave syndrome that seemed to accompany organized action,

---

unify the national economy under a single plan without first bringing electric power to all corners of the land (see, e.g., *Polnoe*, XL, 339-47).

he spoke of a gift his father possessed that was somehow higher than intellect. As Walter the young executive saw it, his father's attainments stemmed not from "the intellect narrowly set on its goal, but visionary intuition, eliminating the goal from its consciousness" (pp. 58-59—the quoted words are Kessler's). In other words, implementing a plan enslaved a man only if he allowed himself to become obsessed with the plan's initial purpose. If, on the other hand, the implementer followed his "intuition," then the plan liberated him. One can see here a double liberation. The planner frees himself from present conditions, and the implementer frees himself from the plan (see pp. 59-64). Walter, it seems, had found a way out of the trap of modern organization by conjuring up the idea of line-over-staff administration (see ch. 3, sec. B).

As we know, the liberating features of line-over-staff organization represent only one side of it. Administrators can easily be discouraged and disoriented by the ultimate futility of acting without articulable purpose or making plans that no one will follow. Walter never lost sight of this negative side. He recognized the unrelenting necessity of throttling line with staff, despite all disadvantages. After several years of working with his father, he found himself enslaved again, this time for good. "I wish nothing," he said in a letter of 1906: "Ruthlessly though I have questioned my inner self, I have never found anything of this world that I wish. I wish what I must, otherwise nothing. And what I must, I see, as a wanderer by night sees by the light of his lantern only a few steps in front of him. That this my life is an oblation, offered gladly and willingly to the powers above, not for reward, nor in hope, this I may say.... That I forfeit the love of my fellow-men in the process I know, and feel it cruelly" (quoted on p. 71).

It is, I think, this nagging despair that makes Rathenau's reaction to World War I intelligible. When war broke out, he plunged joyfully into the hurly-burly of mobilization, and for a few brief months he enjoyed the intoxicating liberty of line-over-staff operation (see, e.g., Rathenau, 1927: I, 158). Events flowed so rapidly that one could hardly notice the contradictions between system and the actions taken in the system's name. Until the end of March 1915 Rathenau reveled in "intuition" (1918: V, 25-28; 1967: 191). Referring to these months, he proclaimed in a speech of 20 December 1915 that Germany had created a centralized, planned economy on the basis of private initiative and mutual trust among her businessmen (1918: V, 57-58). This was a typical specialist statement. When Rathenau said "businessmen" in this context, he had specialists in mind (pp. 132-33). His absurd hymns to private initiative and central planning corresonded exactly to Chaianov's chants about autonomy combined with central administration (see ch. 9, sec. C). Both were unintelligible except to listeners who understood without reflection that mobilization had to go on whether it had any discernible purpose or not.

But Rathenau, unlike Chaianov, did not surrender his self-perception. Only a few weeks after the war began, when he was at the height of his mobilizing exhilaration, he wrote the following lines:

> It is as though there were two people living within me, one growing and the other dying. The dying one is moved by passions and desires and love of pleasure, and with him dies much of the vigor and colour of life, much of its joy and friendliness; but the other grows, that other whom I can scarcely call "I" any longer. For my fate seems no longer to concern it; its ends are impersonal; it makes me the servant of forces over which I have no control. This other is like an alien power, which avails itself of my humble existence for a period in order to carry out its own purposes.... What I create, what I have to give others, is no longer my own. I can no longer give it; it breaks away as it pleases. On whose behalf? I must not ask.... I feel nearer to mankind than before, but to the individual I have nothing to give. (Quoted in Kessler, 1969: 239; see also Rathenau, 1927: I, 161-62)

This is the clearest and most complete statement of the specialist's state of mind I have ever seen. At the height of his success, at the very time when he was helping to establish the course of Germany's wartime development, Rathenau did not forget that he considered the war stupid. He already sensed the bitterness inherent in his work and the frustration that ultimately came to an intellectual who believed he possessed a quality higher than intellect. Whether Germany won or lost the war, Walter would get small satisfaction from his participation. The reason he never had to take refuge in blaming "conservatives," ministers, speculators, or royal courts for Germany's failure or his own was that he knew his work was pointless even before he began it. When, in 1916-17, Ludendorff began to ravage Germany at will to keep his army in the field (ch. 3, sec. B), Walter was sufficiently detached to see the need for it (Rathenau, 1967: 210-11). And while he was encouraging Ludendorff to wreck the organization he, Rathenau, had constructed, he continued to submerge himself in his own public image and to proclaim his faith in the ability of his countrymen to sustain a centralized, planned economy through their local initiative and mutual trust.

Indeed, he erected his faith into a nationalist ideology that transcended the war effort. The German people had undergone a fundamental transformation, he said in a speech of 1917, and there would be no going back to the old ways. Private owners had given way to specialists; capitalism had given way to socialism. Capitalism had not fallen. Rather, it had developed to the point where its members, especially the specialists, were capable of transcending it. This was a triumph, not a collapse. Gigantic industrial enterprises had transcended their ostensibly private owners and all the laws of property. They were now operating solely in order to cope with economic necessity (Rathenau, 1918: V, 215). Specialists have taken over, he crowed, and for these new leaders of industry, economic necessity was a moral command. With such men in control, one could speak realistically of a tightly centralized organization resting on autonomous, self-governing units (pp. 215-40). Men can change, he insisted. They have grown nobler as capitalism and the dominion of specialists have evolved. After the war they will be able to go on sacrificing themselves in order to sustain the national economy, just as they have done hitherto for military victory. Interestingly, he gave only one reason for believing this to be true. He said that if he did not believe it, he would be unable to go on living (pp. 250-51).

Later, after the war, he changed his mind. He recommended *against* the perpetuation of wartime industrial organization in peacetime because, he admitted, society was not ready for a uniform plan. His fellow men had not yet caught up with his vision (Kessler, 1969: 267-70).

Rathanau's perception of himself provides a measure of insight into the Russian agricultural specialists. Their inner conflicts, like his, were not in essence the results of character deficiencies or intellectual feebleness. If a sane, wholesome mind is one that can function adequately in its social context, then their love-hate relationship with system was not a neurosis but a basis for mental health. The specialists were doomed—as Russian government has been doomed since 1861—to lay plans for social change in a mood of frenzied optimism and then to carry them out in bitter disillusionment. Planners and enactors had to endure the erosion of their purposes during the process of implementation; implementers had to stumble through their work without usable guide or intelligible purpose. The possibilities for discord were virtually infinite, yet the carrying out of a reform (mobilization) required continuous cooperation and trust. Only men driven by Rathenau's inner conflict possessed the necessary self-discipline to function harmoniously in a countryside that contradicted and violated every idea they had of reform, benefit, and justice. Only men who shared a common urge to mobilize could rely on one another's desperation and coordinate their efforts into the semblance of an organization. Mere conviction regarding the soundness or rightness of one's ideas or plans was not enough.

As a symbol, Rathenau's electric power bore a striking resemblance to A. V. Chaianov's concept of agronomic science. Metaphorically speaking, Chaianov's *agronom-organizatory* were setting out to electrify the Russian countryside. By introducing sound methods into peasant farming and forming cooperatives, they were creating and distributing power, and this power would transform isolated villages into a vast network of productive enterprises, simultaneously making possible and demanding a central economic organization for distribution and supply. Chaianov's vision required a specialist to work simultaneously in two very different contexts. On the one hand, the *agronom-organizator* had to involve himself in the eccentricities of each village, with its own peculiar customs, feuds, and soils; on the other, he had to conform to the demands of science and systematic organization. The contrast between these two social contexts resembled the one Rathenau saw between a capitalistic patchwork of disparate industrial plants, each rooted in its locale, and an efficient, state-managed system of energy utilization, fueled and coordinated through a system of wires. In both visions, Chaianov's and Rathenau's, the contradiction between the two contexts created strong pressures to resolve it by promising salvation—i.e., agronomic science or electric power—and then destroying all obstacles to system for the sake of this salvation. From this underlying "psycho-sociological" compulsion to "save" sprang the specialists' urge to mobilize: Judaeo-Christian missionary zeal in its modern form.[29]

To sum up, the agricultural specialists welcomed war with joyful anticipation primarily because they were specialists. War fever did not contradict or undermine the passion for agrarian reform but proceeded from it and, in turn, strengthened it. As Fridolin's frustration after years of dealing with zemstvo administrators led him into war work, so did the frustrations and disappointments of war and revolution lead him back to agrarian reform. It would be useful to speak at length of Fridolin's experience as he stumbled through this peculiar odyssey, but he—like other Russian *agronom-organizatory*—does not grant us much insight into his attitudes. This is why I have introduced Walter Rathenau into the account. He, unlike his fellow specialists, could let his urge to mobilize run riot without having to insist that it proceeded from thought. Of course, Rathenau's example proves nothing, but for those who wonder why the specialists of Europe should have loved war in 1914, he presents some interesting material. Better yet, his insights allow us to observe the urge

---

[29]Scholars have shown very little interest in the inclination among modern professionals—including scholars—to save the unenlightened. Books like Eric Hoffer's *True Believer* refer to this phenomenon and attest to its existence, but they are more anxious to condemn than to analyze or explain. They proceed from the professionals' own cherished assumption that "true" specialists should aspire not to save or convert but only to serve and inform. Occasionally one finds a study that views the motives underlying specialist behavior from a broader perspective. Most noteworthy for our purposes is a book edited by G. Benveniste and W. F. Ilchman, *Agents of Change: Professionals in Developing Countries* (1969). This work, which focuses on modern agrarian reform in backward areas, contains a wealth of references to the "predisposition of professionals to elevate the ends of their usual problems and to conceive of the rest of the universe in terms of the extent to which it impedes or facilitates these ends" (p. 35). The editors go so far as to speak of a "religion of development," which is comparable with Christianity, communism, and nationalism (pp. 37-39). See also Hughes (1958: 22-55).

to mobilize in operation before, during, and after the war. We may now see more deeply into such minds as Alexander II's when he found himself freeing the serfs, Alexander III's when he forced his statesmen to embark on peasant reform and build the Trans-Siberian Railroad, Krivoshein's when he abandoned the peasant bank in 1908 and undertook to put *agronom-organizatory* in charge of Russia's peasants, and, of course, Lenin's when he stumbled into the halls of government in October 1917 and abruptly abandoned the trite formulations he had just written down in *State and Revolution*. Rathenau suggests to us that none of the madcap adventures into which these leaders plunged their country could ever have produced any practical result had they not aroused an urge to mobilize that was already incipient—though not always visible—in Russia's capital-city society. War fever represented a culmination of the Russian intellectual's passion for mobilization, and this explains why the movement for agrarian reform did not perish during the disintegration of 1914-21. The reform organization disappeared, but the urge that had built and sustained it grew stronger than ever.

Involvement in Food Procurement

The foregoing section has portrayed the attitude that brought agricultural specialists into the new task of grain supply. Now we are prepared to inquire into their actual work as food collectors.

First of all, the point must be made that the central government considered their service to be of value; that is to say, many specialists actually did collect grain. In December 1916 Rittikh ordered his surveyors to join in the grain procurement campaign (TsGIAL, f. 456, op. 1, d. 110, l. 64) and proposed that all specialists be exempted from military service so that they too could participate (*Ekonomicheskoe*, III, 55-57). Cooperatives—the specialists' cadres of advanced peasants—also served the cause of food distribution. In 1914-15, when selling grain to the government could still be profitable, they were glad to help out. Army contracts "saved" the dairy producers' cooperatives in Siberia. As late as January 1916 the special conference could still express enthusiasm about the contribution being made to the national food supply by cooperatives throughout the empire (*Svedeniia*, 8 Jan. 1916: 41-42). Many credit cooperatives expanded their operations during these halcyon days to include the buying, selling, and storing of grain (Kayden, 1929: 359-63, 67-71, 110-14, 182-83). Many new cooperatives were established (Baker, 1977: 155), doubtless to join in this good work. It was more or less natural, therefore, for Shingarev—the Provisional Government's first MZ—to put his reliance on them to procure grain. According to Shingarev's reasoning, cooperatives were close to the peasants, and they could use their good will to persuade food producers to sell grain to the govern-

ment just as they had in 1914-15 (*Sezd,* 1917: 5). As a sign of his faith in
the specialists' cadres, he took measures (in April) to postpone the con-
scription of co-op staff workers (*IGU,* 1917: 297). On the whole, however, Shingarev's reliance on cooperatives was a forlorn hope. Government grain prices had fallen well below market levels, and official food
purchasing had lost its appeal to farmers. Specialists and cooperatives
fared relatively well in food-consuming areas, where benevolence continued to be an element of government policy (*Prodovolstvie,* 1 Nov.
1917: 12-23), but in food-producing areas they did poorly.

Apparently some cooperatives did participate in the Provisional Government's procurement campaigns. So said reports from Tambov and
Samara in early May 1917 (*Sezd,* 1917: 11). In July the minister of food
supply said he thought that his new food committees were pushing the
cooperatives aside as organizations, but, he added reassuringly, workers
in cooperatives were still playing a leading role as members of the committees (*Prodovolstvie,* 15 July 1917: 25). The cooperatives may have
been more important than the minister believed. By September the ministry was urging its local committees to work through them *as organizations* to collect their quotas (1 Sept. 1917: 14-15). Reports from Kherson,
Bessarabia, and Tavrid gubernias in the late summer said that cooperatives were the core of the food procurement organization (p. 17).

But specialists and cooperatives that participated in food procurement during 1917 were only tightening the noose around their collective
neck. Anyone who involved himself in the conflict between farmers and
consumers found himself in no-man's land. Some political leaders were
blaming the hapless specialists for failing to feed the populace in the
cities; others were accusing them of oppressing peasants in the food-
producing gubernias. Like the land captains of a decade or two earlier,
the *agronom-organizatory* of 1917 could do no right.

In May a congress of food supply plenipotentiaries—virtually all of
them specialists—came close to bringing the conflict out into the open.
Delegates strove to sound as if they all agreed concerning the need for
systematic food collection, but the food-producing areas stood four square
for local control over collectors, whereas food consumers insisted on full
subjugation to agents from the center. V. G. Groman, menshevik and
delegate to the congress from the Petrograd-dominated executive committee of the conference of soviets of workers' and soldiers' deputies,
insisted that cooperatives in food-producing gubernias be strictly subordinated to agents from Petrograd (*Sezd,* 1917: 51-52). Voluntary,
"spontaneous" activity was entirely acceptable to Groman and his ilk so
long as it was confined to Petrograd, but it would not do in food-
producing areas (pp. 22-24, 29-31). As one might expect, plenipotentiaries from the food-producing gubernias could not stomach this. Even
Shingarev, whose home territory was in the black-earth region, was un-

able to maintain a neutral position in the debate, though as MZ it was his duty to bring opposing sides together. He flatly opposed Petrograd's demands for centralization and insisted on autonomy in food-producing areas (pp. 13-15, 24-26). All this was a polite way to discuss basic differences without referring to them directly. Shingarev's side was determined to protect farmers from collectors, not to collect; Groman and other city men wanted a dictatorial organization to take grain from farmers by force.

Not surprisingly, the program adopted by this congress decided nothing and satisfied no one (*Izvestiia po prodovolstvennomu,* June-July 1917: 39). It was too late for conventional (staff-over-line) administration to change the situation in the food-producing gubernias. Out in the black-soil villages a few cooperatives did keep on trying to collect grain (see, e.g., *Prodovolstvie,* 1 Sept. 1917: 13), but they could not come close to meeting the government's needs. Reports had been coming in since July of their members being attacked and beaten up (15 July 1917: 26). In short, neither the government's hammer nor the village's anvil thanked the MZ's agencies for their efforts. Any specialists and cooperatives that actually tried to collect grain in 1917 only discredited themselves with government, peasants, and "workers" alike.

The specialists' failure to collect grain stemmed at least in part from the simple fact that they had evolved as agents of benevolence, and their interaction with peasants on this basis did not permit them to become imposers of unwelcome edicts. Trade they could foster; prosperity they could bring; enlightenment they could spread; but force they could not exert. Some of them, when they attained high positions in Petrograd, showed themselves quite willing to write out stern commands calling for drastic collection measures. Rhetoric of this sort found favor with the Petrograd crowd. In the countryside, however, face to face with the objects of their missionary zeal, not many could bring themselves to take up whips and clubs. In a word, their *interaction* in previous years had formed their minds and set them firmly in their social roles. They could not change overnight, no matter how "necessary" it was, any more than the land captains had been able to switch abruptly in 1906 from preservers of village unity to instigators of village-splitting reforms.

Perhaps the specialists should never have allowed themselves to be drawn out of their priestly positions of scientific detachment into the business of practical management. Had the *agronom-organizatory* stuck to laboratories and conversations about improvement and left the government's dirty work to others, they might not have found themselves committed in 1917 to a pathetic regime that doomed itself to impotence while affecting to be tyrannical. After all, they themselves were very fond of repeating that they were engaged in an inevitably slow process of establishing stable land tenure and introducing systems of individual right. They wanted to survey land before they distributed it, so that there would be no disorderly quarreling over it after the reform was finished. They wanted to compensate owners before taking away their land, which meant they had to assess value. They wanted productive peasants to get the land, so they had to estimate the capabilities of recipients. In short, everything the agricultural specialist wanted to do required an elaborate administration and an enormous span of time. His work had nothing to do with the rapid, crude measures necessary to deal with upheavals. Put a specialist into a political crisis, and he either adheres to his principles, thereby rendering himself unable to act effectively, or he betrays his principles and plays witch doctor.[30]

But the specialists did not err when they ventured into politics, not if it was their purpose to mobilize the peasantry. Not even their attachment to the Soviet regime after 1917 was a mistake, though Soviet power would ultimately wreck their dreams of reform. The accommodations they made from 1906 on represented the best they could do to achieve their purposes under the circumstances they faced. The fact that many of them did accommodate themselves explains why they were still there in the countryside in 1921 and why Lenin had to rely on them. Despite everything, they did succeed in involving themselves in rural society.

The cadres of "advanced" peasants who staffed the cooperatives probably suffered more than specialists from their attempts to serve their government. At least they proved to be less resilient. As we shall see in Chapter 12, the specialists, who needed only their science to sustain them through all storms (and who found it relatively easy to run away from storms), were able to return to the countryside in force in 1921. By contrast, the credit cooperatives simply ceased to exist in the food-producing gubernias. According to one estimate, the total number of rural credit cooperatives dropped from over 15,000 in 1915 to about 600 in 1922 (Gordeev, 1925: 198).[31]

The Quasi-Revival of Land Reform in 1917

Our description of rural administration in 1917 is not quite complete. We must not imagine that the MZ simply ceased to exist after the

[30]David Joravsky has made this point exhaustively and, I think, conclusively with regard to the first 40-odd years of the Soviet era (see 1961: 253-71; 1970: 30-38).

[31]Gordeev's figues are not reliable, but the tendency they reflect was real enough. Kayden indicates that *consumer* cooperatives continued to expand until 1919 (1929: 67-71, 110-14, 182-83, 198-218), but from 1918 on the Soviet government tightened its dominion over them, and by 1921 it had transformed even these relatively hardy institutions into state minions (*Chetyre,* 1922: 102). In effect, they ceased to be cooperatives.

splitting off of the food supply ministry in May and the absorption into it of many specialists and other officials. On the contrary, it too set out to build a new empire in rural Russia. On 19 March 1917 the Provisional Government declared that the MZ would formulate plans for dealing with the peasants' demand for land (Browder, 1961: II, 524-25). Many *agronom-organizatory,* doubtless glad to be free from the unpleasant duty of collecting grain, would now have the opportunity to take up their old role as benefactors. Or so they hoped.

According to the declaration of 19 March, the MZ was to set up a land committee in the central government, and this body would commence gathering data in order to formulate a new land reform designed to distribute land to needy peasants. This was the same cry with which the Stolypin Reform had begun 11 years before (ch. 7, sec. A), but of course the government of specialists did not intend to follow in tsarist footsteps. In particular, it was determined not to blunder haphazardly into its reform. The declaration of 19 March read, in part, "Proper consideration and passage of a land law is impossible without serious preparatory work: the collection of materials, the registration of land reserves, [the determination of] the distribution of landed property, and the conditions and forms of land utilization, and so forth" (p. 525). At the very beginning, then, the Provisional Government's MZ doomed all its efforts to absurdity. Like the tsarist government, it promised the peasants land *and* a systematic legal order; that is, it undertook to satisfy the immediate demands of peasant rebels by legislating programs that would take decades to carry out. Now, however, the specialists were going to try the old act without having anyone around to pull their chestnuts out of the fire.

It took about a month after the 19 March declaration for Shingarev to write up and publish the statute of 21 April, establishing the Chief Land Committee and its local organs. As in the ostensibly democratic food supply organization (see above, sec. D), local committees were set up in gubernias, uezds, and volosts. Elected members voted; administrators did not. There were some new, ostensibly decentralizing and democratic twists in the land committees' structure. On all levels except the volost, each committee was to include representatives from the committees on the next lower level. The Chief Land Committee had one representative from each gubernia, the gubernia committees had representatives from the uezds, and so forth (pp. 528-32). On paper, there was also a little more democracy on the volost level than in the food supply committees. Volost zemstvo assemblies were to elect *all* members of the volost land committees. In April volost zemstvoes did not yet exist, but they were enacted exactly a month later, on 21 May. According to the statutes on zemstvo elections issued on that day, suffrage was to be equal for all males (I, 277-82, 284-90). Seemingly, then, volost zemstvo assemblies would be dominated by rank-and-file peasants, and volost land committees—where they came into being—would be predominantly peasant bodies (pp. 293-94; see also Kostrikin, 1975: 142-45, 331-34).

D. Posnikov, the first chairman of the Chief Land Committee, opened its first session on 19 May with a speech denouncing the Stolypin Reform and its "seizures" of communal land by individuals (Browder, 1961: II, 538-41). He did this in order to contrast the "arbitrary" injustices of the old regime with the humaneness and legality of the new. The new MZ, Victor Chernov, followed Posnikov on the platform with a ringing suggestion that the government would now find "new sources of law" in "the depths and hidden places of the village" and the new reform would emerge from these depths (p. 542). All was well for democracy.

But Chernov's practical moves reflected a somewhat different attitude. An MZ order issued on 9 May, ten days before his oration on law in the depths, had already provided that the new land reform would come from a "census." During the next four months the specialists of the MZ were going to count up the number of people throughout the empire and the number of animals they possessed. The area of their landholdings was to be measured. The data thus collected would be the basis for both land reform and food procurement (pp. 536-38). Here was another rendition of the specialists' hymn. All the people were to join together according to their own traditional customs and march to the tune of systematic administration. Specialists would apportion their land and make off with their harvests systematically. Everyone would be grateful.

The concrete results of this unquenchably optimistic parade of census-takers and surveyors into the countryside would be of great interest to the historian of mobilization, but, alas, they are unknown and probably unknowable. We can say something, however, about the results. Food was not procured in sufficient quantity, land was not rearranged or even identified on any systematic basis, and the local committees set up by Petrograd to perform these functions did not play any significant role in local government.[32]

As we shall see in Chapters 11 and 12, grain collecting and land apportionment could not be divided neatly into separate categories. When official procurers actually tried to do their jobs, they had to seize arable land and redistribute it rapidly, without formality, in order to ensure that

[32]Kostrikin suggests that many volost land committees led peasants into revolutionary action—about 1,100 of them in European Russia during the Provisional Government's brief reign (1975: 306-7). Thus at least some land committees were politically active. Perhaps most of them were. As governing bodies, however, they had little success. Higher-level committees had little or no influence on the actions of their supposed subordinates, and even the active volost committees played only a fleeting role before disappearing or being muscled out by soviets and "committees of the poor" during the year after the Bolshevik Revolution (see ch. 11, sec. C).

someone would work it. Democratically elected land reformers—if there were any—also aspired to seize land, but their purposes proceeded from local politics. Thus the official activities of procurers and land reformers overlapped. In practice, the distinction disappeared altogether. From 1917 on the central government could not tell which committee was doing what. It often behooved procurers to act and speak as if they were serving local interests; likewise, it often behooved land reformers to act and speak as if they were zealously striving to increase harvests. Neither MZ nor minister of food supply could regulate its local agencies or even be sure of their existence, so we must conclude that there was no government-regulated land reform, in 1917 or at any time during the civil war.

I know of only one study that looks into the actions of the Provisional Government's local committees in a particular area, using materials collected in the locales. This is G. A. Gerasimenko's monograph on Saratov gubernia, published in 1974. Gerasimenko observes that soviet executive committees on the volost level often took direct charge of food supply work, thus leaving many food supply committees without function or power (pp. 86-87). These same *ispolkomy* (see Glossary) dominated the volost land committees by electing their own candidates as members (pp. 118-31, 157-58, 243-62). If Saratov is any indication, then, the central government had little to do with the governing of rural Russia in 1917, especially in food-producing areas. The MZ's last-ditch efforts at radical land reform were only significant insofar as they helped to sustain the specialists' presence in the countryside at a difficult time.[33]

The last question is: did any specialists actually remain in the countryside during the dark years from 1917 to 1921? Apparently a fair number did. To be sure, they were fully as inclined to run from violence in 1917 as the land captains had been in 1905. A report from one P. Romanov, head of a Duma committee in the summer of 1917, spoke of this flight during the spring, even before peasant violence became widespread (1926: 42). Gerasimenko (1974: 51-55) tells us that returning soldiers chased agronomists out of local soviet committees between March and May in Saratov gubernia, and this may have inclined many disappointed conversationalists to absent themselves from villages. However, Soviet scholar M. Snegirev has estimated that 2,000 specialists who called themselves *zemleustroiteli* were still out in the uezds in 1918. For the most part, Snegirev says, they were not functioning. They spent their time in offices in uezd towns waiting for the villages to settle down and begin again to call for their services (1947: 12-14). Under the circumstances, holding out in uezd capitals was no small achievement, and, as it turned out, the villages did begin to call for their services after a time (ch. 12, sec. A). The legacy of the Provisional Government's land reform was not entirely

[33]I am grateful to Donald Raleigh for referring me to Gerasimenko's book.

a negative one. The carriers of agrarian reform had rendered themselves helpless by the end of 1917, but they were still present. Sooner or later government-peasant interaction would begin again to assume more orderly forms, and when it did, the specialists would be ready to step forward. The reform organization was down but not out.[34]

---

[34] V. I. Kostrikin, perhaps the most able Soviet investigator of peasant insurgency in 1917, does not interest himself in specialists. In all the 300-odd pages of his latest work (1975), he has nothing whatever to report about the role of agronomists in peasant upheavals. Nevertheless, it is tempting to imagine a fair number of *agronom-organizatory* striving to regain the confidence of their erstwhile cadres by leading them off for a little pillage here and there. Such action would have fit Chaianov's prescriptions for "conversation" well enough. Given the harsh conditions that prevailed in the war between city and country, an agronomist who adopted the cause of food supply in 1914 could easily have thrown it up in 1917 and joined his "people" in resisting the increasingly empty edicts from Petrograd.

CHAPTER **11**

Disintegration, Part Two, 1917-21: The Struggle to Restore Order

> It is enough to recollect how helpless, spontaneous and inciden-
> tal were our first steps, our decrees and resolutions.... It seemed
> to us to be the easiest thing of all. Yet we only proved to our-
> selves the necessity for organization. Many people accused us for
> having attempted a thing we did not know how to carry
> out.... In my opinion it is to our credit that in spite of almost
> incredible difficulties we attempted to solve a problem till then
> unfamiliar to us. This proved our resolution and our desire to
> awaken the active spirit of the proletariat.
>
> Vladimir Lenin (1919)

It is not my purpose to add yet another study of Soviet government organization in its early years to the already long list of them. We need only to study those elements that relate to agrarian reform and food supply: those elements, in other words, in which agricultural specialists were involved and which registered most directly the continuing impact of the peasantry upon the government. What I am trying to show, in brief, is the manner in which the bolshevik regime coped with the countryside, how it gradually arrested the processes of disintegration and brought coherence to the capital-city's hitherto scattered and ineffectual efforts to mobilize.

The next chapter will take up the revival of land settlement and agricultural improvement after 1917 and carry the story of their development to 1930. In the present chapter we are concerned with the context in which agrarian reform was able to revive. There are four main topics: (1) the peasants' attitude toward government during the period 1917-21; (2) some aspects of the bolsheviks' initial perception of government; (3) the bolshevik organization for food procurement during the civil war; and (4) the early evolution of the party's organization in the context of the bolsheviks' desperate efforts to cope with the peasantry. As will be seen, agrarian reform under the Soviet regime and, indeed, the regime itself cannot be comprehended apart from the basic problem of making contact with the peasants and compelling them to provide food for their fellow citizens in the cities.

A. OBSCURITY IN THE COUNTRYSIDE

As we have seen, communication between peasantry and government took the form of fantasies during the decades after the Liberation. After 1906 interaction consisted primarily of struggles on both sides to convert fantasy into reality and vice versa. Capital-city men worked actively to squeeze villages into conceptual frameworks drawn from European imaginings, and by 1914 experience had created relationships that were not entirely fantastic. *Agronom-organizatory* had formed ties with many villages by coming to them with promises of science and credit, and these apostles of capital-city wisdom had begun to find peasants willing to fit themselves into capital-city visions. Dark masses seemed at last to be coming into the light, where capital-city minds could deal with them directly.

When war came, however, progress began to lose its attractiveness in the villages, especially in the black-soil gubernias. The masses once again became dark. The basic reason is obvious. The government had to abandon its reliance on patient benevolence and long conversations and take up once again the old work of exploiting peasants as a resource. Political leaders did not stop orating about their wishes to shower benefits on peasants, but in fact they sent agents to villages to extort grain, horses, recruits, and laborers. Under the circumstances it was natural for the capital cities to resume their old habit of envisioning peasants as crowd-images deduced from ideological preconceptions and statistical quackery. It was equally natural for the peasants to scatter into their old obscurity.

It is my aim here to call attention to darkness, not to shed light on it. The last thing I want to do is to tell the reader "what really happened" in the villages during the period 1914-21. Even supposing I were able, by some trick with computers, to discover a recognizable pattern of behavior or development among food-producing peasants, it would not help us to understand the *agronom-organizatory,* who obviously had no such "knowledge" available to them at the time. Obscurity is our subject: its impact on capital-city behavior and especially on the agricultural specialists. If we are to understand the government's side of its interaction with the peasantry, we must focus our attention on the problem of coping with the unknowable, not on knowing it.

I must emphasize the unknowability of the countryside during 1914-21 because this was a time when administrators, political leaders, and specialists found it not only expedient but necessary to proclaim themselves the "true" voice of the peasants. No man could speak intelligibly of political questions unless he affected to "know" what peasants wanted, or what they were doing, or where they were going. At the beginning of the war the tsar and his generals indulged themselves in the fond belief that peasants were willing to fight Germany and Austria on behalf of Serbia and France. For evidence they could watch troops marching by or lead them into battle. In 1917 "liberal" political leaders cherished the image of patriotic farmers willingly surrendering their produce to the Provisional Government at low prices for the sake of "freedom." For evidence they could listen to the rhetoric that poured forth from ostensible peasant representatives in a variety of soviets and committees. Finally, there were radical political leaders who believed that the countryside was teeming with "poor" peasants demanding a "just" share of land. For evidence they could point to the riots and pogroms of 1917.

These were flights of the capital-city imagination, not information. They all disappointed their believers. In 1917 peasant soldiers were displaying very little interest in Russia's foreign policy, and peasant farmers were showing no inclination at all to pay for their freedom with grain. As to the alleged multitudes who demanded land in 1917-21, a few probably did want to cultivate more soil—in the food-producing gubernias at any rate—but not many of these were poor, and none seem to have been concerned with justice or equality. In short, the above metaphors do not constitute descriptions of peasant behavior. None of them sheds light on rural darkness. On the contrary, the unending verbal battles between their upholders indicate the degree to which rural society was obscure to the capital cities during the war years.

The point here is not that Russia's wartime leaders were stupid, any more than Alexander II was stupid when he blundered into the liberation of the serfs. Rural obscurity was a fact of capital-city life and a basic element in capital-city consciousness, not someone's mistake, or sin, or lack of understanding. We are dealing with men who had to work in the dark or not work at all. I dispose of puerile notions regarding the peasantry not to dismiss the men who had to cling to them while doing their work but to behold more directly the confusion in which would-be agrarian reformers had to operate during the war years.

Alas, it is not so easy to shake off capital-city fantasies about peasant behavior in 1917. No one will quibble if I set aside the patriotic and liberal fantasies of tsarist and "bourgeois" administrators, but I cannot be quite so cavalier about the image of poor peasants grabbing land from the victimizing rich and distributing it equally among themselves. It is still common coin in both Russia and the West, and we cannot properly appreciate rural obscurity in 1917-21 without saying a word about it. If, indeed, the poor were rising and equalizing while the rich went on striving to exploit and oppress, then rural society was quite intelligible, and my statements about obscurity have no relevance to the specialists' experience. The same can be said, I suppose, for the notion that equalizing peasants were throwing off the shackles of tsarist land settlement and restoring the close fraternal relationships of their traditional "communes."

When the bolsheviks seized "power," they were shouting about the rising-equalizing poor. They had joined the populists in proclaiming that rural crowds were taking land from the rich and dividing it among themselves. Even Lenin, who was usually more perceptive than most on this subject, suggested on the day after the Winter Palace fell that if the Provisional Government had responded to the needs of poor peasants, the rural "masses" would not have risen (*Polnoe,* XXXV, 23).

In 1918-19, however, the line changed. The people who had grabbed land before October 1917 turned out to have been rich peasants. Somehow they had duped the crowds of equalizing poor, and now the party would have to go out and take away their ill-gotten gains. On 18 May 1918 a decree went out from the central committee of the bolshevik party (hereinafter referred to as the TsK) proclaiming that the struggle with the village bourgeoisie was "only beginning" (*Resheniia,* I, 65-67).[1] A new "equalization" began forthwith that would be carefully regulated by the party to protect the equalizing poor. Lenin touched on the new equalization in a speech of 8 November 1918 (*Polnoe,* XXXVII, 179-80). The bolsheviks had always disapproved of letting villages divide up land on their own, he said, blatantly contradicting his own shrill cries during the summer of 1917 (see Kostrikin, 1975: 157-58, 323). The party had only advocated spontaneous equalization in October 1917 because a majority of the peasants wanted it. The peasants had been ignorant then, but now they were learning from their own experience, and they would not do anything silly like that again.

In fact, the dark masses were not learning as fast as Lenin hoped. In late 1919 an official newspaper complained that they had been seizing lands without proper plan ever since 1917 and were still at it. Consequently the "strong"—i.e., the rich kulaks—had derived the most benefit. Only now, said the paper, were peasants beginning to see the harm in arbitrary land division (*Derevenskaia,* 3 Oct. 1919: 2). In 1922 P. A. Mesiatsev took a similar stance. He denied that there had been any "real" equalization before the second half of 1918 (1922: 71).

---

[1]See also the decree of 9 May 1918 from the central executive committee (hereinafter called the TsIK) of the All-Russian Congress of Workers', Soldiers', Peasants', and Cossacks' Deputies (*Resheniia,* I, 55-56).

Later, in the 1920s, many party spokesmen gave up this disapproving attitude toward peasant behavior in 1917. They reverted to their original rhapsodies about the great equalization and began again to complain of subsequent subversion by kulaks (e.g., Shestakov, 1927: 84-162; Iakovlev, *Derevnia,* 1924: 32-33), conveniently forgetting that in 1918-19 the party had allegedly been triumphing over kulaks. In 1925 Gordeev went so far as to assert that the so-called equalization of 1918 had actually benefited the kulaks (1925: 107).

Soviet scholars still chant these random liturgies unblushingly. One would think they might have tripped over each other by now, but they avoid this embarrassment by faithfully observing a tacit convention: to wit, none of them ever carries his investigations across 25 October 1917. A scholar may investigate events prior to this fatal line, or he may begin his account after it, but he dares not carry his analysis through the holy day in either direction. Discussions of the massive bolshevik attack on rural soviets in mid-1918 *imply* that kulaks played a predominant role in the riots of 1917, but no student ever presses the matter (e.g., Averev, 1933: I, 4-5; Abramov, 1968: 4). By the same token, glowing descriptions of spontaneous peasant risings in 1917 may *imply* that the party's subsequent attacks crushed an authentic popular revolution, but no student ever says this explicitly. E. A. Lutskii, for example, had only to keep his study focused on 1917, and he could claim, without the slightest sign of embarrassment, that the bolsheviks themselves led the peasant riots of 1917 (1948: 503; see also Kostrikin, 1957: 3-16; 1975: 209-10, 259-63, 314-20). The value of this convention is obvious. It keeps prerevolutionary mythology safely separate from legends proper to early bolshevik rule, thus allowing scholars to study specific events without exposing the painfully obvious contradictions in Soviet historical dogma. Soviet scholars investigate, yet they preserve a continuous and harmonious relationship among peasant upheavals, marxist-leninist ideology, and bolshevik leadership during the Revolution. The rising-equalizing poor somehow remain in the van of the revolutionary movement, and the bolsheviks are always with them. Such is the advantage of careful attention to periodization.

But supposing we set aside the sacred convention and put the prerevolutionary myth together with those of bolshevik rule. We then find that the poor got land in 1917, the government had to take it away from the rich in 1918, and in the 1920s the rich still had it anyway. In other words, Soviet investigators have not yet come up with any useful generalizations about events in the countryside in 1917-21.

To be sure, Soviet scholars do not agree on who the rich and poor were. Leading students of the peasant question have been debating the subject for the last two decades. Dubrovskii represents one side. He has maintained since the 1920s that the rich were mostly kulaks and the poor were landless peasants. Anfimov disagrees. He thinks the rich were predominantly estate owners, while the poor were peasants-in-general (*Osobennosti,* 1962: 5-44, 82-83). Thus, although the participants in the debate do not question the metaphor of equalizing poor rising against exploiting rich, they have not yet identified the two sides. Fortunately for the cause of orthodoxy, this debate has strengthened the metaphor's hold on scholarly imaginations, for all participants have had to accept its essential validity in order to give their undivided attention to discussing its internal structure. The happy result is that the metaphor has been rendered enormously complex, hence much more difficult to abandon.

Not so good for orthodoxy are the remarks of A. K. Kasian (1963: 147-48) and E. A. Lutskii (1970: 435-39, 444-45) to the effect that virtually all statistics used in the perennial quest to distinguish rich peasants from poor ones during the war years are close to worthless. Up to now, however, Soviet scholarship has taken no public notice of this incipient heresy.

Let us leave capital-city pamphlets aside for a moment and consider some evidence. There was a little bona fide reporting on peasant behavior in 1917-21. A few men who studied separate locales apparently wished to observe rather than peddle ideologies. Most of their work was published in the 1920s (e.g., Bolshakov, 1927; Fenomenov, 1925; Khriashcheva, 1926). Generally speaking, it suggests no consistent pattern in village activities but, rather, a wide variety of actions and attitudes in the countryside during the war years. I. P. Stepanov's survey of about 600 villages in Moscow gubernia showed that almost no "equalizations" took place in 1917, when, presumably, the peasants were seizing neighboring lands. In 1918 about 37% of the villages conducted redistributions of the traditional sort on their own lands—which meant a variety of things, usually a reshuffling of strips to assure that land was assigned to families capable of working it. Another 30% did nothing at all to readjust their holdings, and about 28% conducted group land settlement measures to reduce the number of strips in each holding and/or introduce advanced crop rotation schemes. Sixteen villages carried out consolidations of household lots (Stepanov, 1925: 26-27). V. N. Alekseev's study of Kurovo village (in Moscow gubernia) shows that no land adjustment took place during the war years, though the village population increased sharply after 1917 (1923: 7-8). Dyskii's companion study tells of a village where a qualitative redistribution (see ch. 9, sec. A) was completed during the period 1911-17 and was then left unchanged in spite of attempts by a minority of villagers to break away and consolidate their strips into otrub farms (1923: 23-24).

Another example of relatively reliable reporting is a government survey of late 1918 conducted by the people's commissariat of agriculture, i.e., the MZ under its new bolshevik name. The commissariat (hereinafter referred to as the NKZ) asked local administrators to report on the formal procedures adopted in their areas for allotting lands. No agents from Petrograd went out to check on the reports, so the survey did nothing but repeat the accounts local administrators sent in. Not all areas sent in reports; consequently the compilers had to admit that their product consisted only of some tentative remarks "illustrating" local procedures (*Raspredelenie,* 1). If the materials were incomplete and highly tenuous, however, they were presented with compelling modesty. The authors made it a point to avoid ideological stances and stick to evidence.[2]

The NKZ's investigators observed that leading men in each area were dealing with land pretty much as they saw fit, without regard for government policies or party ideologies. Regulations varied widely from one locale to another. For example, rules regarding the disposal of consolidated farms varied widely. In Orel and Viatka gubernias some volosts were taking pains to protect khutors and otrubs from redistribution, whereas in Vladimir some sets of volost rules required khutor and otrub farmers to give up their plots—if necessary, their homes—and return to their old strips (pp. 9-10; *Otchuzhdenie,* 4-6; see also Mesiatsev, 1922: 121-23). Local administrators, it seems, were not making it a point to defy the government, but they saw no pressing reason to obey the government. Nor did their work reflect anything like a typical pattern of action in the villages or even a typical attitude toward economic and social problems.

The investigators did come up with one generalization. Local regulations, they opined, were never aimed at establishing the rights or shares of individuals. Whoever was writing the rules, their primary purpose in almost all cases was to determine who the members of a household were, thereby providing a basis for measuring off the household's share of land (*Sostav,* 4-8, 14-15, 20). Each household head seems to have been striving to maximize his share of land by including more members in his own *dvor* while preventing other households from doing the same. If several households in a village had members who were part-time factory workers, these households would support a rule granting part-time factory workers a full share of village land. Other households, lacking factory workers among their membership, would maintain that such men were not members of any household and hence could not be counted for purposes of claiming shares of land. Each village decided such disagreements in its

[2] I have seen only three volumes of this study: *Sostav (kontingent) nadeliae-mogo zemlei naseleniia* (1918 or 1919), *Raspredelenie zemli v 1918 godu* (1918), and *Otchuzhdenie i ispolzovanie selskokhoziaistvennogo inventaria* (1919). There may have been others, but scholarly works on peasant efforts to redistribute land in 1917-18 have relied entirely on these three booklets. More precisely, scholarly works have relied on Pershin's book, *Uchastkovoe* (1922), and his article, "Formy" (1921), which are based almost entirely on these surveys (see especially 1922: 35-37; 1921: 69-72).

own way, and this is one reason why peasants were adopting such a bewildering variety of views on land "rights" in 1918.

Note that the local rules reflected no more concern for "equality" than for "rights." Individuals and households that were not part of a village's land-shuffling arrangement had no claim on its land except for fields the villagers did not wish to cultivate. In the summer of 1918 peasant "revolutionaries" were still not showing much inclination to help the poor.[3]

Admittedly, local regulations collected via the mail are not the best kind of evidence, but the equalization scenario of bolshevik and populist legend rests on even less solid ground. Chiefly, it comes from two bodies of material: an abundance of obviously faked reports from administrators in the locales, and a census taken in 1919. Let us take a glance at these pillars of conventional wisdom.

As to the reports, consider one from an uezd in Vladimir gubernia. It claimed with breezy assurance that surveyors were busily making maps of *all* village lands and private estates, listing the number of people (on the basis of the census of 1897!) and calculating the area of each arable field (*Agrarnaia,* 1954: 301). Allegedly this was going to allow uezd administrators to distribute all private estates to the peasants and also rearrange their own land, all this before the year was out. The outlandish crudity of this claim is evident in itself. It becomes even clearer when contrasted with relatively honest statements, such as a report from an uezd in Saratov gubernia describing how difficult it was to equalize holdings without immensely complicating the basic business of cultivation (pp. 320-21). Preposterously fake reports of the Vladimir type were typical in 1918; those of the Saratov variety were very rare. Thus it is easy to accumulate "evidence" for massive equalization in 1917-18.

As to the census of 1919, it rests entirely on reports from locales and represents an unusually blatant fraud even by Russian standards. Scholars cite it, however. After all, a census is a census, and it does give support to the poor-rich scenario. Indeed, it concerns itself with little else than identifying poor, middle, and rich peasants. Totals drawn from the reports suggest that in 1917-18 the percentage of very poor and very rich households decreased. "Poor" referred to households with less than four acres of land or none at all; "rich" referred to households with more than 22 acres. Actually, it was not only the rich and poor who shrank in proportion to the rest. Farms of more than 11 acres and less than 22 also decreased proportionately. The only kind of farm that became more

[3]It is of interest that the investigators perceived a general tendency to leave khutors and otrubs alone if the village from which they had been blocked off did not consider them to be obstacles to the cultivation of village land (*Sostav,* 6-7). On the spread of land settlement in 1918, see ch. 12, sec. A.

abundant, according to the census, was the sort that fell between four and 11 acres. In 1916, 59% of peasant households had held this minimal amount of land. In 1919 the corresponding figure was 74%. So say the "data" (Khriashcheva, 1921: 21-22; Kirillov, 1922: 112; Poliakov, 1963: 28-31).

But in 1919 the bolshevik kulak hunt had already been in full swing for over a year. By this time it was vitally necessary for peasants, specialists, and local officials, including party agents, to report small farms, lest they be accused of protecting kulaks and suffer the depredations of grain-grabbing gangs (see Bolshakov, 1927: 90, 100-101; and below, sec. C). If we are to credit the census of 1919, we must believe that in the already difficult years of 1917 and 1918 large numbers of peasant farmers cheerfully undertook to destroy not only their larger farms but also most of their moderate-sized ones in order to replace them with unworkable little patches.

Probably no such equalization ever took place. What did take place in 1917-18, as we shall see presently (sec. C), was a series of devastating raids on the countryside by armed grain-collecting gangs who were formally authorized to take anything they found from peasants who had larger shares of land. By 1919 it was more imperative than ever before for peasants to appear poor. The census of 1919 reflected this fact of life, not reality. As to what reality might have been, the census takers never asked.

Scholars have had very little to say about the violence that accompanied food procurement. One reason is the bolshevik-populist obsession with what they call the peasant "movement"—another variation on the rich-poor theme in the equalization scenario. The peasant "movement" comes to us from the following intellectual procedure. Incidents of violent disruption in the countryside are carefully numbered and, where possible, described. Lists of these incidents are presented, interspersed with assertions about the sweeping nature of each incident, thereby creating an impression of rural Russia in flames. Soviet research along these lines tells us that peasant violence increased for a while in 1914, when the war broke out, and it never stopped entirely thereafter (ch. 9, n. 20). Following the February Revolution, violence and outlawry spread much more rapidly in the countryside, putting all previous upheavals, even those of 1861 and 1905, far behind. Disorder seems to have reached a high point in October 1917 (*Krestianskoe,* 1927: iii-x; Kravchuk, 1971: 88). This presents a tableau that gives comfort to most scholarly preconceptions, both left and right. We see an approaching revolution signaled by growing unrest among the rural poor, and we contemplate yet again the vast historical forces set in motion by poor people struggling against wealth.

It would serve no useful purpose to go through all the nonsense published on this subject and critique it in detail. Consider only one example. A. M. Anfimov finds it aesthetically pleasing to see an upswing in peasant violence prior to the February Revolution (1965: 27). One of the tricks he plays to give substance to this fantasy is to list 27 separate incidents in Kostroma gubernia in February. This brings his total for January-February to 51, a higher monthly rate than had obtained during 1915-16, which permits him to conclude that the February riots in Petrograd had deep roots in the countryside. By his own report, however, the 27 incidents were all part of a single collective refusal by peasants *and zemstvoes* in two uezds to deliver oats to an army grain procurer (pp. 421, 512-13). Now it is interesting to learn that by 1917 tsarist food administrators had been reduced to trying to pull grain out of a net grain-consuming gubernia like Kostroma, but it is ridiculous to refer to obviously specialist-led opposition to these antics as an upswing in a "peasant movement." Peasants did resist grain requisitions ever more openly and successfully as the war went on, but if specialists and landholders were leading the resistance, as often happened, then we cannot speak of the poor rising against the rich (see Figurovskaia, 1968: 45; *Krestianskoe,* 1927: 165; *Prodovolstvie,* 1 Sept. 1917: 28-29). Anfimov's blatant distortion of evidence in this case is typical of Soviet scholarship relating to the peasant "movement."

It has never been fashionable to consider the food producers' resistance to government collectors as revolutionary or even popular, since this would becloud our pretty picture of righteous poor rising in wrath against grasping rich. In fact, however, popular resistance to food collection in the food-producing regions played a key role in setting off the Revolution, and it is important to note that government agents, zemstvoes, and cooperatives all played a key role in fomenting this "movement." Rittikh's forced procurement campaign of late 1916–early 1917 was entrusted to zemstvo directorates, and it was they, not peasants, who took the lead in refusing to obey orders from the capital cities (ch. 10, sec. D). From then on rural violence *centered* on the struggle for food. There were fights between hoarders and government agencies (*Prodovolstvie,* 1 Sept. 1917: 10-13), attacks on estates to force them to cultivate land or give up their grain (see Fleer, 1926: 14; *Ekonomicheskoe,* III, 312-23, 328; *Krestianskoe,* 1927: 247), attacks by food-collecting gangs on villages (e.g., *1917 god v Saratovskoi,* 1961: 259-60, 269, 333; *Prodovolstvie,* 15 Oct. 1917: 19), fights between army and civilian grain purchasers (e.g., *Prodovolstvie,* 15 Oct. 1917: 20), fights between grain purchasers from different gubernias and uezds (pp. 9, 16; see also Kravchuk, 1971: 194-97), etc. None of this constituted a struggle of poor vs. rich, nor did it constitute a peasant "movement." The capital cities were attacking farmers of all sorts, and farmers were trying to hide their harvests.

We cannot slip by without devoting at least one paragraph to the seizure of landed estates. Peasants did seize them in 1917, and their actions did fit the rich-poor scenario, albeit roughly. However, the seizure of estates represented a rather small part of peasant activity. In the previous year a reasonably reliable census had determined that private estate owners held only 10.7% of European Russia's plowland (Osipova, 1974: 31). The vast majority of peasants did not live near enough to an estate to take one over. To be sure, private estates did comprise a somewhat greater portion of European Russia's forests and meadows. Many villages benefited—at least for a while—by gaining free access to firewood, fishing holes, hunting preserves, and grazing land. Most forest land, however, was state property, and if we were to transfigure firewood chopping and poaching into major revolutionary manifestations, we should have to deal primarily with a contest between government and poor, not rich and poor. But in fact no capital-city pamphleteer has ever considered it particularly revolutionary to poach. In the conventional metaphor of the estate-raiding peasant, he took plowland and shared it with his comrades by mutual agreement so that each one got what was coming to him. This seizure and redistribution was what the rural revolution of legend was all about, and my point is that not much of it actually took place in 1917-18. Moreover, villages that did acquire plowland had somehow to put it in the hands of farmers who possessed the necessary animals and equipment to farm it. Landless peasants, refugees from cities, and army deserters all came pouring into villages in 1917, desperately trying to survive the general famine hysteria, and they must have found it expedient to call out slogans about equal land distribution, but what they needed were the products of the soil, not soil itself. Their problem was to eat, not to cultivate, and no one would eat if the land were parceled out to "poor" people who lacked the wherewithal to farm it. Even when plowland was taken over, therefore, it was the wealthier peasants—if anyone—who farmed it, i.e., those who already had land. If there was a "mass" movement among the peasantry in 1917, it had very little to do with landless peasants getting land, the 1919 census notwithstanding. When it came to the peasants' alleged demand to abolish private property, the most important consideration in their minds was the cancellation of their mortgage indebtedness, especially their debts to the peasant bank. But, of course, peasants who worried about mortgages were far from poor.

Now we come to the last of our conventional images: the revival of the commune. We have just discussed the widespread assumption that peasants "equalized" their holdings on a massive scale during the period 1917-21. According to many populist pamphleteers of 1917-18, these peasants were re-establishing the old peasant practice of land redistribution, forcing all those who had broken away from their villages to come back in and bring their land with them. Many scholars have accepted this tableau (see, e.g., Kachorovskii, 1929: 571-76; Taniuchi, 1968: 19), thus replacing the bolshevik picture of rich and poor peasants fighting each other with a united yeomanry standing by their old ways in accordance with Lev Tolstoi's latter-day fantasies.

As I have said, we have no reliable evidence on what peasants were actually doing with their land in 1917-18. Supposing, however, that massive redistributions did take place, reabsorbing khutors into interstripped villages, it seems to me that we do not have to look far for *practical* explanations. From 1917 on the countryside was a dangerous place, and private grain trading was a criminal offense. A peasant who used the latest agricultural methods, thereby producing harvests more bountiful than his neighbors', was not better off than they, only more exposed to peril. His neighbors considered the paying of tribute to a gang of marauders to be a misfortune, not an obligation of citizenship, and they were little inclined to sacrifice their own grain if they could avoid doing so by leading raiders to the storehouses of more productive farmers. It was, therefore, a matter of common sense to blend into the pack, especially when the pack included a fair number of armed deserters and urban cousins who had rejoined their villages and were eager to qualify their households for additional shares of land (see Gerasimenko, 1974: 51-55; Osipova, 1974: 61). It was also not a bad idea to keep all houses in a village in a single cluster and go out to the fields to work in large groups, which is to say that some very good reasons for not farming khutor and otrub lots suddenly became manifest in 1917 and remained so until 1921. Interstripped fields and clustered houses were not "natural" or inevitable, or even desirable, to most peasants, but in a countryside where the group's survival was exactly equivalent to the individual's welfare, they certainly looked more attractive than they had for a long time. At least this is not a bad guess (see Mesiatsev, 1922: 122-24; Pershin, 1922: 39-42; Atkinson, 1973: 153-55). When contemplating the Russian village in 1917-20—especially in the grain-producing gubernias—one should keep in mind the image of a tribe of baboons in an African jungle, huddling together at night so that only the outermost ones will be torn apart by leopards. The most successful baboons are not the strongest, or even the smartest, but the ones who get closest to the center of the pack. The reader will do well to recall R. E. F. Smith's remark about sixteenth-century peasants (quoted above in ch. 5, sec. B): "the small size and low level of technology of the peasant unit contributed to its viability when disaster struck" (1977: 172).

Redistribution had a double edge. It could unite resident households against a hostile world, and it could also serve as a device by which outsiders broke in. Doubtless the large crowd of people who were trying to get back into villages from 1917 on found redistribution immensely appealing. They were not equipped to farm, but they probably wanted to establish a claim to some land so they could then rent it out to authentic farmers and live off the proceeds. This sort of thing had already been taking place on a relatively small scale during Stolypin's day. Paradoxically, the reform had created a demand for redistribution by wiping out most of the debt attached to the land and raising its market value. A few urban cousins had tried to return and cut back into their shares of the newly valuable fields whenever they had gotten wind of redistributions (ch. 6, sec. D). Usually these opportunists had not wished to take up farming. Their purpose in acquiring land through redistribution had been to convert it to private property and sell it. This had not occurred frequently before 1917 because the "rigid" MVD had taken steps to oppose it (ch. 9, sec. A) and because the returning prodigals had not come bearing arms. In 1917-18, however, much larger numbers of erstwhile villagers came pouring back home from the cities and the army, calling themselves members of land-poor households and demanding redistributions, and after October 1917 they had the government on their side (see Kirillov, 1922: 14; Poliakov, 1963: 38; Atkinson, 1973: 156-57; also ch. 12, sec. A). Obviously their purpose was no longer to sell the land they got. What they wanted now was to live off the labor of established farmers until things got better in the cities. It is at least conceivable, then, that some villages reasserted the "traditional" practice of redistribution under the guns of returning "proletarians."

Probably the residents did not welcome their returning cousins with open arms. In a village studied by A. Karunovskaia in Iaroslavl gubernia, it took several years for residents and returnees to agree to a redistribution (1924: 59-61, 69-70, 79-83). According to L. Kritsman, villages generally kept out would-be returnees until the spring of 1918, when bolshevik food-collecting agents began to appear in force (1926: 188), which suggests that redistributions in mid-1918 and thereafter were often imposed upon resident farmers by combined pressure from returnees and procurement gangs.

These inconclusive speculations constitute about all one can say in a general way about redistribution during the civil war. It is hard to discern in the available evidence any sign of resurgent village tradition. Nevertheless, scholars continue to discover and rediscover that redistribution was a living principle in which peasants believed and to which they strove to return, as to some sort of sanctity. Such imaginings leave much to be desired. The millions who fled from Russia's starving cities were not longing for communal landholding, let alone sanctity. Very few of them wished to take up farming again under any system of landholding. What they wanted was simply to stay alive in a time of disintegration (and unrestrained mobilization).

I can see no point in affirming or denying the "resurgence" of the commune. Imagine for a moment that the tsarist government had devoted its last years to installing flush toilets in all the peasant huts of European Russia, together with aqueducts and sewage systems. Doubtless its publications would have trumpeted forth its successes in terms of numbers of peasants renouncing outhouses and taking up the use of toilets. With the onset of war and revolution, the water and sewage systems would have fallen apart and peasants would have reverted to outhouses. So far, so good—but what could one say when confronted with an enthusiast who claimed that the outhouse triumphed in 1917-21, thereby demonstrating the futility of the government's programs and the strength of the outhouse in peasant hearts? I for one do not know how to argue with this kind of assertion. I do not see any point in arguing with it, and I only bring up the very tired subject of the commune once again because it has loomed so large in histories of the peasantry during the war years. Ditto for the peasant "movement" and the rising-equalizing poor. The essential quality of the villages after Rittikh's pathetic gestures at forced procurement was obscurity. The main problem of government during the period 1917-21 was to deal with a peasantry that had made itself invisible. At the end of the period, after more than three years of struggling to assess the resources each village possessed, measure its production, and estimate its income, the Soviet government had made no progress whatever toward these goals (Shlikhter, 1975: 418).

B. THE BEGINNINGS OF SOVIET GOVERNMENT

Formal Structure

The bolsheviks' campaign to take power led them more or less unavoidably to set up an extremely democratic and decentralized government. This proved embarrassing, since, as we have observed, the collapse of both state and national economy had proceeded from the steady deterioration of central direction under Nicholas II and the Provisional Government. Generally speaking, then, the formal structure of the Soviet state evolved from two basic facts of life: existing institutions of government were decentralized, and the government had somehow to be subordinated again to central direction.

The bolsheviks did not do much to reform the executive apparatus of government. The old Council of Ministers became the *Sovet Narodnykh Komissarov,* or Council of People's Commissars (SNK), but this represented only a nominal change. The functions of the commissar-ministers (NKs), and their manner of operating remained much the same as before the Revolution. So did their personnel. At least two-thirds of the specialists who were serving the Soviet regime in 1922 had also served the tsars (Fediukin, 1965: 138; see also Rigby, 1979: 61-64).

The constitutional structure of the state underwent somewhat more drastic changes. Formally speaking, supreme governing power now rested in the people, who expressed their will through their local soviets. Supposedly these local bodies elected deputies to higher-level groups—uezd or city soviets—and these in turn elected deputies to gubernia soviets (or congresses of soviet deputies), which then sent deputies to the "all-Russian" congress of deputies of soviets of workers, soldiers, peasants, and cossacks (to use the longest of several titles assigned to this supreme body). Until 1924 this congress was the supreme governing body of the Russian Socialist Federation of Soviet Republics (RSFSR). In 1924 the USSR was formed, and another echelon was added. The RSFSR and her sister republics sent delegates to the all-union congress (supreme soviet), and this became the supreme governing body.

Each soviet (or congress) at each level spawned its own set of administrative organs, which were invariably managed by an "executive committee" elected by the soviet. The executive committee—*ispolnitelnyi komitet,* hereinafter referred to as the ispolkom—managed the soviet's (or congress's) affairs, carried out its orders, and enforced its laws. The ispolkom of the all-Russian congress was the central ispolkom of the RSFSR (after 1924 the USSR), and it was this body, usually referred to as the TsIK, that hired and fired NKs.

This structure of congresses was potentially either decentralized or centralized. Had it been decentralized in fact as it was in appearance, each local ispolkom would have been primarily responsible to the soviet that elected its members, and local administrators would have taken their orders from the ispolkom that hired them. But the Soviet state did not operate very long in this fashion. The bolsheviks rapidly established the operating principle that administrative organs on each level took their orders from corresponding executive organs at higher levels, and by the end of 1918 the ispolkoms themselves had become increasingly subordinated to higher-level ispolkoms. Local soviets continued to go through the motions of electing their committees, but the only orders they could issue had to do with exclusively local concerns, and even these modest assertions of prerogative had to be approved by higher echelons to make sure they conformed to decrees and ordinances from the center. So it has been in the USSR ever since.

The main agency for centralizing the regime of soviets was the bolshevik party, though in 1917 this group of crowd pleasers seemed an ill-suited device for the purpose. Initially, party leaders influenced local institutions by working through party members within each soviet and/or ispolkom, using them to manipulate their nonparty colleagues according to dictates from central party headquarters, i.e., the party secretariat. The principal means for exercising influence in this fashion were the local "cells," which in the early days were made up of any people in any locale who were pleased to call themselves bolsheviks. The cells were linked with the party as a whole in much the same way as the soviets were linked with the central government. Each cell elected a "committee" to manage its affairs, and it also periodically elected delegates to higher-level conferences or congresses. Supposedly these bodies formulated general policies and plans for their respective territories and elected delegates to conferences and congresses on yet higher levels. Each conference-congress elected a permanent committee to conduct its affairs on a regular basis. At the top, of course, was the All-Russian Party Congress. Prior to 1921 this body met annually; from 1921 to 1928 it met every other year. It too elected a "central committee," the TsK, and the TsK set up the party secretariat to conduct its affairs. In the absence of any other agencies, the secretariat acted directly through its cells, even though, at first, it had no idea who the members were.

Since the party organization resembled that of the soviets, it also embodied the same dual potential for centralized or decentralized operation. Before seizing power, it had been relatively decentralized. To be sure, the bolsheviks accepted Lenin's old dictum that edicts of the All-Russian Party Congress were a law unto the local cells. No one could oppose this law except at congress meetings. But if the cells could not go against directives from the center, they still managed their own affairs. Party leadership did not attempt to direct their actions on a regular basis. Before the Revolution, when the bolsheviks had nothing to do but stir up rebellion, the only constraint central authority needed to exercise over its members was in the matter of doctrine.

After October 1917 the party found itself in "power" over a conglomeration of local soviets, ispolkoms, and administrative organs that had lost the ability to coordinate with each other or operate on their own. Worse, their personnel were generally hostile to central government of any kind and to the bolsheviks in particular. Under the circumstances, the party secretariat could not rely on cells to do its work. Lenin and his colleagues could not rebuild a government and national economy in Russia—to say nothing of restoring order—on no other basis than the friendly cooperation of their followers in each locale. Therefore, the secretariat undertook to direct Russia by sending out plenipotentiary agents with full power to command local cells to do their bidding. Indeed, everyone had to work under their direction—soviets, NK organs, army divisions, and whomever else they encountered. During the civil war the secretariat resorted to these frenzied line-over-staff methods quite often, and before long a more or less regular organization of them emerged. This was the party *apparat*.

In a later section I shall dwell at some length on the establishment of the apparat. Suffice it here to remind the reader that the bolsheviks' postrevolutionary passion for centralized organization was quite understandable under the conditions of 1917. The apparat did not originate in Lenin's psychological peculiarities, whatever they may have been, or in marxist ideological formulations, or in any aspect of "revolutionary" activity prior to 1917. It came into being in 1917 because civil administration in Russia had been disintegrating for more than three years—ever since Nicholas II permitted his army to push it out of the way—and because disintegration called forth a renewed urge to mobilize.

The Role of Bolshevik Ideology in Mobilization

If I ignore marxism and return directly to the problem of food supply at this point, I shall be in danger of implying that marxism had nothing to do with the bolsheviks' success at arresting disintegration in Russia. I might even be understood to mean that the Soviet state itself owed nothing to Marx, since Marx, after all, had very little to say about agrarian reform and famine hysteria, let alone the influence of dark peasant masses on administrations. I hasten to declare, therefore, that the Soviet state owed a great deal to Marx and especially to Lenin's use of Marx's writings.

On the other hand, it seems to me that most students of revolutionary history have not grasped Marx's contribution, or Lenin's either, mainly because they give too much attention to the concept of revolution. Taking one thing with another, revolution was one of Marx's least meaningful ideas. We shall do well to free ourselves, at least for a moment, from his rhetoric about downtrodden masses leading the way to heaven on earth and speak instead of his impact as a prophet of mobilization. What I should like to do here is to follow Max Weber's manner of dealing with capitalism and to set aside Marx's ideological formulations so as to perceive the "spirit" behind them.

Marx and Mobilization

One gets the impression that Marx never thought very deeply about administration. He spoke of it only rarely and superficially, and Engels mentioned it only to dismiss it as unimportant. "With six clerks," said Engels in a letter to Marx dated 20 July 1851, "I could organize an infinitely more simple, better arranged and more practical branch of administration than I could with sixty government councillors and bureaucratic financial advisors" (Marx, *Correspondence,* 68). In effect, however, Marx's concept of the dictatorship of the proletariat embodied a concept of administration, one that resembles very closely my model of line-over-staff organization. Mass leaders, said Marx in his *Holy Family,* should deal directly with their masses and not attempt to impose rules and procedures on them. A proper leader of the proletariat had to be free not only from doctrine but from law and regulation as well. The "dictator" and his agents had to determine the way revolution should develop as they went along through interaction with the masses. As Lenin once put it, "The scientific concept 'dictatorship,' means nothing more nor less than unrestricted power, absolutely unimpeded by laws or regulations and resting directly upon force" (*Selected Works,* VII, 252).[4] Marx's writings did two things relating to the concept of mobilization: (1) they identified capitalism as a mobilization of the people of the world so thoroughgoing that it would ultimately break down all cultural individuality; and (2) they predicted that the proletariat would take over this irreversible movement because the capitalists themselves would be unable to cope with their own creation. The capitalists were destroying culture, including the family, with an absolutely irresistible combination of technology and greed, but greed, protected by property rights, could not manage the vast machinery of production and distribution it was creating. Capitalists were not fully aware of the machine they were erecting. They did not and could not perceive that they were becoming mere cogs, for each one of them fancied that he owned his role in the world exchange. But as the machine grew more refined and complex, it became increasingly vulnerable to the idiosyncrasies of its participants, and therefore the time would come when the cogs would destroy the machine. Sooner or later the whole apparatus would fall to the "proletariat," i.e., men purged of greed and of every remnant of cultural individuality by their long experience as slaves to machines.

Never mind that Marx's specific predictions about the development of capitalism were faulty. In his uncompromising acceptance of mobilization, he came much closer than most of his myopic contemporaries to understanding the spirit of modern society. Never mind that he sometimes spoke foolishly of communist society as a utopia in which men would not suffer from scarcity and would therefore enjoy the leisure to fulfill the possibilities in their personalities (see, e.g., Marx, *Capital,* III, 799-800). If this silly pap were all he said about the goal of revolution—if he had really believed leisure to be the ultimate aim of human striving—then obviously we could not refer to the communist world as a mobilized one. But Marx also described communist society as one in which each member gives what he can and receives what he needs. He does not claim rights but only acknowledges obligations. Marx would not have admitted it, but in fact his ideal communist society did not eliminate bourgeois society but restored it to its original ethical ideals. Communism strives to cope with modern bourgeois society's practical necessities by reasserting

[4]Two excellent accounts of bolshevik line-over-staff operation in Petrograd in 1917 are Alex Rabinowitch's seminal studies, *Prelude to Revolution* (1968) and *The Bolsheviks Come to Power* (1976).

the cardinal principle of capital accumulation: one must serve without thought for personal gain (see Little, 1978: 70-96, 173-95). The man who gives what he can and takes only what he needs has not ceased to be a commodity. On the contrary, he has become a perfect commodity in the world market. He makes a virtue of selling himself as cheaply as he can and lending himself readily to exploitation (distribution). The member of communist society who earnestly believes he should act this way is happy and proud to be a cog in the universal machine of production and distribution, and this happiness constitutes his own salvation as well as that of his fellow commodities. Only in a world inhabited by willing slaves, resolutely affirming their unrelenting responsibility for the circulation of goods, could the state wither away and leave all men free to cope with necessity in a spirit of joyful acceptance.

This was mobilization with a vengeance. Few thinkers have come as close as Marx to looking directly at the consequences of modern economic development. It was his perception of the central role of mobilization in this development that constituted the essence of his contribution to the formation of the Soviet state.[5]

The Bolsheviks' Use of Marxism

When the bolsheviks seized what they took to be power in Petrograd, they were not saying much about Marx's doctrines. Their ideological appeal consisted primarily of the slogan "peace, bread, and land." Peace proved to be unrealizable for more than three years; bread and land implied contradictory state policies. Handing out land to grain farmers and letting them use it as they pleased meant starving the cities; feeding cities meant forcing farmers to produce grain and sell it for an unprofitably low price. Be this as it may, peace, bread, and land were no more fatuous in late 1917 than victory, inflation, and the prompt payment of rent, which had been the goals of preceding regimes. Bolshevik slogans

---

[5] Marx's meandering denunciations of Hegel's disciples and French radicals in *The Holy Family* (1956) only hint at the above formulation. The critical essays in this volume, some from Marx and some from Engels, have no apparent connection except a persistently anti-intellectual tone. No single quotation can properly sum them up, but Marx's gut attitude peeks through in the following: "Since the abstraction of humanity...is practically complete in the full grown proletariat;...since man has lost himself in the proletariat; yet at the same time has not only gained theoretical consciousness of that loss, but through...*need*...is driven directly to revolt;...it follows that the proletariat can and must free itself" (p. 52). Marx and Engels devoted most of *The Holy Family* to heaping ridicule upon intellectuals who aspired to self-consciousness as an end in itself. The intellectual's self, according to Marx, is only a grotesque fantasy that demonstrates his own personal alienation.

were meaningful even if their basis in doctrine was shaky and their promises unrealizable.

But our primary interest does not lie in the pleasing of crowds. We wish to know, rather, the role bolshevik ideology played in the formation of bolshevik government organization. From this point of view, the key feature in bolshevik ideology was Lenin's emphasis on Marx's implied commandment to *avoid* formulating concepts about revolution and to lead revolutionary masses in whatever direction they seemed capable of going. "At the present moment," Lenin said in mid-September 1917, "it is impossible to remain loyal to Marxism and to the revolution *without regarding insurrection as an art*" (*Selected Works,* VI, 223; italics in the original). He meant that party leaders should stop worrying about doctrine and focus their attention on actual conditions. In the fall of 1917, when there was no force in Russia capable of stopping crowds, Lenin believed that a proper revolutionary should respond to them rather than trying to do the correct thing (pp. 218-23).

We must consider two questions: (1) was bolshevik ideology marxist, and (2) did it produce the Soviet government?

In October 1917 most learned marxists believed that bolshevik slogans and tactics were not marxist. If Marx's teaching be understood to consist of doctrines and prescriptions to be followed and interpreted, the way rabbis follow and interpret the Torah, then the learned marxists were probably correct. Marx, however, was quite unlike most of his disciples in that he himself was not a disciple. His ideology was in essence a call to action, not a prescription for it, and his basic directive to all intellectuals was to *respond* to "workers," not to plan their movements for them. He did say that capitalism had to collapse in a certain way before it could be overthrown, but in practice he was willing to accept any form of social upheaval as *the* revolution, quite without regard for conditions in the stock market. He ended his *Communist Manifesto,* which he wrote just before 1848, with a prediction of a proletarian revolution in Germany in the very near future. In 1871 he described the Paris Commune as an authentic revolution, though he only knew what he read in the newspapers about it. In both cases his analyses flagrantly violated his ideas on how history produced revolutions.

In sum, Marx's basic law for intellectuals was to take masses as they were and to recognize a collapsing state when they saw one, whether or not its disintegration followed pre-established patterns. In 1917, had he been alive, he doubtless would have done as Lenin did in Petrograd. Capitalism had not matured on schedule, but in fact the state was breaking down. Armed crowds were in the streets demanding to be mobilized. One had either to go before the people and lead them or withdraw from the scene, and when one goes before armed crowds in Russia, one does not recite prescriptions written by a German philosopher. One tries to find out what the masses will follow and then one says it. A marxist may say virtually anything to a crowd with conviction, because he believes in advance that the crowd is right. It has to be right, especially if there is no force capable of stopping it. Lenin sensed this. Initially he did not get his revolutionary program from the Petrograd crowd, but in the fall of 1917 he was able to grasp that the crowd was indeed following him. Unlike most of Marx's learned disciples, with their heads buried in *Capital,* he was aware that collapsing governments and crowds are facts, not corollaries to theoretical propositions. His ideology, then, was quite orthodox. Lenin was not a disciple but a leader, which was, after all, what Marx had called upon intellectuals to be.

We may say, then, that bolshevik ideology, or rather the bolshevik *approach* to ideology, did have much to do with producing the Soviet state. True, one can read any number of bolshevik proclamations and convince oneself that bolshevik words and actions were entirely unrelated —that nothing could be further removed from the reality of the Soviet state than prerevolutionary communist ideology. One of Lenin's most famous works, *State and Revolution,* written only a few weeks before the October coup in Petrograd, indicated a puerile disregard for administrative policies and problems. A typical pearl: "The great majority of functions of the old 'state power' have become so simplified and can be reduced to such simple operations of registration, filing and checking that they can be easily performed by every literate person" (*Selected Works,* VII, 42). We cannot doubt that Lenin meant every word of this. In August 1917, when he feared arrest and assassination, he asked a comrade to make sure that his manuscript was published (Rabinowitch, 1976: 37). He published it himself after he had come to power, though by then he was demonstrating each day what monstrous twaddle it contained. But this only illustrates my point. Lenin shifted his concept of the state as often and as sharply as seemed necessary to mobilize his people. "In order to obtain the power of state," he said on 22 April 1917, "the class conscious workers must win the majority to their side.... We are not in favor of the seizure of power by a minority" (*Selected Works,* VI, 29). In a writing dated *one day* later, he added, "We must look forward to the new democracy which is in process of being born, and which is already ceasing to be a democracy. For democracy means the rule of the people, whereas the armed people cannot rule over themselves. The term democracy...has now, since March 1917, simply become a *blinker* covering the eyes of the revolutionary people" (p. 74, italics in the original). In short, Lenin's marxism consisted mainly of being able to stand ideas on their heads while keeping his own feet. Under his leadership the Soviet state evolved as an organization capable of shifting rapidly from one premise to another. Lenin worked and thought within the framework of a line-over-staff organization, and in this sense his marxism played a fundamental role in the forming of the Soviet state.

Admittedly Lenin took great pains to keep up an appearance of doctrinal consistency. This too, however, was part of the business of responding to the "people." If the masses really exist as a recognizable entity—and marxism makes very little sense if they do not—then anyone who ventures to mobilize them must continuously give them the impression that he possesses some concept of the paths they have followed and the goal that lies ahead. The concept may change from time to time, but at any one point it must appear to be reasonably coherent and purposeful. In other words, a mass government must present at least as good a simulation of continuity as a daily newspaper. It must preserve a facade of consistency and, complementarily, it must crush all public criticism directed against the facade. Not a beautiful prospect for intellectuals, but it is no less beautiful than an intellectual who denounces mass leaders while piously proclaiming his concern for masses. Lenin never lost sight of his dependence on the masses and *therefore* he gave them endless pages covered with rabbinical prose about the purposes of his government without ever allowing his prose to obstruct his perception.

This is not to deny that the early bolshevik mode of government was a result of organizational evolution under the tsars. Insofar as successive waves of mobilization and systematization were an essential and highly noticeable feature of Russian government, the bolsheviks were continuing an old tradition. Even so, marxist ideology—in particular, Lenin's marxist ideology—was a significant motivating and organizing force. In 1917 a great variety of political leaders joined the struggle to govern in the absence of an effective system, but the bolsheviks were the only ones apart from the tsarist general staff who called unequivocally for line-over-staff administration. Tsarist experience did not automatically produce the bolsheviks, but it did lead to a situation in which bolshevik ideology suddenly began to make practical sense. The bolsheviks created an effective government not only because they were Russian but also because marxist ideology gives expression to a consuming urge to mobilize.

It is tempting to see in the marxist-leninist demand for absolute self-renunciation among intellectuals a return to the ideals of the Russian gentry. One might also refer to Chernyshevskii's model hero, who was certainly of Russian origin. In spite of the native elements in Lenin's thought, however, we must still recognize the importance of Marx's thought as such. Marx was not merely congenial to the mobilizing Russian servitor-gentry of the capital cities. He offered to Russians an intellectual apparatus that lifted their urge to mobilize to a spiritual plane and spread it out to global dimensions. Marx's thought not only conveyed the gentry's traditional scorn for bourgeoisie, intellectuals, bureaucracy, and private enterprise, but it also competed with the world's religions and philosophical systems on their own ground and offered appropriate satisfactions on this ground to anyone who needed them. In particular, Marx's flat command to renounce private property brought with it a basic corrective to gentry ideology that not even such radicals as Paul I, Arakcheev, or Pazukhin had ventured to recommend. Lenin was not merely a Russian who utilized Marx; he was to some extent a Russian transformed by Marx. It is probably true that Russian soil was the very best there was for the seeds of Marx's prophecy, especially after its preparation during the course of tsarist agrarian reform and wartime food procurement. But even the best of soils does not *produce* seed.

C. BOLSHEVIK FOOD PROCUREMENT

Having noted in a general way that the bolsheviks employed line-over-staff organization in their efforts to restore order in Russia and remobilize the population, we are now prepared to take up a more specific topic: bolshevik efforts to feed the populace. This marks an abrupt departure from the topic of the immediately preceding section. Marxist ideology certainly offered no instructions for a campaign against famine hysteria. Food supply was a problem strictly from Russia's own experience, and all bolshevik programs to procure grain had already begun at least on a small scale before the October Revolution. Any government that undertook to procure food in 1917-18 would probably have had to act in much the same way as the bolsheviks in order to survive, regardless of its rhetorical configuration. From now on, then, we stop talking about what the bolsheviks were inclined to do and focus instead on what they had to do.

Existing Agencies

In the first months of bolshevik power most state agencies and local institutions of the tsarist and provisional government continued to function wherever they still existed. When an agency worked well, the bolsheviks kept it going indefinitely. This was the case with the state salt monopoly. One A. S. Salzakin had been managing it for the MZ since 1915, and he actually had had some success at distributing salt. He continued his work without interruption until at least a year after the October Revolution as an agent for the NK of food supply (Orlov, 1918: 267-68). The sugar monopoly was also performing reasonably well in October 1917, and it probably would have continued indefinitely under the bolsheviks had it not been lost to the Germans when they occupied the Ukraine (pp. 248-49; see also Zaitsev, 1930: 174-97).

It seems, then, that the bolsheviks had no objection to working with the procurement agencies of their predecessors and following their policies. Where possible, they used old government agencies as instruments of a centralized organization, and, where necessary, they allowed autonomous operation. In most areas zemstvoes and town dumas continued to form the core of local procurement administration until late January 1918. It was only in February that the party began making deliberate efforts to dismantle these old institutions (Chebaevskii, 1957: 226-27, 233), and even this was a very limited operation. Most of the old personnel worked on under "sections" of local soviets (pp. 245, 249-51). Admittedly Soviet administration made strenuous efforts from the very first to influence peasant soviets by infiltrating "proletarians" into them (pp. 230-31), but even this tactic did not differ in form from the methods employed by previous food procurers. A. A. Bobrinskii, MZ in the fall of 1916, had also striven to put the "right people" in charge of his pseudo-autonomous food supply organs, and the liberal Shinagarev had followed essentially the same line in early 1917, when he tried to pack his local committees with specialists (ch. 10, sec. D). The bolsheviks had all the more reason to resort to such tactics, since they, unlike their predecessors, had not only the opposition of local institutions to contend with but that of the central offices as well. Officials in the ministry of food supply conducted a running battle against their new overlords. They actually went on strike in December 1917. Nevertheless, the bolsheviks continued to use them as long as possible.

The state grain monopoly followed a very uneven course after the bolshevik takeover, mainly because it was not working very effectively. During the first eight months of 1917 it had made only one-third of its scheduled deliveries. After October performance deteriorated yet further. Grain deliveries fell off sharply in December 1917, and they remained low through February 1918. In March and April the ratio of actual to scheduled deliveries rose a little, but in May and thereafter the decline in grain shipments turned into a virtual stoppage (Orlov, 1918: 324-39). Yet even in a clearly failing enterprise like this the new regime clung to the policies and offices of its predecessors as long as it could. As will be seen, serious innovations in grain procurement did not begin until the spring of 1918.

It would be a serious error to blame the chronic grain shortage of 1917-18 entirely on weaknesses in government organization. A major part of the problem was the physical loss of grain-producing territories. A cossack gang had already seized Orenburg before the October coup; the Germans took the Ukraine and the Black Sea shore in March-April 1918; the "whites" took over the Don and Kuban regions in May, and in July the Czech Legion cut off Siberia and much of the trans-Volga region. By August the only net-producing gubernias left to the bolsheviks were in the north Caucasus (Stavropol gubernia and the Terek oblast), the trans-Volga region around Ufa, and the central black-earth region.

Certainly these were serious losses. They would have created a grain shortage by themselves even if the bolshevik regime had inherited the best of food-procuring organizations from its predecessors. Even more serious than the loss of acreage, however, was the government's inability to collect grain in the territories it ostensibly controlled. N. Orlov, who published a study for the NK of food supply in July-August 1918, was forced to conclude that if the cities had actually been depending on the government's grain monopoly since the Revolution, most of the urban population would have already starved to death (pp. 284-87).[6]

In fact, most of the population had not starved. The explanation, said Orlov, lay in "bagmen" *(mesochniki)*, individuals who carried grain illegally from producing farms to cities and grain-consuming areas. Usually they moved by train. Some sold their loads at a profit; some were only feeding themselves and their families. The bagmen were able to operate, despite increasingly draconic laws against them, because local soviets and supply organs in the producing areas, and in the cities as well, not only tolerated but actively helped them. This was not remarkable. Soviets and committees had to cope with a population of would-be hoarders who had become extremely distrustful of collective efforts made ostensibly for the common good, and they probably observed that bagmen were unearthing more hoards than government agencies could hope to find.

The bagmen succeeded in doing what no regime was able to do throughout the period of disintegration. They delivered manufactured goods to grain farmers and got grain in return. When a bagman reached a food-producing village, he was carrying manufactured goods with him. Unlike the state's administrators, he did not ask anyone to be patient or have faith while he took their grain for a fraction of its value. He simply displayed his goods. No one had to believe that he was doing his best to distribute everything fairly. If the peasants wanted his goods, they simply brought out some grain and an arrangement was made. On this basis circulation of goods could continue despite the general inclination to hoard (Vladimirov, 1920: 3-14).

The phenomenon of the bagmen offers a particularly clear illustration of the bolsheviks' reliance on the procurement policies of their

[6]N. Orlov was a Soviet food supply official. His book is as reliable a source as one can find on the subject of bolshevik food procurement in 1917-18. The government did not allow it to be printed except with an official introduction denouncing his views but admitting that his work constituted the first systematic study of the supply question. Orlov inserted an apology that must have been sarcastic. He confessed that he had based his study on evidence, not theory, and this defect rendered the book less valuable than it might have been (1918: 2).

predecessors. Tsarist and provisional governments had striven—without success—to regulate factories and markets in order to keep up the flow of goods between city and country.[7] Along the same line the bolsheviks mounted a grain procurement campaign in western Siberia during the winter of 1917-18 that involved a massive delivery of manufactured goods to consumer cooperatives there. Thus it must have seemed quite practical to all manner of local government organs under all manner of regimes to encourage the efforts of individuals who were actually achieving the government's purposes. Bagmen were already playing a vital role in grain distribution before the October Revolution, and government agencies had helped them along from the beginning (Strizhkov, 1973: 36-48).[8]

The earliest record I have seen of a local official openly encouraging illegal grain distribution dates from tsarist times. It is in a letter of 17 February 1917 from the governor of Tver to the Special Conference on Food Supply. The governor requested permission for a factory of 40,000 workers to send out small parties to several black-earth gubernias to buy food for their fellows (TsGIAL, f. 457, op. 1, d. 603, l. 109). Under the Provisional Government the phenomenon spread rapidly, though the word "bagman" had not yet come into general use. The journal of the Provisional Government's food ministry referred to "illegal" grain carriers a number of times during the fall of 1917 (e.g., *Prodovolstvie*, 1 Nov. 1917: 14-16; 15 Oct. 1917: 15-16; 1 Sept. 1917: 16-18). On 18 October, only a week before the Revolution, the ministry conducted a conference on the subject of private grain traders. It was reported that "tens of thousands" of them were carrying grain out of Tambov, Kursk, and other black-earth gubernias, terrorizing railroad employees and causing general disruption (1 Nov. 1917: 26). Still, the ministry did very little to discourage traders. On the contrary, it expressly permitted grain-consuming gubernias to send agents to the black-earth regions to buy grain on their own (15 Oct. 1917: 8-9). Local soviets took part in the freewheeling hunt for grain. Workers' soviets in the cities of the black-earth gubernias were openly sending out their own agents to get grain even before autumn, and they did not trouble to ask the central government's permission (1 Sept. 1917: 19).

Initially the bolsheviks imitated their predecessors and cooperated with the bagmen (Orlov, 1918: 315, 341). According to Vladimirov (1920:

---

[7]See *Izvestiia osobogo* (1 Sept. 1916: 85), *Prodovolstvie* (1 Sept. 1917: 24-26), and also the MZ's speeches of May 1917 in *Sezd* (1917: 6, 10).

[8]Bolshevik efforts to send manufactured goods to villages in early 1918 are described in Orlov (1918: 185-240, 279), Kayden (1929: 182-83), Alekseev (1966: 137), and Baburin (1957: 342). Some authorities (e.g., Kayden) imply that the campaign in western Siberia actually succeeded in delivering goods to farmers and bringing back a fair amount of grain to the capital cities, but Baburin and Alekseev seem to doubt this.

9-20), this cooperation did not cease even after the Soviet government proclaimed its official hostility toward them. Vladimirov is probably correct. A typical report from a party agent in Nizhnii Novgorod in August 1918 protested indignantly that even party organs were allowing private grain traders to carry on their work without restraint (*Perepiska,* IV, 175-76).

It is clear, then, that the bolsheviks had no policy of their own regarding food supply when they took "power." Notwithstanding their dramatic demand for bread in October 1917, they only began to develop a distinctive approach to grain procurement in 1918, when the existing agencies virtually ceased to operate (Orlov, 1918: 53-54).

New Approaches

The man chiefly responsible for introducing and carrying out the Soviet government's first new grain procurement measures in May-June 1918 was A. D. Tsiurupa, NK of food supply from early 1918 until 1922. One indication of the importance of Tsiurupa's work is the size of his NK. It was already the bulkiest of all the domestic ministries under the Provisional Government, and by 1920 it commanded a staff of at least 40,000 plus a small army of 20,000 roving the countryside in armed bands, *otriady* (Sviderskii, 1920: vii, 87-89). Supposedly Tsiurupa's men were an elite group, with members carefully selected by central offices and identified by documents issued under close supervision. The NK's official history claims that by 1920 only 42% of its personnel were holdovers from prebolshevik regimes. More important, over 67% had not gone beyond the sixth grade in school—evidence, the history says proudly, of their working-class origin (pp. ix-x; see also *Chetyre,* 1922: 111).[9]

The decree of 9 May 1918 explicitly granted Tsiurupa dictatorial powers to perform two functions: procure grain from producers, and ration it out to consumers. It reaffirmed the Provisional Government's regulations regarding the government's monopoly on grain, except that it drastically increased penalties for hoarding. Under the 9 May decree a hoarder lost his grain without compensation and could be jailed for up to ten years. Half his hoard went to the man who informed on him (*Iz istorii,* 1960: I, 279-82; see also *Resheniia,* I, 56; Sviderskii, 1920: v-vi).

[9]The above estimate of the size of Tsiurupa's organization is the most modest I have seen. The highest is that of Baburin, who claims it reached 300,000 men in Nov. 1921 (1957: 367). It is doubtful, however, that the NK ever had this many men serving it at any one time, especially as late as Nov. 1921. According to Iu. K. Strizhkov, who seems to have done more research on the matter than any other scholar, as many as 250,000 men collected food for Tsiurupa and for the military at one time or another during the period 1917-21 (1973: 299). In any case, the army's food-collecting organization and Tsiurupa's NK both dwindled away speedily after Mar. 1921 (pp. 288-300).

As we have seen, the tsarist government had merely taken hoards at reduced prices, and the Provisional Government had taken them without imposing any punishment at all (ch. 10, sec. D).

About three weeks later the decree of 27 May carried dictatorship a vital step further by expressly depriving *all* local autonomous bodies of any prerogatives in matters relating to the collection and distribution of grain. All bodies engaged in grain supply were to be subordinated to central authority. "Kulaks" were to be weeded out of soviets and local supply organs; soviets were to be "connected" to Tsiurupa's local organs; the NK of supply was to construct "ties" between collecting agencies in grain-producing areas and "working people" in grain-consuming areas (Sviderskii, 1920: vii).

The "connecting" of soviets with supply organs did not mean democratization. It meant, rather, that villages and volosts would be held collectively responsible for meeting quotas assigned to them by the NK's uezd offices (p. 17). Officials from the NK were to attend and direct soviet meetings to ensure that members had a "proper understanding" of the government's demands. These agents would even "help" individual households when necessary. Local soviets would still have the "right" to elect uezd food supply officials, but elected candidates had to be approved by the NK and were strictly obliged to carry out orders from the center (p. 18). Just in case the "autonomous" soviets and their appointees did not exhibit sufficient zeal in their work, *informatory* were appointed at the gubernia level—official spies who would report to the NK's central offices on activities in the locales (pp. 5-6).

As for the construction of ties between collecting agencies in grain-producing areas and working people in consuming areas, this consisted of forming armed *otriady* (gangs) in cities and factories to go out to the countryside and grab grain any way they could (Averev, 1933: I, 25; II, 80-81; see also Orlov, 1918: 73-74, 101, 305). The *otriady* were rough and ready crews who had little regard for technical expertise or any system of rules or procedures—in short, line units completely free of staff control. The measure of a leader's performance was simple enough: the weight of grain his gang brought in. The NK's official history all but asserts that food gathering knew no further refinement. What else does the author mean when he acknowledges that the primary defect in the NK's food gathering was a practical disregard for the economic status of its victims? The *otriady* simply left it up to the villages to decide which peasant would give how much. A poor man's grain weighed as much as a rich man's (Sviderskii, 1920: 29; see also Alekseev, 1966: 140-43).[10]

---

[10]The introduction to the history claims that *"krupnye"* (big) households had consistently to bear a heavier burden than other types (Sviderskii, 1920: viii-ix; Andreev, 1976: 18-19).

Lenin took a personal interest in the *otriady*. In May 1918 he wrote directly to a number of industrial and urban organizations in the capital cities, inviting them to form *otriady* and send them to food-producing villages to get grain. Half of what they got would go to their parent organizations; the other half would go to the NK of food supply (Kulyshev, 1972: 50). Lenin's letter produced fast results. On 2 June an *otriad* of 400 men was on its way (pp. 19-21, 27), and by the end of September Petrograd alone had sent out over 7,300 men under Tsiurupa's auspices (pp. 35, 54). From then on these government-sponsored bagmen would go out in groups of various sizes, ranging from small units of 20-30 men to battalion-size groups of several hundred (pp. 27-43). Petrograd generally sent out larger units; Moscow and other towns employed smaller ones (Strizhkov, 1973: 118). Clearly the government's armed detachments were operating on a much more ambitious scale than ever before. The terms of Lenin's invitation became law in August 1918 (*Agrarnaia*, 1954: 190), and spontaneous raiding became an established order.

The bolsheviks were much more open than their predecessors about the use of armed gangs, but even in this matter they were following methods and tendencies already familiar to both government and peasantry. What Tsiurupa and Lenin did in May was to strengthen the formal administration left over from the Provisional Government by amalgamating it with gangs that were already raiding villages on their own. They had begun forming spontaneously well before October 1917 and had marched out to seize carts, horses, and grain wherever they could get away with it. In effect, they were bagmen who stole instead of buying, and, as we have seen, the Provisional Government had actually encouraged this sort of thing in its last, desperate days. The peasants had resisted. In the fall of 1917 there had already been some battles (ch. 10, sec. D). In early 1918 there were more (Kulyshev, 1972: 36-39, 44-47, 77-84; Strizhkov, 1973: 36-48), though of course the latter were no longer part of the peasant "movement." Unable to stop this guerrilla warfare, the bolsheviks simply made the best of it by converting gangs of militant bagmen into government agencies.

For all their brute power, *otriady* were not enough by themselves to supply Russia's cities. They could not cover much of the countryside, and in any case they were at a disadvantage in unfamiliar territory. Once aroused, native gangs could fight more effectively, and peasants had a variety of passive techniques for frustrating collection. A common one was simply to leave grain without threshing it, thereby forcing an *otriad* to remain in each village for a relatively long period of time and rendering it vulnerable to ambush (*Iz istorii*, 1960: I, 279-80). Then, too, *otriady* were difficult to control. They could easily take to plundering on their own, and their members may have found it easy to desert and join villages they were supposed to be attacking. In any case, there was not enough military force in the cities to keep up a steady supply of grain while also fighting a civil war. The bolsheviks would have to do something besides attacking the villages; so it seemed in May 1918.

They did do something else, or at least they tried. At the same time Tsiurupa was organizing *otriady* to displace the private bagmen, the government also made a direct appeal to "poor" peasants to help with grain collection. The bolsheviks had always spoken sympathetically of the rural poor, but until the dark days of 1918 they had confined themselves to adopting populist (Socialist Revolutionary) slogans. In other words, they had agreed to act on the vague assumption that all peasants were poor and would therefore be sympathetic toward a genuinely revolutionary government. Villages could be treated as units and even entrusted with governmental functions. One of the Soviet government's first official acts was to proclaim village autonomy and invite villages to take over the countryside. To be sure, *otriady* were already going out to get grain in 1917, but they did not yet have explicit instructions to dismantle villages. In May, however, the bolsheviks abandoned the villages as institutions. They concluded that populists could no longer be trusted as intermediaries between government and peasants (see below, sec. D) and that food-producing villages were irretrievably hostile to any and all governments. Instead of treating villages as united groups of oppressed masses, they now called upon "poor" peasants in each village to raise their heads against the kulaks who dominated villages institutions and were using these institutions to serve sordid ends. The proletariat would help. Ia. M. Sverdlov, chairman of the TsIK, proclaimed in a report of 20 May 1918 that the government's purpose would now be to plunge villages into civil war. "If we cannot split the villages into two irreconcilably hostile camps," he warned, "if we cannot unite the village poor against the rich, then we are going to live through some very bad days" (1959: II, 212-14). Four days later Lenin sent his first letter to the Petrograd workers inviting them to go get their own grain (Kulyshev, 1972: 19-21), and in it he advised them to organize the rural poor into committees in order to get their help. Shortly thereafter, on 11 June, with the new *otriady* already in the field, a decree from the SNK ordered rural inhabitants *in grain-producing areas* to establish committees of the rural poor on their own (*Resheniia*, I, 91-94). Each village was to have its own *kombed,* if its members knew what was good for them. With the advent of the *kombedy,* we may speak at last of an authentic bolshevik innovation. The tsarist and provisional governments had never tried anything like them.

Like the *otriady,* the *kombedy* were agencies of a line-over-staff organization. Uezd *kombedy* existed, but they generally did not operate in the countryside, and they were never able to exercise more than cursory supervision over practical affairs. The *kombedy* that did the actual collecting were the ones on village and volost levels, and they operated with the same freedom (and under the same difficulties) as the *otriady*. All rhetoric about democracy aside, the volost and village *kombedy* were not subject to control by the local population. On the contrary, they were almost invariably the preserve of nonfarmers who had only recently arrived in the locales. According to an official study of Tambov gubernia, local peasant farmers made up slightly over half of the village-level *kombedy*, but volost committees were more than half soldiers, officials, and workers. The executive officers *(kaznachei)*, who did most of the field-work, were 90% nonfarmers and nonresidents (Averev, 1933: I, 21-22). In effect, then, the *kombedy* were little more than *otriady* that had settled down, and perhaps the two forms of organization were even less distin-guishable in practice than this. *Kombedy* could actually become *otriady*. We have an order from the Tambov gubernia food supply organization, directing *kombedy* in the area to form *otriady* from among their members (II, 170-71). More commonly, *otriady* became *kombedy*. During the latter half of 1918 the *otriady* made it a policy to settle small groups of their members in various areas. Usually they took in a few members from among the local peasants, and an SNK decree of 4 August expressly commanded all *otriady* to take on peasant members (*Agrarnaia*, 1954: 188-89). These commonly called themselves *kombedy*. In a speech of 6 November 1918 Sverdlov claimed that the *kombedy* had been organized at the initiative of the proletariat (1959: III, 58), which suggests heavy *otriad* participation. In the Ukraine, where *kombedy* were first introduced in early 1919 following the bolsheviks' takeover there, these ostensibly peasant groups were "reinforced" by 3,000 urban workers from the north (Adams, 1963: 231). In other words, they were *otriady* in all but name from the beginning. Strizhkov comes close to making this same generali-zation about the *kombedy* of 1918 (1973: 93-95).

Whatever each *kombed-otriad* may have been in its separate locale, all of them were line-over-staff agencies, armed by the central government with unlimited power for the purpose of procuring grain. One result was that they very often took over the entire apparatus of local government (Lepeshkin, 1957: 190). They made laws, implemented them, conducted trials of offenders, and punished the convicted. They even enjoyed the prerogative of financing themselves out of their own collections, a practice officially disapproved of in Russian administration ever since Peter's time (Averev, 1933: II, 248, 250-69). In short, their authority was far more arbitrary than that of the land captains or even the governors-general of Catherine's day.

Far from disapproving of the committees' vast powers, bolshevik leaders initially encouraged them to expand their sphere of action and to take over the soviets, those "spontaneous" products of the halcyon days of 1917, when Lenin had been overjoyed to see rioting "poor" peasants forcing the dismemberment of capitalism (see *Collected Works*, XXV,

274-82). "Kulaks" predominated in the rural soviets, said Sverdlov in a speech of 20 May 1918, and they would have to be driven out (1959: II, 212-14). And so they were. A characteristic report from a military commissar in September 1918 described a Tatar village in which a majority of the inhabitants were allegedly kulaks. An army unit had had to attack it with machine guns and artillery in order to establish a *kombed* there and compel the people to elect a new soviet (*Perepiska*, IV, 446-47).

As in all line-over-staff organizations, staff quickly began to reassert itself. The *kombedy* only got going on a large scale in September (see Averev, 1933: I, 16-17), and already their freewheeling ways were beginning to irritate the central offices. On 14 October Sverdlov publicly complained of their arbitrary interference in the soviets, and he called for their abolition (1959: III, 40-42). But Sverdlov's complaint was premature. The *kombedy* still had a task to perform. On 11 November the sixth congress of soviets called for new elections in the rural soviets that would cleanse them of kulaks, and during December 1918 and January 1919 elections were duly held. The *kombedy* supervised. They saw to it that the right people got the votes. Presumably the soviets were then able to assume their former role in government with a new perspective—that of their new leaders from the *kombedy-otriady*—and at this point the *kombedy* themselves were officially abolished (Averev, 1933: I, 32-42; Lepeshkin, 1957: 190-97). Just in time, apparently—some people were saying that kulaks had already infiltrated their ranks (Averev, 1933: I, 4; Lepeshkin, 1957: 194).

The abolition was not carried out immediately. Orders continued to emanate from the party's central committee calling for the establishment of *kombedy* in this or that locale. They were introduced on a large scale in the Ukraine in 1919 and again in 1920. Apparently many of them remained active in areas that had been under bolshevik rule since the Revolution (see, e.g., Averev, 1933: II, 17).

To sum up this unavoidably chaotic account of Soviet grain administration after May 1918, we may say that during the civil war raiding parties attempted to become local governing institutions. At first this was in accord with the desire of the central government, but by the end of 1918 Moscow was beginning to call for order in the countryside. Confusion did not actually end, not in the grain-producing gubernias at any rate, but it seems that the *otriady* generally gave up their pretense at being peasant groups in early 1919 and began instead to call themselves proletarian enlighteners of the peasantry. Instead of inviting peasants to join them, they began to consider themselves "agitators," whose function it was to lead peasants. *Otriady* were not only to seize grain, said a typical decree, but also to set up reading rooms in the villages (Kulyshev, 1972: 71-73). One gathers that by this time local soviets and/or villages had become more satisfactory agencies for food procurement. Tsiurupa's agents could now confine themselves to imposing quotas and allow local people to manage their own collections. In short, the new approach to rural administration had been temporary. The *kombedy* had constituted an extended raid, not an invasion. Local society had been more or less subjugated but not taken over. It would be another 12 years before the state would have the strength to destroy peasant society.

We have left out of account the civil war itself. In large areas of Russia, especially the food-producing areas, villages suffered not only from bolshevik procurement gangs but also from other marauders. The white armies had also to collect grain, and in addition there were a variety of "green" gangs, ostensibly defenders of peasant autonomy but also, of necessity, procurors of grain from them. Procurement being what it was, greens were often as cruel and destructive as whites and reds (Radkey, 1976: 321-22). Even worse than cruelty and extortion were the epidemics of typhus and syphilis these multicolored gangs brought with them. It is possible that the violence done to villages in the combat zones was not substantially more devastating than the depredations of Tsiurupa's food collectors. Even if this were true, however, the violence of war must have inspired somewhat greater fear than that of the bolsheviks, mainly because its destructiveness was random. It made peasant farmers in the combat areas—which were almost all food-producing areas—more keenly aware of a need for orderly government, however stifling and oppressive it might be. This fact of life probably made Tsiurupa's grain collectors somewhat less objectionable than their opponents. To be sure, whites and greens did not have grain-consuming areas to feed, so they did not need to collect so much grain. On the other hand, Tsiurupa's gangs were more inclined to be businesslike. They were made up of men whose families were starving, and it could not have been very difficult to persuade them to get grain without actually destroying the producers outright or subjecting them to erratic vandalism. Because the bolsheviks were hungrier than their rivals, they were relatively good administrators, capable of reducing their operations to regular, predictable extortion. Therefore they were more endurable to peasants whose basic desire was to be left alone. In the long run, *random* destruction in the south and east, together with famine in the north and west, strengthened bolshevik rule.[11]

[11]It is significant that many Mennonite peasants in the Ukraine welcomed the bolsheviks. They had little love for communist ideology, but in 1919-20 they recognized the Soviet government—especially its Cheka agents—as the only force capable of protecting their hitherto prosperous farms from covetous Ukrainian neighbors and local thugs like Makhno (see, e.g., Toewes, 1967: 66, 76-77, 110-17). Mennonites were not typical peasants, but their desire for protection, however oppressive, must have been widespread in the combat zones.

Not surprisingly, Tsiurupa's organization lost whatever appeal it might have had to farmers in grain-producing areas as soon as the war died down. In late 1920 and early 1921 large-scale peasant outbreaks in Tambov and western Siberia implied that forced procurement was no longer having a pacifying effect (see Andreev, 1976: 38-40; Strizhkov, 1973: 273; Radkey, 1976: 227-29). When Lenin perceived this in February 1921, he began to dismantle Tsiurupa's NK (Strizhkov, 1973: 288-300).[12]

Bolshevik grain procurement methods were not successful in the ordinary meaning of the term. They did incalculable harm to Russian agriculture, and they obviously failed to supply the grain Russia's consumers needed. In 1920, the procurement organization's biggest year, it still did not provide much over 40% of what it considered to be a necessary grain supply. Bagmen brought in the rest (Sviderskii, 1920: iv-v, 31; Strizhkov, 1973: 179, 193, 267-70, 288). I maintain, however, that no degree of inadequacy demonstrates the "wrongness" of forced grain procurement or even its failure. Forced collections began *before* the February Revolution, and they continued under specialist rule during the following months. They were first introduced by men devoted to the institutions of private property, and their most extreme form—inciting factory workers to attack villages directly—first became government policy under a regime of liberals and socialists. Thus bolshevik methods, even the new measures introduced in the summer of 1918, did not proceed from marxist ideology or even from choice. They were, rather, a direct outgrowth of the experience of agricultural specialists in interaction with peasants under the circumstances of a general European war. Similarly, the phenomenon of bagmen, far from representing a resurgence of private enterprise against communist bureaucracy, actually expressed a more basic opposition to centrally directed mobilization of any kind—capitalist, communist, or specialist—in a time of famine hysteria. It follows that neither the inadequacies of state procurement in 1917-21 nor the emergence of bagmen proceeded from specifically bolshevik errors or weaknesses. It is even incorrect to assume that bolsheviks were more determined and consistent than their predecessors. Nicholas II and his generals were just as resolved to be ruthless in the summer of 1915 as Lenin was in 1918. The basic novelty in bolshevik methods lay in the extremity of the situation the bolsheviks faced, not in their inclinations or policies.

[12]The NK's own account of its achievements up through 1920 gives no hint of Lenin's impending attack. Grain procurement, it said, had been an "undoubted" success (Sviderski, 1920: v), and the author went on to describe various improvements the organization was about to introduce in order to make forced procurement and rationed distribution an even more gigantic enterprise (pp. 10-13).

D. THE PARTY APPARAT

Formation

The question remains: how did the bolsheviks exercise control over their gangs in order to make them relatively orderly? I have suggested some partial answers: the gimmick of the *kombedy,* pressure and support from the hungry inhabitants of grain-consuming gubernias, and prolonged, random devastation in food-producing gubernias. Thus far, however, we have ignored the bolshevik party organization itself, the famous apparat.

According to E. N. Gorodetskii (1971: 147-152), the history of the apparat began in April 1917, when a number of delegates from local "cells" throughout Russia assembled in Petrograd at the invitation of capital-city party leaders. At that point the party had no formal organization. It consisted merely of separate groups—cells—who identified themselves, most of them for the first time, by sending delegates to the conference. At the April conference the assembled delegates elected several of their number to a central committee (TsK). A central committee had existed before, but its members had always conducted their affairs from abroad and had never attempted to engage in practical management. The new committee, basing itself on an almost entirely new membership, would now affect to manage and direct. As yet, the TsK had virtually nothing to work with but the cells themselves, and it knew nothing about these cells except what their delegates chose to report. Central direction, therefore, consisted mainly of sending out requests and suggestions to unknown recipients and hoping for good results. In late July 1917 the sixth party congress was held. Its participants agreed to appoint Iakob Sverdlov to be secretary of the TsK. Sverdlov had been a delegate from the Ural region to the April conference and had been elected to the TsK at that time. It was he who, following the July congress, would establish the apparat.[13]

Sverdlov introduced such basic practices as keeping minutes of TsK meetings and maintaining a record of the TsK's correspondence with groups purporting to be cells. At this stage he demanded little of the cells. When a group wrote to him to declare its affiliation, he usually answered that they were welcome to the party, provided only that they agreed to abide by the resolutions of the sixth congress (e.g., Sverdlov, 1959: II, 63). He did want to know who their members were. On 25 October, the day of the Revolution, he sent out cards to the cells for

---

[13] A more recent account suggests that Sverdlov took charge of the secretariat as early as Apr. 1917 and began immediately to use it as an instrument of control over the cells (Duval, 1973: 47-57).

individual members to fill in and send back to his office (*Perepiska*, IV, 74-76). On the whole, however, he was realistic enough not to press the point. It would be about a year before he began to receive such information in anything like regular fashion. One of his circulars of late 1918 complained that most local party organs were not even telling him how many people they had, let alone who they were (V, 22-24).

Informality in party management was especially undesirable in late 1917 because the vast majority of members were newcomers. Of the 200,000 or more alleged members of cells that sent delegates to the sixth congress in July, only about 23,000, less than 12%, had been in the party prior to the February Revolution. In October, when the party suddenly found itself compelled to deal with a vast and disorderly pile of government agencies and local institutions, the leaders could not hope to reassemble the mess into an administration by relying on unknown supporters to do the right thing on their own. The party had somehow to lead. It had to keep watch on the soviets, whose membership, until the latter part of 1918, was predominantly antibolshevik. It had to involve itself directly in gathering grain, running trains, and mobilizing armies. Whatever needed doing in Russia, the party's TsK had to see to it. This meant that Sverdlov had to see to it.

The new secretary began his work in the simplest way: by sending out plenipotentiary agents to cope with specific problems as they arose. They operated apart from any government department, local institution, or party cell, drawing all their power from their instructions, which they received from an office inhabited by Sverdlov and less than a half-dozen assistants. According to one of Sverdlov's reports, 30 to 40 such agents went out on missions for the TsK as early as August 1917. Only 12, however, were actually under his orders (Sverdlov, 1959: II, 36). These dozen or so line-over-staff agents were the earliest manifestation of the party apparat.

After October the number of Sverdlov's agents increased dramatically, though his office staff remained minuscule (Gorodetskii, 1971: 178, 222). Their functions and authority expanded to cover all areas of government, but they continued to operate as arbitrary line officers, each one of them empowered to take any measure he deemed necessary to carry out Sverdlov's commands. Thus Sverdlov's organization did not change its basic nature after October but only expanded its influence.

In November 1917 Sverdlov became chairman of the TsIK as well as party secretary, assuming thereby a dual position that rendered him virtually invulnerable to opposition until his death in March 1919. His authority as chief of state did not render him responsible to the government, for he had a "higher" responsibility to the party. Conversely, his authority as administrative head of the party did not make him responsible to its membership, for he faced a "higher" necessity as head of state.

In effect, he answered only to Lenin, and Lenin answered to no one. Sverdlov's agents partook of his power and also his non-answerability. The "secretary" had only to scribble a command and give it to a man, and no staff or law or institution had any legitimate grounds for standing in his way. On the contrary, all individuals and organizations were obliged to obey him.[14]

After the Brest-Litovsk peace (3 March 1918), line-over-staff agents from the TsK became the main unifying force of Soviet government. The party suddenly lost what little outside support it had enjoyed; now it would have to manage the country all by itself. In a speech to the seventh party congress on 8 March, less than a week after Brest-Litovsk, Sverdlov noted that hitherto the party had supported "spontaneous" local soviets and relied on their support, but now it would have to act on its own. What had previously been done through party members holding positions as government executives or members of soviets was now to be done by agents of the TsK (Sverdlov, 1959: II, 145). By the same token, the party itself would now have to become the instrument of the TsK. As Sverdlov said in a report of 23 March, cells and their committees had to realize that the TsK had the prerogative to send commands to *any* party worker, ordering him to go anywhere at any time without consulting the cell of which he was a member (pp. 151-57). Moreover, the party's agencies had to be subordinated to the TsK. In December 1917 the secretary had expressed concern that bolshevik delegates to the forthcoming constituent assembly would not obey his dictates (pp. 90-91). In March 1918 he told the seventh congress with considerable satisfaction that the TsK had at last acquired full authority over the party newspaper *(Pravda)* and had even brought the formerly all-powerful military-revolutionary committees under control (pp. 133-34). In early 1919 he was still raging at the failure of some party leaders to follow TsK directives, but apparently he had at least persuaded everyone that the TsK *should* be the highest authority in the party. So he claimed in a report of 16 January (III, 120-24). By then Sverdlov had long since rejected the idea that party cells were anything other than agencies of the TsK. In the fall of 1918 he was warning the secretaries of local party committees to carry out instructions from higher-level secretaries without alteration *(Perepiska,* V, 16). On the other hand, he said in some orders of October that they were not to communicate directly with the TsK but only via their immediate superiors, i.e., the secretaries on the next higher echelon of party committees (IV, 66-68).

[14]Sverdlov's authorizations could cover any subject from the loftiest to the pettiest. They carried weight on any echelon of any organization. See, e.g., his note to a local agency of the union of zemstvoes and towns, dated 8 Sept. 1918, ordering the agency to assist the bearer of the note in obtaining tobacco (1959: III, 201; see also pp. 200-214).

There is more than a hint here that by the end of 1918 the party secretary was seeking to regularize the activities of his random plenipotentiaries with a more systematic organization, and his method for achieving this end was to render the party itself into a bureaucratic administration.

Sverdlov's inclination to rely on line-over-staff administration made him impatient with the tedious formalities of collegial administration, and he undertook from the beginning to reduce meetings of the government's TsIK and the party's TsK to mere ritual performances. As early as 21 February 1918 he peremptorily ordered the members of the TsIK not to waste time debating his proposal to limit their meetings to once a month. After all, he said, the committee's membership had reached an unwieldy total of 200, most of whom were executives with little time to spare for meetings (1959: II, 124-27). "We are living in a time of deeds, not words," he said (p. 127). Somewhat more severe was his recommendation a month later to the seventh party congress to the effect that the TsK should be reduced from 21 to 15 members and thereafter confine itself to one meeting a month (pp. 143-44). Sverdlov also had something to say about the representative nature of collegial governing bodies. In a report to the TsIK on 23 December 1918, he told regional officials that they would do well to come to Moscow now and then to keep in touch. They would even be allowed to attend meetings of the councils in the various NKs. Under no circumstances, however, would they have a right to vote. Each voting member of these councils was personally confirmed by the SNK, and it would "contradict our whole constitution" to allow any mere representatives to participate (III, 95). Alexander III could not have said it better.

Like all line-over-staff administrators, Sverdlov feared that his agents might use their arbitrary powers too crudely. A note from him dated 3 September 1918 urged one of his plenipotentiaries to use "maximum tact" when removing government officials from their positions and not to resort to this extreme remedy unless it was necessary (p. 11). But Sverdlov's own attacks on both party and government did not slacken, nor did they often express even a minimal degree of tact. On 1 January 1919 he sent off a telegram to the Ural regional party committee, telling them that a *"kommisiia"* was coming to investigate the loss of Perm to white armies. It would take "all necessary measures" to straighten out local government and party agencies (p. 102). The *kommisiia* consisted of Joseph Stalin and Felix Dzerzhinskii, perhaps the most effective troubleshooters the TsK had, though not well known for tact.[15] On this occasion they did not disappoint Sverdlov. Ten days after he sent them off, on 11

[15]Americans involved in the famine relief campaign of 1921-22 testified to Stalin's and Dzerzhinskii's administrative capabilities (Fisher, 1935: 205-9; Weissman, 1974: 196).

January, he authorized them to abolish the Ural regional committee (p. 111). Much as he wanted his agents to avoid unnecessary harshness, Sverdlov had no way to ensure that they would. He needed resolute agents, capable of dealing firmly and rapidly with the unforeseen, and, unlike Chaianov, the party secretary could not pick his mobilizers on the basis of their conversational abilities.

While Sverdlov was struggling to mobilize the party into an administration, he also had to deal with a growing split between bolsheviks and left socialist revolutionaries that extended through soviets on all levels and into the government administration as well. The Brest-Litovsk peace (3 March 1918) started the formal split. The left SRs did not approve of Lenin's drastic concessions to the Germans. Doubtless they also took exception to the fact that the party TsK, not the regular Soviet government, had made the peace. Shortly after the SRs heard the news, their NKs resigned from the SNK. Next, all SR members of the TsIK resigned, and in early July all SR delegates to the fifth congress of soviets walked out (!I, 236). A few days later a left SR assassinated the German ambassador, and the fifth congress, still in session, responded by voting to ban all left SRs from all soviets (p. 254). It was against this background of mounting hostility between the two major parties in government that the bolshevik leaders conducted their campaign to undermine local soviets and replace them with party committees.[16]

Sverdlov certainly did not do much to prevent the rupture. He claimed in a huffy speech of 16 March 1918 that the left SRs had already split with the bolsheviks in spirit some months before the Brest-Litovsk peace (p. 148), and he called upon party committees to disband uncooperative soviets on their own authority (p. 145). On 1 April, with left SRs still sitting in the TsIK, he informed this distinguished group that the SNK's decrees would now be subject to the scrutiny of the party's TsK before they were published. He added coolly that the SNK had been enacting laws on its own without consulting the TsIK and would continue doing so in the future; that is, it would act not only as the executive agency of the supreme governing body of the country but also as a legislative body on its own, subject only to the party's central committee. It was a waste of time, he said, to discuss a matter twice over in both the

[16]Members of opposition parties who publicly renounced their affiliation could continue to occupy government posts. Jacob Blumkin, one of the SRs who assassinated the German ambassador, was pardoned and then hired by the Cheka. He continued to serve in the Soviet secret police until the late 1920s (Deutscher, 1965: 403). Similarly, Andrei Kolegaev, a leading left SR and NK of agriculture during the first months of Soviet rule, joined the bolsheviks in Nov. 1918, after having opposed them in March. During the remainder of the civil war he played an active role in food procurement. I am indebted to Mr. Alex Cummins for pointing out Kolegaev's example to me.

TsIK and SNK. In fact, said the chairman of the TsIK, it would be good to cut down still further on the range of questions the TsIK had to consider. He also informed the TsIK that a local soviet could not order its bolshevik members to do anything unless their party cell approved (pp. 161-64). With Sverdlov firing off remarks like these, the left SR members would doubtless have felt uncomfortable even if there had been no Brest-Litovsk.

Sverdlov used the defection of the left SRs to eliminate every vestige of opposition from the TsIK. On 14 June 1918 a TsIK order went out over his signature expelling all mensheviks and SRs from the TsIK and from all soviets (*Iz istorii*, 1960: I, 193-94). This was an unusually insignificant piece of legislation. It was unnecessary, since almost none of these people remained in the soviets. It was ineffective, since a few of them were still there as late as 1920. It is of interest, however, as a reflection of the first party secretary's mode of governing.

Sverdlov's chief instruments for rooting political opponents out of rural soviets were the *kombedy*. We have seen that these bodies were agencies for collecting grain, but Sverdlov had no reservations about using them as party organs. They were to operate "entirely under Party leadership," said a circular letter sent directly from the TsK to the *kombedy* (p. 207), and Sverdlov never departed from this view. Communications between *kombedy* and TsK kept up at a brisk rate, and they usually sounded as if Tsiurupa's NK did not exist. One typical letter, dated 18 October 1918, four days *after* Sverdlov's speech recommending the abolition of the *kombedy* (Sverdlov, 1959: III, 40-42), reminded party committees that *kombedy* should work under the "flag" of the party (*Perepiska*, IV, 305). A report from Moscow dated 25 October 1918 proudly assured Sverdlov that the *kombedy* were party cells in all but name. The members did not distinguish food collection from party work (pp. 377-78).

To sum up our account of Sverdlov's approach to administration: he relied on line-over-staff agents to deal with problems demanding immediate attention, while at the same time he strove to develop the entire party into an administrative organization through which he—as head of the TsK—could manage the government. To achieve the latter end, he subordinated all central party agencies to his office and tried to do the same with the party committees, along with their cells. In the end, however, no hierarchical organization emerged. Sverdlov did not treat his party committees as a single system that would operate by its own rules. He only used them to gain access to the cells, with the purpose of finding men among their membership whom he could employ as line-over-staff agents. By the time he died, Sverdlov had constructed a surprisingly large network of personal agents, many of whom had in turn established their own networks, extending in random fashion through government offices, army units, industrial enterprises, and even peasant villages. But there was as yet nothing resembling a hierarchical organization. In its original form the party apparat possessed no regularized structure at all, but only signified a continuous struggle to keep party leaders in active contact with government administration and national economy. This extreme form of line-over-staff organization never allowed any central office to manage a system. I have spoken at length in the preceding section about such phenomena as the "agencies" of Tsiurupa's NK of food supply, and such terms were widely used during the civil war. In practice, however, no self-styled agent of this NK or any other really enjoyed the luxury of having only one chief or performing one set of functions. The *kombedy* were as much agencies of party and army as they were Tsiurupa's subordinates. The same can be said for Sverdlov and his men. They held awesome powers in the sense that people feared them, but they had no systematic control over the employment of these powers. Thus they were feared but also terribly vulnerable. Ostensibly answerable to Sverdlov, they were in fact answerable to anyone who might cause them to fail in the many and varied enterprises in which their missions involved them. There were many such men in Soviet administration during the civil war, for no one knew from one day to the next who might become a part of Sverdlov's agencies or what Sverdlov's agencies might find themselves doing.[17]

Significance

Sverdlov's mode of administration, especially his abiding horror of formal opposition and discussion, bore no relation to Lenin's old idea of democratic centralism, which prevailed in the party before the fall of 1917. Democratic centralism was, after all, democratic. Lenin insisted on this quite frequently. In May 1905, for example, he wrote: "It must be clear to anyone who understands the principles of Party organization ...that discipline in relation to the Council is determined by the submission of the Council to its constituents; i.e., to the committees and the whole body of the Party as represented by the Party Congress. Those who disagree with these elementary principles must inevitably draw the

[17]Thomas Rigby's excellent study of the SNK points out that, under Lenin's direction, it did most of the actual work of government administration during the civil war, and this seems convincing to me. Sverdlov's tiny office could not actually run everything in the RSFSR. On the other hand, Sverdlov's agents could and did involve themselves in any matter on any occasion, and it was their use of this persistently personal power, in the TsK's name, that ultimately gave the Soviet government its characteristic features. As Rigby concludes, the SNK's central position in management depended on Lenin's presence at its head. As soon as the master fell ill and retired from active work, the TsK's line-over-staff agents became the undisputed center of government (1979: 200-223).

absurd conclusion that delegates are not responsible to their constituents, but vice versa" (*Selected Works,* III, 441). Nothing here implies Sverdlov's use of line-over-staff agents to push local cells around, nor is there any suggestion that participants in party congresses should not oppose proposals made by party leaders. Lenin's centralism only consisted of forbidding cells to impose mandates on their delegates to congresses or to oppose the decisions of congresses once they were made by majority vote. Discussions at congresses were to be unconstrained by any predetermined positions, including, supposedly, the leaders' own, and delegates were to be free to negotiate compromises. Once the congress voted on a matter, its majority decision was law. All cells and agencies had to abide by it. Democratic centralism, then, was a governing system in which the party congress was the highest authority in the party. Sverdlov was no democratic centralist. The party apparat did not emerge from prerevolutionary bolshevik concepts.

Sverdlov's methods arose primarily out of desperation. Leaving aside a variety of psychological explanations for Sverdlov's (and Lenin's) frenzies, we may say that the peace of Brest-Litovsk in March, followed by the virtual cessation of food deliveries in May and the "uprising" of the Czechoslovak Legion in June, put the bolsheviks into a state of peril far more extreme than anything the tsarist or provisional governments had known. Peace had cost them not only the left SRs' support but also that of a great many bolsheviks. At the seventh party congress, held in early March, a few days after the peace was signed, Sverdlov proclaimed that party membership had increased 50% since July 1917, when he had claimed over 200,000 (1959: II, 132-33). Delegates at the congress, however, represented only 169,000 members (p. 131). This was the time when Sverdlov began shrieking about the collapse of party organization (see, e.g., pp. 151-57). From March until the end of the year his messages were punctuated with remarks about being on the edge of annihilation. In a speech of 21 June he said that the Soviet government had never been in such a critical position (p. 224). On 20 October he said, "We have perhaps never been so close to catastrophe as now" (III, 47).

We can get an impression of Sverdlov's own vision of his work from a speech he made on 16 September 1918. He said that the party apparat had no form. He and other bolshevik leaders had been so busy organizing the government that they had had no time to think about the party itself. Now, he said, the party would have to begin organizing itself (p. 19). Strange words from the man who had just spent a year building the party into an instrument of government, whose work along these lines would be a model for such future leaders as Mao Tse Tung. Actually he and his associates had hardly touched the government organization except to kick at it. On the other hand, they had reformed the party from top to bottom. They had, in effect, adopted a mode of collective action that allowed Sverdlov's agents to *wield* the government, or at least parts of the government. Sverdlov, however, was utterly unaware of this. All the time he had been forcing the government to act, he had conceived of his activity as a process of reorganizing.

He went on to describe what he thought the party apparat should do, now that it was going to get organized. How excited his listeners must have been. One of the world's greatest, most innovative mobilizers—the man who had preserved a semblance of organization in Russia in the face of crises that had already brought down two governments—was going to set forth his own special theory of organization. Alas, the audience heard nothing but a string of banal chinovnik clichés that could just as well have come from a simple office manager haranguing his clerks. Sverdlov recommended the establishment of a single line of command, running from Moscow down to regional centers *(oblasti)* and thence to gubernias, uezds, volosts, and villages. On each level would be a cell or assembly of cells. Each of these would have its committee, each committee would have administrators, and each administrator would have his own separate function, for the performance of which he would be responsible to the equivalent administrator on the next highest level. What would this magnificent staff-over-line machinery achieve? Sverdlov answered this question in a TsK memorandum. His new hierarchy would ensure the rapid and correct implementation of orders from Moscow and would keep Moscow informed of local developments. In particular, it would collect grain effectively (p. 22). This from the man who had given his life to an all-out attack on bureaucratic hierarchy and who, for the previous year, had managed to hold Russia together without any staff at all, let alone hierarchy. As Sverdlov saw it six months before his death, the ideal result of all his labors would be to restore the same ponderous, unworkable tangle of paper and de facto irresponsible officials that the "liberators" of the 1860s had explicitly renounced and from which the tsarist government had been laboring to extract itself ever since. We may conclude that Sverdlov had no relevant concept of administration at all in his mind while he was assembling his apparat. When he undertook to set one forth, he could do no better than repeat platitudes.

But if Sverdlov did not realize what he was doing when he founded the party apparat, we may still say that he and Lenin were highly successful mobilizers. True, the economy was perhaps even closer to collapse in 1921 than it had been in 1918. Coal production had fallen to less than one-seventh of its 1916 level, steel production to 2%, and railroad traffic to 10%. The grain shortage was as critical as ever (Stalin, 1952-54: IV, 310). Procurement gangs were not only rousing peasants to violence but also, by indiscriminate use of extreme measures, driving them to cut grain production down to subsistence levels—the farmer's last defense against unrestrained tribute collection. There were still no effective agencies of rural administration or institutions of government. Soviets, committees of the poor, and rural party cells had all been swallowed up in the persistent amorphousness of the countryside. Insofar as these administrative metaphors actually had any concrete existence in 1921, they were only gangs, separate from peasantry and administration alike. So said Ia. A. Iakovlev, an unusually alert party inspector (see, e.g., Iakovlev, *Derevnia,* 1924: 71, 85-86, 91, 131-34; 1925: 3-11). Nevertheless, Russia had survived, and this was no small accomplishment. The bolsheviks' performance in the absence of any workable plan or reliable information reminds us that these entities, though highly valued by all who have governed Russia since the seventeenth century, were *never* the most vital ingredients of government. They were—and are—only the language of government.

Obviously the bolsheviks felt the need for such a language. Two years after Sverdlov's death his apparat had grown very large, and although it still operated arbitrarily, it was rapidly acquiring the trappings of a hierarchy with functional subdivisions. A profusion of plenipotentiaries were still running into each other on all echelons of government administration, but the secretariat was now striving much harder than before to bottle everyone up in regulations. In the fall of 1920 the party established "control commissions" to protect its cells against arbitrary incursions by the apparat and to inculcate some sense of mutual respect among the apparat's agencies (Schapiro, 1960: 256-58).

Alas, hierarchies were no easier to manipulate in 1920 than they had ever been. As the tsars of the early nineteenth century had learned, a government may establish a language for itself by fiat, but it cannot impose the use of this language on its subordinates. Control commissions quickly evolved into a hierarchy of their own, and the famous tenth party congress of March 1921 could offer no better antidote to the wild competition between separate, all-powerful hierarchies than a greater degree of centralized regimentation. The bolsheviks had achieved much with their line-over-staff work prior to 1921, but they would be a very long time changing the habits and relationships their achievements had formed.

It was at this point that Lenin decided to give up his effort to invade the villages. Tsiurupa's thugs were disbanded or given new tasks, and food-producing peasants were freed from the annoying obligation of contributing all produce they did not need to the state. Henceforth farmers could give up a certain portion of their crops and keep everything else for themselves. So the government promised.[18]

---

[18] In fact, Soviet tax collectors, most of whom were veterans of Tsiurupa's campaign, never succeeded in setting up a tax system based on wealth and income. V. A. Tsybulskii (1965: 46-59) traces the government's frenzied attempts in 1921-24 to arrive at an equable basis for taxing peasants, and his account

But Lenin did not abandon the apparat. He restricted its operations to a relatively small arena, but only because he wanted to organize it in more thoroughgoing fashion. In his last years Lenin was still trying to employ system to wield the party, not to make it possible for party institutions to work together in a uniform framework. In 1921 the party leader purged the party of members who did not show promise as instruments of rule. He also persuaded the tenth congress to outlaw "factions," which meant in effect that members were forbidden to work together for any purpose except the implementation of TsK orders. The country was no longer under siege, but the party still was (Schapiro, 1960: 231-33, 249-58). The peasants had grown even "darker" than in 1917-18, and the bolsheviks' compulsion to form an instrument of mobilization using an elite corps of line-over-staff agents had not diminished.

Sverdlov's organizational work and the emergence of the apparat are important here, chiefly because they form the context within which agricultural specialists and peasants had to interact with each other during the 1920s. Before 1921 famine hysteria and the rise of the apparat complemented each other and found expression, so to speak, in the desperate campaign to get grain. When Lenin brought the campaign to a halt, agricultural specialists and apparatchiki had already gained considerable experience in dealing with each other, and their relationships lingered. One form of mobilization continued to conflict with and complement the other.

Before we leave the subject, it deserves pointing out that Sverdlov's accomplishments show us the relationship between systematization and the urge to mobilize in dramatically naked form. The bolsheviks were a group of men who did not know enough about administration to run a grocery store competently, yet within a year after assuming power, they had learned by heart all the proper phrases bureaucrats use when they talk about themselves. The bolsheviks had never heard these phrases before except from the mouths of men they loathed; system was both unknown and useless to them. But when they took power, their puerile mouthings about the proletariat gave way within hours to direct expressions of a consuming passion to mobilize, and within a year their efforts

shows how hopelessly unrealistic they were. Rural agencies collected taxes, but their activities had no apparent connection with the government's commands, nor were they based on anything resembling a uniform system. Party resolutions from 1922 to 1926 went on repeating inanely the same complaint: no one had yet discovered a usable basis for assessing taxes in the countryside (*Resheniia*, I, 306, 309, 363-65, 405, 520-21). Taxation did not replace forced procurement after 1921 but only relaxed it. The only significant actions taken in this regard in Mar. 1921 were the reduction of the annual quota for state grain purchases from 7.6 to 4.3 million tons (Strizhkov, 1973: 288) and the legalization of private trading.

to mobilize had set them to babbling the rituals of bureaucracy with an intensity of feeling that would have done honor to any vice-president.

The bolsheviks' performance testifies to the profound change in Russian culture since Peter I. Faith in system not only had prevailed in the government but had transcended any mere organization and firmly implanted itself in capital-city society. Sverdlov's experience offers us perhaps the clearest indication we have that the urge to mobilize had been the moving force behind systematization ever since Peter's time.

E. THE AGRICULTURAL SPECIALISTS IN 1921

Lenin's decision of March 1921 to let the bagmen have it their way created new opportunities for agricultural specialists. As Fridolin, the zemstvo agronomist, put it, NEP (see Glossary) brought new conditions and a new spirit to agricultural improvement. He himself returned to Moscow to take up agronomy again, after holing up in a village and avoiding administration entirely for three years (1925: 110). With Tsiurupa's gangs benched, agronomists, statisticians, teachers, et al. could once again take up their conversations with peasants without suffering undue interference from the government. They were still subject to the whims of the apparat, of course, but it happened to be the apparat's whim to let them work on their own, and this whim was to persist for nine years. For all practical purposes, the bolsheviks withdrew from villages and NKZ alike, leaving the specialists to manage rural Russia without outside supervision. All the specialists had to do to secure their position was promise to raise agricultural productivity while refraining from open opposition to the regime.

As we have seen, the specialists' position in government administration had undergone several dramatic changes since 1914. Before the war began, the MZ had been supplying them with funds and encouraging them to organize themselves. Their programs for agricultural improvement had expanded steadily; they and the cooperatives had gained wider autonomy. Their hostility toward "bureaucracy" remained strong in 1914, but they were working within the ministerial system. Between 1914 and February 1917, they moved far more rapidly than before into government administration by taking responsibility for food supply. *Agronomorganizatory* worked closely with the army and MZ on a scale hitherto unimaginable, selling to the one and drawing subsidies from the other. So quickly were they and other forms of specialist able to move into a dominant administrative role that in February 1917, when specialists took over the government, the entire MVD hierarchy was dismissed, leaving the *agronom-organizatory* virtually alone in the countryside.

Judging from the unseemly haste with which the MVD-police apparatus was dismantled, the specialists were sure of their ability to govern on their own. In fact, however, they were following in the footsteps of the general who had dumped Nicholas II: they were eliminating their scapegoats. Before they realized what was happening, they were caught in the middle of social conflicts that reduced their programs for harmonious progress to nonsense. Until 1921, when the central government once again surrendered the countryside to them in return for their shrill promises of salvation through science, they ceased to play a dominant role in government-peasant interaction.

This peculiar history did not return the specialists to the same position they had occupied in 1914. By 1921 their place in government organization had undergone a fundamental change, the chief result of which was that they were no longer able to *influence* government administration. In 1914 they had been not only receiving subsidies in ever-increasing amounts but also expanding their role in government and persuading statesmen to make basic changes in government administration. In the 1920s this was no longer the case. The nature of bolshevik organization made it virtually impervious to the sort of infiltration that Krivoshein had been encouraging during the tsarist government's last years. The apparat had taken its hands off the countryside, but, as I have said, its agents continued to work outside law and ideology to carry out personal commands. The party was uniquely capable of making dramatic changes in policy, but it persistently eluded any commitment to a particular organizational structure. There being no structure, the specialists had nothing to influence. They could not *establish* a position in relation to the line-over-staff apparat, mainly because the agents of this apparat were not themselves established in any identifiable institutional position.

On the other hand, it must be said that the gap between specialist and apparat was only an underlying reality, not an inevitable or unchanging one. So long as the specialists refrained from treading on ideological sore points, they had things their own way, and since bolshevik ideology was in many respects congenial to them, it was not difficult to minimize conflict. Specialists who wished to immerse themselves in villages and blend their science with peasant practice could do so while singing hymns to social and economic advance; those who wished to collect information and concoct programs could predict results, estimate costs, and rhapsodize about scientific advances. All these refrains were pleasing to bolsheviks. As long as the specialists had only to sing, the bolsheviks let them work. On the whole, specialists prospered in the 1920s, just as they had during the war years prior to February 1917. During both these periods the government wanted mobilization so badly that it was willing not only to sanctify science but also to stay out of the scientists' way. 1921 was indeed a good year for the *agronom-organizatory.*

CHAPTER 12

Land Reform in the 1920s

Imposture is of sanative, anodyne nature, and man's Gullibility
not his worst blessing. Suppose your sinews of war quite broken;
I mean your military chest insolvent, forage all but exhausted;
and that the whole army is about to mutiny, disband, and cut
your and each other's throats,—then were it not well could you,
as if by miracle, pay them in any sort of fair-money, feed them on
coagulated water, or mere imagination of meat; whereby, till the
real supply came up, they might be kept together and quiet? Such
perhaps was the aim of Nature, who does nothing without aim, in
furnishing her favorite, Man, with this his so omnipotent or
rather omnipatient Talent of being Gulled.

Professor Teufelsdröckh, in
Thomas Carlyle's *Sartor Resartus* (1893: 77)

As everyone knows, a theory that is a real theory will give practical men strength through proper direction.

Joseph Stalin in a speech before
the first conference of marxist
agrarian specialists, December 1929

One final task and the story is done. Having contemplated the downfall of agrarian reform, the withdrawal of peasant farmers into darkness,
and the re-establishment of centralized government, we have now to pick
up once again the story of the specialists and to trace their last efforts at
agrarian reform. Two topics are to be discussed in this chapter: Soviet
legislation on agrarian reform down to 1930, and the role played by
agronom-organizatory in implementing this legislation. The first tells us
something about the administrative framework within which the specialists worked and the purposes they hoped to achieve. The second provides
some insight into what they did and the result of what they did. It is not
to be expected that an account so narrowly focused will constitute by
itself an explanation of the cataclysmic events of 1929-30, but I do hope
that the story of the specialists' last try at mobilization will shed some
light on them.

A. SOVIET LEGISLATION ON LAND SETTLEMENT

Legislation continued to have very little influence in the countryside throughout the 1920s. Laws emanating from the capital cities must have produced an impact here or there, but their terms were not enforced for their own sake and they never achieved the purposes of their enactors. We study them here only because they reflected, albeit dimly, what their enactors wanted to achieve. Even if law did not direct agrarian reform during the 1920s, legislation regarding the rural economy did express the aspirations and pretensions of would-be reformers, both bolshevik and specialist.

In the following pages we shall see that the bolsheviks had one view of agrarian reform and the specialists another. The party's view has been much studied and is relatively well known, since it was the Soviet government's official view (see, e.g., Jasny, 1949; Danilov, 1957). Less well known is the attitude of the specialists, since they tried to obscure their differences with the party and they ultimately failed to impose their brand of agrarian reform on the villages. The specialists' view is significant, however, for it did work its way into Soviet legislation on agrarian reform for a time. This in itself is interesting and deserves study. Equally interesting is the marked change in the specialists' perception of legal order that comes through in their legislation. It will be recalled that before their experience with war and revolution, the *agronom-organizatory* had often found themselves at odds with the upholders of legality. In Krivoshein's day the MZ's minions repeatedly expressed irritation at the constraints imposed upon them by law courts and MVD agents (ch. 9, sec. B and C). During and after 1917 they seem to have acquired a greater respect for legal-adminstrative system. It would be the wildest of exaggerations to suggest that they became consistent legalists, but during the decade from about 1919 to 1929 it certainly served their purposes to make a stand for legality. As we shall see, they made their stand in the offices of the NKZ (people's commissariat for agriculture), which the bolsheviks allowed them to dominate from about 1919 until late 1929. Much of the legislation we shall study in the following section originated in this office, and, for a few years at least, it actually favored the specialists' brand of mobilization rather than the party's.

The Bolsheviks' Concept of Land Reform

The basic aim of bolshevik legislation on land never changed after 1917. To party leaders, agrarian reform always meant collectivization: dividing up the countryside into large-scale productive enterprises whose members would understand their roles not by their family relationships with each other or the share of land each household worked but by the productive *functions* each of them performed. Somehow city workers were to teach peasants how to live and labor as members of enterprises. This was understandable as a general statement. In some respects, however, the proposed enterprises were ambiguous, especially with regard to the question of authority. The two primal forms of enterprise, *kolkhoz* (collective farm) and *sovkhoz* (state farm), were both supposed to be managed democratically by their participants. On the other hand, the bolsheviks cherished the expectation that these enterprises would operate according to commands from the central government. Before 1922 and after 1929 Soviet law expressly provided that they would. Collectivized peasants, it seems, were to be free to manage their own enterprises so long as they followed the state's commands. So the bolsheviks said.

This nonconcept of political order is familiar to us. During and after the Stolypin era agricultural specialists spoke with enthusiasm of democratic cooperatives that would run smoothly as instruments of a centralized administration. Indeed, the simplest form of kolkhoz, the so-called TOZ, first took form in the brain of an agricultural specialist, one A. N. Minin, in 1913. Minin originally regarded his creation as an advanced form of cooperative, not a primeval collective farm, but the latter concept gained ascendancy during the civil war. When it came to political thought, bolsheviks and specialists spoke much the same language.[1]

Two general principles underlay the operation of the bolsheviks' agricultural factories: each able-bodied member had to work if he wanted to eat, and his work had to be as productive as possible. By themselves these were relatively clear aims, but they always came out in company with a flood of rhetoric about eliminating personal wealth. The bolsheviks never said outright that they wanted all peasants to be poor. On the contrary, they promised endlessly that they would make the countryside prosper. As we shall see, however, all their laws and policies conveyed a bizarre desire to make poor farmers productive while keeping them poor. Even the statutes published after 1921 indicated that wealth was reprehensible, while poverty, on the other hand, was an unmistakable sign of honesty, reliability, and diligence. More to the point, wealth implied disloyalty to the state, whereas poverty signified patriotism. Thus on the one hand peasants were encouraged to increase productivity, while on the other they were cautioned—in effect—against doing anything to remedy their poverty. During the war years the Soviet government consistently encouraged both peasants and workers to form kolkhozy and sovkhozy. When it could, it even subsidized collective farms and pro-

---

[1]TOZ is an acronym for *tovarishchestvo obshchestvennoi obrabotki zemli,* which translates roughly into "association for collective farming." Minin's presentation of the idea and the debate he set off are in *Trudy* (n.d.: II, 47-59).

vided them with equipment. At the same time, however, it ordered these ostensible supporters of bolshevism to surrender all their produce to the state except what they needed to sustain and develop their enterprises. In other words, Soviet law required peasants who formed productive enterprises to remain as poor as those who refused.[2]

On the face of it, Soviet legislation on land reform and agricultural improvement was impractical. It was the height of fatuity to expect the peasantry of Russia to take up untraditional tasks under novel circumstances and to receive nothing in return except closer supervision. But we have seen in Chapter 11 that 1918-20 was not a time when the bolsheviks *did* many things they thought to be impractical. The question arises: what was the practical purpose of collectivization?

One obvious answer is propaganda. Lacking the capability to bring actual benefits to their subjects, the bolsheviks continued to offer them fantasies. Lenin once said to Ia. A. Iakovlev: "It will not do to brush aside revolutionary fantasies and the revolutionary enthusiasm that goes with them. There is often more authentic realism in them than in the deliberate calculations of 'practical men'" (Iakovlev, *Za*, 1929: 123). Nor was Lenin averse to making this point in public. In his speech of 23 March 1919 he openly acknowledged that the government's decrees on land and land reform were unenforceable and were only meant as a form of propaganda (*Agrarnaia*, 1954: 210-11; see also pp. 390-92). In a similar vein Sverdlov sent off a telegram to some would-be revolutionaries in Berlin on 11 November 1918, promising them that trainloads of grain were on the way, though at the time many of his own cities were starving (1959): III, 61).

But collectivization served a practical purpose during the civil war quite apart from its inspirational qualities. Basically, it was a food supply measure. It called upon starving men, women, and children in food-consuming areas not only to grab grain but to grow it for themselves. This made perfectly good sense to hungry people, even if the state did take all of their harvests except what they needed to survive.

Ostensibly, of course, collectivization was a land reform, not a food supply measure. It was to be carried out by the NKZ's specialists, whereas food supply was the business of Tsiurupa and his proudly uneducated *otriady*. In reality, however, land reform was subordinated to the more pressing problem of food supply until the end of 1920, when the Soviet

[2]See, e.g., the laws of 14 and 15 Feb. 1919. The former is in *Resheniia* (I, 109-26), the latter in Kazantsev (1954: 50-51). Articles 39 and 44 of the former and article 4 of the latter ordered state farms to turn over all produce beyond their basic needs to state procurement agencies. Articles 69-70 and 126-28 of the 14 Feb. law imposed the same command on collective farms.

government found itself for the first time in secure possession of its food-producing regions. Scholars have generally treated formal distinctions between the NKZ's land reform and Tsiurupa's grain grabbing as if they were real. Studies of land reform and agricultural improvement in 1917-20 have treated early bolshevik legislation on collectivization as if it actually constituted an attempt to transform rural Russia into garden-factories (e.g, Sharapov, 1961, and Gerasimiuk, 1965). Such studies, though sometimes informative in detail, are beside the point. Until 1920 at the earliest, collectivization meant little more than food procurement measures that specialists could presumably perform more effectively than thugs.

The bolsheviks used several terms to describe their rural enterprises, each of which was supposed to identify a different type. In practice, they lacked precise meaning. Official definitions varied from one document to another, and each term was applied to a wide variety of peasant groups. Nevertheless, a few generalizations are possible. The law of 14 February 1919 set forth the first legal descriptions. It identified two general types: sovkhozy and kolkhozy. The sovkhoz was owned by the state, and, although its management was democratic in form, the members were government employees (*Resheniia*, I, 109-26, arts. 29-55). The kolkhoz, on the other hand, was supposed to be held and managed entirely by the people who resided on its land. At first, the kolkhozy were of two general types: the *kommuna,* in which *all* land, stock, and machinery was held in common (arts. 60-93; see also *Agrarnaia,* 1954: 433-41), and the TOZ, which could be any kind of producers' cooperative that fell short of a thoroughgoing *kommuna* (*Resheniia*, I, arts. 94-134). A third type, the artel, was formally recognized and described as a distinct and more thoroughly collectivized form of TOZ in a "model *ustav*" published by the NKZ on 19 May 1919 (*Agrarnaia, 1954*: 462-70). From then until 1930 it was customary to speak of three general types of kolkhoz: *kommuna,* artel, and TOZ.

I have suggested that in 1917-20 the underlying practical purpose of most rural factories was to keep their members alive, but it must be admitted that a few of them functioned successfully as authentically communistic enterprises. According to an NKZ-sponsored study of 1922, the most successful and enduring *kommuny* were those run by Orthodox monks and Old Believers, men who actually believed in ideal communism and were also capable farmers. In addition, a few artels were formed by groups of moderately wealthy farmers who deemed it wise to combine their efforts in productive enterprises (Kirillov, 192: 191; see also Wesson, 1963: 64-78). After October 1918 a few sovkhozy—less than 40—took over former estates that had been organized as modern farms by their ex-owners prior to the Revolution and kept intact thereafter. Some of these developed into productive enterprises (Kirillov, 1922: 168; Knipovich, 1921: 30).

For the most part, however, the "collectives" of 1917-20 were either groups of desperate people who had nowhere else to go or shrewd peasants who applied bolshevik labels to their land arrangments without making any real changes (see, e.g., Kirillov, 1922: 190). In January 1921 the *average* artel had only 50 or 60 members—men, women, and children—and it held less than three acres per person (p. 188). Most sovkhozy must have been equally small and crowded. Official figures vary, but one oft-cited authority tells us that in 1920 all the sovkhozy in 40 gubernias possessed a grand total of only 2.4 million acres of arable land (Knipovich, 1920: 13). Another official account, based on reports of party inspectors, points out that despite their inadequacies these sovkhozy kept alive about a half-million refugees from the cities (Kirillov, 1922: 168). Assuming that only urban unemployed occupied the sovkhozy in 1920, this comes to a maximum of five acres for each person on the state farms. During the civil war the actual land area in the vast majority of sovkhozy must have been much smaller, for the huge sovkhozy of the southern and southeastern gubernias had not yet been established. At the end of 1918 two-thirds of the sovkhozy were in the central industrial region and Petrograd gubernia (Knipovich, 1921: 32-34), and these sovkhozy, on the average, probably had less plowland per capita than the artels. They were little more than oversized shantytowns struggling to survive on fields the local peasants did not consider worth cultivating. Even if a particularly tough gang of refugees somehow compelled a local village to give up some reasonably fertile land, they still lacked tools, seed, and work animals, and they surely had very little interest in agriculture. Before 1921, then, sovkhozy may have been collective enough and they may have brought relief to their wretched inhabitants, but they had little to do with agricultural improvement (*Sbornik zakonopolozhenii,* 1927: 142-43; Kirillov, 1922: 161-68; Knipovich, 1920: 10-14).

On the other hand, we must acknowledge that the idea of collectivization had a certain appeal to would-be land reformers. It was simple. Collective farms could be created without paying any attention whatever either to peasant custom or private right, those two formidable obstacles to progress that had made the Stolypin Reform so complex and rendered the Provisional Government unable to function effectively in the countryside. From a technical point of view, it was infinitely easier to plow up large units of land without regard for individual claims than it was to identify each family allotment, measure its value in the peasants' traditional terms, and then painfully transpose it from scattered strips to a consolidated farm. Then, too, a capital-city administrator could not help but prefer to supervise and tax large productive units and not have to deal with separate farmers. Thus collective farms had a dual appeal to authentic agrarian reformers. They represented a social ideal for rhetorical purposes, and at the same time they seemed to simplify the technical problems of land reform and state control.

The tsarist regime had toiled for over a century to establish private property in Russia in the belief that the experience of owning would inculcate in the population a sense of civic duty. We have seen the difficulties this made for rural administrators, and we have noted that as specialists took over the Stolypin Reform, they grew less patient with legal technicalities and more concerned with improving agriculture. It might be an exaggeration to call the bolshevik approach to land reform an outgrowth of specialist attitudes, but on paper collectivization did offer an abrupt resolution to many of the dilemmas and technical perplexities that had irked specialists. This was one reason why capital-city bolsheviks found it attractive quite apart from its practical value as a famine relief measure. Moreover, the close connection between bolshevik and specialist purposes explains in part why they were able to work together in the same administration despite sharp ideological differences. Both were mobilizers of peasants. Both wanted to transform peasants into producers.

The Elimination of Private Property, 1917-18

The bolsheviks published their first land reform on 26 October 1917, only one day after taking power. It was a relatively simple statement abolishing private property in land and, in effect, calling upon "individual villages and settlements" to divide the land in their vicinity to suit themselves (*Resheniia*, I, 15-17). At a single stroke the new rulers eliminated all the technical and legal problems of land settlement and reduced agrarian reform to a matter of persuading peasants to take measures to increase their productivity. The "fundamental law on the socialization of land," published on 27 January 1918, confirmed the hastily written October decree and added to it a proviso that local soviets should do what they could to "accelerate the transition from unproductive systems of field cultivation into more productive ones" (*Agrarnaia*, 1954: 136). By this the January law meant primarily the replacement of interstripped village fields and individual plots by collective farms (pp. 135-45).

We need not dwell on the contents of these laws. Aside from some pious appeals to peasant soviets to avoid any actions that would lower production, such as the provision in the October decree ordering villages to leave modern farms and enterprises intact, the bolsheviks had nothing to say about the *process* by which land was to be rendered more productive. Their initial laws had the political purpose of winning peasant support, and their method of doing this was to repeat some vague aims put forward by the SRs in the summer of 1917. It seems, then, that the initial laws on the socialization of land did not reflect bolshevik ideas.[3]

Ostensibly, of course, the main purpose of these early laws was to equalize landholdings—to take from the rich and give to the poor. The January law set forth a basis for calculating the share of confiscated land to go to each deserving family, and it suggested vaguely the kinds of families that were most deserving. Here, however, the law departed sharply from physical realities in the countryside. It said nothing about *how* peasants were to occupy and farm their new lots along with the village strips they already held (see *Agrarnaia*, 1954: 139-41). This was no obstacle to peasants who had no land at all, nor was it a serious problem in cases where confiscated land adjoined or intermixed with village land. In many cases, however, peasants who possessed strips in the village had somehow to go on farming them and also to take up the cultivation of new ones several miles away. Thus, although the peasants' land grabbing threatened to multiply their difficulties with interstripping, the government did not propose any procedures for dealing with these difficulties. Worse, the January law actually forbade peasants to cope with their new problems on their own. The normal peasant way to minimize the absurdities of interstripping was for individuals to trade off strips or rent them to each other, but the new law prohibited both the renting or private exchange of land. Worst of all, it also required holders of farmland to cultivate it on pain of losing it (pp. 143-44). In sum, "equalization" had the practical effect of giving peasants land they could not farm, ordering them to farm it, and forbidding them to dispose of it in any other way. That is, the January law would have had this practical effect if anyone in the volosts had paid any attention to it. The point here is not that these laws did harm but that they did not say

[3] The introduction to the October decree on land (*Resheniia*, 1, 15) stated that it was based primarily on 242 separate instructions *(nakazy)* brought forward by various delegates to the first congress of soviets of peasant deputies, which had been held in June 1917. The executive committee of this congress had published a "model *nakaz*" that supposedly summarized all 242 of them (Shestakov, 1922: 152-59). In August Lenin said that the model was by no means a perfect expression of peasant thinking but he considered it to be the best available one, and he decided to use it as a basis for bolshevik land policy (*Agrarnaia*, 1954: 94-99). The peasant congress had been dominated by right SRs (Shestakov, 1922: 121-22, 132), and it follows that the bolshevik decree on land was an expression of SR views. Lenin admitted as much a few months later (*Agrarnaia*, 1954: 115; see also Sharapov, 1961: 113-15). As to the fundamental law of Jan. 1918, it was drafted by left SRs in the NKZ (Lutskii, 1949: 230). In a speech of 8 Nov. 1918 Lenin explicitly renounced the January law as well as the October decree, claiming that the bolsheviks had opposed these measures from the beginning and had only tolerated their enactment out of respect for peasant demands (*Agrarnaia*, 1954: 174).

anything meaningful either about "equalization" or about agricultural improvement (Spektor, 1925: 3-5; Knipovich, 1921: 29).

To be sure, the January law did affect to describe an *organization* for land reform. It ordered local soviets to set up executive offices— "land sections"—to take responsibility for all matters connected with land use. Volost land sections were to do the actual work of reform. Like other administrative offices, they did not work for their own soviets but for the corresponding office on the next higher echelon, the uezd soviet's land section. Appeals against the volost section's decisions went to the uezd and from there to the gubernia, not to the local soviet or its ispolkom (*Agrarnaia,* 1954: 143). It is hard to tell if this fake autonomy represented an SR or a bolshevik idea, since it was congenial to both groups. In any case, land sections of soviets formed a paper basis for a land reform organization.

In fact, of course, the government had no organization at all for dealing with land problems in early 1918. Central NKs had no reliable way of knowing what local soviets were doing. The idea of land sections attached to local soviets was quite new. In November-December 1917 the bolsheviks had been trying to set up "land committees" to carry out land reform through a hierarchy of elected collegial bodies *entirely separate from the soviets* (pp. 129-33). Apparently these committees had not only failed to satisfy the party but had not even come into existence. The January law disregarded them entirely. As of early 1918, then, there was no agency in rural Russia capable of compelling volost soviets even to establish land sections, let alone accept the authority of higher-level sections. The emergence of an operational organization for land reform began only in April 1918, when S. P. Sereda, a bolshevik and also a specialist, was appointed NKZ (Lutskii, 1949: 236).

It should be kept in mind that the bolsheviks' ignorance of village reality did not distinguish them from anyone else in the capital cities. If, as Lenin claimed, the initial laws on "equalization" were a product of the SR party and the peasant congresses of 1917, it follows that neither the SR nor the peasants themselves were capable of enacting laws that dealt with real peasant problems. The villages had indeed receded into the darkness.

The Beginnings of Neo-Stolypin Land Settlement

Land Settlement in 1918

The bolshevik government began to acquire intelligible ideas about agrarian reform only as the party brought agricultural specialists into high positions in government. To judge from the NKZ's work under Sereda's management, he was a believer in practical agrarian reform, and he intended to make his NK the agency for carrying it out. His first steps, however, had nothing to do with agricultural improvement. Instead of separating his office from Tsiurupa's assaults on villages, he joined the food procurement campaign. The law of 2 May 1918 transferred responsibility for sowing Russia's arable land from Tsiurupa's NK of food supply to the NKZ (*Agrarnaia,* 1954: 153). Beginning in the summer, NKZ orders to local land sections empowered them to *force* peasants to cultivate land (e.g., pp. 186-87). Sereda himself went out in August 1918 to manage Tsiurupa's *otriady* in an uezd of Orel gubernia, whence most of Moscow city's grain was coming at that time, and he stayed there through December (Alekseev, 1966: 141-42). Thus Sereda brought his organization back into the dirty business of procurement, in effect giving up Shingarev's attempt of the previous year to separate land reform from food supply. But Sereda was a specialist at heart, and he seems to have had more than food supply in mind. By joining Tsiurupa and acquiring official functions for the NKZ, he was getting himself on a bandwagon, so to speak, preparing a basis on which he could begin to formulate programs of his own. Under the conditions of 1918 no one in the countryside could expect to exercise any authority except in the name of urgent government needs, such as food procurement and recruiting. Sereda was only doing what was necessary to exist as an organization. To some extent, his ploy worked. While the NKZ was proclaiming its dedication to food supply, it was also acquiring some functions more appropriate to agricultural improvement. On 3 July, for example, it assumed the task of supplying seed to farmers (pp. 180-81; see also pp. 147-49).

It is doubtful that the NKZ's land sections actually forced anyone to cultivate land. Many sections reported significant successes at increasing sown acreage, but this was blatant falsification (see, e.g., *Agrarnaia,* 1954: 312-13). If anyone actually compelled peasants to plow, plant, or harvest in 1918-21, it was Tsiurupa's *otriady* and the army, not the would-be scientific reformers of the NKZ.[4] The NKZ's responsibility for land cultivation was only significant because it put the specialists in a solid position to take up their old work for land settlement.

There was no hope for a *formal* program of land settlement in 1918. The bolsheviks felt the need to purge "SRs" out of soviets and government agencies in rural Russia (ch. 11, sec. D), and many agricultural specialists were associated with the SRs. To be sure, government agencies often proclaimed their need for specialists. In April 1918 a circular from the "agricultural section" of the Perm gubernia ispolkom ordered its local organs to retain their staffs of agronomists and pay them salaries commensurate with what they had received from the zemstvoes and the

---

[4]An SNK decree of 4 Aug. 1918 called upon *otriady* to do the harvesting themselves when they thought it necessary (*Agrarnaia,* 1954: 188-89).

old MZ (*Agrarnaia*, 1954: 273). On 2 August the SNK called upon land sections of gubernia ispolkoms to draw as many agronomists and other agricultural specialists into their work as they could (p. 187). Apparently, however, specialists were still under a cloud. The next day, 3 August, the NKZ warned the Orel gubernia "commissariat of agriculture" that it should not allow specialists to vote in its "college" (pp. 187-88). In July an NKZ circular had told its organs that they were employing too many surveyors and ordered them to get rid of all but a few. Surveyors were to be used primarily to help out with the forming of collective farms, but they were not to get involved even in this good work unless it was absolutely necessary (pp. 183-86).[5] In the summer of 1918, then, relations between specialists and bolsheviks were still less than harmonious.

But if specialists were under suspicion, the above circulars and orders do make it obvious that they were not entirely absent from local government offices in 1918. Their numbers had fallen off since 1913; on the other hand, there were far more of them than there had been in 1906, when the tsarist government ventured to initiate its land reform. Then, too, many peasants had had experience with land settlement by 1918. Thus a reform of sorts could at least begin, even if only on a small scale.[6]

The question is: how were specialists to carry out measures of land settlement in 1918? If an *agronom-organizator* desired to make his services available, what agency or institution was he to employ? The answer, it seems, was the village. With *kombedy* and *otriady* tearing up both cooperatives and soviets, the village was the only institution capable of managing and improving agriculture. This is probably the reason the NKZ attempted to utilize villages to bring whatever order they could into land use. To introduce measures of group land settlement—including the amalgamation of newly seized land with old strips—the agricultural spe-

[5]The earlier law of 11 Dec. 1917 had transferred the survey office from the NK of justice to the NKZ (Kirillov, 1922: 20).

[6]As noted earlier, 2,000 specialists were at work in the uezds in 1918 (ch. 10, sec. E). According to Mesiatsev (1922: 136), their number reached 4,200 by 1920. Kirillov, another NKZ scholar, tells us that the fieldwork schedule for 1919 sent approximately 3,000 surveyors into the field in 32 gubernias (1922: 141), though he notes that they did not stick very long at their jobs owing to low pay (p. 143). Berzin (1921: 163) tells us that there were 3,500 "surveyor-*zemleustroiteli*" working for the NKZ by the end of 1919.

The NKZ sometimes claimed to have many more specialists in the field than the above figures show. One official asserted in 1920 that 16,000 specialists were at work (Knipovich, 1920: 24, 38). A recent Soviet scholar (Sharapov, 1961: 119-20) accepts this estimate and adds 2,000 more for good measure; see also Gerasimiuk (1965: 96-97) for an equally imaginative estimate. These higher figures are fantastic. They only illustrate the government's habitual way of talking in 1920. Lower estimates are not more reliable, but they are more probable.

cialists found it temporarily expedient to foster old-fashioned communal redistributions.

The land laws of October 1917 and January 1918 had not provided for communal redistribtuions. So far as I know, only one law mentioned them prior to the spring of 1918. This was the statute on land committees of 4 December 1917 (arts. 16-18; Kazantsev, 1954: 21). But the mention was very brief, and this statute, as said before, was very quickly forgotten. It was only in the spring of 1918 that the party's propaganda suddenly began to depict redistributions in a favorable light as a means to struggle *against* the ever-present kulaks (Lutskii, 1949: 236). We have seen how important antikulak rhetoric was to bolshevik leaders as a device to justify grain grabbing. For the specialists, however, it was primarily a cover under which they could help farmers eliminate the worst distortions created by the land grabbing of 1917. The NKZ did not speak openly of these matters in 1918, but we already know that specialists who favored redistribution in Stolypin's day saw it as a means to introduce group land settlement (ch. 9, sec. A). We also know that in the summer of 1919 specialists in the NKZ's capital-city offices did begin to call openly for land settlement. On 1 July the NKZ put out an order condemning any redistribution that did not accomplish land settlement purposes. Henceforth, said the order, villages would have to secure permission from specialists in the volost land section before undertaking redistributions (Kazantsev, 1954: 83-84). On 30 April 1920 the government as a whole followed the NKZ's lead and published the same message in the form of an SNK decree (pp. 88-90). Thus it is not far-fetched to assume that the relatively subdued specialists of 1918 were utilizing rhetoric about communal redistributions simply to sidestep SR nonsense about equalization and bolshevik pressure for collectivization.

We have seen that there is little reliable evidence regarding peasant landholding in 1918 (ch. 11, sec. A), but we have a few indications that land settlement was already getting underway. For one thing, Pershin has attested to this (1922: 38-42; Bochkov, 1956: 130-31), and so have a number of other scholars, e.g., Bogoraz (1924: 15-16).[7] For another, several reports submitted in late 1918 by land sections of uezd and gubernia soviets referred explicitly to a growing desire among local peasants to decrease the number of their strips and increase their size, this at a time when such statements were not yet finding favor with bolshevik leaders (*Agrarnaia,* 1954: 350-52, 361-64; Kirillov, 1922: 48-54). Other local sections suggested flat out that communal redistributions could be utilized to lessen the number of strips and the distance between them (*Agrarnaia,* 1954: 320-21, 342-43). It is probably, then, that in 1918 many of the NKZ's specialists in the field were already utilizing their *formal* functions—

[7]Pershin was the author of the pages I have cited above in Bochkov.

equalizing, collectivizing, and forcing the expansion of cultivation—to work for land settlement.

Apparently the way was being made easier for these closet Chaianovites by the party itself. In November 1918 the NKZ ventured to call on food-collecting gangs to make sure that local land sections included specialists (pp. 224-27). In December a congress of delegates from land sections and other rural government organs was able to meet and draw up resolutions that would serve as a basis for the first Soviet law on land settlement. An NKZ order of 10 May 1919 gave specialists broad decision-making powers in land sections (Kazantsev, 1954: 65-80), and in July of the same year Sereda felt sufficiently self-assured to forbid any redistribution of land that was not approved by a surveyor (pp. 83-84). By this time, land sections were deluging the central offices with reports to the effect that the shortage of surveyors was one of the biggest obstacles to "collectivization" (Kirillov, 1922: 72-75). This must have meant land settlement, for collectivization required no surveyors (nor did communal redistribution for that matter—see ch. 9, sec. A). By the spring of 1919 the specialists were definitely on the bolshevik bandwagon, and, by and large, they were doing what they wanted to do.

The First Soviet Laws on Land Settlement

Soviet legislation on "socialist" land settlement was strongly influenced by the bolsheviks' vaguely fourrierist fantasies about collective labor. The law of 14 February 1919 and succeeding measures demanded that the specialists devote their efforts first and foremost to the formation of state and collective farms. Of the 138 articles in the 14 February law, 112 were concerned with the business of forming sovkhozy and kolkhozy. Otrubs and khutors were mentioned only to be rejected. Article 3 explicitly denounced them as "traditional and outdated" (*Agrarnaia*, 1954: 418). Lenin had taken this line in a speech of December 1918, when he said it was time to wipe out the "little peasant farm" (pp. 381-87).

Lenin's injunctions and official rhetoric notwithstanding, the legislation of early 1919 allowed for a variety of land settlement measures other than collectivization. Articles 13 and 15 of the 14 February law provided for two types of group land settlement: the disentanglement of villages that were interstripped with each other, and the breakup of large villages into smaller ones, each occupying a separate plot (p. 419). An NKZ instruction of 11 March set forth detailed provisions for redividing land among the villages in a volost. Ostensibly this operation was to serve the noncause of equalization and also produce large numbers of *kommuny*, but provisions for it were ambiguous enough to be used as a cover for any form of group land settlement (pp. 441-61; see especially arts. 27-114).

The 14 February law did more than merely *allow* specialists to perform tasks other than collectivization. It actually discouraged collectivization. Article 4 declared that the highest consideration in land settlement work was to increase productivity (p. 418). Uplifting the poor and struggling for perfect equality were all very well, but productivity came first. Moreover, individual households were not to be pushed into collectives against their will. Articles 10 and 97 forbade both state agencies and villages to collectivize a household's land without the members' consent (pp. 418, 427). The instruction of 11 March went even further. It explicitly protected extant otrubs and khutors against seizure (pp. 453-54). We may say, then, that in early 1919 the beautiful simplicity of collectivization was already lost. Once again, government agencies would have to confront the question of who held what land, and this meant that collectivization would offer no real advantage to food procurers. We have already seen that it offered no advantage to farmers, and so the effect of the NKZ's laws of 1919 was to render collectivization pointless for all concerned. The 14 February law had no particular impact on the roaring chaos in rural Russia, but its formal enactment signified a successful reassertion of the specialist brand of land reform in the halls of government.

The enactments of early 1919 also set up a paper organization for *implementing* land settlement. According to the NKZ order of 10 May 1919 (Kazantsev, 1954: 65-80), each land section of each gubernia and uezd ispolkom was to set up a subsection for land settlement. The head of this subsection was to be appointed by the land section, subject to the ispolkom's approval, *but he had to be a specialist.* On the volost level there was no special subsection; the volost land section handled all land affairs, including land settlement, as a unit (see arts, 4, 15, 87, and 99). Nevertheless, specialists in land settlement subsections on higher levels could conceivably wield a fair amount of influence in the volosts. Land sections, it will be recalled, were supposedly independent of their soviets and ispolkoms and subject entirely to the corresponding offices on the next higher echelon.

The new organization bore a marked resemblance to the old tsarist land settlement administration. Land settlement subsections did their work under very loose supervision by the central NK. Projects were to be prepared and implemented by volost and uezd sections, and their decisions could not be appealed except to higher-level sections, ultimately to the NKZ (*Agrarnaia,* 1954: 419). The old system of gubernia fieldwork schedules was reintroduced. Land settlement subsections of uezd soviets drew up lists of projects that were ready to go on the schedule, and land settlement subsections of gubernia soviets made up the actual schedules (pp. 443-45). In one way the new organization was yet more centralized than Krivoshein's had been. At the volost level, land sections fully subordinated to the center now did the work formerly done by the relatively freewheeling zemstvo specialists and their credit cooperatives.

Another major difference between tsarist legislation and the 1919 enactments was that the latter encouraged the use of force much more directly than the former had. The NKZ's 11 March instruction included the old idea that one-fifth of a village's members—or, in larger villages, any group of at least 50 households—could consolidate their strips in a single area against the wishes of their neighbors (p. 452). The instruction went further to provide that any measure of group land settlement could be introduced *unless* three-fourths of all the peasants affected by it protested, and even this massive discontent would not stop the project if the uezd soviet's land section did not attest to the project's detrimental *economic* effect (p. 452). Then there were the redivisions of volost land among villages. When a land section undertook one of these, the instruction allowed it to reduce interstripping by carrying through a general redistribution of all unconsolidated (!) land in the volost *no matter how many people opposed it* (p. 452). It is also worth noting that the NKZ's instruction provided for forced resettlement of peasants to other areas within their gubernias if the local land settlement agency decided this was necessary to relieve congestion and achieve the equal distribution of land (p. 460). One more item: the NKZ's commands of 1919 reflected greater enthusiasm in the capital cities for land settlement than Krivoshein's edicts had ever shown. Instead of setting up one fieldwork schedule each year, the NKZ ordered gubernia land settlement subsections to work one up every six months. Fieldwork was to go forward in both summer and winter (p. 419). In the countryside surveyors who tried to drive stakes into snow and frozen ground probably did not share Moscow's dedication, but we cannot doubt the zeal for tsarist land settlement that prevailed among the unleashed Chaianovites in the NKZ's central offices. According to the law of February 1919, peasants were actually better protected against collectivization than they were against land settlement!

It is of interest that these Chaianovs and Pershins, who spoke so glibly of tsarist brutality, rigidity, and arbitrariness, should have exhibited so little tolerance of peasant opposition. I do not know exactly what was in their minds in 1919, but they must still have harbored the conviction that any administrative arrangement would be all right so long as specialists ran it. Probably one explanation for their disregard for peasant rights in 1919 lay in their persistent disdain for the legislative process itself. Their enactments reflected a willingness to write high-sounding jibberish into statutes that even Lenin did not surpass. For example, articles 21-28 of the February law directed volost-level land sections to map out and record every plot of land in their volosts, listing its area and its owner (pp. 419-20; see also pp. 445-47). In fact, no administration had ever been able to make any such chart or complete any such records, and the specialists knew it. Even the capital-city specialists knew it. Yet, like the MVD's land section in the 1890s, they did not hesitate to stick any hymn or slogan into their laws if it gave their archives an orderly and purposeful appearance. It is no exaggeration, then, to assert that the specialists in the NKZ's central offices were not averse to pushing peasants around in the name of technical progress. Moreover, they were also loath to allow peasants to do anything on their own. The March instruction forbade villages to initiate land reform projects, even if all participants approved, unless their proposals conformed to the government's requirements as interpreted by local specialists (pp. 442-44).

Whatever we may think of the specialists of 1919, they were certainly in charge. Having established itself firmly on paper in February-March 1919, the cause of land settlement continued to advance. At the eighth party congress, which met immediately after the 11 March instruction had been issued, the assembled party elite resolved that *agronom-organizatory* should receive higher pay. Never mind that unequal pay violated Lenin's erstwhile principles and that apart from these principles the collectivization campaign of 1918-21 made no sense; the country's economic needs took precedence over administrative consistency (*Resheniia*, I, 135). Nor was this the eighth congress's only assault on equality. The party also resolved to take a more positive view of middle peasants, i.e., authentic farmers. From now on, people who cultivated their land effectively were not only to be tolerated but also protected and supported by the government. In particular, the eighth party congress declared, interstripping was to be eliminated, agriculture was to be improved, and there was to be an end of arbitrariness in rural administration (pp. 141-44)—a curious view for the party to express in March 1919, only two months after the government had issued a law extending its methods of grain seizure from kulaks to middle peasants.[8]

Lest the reader be inclined to dismiss the rhetoric of the eighth congress as mere circus performing, I should note that it marked a drastic departure from the proclamation for instant socialization that had resounded through most of the previous year. To be sure, socialist ideology never ceased to echo through the capital cities. Even in late 1920 the extraordinarily malleable eighth congress of soviets proclaimed its willingness to consider the introduction of a system of government-supervised grain planting. Apparently the delegates regarded the work of Tsiurupa's gangs so highly that they were prepared to extend procurement into a general takeover of peasant farms (Prokopovich, 1924: 114-16).[9] But the bolsheviks did not allow their unceasing cant to block moves toward

[8]This was the law of 11 Jan. 1919, which had formally established the government's grain procurement system on the basis of unrestrained seizure of all grain beyond each village's survival needs (Kulyshev, 1972: 70-71).

[9]The SNK enacted a law providing for forced sowing as late as July 1921 (Kazantsev, 1954: 128-29).

practical agrarian reform. A decree of 23 December 1919 granted special benefits to experts in scientific fields vital to the state's interests: higher pay, exemption from military service, better quarters, and, in general, "greater contentment" (*Resheniia*, I, 156). In April 1920 the party resolved to pay higher wages to workers who were more productive (pp. 169-71). Finally, delegates to the ninth congress of soviets in December 1921 approved a resolution calling for a drastic relaxation of the rules on land settlement. The land should remain nationalized, said the congress, but collectivization would no longer have to be the immediate purpose of the government's work. Villages should have the right to decide their own manner of land usage. If peasants wanted consolidated individual farms, so be it (p. 268; see also Danilov, 1958: 192). By 1922 the bolsheviks' formal acceptance of private greed in Russia was turning into ringing enthusiasm.

Consider the experience of the American famine relief program in 1921-22. According to Benjamin Weissman, American food distributors encountered opposition primarily from wealthier peasants, who protested that they could not sell their grain as long as the Americans continued to hand it out gratis. Producing farmers refused to allow relief officials to use their horses and carts, and at the same time they submitted requests to Soviet authorities to throw the Americans out. The authorities were sympathetic to these erstwhile kulaks. They refused to support the American requests for horses. Some American agents responded by rallying poor peasants to take horses by force from their wealthier neighbors. While this interesting manifestation of American imperialism was taking place, the Soviet government was taxing famine areas at the same rate as the rest of the country, exporting more grain than the Americans were bringing in, and moving cautiously to edge the Americans out (Weissman, 1974: 144-46, 156-61). On 8 September 1922 Lev Kamenev, a leading bolshevik noted for his relative mildness and his insistence on adhering to marxist doctrine, told an American relief administrator that the Soviet government did not intend "to feed great numbers of people and create chronic paupers but rather to make everyone get to work" (p. 156). In public the bolsheviks continued to speak of their concern for the poor. What Russian statesman has ever dared to do otherwise? Practically speaking, however, mobilization had enjoyed yet another of its many victories over its ideologies.

The Land Laws of 1922

The legislation of 1922 brought the trend toward practical land settlement to its culmination. The new laws were practical not only in their aims but in their recognition of the limits to government power in the countryside. For the most part they reflected a return to prewar programs, or, let us say, a return to prewar tendencies. The NKZ instruction of 13 March 1922 offers us a symbol of the prevailing trend. It flatly advised surveyors involved in land settlement to follow old tsarist government regulations until the Soviet administration could prepare its own (*Sbornik zakonopolozhenii,* 1927: 57).

The first of the new laws on land settlement was the "law on land use," which came out on 22 May 1922 (*Direktivy,* 1957: I, 334-40). It was a relatively short statement, comparable in length and purpose to the decree of 9 November 1906 in Stolypin's day (see ch. 7, sec. A). Its authors seem to have assumed that everyone had a fairly clear idea of what land settlement was by this time, for they included very few specific provisions. Taken together, their product embodied three general ideals: village autonomy, individual freedom, and the solidarity of the household as a working unit. I say these were ideals, because it would be far from correct to assume that the May law really put them in force. All it did was to indicate that some government officials considered them desirable.

The first of these ideals, village autonomy, was expressed in provisions allowing a village to choose the manner in which its land would be used (arts. 1-3) and to carry out its own land reforms if it wished (art. 11). The village's "choice" no longer had the same legal definition as in tsarist times. It now meant the decision of a simple majority in the village assembly. Majority would now be the basis for all acts of land reform in villages and collective farms alike. The latter were to be as free to change their status as the former; kolkhozy could switch back to villages of separate household farms as easily as villages could elect to collectivize. The village assembly also received a new membership. The vote would no longer be restricted to heads of household but would now include all adults belonging to households in the village.

Presumably land reform would now be a relatively safe venture for a village. In effect, the new law renounced the "equalization" provisions of 1917-19 by guaranteeing that no government action could diminish a village's land. Group land settlement projects could be imposed on a village by some portion of its own members or by other villages—as in tsarist times— but these projects could not change the *amount* of land belonging to each village (arts. 32-34). Generally speaking, the laws of 1922 gave villages a legal *right* to their land apart from the exigencies of land settlement. The land codex of 30 October 1922, which incorporated the 22 May law, had only one provision for something that could be construed as government seizure of village land: article 46 allowed the government to settle outsiders on *unused* land without a village's consent (Kazantsev, 1954: 160). But this was not a significant threat to village autonomy. Stolypin's law of 5 October 1906 had been far more more dangerous (see ch. 6, sec. D). It will be recalled that this grant of "rights" had given outsiders the privilege of buying land from individual villagers without securing the village's consent. Now, in 1922, the Soviet government was guaranteeing each village the right (on paper) to keep its land so long as its members worked it. The only harm land reform could conceivably do to a village under the 1922 laws was to *rearrange* its lands.

The legislation of 1922 gave villages so much control over their members' land that one is tempted to see in it a return to pre-Stolypin guardianship. Before 1905, it will be recalled, the tsarist government had tried to keep villages strong not for the sake of autonomy but to use them as a force for order. This, however, was not what the Soviet government was doing. Villages were "dark" in 1922, not instruments of rule. The only institution resembling an instrument of rule in the countryside was the volost soviet, and this stronghold of outsiders had little contact with villages. Thus granting a village the power to govern meant that the village assembly really would govern. The only important similarity between the village depicted in the legislation of 1922 and the pre-Stolypin variety was that both types could control the use of the village's land so long as its fields were divided into strips.

The law of 22 May also referred to land settlement. It returned to the relatively benign principle of Krivoshein's day that only villagers could initiate projects of land reform. Before an *agronom-organizator* could swing into action, a village assembly had to submit a statement of its majority-approved plans to the uezd land section, or a minority of one or more had to appeal for a separation. Then, and then only, specialists would come and "help" the villagers conduct their rearrangement, making sure that the government's technical rules were observed. It would be hard to guess how much influence land settlement subsections actually exerted on the conduct of reform projects during the 1920s. The law did make one thing relatively clear, however. When it came to determining each household's share of land, specialists had to defer to the village assembly's judgment unless a villager or group of villagers made formal protest against the majority decision. Note that minorities and individual peasants could not block a reform project once a majority had approved it. It may be said, then, that the May law gave the village assembly very broad powers over individual households, at least in theory.

On the other hand, the significance of the assembly's powers was limited—again, in theory—by the extreme ease with which minority groups in a village could break away and form their own villages. As in earlier laws a group of at least 50 households, or one-fifth of the households in a village of less than 250 households, could consolidate their land in a separate area at any time without the consent of the village from which they were splitting (*Direktivy,* 1957: I, 335). In effect, the land settlement provisions in the laws of 1922 seriously undermined the village autonomy implied in other clauses. A village could not lose its land by government fiat, but it had no legal basis for maintaining itself as an institution or system of cultivation against the opposition of its own members. A majority could change the whole village around every year; a succession of minorities could force frequent redistributions of strips by splitting off into separate villages. In this sense, early NEP legislation may have done more to restore tsarist agrarian reform than to protect villages.[10]

The second ideal, individual freedom, reposed in some clauses regarding the right of each villager to consolidate his share of a village's land. He could do this with the village's consent at any time, and he could do it without the village's consent if vacant land was available or if the village engaged in some formal rearrangement of its land (arts. 5-8). Once a villager consolidated his land and "improved" it, the village assembly lost all power to compel him to exchange it for other lots, always assuming that he continued to cultivate it (art. 10). In theory, then, the May law made it relatively easy for a peasant to secure his own integral farm and keep it. Indeed, the laws made it impossible for a household to achieve security of tenure in any way except by consolidation, since bolshevik law, following the tsarist model of 29 May 1911 (ch. 9, sec. B), offered no legal basis for individual ownership on interstripped land.

The third ideal, household solidarity, was not explicitly required or guaranteed in the May law. Indeed, the provision for allowing all members of households to vote in village assemblies implied a desire to weaken the household as an institution. Nevertheless, the enactors evidently regarded the household as the only institution other than the kolkhoz and sovkhoz capable of assuring some measure of stability in land use. The Soviet government did not necessarily believe in large families in 1922, but it enacted several provisions that tended to strengthen and stabilize the household as a productive enterprise. Articles 19-31 allowed a household to rent out its land or hire workers to cultivate it in cases where its own members were temporarily unable to do the work. Article 14 provided that if a household member went outside the village to work, he would still be listed as one of the household's "eaters," thereby entitling the household to an additional share of the portion of village land that was interstripped. If a departer entered government service, civil or military, he could be maintained on the household list throughout his career.

[10]One article in the May law implied a desire to limit the number of times a village's land could be subject to rearrangement in order to allow the departure of its members. It was, however, too vague to be enforceable (art. 8; *Direktivy,* 1957: I, 335).

If he got some other kind of job, he could stay on the list for six years or more.[11] These articles were inserted into the law as exceptions to the old ideological commandments against renting land and hiring labor. Supposedly the commandments would continue in force in a general way, but farm households would enjoy a certain immunity.

The essential message of the May law was that the central government wanted the thugs left over from Tsiurupa's campaigns to stay out of agrarian reform. It did not resolve any of the old contradictions inherent in the Stolypin Reform. Its authors did not face the fact that free individual and autonomous village were flatly contradictory terms in rural Russia, which suggests that provisions for individual freedom would be the deadest of letters for anyone desiring to farm land. The consolidation of household lots could not really go forward without village consent (though this is not to say that it did not go forward). The law also failed to establish a legal basis for stable land tenure, since it offered no very clear guide for resolving disputes over land use. Needless to say, the law also failed to address itself to the old problem of Stolypin's time: how to draw a sharp line between consolidated farms and those which were still subject to village custom. It did not say precisely at what point a consolidated farm ceased to be a process of change and became an enterprise enjoying firm legal protection against interference by government agencies and/or its own neighbors. What the law did do was to leave local specialists on their own to interact with the peasantry according to their own lights, provided they were able to secure peasant cooperation.

The most elaborate attempt to subject landholding to law was the "land codex" of the RSFSR, published on 30 October 1922 (Kazantsev, 1954: 155-79). This was one of several "codices" turned out at about this time (Lepeshkin, 1959: 13). The bolsheviks, like Peter I in his day, had suddenly perceived the disadvantages of shotgun legislation and were trying to set up fundamental laws, frameworks into which all future enactments would have to fit or to which they would be amendments. In the land codex, for example, preliminary articles stated that earlier statutes contradictory to the codex would no longer be in force, a refinement hitherto lacking in Soviet law. Better yet, the codex set forth a formal procedure necessary to amend its provisions. No longer could a mere memorandum from an NK change the law. Only the TsIK would have this authority (Kazantsev, 1954: 155-56).

If the codex was a step toward a uniform system, however, it was still a crude effort. One misses, for example, the pre-World War I custom

---

[11]The law provided for a period of time equivalent to two crop rotations. Ordinarily this was six years, but in villages with more elaborate rotation systems it could be longer.

of precisely identifying administrative bodies, to say nothing of their functions and membership. Like almost all early Soviet legislation, the codex spoke freely about the responsibilities of a variety of local agencies. There were land settlement institutions (art. 167), organs of land registration (art. 200), land commissions (art. 206), land organs (art. 7), and land administrations (art. 222). But most of these names were not formal titles of officially designated bodies. They were, rather, descriptive terms that referred to land sections of ispolkoms and, on the uezd and gubernia levels, land settlement subsections of land sections. Curiously, these more formal titles almost never appeared in the codex. The codex did not establish an administrative hierarchy of the offices that were to manage land and land reform, nor did it prescribe their membership or functions. The only land reform agency mentioned in the codex whose membership was clearly defined in the codex itself was the land commission (pp. 177-78).

The land commission was created by the law of 24 May 1922 (pp. 144-45). It was a quasi-judicial tribunal on the volost level with superior instances in the uezds and gubernias. These courts of land reform were to operate separately from the quasi-executive land settlement subsections, and they, rather than the subsections, were to resolve disputes arising among land-settling peasants. A very orderly concept, the commission. In the absence of statutes identifying land rights, it could, nevertheless, render decisions in specific cases, and over a period of time, as some of these decisions were appealed through uezd and gubernia instances to the NKZ, final pronouncements emanating from this august office would have the force of law throughout the nation. High-level decisions regarding specific cases, rendered with due regard for consistency, properly recorded, publicized, and annotated, could conceivably develop into a body of precedents that would constitute in themselves a uniform land law having some connection with reality.

Even the commission, however, found itself in an ambiguous position. The law of 24 May had identified it well enough but had not troubled to define its relationships with other government organs. Nothing was said about the division of functions between commissions and land settlement subsections. The October codex should have repaired this flaw. Strangely, it did exactly the opposite. It not only left the flaw unrepaired but gave it explicit, legal form. On the one hand, the enactors of the codex preserved the land commissions intact by taking the descriptive clauses from the 24 May law and dumping them without change into the codex as articles 206-21. On the other, they introduced articles 188-90 (p. 175), which provided vaguely that land settlement "institutions" would resolve disputes arising from *their* projects—meaning, obviously, that land settlement subsections were to constitute tribunals in themselves. It seems that the compilers of the codex simply did not notice the relationship between commissions and subsections. They were not aware that a division between executive and judicial bodies might lead to the creation of a system of land tenure. Evidently they only troubled to describe the commissions because it was easy to stick the law of 24 May into their pile of clauses. In any case, the laws of 1922 did not tell land sections, land settlement subsections, and commissions who was to do what.[12]

It is worth noting that the codex added a few provisions in support of the trend toward stabilizing the household farm. A household in any kind of village or collective farm was explicitly forbidden to subdivide its land if the division would create farms too small to be economically viable. Gubernia land sections were empowered to establish minimum permissible sizes for khutor and otrub farms. Interstripped villages, both communal and noncommunal, were "allowed" to set such limits for their households if they wished (arts. 74-86; pp. 162-63). Admittedly this fell far short of an open commitment to individual land settlement, but the codex gave all the force paper could give to the inclinations of local specialists to establish peasant households as productive units. The trumpeting about collectivization never let up, but in 1922 the government seemed to be preparing to allow the *agronom-organizatory* to muffle it and to embark on their own style of mobilization.

It is of more than passing interest that the specialists of 1922 should have been so concerned with legality. In Stolypin's day they had been impatient with MVD agencies and law courts whenever these bodies had insisted on the formalities associated with private property. Judging from their apparent concern for peasant households, one might be tempted to conclude that specialists changed their minds under the bolsheviks and become advocates of land ownership. Speaking generally, this would be a bad guess. The codex of 1922 depicted a household farm primarily as a productive unit, not as someone's domain. The *agronom-organizatory* were as anxious to mobilize peasants under the Soviet regime as they had been in tsarist times, and they still put their faith in the same methods. A household farm whose operator belonged to a cooperative still appeared to them as the most likely unit for the mobilization of farmers. The specialists' ideal farmers did not *own* their farms. They *held* their khutors or otrubs only as long as they farmed them according to prescriptions handed down by local agronomists. Such was the gist of the 1922 codex, and in

[12] A number of laws in the 1920s were published in the form of amendments to the clauses regarding the commissions, indicating that commissions were indeed operating and that their work was calling forth changes in their organization. The law of 5 May 1925 (Kazantsev, 1954: 648-50) brought the commisions to the apex of their paper power. Among other things, it required them to confirm all land settlement projects, even undisputed ones. The RSFSR law of 10 Oct. 1930 abolished the commissions (pp. 509-10). Whatever the commisssions did, then, we can be certain that they came into existence and functioned.

this sense it was a direct descendant of Krivoshein's law of 29 May 1911 (ch. 9, sec. B). Interestingly, German officials followed a similar approach when they attempted to organize food procurement in the Ukraine during the summer of 1918. They considered the household farm cultivated by its possessor to be the most effective unit for compelling peasants to deliver grain (Palij, 1971: 74).

Changes in the Laws after 1922

From 1922 until 1928 Soviet legislation indicated no observable trends in agrarian reform. The codex suffered no basic changes, though, to be sure, a number of amendments were enacted (Kazantsev, 1954: 638-79). In particular, the decree of 28 June 1926 liberalized a household's right to rent out its land or hire labor to work it, and a number of decrees in 1925-27 assigned land commissions and ispolkoms somewhat more active roles in land settlement (pp. 648-50, 665-68). Special provisions were also added from time to time to apply to this or that autonomous republic. In the main, however, legislation favored neither household nor collective farms. This does not mean that no significant changes took place in agrarian policy or rural administration during the period 1923-27, only that they were made without referring to the codex or consulting with the NKZ. The codex, after all, was only a law of the RSFSR, not the entire Soviet Union. It was enacted only a little more than a year before the USSR acquired constitutional form; thus, although most of its provisions were applied throughout the USSR, it never became a USSR law. Similarly the NKZ was only an agency of the RSFSR. No corresponding agency was established at the USSR level until late in 1929.[13]

In 1927-28 a trend did become perceptible in legislation on agrarian reform. Land settlement ceased to be described as something to be worked out in the locales by peasants and freewheeling specialists and began to take on the appearance of a program to bring peasants into collective and state farms.

The first clear—albeit small—legislative step in this direction was the USSR law of 16 March 1927, which ordered that land settlement projects carried out on collective farms or for the purpose of forming them were to be financed entirely by the state (p. 254). This was not yet an all-out campaign for collectivization. A year later, however, the USSR law of 2 March 1928 expressly ordered land organs throughout the union to give all their support to collectives. From now on, consolidation of individual farms was to have the lowest priority on fieldwork schedules,

[13]The USSR law of 12 Nov. 1923 established ten NKs at the union level (*Direktivy,* 1957: I, 408). None of them was agriculture.

and it was not to be tolerated at all if it gave any support to "kulaks" (pp. 289-90). After this general pronouncement from the USSR, the RSFSR began to stir. On 30 April 1928 its SNK amended the land codex of 1922 to remove all restrictions on consolidations into integral collective farms. Would-be joiners of collectives could demand the separation of their strips whenever they wished, and similar operations could be repeated any number of times regardless of their effect on remaining villagers (pp. 672-73). Note that at this time, in early 1928, the government was still showing enough concern for legal system to issue its new laws in the form of amendments to the old.

The most important legal enactment in the campaign to eliminate interstripping on collective farms came in December 1928. This was the "general basis for land use and land settlement," published by the SNK of the USSR on the 15th (pp. 299-307). The "general basis" was a code of sorts, though it was far shorter and more general than the RSFSR codex of six years earlier. It reflected, however, a complete lack of concern for the formalities of codification. It did not trouble to rescind the 1922 codex, nor did it call upon the RSFSR to do so. Apparently its enactors did not worry about the problems of local officials, who would have somehow to deal with both codex and new "basis," though these two laws contradicted each other in both spirit and letter. Indeed, it is safe to surmise that December 1928 marks the end of the period during which rural administrators could conceivably have worked under something resembling a system of law. Thenceforth, "law" came to mean only what the most influential official in a given area said it was. To be sure, statutory law had been vague in earlier years. Now, however, it was flatly self-contradictory. It could no longer serve as a basis for coherent discussion, let alone action.

It will be useful to say a few words about the contents of the 15 December law, since it marked a distinct stage in the trend toward forced collectivization. In essence, it was a disorderly pile of vague clauses, only some of which contained provisions for intensifying the government's pressure to collectivize. Many clauses continued the business of regulating land arrangements apart from collectives, and article 15 even repeated the principle that peasants were to be free to choose their manner of using their land. There were several collectivizing clauses. Article 18 assigned top priority in fieldwork schedules to collective farms desiring to consolidate their land (p. 302). To be precise, article 18 said "outside all priorities" *(vneocherednyi)*. Projects for reducing interstripping on collective farms would not merely be put first on schedules but could be taken up at any time regardless of schedules. Article 30 extended certain privileges to collective farmers: lower taxes, easier credit, the right to acquire state lands, and priority over noncollectivized peasants in receiving machinery, fertilizer, and seed from the government. Most important, villagers who broke away from their neighbors to form kolkhozy were to receive the village's best fields. Article 36 granted similar privileges to state farms (p. 304). In short, the December law openly granted extensive privileges to collectivizing villagers—more extensive even than the ones Soviet scholars accuse the tsarist government of having granted to individual consolidators (see ch. 7, sec. E).

The December law did more than give collectives preferential treatment. It also furthered two other trends: the weakening of the village assembly, and the tendency toward forced land settlement.

Let us take up the village assembly first. In late 1927 a variety of laws had begun to call upon village soviets to play an active role in land settlement (see pp. 663-68), and the law of December 1928 not only expanded their powers to do this but also weakened village assemblies. Article 16 gave village soviets the right to initiate land settlement projects (p. 302), and article 51 gave them such broad powers of supervision over village assemblies as to leave the assemblies' autonomy entirely at the soviets' discretion (p. 306). Finally, article 49 decreed that the right to vote in the village assembly or be elected to village office was to be restricted on the same basis as in the soviet, a measure which, if observed, virtually eliminated the difference between assemblies and soviets and rendered the former superfluous.

A word about village and volost soviets. They were never democratic during the 1920s. There was never a time when party agents did not dictate to them at will. In NEP's early years the party was more or less passive in rural areas, and the soviets manifested an aimless indifference to peasant life. A series of reports from the office of workers' and peasants' inspection indicated that in 1923-24 the turnout for elections to volost soviets had been very low and election results had been faked (Iakovlev, 1925: 3-6, 13-17, 77). As a result, the percentage of delegates who were party members was consistently high, which is to say that veterans of the Red Army and Tsiurupa's gangs were continuing to dominate village and volost soviets (Iakovlev, *Nasha,* 1924: 43, 109-110, 140-50; Lewin, 1966: 424; Fainsod, 1958: 138-41).

Measures were enacted in the mid-1920s to make rural soviets more truly representative. In one Tver volost this meant that in 1925 the number of ispolkom members who were local residents increased *for the first time* to the point where they were in the majority (Bolshakov, 1927: 176-79). Perhaps soviets generally came a little closer to being local institutions in 1925-26. In 1927, however, they quickly fell back to their role as agencies of the central government. Thus the replacement of village assemblies by soviets in 1928 signified the installation of government administrators as managers of villages—managers from the outside who knew virtually nothing of village life in general or of agriculture in particular. Soviet law was not only "encouraging" the formation of collective farms in December 1928 but also subverting the villages' ability to resist government pressure of any kind.[14]

Meanwhile, land settlement was becoming increasingly a matter of government dictation rather than encouragement. In early 1927 the party began making harsh demands for simpler and speedier measures. The fourth congress of soviets of the USSR adopted a resolution on 26 April setting up a hue and cry after local agencies that took too much time to complete land settlement projects (Kazantsev, 1954: 256-57). From then on clauses began to appear regularly in the statutes demanding faster work. On 15 December 1928, the same day the "bases" for land settlement came out, another USSR law, this one devoted to raising agricultural productivity, explicitly ordered the republics to set deadlines for the completion of land settlement projects already in process (*Direktivy*, 1957: I, 862-63).

Summary

The legal grounds for forced collectivization were in place by the end of 1928. Households, villages, and individual farmers had all lost the last vestige of their paper protection. The laws now made it explicit that legal rules only existed insofar as government agents chose to honor them. Collective farms enjoyed rights and even substantial prerogatives, but they did not rest primarily on the content of statutes. The basic quality in all rural life after December 1928 was the meaninglessness of all statutes and the overriding importance of the aims being pursued by persons in authority. The most significant element in rural administration now was the identity of the administrators, and in 1929 the big question was: who would they be? Would agrarian reformers continue to be specialists, concerned primarily with long-term agricultural improvement? Or would they be democratically elected peasants, anxious to keep outsiders from breaking up their villages? Or would they be bolshevik enthusiasts, concerned with immediate measures to get cheap grain to the towns? This, of course, had long been the key question around which rural government revolved, but in 1929, with the disappearance of legal-administrative system, it became the only question.

We have seen that Soviet legislation on land reform had never ceased to contain expressions of bolshevik ideals. After 1919, however,

[14]Concerning the random nature of party interference in volost and "village" soviets and, in turn, the gap between soviets and villages, see Lepeshkin (1959: 74-80, 110-12, 176-77, 276-78, 327), Fenomenov (1925: II, 34-35, 38, 43, 95), Burov (1926: 26-27, 57-58, 179-81, 236-41), Iakovlev (*Nasha*, 1924: 156-64; *Borba*, 1929: 62, 95), and Bolshakov (1927: 428-33). An RSFSR statute of 30 July 1930 completed the process of weakening villages by abolishing them altogether (Kazantsev, 1954: 504-5).

the influence of Krivoshein's old land settlement organization began to make itself felt. It had been tied up with grain procurement from 1914 on and, as a result, had remained active in the countryside until 1921 despite the virtual cessation of land reform. With the end of forced procurement in 1921-22, specialists took over the business of agrarian reform and it became possible to work toward the establishment of a legal-administrative system in the countryside. This the specialists did after a fashion until 1927-28, when the party once again began to turn to force.

The theoretical basis for land reform in the quasi-system of 1923-28 was the peasants' voluntary action, but the codex of 1922 provided that this action would have to be acceptable to specialists in the local organs of government administration. In other words, the legislative modus operandi of agrarian reform in the mid-1920s was essentially the same as that which had developed under the tsarist regime. The specialists of the 1920s differed from those of the tsarist period only in the greater freedom of action they enjoyed on paper. At the end of 1928 statutes on land reform virtually ceased to embody an operating system, but since they were only a reflection of the specialists' dominant position in rural government, breakdown was not in itself an important event. What was important, as we shall see in the following section, was the development this breakdown marked: the rapid decline in the specialists' position after 1928 and the end of their style of reform.

B. AGRICULTURAL SPECIALISTS UNDER THE BOLSHEVIKS

We turn now to the question of what the *agronom-organizatory* actually did during the 1920s. I have suggested that a fair number of them were still out in the "dark" villages at the end of the civil war. After all Tsiurupa's ravaging, laws and commands from the capital city carried less weight than ever in the countryside, but the specialists, it seems, had been able to maintain a certain position. Thus the specialists' relationship with the peasantry during the 1920s is doubly interesting. It not only allows us to look more deeply into the interaction between government and peasantry that commenced with the Stolypin Land Reform but also sheds some light on the situation the party had to face when it undertook to deal with peasants on its own.

The Alliance of Rhetoric

Specialists in the Government Organization

In 1914 about 5,000 agronomists and 7,600 surveyors were active in peasant land reform. They served under various agencies. Surveyors worked for the ministry of justice, the administrative directors and most of the agronomists were under the MZ, and some agronomists worked for the zemstvoes. In the early 1920s an estimated 7,000 specialists were again at work (Bochkov, 1956: 151), this time all of them under a single organization, the NKZ. Their ranks swelled rapidly in the following years, and in 1928 there may have been more than 17,000 of them (*Spravochnik*, 1928: 223-24).[15]

Specialists who had begun their service under the tsar dominated the NKZ. Most middle and high-level servitors in the old MZ retained their positions in the new organization throughout the revolutionary years of 1917-18, and in January 1928 they still occupied about half the positions in the land settlement organization at the uezd level and above (p. 226). Until late 1929 specialists trained in tsarist land reform wrote the laws, circulars, and plans that expressed the Soviet government's agricultural policies. More, they staffed the faculties of agronomic science and rural economics in institutions of higher and middle education. They ran the agricultural section of the state planning commission, and in 1927-28 it was they who turned out the first five-year plan for agriculture (Moshkov, 1966: 67-68). These men were very active throughout the 1920s in producing scholarly works. Pershin published his outstanding book on the Stolypin Reform in 1928 *(Zemelnoe ustroistvo dorevoliutsionnoi derevni)*, and studies by Russian agricultural economists like Chaianov attracted worldwide attention (Chayanov, 1966: v-vi, xxx-xxxiii). As for specialists who began their careers after the Revolution, many of them were men of "advanced" political views, but they acquired their technical training and their ideas on agricultural productivity at the hands of their tsarist predecessors.

It is not so surprising, therefore, that land settlement should have continued through the 1920s and even speeded up. Land settlement projects in 1907-13 had covered a total area of less than 44 million acres, of which 8 million were completed during the year 1913 (ch. 5, sec. A). Had the specialists of the 1920s gone on performing at the 1913 level, they would have covered about 40 million acres during the five years from 1921 to 1926. But a recent Soviet study says they actually covered 200 million acres during these years (Bochkov, 1956: 147-48), and this is close to what specialists were claiming at the time. According to a report made in 1929, the area covered in the RSFSR alone by the end of 1928 totaled almost 400 million acres (*Stenograficheskii*, 1929: 492).[16]

[15] Another estimate gives the number of specialists in operation at the end of 1928 as 7,900 (*Stenograficheskii*, 1929: 40). Surveyors, it will be recalled, came under the NKZ in Dec. 1917 (n. 5).

[16] When the same land area was subject to land settlement more than once, it was counted into the above total each time (p. 493). Thus the actual area affected by land reform in the 1920s was somewhat less than 400 million acres, even if the *zemleustroiteli* were as energetic in fact as official figures indicate.

In part, these high figures reflect the Soviets government's small concern for the annoying intricacies of land rights, which made things simpler for land reformers in the field. They also reflect the generally more modest nature of the projects undertaken in the 1920s. Most of them involved group land settlement, chiefly the disentangling of villages (though there was probably a vast amount of covert khutor and otrub forming during the course of these ideologically acceptable projects). Then, too, land settlement subsections were inclined to exaggerate their achievements. One thing is obvious, however: agricultural specialists went on working actively on land settlement under the bolsheviks, *and they were very proud of it.* If they completed only one-third of the projects they claimed, the programs that began in 1906 went forward in the 1920s at least as rapidly as they had in 1913.

Bolshevik Weakness in Rural Government

The bolsheviks suffered throughout the 1920s from an almost total lack of operational relationships with the villages. To be sure, there were party members at work who were of peasant origin, but the vast majority of these were petty administrators, holding positions in volost-level organizations far from their own home villages. In Tula gubernia in the early 1920s, 93% of the party members of peasant origin were working in volosts far from their homes, and this was typical of the RSFSR in general (Iakovlev, *Nasha,* 1924: 163). It seems that when peasants joined the party, they lost contact *and any desire for contact* with their own villages and with peasant society in general. Working as alien administrators, they rarely went out even to visit the villages under their official jurisdiction, let alone participate in their development (pp. 109-10, 156-64; see also Iakovlev, 1925). By 1929 the situation may have improved slightly. Of 333,000 party members in rural cells, 124,000 were alleged to be practicing farmers. Nevertheless, the party still considered its connections with the peasants to be very weak (Lewin, 1966: 111-17).

What was true of ostensibly peasant party cells was equally true of the formal apparatus of rural government. Rural soviets and ispolkoms neither represented nor governed the villages (sec. A). Soviets were not averse to interfering arbitrarily in villages, but their sporadic invasions did not make them effective agencies of government policy. On the whole, soviets and ispolkoms left the peasants to themselves, interfering in villages only when someone made a specific complaint or openly opposed their authority. One is reminded of the *stanovye* of tsarist times (ch. 3, sec. C).

Specialists in the Countryside

Bolshevik weakness in rural Russia left the agricultural experts a clear field. They constituted the only group capable of bringing the peasantry into the national economy, and therefore the bolsheviks needed them. This need was the foundation for a patently self-contradictory but practical alliance between the dictatorship of the proletariat and agrarian reform.

The alliance began in the midst of civil war and general economic disintegration, when no one in Russia worried much about the absurdity of what he was doing or saying. As we have seen, bolshevik leaders kept up a remarkable flow of promises and directives, putting their hopes in the more or less sound principle that if positive action is utterly impossible for a government, its need to resort to rhetoric is all the greater (sec. A). Confronted with a fantasy government, agricultural specialists attached themselves to it by adopting the ridiculous but tactically sound dogma that collectivization would raise agricultural productivity. This idea received formal expression in the law of 14 February 1919, which, as we have seen, gave the NKZ control over collectivization and at the same time set forth guidelines for the process of land settlement (sec. A). From then on the specialists' measures for land settlement and agronomic aid, designed primarily to raise productivity, could be advertised as collectivization or "progress toward collectivization." Opposition to land settlement, on the other hand, could be denounced as a deterrent to collectivization or "not true, Leninist collectivization" (Knipovich, 1920: 23-24).[17] Specialists could adopt bolshevik rhetoric without fear, and some of them could even believe it in a general way, because, as we have seen, it was irrelevant to the technical problems of agricultural production and had no concrete meaning for the vast majority of peasants, once the civil war was over and forced procurement had been abandoned.

The alliance of rhetoric worked very well for all parties concerned. Peasants enjoyed a measure of freedom from external constraint, specialists conducted their conversational reforms with some success, and the bolsheviks could forget about their embarrassing failure to mobilize the dark masses under their own leadership. By affecting to accept the bolsheviks' preposterous slogans about a class of productive poor who would labor dilegently without hope of material reward, the *agronom-organizatory* freed themselves from thug rule and carried forward the good work of agricultural improvement. There was, however, a basic disadvantage in the alliance. Its foundation was a tacit agreement by both sides *not* to communicate meaningfully with each other, and as time went by, this lack of communication allowed both sides to widen the gap between their practical aims without doing anything to compromise their differences. The existence of the alliance ruled out any discussion of real problems or even any recognition of them. *Agronom-organizatory* could easily remain indifferent to all problems and considerations save their old

[17]Quoted phrases are taken from the law of 14 Feb. 1919.

programs of land settlement, which, they were sure, would ultimately bring prosperity and pacify the bolsheviks; the party could easily forget that it had no means to administer rural Russia except the specicalists. In the end, therefore, the separation between the two sides widened even as they cooperated. The alliance proved fatal precisely because it worked so well. Specialists learned to scorn their masters and ignore the wider problems of government, and as their influence in the countryside grew, so did the party's mistrust.

We have now to trace the widening of the gap between party and specialists. To be more precise, we shall take a few glances at this widening, for available evidence permits no more. Chiefly, we can get a few glimpses of the specialists' growing success with land settlement and their ever greater need to disguise their work with bolshevik rhetoric.

The essential point is that the reforms the NKZ carried out in the 1920s did not differ appreciably from those the tsarist MZ had been working on in 1914. The basic element in the specialists' work was their determination to focus all the powers of science on that old and much-studied problem inherent in interstripping: the waste of effort entailed in peasant ownership of fields that were far from each other and from their dwellings. In the 1920s most articulate specialists agreed that the chief practical aim of land settlement was to minimize the distance between peasant homes and fields, which is to say that they adopted a purpose, derived from tsarist land settlement, that covertly militated against collectivization and in favor of consolidated household farms. No one ventured to say in public that individual consolidated farms were the best form of landholding, but specialists generally insisted that peasants who did establish such farms should have their homes and fields adjacent; that is, they echoed Kofod's demand that consolidating households take up khutor farms rather than otrubs, despite the difficulty and expense of building new dwellings. No one dared to deny openly that collective farms were superior forms of landholding, but most specialists stressed the need to keep kolkhozy small so that members would have easy access to their fields. With a little ingenuity, then, an *agronom-organizator* could set up clusters of otrubs or khutors and call them kolkhozy (see Iakovlev, *Nasha,* 1924: 54). For example, the dwellings of four households could be placed together at the center of a square area, and each would farm the quarter of the square in which its dwelling was located. This arrangement was a product of capital-city drawing boards in Stolypin's day, when reformers called it four khutors. But one could also call it a section of a village or a small TOZ, depending on one's taste. Such a perfect blending of actual household farm with collectivist jargon probably did not often translate into reality, but many other, less perfect combinations were possible. One NKZ official referred with approval to a widespread movement during 1920-21 in Smolensk gubernia to form five-khutor clusters, in which homesteads were built close together and the five separate fields spread out around them (Mesiatsev, 1921: 7). All this made perfectly good sense as long as official discussions of agricultural improvement hinged on the basic purpose of minimizing the distance from home to field and dismissed all other considerations as peripheral. I am not sure that the specialists took this tack with the conscious aim of deceiving their bolshevik masters. Maybe they really believed what they said.

As noted before, most reform projects in the 1920s appeared in the records as group land settlement operations that divided villages into consolidated portions *(vyselki),* each belonging to a few households. Since the manner of land division within each *vyselka* was left up to the settlers themselves, they could divide their fields into strips in the traditional manner. Alternatively, they could collectivize into a kolkhoz, consolidate into khutors, or adopt some partial reform such as strip widening or an improvement in crop rotation (Vasilchenko, 1924: 7-22). Official records did not reveal what the peasants were actually doing with their land. No one could tell what actual reforms in land usage took place on the *vyselki* except by going to each village and looking at the result (see Pershin, 1921: 58-59, 67-68; *Sbornik po voprosam,* 1927: I, 46-48). the *vyselka,* it seems, was an excellent device for sustaining the alliance of rhetoric. Local specialists could work closely with peasants in any direction they liked and they could apply any label to what they did that seemed politic.

The most striking evidence for this general feature of specialist-dominated land settlement may be found in the angry speeches given by some rebellious specialists at a meeting held in Moscow in December 1929. The participants called themselves "marxist agrarian reformers" *(agrarno-marksisty).* They were mostly young men who had had some training in agronomy and were in the process of purging the *"neonarodnik"* specialists. Neonarodniks, said the self-proclaimed marxists, dominated the NKZ and all the mechanisms of agrarian reform. One typical *agrarno-marksist,* V. Matiukhin, denounced what he took to be Chaianov's approach to reform and accused the NKZ of having permitted this approach to prevail in Russian practice ever since the Revolution. So-called collectivization, cried Matiukhin, had been primarily a matter of setting up individual farms (*Trudy,* 1930: I, 165-68). Several other *agrarno-marksisty* supported Matiukhin's assertion. One conferee noted angrily that O. Khauke, an old tsarist student of agrarian reform, had just published an article openly claiming that collectivization was essentially a continuation of the Stolypin Land Reform (pp. 181-84). Yet another *agrarno-marksist* was infuriated at the lectures B. S. Martynov was giving at Leningrad University. This old advocate of consolidation and private property (see ch. 9, sec. B) was describing kolkhozy as if they were and should be clusters of individual farms (pp. 341-44).

A fair amount of evidence indicates that the outraged *agrarno-marksisty* had right on their side. Many laws and orders from the NKZ reflected a remarkable willingness to continue tsarist programs. It will be recalled that an NKZ instruction of March 1922 advised surveyors to follow tsarist regulations until the Soviet administration could prepare its own. A year later an NKZ circular listed the general types of socialist land settlement, and they were still essentially the same as tsarist measures (see *Sbornik zakonopolozhenii,* 1927: 87). As said before, the RSFSR law of 9 October 1925 expressly encouraged specialists to form individual consolidated plots whenever land-settling peasants preferred them to collectivization (p. 35). In 1927 the party began to voice dissatisfaction with the specialists' failure to push collectivization, but the party instruction of 20 October 1927 had to admit that Soviet law still contained no guide for applying land settlement work to collective farms. The instruction recommended, as the best set of rules available, a project code of land settlement procedures that had been drawn up in the Ukrainian SSR by Pershin (*Spravochnik,* 1928: 45), but Pershin's project represented no serious departure from tsarist programs and regulations (see pp. 45-55). Finally, it is worth mentioning that a widely used instruction book for guiding the formation of *vyselki* during the 1920s briefly repeated the standard line that collectives were a superior type of land-holding (Rzhanitsyn, 1927: 129-35), but the author offered no descriptive remarks on the business of forming them. Almost all of his book—125 of its 135 pages—was devoted to describing tsarist forms of land settlement.

Another indication of the specialists' true purposes may be found in the official record of their efforts to form collective farms. The laws of 1919-22 required collectivizing peasants to work within a framework of legal rights. Until 1929 they had to establish their kolkhozy and sovkhozy by determining external boundaries in agreement with noncollectivized neighbors and making specific arrangements among themselves for the disposition of their strips. In short, they required the services of *agronom-organizatory.* A collective farm without land settlement was just a group of interstripped peasants, in most cases still tangled up with noncollectivized neighbors as well as their own comrades. Thus the contribution of local specialists was a crucial factor in carrying out collectivization. If specialists took no interest in collective farms, it meant either one of two things: "collectivized" peasants had no real interest in changing their way of life, or the specialists were determined not to support collectivization. The question is: did the specialists help collective farms to take form during the period of quasi-legality before the party reasserted its dominance in rural Russia?

The answer is no. Ostensibly socialist land settlement throve on the pretext that it was furthering the cause of collectivization, but in fact specialists generally allowed sovkhozy and kolkhozy to flounder along on their own. According to an official report for the RSFSR, covering the period up to the end of 1928, all varieties of land settlement touched only 23.7 million acres of kolkhoz and sovkhoz land (*Stenograficheskii*, 1929: 485), which compares very poorly with the 400 million acres that supposedly represented the total area affected by land settlement in the RSFSR (p. 492). The specialists' inclination to ignore the collectivized sector appears all the more pronounced if we keep in mind that they did most of the 23.7 million acres during the single year 1928. I have no figures on sovkhozy, but of the 23.7 million collectivized acres covered by specialists, 11.5 million were on kolkhoz land, and of these only 3.6 million were subject to reform prior to 1928 (p. 335). Before 1928 *agronom-organizatory* did virtually nothing for collective farms; during 1928 they did a little.

It is true that kolkhozy and sovkhozy covered only a small area in toto. The most passionate devotion to collectivization would not have allowed the specialists to cover more ground than was there. But the 23.7 million collectivized acres actually touched by land settlement did not even cover all the collectivized area. As of late 1927 less than half the acreage in kolkhozy and only 77% of sovkhoz land had benefited from their ministrations (p. 253; *Spravochnik*, 1928: 26). By 1 November 1928 specialists had touched only 75% of kolkhoz land (*Stenograficheskii*, 1929: 485). Keep in mind that these figures refer to land settling of all types. Only a small portion of them represented the complete consolidation of collectives into integral areas, separate from their neighbors. As we shall see presently, most land settlement operations on collectivized land were far from complete. Then, too, these figures are probably inflated. Specialists and peasants alike found it advantageous to show enthusiasm for socialization.

Be this as it may, in 1929 *most* collective farms and even many state farms were still little more than groups of peasants who called themselves TOZs, artels or sovkhozy but who did nothing to change their methods of land use or distribution. Seemingly interested only in the financial benefits for which collectives were eligible, they continued to live in their old villages and hold their land in scattered strips along with their uncollectivized brethren (Lewin, 1966: 102-3, 242-44). An NKZ report of 1929 noted that most sovkhoz workers were hired temporarily, by the day or season, and over 60% of the regularly employed farmers were peasants who worked their own plots in the surrounding area and labored part of the time on sovkhoz land—much the same arrangement as had obtained on the private estates of prerevolutionary days (*Materialy*, 1929: I, 63-64). Many sovkhozy had taken form on these estates. One NKZ report of 1929 hinted strongly that they simply continued the old sharecropping arrangements (pp. 52-53).

As I have suggested, land settlement on collective farms could actually disguise the forming of otrubs and khutors. This is perhaps the most interesting of the specialists' many ways of duping their bolshevik masters. Although it affected only a tiny portion of the peasant population, it shows more clearly than the relatively obscure *vyselki* of the noncollectivized sector just how far specialists and peasants could carry their cryptic cooperation.

Consider the sovkhozy. A reference work for agricultural specialists, published in 1928, insisted that land settlement on state farms should not consist of "the cutting away of separate plots from sovkhoz land for 'rational' land use by individual peasants, *as has been done up to this time*" (italics mine). Instead, sovkhoz lands should be consolidated into a single area to be farmed as a unit (*Spravochnik*, 1928: 29). Sovkhozy, then, were often clusters of otrubs or khutors in disguise.

As for the kolkhozy, an NKZ official from the lower Volga observed in January 1929 that *most* of the tiny collectives in his area were really otrubs (*Stenograficheskii*, 1929: 393), and at the same time a high-level NKZ administrator expressed his disapproval of the fake kolkhozy being formed in Smolensk gubernia by farmers who actually lived on khutors (p. 404). Data from a field survey conducted in October 1927 indicated that TOZ members were farming only 2.9% of their *sown* land collectively, and for artel members the figure was only 13.5%. Only the *kommuny* had actually collectivized all their sown land (*Materialy*, 1929: I, 84). These figures, taken from small random samples, conflicted sharply with official tabulations of reports from local agencies. In 1926, only one year before the above figures were compiled, the administration's figures showed TOZ members farming 33% of their land collectively, while the corresponding figure for artels was 55.5% (Wesson, 1963: 140). But this is no reason to disregard the survey of October 1927. For one thing, official figures were not exactly comparable to the survey. They covered all varieties of land, whereas the survey concerned itself only with sown land. Some of the difference between the two sets of figures could be accounted for by subtracting collectivized forests and meadows—most of which were already held in common in traditional villages—from the total collectivized area. Then, too, official tabulations exaggerated the extent of collectivization. According to Lewin, information gleaned from routine reports from locales was highly unreliable in the late 1920s (1966: 98-99).

The most interesting phase of the specialists' work with kolkhoz land settlement came in 1928-29, when the party exerted itself to speed up and "improve" collectivization. Little TOZs would no longer do. The party demanded big artels and *kommuny*. It wanted authentic rural factories, not warmed-over villages, and it wanted them fast (Moshkov, 1966: 41-42). But bolshevik pressure failed to halt the trend toward consolidated individual farms on "collectivized" land. In 1928 specialists who worked on collective farms concentrated more than ever on the formation of small TOZs. Many kolkhozy formed in 1928 were so small they represented little more than large families. The average sown area of the TOZs formed in this year was 71.5 acres; that of artels, 114 acres; and that of *kommuny*, 180 acres (*Materialy*, 1929: I, 81-82). These averages were much smaller than corresponding averages for all kolkhozy that had been formed since the Revolution and still existed at the end of 1928. The average for all extant TOZs at the end of 1928 was 96 acres of sown land; for artels, 129; for *kommuny*, over 300 (*Stenograficheskii*, 1929: 481; see also Lewin, 1966: 378-79). Moshkov asserts that TOZs formed in 1928-29 were larger on the average than those formed earlier, but his only sources are two publications of the early 1930s that cannot be considered reliable (1966: 42).

The new TOZs were not only smaller but also less collectivized; that is, the members surrendered an even smaller portion of their land to collective holding and common cultivation (*Stenograficheskii*, 1929: 482). We are forced to conclude that the majority of peasants who formed TOZs in 1928 were actually consolidating their land into household farms. If it be true or even half true that they had subjected three-fourths of their arable land to land settlement by the end of 1928 (p. 485), and if it be true that they continued in 1928 to farm less than 10% of it collectively (p. 482; see also *Materialy*, 1929: I, 84), it follows that most of the consolidated or semiconsolidated sown land within "collective" farms was held and worked as otrubs or semi-otrubs.

The nature of the TOZ-otrub clusters must have varied widely. The most usual "collectivization," however, seems to have been the simplest. The members continued to live together with nonmembers in the old village cluster of houses, while their strips in each of the village fields were combined into one lot. The "collective" consisted of a number of relatively wide sections in each field, constituting little fields in themselves. From the traditional villager's point of view, then, each of the village's fields would be divided into two parts. At one end would be the strips of uncollectivized villagers, at the other, a consolidated lot. In the consolidated part the members eliminated their strips and, supposedly, worked the land as a team. When they actually functioned in this manner, they were in fact a collective farm of sorts (see Bochkov, 1956: 172-73). Alternatively, however, each member of the "collective" could take one or two lots and farm them as his own otrub, in which case there would be no collective at all but simply a village that had gone part of the way toward forming integral household lots. The figures presented above suggest that this was indeed the dominant tendency throughout the 1920s and especially during 1928-29. One can imagine how difficult it was for a party hack making an occasional visit from a volost center to detect this sort of thing and how little benefit he would have derived from making a fuss about it even if he did detect it.

Thus the collectivization boondoggle of 1919-29. There is no evidence apart from standard bolshevik denunciations of bourgeois specialists to indicate that the specialists were consciously conspiring among themselves to hoodwink the party or to "seize power." The only explanation for their conduct that makes sense to me is simply that it stemmed from attitudes toward the peasants that individual specialists acquired as they did their jobs. Each *agronom-organizator* perpetrated frauds more or less consciously on specific occasions, usually in order to carry out this or that practical project for improving agriculture. By and large, the specialists seem to have believed sincerely and even fanatically that their work was actually bringing the bolshevik regime the support it desired. Scientific-democratic land reform would increase agricultural productivity, and this would solve the government's economic problems. Sooner or later the bolsheviks would open their eyes to reality as farmers saw it, and the need for an alliance of rhetoric would fade away.

The Party Breaks with the Specialists

Bolshevik indifference to the peasantry depended on the ability of rural Russia to furnish enough grain to satisfy the government's needs. Unfortunately for all concerned, grain supply to the cities began to fall off noticeably in early 1928 (Lewin, 1966: 260-61, 340-41), and this, perforce, marked the beginning of the end of the alliance of rhetoric. Grain procurement campaigns began again, and the rhetoric of "socialist" land settlement crumbled rapidly just as the agrarian reform it had sheltered was reaching significant proportions. I have seen no evidence that the bolsheviks intended to make forced grain procurment the basis for a clash with the specialists. On the contrary, they probably did not fully realize how far their determined interference into rural politics would take them until they had become heavily involved (see pp. 245-50, 393). Procurement campaigns began in January 1928, but it was only at the end of 1929, almost two years later, that open conflict broke out between specialists and goverment.

Scholars have discussed the background to the urban grain shortage of 1928-29 in great detail (e.g., Karcz, 1967; Erlich, 1960; Millar, 1970; Dohan, 1976). Interpretations vary, but everyone agrees that the peasants became increasingly reluctant to market their produce in 1927, when the government began taking measures to hold down the price of grain. Grain prices had begun to rise in 1926, presumably because the party had decided in the previous year to accelerate Russia's industrial development. Russia's manufacturing facilities were directed to the production of industrial goods, thereby creating a scarcity of consumer goods, which, in turn, inflated the prices peasants paid for them. When the government acted to keep grain prices down, while allowing the prices of manufactured goods to rise, the peasants began increasingly to consume their produce on their own farms (or peddle it on the black market) instead of selling it to the state (Moshkov, 1966: 29-30). The market suffered further dislocation in 1928 because grain prices were held down while the price of meat was allowed to rise. Peasants thus had more than one reason to divert grain from the market to their animals. Isaac Deutscher and Alec Nove, among others, have suggested that although the decisions and experiments leading up to this state of affairs were not necessarily the best possible ones, they were by no means uniformly unintelligent, given the circumstances the regime had to face and its extremely limited ability to ascertain what was going on in the countryside (Deutscher, *Unarmed,* 1965: 208-46; Nove, 1964: 20-25). Intelligent or unintelligent, the party's commitment to forced industrialization produced serious economic dislocations, which apparently the party leaders had not foreseen (Karcz, 1967: 421-27; Lewin, 1966: 223). When grain export fell to practically nothing by the end of 1927 and the cities began to run short of grain, the government was caught flatfooted (Moshkov, 1966: 52; Dohan, 1976: 605-19).

The party does not seem to have realized the seriousness of its grain supply problem until early 1928. Discussions during the fifteenth party congress in December 1927 reflected no awareness of it, although reports of a bad harvest were coming in from grain-producing areas while the delegates were still meeting (Lewin, 1966: 177-90, 193-96; Moshkov, 1966: 33-34). When forced procurement began, therefore, it materialized in random fashion, without authorization or plan, to say nothing of coordination with existing rural agencies. In February 1928 Stalin simply moved into Siberia, where the harvest had been good in 1927, and took up once again the wartime practice of unleashing gangs upon villages to confiscate "kulak" grain hoards (Lewin, 1966: 196-207).

Stalin's ad hoc invasion brought in enough grain to satisfy immediate needs in early 1928, but in the following months the peasants responded, as they had under war communism, by planting less grain and/or hiding what they harvested (Moshkov, 1966: 31-35). In 1929 urban food shortages again became serious, and rationing had to be introduced in the large cities (p. 52; Lewin, 1966: 345-48). Strikes broke out in some towns in early 1929, probably as a result of the government's short-lived attempt in late 1928 to coax more grain from the peasants with higher food prices (Moshkov, 1966: 51; Lewin, 1966: 341, 393-95). In the countryside forced procurement campaigns expanded in scope and intensity, and by the late summer of 1929 more than 100,000 of the urban loyal were out in the villages hounding peasants (Moshkov, 1966:

66-69; Lewin, 1966: 343-49).[18] New decrees on grain confiscation allowed the new *otriady* very broad powers, mainly by applying the metaphor "kulak" to anyone who had grain in storage (Moshkov, 1966: 63-65).

In the short run the new *prodrazverstka* was effective. Harvests in 1929 were slightly smaller than those of the year before—78.9 million tons of grain as compared to 80.6 million in 1928 (pp. 19-20)— yet 16 million tons came into the government's distribution system in 1929, as opposed to only 11 million in 1928 (Lewin, 1966: 366-67). Nevertheless, it gradually became clear that forced procurment would not be enough. Despite the accumulation of normal grain reserves by the end of 1929, the threat of peasant resistance now loomed larger than ever. In the RSFSR alone 702 instances of rural violence were reported for 1928, and 1,002 for the first nine months of 1929. Three hundred government agents lost their lives fighting peasants during 1927-29 (pp. 219-21, 349-50; Osokina, 1978: 103). More ominous than scattered violence was the threat of a large-scale decrease in sown area. Reports from the countryside in late 1929 indicated that if the peasants were left to themselves in the spring of 1930, they would sow much less than they had in the previous year (Moshkov, 1966: 75-81; Lewin, 1966: 394-95). Moshkov tells us that this was when the party once again had to decide whether to give up its forced procurement and withdraw from the countryside, as it had in 1921, or to form a permanent organization in the villages that would not only procure grain but also see to its planting, growing, and harvesting (1966: 65-67).

The government's first attempts to make peasants sow more land came in early 1928. They were less than effectual. The best the party could do was send out vague orders to local soviets to "agitate" among the peasants about extending their planting. Local leaders were to gather peasants together and persuade them to sign agreements—*kontrakty*—to sow more land (Lewin, 1966: 239-40). In the ensuing year the government introduced a much more elaborate campaign. Peasants were to sign agreements to sow certain fields using improved methods. They would agree to sell part of the harvest to the government at a fixed price, and in return the government would advance seeds, tools, and credit. Alas, the government failed to make its promised advances, and the "agreements" quickly evolved into a basis for forcing peasants to cultivate more land (pp. 240-41, 360-61).

But contracts would not force peasants to cultivate land by themselves. Village fields would have to be organized in such a way as to

[18]V. P. Danilov, a Soviet scholar with obvious poetic talent, refers to the *otriady* of early 1929 as machinery repairmen who also did political-cultural work (1957: 278-79).

make them susceptible to central management, and the best vehicle for achieving this purpose was the collective farm. In December 1929 the party mounted a campaign to force peasants into collectives en masse, and at this point the boondoggle ceased abruptly. Collectivization became an unusually thoroughgoing technique of forced grain procurement (Bogdenko, 1963: 20-25; Vyltsan, 1965: 4-6, 11-13).

Stalin had understood collectivization to be essentially a food supply measure at least as early as May 1928, when he "conversed" with some students about the grain problem. Individual peasants do not market grain, he had said; kolkhozy and sovkhozy do (1933: 13-20). Authentic kolkhozy and sovkhozy turned *all* their marketable produce over to state agencies and cooperatives, and for this reason the party's proper aim was to urge individual peasants into collectives (pp. 24-27). According to Stalin's quaint logic, the spread of authentic collectives would smooth conflicts between peasants and workers. Farmers and factory laborers would at last form a perfect union, which, Stalin said with evident satisfaction, would secure the workers' leading position and eliminate classes (pp. 39-40). Tsiurupa's old theory lived again. Peasants would feed workers for nothing, and they would like it.

Considered solely as an administrative method of imposing quotas of grain production and delivery on unfriendly villages, there can be no doubt that the forming of collectives was a sound idea. N. Orlov, a reasonably intelligent food supply official during the years of war communism (see ch. 11, n. 6), advanced the following consideration in a study of 1918: "Our most urgent task, dictated by severe necessity, is to make the urban and industrial population independent of the villages, as far as the supply of foodstuffs is concerned.... The more 'grain factories' are erected...the stronger will be the hold of the working class inside the hostile domain of the peasantry" (quoted in Sorokin, 1920: I, 619). Agricultural administrators attached to the German occupation forces of 1941-43 took a similar view. They noted that the collective farm was an admirable means to compel peasants to produce and deliver grain, and they tried to keep kolkhozy in operation in much of the territory they occupied (Schiller, 1943: 3). In December 1929, then, collectivization did have practical significance. The trouble was that the decision to use collectivization as a means to attack the peasantry brought the party into open conflict with the specialists. Collectivization, after all, had been their affair since 1919, and long before then they had rejected force as a means to mobilize peasants. As we saw in Chapter 10 (secs. D and E), *agronom-organizatory* could not go about their reforming unless they first persuaded themselves that they were acting in the peasants' interests.

There was no escaping the confrontation. The specialists were no dissident group, to be denounced at a congress or dismissed in disgrace. True, their point of view could be and was rejected when their advocates ventured to express it. Nikolai Bukharin, for example, was shouted down in a meeting of the TsK in November 1928, when he claimed that compulsory measures were destroying the peasants' incentive to produce and leading to the "degradation" of agriculture. In early 1929, still unbowed, he wrote: "We shall conquer on the basis of scientific economic management or we shall not conquer at all" (Lewin, 1966: 300; see also Moshkov, 1966: 38-39). Such outright opposition to the bolshevik approach to mobilization made the business of defeating him very easy, given the nature of party organization. But crushing specialists was an entirely different matter. They were a functioning link in the machinery of state and the only operational contact between central government and peasants. One could not conceivably undertake an agrarian reform without their participation. The state could *procure* grain without their help. Tsiurupa had demonstrated that any thug from the city could find grain hoards. But Tsiurupa's experience had also indicated that forced procurement was ultimately self-defeating. If the party was to invade the villages again, in the midst of a massive economic mobilization, it would have to *manage* the villages, and this was not a task for thugs, not if productivity was the aim. The party could not hope to supervise planting, cultivating, and harvesting effectively without the specialists' help. Discharging specialists en masse on the grounds that they would not collectivize properly would make about as much sense as dismissing all the officers and men in the army because they could not fight properly.

But the party had no way of coping with the specialists. Their manner of opposing central authority through an alliance of rhetoric made them impervious to open debate or negotiation. The specialists did not debate; they simply agreed—rhetorically—with everything the bolsheviks told them to say. How could two parties negotiate if they agreed on every point? Indeed, lacking any formal organization, the specialists could not have negotiated as a group even if they had wanted to. They had been echoing communist slogans for over a decade, and in 1929 many of them, notably Iakovlev, were continuing to agree with every new emanation from the party no matter how outlandish it sounded. Meanwhile, in the countryside, in the midst of search-and-seize gangs and openly hostile party activists, they were pushing tsarist-style land reform as if there had never been a revolution. What could bolshevik grain procurers do with them except wipe them out of the way?

Forced Collectivization: The End of Agrarian Reform

No law explicitly banished agricultural specialists from the countryside or forbade them to continue working. What happened, rather, was that a series of decrees produced the cumulative effect of depriving their positions of any authority and making land reform according to their lights impossible.

The first official step in this direction was an order of 7 January 1930 (*Spravochnik*, 1931: 146-47), directing that land settlement projects in the individual sector—i.e., the great majority of them—be abandoned abruptly and all effort concentrated on consolidating collective farms into integral areas. Existing land settlement procedures and technical requirements were to be disregarded. A project for forming a collective would now require only the approval of its chairman-to-be, the local ispolkom, and an agricultural specialist. *No authority higher than the raion level had to approve it or even hear about it,* which meant, in effect, that local specialists could no longer protest projects to their superiors in the NKZ's hierarchy of land settlement subsections.[19]

The January edict did not expressly eliminate the local specialists' prerogative of vetoing collectivization projects. An *agronom* could still refuse to sign a project, and in theory this left him with a certain amount of influence. Practically speaking, however, the specialists were now help-less. Local ispolkoms did not have to obtain a particular expert's signa-ture. Any expert would do. If one *agronom* ventured to oppose a project even with party procurers and collectivizers standing around ominously, the ispolkom had only to find another. Given the drastic simplification of requirements for land settlement and the party's pressure on all branches of the government to get on with collectivization, it could not have been difficult to circumvent specialist opposition—if there was any. A few days later the specialists' position was made even weaker. An order of 18 January explicitly stripped them of direct executive authority *(rukovod-stvo)* over land reform and put it in the hands of local ispolkoms.[20]

The final formal step toward the streamlining of collectivization came with the statute on artels of 1 March 1930. This document pro-vided that *zemleustroiteli* would henceforth have only one injunction to follow: eliminate "all boundary lines separating land allotments of artel members," thus combining "all fields in a single land mass" (Kazantsev, 1954: 467-68). Now, of course, there would be no need for specialists. All it took to implement the statue on artels was a plow.

The abrupt exclusion of specialists from land reform does not seem to have been a carefully planned affair. A brief consideration of the rise and fall of the agronomists' prerogatives in land settlement projects dur-

---

[19]The *raion* was a new territorial unit dating from the early 1920s. It was roughly equivalent to but much bigger than a volost.

[20]So said the circular of 6 Mar. 1930, which was based on the order of 18 Jan. The former is printed in *Spravochnik* (1931: 143-46).

ing the late 1920s suggests that the bolseviks did not become fully aware of their impending break with technocracy until 1929.

Legislation began to assign *rukovodstvo* over land settlement projects to specialists in the mid-1920s. At that time statutes were still vague on the subject of responsibility for implementing land settlement projects. Some orders from local organs, however, suggest that many specialists were already exercising *rukovodstvo* in practice. A memorandum of 30 April 1925 from the Moscow gubernia offices ordered volost ispolkoms to confine themselves to "general oversight" over land settlement and to leave *"rukovodstvo"* to the specialist-dominated "land organs" (*Sbornik zakonopolozhenii,* 1927: 151). In 1928 the law became more specific. In the early part of the year a draft statute on land settlement, approved by the TsIK of the USSR, expressly assigned *rukovodstvo* over land settlement projects to agricultural specialists (Miliutin, 1928: 59). This project became the law of 15 December 1928, which, it will be recalled, destroyed village autonomy and opened the way to direct party rule in the villages (sec. A). From the specialists' point of view, this bizarre law had contradictory effects. It entrenched their administrative role in land settlement while simultaneously mounting an attack on their real source of power, the villages themselves. It seems, then, that at the end of 1928 the party still did not realize that its moves to speed up collectivization were going to bring on a break with the specialists. This is probably why the break came so suddenly. Instead of gradually slipping out of their administrative position, the specialists experienced a steady improvement, followed in January 1930 by an abrupt fall.

With no function left to them except that of a rubber stamp, many specialists quit (Bochkov, 1956: 194). It is impossible to say exactly how many left and how many stayed at their posts in the countryside, but it must have been extremely difficult to stay. It will be recalled that a conference of *"agrarno-marksisty"* met in December 1929 to denounce the "neonarodism" that prevailed among both practicing and academic specialists (sec. B). One spokesman at the conference complained that only 9% of the 5,000 scientists at work in Soviet agricultural institutions were party members (*Trudy,* 1930: I, 249-50). Yet another noted angrily that only 3,200 of a total of 25,000 practicing agronomists in the USSR were associated with kolkhozy and sovkhozy (II, 390-97). I suspect that very few operating specialists found favor in the bolsheviks' eyes. In the face of this crashing wave of the future, the *agronom-organizatory* who did stick with the NKZ must have kept a low profile.

With the specialists out of the way, the party had somehow to replace them with its own engine of mobilization. Its first step, predictably, was to reform its own ranks. In 1929-30 it carried out a combination purge and recruiting campaign that struck especially hard at its rural cells. The ostensible purpose was to get "careerists" out and more "poor toilers" in (Mitrofanov, 1930: 4). The actual result, it seems, was to drum out many members of peasant origin and replace them with city workers.[21]

This was a beginning, but it was not yet an administration capable of implementing a land reform. It will be recalled that carrying out a mere grain procurement campaign had required 100,000 activists from the city in late 1929. In 1930 the total number of party activists, enlightened machine repairmen, and other urban types who went to the villages reached 180,000, and many of these stayed on for several months (Moshkov, 1966: 84-86). It is impossible to say how much of this crowd worked on collectivization. Division of labor was not an important element in rural organization in 1930, anymore than it had been during the gang wars of 1918. Squadrons sent out to do one job often ended up doing another. A report from one locale complained that the party's purge teams were being drafted into sowing and collectivizing campaigns by local authorities and were not really purging anyone (Mitrofanov, 1930: 12). But we do not need to know exactly what the crowd of urban loyal were doing in the villages in 1930. The point is that it was this crowd, not any administration, that carried out forced collectivization.

In the early months of 1930 many of the loyal were engaged in forced sowing, i.e., procuring seed wherever they could find it and driving peasants onto anything that looked like a field to plant it. Their method seems to have been to descend on villages in gangs and go from house to house, confiscating whatever seed they found. Moshkov reports a typical event wherein about 200 activists spent a day in a village to the north of the Caucasus Mountains "persuading" villagers to hand over their stores. Decisive measures of this sort made the sowing campaign quantitatively successful. Sown area reached a record high in 1930. On the other hand, the sharp drop in productivity per unit area in 1931-34 suggests that disorderly attacks on villages by gangs of ignoramuses not only wasted seed on unproductive land but also disrupted crop rotation for years to come (Moshkov, 1966: 110-12, 223-30; Bochkov, 1956: 190-93, 198-99, 213-18). Arbitrary grain confiscation left many peasants with-

---

[21]The party expelled 10.4% of its total membership during the purge. In the rural cells 18.5% of the peasant members were thrown out, as opposed to 8.6% of the members classified as "workers" (Mitrofanov, 1930: 56-57). Somewhat more new members were taken in than were expelled, and the vast majority of the recruits were city workers or officials (p. 63). Party membership in collective farms doubled while this was going on (p. 48), so it is very likely that urban elements substantially increased their influence in rural party cells. This was especially true of the grain-producing areas, where, as we shall see, collectivization went forward much faster than elsewhere.

out feed for their animals, and many of them had to be slaughtered (Moshkov, 1966: 77-78).

The most significant activity of 1930, however, was not the purging of party cells or forced planting but forced collectivization. Collectivization entered its massive stage in November 1929, when the TsK decided to send 25,000 industrial workers to villages in grain-producing areas.[22] These were to conduct *(rukovodit)* collectivization in such a way as to complete the process before spring planting in 1930. They were to travel to the villages with their families at government expense, and as long as they remained active they were to continue to receive their salaries from the enterprises at which they had been employed (*Spravochnik*, 1931: 74-77). Many of them must have stayed on a while, for an order from the SNK of the USSR of 4 September 1930 called upon their parent enterprises to pay their salaries yet another year (pp. 84-85). According to Moshkov, 19,600 of the "25,000" actually arrived in the villages in early 1930, and their number subsequently increased to 35,000 (1966: 85). Apparently this was not enough. On 1 February 1930 the army announced that it would send 100,000 volunteers, selected for their "political literacy," to the villages of the grain-producing regions to *rukovodit* the formation of kolkhozy (*Spravochnik*, 1931: 91), and an order of 16 February called for 7,200 members of urban soviets to volunteer for a year's service as *rukovoditeli* in the villages (pp. 85-86). No effective provision was made concerning the volunteers' technical qualifications and nothing specific was said about the manner in which these new reformers were to be employed. For the central government, it sufficed if they were experienced organizers and "politically literate." Their instructions were simply to go to the villages and *rukovodit* (pp. 74-75, 85-86, 91).[23]

Crash campaigns for sowing, procurement, and collectivization continued for well over a year in the grain-producing regions. The last forced sowing by an officially proclaimed campaign came in the spring of 1931. Collectivization and grain procurement ceased to be called campaigns only after 1932. The party conducted its last big rural purge in 1933. Only in 1934 did a new, USSR-level NKZ begin to assume a measure of control over agriculture through normal administrative methods (Moshkov, 1966: 74-220; Miller, 1966: 475-96).[24]

[22] Bogdenko (1963: 20-25) lists the areas within the grain-producing regions in which *"sploshnaia"* (all-out) collectivization was carried forward in early 1930.

[23] The order to the army did go into somewhat greater detail. It suggested that soldier-reformers know something about tractors and combines, that they be able to manage kolkhozy, and that they be "fighters" for kolkhoz transformation (*Spravochnik*, 1931: 91).

[24] The USSR-level NKZ was formally established at the end of 1929, but it does not appear to have had rural agencies of its own before 1934.

To sum up, forced collectivization was, among other things, a process whereby the party unleashed a mob of somewhat less than 200,000 urban workers and soldiers upon villages in the grain-producing regions. Factory workers joined schoolteachers and soldiers and set out with orders to attack villages and destroy/reform village society. Thousands of Arakcheevs rubbed elbows with thousands of Chernyshevskiis and undertook to teach peasants how to live, though very few members of the new *otriady* had the vaguest idea how to harness a horse to a plow. Under the circumstances it is difficult to generalize about what actually happened in the villages in 1930-32. Our only evidence consists of anecdotes. As M. L. Bogdenko and I. E. Zelenin said in 1963, historians have not yet attempted to study "the internal development of the kolkhozy and sovkhozy" (1963: 197). The peasant farm "lies outside the field of vision of the historian" (p. 210).

It will bear emphasizing that state-incited violence in the early 1930s sprang not so much from the orders of this or that party leader as from the nature of the process. The choice facing the bolsheviks in 1929 was not between one policy and another. It was not a matter of deciding which aims to pursue, which regulations to impose, or which powers to vest in the government's agents. The government had no agents in the countryside. The first step was to sweep them out of the way. The question was not *how* to collectivize, because there was no articulable way to do the job. The party had opted for rapid industrialization in 1925. Four years later its leaders felt that if they renounced their decision, they would lose both their unity and their leading position. They believed that if the party lost its dominant position, the Soviet Union would fall apart again into the chaos of 1917, whence the apparat had emerged to begin with. Right or wrong, this was their collective view, and it followed that the government would have to act in the countryside in the absence of a systematic organization.[25]

Conclusion

It seems narrow and petty to me to dismiss bolshevik actions during the 1920s as mistakes or departures from some a priori rectitude. The alliance of rhetoric with Chaianov's *agronom-organizatory* ended in di-

[25]Concerning the party leaders' acceptance of Stalin in 1928-29, see, e.g., Ulam (1973: 316-18, 333-35). Ulam, like most Western writers, is reluctant to acknowledge any elements in Soviet politics except leaders grabbing for "power," but occcasionally he lets slip a hint that experienced party leaders who knew Stalin quite well recognized a practical, national need for his authority. These "power grabbers" seem to have considered the state's need for Stalin to have been sufficiently urgent to make them willing to risk—and ultimately sacrifice—their lives for him.

saster, but it was not senseless or irresponsible. If the bolsheviks had little more than rhetoric and gangs of thugs to hold the country together during the early years of their reign, and if they realized in 1921 that thugs could not do the job alone, then their alliance with specialists can be seen as a promising device for pulling the disparate elements of state and society together. Likewise, it would be fatuous to condemn the agricultural specialists. They seem on the whole to have been brave, dedicated men. More to the point, they were competent. One could argue that they allowed their specialized knowledge to blind them to the broader reality around them. From hindsight, it is tempting to judge the Chaianovite *agronom-organizatory* for deluding themselves into believing that their work was based solidly in science. But, as we have seen numerous times in the preceding chapters, agrarian reformers cannot operate without delusions. To accuse agrarian reformers of basing their programs on fantasy is like accusing men of having two legs. The really impressive thing about the specialists is the scale of their accomplishment. It was their very success at interacting with the peasantry that called forth their destruction. Surveyors and agronomists did their work so well that they all but formed a government out of Russia's old villages. If they had been nothing but dupes or hypocrites, they would not have troubled even to remain in rural Russia after 1917, let alone work for reforms that their masters considered subversive.

As to forced collectivization, it was far from inevitable or "right," but if we regard it solely according to the criterion of social progress, we come face to face with the curious fact that it was successful. Stalin had no virtuous gentry or scientific specialists to carry out his commands, yet it was he who finally communicated the state's purposes to the peasantry and compelled them to change their way of life. Why was it that Stalin and his howling mob of ignoramuses succeeded? Because the basic purpose of a modern state—any modern state—is mobilization, not liberation. What is called liberation and social progress is never in fact a movement toward individual freedom but an expression of a persistent urge to destroy all social orders that stand in the way of mobilization. Stalin's crowd was inefficient and, indeed, undirectable, but its members were comparatively free from archaic fantasies about individual freedom. This was why, despite its evident limitations, it did indeed impose social change on the villages.

CHAPTER 13

Nikolai Gogol on the
Tragedy of Agrarian Reform

If I skip the last few years, I'm forced to admit that man is somehow beautiful and his creation somehow wise.... He seeks out
and creates every moment new idols for himself and cannot realize that he himself is better than all his creations.

Firsov, in Leonid Leonov's
The Thief (1960: 359)

The preceding chapters have discussed agrarian reformers, men who
believed or made believe that they knew what agrarian reform should
accomplish. I have tried to make the point that their belief-affectations
were their problem, not their guide. Government agents seeking to modernize rural Russia had always to contend with painful contradictions
between the aims they persuaded themselves to pursue and those their
action generated. Law, virtue, theory, science, and/or data never presented a path leading toward a goal but instead drove their devotees into
situations wherein, to some degree, they had to realize that they did not
know what to do. This realization may come to any man in any society,
but a reformer is a special kind of person. He believes that he above all
men should know what "advance" is, and if somehow he arrives at the
conclusion that he does not *and cannot* know, he actually ceases to exist
as a separate person. If one day it comes to him that his reform measures, however successful, are not contributing to progress, he can no
longer conceive of himself. So said Walter Rathenau, the greatest reformer
of them all (ch. 10, sec. E).

Surely the reader has noticed in the foregoing pages that whenever
would-be reformers found themselves at odds with their own ideal purposes, their efforts to improve awakened in them an urge to attack. They
set out intending to save and ended by trying to destroy. This generalization holds true even for the relatively gentle specialists. Having failed to
storm the villages at first visit, they resigned themselves to years of
patient conversation before their purpose would be accomplished, but

their purpose, though benign, was still the destruction of village society and the remodeling of peasants after capital-city notions of mankind. All serious reformers ended up at odds with themselves. Their efforts to achieve goals invariably evolved into losing struggles to make sense of their goals. To put it in my terms, their determination to mobilize peasants caused them to redouble their efforts to systematize themselves, which in turn intensified their urge to mobilize.

Consider Pavel Ivanovich Chichikov, the main character in Nikolai Gogol's famous novel, *Dead Souls*. Chichikov was certainly no agrarian reformer, but he will do for a model of a more or less modern man who undertakes to deal with rural Russia on its own terms. In Chichikov's day, before the Liberation, one measure of a man's wealth and social status was the number of serfs he owned, so Chichikov sought to acquire credit and esteem for himself by assuming ownership of serfs. He could not afford to buy an estate, so he traveled about picking up serfs who had died since the previous census. He could buy large numbers of them cheap, for their owners had to pay taxes on them until the next census, and this could mean anywhere between five and twenty years. In Gogol's novel most estate owners were quite happy to be relieved of their dead serfs, and therefore Chichikov was able to pose for a time as a man of means.

In many respects the various types of agrarian reformer we have studied were Chichikovs. Like Gogol's character, they coped actively and creatively with the burdens imposed upon them by their culture. They were comical, as Chichikov was, but they also acquired a certain stature, as Chichikov did, because of the unusual difficulties they experienced, their perseverance in the face of continual defeat, and the highly original devices they employed to keep themselves going.

Over and over again capital-city legislators enacted reform programs that quickly turned into obstacles to reform. As a result, would-be reformers in the countryside repeatedly found themselves being swept aside by new waves of mobilizers promising to undo the harm done by their "reactionary" predecessors. Land captains worked to establish regular administration in the villages, specialists pushed these administrators aside to establish their "advanced" protégés on productive farms, and at last the bolsheviks destroyed the specialists' farms in order to bring rural Russia under a centralized administration. Each set of rural agents prepared the way for their own downfall at the hands of their successors. Worse, they were commanded to help the arrogant newcomers dismantle their own creations and to betray their supporters among the peasantry. Land captains had to help undermine their volost elders; specialists were ordered to help seize the farms of their advanced followers. Even the victorious bolsheviks suffered this fate. In fact, they suffered it several times. In 1917 Lenin had to renounce his holiest beliefs when he seized power. In 1921 the party apparat had to abandon its crusade for communism and allow its enemies, the bagmen, to prevail. Almost all the bolshevik leaders had ultimately to pay for "victory" with their lives and reputations.

It seems to me that the ususal images of gradually rising GNPs and literacy rates tell us less about Russian agrarian reform than the biblical story of Abraham, whose god at long last gave him a son and then ordered him to kill him. In the end Abraham's god withdrew his command, but the point is that Abraham, like Russia's peasant reformers, had to live all his days in mortal fear that he would be ordered to destroy his own creation. Supposedly Abraham could endure his agony, because he understood from the beginning that his world and his very self were the playthings of an arbitrary power. Not so Russia's reformers. No such explanation was available to them. For modern men arbitrary power is something to curse and overthrow, not a reality to which they gladly submit. Russia's would-be agrarian reformers had no intellectual basis for reconciling themselves to their failures.

Yet they managed to struggle on, seemingly without any direction at all, concocting fantasies and uniting behind them from decade to decade. More to the point, they *had* to struggle on, mobilizing and systematizing, precisely because they possessed no concept that could reconcile them to the absurdities and catastrophes inherent in all their programs. There was nothing left to them but their action. On the whole, they performed quite as well as Abraham. They did not lose faith. There is no small measure of grandeur in the history of Russian agrarian reform from 1861 to 1930.

In this sense, Chichikov too was a tragic figure, or so Gogol meant him to be. Long before the era of state-managed agrarian reform, Gogol was able to portray the role into which such reforms would force their agents, and he tried—albeit with less success—to convey the heroism in men who could play this ostensibly sordid role. Already in the supposedly motionless days of Nicholas I, Gogol sensed that his country was hurtling into some sort of progress whether anyone desired it or not, and he wanted his readers to observe that it would be Chichikov who would lead. This is why he wanted them to suffer with Chichikov, not merely to laugh at him. He wanted to show that there was more to Chichikov than met the eye. "Perhaps the passion that drove Chichikov was something beyond him," said Gogol. "Perhaps there was something in his barren existence that would later make men fall to their knees and kiss the dust in admiration of heavenly wisdom" (1961: 273). Somehow Chichikov ended up thundering down a road in a cart making people step out of the way, and so would rural Russia go roaring into the modern world without the vaguest idea where she was going, and other countries, "casting worried and sidelong glances," would "step out of the way" (p. 277). A nation of peasants would be grabbed out of their traditional society by

Chichikov-like leaders whose hopeless but determined struggles not to be themselves would hold them together even as they undertook to destroy their society and each other. Somehow Chichikov had to be heroic.

Admittedly Gogol failed to convey Chichikov's tragic stature with his art. To be fair, however, we should consider the difficulty of the task. He never tried it in any other work. His other heroes are either swashbuckling cossacks, storming about under the influence of mighty passions, or petty clerks, terrified by the most trivial matters of form. He wished to combine both types in Chichikov; his story failed to do this, so he resorted to lecturing. Having failed to make Chichikov appear heroic, he simply told his readers to find the herosim for themselves—for if they could not find it in Chichikov, they would never find it in themselves.

Which is approximately the sort of lecture I should like to deliver here at the end of this long book about agrarian reformers in Russia. But I shall not, for I cannot improve on Gogol. Suffice it to say that Russian government and society have been much maligned and misunderstood by scholars who insist on describing her history according to stale formulae of self-interest and the struggle for "power." Chichikov had much more— and much less—than these matters on his mind.

Glossary

Agronom-organizator. Agronomist-organizer. Term used by Chaianov and other agricultural specialists around the time of World War I to refer to agronomists who not only helped peasant farmers with expertise but also led them into social reform. See Chapter 9 (sec. C).

Allotment Land. Land received by peasants after 1861 under the terms of the Liberation. These terms varied from one place to another, from one decade to another, and from one type of peasant to another, but they all included the proviso that recipients of allotment land had to pay the government for the land over a period of several decades. Tsarist law distinguished between allotment land and land purchased by peasants, either groups or individuals. Supposedly, purchased land was not affected by legislation having to do with allotment land. See also Redemption Debt.

Apparat. The administrative organization of the Russian communist party. It grew up after the Revolution to become an important element in the government of the USSR. See Chapter 11 (sec. D).

Arbitrator. *Mirovoi posrednik.* Official appointed by the ministry of internal affairs in 1861 to oversee the implementation of the Liberation in his territory. Within a few years he became, in effect, a supervisor over the new peasant organs of government. See Chapter 3 (sec. C).

Artel. A term used in the nineteenth century and earlier to refer to labor gangs and just about any kind of economic association. From 1918 on Soviet law used the term to describe a type of collective farm. See Chapter 12 (sec. A).

Article 87 (of the Fundamental Laws of 1906). This clause allowed the tsar to promulgate decrees while the legislative bodies—the State Duma and State Council—were not in session. These decrees were to have the force of law until or unless the legislative bodies voted them down.

Bagmen. *Mesochnik.* A term used during the civil war to refer to someone who illegally brought grain to cities and grain-consuming areas. See Chapter 11 (sec. C).

Chief Committee for the Management of Rural Society. Until its dissolution in 1882 this group of leading statesmen, including most of the ministers, was the supreme body for directing the Liberation. From 1856 to 1858 it was called the Secret Committee on Peasant Affairs, and from 1858 to 1861 it was the Chief Committee on Peasant Affairs.

Chief Committee on Peasant Affairs. See Chief Committee for the Management of Rural Society.

Chin. Russian word used from the early 1700s to 1917 to connote rank in government service. It conferred social position as well as official prerogatives.

Chinovnik. Government servitor holding one of the official ranks; equivalent to a commissioned officer in the army.

Collective Farm. Strictly speaking, an English equivalent for *kolkhoz.* In this book I have sometimes used it to include both *kolkhozy* and *sovkhozy.* For definitions, see Chapter 12 (sec. A).

Committee of Ministers. One of the "supreme organs" of the tsarist government from the early nineteenth century until 1905, when it was superseded by the Council of Ministers in its new form. The committee could legislate and also coordinate its members for executive operations, but it did not perform either of these functions on a regular basis. Its membership was not restricted to ministers; the tsar could appoint anyone he liked. See Yaney (1973: 194-96, 250-58, 275).

Commune. See the discussion in Chapter 5 (sec. B).

Consolidation. As used in this book, the rearrangement of a peasant's farm to replace scattered strips with a single plot of land.

Council of Ministers. A body carrying this name existed in the tsarist government from 1864 until 1905, but it had no regular function. From 1905 on it was something like the tsar's cabinet, though it lacked the firm prerogatives such bodies usually possess in European governments.

Desiatina. Traditional Russian measure of area, equivalent to 2.7 acres. See the discussion in Chapter 5 (sec. B).

Doklad. Report. I use this term in Chapter 2, chiefly sec. D, to signify the report of the Valuev commission. The full title of this report, three lines long, is given in the bibliography. Concerning the meaning of references made to the *Doklad,* see Chapter 2 (nn. 21, 23, 24).

Dopolnitelnyi. Supplementary.

Duma. In this book I use *Duma* to refer to the State Duma, the lower house in the legislature set up in 1905-6.

Dvor. Household. Concerning the role of the household in the peasants' sociopolitical order, see Chapter 5 (sec. B).

Dvorianin (pl. *dvoriane*). See Gentry.

Fiscal Chamber. Gubernia-level organ of the MF. After 1866 it ceased to hold final authority and became a consultative body to the fiscal administrator. See Yaney (1973: 70, 73, 219, 325-27).

Fundamental Laws of April 1906. The constitution (or pseudo-constitution) of Russia from 1906 until February 1917.

Gentry. Word used here to describe Russia's nobility. From the early 1700s on a man could either inherit gentry status or earn it by rising to a certain *chin* (rank) in the government service. Gentry who inherited their status still had to attain a *chin* and own a certain amount of land in order to participate in their local assemblies. There was a lower order—the so-called personal gentry—who enjoyed the privileges of gentry status but did not pass them on to their offspring.

Gentry Marshal. *Predvoditel dvorianstva.* Originally set up in the 1760s as the leading representative of the gentry in each uezd and gubernia. In practice, however, he was much more a government official than an advocate of local interests. Until March 1917 the marshal could play a leading role in local government. See Yaney (1973: 69-71, 74, 342-45).

Gubernia. Strictly speaking, the Russian word is *guberniia*. Sometimes it is translated as province. Imperial Russia had about 80 of them, of which about 50 made up European Russia (excluding Finland and Congress Poland). See Figure 1.

Gubernia Board. *Gubernskoe prisutstvie.* Collegial body of gubernia-level officials established in 1889 to manage peasant affairs. See Yaney (1973: 325-26, 368-69, 376-79).

Gubernia Board for Peasant Affairs. *Gubernskoe po krestianskim delam prisutstvie.* Collegial body of gubernia-level officials that managed peasant affairs from 1861 until 1889.

Ispolkom. Ispolnitelnyi komitet (executive committee). Basic unit of administration in the Soviet government—in theory. It is the governing body for each soviet and congress of soviets, elected by its soviet (or congress) to handle affairs during the time between sessions. See Chapter 11 (sec. B).

IGU. Izvestiia glavnogo upravleniia zemleustroistva i zemledeliia. Weekly journal of the ministry of agriculture.

IZO. Izvestiia zemskogo otdela. Monthly journal of the land section in the ministry of internal affairs.

Justice of the Peace. *Mirovoi sudia.* Title of local judges set up in 1864. They were elected by uezd zemstvoes. See Chapter 2 (n. 8).

Kazennaia Palata. See Fiscal Chamber.

Khodok. Literally traveler. Used in this book to refer to scouts sent ahead by peasant families who planned to move to new lands. See Chapter 4 (sec. C).

Kolkhoz. Kollektivnoe khoziaistvo (collective farm). See Chapter 12 (sec. A).

Kombed. Komitet derevenskoi bednoty (committee of the village poor). A unit set up at the government's instigation during the summer of 1918. Ostensibly its purpose was to reform peasant society by distributing wealth, but in fact it was an agency for grain procurement. See Chapter 11 (sec. C).

Komissiia. Commission. Used in this book to refer to the commission on gubernia and uezd institutions. See Chapter 2 (sec. B).

Kommuna. A term used during the period 1918-30 to describe an extreme form of collective farm on which *all* property—land, animals, machinery, etc.—was held collectively. See Chapter 12 (sec. A).

Kulak. Literally fist. Used by peasants and intellectuals to refer pejoratively to a rich peasant.

Land Captain. *Zemskii nachalnik.* An agent of the ministry of internal affairs (land section) who managed peasant affairs during the period 1889-1917. See Chapters 3 and 4.

Land Section. *Zemskii otdel.* A department in the ministry of internal affairs, established in 1858 to help enact the Liberation. It was expanded into an executive agency for handling peasant affairs, and in 1889 it became the head office for the newly established land captains.

Land Settlement. *Zemleustroistvo.* As used here, the general term for land rearrangements carried out under the Stolypin Reform. See Chapter 5 (sec. A).

Land Settlement Commissions. Gubernia and uezd agencies established in 1906 to conduct land reform in European Russia. See Chapter 7 (sec. A).

Land Settlement, Group. *Gruppovoe zemleustroistvo.* A term used in Stolypin's day and thereafter to refer to land rearrangements involving village land that fell short of full consolidation. See Chapter 5 (sec. A).

Land Settlement, Individual. *Edinolichnoe zemleustroistvo.* A term used in Stolypin's day to refer to the consolidation of a peasant farm into an integral plot of land. There were two general types. Personal *(lichnoe)* land settlement referred to operations in which only a few (or only one) households in a village underwent consolidation. Village *(obshchestvennoe)* land settlement was involved when all the households in a village acquired integral farms at once. See Chapter 5 (sec. A).

Liberation. The formal abolition of serfdom. Tsar Alexander II signed the initial statutes providing for it on 19 February 1861, and these statutes were published on 5 March. They were put into effect and extended to state and crown peasants during the period 1861-87.

Marshal. See Gentry Marshal.

MF. Ministry (minister) of finance.

MVD. Ministry (minister) of internal affairs *(ministerstvo vnutrennikh del).*

MZ. Ministry (minister) of agriculture *(ministerstvo zemledeliia).* Actually the organization (and minister) to which I refer here as the MZ was only called this officially in the period 1915-17. Its offical name from 1894 to 1905 was ministry of agriculture and the state domains. From 1905 to 1915 it was called the chief administration of land settlement and agriculture. In October 1917 the bolsheviks renamed it the people's commissariat of agriculture (NKZ).

Mir. See the discussion in Chapter 5 (sec. B).

Mirovoi posrednik. See Arbitrator.

Mirovoi sudia. See Justice of the Peace.

Nadel, nadelnaia, See Allotment Land.

Nakaz. Instruction. The word can be used to refer to a government order or a report brought to the government by a representative from some locale.

Narodnik. Populist. Name given to a variety of political activists during the late nineteenth century who advocated reform or revolution for the peasantry. By 1900 it had come to imply opposition to marxism.

NKZ. Narodnyi Komissariat Zemledeliia (people's commissariat of agriculture). Name for the ministry of agriculture after the Bolshevik Revolution (and prior to World War II).

Neonarodnik. Pejorative term used in the 1920s by the bolshevik government to denounce advocates of gradual peasant reform. See Chapter 12 (sec. B).

Nepremmenyi chlen. See Permanent Member.

NEP. New Economic Policy. Conventional term used to describe the Soviet regime from 1921, when war communism ended, to the end of 1929, when forced collectivization began.

Obshchestvo. Society, association. See *Selskoe Obshchestvo.*

Obshchina. Commune. See the discussion in Chapter 5 (sec. B).

Okrug, okruzhnyi. Region, regional. In governmental jargon, an administrative subdivision the size of one or two gubernias.

Otriad. Detachment. Used in this book to refer to food-collecting units (gangs) sent out to the villages by the Soviet government during the years of war communism.

Party. Term used in this book to refer to the Communist Party of the Soviet Union (bolshevik).

Peasant Captain. *Krestianskii nachalnik.* Official appointed by the land section of the ministry of internal affairs to manage peasant affairs in Siberia. By 1905 there were about a hundred of them. See Chapter 4 (sec. A).

Peasant Land Bank. Agency set up in 1882 to lend money to peasants who wished to buy land. See Chapter 4 (sec. D).

Peredel. See Redistribution.

Pereselenie. See Resettlement.

Permanent Member. *Nepremmenyi chlen.* The title of the active administrator in a gubernia or uezd commission or board. Usually the chairman of such bodies was the governor or gentry marshal, but the permanent member did the actual work of managing.

Personal Gentry. See Gentry.

Pochetnyi. Honorary.

Police Captain. See *Stanovoi.*

Police Commandant. *Ispravnik.* The uezd-level agent of the MVD. Along with the uezd gentry marshal, he was something like the uezd head of government, but his authority over agencies from other ministries was minimal, and therefore it dwindled after the 1870s as more agencies were set up in the uezds. See Yaney (1973: 69-71, 207, 343-45).

Polozhenie. Statute.

Popechitelstvo. Guardianship. Often used in a general way to refer to an official's (or office's) paternalistic relation to the people over whom he had jurisdiction.

Populist. Refers to radical groups and individuals who believed that virtue and/or revolutionary impulse resided in the peasantry or should be inculcated there. See also *Narodnik; Neonarodnik;* SRs.

Prilozhenie (pl. *prilozheniia*). Appendix.

Prodrazverstka. System of procurement in which all surplus is taken. As used here, it refers to a number of grain procurement campaigns by the Russian government beginning in late 1916. See chapters 10 (sec. D) and 11 (sec. C).

PSZ. Polnoe Sobranie Zakonov. The "full collection" of the laws of the Russian Empire. This was a chronological list of government enactments from 1649 on. It was first compiled in the 1830s, and from then until 1914 additional volumes were published each year. It was divided into three sets: the first *(Pervoe—PPSZ),* second *(Vtoroe—VPSZ),* and third *(Trete—TPSZ).*

Qualitative Redistribution. *Kachestvennyi peredel.* A rearrangement of a village's land, usually carried out according to traditional procedures, in which the aim was to modernize farming methods. See Chatper 9 (sec. A).

Raion. Unit of territory introduced during the 1920s. It was (and is) usually larger than a volost and smaller than an uezd.

Redemption Debt. The peasants' debt to the government, ostensibly in payment for their allotment land. Under the terms of the Liberation the government paid for the ex-serfs' land and sold state lands to the former "state" peasants, thereby freeing all peasants from the necessity of paying rent on their lands. In return, the peasants undertook to pay for this land over a 49-year period. Until about 1900 villages were held collectively responsible for making these payments, so they enjoyed considerable authority over their member households. The debt was canceled in 1905; the last payments were made in 1906.

Redistribution. *Peredel, razverstanie.* The traditional practice of land rearrangement in Great Russian villages, conducted for the purpose of keeping equivalence between each household's share of the village's obligations (taxes, debts, service, etc.) and the amount of land it farmed.

Resettlement. *Pereselenie.* As used here, the term refers generally to the movement of peasants to Siberia to settle there, primarily during the period 1880-1914. It could refer to any movement of peasants to new lands, but usually it meant Siberia. See Chapter 4 (sec. C).

Rukovodstvo (verb *rukovodit*). Direct management of and responsibility for the performance of some task; discharge of some duty. See Chapter 12 (sec. B).

Sbornik. Collection.

Selskoe Obshchestvo. Official term for village. This institution was not always a single cluster of dwellings, nor did it always correspond to the communities to which peasants belonged, but it possessed a more or less meaningful legal identity from 1861 until 1930. The law recognized two general types: *obshchinnoe* (communal) and *podvornoe* (literally household). In the former, the village owned the land (except for dwelling areas) and had the legal power to redistribute it among the member households if and when two-thirds of the household heads voted to do so. In the latter, each household possessed its own strips of plowland, and only meadows and wooded land could be held in common. See Chapter 5 (sec. B).

Skhod. Village assembly.

SNK. *Sovet Narodnykh Komissarov* (Council of People's Commissars). Soviet equivalent of the Council of Ministers until World War II.

Sobranie. Assembly. This became the official term for the village assembly (replacing *skhod*) in the 1920s. Also used to mean collection (as in *Polnoe Sobranie Zakonov*).

Soul Tax. *Podushnoe.* Tax levied on each male from Peter I's time (1720s) until its abolition in 1885 (as of 1 January 1887). Privileged classes, chiefly merchants, gentry, and clergy, were exempt. Actual levies were made by village authorites (or serfowners) in accordance with local practice. Assessments on each village were based on the latest census, which was usually inaccurate and, in any case, could be a decade or more out of date.

Soveshchanie. Conference.

Soviet (Russian spelling, *Sovet*). Council.

Sovkhoz. State farm. Ideally, this was (and is) a farm managed like a factory. The farmers do not own it, either individually or collectively, but instead work on it for wages. Instead of working particular fields, they perform particular functions. See Chapter 12 (sec. A).

SRs. Socialist Revolutionaries; a political party that existed from 1904 until 1918. It was loose enough to include most variants of populist, from terrorist assassins to radical Duma members. They would have played a leading role

in the Provisional Government after May 1917, had they been capable of
organizing themselves, for large numbers of servitors, probably a majority,
were at least sympathetic with them if not actually members. The party split
into left and right wings in October 1917. The "left" SRs supported Lenin
when he led the bolsheviks into the halls of government. Both left and right
wings were driven out of Lenin's new government within a year.

Stanovoi. Police captain. His full title was *stanovoi pristav.* See Chapter 3 (sec.
C).

State Control. *Staats Kontor.* Administrative body in the tsarist government
that audited accounts. It was equivalent in status to a ministry.

Svod. Compilation.

Third Element. Term used at the time of the Stolypin Reform to refer to salaried employees of the zemstvoes. The first element consisted of government
officials *(chinovniki),* and the second, elected members of zemstvo assemblies.

TOZ. See Chapter 12 (n. 1).

TPSZ. See *PSZ.*

Trudy. Works.

TsGIAL. *Tsentralnyi Gosudarstvennyi Istoricheskii Arkhiv Leningrada* (Central State Historical Archive in Leningrad). Citations of materials in this
archive are identified first by *fond* (f.), then usually by *opis* (op.), then by the
individual *delo* (d.), which is usually a separate volume or box, and last by
the *list* (l.) number. A *list* is a page with only one number for both sides.

TsIK. *Tsentralnyi Ispolnitelnyi Komitet* (central executive committee). Theoretically, the supreme administrative body in the Soviet Union in its early
years. Its members were elected by each All-Russian Congress of Soviets to
operate continuously as head of government while the congresses were not
in session. It appointed the people's commissars (ministers) and, to some
extent, oversaw their work. See Chapter 11 (sec. B).

TsK. *Tsentralnyi Komitet* (central committee). The supreme administrative body
of the Communist Party of the Soviet Union. Theoretically, its members
were (and are) elected by each All-Russian Party Congress to operate continuously as a directorate of the party while the congresses were (are) not in
session. See Chapter 11 (sec. B).

Uchastok. Part. As used here, it refers to administrative subdivisions of uezds
in tsarist times. Usually, each one included a half-dozen volosts, and there
were four to 12 of them in each uezd.

Uezd. Administrative subdivision of a gubernia. In the early 1900s European
Russia contained about 460 of them, with an average population of 200,000-
300,000.

Uezd Congress. *Uezdnyi sezd.* Governing body that oversaw the work of the
land captains. See Chapter 4 (sec. B) and Yaney (1973: 326).

Ukreplenie (verb *ukrepit*). Literally an act of strengthening or fortifying. In Stolypin's day it was used to mean a legal action taken by a household head in a
communal village to acquire his share of village land as his own personal
property.

Usadba. The part of a peasant household's land on which the dwelling stood. In
all villages, even communes and collective farms, this was the household's
personal property.

Village.   See *Selskoe Obshchestvo.*

Village Assembly.   See *Skhod; Sobranie.*

Volost.   Historically a term connoting a geographic area governed by an administrative office. After the Liberation it was a cluster of peasant villages governed by officials elected from among the peasant inhabitants.

VPSZ.   See *PSZ.*

Vyselka.   As used here, an integral plot of land occupied by a group of peasant households after they split away from a traditional village and formed their own settlement. See Chapter 12 (sec. B).

Zemleustroistvo.   See Land Settlement.

Zemleustroitel.   Government agent, usually a surveyor, who personally directed a land settlement project.

Zemskii Nachalnik.   See Land Captain.

Zemskii Otdel.   See Land Section.

Zemstvo.   Institution of local government in most gubernias of European Russia. Its basic unit was an elected assembly in each uezd. Gubernia-level assemblies were made up of delegates from the uezd assemblies. They were established in 1864 in 34 gubernias and granted a measure of freedom to act on their own, apart from the central government's direction, but it was only a small measure. For details, see Yaney (1973: 230-31, 346-60).

Selected
Bibliography

Abbott, R. J. "Police Reform in Russia, 1858-1878." Ph.D. dissertation. Princeton University, 1971.

Abramov, P. N. "K istorii pervogo etapa oktiabrskoi revoliutsii v derevne (oktiabr 1917-mai 1918)." *Istoricheskie zapiski,* LXXXI (1968).

Adams, Arthur. *Bolsheviks in the Ukraine.* New Haven, Conn., 1963.

Agrarnaia politika sovetskoi vlasti (1917-1918 gg.). Moscow, 1954.

Agronomicheskaia pomoshch v Rossii. St. Petersburg, 1914.

Aleksandrov, V. A. *Selskaia obshchina v Rossii.* Moscow, 1976.

Alekseev, Iu. P. "Ekspeditsii A. G. Shlikhtera i S. P. Seredy za 1918 g." *Istoriia SSSR* (1966).

Alekseev, V. N. *Opyt monograficheskogo opisaniia der. Kurovo Demitrovskogo uezda.* Moscow, 1923.

Andreev, V. M. "Prodrazverstka i krestianstvo." *Istoricheskie zapiski,* XCVII (1976).

Anfimov, A. M., ed. *Krestianskoe dvizhenie v Rossii v gody pervoi mirovoi voiny, iiul 1914 g.-fevral 1917 g.: Sbornik dokumentov.* Moscow, 1965.

————. *Krupnoe pomeshchiche khoziaistvo evropeiskoi Rossii.* Moscow, 1969.

————. *Rossiiskaia derevnia v gody pervoi mirovoi voiny.* Moscow, 1962.

Antsiferov, A. N. et al., eds. *Russian Agriculture during the War.* New Haven, Conn., 1930.

Aperçu des travaux des commissions agraires pendant la première année de leur fonctionnement. St. Petersburg, 1908.

Arnold, Thurman. *The Symbols of Government.* New Haven, Conn., 1935.

Atkinson, D. "The Statistics on the Russian Land Commune, 1905-1917." *Slavic Review,* XXXII (Dec. 1973).

Augé-Laribé, Michel, and Pierre Pinot. *Agriculture and Food Supply in France during the War.* New Haven, Conn., 1927.

Augustine, Wilson R. "Notes toward a Portrait of the Eighteenth-Century Russian Nobility." *Canadian-American Slavic Studies,* IV (Fall 1970).

Averev, V. N. *Komitety bednoty, sbornik materialov.* 3 vols. Moscow, 1933.

Baburin, D. S. "Narkomprod v pervye gody sovetskoi vlasti." *Istoricheskie zapiski,* LXI (1957).

Baker, Anita. "Community and Growth: Muddling Through with Russian Credit Cooperatives." *Journal of Economic History,* XXXVII (Mar. 1977).

————. "The Development of Cooperative Credit in Rural Russia, 1871-1914." Ph.D. dissertation. Cornell University, 1973.

"Banki." In Brokgaus and Efron, *Entsiklopedicheskii*, II, 927-28.

Barnard, Chester I. *Functions of the Executive*. Cambridge, 1938.

Barykov, F. L., et al., eds. *Sbornik materialov dlia izucheniia selskoi pozemelnoi obshchiny*. St. Petersburg, 1880.

Beer, V. A. *Kommentarii novykh provintsialnykh uchrezhdenii 12 iiulia 1889 goda*. 2 pts. Moscow, 1894-95.

Belk, Fred R. "The Great Trek of the Russian Mennonites to Central Asia, 1880-1884." Ph.D. dissertation. Oklahoma State University, 1973.

Benckendorff, C. *Half a Life*. London, 1954.

Benet, Sula, ed. *The Village of Viriatino*. New York, 1970.

Benveniste, Guy, and Warren F. Ilchman, eds. *Agents of Change: Professionals in Developing Countries*. New York, 1969.

Berkevich, A. B. "Krestianstvo i vseobshchaia mobilizatsiia v iiule 1914 g." *Istoricheskie zapiski*, XXIII (1947).

Berzin, A. "Itogi i blizhaishie perspektivy zemleustroistva." In *O zemle* (1921).

Bilimovich, A. D. "Land Settlement and the War." In Antsiferov, *Russian Agriculture* (1930).

Bing, E. J., ed. *Letters of Tsar Nicholas and Empress Marie*. London, 1937.

Biriukovich, V. "Po povodu uchrezhdeniia ministerstva zemledeliia." *Vestnik Evropy* (June 1894).

Bochkov, N. V., ed. *Istoriia zemelnykh otnoshenii i zemleustroistva*. Moscow, 1956.

Bogdenko, M. L. "K istorii nachalnogo etapa sploshnoi kollektivizatsii selskogo khoziaistva SSSR." *Voprosy istorii*, XXXVIII (1963).

————, and I. E. Zelenin. "Osnovye problemy istorii kollektivizatsii selskogo khoziaistva v sovremennoi sovetskoi istoricheskoi literature." In *Istoriia sovetskogo krestianstva* (1963).

Bogoraz, V. G., ed. *Revoliutsiia v derevne*. Moscow, 1924.

Boianus, A. K. *Otchet po zemskomu otdelu*. St. Petersburg, 1911.

Bolshakov, A. M. *Derevnia, 1917-1927*. Moscow, 1927.

————, ed. *Istoriia khoziaistva Rossii*. 3 vols. Moscow, 1926.

Borisov, V. M. "Torkhovskaia obshchina." In Barykov, *Sbornik* (1880).

Boshko, V. I. *Grazhdanskaia pravosposobnost krestian v oblasti zemlevladeniia*. Kiev, 1917.

Brokgaus, F. A., and I. A. Efron. *Entsiklopedicheskii slovar*. 41 vols. plus 2 supplementary vols. St. Petersburg, 1891-1907.

————. *Novyi entsiklopedicheskii slovar*. 29 vols. St. Petersburg, 1911-16.

Browder, Robert, and Alexander Kerensky, eds. *The Russian Provisional Government*. 3 vols. Stanford, Calif., 1961.

Brown, Alvin. *The Armor of Organization*. New York, 1953.

Brunst, V. "Delo rasprostraneniia selsko-khoziaistvennykh znanii v razlichnykh stranakh i vozmozhny li u nas vidy etogo roda agronomicheskoi raboty." *Iugo-vostochnyi khoziain* (Oct. 1910).

————. "Departament zemledeliia, zemstva i sel.-khoz. obshchestva." *Vestnik selskogo khoziaistva*, XXI (1914).

Brzheskii, N. *Ocherki iuridicheskogo byta krestian*. St. Petersburg, 1902.

Buchanan, H. Ray. "Soviet Economic Policy for the Transition Period: The

Supreme Council of the National Economy, 1917-1920." Ph.D. dissertation. Indiana University, 1972.

Bukshpan, Ia. M. *Voenno-khoziaistvennaia politika.* Moscow, 1929.

Burch, R. J. "Social Unrest in Imperial Russia: The Student Movement at Moscow University, 1887-1905." Ph.D. dissertation. University of Washington, 1972.

Burov, Ia. *Derevnia na perelome.* Moscow, 1926.

Busygin, E. P., et al. *Obshchestvennyi i semeinyi byt russkogo selskogo naseleniia srednego povolzhia.* Kazan, 1973.

Carlyle, Thomas. *Sartor Resartus.* London, 1893.

Chaianov, A. V. *Oeuvres choisies de A. V. Cajanov.* 8 vols. The Hague, 1967.

―――. "Optimalnye razmery selsko-khoziaistvennykh predpriatii." In *Problemy zemleustroistva* (1922).

―――― (spelled Chayanov). *Theory of Peasant Economy.* Homewood, Ill., 1966.

Chebaevskii, F. V. "Stroitelstvo mestnykh sovetov v kontse 1917 i pervoi polovine 1918 g." *Istoricheskie zapiski,* LXI (1957).

Chekhov, Anton. *The Island.* New York, 1967.

Cherniavsky, M., ed. *Prologue to Revolution.* Englewood Cliffs, N.J., 1967.

Chernukha, V. G. "Pravitelstvennaia politika i institut mirovykh posrednikov." In Nosov, *Vnutrenniaia* (1967).

―――. "Problema politicheskoi reformy v pravitelstvennykh krugakh Rossii v nachale 70-kh godov XIX v." In Nosov, *Problemy* (1972).

―――. *Krestianskii vopros v pravitelstvennoi politike Rossii.* Leningrad, 1972.

―――. *Vnutrenniaia politika tsarizma.* Leningrad, 1978.

Chernyshev, I. V. *Agrarno-krestianskaia politika Rossii za 150 let.* Petrograd, 1918.

―――. *Krestiane ob obshchine nakanune 9 noiabria 1906 goda.* St. Petersburg, 1912.

Chetyre goda prodovolstvennoi raboty. Moscow, 1922.

Confino, Michael. *Domaines et seigneurs en Russie vers la fin du XVIIIe siècle.* Paris, 1963.

―――. *Systèmes agraires et progrès agricole.* Paris, 1969.

Coquin, F. *La Siberie: Peuplement et immigration paysanne au XIX siècle.* Paris, 1969.

Croce, Benedetto. *History, Its Theory and Practice.* New York, 1923.

Crozier, Michael. *The Bureaucratic Phenomenon.* Chicago, 1964.

Curtiss, John S., ed. *Essays in Russian and Soviet History.* New York, 1963.

Czap, Peter. "The Influence of Slavophile Ideology on the Formation of the Volost court of 1861 and the Practice of Peasant Self-Justice between 1861 and 1889." Ph.D. dissertation. Cornell University, 1959.

―――. "P. A. Valuyev's Proposal for a Vyt Administration, 1864." *Slavonic Review,* XLV (July 1967).

Danilov, V. P. *Sozdanie materialno-tekhnicheskikh predposylok kollektivizatsii selskogo khoziaistva v SSR.* Moscow, 1957.

―――. "Zemelnye otnosheniia v sovetskoi dokolkhoznoi derevne." *Istoriia SSSR* (1958).

Dashkevich, L. V. *Gosudarstvennye izbiratelnye zakony. Agrarnyi perevorot.* Moscow, 1909.

Davies, R. W. *The Development of the Soviet Budgetary System.* Cambridge, 1958.

Deiatelnosti selsko-khoziaistvennoi komissii 3-i gosudarstvennoi dumy za period s 26 oktiabria 1910 g. po 5 maia 1911. 2 vols. St. Petersburg, 1911.

Delvig, A. I. *Moi vospominaniia.* 4 vols. Moscow, 1912-13.

Demchenko, G. V. *Sudebnyi pretsedent.* Warsaw, 1903.

Derevenskaia kommuna. Government newspaper in civil war era.

Desiatiletie zavedyvaniia mezhevym upravleniem zemlemernoiu chastiu zemleustroitelnykh kommisii, 1906-1916. Petrograd, 1916.

Desiatyi sezd RKP (b), Mart 1921: Stenograficheskii otchet. Moscow, 1963.

Deutscher, Isaac. *The Prophet Armed.* New York, 1965.

_____. *The Prophet Unarmed.* New York, 1965.

Devons, Ely. *Essays in Economics.* London, 1961.

Diakin, V. S. *Russkaia burzhuaziia i tsarizm v gody pervoi mirovoi voiny.* Leningrad, 1967.

_____. "Stolypin i dvorianstvo." In Nosov, *Problemy* (1972).

Dinnik, N. "Stavropolskaia guberniia." In Brokgaus and Efron, *Entsiklopedicheskii,* XXXI, 391.

Direktivy KPSS i sovetskogo pravitelstva po khoziaistvennym voprosam (1917-1957 gody). Sbornik dokumentov. 4 vols. Moscow, 1957.

Dmitriev, K. D. *Dokladnaia zapiska v zemskiia upravy i Gospodam Predvoditeliam Dvorianstva.* Moscow, 1904.

_____. *Obezpechennyi dokhod s imeniia bez kapitala na vedenie khoziaistva.* Moscow, 1894.

Dohan, Michael R. "The Economic Origins of Soviet Autarky 1927/28-1934." *Slavic Review,* XXXV (Dec. 1976).

Doklad vysochaishe utverzhdennoi (26 Mai 1872) komissii dlia issledovaniia nyneshnego polozheniia selskogo khoziaistva i selskoi proizvoditelnosti v Rossii. St. Petersburg, 1873.

Dokuchaev, V. V. *Russian Chernozem.* Jerusalem, 1967.

Dolgorukov, P. D., and S. L. Tolstoi, eds. *Krestianskii stroi.* 3 vols. St. Petersburg, 1905.

Dopolnitelnyi sbornik zakliuchenii po voprosam otnosiashchimsia k peresmotru zakonodatelstva o krestianakh. St. Petersburg, 1897.

Dovnar-Zapolskii, M. "Ocherki semeistvennogo obychnogo prava krestian Minskoi gub." In *Etnograficheskoe obozrenie* (1897): XXXII, 82-142; XXXIII, 1-16.

Dovring, F. *Land and Labor in Europe, 1900-1950.* The Hague, 1956.

Druzhinin, N. M. *Gosudarstvennye krestiane i reforma P. D. Kiseleva.* 2 vols. Moscow, 1946, 1958.

Dubrovskii, S. M. *Krestianskoe dvizhenie v Revoliutsii 1905-1907 gg.* Moscow, 1956.

_____. *Stolypinskaia zemelnaia reforma.* Moscow, 1963.

Duisburg, A. "Zabytyi krai." In Bogoraz, *Revoliutsiia* (1924).

Duval, C., Jr. "The Bolshevik Secretariat and Yakov Sverdlov: February to October 1917." *Slavonic Review,* LI (Jan. 1973).

Dyskii, K. K. *Opyt monograficheskogo opisaniia der. Burtsevoi Volokolamskogo uezda.* Moscow, 1923.

Efimenko, A. *Issledovaniia narodnoi zhizni.* Moscow, 1884.

Ekonomicheskoe polozhenie Rossii nakanune velikoi oktiabrskoi sotsialisticheskoi revoliutsii. 3 vols. Moscow, 1957-67.

Elenev, F. P. *V zakholusti i v stolitse.* St. Petersburg, 1870.

Emin, A. *Turkey in the World War.* New Haven, Conn., 1930.

Engelgardt, A. I. *Iz derevni.* Moscow, 1937.

Erlich, A. *The Soviet Industrialization Debate: 1924-1928.* Cambridge, Mass., 1960.

Ermolov, A. A. *Nashi neurozhai i prodovolstvennyi vopros.* St. Petersburg, 1909.

_____. *Neurozhai i narodnoe bedstvie.* St. Petersburg, 1892.

Eroshkin, N. P. *Ocherki istorii gosudarstvennykh uchrezhdenii dorevoliutsionnoi Rossii.* Moscow, 1960.

Etnograficheskoe obozrenie. 55 vols. Moscow, 1889-1902.

Ezhegodnik po agrarnoi istorii vostochnoi Evropy, 1963 g. Vilna, 1964.

Ezhegodnik po agrarnoi istorii vostochnoi Evropy, 1964 g. Kishinev, 1966.

Ezhegodnik po agrarnoi istorii vostochnoi Evropy, 1965 g. Moscow, 1970.

Ezhegodnik po agrarnoi istorii vostochnoi Evropy, 1968 g. Leningrad, 1972.

Fainsod, Merle. *Smolensk under Soviet Rule.* Cambridge, Mass., 1958.

Falls, Cyril. *The Great War.* New York, 1959.

Fediukin, S. A. *Sovetskaia vlast i burzhuaznye spetsialisty.* Moscow, 1965.

Feldman, G. D. *Army, Industry and Labor in Germany, 1914-1918.* Princeton, N.J., 1966.

Feldman, R. S. "Between War and Revolution: The Russian General Staff, February-July 1917." Ph.D. dissertation. Indiana University, 1967.

Fenomenov, M. Ia. *Sovremennaia derevnia.* 2 vols. Moscow, 1925.

Feoktistov, E. M. *Vospominaniia za kulisami politiki i literatury.* Cambridge, 1975.

Field, Daniel. *Rebels in the Name of the Tsar.* Boston, 1976.

Figurovskaia, N. K. "Bankrotstvo 'Agrarnoi reformy' burzhuaznogo vremennogo pravitelstva." *Istoricheskie zapiski,* LXXXI (1968).

Fisher, H. H. *Famine in Soviet Russia, 1919-1923.* Stanford, Calif., 1935.

Fleer, M. G. "Vremennoe pravitelstvo v borbe s agrarnoi revoliutsiei." *Krasnaia letopis,* II (1926).

Fortunatov, A. "O vosmi nastavnikakh." *Vestnik vospitaniia,* XXVIII, nos. 8-9 (Nov.-Dec. 1917), 140-74.

Foster, G. M. *Traditional Cultures and the Impact of Technological Change.* New York, 1962.

Fridolin, S. P. *Ispoved agronoma.* Moscow, 1925.

Garmiza, V. V. *Podgotovka zemskoi reformy 1864 goda.* Moscow, 1957.

Gerasimenko, G. A. *Nizovye krestianskie organizatsii v 1917—pervoi polovine 1918 godov.* Saratov, 1974.

Gerasimiuk, V. R. "Upravitelnoe raspredelenie zemel v evropeiskoi chasti Rossiiskoi Federatsii v 1918 g." *Istoriia SSSR* (1965).

Gerbe, V. *Vtoroe raskreposhchenie.* Moscow, 1911.

Gessen, V. M. *Voprosy mestnogo upravleniia.* St. Petersburg, 1904.

Gindin, I. G. *Gosudarstvennyi bank i ekonomicheskaia politika tsarskogo pravitelstva (1861-1892 gody).* Moscow, 1960.

Gleason, William E. "The All-Russian Union of Towns and the All-Russian Union of Zemstvos in World War I: 1914-1917." Ph.D. dissertation. Indiana University, 1972.

Glinka, K. D. *Great Soil Groups of the World and Their Development.* Washington, D.C., 1927.

Gluckman, Max, ed. *The Allocation of Responsibility.* Manchester, 1972.

1917 god v Saratovskoi gubernii. Saratov, 1961.

————. *1917 god v selskokhoziaistvennom otnosheniem po otvetam, poluchennym ot khoziaev.* Journal published annually by the department of agriculture. St. Petersburg, 1882-1916. The first word in the title of each issue is the year of publication.

Gogol, Nikolai. *Dead Souls.* Trans. A. R. MacAndrew. New York, 1961.

Golitsyn, A. D. "Vospominaniia." Unpublished ms. Russian Archive, Columbia University.

Golovin, K. *Muzhik bez progressa ili progress bez muzhika.* St. Petersburg, 1896.

Golovine, N. N. *The Russian Army in the World War.* New Haven, Conn., 1931.

Gordeev, G. S. *Selskoe khoziaistvo v voine i revoliutsii.* Moscow, 1925.

Gorodetskii, E. N. *Sverdlov.* Moscow, 1971.

Gosudarstvennaia Duma. *Stenograficheskie otchety, 1906 god, sessiia pervaia.* 2 vols. St. Petersburg, 1906.

————. *Ukazatel k stenograficheskim otchetam, 1906 god, sessiia pervaia.* St. Petersburg, 1907.

Grant, Steven A. *"Obshchina* and *Mir." Slavic Review,* XXXV (Dec. 1976).

————. "The Peasant Commune in Russian Thought, 1861-1905." Ph.D. dissertation, Harvard University, 1973.

Gratz, Gustav, and Richard Schuller. *The Economic Policy of Austria-Hungary during the War.* New Haven, Conn., 1928.

Grinevetskii, V. I. *Poslevoennye perspektivy russkoi promyshlennosti.* 2d ed. Moscow, 1922.

Gronsky, Paul P. *The War and the Russian Government.* New Haven, Conn., 1930.

Gurko, V. I. *Features and Figures of the Past.* Stanford, Calif., 1939.

————. *Ustoi narodnogo khoziaistva Rossii.* St. Petersburg, 1902.

Haimson, L. H., ed. *The Politics of Rural Russia, 1905-1914.* Bloomington, Ind., 1979.

Hasegawa, T. "The February Revolution of 1917 in Russia." Ph.D. dissertation. University of Washington, 1969.

Hoffer, E. *The True Believer.* New York, 1958.

Hough, J. F. *The Soviet Prefects.* Cambridge, Mass., 1969.

Hughes, Everett C. *Men and Their Work.* Glencoe, Ill., 1958.

Huizinga, Johan. *Homo Ludens.* Boston, 1955.

Iakovlev, Ia. A. *Borba za urozhai.* 2d ed. Moscow, 1929.

————. *Derevnia kak ona est.* 2d ed. Moscow, 1924.

————. *Nasha derevnia.* Moscow, 1924.

————, ed. *Selsovety i volispolkomy.* Moscow, 1925.

————. *Za kolkhozy.* Moscow, 1929.

Ianson, Iu. E. *Opyt statisticheskogo issledovaniia o krestianskikh nadelakh i platezhakh.* 2d ed. St. Petersburg, 1881.

Iaroshevich, A. I. *Ocherk khutorskikh khoziaistv Kievskoi gubernii.* Kiev, 1911.

Iarotskii, V. G. "Rezultaty operatsii Krestianskogo Pozemelnogo Banka." *Iuridicheskaia letopis,* III (May 1892).

Ihering, Rudolf von. *The Struggle for Law.* Chicago, 1879.

Ilchman, Warren F., and Guy Benveniste. "Dilemmas of Professionals Abroad." In Benveniste and Ilchman, *Agents* (1969).

Instruktsiia dlia proizvodstva zemlemernykh rabot pri zemleustroistve. St. Petersburg, 1913.

Istoricheskoe obozrenie piatidesiatiletnei deiatelnosti ministerstva gosudarstvennykh imushchestv, 1837-1887. 5 vols. St. Petersburg, 1888.

Istoriia sovetskogo krestianstva i kolkhoznogo stroitelstva v SSSR. Moscow, 1963.

Itogi rabot za poslednoe piatiletie, 1909-1913. St. Petersburg, 1914.

Itogi zemleustroistva. St. Petersburg, 1912.

Iugo-vostochnyi khoziain. Monthly journal of the Imperial Don-Kuban-Terek agricultural society. 1904- .

Iuzhno-russkaia selsko-khoziaistvennaia gazeta. Weekly journal of the Kharkov agricultural society.

Iz istorii grazhdanskoi voiny v SSSR. 3 vols. Moscow, 1960.

Izvestiia Glavnogo Upravleniia Zemleustroistva i Zemledeliia. Weekly journal of the ministry of agriculture. 1894-1917.

Izvestiia Kantseliarii Komiteta po Zemleustroitelnym Delam. 1913-14.

Izvestiia osobogo soveshchaniia dlia obsuzhdeniia meropriiatii po prodovolstvennomu delu. 1916-17.

Izvestiia po prodovolstvennomu delu. 1917.

Izvestiia Zemskogo Otdela. Monthly journal of the land section in the ministry of internal affairs. 1904-17.

Jasny, Naum. *The Socialized Agriculture of the USSR.* Stanford, Calif., 1949.

Johnson, Paul. "I. D. Delianov and Russian Educational Policy." Ph.D. dissertation. Emory University, 1971.

Joll, James. *Three Intellectuals in Politics.* New York, 1960.

Joravsky, David. *The Lysenko Affair.* Cambridge, Mass., 1970.

—————. *Soviet Marxism and the Natural Sciences (1917-1932).* New York, 1961.

Kachorovskii, K. R. *Russkaia obshchina.* St. Petersburg, 1900.

————— (spelled Kachorovsky). "The Russian Land Commune in History and Today." *Slavonic Review,* VII, no. 2 (1929).

Karcz, J. "Thoughts on the Grain Problem." *Soviet Studies,* XVIII, no. 4 (Apr. 1967).

Karpov, N. *Agrarnaia politika Stolypina.* Leningrad, 1925.

Karunovskaia, A. "Selo Novoselka-Ziuzino Rostovskogo uezda." In Bogoraz, *Revoliutsiia* (1924).

Kasian, A. K. "Comment." In *Istoriia sovetskogo krestianstva* (1963).

Kataev, M. M. *Mestnyia krestianskaia uchrezhdeniia, 1861, 1874, i 1889 gg.* 3 pts. St. Petersburg, 1911.

Kaufman, A. A. *Pereselenie i kolonizatsiia.* St. Petersburg, 1905.

Kayden, E. M., and A. N. Antsiferov. *The Cooperative Movement in Russia during the War.* New Haven, Conn., 1929.

Kazantsev, N. D., and O. I. Tumanova, eds. *Sbornik dokumentov po zemelnomu zakonodatelstvu SSSR i RSFSR.* Moscow, 1954.

Kechedzhi-Shapovalov, M. V. *Voina i khoziaistvo Germanii.* Petrograd, 1914.

Keep, J. L. H. *The Russian Revolution.* New York, 1976.

Keller, P. C. *The German Colonies in South Russia: 1804 to 1904.* 2 vols. 1968, 1973.

Kessler, Harry. *Walter Rathenau, His Life and Work.* New York, 1969.

Khauke, O. A. *Krestianskoe zemelnoe pravo.* Moscow, 1913.

Khizhniakov, V. "Zemstvo i kooperatsiia." *Vestnik selskogo khoziaistva* (2 Mar. 1914).

Khriashcheva, A. I. *Gruppy i klassy v krestianstve.* 2d ed. Moscow, 1926.

————. *Krestianstvo v voine i revoliutsii.* Moscow, 1921.

Khutor. Private journal, edited by P. N. Elagin, formerly editor of *Derevnia* and *Krestianskaia gazeta.* 1906-

Khutorianin. Weekly journal of the Poltava agricultural society.

Kimball, Alan. "The First International and the Russian Obshchina." *Slavic Review,* XXXII (Sept. 1973).

Kirillov, I. A. *Ocherki zemleustroistva za tri goda revoliutsii.* Petrograd, 1922.

Kisel-Zagorianskii, N. N. "Les memoires du General N. N. Kisel-Zagorianskii." Unpublished ms. Russian Archive, Columbia University.

Knipovich, B. N. "Napravlenie i itogi agrarnoi politiki 1917-1920 gg." In *O zemle* (1921).

————. *Ocherki deiatelnosti narodnogo komissariata zemledeliia za tri goda: 1917-1920.* Moscow, 1920.

Koch, F. C. *The Volga Germans.* London, 1977.

Kofod, A. A. *Khutorskoe rasselenie.* St. Petersburg, 1907.

————. *Krestianskie khutora na nadelnoi zemle.* 2 vols. St. Petersburg, 1905.

————. *Russkoe zemleustroistvo.* 2d ed. St. Petersburg, 1914.

Kokovtsov, V. N. *Out of My Past.* Stanford, Calif., 1935.

Kolobov, V. *Lichnoe krestianskoe zemlevladenie v Moskovskoi gubernii v 1907-1912 gg.* Moscow, 1913.

Kompaneets, M. *Uchenye agronomy Rossii.* 2 vols. Moscow, 1971, 1976.

Konfidentsialno Tsirkuliarno gubernatoram. Listed in the catalog of Leningrad Public Library under Rossiia, Ministerstvo Vnutrennikh Del, Zemskii Otdel po 4 deloproizvodstvu.

Kostrikin, V. I. "Iz istorii zemelnykh komitetov riazanskoi gubernii (Mart-oktiabr 1917 g.)." *Trudy moskovskogo gosudarstvennogo istoriko-arkhivnogo instituta,* IX (1957).

————. *Zemelnye komitety v 1917 godu.* Moscow, 1975.

Krasovskii, V. E. "Undorovskaia obshchina." In Barykov, *Sbornik* (1880).

Kratkii ocherk deiatelnosti Ministerstva Vnutrennikh Del za dvadtsatipiatiletie 1855-1880 g. St. Petersburg, 1880.

Kratkii ocherk vozniknoveniia i razvitiia vazhneishikh faktov deiatelnosti Zemskogo Otdela Ministerstva Vnutrennikh Del. St. Petersburg, 1908.

Kratkii ocherk za desiatiletie 1906-1916. Petrograd, 1916.

Kravchuk, N. A. *Massovoe krestianskoe dvizhenie v Rossii nakanune Oktiabria.* Moscow, 1971.

"Krestianskii Pozemelnyi Bank." In Brokgaus and Efron, *Entsiklopedicheskii,*

XVI, 726-28; supplementary vol. I, 781.

Krestianskoe dvizhenie v 1917 godu. Moscow, 1927.

"Krestianskoe pravo." In Brokgaus and Efron, *Entsiklopedicheskii,* XXIII, 328-29.

Kritsman, L. *Geroicheskii period Velikoi Russkoi Revoliutsii.* 2d ed. Moscow, 1926.

"Krivoshein." In Brokgaus and Efron, *Novyi,* XXIII, col. 344-45.

Krivoshein, K. A. *A. V. Krivoshein.* Paris, 1973.

Kryzhanovskii, S. E. *Vospominaniia.* Berlin, 1938.

Kucherov, Samuel. *Courts, Lawyers and Trials under the Last Three Tsars.* New York, 1957.

Kulyshev, Iu. S. *Borba za khleb.* USSR, 1972.

Kurlov, P. G. *Konets russkogo tsarizma.* Moscow, 1923.

Lazarevskii, N. I. *Lektsii po russkomu gosudarstvennomu pravu.* 2d ed. 2 vols. St. Petersburg, 1910.

Leikina-Svirskaia, V. R. *Intelligentsiia v Rossii vo vtoroi polovine XIX veka.* Moscow, 1971.

Lenin, Vladimir I. *Collected Works.* 45 vols. Moscow, 1964-70.

————. *Polnoe sobranie sochinenii.* 5th ed. 55 vols. Moscow, 1958-65.

————. *Selected Works.* 12 vols. New York, 1943.

Leonov, L. *The Thief.* New York, 1960.

Leontev, A. "Volostnyi sud i obychnoe pravo." *Zhurnal iuridicheskogo obshchestva pri S-Peterburgskogo Universiteta,* XXIV (Nov. 1894).

Lepeshkin, A. I. *Mestnye organy vlasti sovetskogo gosudarstva: 1917-1920.* Moscow, 1957.

————. *Mestnye organy vlasti sovetskogo gosudarstva: 1921-1936.* Moscow, 1959.

Lewin, Moshe. *Lenin's Last Struggle.* New York, 1968.

————. *La paysannerie et le pouvoir soviétique, 1928-1930.* Paris, 1966.

Litoshenko, N. A. "Morakhovskaia obshchina." In Barykov, *Sbornik* (1880).

Little, Lester, *Religious Poverty and the Profit Economy in Medieval Europe.* Ithaca, N.Y., 1978.

Litvak, Boris G. "O nekotorykh chertakh psikhologii russkikh krepostnykh pervoi poloviny XIX v." In B. F. Porshnev, ed., *Istoriia i psikhologiia.* Moscow, 1971.

————. "Ob izmeneniiakh zemelnogo nadela pomeshchichikh krestian v pervoi polovine XIX v." In *Ezhegodnik...1963* (1964).

————. *Opyt statisticheskogo izucheniia krestianskogo dvizheniia v Rossii XIX v.* Moscow, 1967.

Liubimov, D. N. "Russkaia smuta, nachala deviatisotnykh godov." Unpublished ms. Russian Archive, Columbia University.

Long, James W. "The Economics of the Franco-Russian Alliance, 1904-1906." Ph.D. dissertation. University of Wisconsin, 1968.

Lutskii, E. A. "K istorii konfiskatsii pomeshchichikh imenii v 1917-1918 godakh." *Izvestiia Akademii Nauk SSSR, Seriia istorii i filosofii,* V, no. 6 (1948).

————. "Metodika statisticheskogo izucheniia izmenenii v zemlepolzovanii klassovykh grupp krestianstva v itoge agrarnoi revoliutsii 1917-1918 gg." In *Ezhegodnik...1965* (1970).

————. "Peredel zemli vesnoi 1918 goda." *Izvestiia Akademii Nauk SSSR,*

Seriia istorii i filosofii, VI, no. 3 (1949).

M-ov, C. "Melkii kredit i zemstvo." *Vestnik selskogo khoziaistva* (2 Mar. 1914).

Macey, David A. J. "The Russian Bureaucracy and the 'Peasant Problem': The Pre-History of the Stolypin Reforms, 1861-1907." Ph.D. dissertation. Columbia University, 1976.

Maenchen-Helfen, Otto J. *The World of the Huns.* Berkeley, Calif. 1973.

Maiborodov, Vladimir. "Moia sluzhba pri Starom Rezhime i vo vremia smuty 1904-1920." 2d of 5 folders. Unpublished ms. Russian Archive, Columbia University.

Malin, James C. *Confounded Rot about Napoleon.* Privately published. 1961.

————. *The Grasslands of North America.* Privately published. 4th printing, 1961.

Maltseva, N. A. "O kolichestve krestianskikh vystuplenii v period stolypinskoi agrarnoi reformy." *Istoriia SSSR* (1965).

Mamulova, L. G. "Zemskaia kontrreforma 1890 g." *Nauchnye doklady vysshei shkoly: Istoricheskie nauki* (1960).

Marshall, S. L. A. *Men against Fire.* New York, 1947.

Martynov, A. P. *Moia sluzhba v otdelnom korpuse zhandarmov.* Stanford, Calif., 1972.

Martynov, B. S. *Poniatie zemleustroistva.* Petrograd, 1917.

Marx, Karl, and Frederick Engels. *Capital.* 3 vols. Moscow, 1961-62.

————. *The Holy Family.* Moscow, 1956.

————. *Selected Correspondence.* Moscow, n.d.

Materialy po perspektivnomu planu razvitiia selskogo i lesnogo khoziaistva, 1928/1929-1932/1933. 2 pts. Moscow, 1929.

Mayer, Arno J. *Politics and Diplomacy of Peacemaking.* New York, 1967.

McKay, J. P. *Pioneers for Profit.* Chicago, 1970.

Meiendorf, A. F. (spelled Meyendorf). "A Brief Appreciation of P. A. Stolypin's Tenure of Office." Unpublished ms. Russian Archive, Columbia University.

————. *Krestianskii dvor.* St. Petersburg, 1909.

Melnikov, N. "Russkoe zemstvo v proshlom i nekotoryia mysli ob ego budushchem." Unpublished ms. Russian Archive, Columbia University.

Melville, Herman. *Pierre.* New York, 1963.

Mendelssohn-Bartholdy, A. *The War and German Society.* New Haven, Conn., 1937.

Mendras, H. *The Vanishing Peasant.* Cambridge, Mass., 1970.

Mertvago, A. P. *Ne po tornomu puti.* 3d ed. St. Petersburg, 1900.

Meshcherskii, A. P. *Ispolshchina i krestianskie zarabotki.* St. Petersburg, 1902.

Meshcherskii, Vladimir P. *Moi vospominaniia.* 3 vols. St. Petersburg, 1897-1912.

Mesiatsev, P. "Blizhaishie puti zemelno-khoziaistvennogo stroitelstva." In *O zemle* (1921).

————. *Zemelnaia i selsko-khoziaistvennaia politika v Rossii.* Moscow, 1922.

Mezhov, V. I. *Krestianskii vopros v Rossii.* St. Petersburg, 1865.

Meznev, M. "Zakonoproekt ob otgranichenii zemel." *Zemlemernoe delo* (Sept. 1916).

Michelson, A. M., et al. *Russian Public Finance during the War.* New Haven, Conn., 1928.

Mikhalenko, A. M. "Zaozerskaia selskaia obshchina." In Barykov, *Sbornik* (1880).

Miliutin, V. P. *Novyi zakon o zemleustroistve i zemlepolzovanii.* Moscow, 1928.

Millar, James. "A Reformulation of A. Chayanov's Theory of the Peasant Economy." *Economic Development and Cultural Change,* XVIII (Jan. 1970).

Miller, Robert F. "The Politotdel: A Lesson from the Past." *Slavic Review,* XXV, no. 3 (Sept. 1966).

Milward, A. S. *The German Economy at War.* London, 1965.

Minarik, L. P. "Kharakteristika krupneishikh zemlevladeltsev Rossii kontsa XIX-nachala XX v." In *Ezhegodnik...1963* (1964).

Mitrofanov, A. Kh. *Itogi chistki partii.* Moscow, 1930.

Morgan, G. G. *Soviet Administrative Legality.* Stanford, Calif., 1962.

Moshkov, Iu. A. *Zernovaia problema v gody sploshnoi kollektivizatsii selskogo khoziaistva SSSR 1929-1932 gg.* Moscow, 1966.

Mosse, W. E. "Stolypin's Villages." *Slavonic Review,* XLIII (June 1965).

Mozzhukhin, I. V. *Zemleustroistvo v Bogoroditskom Uezde, Tulskoi Gubernii.* Moscow, 1917.

Naumov, A. N. *Iz utselevshikh vospominanii: 1868-1917.* 2 vols. New York, 1954.

Nifontov, A. S. "Statistika krestianskogo dvizheniia v Rossii 50-kh godov XIX v. po materialam III otdeleniia." In *Voprosy istorii selskogo* (1961).

Nikolskii, A. *Zemlia, obshchina i trud.* St. Petersburg, 1902.

Nosov, N. E., ed. *Problemy krestianskogo zemlevladeniia i vnutrennei politiki Rossii.* Leningrad, 1972.

————, et al., eds. *Vnutrenniaia politika tsarizma.* Leningrad, 1967.

Nötzold, J. *Wirtschaftspolitische Alternativen der Entwicklung Russlands in der Ära Witte und Stolypin.* Berlin, 1966.

Nove, Alec. *Economic Rationality and Soviet Politics.* New York, 1964.

Novikov, A. *Vtoroi sbornik statei.* St. Petersburg, 1902.

O rasprostranenii Zakona 13 iiulia 1889 goda na Irkutskuiu i Eniseiskuiu gubernii. Listed in the catalog of the Leningrad Public Library under Rossiia, Gosudarstvennyi Sovet, Departament Zakonov, Materialy, vol. CCXI (1892), d. 11.

O zemle: Sbornik statei o proshlom i budushchem zemelno-khoziaistvennogo stroitelstva. Moscow, 1921.

Obsledovanie zemleustroennykh khoziaistv proizvedennoe v 1913 godu v 12 uezdakh Evropeiskoi Rossii. Petrograd, 1915.

Obzor deiatelnosti osobogo soveshchaniia dlia obsuzhdeniia i obedineniia mero-priatii po prodovolstvennomu delu 17 avgusta 1915 g.-17 fevralia 1916 g. Petrograd, 1916.

Obzor deiatelnosti uezdnykh zemleustroitelnykh kommisii (1907-1908 gg.). St. Petersburg, 1909.

Obzor deiatelnosti uezdnykh zemleustroitelnykh kommisii na 1 iiulia 1909. St. Petersburg, 1909.

Obzor deiatelnosti za 1913 god. Published by the MZ. St. Petersburg, 1914.

Obzor deiatelnosti za 1914 god. Published by the MZ. Petrograd, 1915.

Ocheredyne zadachi vedomstva zemledeliia v sviazi s voinoiu. Published by the

MZ. 1916.

Ocherk piatidesiatiletnei deiatelnosti ministerstva gosudarstvennykh imushchestv, 1837-1887. St. Petersburg, 1887.

Ocherk rabot po zagotovleniiu pereselencheskikh uchastkov: 1893-1899. St. Petersburg, 1900.

Oganovskii, N. V. *Individualizatsiia zemlevladeniia v Rossii i ee posledstviia.* Moscow, 1917.

————. "Obshchina i zemelnoe tovarishchestvo." In *O zemle* (1921).

Oldenburg, S. S. *Tsarstvovanie Imperatora Nikolaia II.* 2 vols. Belgrade, 1939.

Orlov, N. *Deviat mesiatsev prodovolstvennoi raboty sovetskoi vlasti.* Moscow, 1918.

Orlov, V. P. *Formy krestianskogo zemlevladeniia v Moskovskoi gubernii.* Moscow, 1879.

Osipova, T. V. *Klassovaia borba v derevne v period podgotovki i provedeniia oktiabrskoi revoliutsii.* Moscow, 1974.

Osnovnye voprosy agrarnoi reformy na 2-m vserossiiskom sezde ligi agrarnykh reform. Moscow, 1917.

Osobennosti agrarnogo stroia Rossii v period imperializma. Moscow, 1962.

Osokina, V. Ia. *Sotsialisticheskoe stroitelstvo v derevne i obshchine: 1920-1933.* Moscow, 1978.

Otchet deiatelnosti selskokhoziaistvennogo soveta v pervuiu ego sessiiu. St. Petersburg, 1895.

Otchetnyia svedeniia o deiatelnosti zemleustroitelnykh komissii. Petrograd, 1915.

Otchuzhdenie i ispolzovanie selskokhoziaistvennogo inventaria. Moscow, 1919.

Otdel zemelnykh uluchshenii v 1909-1913. Petrograd, 1914.

Owen, L. A. *The Russian Peasant Movement, 1906-1917.* London, 1937.

Padenie tsarskogo rezhima. 7 vols. Leningrad, 1924.

Palij, M. "The Peasant Partisan Movement of the Anarchist Nestor Makhno." Ph.D. dissertation. University of Kansas, 1971.

Pavlovsky, G. *Agricultural Russia on the Eve of the Revolution.* London, 1930.

Pazukhin, A. D. *Sovremennoe sostoianie Rossii i soslovnyi vopros.* Moscow, 1886.

Perepiska sekretariata TsK RKP(b) s mestnymi partiinymi organizatsiiami. 8 vols. Moscow, 1957-74.

Pershin, P. N. "Formy zemlepolzovaniia." In *O zemle* (1921).

————. "Krestianskie zemelnye komitety v period podgotovki velikoi oktiabrskoi sotsialisticheskoi revoliutsii." *Voprosy istorii,* XXIII (1948).

————. *Obshchina i khutora Krasnoufimskogo Uezda Permskoi Gubernii.* St. Petersburg, 1918.

————. *Uchastkovoe zemlepolzovanie v Rossii.* Moscow, 1922.

————. *Zemelnoe ustroistvo dorevoliutsionnoi derevni.* Moscow, 1928.

Pestrzhetskii, D. I. *O prepodavanii uzakonenii o krestianakh.* St. Petersburg, 1905.

————. *Opyt agrarnoi programmy.* St. Petersburg, 1906.

————, ed. *Sbornik postanovlenii, otnosiashchikhsia k grazhdanskomu pravu lits selskogo sostoianiia.* St. Petersburg, 1898.

Petrazhitskii, Lev. *Law and Morality.* Cambridge, Mass., 1955.

Phillipot, R. "L'aggravation des famines et la legislation des subsistences en

Russie, 1861-1914." *Revue historique,* CCIX (Jan. 1953).

Pobedonostsev, K. P. *Pisma Pobedonostseva k Aleksandru III.* 2 vols. Moscow, 1926.

Pogrebinskii, A. P. "Selskoe khoziaistvo i prodovolstvennyi vopros v Rossii v gody pervoi mirovoi voiny." *Istoricheskie zapiski,* XXXI (1950).

Polanyi, Karl. *The Great Transformation.* Boston, 1957.

Poliakov, Iu. A. "Sotsialno-ekonomicheskie itogi agrarnykh preobrazovanii oktiabrskoi revoliutsii (1917-1920 gg.)." In *Istoriia sovetskogo krestianstva* (1963).

Polianskii, N. N. *Tsarskie voennye sudy v borbe s revoliutsiei 1905-1907 gg.* Moscow, 1958.

Polner, T. J., et al. *Russian Local Government during the War and the Union of Zemstvoes.* New Haven, Conn., 1930.

Polovtsov, A. A. *Dnevnik A. A. Polovtsova.* 2 vols. Moscow, 1966.

Popov, A. "Krestiane-zemlevladeltsy." *Selskoe khoziaistvo i lesovodstvo,* CXCIII, no. 4 (Apr. 1899).

Pravitelstvennyi Vestnik. Prerevolutionary government daily newspaper.

Preobrazhenskii, E. A., ed. *Russkie finansy i evropeiskaia birzha v 1904-1906 gg.* Moscow, 1926.

Preyer, W. D. *Die russische Agrarreform.* Jena, 1914.

Problemy sotsialno-ekonomicheskoi istorii Rossii. Moscow, 1971.

Problemy zemleustroistva. Moscow, 1922.

Prodovolstvie i snabzhenie. Organ of the Provisional Government's ministry of food supply. 1917.

Programma ispytaniia na dolzhnost Zemskogo Nachalnika. St. Petersburg, 1914.

Prokopovich, S. N. *The Economic Condition of Soviet Russia.* London, 1924.

_____. *Mestnye liudi o nuzhdakh Rossii.* St. Petersburg, 1904.

Protokoly delegatskogo soveshchaniia Vserossiiskogo Krestianskogo Soiuza 6-10 noiabria 1905 g. v Moskve. Moscow, 1906.

Protokoly tsentralnogo komiteta RSDRP(b): Avgust 1917-Fevral 1918. Moscow, 1958.

Prugavin, V. S. *Russkaia zemelnaia obshchina v trudakh ee mestnykh issledovateli.* Moscow, 1888.

Rabinowitch, Alex. *The Bolsheviks Come to Power.* New York, 1976.

_____. *Prelude to Revolution.* Bloomington, Ind., 1968.

Raboty komissii ob uezdnykh uchrezhdeniiakh. 2 vols. St. Petersburg, 1859.

Radkey, Oliver H. *The Unknown Civil War in Soviet Russia.* Stanford, Calif., 1976.

Raimov, R. M. "Agrarnaia revoliutsiia v Bashkirii, 1917-1923 gg." *Istoricheskie zapiski,* XXXII (1950).

Ransel, David L., ed. *The Family in Imperial Russia.* Urbana, Ill., 1978.

Raspredelenie zemli v 1918 godu. Moscow, 1918.

Rathenau, Walter. *Briefe.* 2 vols. Dresden, 1927.

_____. *In Days to Come.* New York, 1921.

_____. *Gesammelte Schriften.* 5 vols. Berlin, 1918.

_____. *Tagebuch 1907-1922.* Düsseldorf, 1967.

Redlich, F. "German Economic Planning for War & Peace." *Review of Politics,* VI (July 1944).

Redlich, J. *Austrian War Government*. New Haven, Conn., 1929.

Rempel, D. G. "The Mennonite Colonies in New Russia." Ph.D. dissertation. Stanford University, 1933.

Renouvin, Pierre. *The Forms of War Government in France*. New Haven, Conn., 1927.

Resheniia partii i pravitelstva po khoziaistvennym voprosam. 10 vols. Moscow, 1967-76.

Revoliutsiia 1905-1907 gg. v Rossii. 15 vols. Moscow, 1955-65.

Rigby, T. H. *Lenin's Government*. London, 1979.

Rittikh, A. A. *Krestianskoe pravoporiadok*. St. Petersburg, 1904.

———. *Krestianskoe zemlepolzovanie*. St. Petersburg, 1904.

———. *Zavisimost krestian ot obshchiny i mira*. St. Petersburg, 1903.

Robbins, Richard G. *Famine in Russia, 1891-1892*. New York, 1975.

———. "Russia's Famine Relief Law of June 12 1900: A Reform Aborted." *Canadian-American Slavic Studies*, X (Spring 1976).

Robinson, Geroid T. *Rural Russia under the Old Regime*. New York, 1932.

Romanov, P. "Mart-mai 1917 g." *Krasnyi Arkhiv*, XV (1926).

Roosa, Ruth. "Russian Industrialists Look to the Future: Thoughts on Economic Development, 1906-1917." In Curtiss, *Essays* (1963).

Rose, J. W. "The Russian Peasant Emancipation and the Problem of Rural Administration: The Institution of the Mirovoi Posrednik." Ph.D. dissertation. University of Kansas, 1976.

Rosenberg, William. *Liberals in the Russian Revolution*. Princeton, N.J., 1974.

Rzhanitsyn, A. A. *Dlia chego i kak nado proizvodit peredely zemli*. Moscow, 1925.

———. *Vnutriselennoe zemleustroistvo*. 3d ed. Moscow, 1927.

Sanakoev, M. P. *Deiatelnost krestianskogo pozemelnogo banka v Gruzii, 1906-1917 gg.* Tbilisi, 1971.

Santoni, Wayne D. "P. N. Durnovo as Minister of Internal Affairs in the Witte Cabinet." Ph.D. dissertation. University of Kansas, 1968.

Savich, Georgii G. *K voprosu o melkoi zemskoi edinitse: Selo Pavlogo i ego obshchestvennoe ustroistvo*. St. Petersburg, 1906.

———, ed. *Novyi gosudarstvennyi stroi Rossii*. St. Petersburg, 1907.

Sbornik po voprosam zemleustroistva. 2 pts. Moscow, 1927.

Sbornik pravil i instruktsii po Krestianskomu Pozemelnomu Banku, 1883-1908. St. Petersburg, 1908.

Sbornik uzakonenii o krestianskikh i sudebnykh uchrezhdeniiakh obrazovannykh po zakonu 12 iiulia 1889 goda. 6th ed. 2 pts. St. Petersburg, 1901.

Sbornik zakliuchenii gubernskikh soveshchanii po proektu nakaza zemskim uchastkovym nachalnikam. 2 pts. St. Petersburg, 1899.

Sbornik zakonopolozhenii i rasporiazhenii po zemleustroistvu. Moscow, 1927.

Schapiro, Leonard. *The Communist Party of the Soviet Union*. New York, 1960.

Schiller, Otto. "The Farming Cooperative: A New System of Farm Management." *Land Economics*, XXVII (Feb. 1951).

———. *Ziele und Ergebnisse der Agrarordnung in den besetzten Ostgebieten*. Berlin, 1943.

Selskoe Khoziaistvo i Lesovodstvo. Journal of the department of agriculture in the MZ.

Selskokhoziaistvennoe vedomstvo za 75 let: 1837-1912. St. Petersburg, 1914.

Semenov, P. P. "Muraevenskaia volost." In Barykov, *Sbornik* (1880).

Semenov, S. T. *Dvadtsat piat let v derevne.* Petrograd, 1915.

————. *V rodnoi derevni.* Moscow, 1962.

Semenova, Olga P. *Zhizn Ivana—ocherki iz byta krestian odnoi iz chernozemskoi gubernii.* St. Petersburg, 1914.

Semevskii, V. I. *Krestiane v tsarstvovanie Imperatritsy Ekateriny II.* 2d ed. 2 vols. St. Petersburg, 1903.

Sezd upolnomochennykh predsedatelia obshchegosudarstvennogo prodovolstvennogo komiteta. Petrograd, 1917.

Shannon, F. A. *The Farmer's Last Frontier.* New York, 1963.

Shapkarin, A. V., et al., eds. *Krestianskoe dvizhenie v Rossii: iiun 1906 g.-iiul 1914 g.* Moscow, 1966.

Sharapov, G. V. *Razreshenie agrarnogo voprosa v Rossii posle pobedy oktiabrskoi revoliutsii.* Moscow, 1961.

Shcherbina, F. A. *Krestianskie biudzhety.* Voronezh, 1900.

Shestakov, A. V. *Ocherki po selskomu khoziaistvu i krestianskoe dvizhenie v gody voiny i pered oktiabrem.* Leningrad, 1927.

————, ed. *Sovety krestianskikh deputatov i drugie krestianskie organizatsii.* Moscow, 1922.

Shidlovskii, S. I. *Obshchii obzor trudov mestnykh komitetov.* St. Petersburg, 1905.

————. *Vospominaniia.* 2 vols. Berlin, 1923.

————. *Zemelnye zakhvaty i mezhevoe delo.* St. Petersburg, 1904.

Shipov, Dmitrii N. *Vospominaniia i dumy o perezhitom.* Moscow, 1918.

Shlikhter, A. G. *Agrarnyi vopros i prodovolstvennaia politika v pervye gody sovetskoi vlasti.* Moscow, 1975.

Shlippe, F. von. "Memoirs" (in Russian). Unpublished ms. Russian Archive, Columbia University.

Shuvaev, K. M. *Staraia i novaia derevnia.* Moscow, 1937.

Shvanebakh, P. Kh. "Zapiski sanovnika." *Golos Minuvshego* (1918).

Sidelnikov, S. M. *Agrarnaia politika samoderzhaviia v period imperializma.* Moscow, 1980.

————, ed. *Agrarnaia reforma Stolypina.* Moscow, 1973.

————. "Zemelno-krestianskaia problema samoderzhaviia v predumskii period." *Istoriia SSSR* (1976).

Simms, James Y. "The Impact of the Russian Famine of 1891-2." Ph.D. dissertation. University of Michigan, 1976.

————. "The Crisis in Russian Agriculture at the End of the Nineteenth Century: A Different View." *Slavic Review,* XXXVI (Sept. 1977).

Simonova, M. S. "Agrarnaia politika samoderzhaviia v 1905 g." *Istoricheskie zapiski,* LXXXI (1968).

————. "Borba techenii v pravitelstvennom lagere po voprosam agrarnoi politiki v kontse XIX v." *Istoriia SSSR* (1963).

————. "Mobilizatsiia krestianskoi nadelnoi zemli v period stolypinskoi agrarnoi reformy." In *Materialy po istorii selskogo khoziaistva i krestianstva SSSR: Sbornik V.* Moscow, 1962.

————. "Politika tsarizma v krestianskom voprose nakanune revoliutsii 1906-

1907 gg." *Istoricheskie zapiski,* LXXV (1965).

_____. "Problema 'oskudeniia' tsentra i ee rol v formirovanii agrarnoi politiki samoderzhaviia v 90-kh godakh XIX-nachale XX v." In *Problemy sotsialno-ekonomicheskoi istorii* (1971).

Sistematicheskii katalog izdanii imeiushchikhsia v sklade departamenta zemledeliia. St. Petersburg, 1912.

Skliarov, L. F. *Pereselenie i zemleustroistvo v Sibiri v gody stolypinskoi agrarnoi reformy.* Leningrad, 1962.

Smith, C. H. *The Coming of the Mennonites.* Berne, Ind., 1927.

Smith, R. E. F. *Peasant Farming in Muscovy.* Cambridge, 1977.

Snegirev, M. "Velikaia oktiabrskaia sotsialisticheskaia revoliutsiia i raspredelenie zemel v 1917-1918 gg." *Voprosy istorii,* XXII (1947).

Sobranie upolnomochennykh v Moskve 7-9 sentiabria 1915 g. Moscow, 1916.

Sobranie uzakonenii i rasporiazhenii pravitelstva izdavaemoe pri Pravitelstvuiushchem Senate. St. Petersburg, 1863-1917.

Solomon, Susan G. *The Soviet Agrarian Debate.* Boulder, Colo. 1977.

Solovev, Iu. B. "Pravitelstvo i politika ukrepleniia klassovykh pozitsii dvorianstva v kontse XIX veka." In Nosov, *Vnutrenniaia* (1967).

Sorokin, P. A., et al., eds. *A Systematic Sourcebook in Rural Sociology.* 3 vols. Minneapolis, 1930.

Sostav (kontingent) nadeliaemogo zemlei naseleniia. Moscow, 1918 or 1919.

Sovremennoe polozhenie taksirovki predmetov prodovolstviia v Rossii i mery k ee uporiadocheniiu. Petrograd, 1915.

Spektor, G. V. *Piat let zemleustroistva v Samarskoi gubernii.* Samara, 1925.

Spiridovich, A. *Les dernières années de la cour de Tsarskoie-Selo.* Paris, 1928.

Spravochnik po kolkhoznomu stroitelstvu. Leningrad, 1931.

Spravochnik zemleustroitelia. Moscow, 1928.

Spuler, Bertold. *The Mongols in History.* New York, 1971.

Stalin, Joseph. *Works.* 16 vols. Moscow, 1952-54.

_____. *Na khlebnom fronte.* Leningrad, 1933.

Starr, S. F. *Decentralization and Self-Government in Russia, 1830-1870.* Princeton, N.J., 1972.

Statisticheskie svedeniia po zemelnomu voprosu v evropeiskoi Rossii. St. Petersburg, 1906.

Stein, Lorenz von. *Gegenwart und Zukunft der Rechts und Staatswissenschaft Deutschlands.* Stuttgart, 1876.

_____. *History of the Social Movement in France, 1789-1850.* Trans. Kaethe Mengelberg. Totowa, N.J., 1964.

Stenograficheskii otchet IV soveshchaniia zemorganov 5-12 ianvaria 1929 goda. Moscow, 1929.

Stepanov, I. P. *Travoseianie na krestianskikh zemliakh v Moskovskoi gubernii.* Moscow, 1925.

Stishinskii, A. S. *Obiasnitelnaia zapiska k proektu polozheniia ob uluchshenii i rasshirenii krestianskogo zemlevladeniia.* Stanford, Calif., n.d.

Stolypin, Petr A. "Izvlechenie iz otcheta za 1904 g." *Krasnyi Arkhiv,* XVII (1926), 83-87.

Stone, Norman. *The Eastern Front, 1914-1917.* New York, 1975.

Strakhovskii, I.M. "Krestianskii vopros v zakonodatelstve i zakonosoveshchatelnykh kommisiiakh posle 1861 goda." In Dolgorukov and Tolstoi *Krestianskii stroi* (1905), I, 389-404.

—————. *Krestianskiia prava i uchrezhdeniia.* St. Petersburg, 1903.

Strizhkov, Iu. K. *Prodovolstvennye otriady gody grazhdanskoi voiny i inostrannoi interventsii, 1917-1921.* Moscow, 1973.

Struve, Peter B., ed. *Food Supply in Russia during the World War.* New Haven, Conn., 1930.

Svedeniia o snabzhenie Petrograda i Moskvy prodovolstvennymi produktami. Petrograd, 1916.

Sverdlov, Iakob M. *Izbrannye proizvedeniia.* 3 vols. Moscow, 1959.

Sviderskii, A. *Tri goda borby s golodom.* Moscow, 1920.

Svod otzyvov gubernskikh prisutstvii po krestianskim delam i zakliuchenii gubernatorov po proektu preobrazovaniia podushnoi sistemy sborov sostavlennomu v ministerstve finansov. 2 vols. St. Petersburg, 1873-74.

Svod trudov mestnykh komitetov o nuzhdakh selskokhoziaistvennoi promyshlennosti po 49 guberniiam Evropeiskoi Rossii. 23 vols. St. Petersburg, 1905.

Svod tsirkuliarnykh rasporiazhenii i raziasnenii Ministerstva Vnutrennikh Del po vedomstvu Zemskogo Otdela. St. Petersburg, 1903.

Svod vysochaishikh otmetok po vsepoddaneishim otchetam za 1895-1901. 7 vols. St. Petersburg, 1897-1904.

Svod zakliuchenii gubernskikh soveshchanii po proektu pravil ob otgranichenii krestianskikh nadelov i ob ikh razverstanii s chrezpolosnymi ugodiami smezhnogo vladeniia. St. Petersburg, 1906.

Svod zakliuchenii gubernskikh soveshchanii po proektu polozheniia o nadelnykh zemliakh. St. Petersburg, 1906.

Svod zakliuchenii gubernskikh soveshchanii po voprosam otnosiashchimsia k peresmotru zakonodatelstva o krestianakh. 3 vols. St. Petersburg, 1897.

Szeftel, Marc. "Nicholas II's Constitutional Decisions of Oct. 17-19, 1905 and Sergius Witte's Role." In *Album J. Balon.* Namur, Belgium, 1963.

Taniuchi, Y. *The Village Gathering in Russia in the Mid-1920's.* Birmingham, 1968.

Timasheff, Nicholas S. "Revoliutsionnaia zakonnost." *Russian Economic Quarterly,* IV (1925).

Tiukavin, V. G. "Formy zemlevladeniia v Sibiri v nachale XX veka." In *Ezhegodnik...1964* (1966).

Toewes, J. B. *Lost Fatherland.* Scottsdale, Pa., 1967.

Les travaux des commissions agraires (1907-1911). St. Petersburg, 1912.

Treadgold, Donald W. *The Great Siberian Migration.* Princeton, N.J., 1957.

Trete Polnoe Sobranie Zakonov Rossiiskoi Imperii. 33 vols. St. Petersburg, 1885-1916.

Trudy komissii o gubernskikh i uezdnykh uchrezhdeniiakh, Chast pervaia. 1st ed. 4 books. St. Petersburg, 1860.

Trudy komissii po podgotovke zemelnoi reformy. Petrograd, 1917.

Trudy kommisii po preobrazovaniiu volostnykh sudov. 7 vols. St. Petersburg, 1873-74.

Trudy mestnykh Komitetov o nuzhdakh selskokhoziaistvennoi promyshlennosti. 58 vols. St. Petersburg, 1903.

Trudy 1-go Vserossiiskogo selsko-khoziaistvennogo sezda v Kieve 1-10 sentiabria 1913 g. 7 vols. Kiev, n.d.

Trudy pervoi vsesoiuznoi konferentsii agrarnikov-marksistov. 2 vols. Moscow, 1930.

Trudy redaktsionnoi kommisii po peresmotru zakonopolozhenii o krestianakh. 6 vols. St. Petersburg, 1903-4.

Trudy sezda deiatelei agronomicheskoi pomoshchi mestnomu khoziaistvu (10-19 fevralia 1901 g.). Moscow, 1901.

Trudy sezda nepremennykh chlenov gubernskikh prisutstvii 24 oktiabria-1 noiabria 1907. St. Petersburg, 1908.

Trudy sezda nepremennykh chlenov gubernskikh prisutstvii i zemleustroitelnykh komissii 10-23 ianvaria 1909 g. St. Petersburg, 1909.

Trudy vysshego seminariia selsko-khoziaistvennoi ekonomii i politiki. Moscow, 1921.

Trutovskii, V. *Sovremennoe zemstvo.* Petrograd, 1914.

Tsentralnyi Gosudarstvennyi Istoricheskii Arkhiv Leningrada (TsGIAL)
    f. 408:   Committee for Land Settlement Affairs
    f. 456:   Administration for the Army's Food Supply
    f. 457:   Special Conference for the Discussion and Coordination of Measures for Food Supply
    f. 592:   Peasant Land Bank
    f. 1090: Shingarev, Andrei Ivanovich
    f. 1149: State Council, Department of Laws
    f. 1276: Council of Ministers (1905-17)
    f. 1278: State Duma
    f. 1282: Chancellery of the MVD
    f. 1291: Land Section of the MVD
    f. 1316: Commission on Gubernia and Uezd Institutions
    f. 1317: Special Commission to Compile Projects for the Reform of Local Administration (Kakhanov commission)

Tsimmerman, R. E. (pseud., R. Gvozdev). *Kulachestvo-Rostovshchichestvo, ego obshchestvennoe-ekonomicheskoe znachenie.* St. Petersburg, 1898.

Tsirkuliary po voprosu o pereselenii krestian i meshchan na kazennye zemli i drugie materialy. St. Petersburg, MVD, Land Section, 1882-95. This is the heading in the catalog of the Leningrad Public Library.

Tsybulskii, V. A. "Nagolovaia politika v derevne v pervye gody NEPa." *Voprosy istorii,* XL (Oct. 1965).

Tucker, Robert C., ed. *The Marx-Engels Reader.* New York, 1972.

Ulam, Adam. *Stalin.* New York, 1973.

Uspenskii, Gleb. "From a Village Diary." In Thomas Riha, ed. *Readings in Russian Civilization.* 3 vols. Chicago, 1969. II, 358-67.

Vaganov, O. A. "Zemelnaia politika tsarskogo pravitelstva v Kazakhstane (1907-1914 gg.)." *Istoricheskie zapiski,* XXXI (1950).

Vasilchenko, V. *Dlia chego nuzhno krestianiu zemleustroistvo.* Moscow, 1924.

Vasilchikov, A. *Zemlevladenie i zemledelie v Rossii i drugikh evropeiskikh gosudarstvakh.* 2d ed. 2 vols. St. Petersburg, 1881.

"Vasilchikov." In Brokgaus and Efron, *Novyi,* IX, col. 681.

Vaskovskii, E. V. *Rukovodstvo k tolkovaniiu i primeneniiu zakonov.* Moscow, 1913.

Vdovin, V. *Krestianskii Pozemelnyi Bank (1883-1895 gg.).* Moscow, 1959.

Veniaminov, P. *Krestianskaia obshchina.* St. Petersburg, 1908.

Verpakhovskaia, E. *Gosudarstvennaia deiatelnost P. A. Stolypina.* 3 vols. St. Petersburg, 1911.

Veselovskii, B. B., ed. *Agrarnyi vopros v Sovete Ministrov, 1906 g.* Moscow, 1924.

_____. *Istoriia zemstva za sorok let.* 4 vols. St. Petersburg, 1909-11.

Veselovskii, S. B. *Issledovaniia po istorii klassa sluzhilykh zemlevladeltsev.* Moscow, 1969.

Vestnik selskogo khoziaistva. Weekly journal of the Moscow agricultural society. 1899-1917.

Vinogradoff, Eugene. "The Russian Peasantry and the Elections to the Fourth Duma." Ph.D. dissertation. Columbia University, 1974.

Vladimirov, M. *Mesechnichestvo i ego sotsialno-politicheskie otrazheniia.* Kharkov, 1920.

Volkov, N. T., ed. *Sbornik polozhenii o selskom sostoianie.* Moscow, 1910.

Volobuev, P. V. *Ekonomicheskaia politika vremennogo pravitelstva.* Moscow, 1962.

von Dietze, C. *Stolypinsche Agrarreform und Feldgemeinschaft.* Leipzig, 1920.

Von Laue, Theodore. *Sergei Witte and the Industrialization of Russia.* New York, 1963.

Vonzblein, M. "Obzor zemsko-agronomicheskikh meropriatii." *Vestnik selskogo khoziaistva* (2 Mar. 1914).

Voprosy istorii selskogo khoziaistva, krestianstva, i revoliutsionnnogo dvizheniia v Rossii. Moscow, 1961.

Voshchinin, V. "Pereselenie." In *O zemle* (1921).

Vtoroe Polnoe Sobranie Zakonov Rossiiskoi Imperii. 55 vols. St. Petersburg, 1830-84.

Vyltsan, M. A., et al. "Nekotorye problemy istorii kollektivizatsii v SSSR." *Voprosy istorii,* XL (Mar. 1965).

Warriner, Doreen. *The Economics of Peasant Farming.* 2d ed. New York, 1965.

Weber, Eugen. *Peasants into Frenchmen.* Stanford, Calif., 1976.

Weber, Max. "Bureaucracy." In H. Gerth and C. W. Mills, eds., *From Max Weber.* New York, 1958.

_____. *Sociology of Religion.* Boston, 1963.

Weissman, Benjamin M. *Herbert Hoover and Famine Relief to Soviet Russia: 1921-1923.* Stanford, Calif., 1974.

Weissman, Neil B. "State, Estate and Society in Tsarist Russia: The Question of Local Government, 1900-1908." Ph.D. dissertation. Princeton University, 1976.

Wesson, R. *Soviet Communes.* New Brunswick, N.J., 1963.

Witte, Sergei Iu. "Pisma S. Iu. Vitte k D. S. Sipiaginu (1900-1901)." *Krasnyi Arkhiv,* XVIII (1926), 30-48.

_____. *Samoderzhavie i zemstvo.* 2d ed. Stuttgart, 1903.

_____. *Vospominaniia.* 3 vols. Moscow, 1960.

_____. *Zapiska po krestianskomu delu.* St. Petersburg, 1904.

Wolters, Margarete. *Aussenpolitische Fragen vor der vierten Duma.* Hamburg, 1969.

Yaney, George. "Bureaucracy and Freedom: N. M. Korkunov's Theory of the State." *American Historical Review,* LXXI (Jan. 1966).

————. "Some Aspects of the Imperial Russian Government on the Eve of the First World War." *Slavonic Review,* XLIII (Dec. 1964).

————. *The Systematization of Russian Government.* Urbana, Ill., 1973.

Young, Arthur. *Travels in France during the Years 1787, 1788, and 1789.* New York, 1969.

Zagorsky, S. O. *State Control of Industry during the War.* New Haven, Conn., 1928.

Zaionchkovskii, P. A. *Rossiiskoe samoderzhavie v kontse XIX stoletiia.* Moscow, 1970.

Zaitsev, K. I., and N. V. Dolinsky. "Organization and Policy." In Struve, *Food Supply* (1930).

Zakon 14 iiunia 1910 g. St. Petersburg, 1914.

Zapiska ot Ministerstva Vnutrennikh Del k chlenam glavnogo komiteta ob ustroistve selskogo sostoianiia 27 Marta 1873.

Zarudnyi, M. I. *Zakony i zhizn.* St. Petersburg, 1874.

Zavadskii, I. "Selskie uchrezhdeniia melkogo kredita i agronomicheskaia pomoshch naseleniiu." *Iugo-vostochnyi khoziain* (Sept. 1911), 42-53.

"Zemelnyi kredit." In Brokgaus and Efron, *Novyi,* XVIII, cols. 448-50.

Zemlemernoe delo. Monthly journal of the Society of Russian Surveyors. 1907-

Zemleustroistvo. St. Petersburg, 1911.

Zemleustroistvo (1907-1910 gg.). St. Petersburg, 1911.

Zenkovskii, A. V. *Pravda o Stolypine.* New York, 1956.

Zhidkov, G. P. "Nekotorye osobennosti agrarnoi revoliutsii na Altae v 1917 g." In *Ezhegodnik...1968* (1972).

Zinovev, P. "Borokskaia obshchina." In Barykov, *Sbornik* (1880).

Zlatovratskii, N. N. "Pustynskaia obshchina." In Barykov, *Sbornik* (1880).

Znosko-Borovskii, A. A., ed. *Polozhenie o zemleustroistve.* St. Petersburg, 1912.

Zyrianov, P. N. "Sovremennaia anglo-amerikanskaia istoriografiia stolypinskoi agrarnoi reformy." *Istoriia SSSR* (1973).

Index

Note on the Author

GEORGE YANEY received his Ph.D. from Princeton University in 1961. Since 1960 he has been affiliated with the University of Maryland, where he is a professor of history. He has received several grants and fellowships, including Fulbright grants for study in the USSR in 1975 and 1977. His publications include many journal articles on various aspects of Russian society and a book, *The Systematization of Russian Government* (University of Illinois Press, 1973).